COASTAL SHIPS AND FERRIES

2nd Edition

David Hornsby

Ian Allan
PUBLISHING

Contents

First published 1964
This edition 2010

ISBN 978 0 7110 3482 2

Published by Ian Allan Publishing

an imprint of Ian Allan Publishing Ltd, Hersham, Surrey KT12 4RG.
Printed in England by Ian Allan Printing Ltd, Hersham, Surrey KT12 4RG.

Visit the Ian Allan Publishing website at www.ianallanpublishing.com

Distributed in the Unites States of America and Canada by BookMasters Distribution Services.

Code 1006/B

Mixed Sources
Product group from well-managed forests and other controlled sources
www.fsc.org Cert no. SGS-COC-005526
© 1996 Forest Stewardship Council
FSC

Front cover: **Brittany Ferries.** Cap Finistere. *Marcel Mochet*
Back cover, top: **Kustvaartbedrijf Moerman BV.** Roelof. *Hans Kraijenbosch*
Back cover, bottom: **Reederei Ernst Komrowski.** BBC Konan. *Hans Kraijenbosch*
Half title: **Viking Line Ab.** Mariella. *Marko Stampeh*
Title page: **Kapitan Siegfried Bojen.** Okko Tom Brook. *David Walker*

Preface

This new edition of *Coastal Ships & Ferries* lists the fleet information of the major ferry and coastal operators based in northern European waters and is intended to sit alongside the companion volume of 'Ocean Ships' on the enthusiast's bookshelf.

During the interval of over a decade since the last edition of *Coastal Ships & Ferries*, mergers/takeovers, market competition and the general economic conditions in northern Europe have ensured that little remains of the previous edition of the book.

A number of ferry companies have merged and some ferry routes have seen a reduction in operators, where there has previously been stiff competition. However, on some routes the high demand for carrying large numbers of road freight vehicles has seen a continuing move towards the hybrid Ro-Pax type of ferry with a substantial freight capacity, but with more limited passenger facilities than full passenger ferries.

This decade has also seen the near-extinction of the small 'paragraph' coasters of the 1960s and '70s and the disappearance of vast numbers of former Russian sea/river coasters to the eastern Mediterranean, Black Sea and other distant parts of the world. Many new owners, particularly from the Baltic states, have entered the market, while the traditional western coaster owners or managers have, in many cases, expanded both the number and size of their vessels, some even now operating large deep-sea ships listed in *Ocean Ships*. When the previous edition was published, container feeder ships operating in the Baltic and North Seas were still mainly 300-600 TEU, whereas today 800-1200 TEU is normal and even larger vessels are in use or are planned.

The definition of which coastal cargo vessels should be included in the new edition has also presented a problem and continues the argument as to what is a coastal vessel. It is now normal to find 100,000 deadweight tonne tankers operating solely between the North Sea/Baltic production fields to northern European oil terminals. Conversely, many smaller northern European owned 'coastal' vessels can be found trading in the Far East, Australasia and across the Atlantic to North America. This edition aims to cover the fleets of the main owners, managers and operators based in northern Europe with vessels up to about 10,000 deadweight tonnes.

Reviewers of *Ocean Ships* have suggested that container capacity should be included. However, it is very apparent there can be very significant variations on published container capacity figures between the shipping registers, ship-owners and shipbuilders. Some refer to the theoretical maximum number of 20-foot equivalents (TEU) including empties that can be carried, while others indicate the number of loaded containers. In this edition, container ships continue to show the deadweight tonnage and the number of loaded TEU capable of being carried can be estimated by dividing the deadweight tonnage by the industry average of 14 tonnes per loaded TEU.

It has also been suggested that vessel IMO numbers should be included, as these normally remain with a vessel for life. However, the space required to include this additional column of information would mean either omitting some fleets or enlarging the book (and cost), while the display of individual IMO numbers would be of limited use without a separate IMO number index taking up even more space.

Thanks are due to many friends and correspondents for their comments and suggestions, also to the photographers who have again provided such a wide range of colour illustrations to enhance the appearance of the book.

Most importantly, now that our children have 'flown the nest' and our first granddaughter has arrived, apologies to my tolerant wife for the disruption to our social life and to the house during the many hours spent working on the book.

David Hornsby
Southampton, England
April 2010

Disclaimer

The publishers, the shipping companies and the Author accept no liability for any loss or damage caused by any error, inaccuracy or omission in the information published in this edition of *Coastal Ships and Ferries*.

Glossary

The companies in each section are listed in alphabetical order under the main company name, followed by the country of origin. Individual 'one-ship' owning companies are not given, but in some cases subsidiary fleets are separately listed. Other significant variations in ownership, joint ownership or management are generally covered by footnotes. Funnel and hull colours normally used are given for some of the principal companies or managers, although these may vary when a vessel is operating on a particular service, or on charter to another operator.

Name   registered name
        all vessels are single screw motorships unless indicated after the name as having more than one screw or other types of main propulsive machinery, as follows
        gt   *gas turbine*
        me   *diesel with electric drive*
        wj   *water-jet propulsion system*

Flag

Ant	Netherlands Antilles	Dma	Dominica	Kna	St Kitts & Nevis	Pol	Poland
Atf	Kerguelen Islands	Dmk	Denmark	Lbr	Liberia	Prt	Portugal
Atg	Antigua and Barbuda	Esp	Spain	Lka	Sri Lanka	Rus	Russia
Bel	Belgium	Est	Estonia	Ltu	Lithuania	Sgp	Singapore
Bhs	Bahamas	Fin	Finland	Lux	Luxembourg	Sle	Sierra Leone
Blz	Belize	Fra	France	Lva	Latvia	Svk	Slovakia
Bmu	Bermuda	Fro	Faroe Islands	Mda	Moldova	Svn	Slovenia
Brb	Barbados	Gbr	United Kingdom	Mhl	Marshall Islands	Swe	Sweden
Che	Switzerland	Geo	Georgia	Mlt	Malta	Ton	Tonga
Cok	Cook Islands	Gib	Gibraltar	Mmr	Myanmar (Burma)	Tuv	Tuvalu
Com	Union of Comoros	Hkg	Hong Kong (China)	Nis	Norwegian International	Vct	St. Vincent and
Cpv	Cape Verde	Iom	Isle of Man (British)	Nld	Netherlands		Grenadines
Cym	Cayman Islands	Irl	Irish Republic	Nor	Norway	Ukr	Ukraine
Cyp	Cyprus	Ita	Italy	Pan	Panama	Vut	Vanuatu
Deu	Germany	Jam	Jamaica	Phl	Philippines		
Dis	Danish International	Khm	Cambodia	Pmd	Madeira		

Year   *year of completion - not necessarily of launching or commissioning.*
GT   *gross tonnage - not weight, but volume of hull and enclosed space under 1969 International Tonnage Convention*
DWT   *deadweight tonnes - maximum weight of cargo, stores, fuel etc — one tonne (1000 kg) equals 0.984 ton (British)*
LOA   *overall length (metres); (- -) length between perpendiculars*
Bm   *moulded breadth of hull (metres) – some ferries and ro-ro vessels may have sponsons and be wider on waterline.*
Draft   *maximum laden draft (metres)*
Kts   *service speed in knots in normal weather and at loaded draft — one knot equals 6,050ft per hour or 1.146 mph.*

Supplementary information on Ferry Section

Pass   *maximum number of passengers (berthed, drivers or deck passengers)*
Car   *number of cars carried (approximate only depending on mix of goods vehicles – see below)*
HGV   *number of lorries, trailers or (r) rail vehicles carried (approximate figure depending on mix)*
Type   *general description of type of vessel*

Ferry Section type
F   *Freight ferry, some with limited driver accommodation*
P   *Passenger ferry*
R   *Train ferry*
T   *Twin-hull ferry*

Cargo vessel type   *general description of type of vessel*

B	*bulk carrier*	*C/ro*	*general cargo with roll-on ramp*	*Ro*	*roll-on, roll-off (often with container*
Bu	*bulk - self discharging*	*Cs*	*general cargo with slurry tanks*		*capacity*
C	*general cargo*	*hl*	*heavy-lift vessel*	*Rop*	*roll-on with pallet loading*
Cc	*general cargo with some*	*hls*	*heavy-lift / semi-submersible*	*T*	*product or bunkering tanker*
	container capacity	*Lng*	*liquefied natural gas*	*Ta*	*asphalt/bitumen tanker*
CC	*fully cellular container*	*Lpg*	*liquefied petroleum gas*	*Tch*	*chemical tanker*
Ce	*cement carrier*	*Lv*	*livestock carrier*	*V*	*vehicle carrier*
Cn	*nuclear fuel carrier*	*R*	*refrigerated cargo*		
Cp	*general cargo — pallet loading*	*Rc*	*refrigerated with containers*		

Remarks:

conv   *converted from other ship type (with former type and date where known)*
ex: *previous names followed by year of change to subsequent name*
l/a   *name at launch or 'float-out' prior to completion*
l/d   *name allocated when laid-down at commencement of construction*
pt: *part of ship*
len   *date hull lengthened*
sht   *date hull shortened*
wid   *date hull widened*
NE   *date re-engined*
teu   *twenty-foot equivalent unit (one teu equals about 14 tonnes deadweight)*

PART ONE
Northern European Ferries

P&O Ferries. Norsky. *Hans Kraijenbosch*

Name		Flag	Year	GT	Loa	Bm	Kts	Pass	Car	HGV	Type	Remarks

Anedin-Linjen Sweden

Funnel: White with narrow pale blue band above blue band and badge below black top.
Hull: White with blue 'Anedin-Linjen' aft, blue boot-topping.
History: Founded in 2002 to operate 'duty-free' day cruises.
Web: www.anedinlinjen.se
Routes: Day cruises from Stockholm to Mariehamn.

Name		Flag	Year	GT	Loa	Bm	Kts	Pass	Car	HGV	Type	Remarks
Birger Jarl		Swe	1953	3,564	92.7	14.2	12	1287	-	-	P	ex Baltic Star-02, Minisea-78, Bore Nord-77, Birger Jarl-73 (NE-82/89)

Baltic Scandinavia Lines AS Estonia

Funnel: Blue with upward pointing blue arrow on yellow disc.
Hull: Yellow with red boot-topping.
History: Founded 2005.
Web: www.bsl.ee
Routes: Kapellskär – Paldiski; Härnösand – Kaskö;

Name		Flag	Year	GT	Loa	Bm	Kts	Pass	Car	HGV	Type	Remarks
Gute *	(2)	Swe	1979	7,616	139.3	16.5	15	88	-	60	F	ex Sea Wind II-98, Sally Sun-95, Gute-92 (len-04)
Via Mare	(2)	Est	1975	8,023	117.9	19.9	18	107	30	76	F	ex Begona-05, Regina I-02, European Pathfinder-02, Panther-98, European Clearway-96

* chartered from Rederi AB Gotland, Sweden (see under Destination Gotland)

Basto Fosen Norway

Funnel: Buff with narrow red, white and red bands below narrow black top.
Hull: Dark blue with black boot-topping.
History: Founded 1995.
Web: www.basto-fosen.no
Routes: Moss – Horten.

Name		Flag	Year	GT	Loa	Bm	Kts	Pass	Car	HGV	Type	Remarks
Basto I		Nor	1997	5,505	109.0	18.0	14	550	200	18	P	
Basto II		Nor	1997	5,505	109.0	18.5	14	550	200	18	P	
Basto III	(2)	Nor	2005	7,310	116.6	19.0	17	550	212	-	P	

Bornholmstrafikken Denmark

Funnel: Turquoise with white vertical wave symbol on lighter turquoise broad band.
Hull: Turquoise with 'BORNHOLMS TRAFIKKEN' on white superstructure, red boot-topping.
History: Founded 1866 as 'Dampskibsselskabet paa Bornholm af 1866 A/S' until taken-over by the State in 1973.
Web: www.bornholmstrafikken.dk
Routes: Ronne - Koge; Ronne - Ystad; Ronne – Sassnitz (Mukran);

Name		Flag	Year	GT	Loa	Bm	Kts	Pass	Car	HGV	Type	Remarks
Dueodde	(2)	Dmk	2005	13,906	124.9	23.4	18	400	280	92	P	
Hammerodde	(2)	Dmk	2005	13,906	124.9	23.4	18	400	280	92	P	
Povl Anker	(2)	Dis	1978	12,131	121.2	21.5	17	1500	270	30	P	
Villum Clausen	(gt2wj)	Dis	2000	6,402	86.6	24.0	41	1037	215	0	T	

Brittany Ferries France

Funnel: White with blue over orange bands, interrupted by similar 'flag'.
Hull: White with blue above orange bands.
History: Founded 1973 as BAI SA (Bretagne-Angleterre-Irelande) and commenced operations later the same year.
Web: www.brittanyferries.com
Routes: Plymouth – Roscoff; Plymouth – Santander; Portsmouth – Caen; Portsmouth – St Malo; Portsmouth – Santander; Roscoff – Cork; Portsmouth – Cherbourg (seasonal); Poole – Santander (freight)

Name		Flag	Year	GT	Loa	Bm	Kts	Pass	Car	HGV	Type	Remarks
Armorique		Fra	2009	29,468	167.0	32.0	23	1500	470	65	P	
Barfleur	(2)	Fra	1992	20,133	157.7	23.3	19	1212	304	66	P	
Bretagne	(2)	Fra	1989	24,534	151.2	26.0	19	2056	580	84	P	
Cap Finistere	(2)	Fra	2001	32,728	203.9	25.0	28	1608	140	110	P	ex Superfast V-10
Condor Vitesse	(4wj)	Bhs	1997	5,007	86.6	26.0	40	754	185	0	T	ex Incat 044-98
Cotentin	(2)	Fra	2007	22,542	165.0	26.8	23	160		120	F	
Mont St. Michel	(2)	Fra	2002	35,586	173.4	28.5	21	2120	600	175	P	
Normandie	(2)	Fra	1992	27,541	161.4	26.0	20	2120	680	-	P	
Normandie Express	(4wj)	Fra	2000	6,581	97.2	26.2	40	900	260	-	T	
Normandie Vitesse		see Condor Vitesse under Condor Ferries										
Pont-Aven	(2)	Fra	2004	41,748	184.6	30.9	26	2,400	65-	-	P	

Brittany Ferries. Armorique. *Mike Lennon*

Brittany Ferries. Cotentin. *Oliver Sesemann*

Brittany Ferries. Mont St. Michel. *Allan Ryszka Onions*

Name		Flag	Year	GT	Loa	Bm	Kts	Pass	Car	HGV	Type	Remarks

Caledonian Maritime Assets Ltd — UK

CalMac Ferries Ltd
Funnel: Red with red lion rampant on yellow disc, black top.
Hull: Black with white 'Caledonian MacBrayne', red boot-topping.
History: Founded 2006 as subsidiary of Scottish government-owned Scottish Transport Group to take over routes of Caledonian MacBrayne Ltd, which started as David Hutcheson & Co in 1851.
Web: www.calmac.co.uk
Routes: Operates 25 routes off western Scotland, including Ardrossan - Brodick; Gourock - Dunoon; Kennacraig - Islay - Colonsay; Mallaig - Syke; Mallaig - Barra - South Uist; Oban - Barra - South Uist; Oban - Colonsay; Oban - Mull - Coll - Tiree; Bute - Largs - Arran; Ullapool - Lewis; Skye - Harris; Wemyss Bay – Bute; * Ballycastle – Cambeltown;

Name		Flag	Year	GT	Loa	Bm	Kts	Pass	Car	HGV	Type	Remarks
Argyle	(2)	Gbr	2007	2,643	72.0	15.3	14	450	60	-	P	
Bute	(2)	Gbr	2005	2,643	72.0	15.3	14	450	66	-	P	
Caledonian Isles	(2)	Gbr	1993	5,221	94.3	15.8	15	1000	110	0	P	
Clansman	(2)	Gbr	1998	5,499	101.0	15.8	16	634	90	-	P	
Coruisk	(2)	Gbr	2003	1,599	65.0	14.0	14	250	40	-	P	
Hebridean Isles	(2)	Gbr	1985	3,040	85.2	15.8	15	510	-	10	P	
Hebrides	(2)	Gbr	2001	5,506	99.4	15.8	16	650	103	-	P	
Isle of Arran	(2)	Gbr	1984	3,296	84.9	15.8	15	800	80	0	P	
Isle of Lewis	(2)	Gbr	1995	6,753	101.3	18.0	18	968	122	0	P	
Isle of Mull	(2)	Gbr	1988	4,719	90.1	15.8	15	1000	33	10	P	
Lord of the Isles	(2)	Gbr	1989	3,504	84.6	15.8	16	536	60	0	P	
Muirneag *		Gbr	1979	5,801	105.6	18.8	16	0	0	63	F	ex Belard-02, Mercandian Carrier II-85, Carrier II-85, Mercandian Carrier II-84, Alianza-83, Mercandian Carrier II-83

* chartered from Harrisons (2002) Ltd and managed by ASP Ship Management Ltd.
Also operates 17 smaller vessels.

Northlink Orkney & Shetland Ferries Ltd
Funnel: Pale blue with white 'N' on dark blue disc with pale blue/red top/bottom wedges.
Hull: Pale blue with black/white 'www.northlinkferries.co.uk', narrow white line above black boot-topping.
History: Founded 2000 by subsidiary of Scottish government-owned Scottish Transport Group.
Web: www.northlinkferries.co.uk
Routes: Aberdeen – Kirkwall; Lerwick – Kirkwall; Stromness – Scrabster;

Name		Flag	Year	GT	Loa	Bm	Kts	Pass	Car	HGV	Type	Remarks
Hamnavoe	(2)	Gbr	2002	8,780	112.0	18.5	19	600	110	0-	P	
Hascosay	(2)	Gbr	1971	6,136	118.4	16.0	14	12	0	46	F	ex Sea Clipper-02, Transbaltica-01, Sea Clipper-98, Commodore Clipper-96, Euro Nor-91, Misida-90, Normandia-86, Juno-79
Hjaltland	(2)	Gbr	2002	11,720	125.0	19.5	24	900	149	0	P	
Hrossey	(2)	Gbr	2002	11,720	125.0	19.5	24	900	149	0	P	

Celtic Link Ferries Ltd — Ireland

Funnel: Green with white 'CL' symbol.
Hull: Dark blue with green 'Celtic Link' and company logo on white superstructure or hull.
History: Founded 2005.
Web: www.celticlinkferries.com
Routes: Rosslare – Cherbourg.

Name		Flag	Year	GT	Loa	Bm	Kts	Pass	Car	HGV	Type	Remarks
Diplomat	(2)	Bmu	1978	16,776	151.0	23.6	17	112	-	160	F	ex European Diplomat-05, Pride of Suffolk-01, Baltic Ferry-92, Stena Transporter-80, Finnrose-80, Stena Transporter-79

Also operates **Norman Voyager** chartered from LD Lines qv

Clipper Group — Denmark

History: The parent Company was founded in 1972 and has a 30% shareholding in Mols-Linien A/S. The Company also owns the Danish operator Sydfynske A/S (formerly Scandlines Sydfynske A/S) operating 7 vessels on three routes and Nordic Ferry Services A/S jointly with Bornholmstrafikken A/S.

Seatruck Ferries Shipholding Ltd, UK
Funnel: White with white 'C' symbol on dark blue oval.
Hull: Dark blue with white 'SEATRUCK', red boot-topping. .
History: Founded 1996 and acquired by Clipper in 2002. Celtic Link's Dublin–Liverpool route was acquired in 2007.
Web: www.clipper-group.com; www.seatruckferries.com
Routes: Warrenpoint – Heysham; Dublin – Liverpool.

Name		Flag	Year	GT	Loa	Bm	Kts	Pass	Car	HGV	Type	Remarks
Arrow	(2)	Mlt	1998	7,606	122.3	19.8	17	12	0	70	F	ex RR Arrow-07, Varbola-05, Dart 6-99, Varbola-99
Clipper Pace		Cyp	2009	14,759	142.0	23.0	22	12	0	120	F	
Clipper Panorama		Cyp	2008	14,759	142.0	23.0	22	12	0	120	F	
Clipper Pennant		Cyp	2009	14,759	142.0	23.0	22	12	0	120	F	

Brittany Ferries. Normandie Express. *Allan Ryszka Onions*

Celtic Link Ferries. Diplomat. *Allan Ryszka Onions*

Name		Flag	Year	GT	Loa	Bm	Kts	Pass	Car	HGV	Type	Remarks
Clipper Point		Cyp	2008	14,759	142.0	23.0	22	12	0	120	F	
Clipper Racer	(2)	Mlt	1997	7,606	122.3	19.8	16	0	0	70	F	ex Triumph-08, RR Triumph-07, Lehola-05
Clipper Ranger	(2)	Mlt	1998	7,606	122.3	19.8	17	0	0	70	F	ex Challenge-08, RR Challenge-07, Lembitu-05, Celtic Sun-01, Lembitu-00, Dart 7-99, Lembitu -99
Moondance	(2)	Bhs	1978	5,881	116.3	17.4	15	0	37	71	F	ex Merchant Victor-97, Emadala-90
Shield *	(2)	Mlt	1999	7,606	122.3	19.8	17	0	0	70	F	ex RR Shield-07, Leili-05, Port Everglades Express-04, Leili-02

chartered-out to NorseLink.
Also see Mols-Linjen and DFDS

Cobelfret NV Belgium

Funnel: Yellow with red 'C' on white diamond on blue band.
Hull: Light grey with blue 'cobelfret ferries', red boot-topping.
History: Founded 1928 and acquired Dart Line in 2006. Also operates C2C container feeder routes as joint venture with ECS.
Web: www.cobelfret.com
Routes: Network of freight services from Zeebrugge to Esjberg, Gothenburg, Killingholme, Ipswich, Purfleet and Dublin, also Rotterdam to Dublin, Killingholme, Purfleet and Ipswich.

Name		Flag	Year	GT	Loa	Bm	Kts	Pass	Car	HGV	Type	Remarks
Aquiline		Bel	1980	22,748	177.0	26.5	20	0	0	213	F	ex Dart 9-06, Gu Bei Kou-99
Catherine		Lux	2002	21,287	182.2	25.8	18	12	0	212	F	ex Romira-02
Celandine	(2)	Bel	2000	23,987	162.5	25.2	17	12	0	157	F	
Celestine	(2)	Bel	1996	23,986	162.5	25.2	17	0	654	157	F	ex Sea Crusader-03, Celestine-96
Cervine	(2)	Bmu	1985	9,088	120.0	21.0	14	12	49	94	F	ex Dart 4-06, Sally Eurolink-97, Bazias 4-93, Balder Bre-85
Clementine	(2)	Bel	1997	23,986	162.5	25.2	17	12	654	157	F	
Cymbeline	(2)	Lux	1992	11,866	147.0	21.0	17	0	0	122	F	
Eglantine	(2)	Lux	1990	10,035	147.4	21.0	14	0	0	122	F	
Mazarine		Lux	2009	25,593	195.4	26.2	19	0	0	180	F	
Melusine	(2)	Bel	1999	23,987	162.5	25.2	18	0	654	157	f	
Palatine		Lux	2009	25,235	195.4	26.2	19	0	0	180	F	
Pauline	(2)	Lux	2006	49,166	203.0	31.0	21	12	0	305	F	
Phocine	(2)	Bmu	1984	9,088	120.0	21.0	14	12	49	94	F	ex Dart 3-06, Merle-00, Sally Euroroute-96, Bazias 3-93, Balder Sten-85
Ranine	(2)	Mlt	1978	7,635	141.3	17.4	15	12	87	91	F	ex Flanders Way-09, Gabrielle Wehr-01, Sari-93, Gabrielle Wehr-92, Tor Anglia-85, Gabrielle Wehr-82 (len-82)
Serpentine		Bel	1980	22,748	177.0	26.5	18	0	0	213	F	ex Dart 8-06, Xi Feng Kou-99
Symphorine	(2)	Lux	1988	10,030	147.3	21.0	14	0	0	122	F	
Taurine	(2)	Mlt	1977	7,628	141.3	17.4	15	12	67	91	F	ex Anglian Way-09,Thomas Wehr-01, Hornlink-94, Fuldatal-94, Santa Maria-93, Maria-93, Thomas Wehr-93, Dana Germania-86, Tor Neerlandia-85, Thomas Wehr-82, Wacro Express-78, I/a Thomas Wehr
Undine	(2)	Lux	1991	11,854	147.4	21.0	15	0	0	122	F	
Ursine	(2)	Bel	1979	16,947	170.3	21.0	16	12	186	140	F	ex Britta Oden-06, Tor Scandia-98, Britta Oden-88 (len-88)
Valentine	(2)	Bel	1999	23,987	162.5	25.2	18	0	635	157	F	
Victorine	(2)	Bel	2000	23,987	162.5	25.2	18	12	635	157	F	
Yasmine	(2)	Lux	2007	49,166	203.0	31.0	21	12	0	305	F	

Newbuildings: Eight further large ro-ro vessels on order for 2010-11 delivery.
managed by subsidiary EuroShip Services Ltd.
Also operates chartered-in vessels including from Wagenborg Shipping BV and Russ

Color Line AS Norway

Funnel: White with small blue over green, yellow and red waves inside large blue 'C'.
Hull: Blue with white 'Color Line'; fast ferries - white with 'ColorLineExpress'.
History: Founded in 1990, although roots back to 1890 through Jahre Line and Norway Line. Also in 1990 acquired the ferry business of Fred Olsen, followed in 1996 by Larvik Line and Scandi Line in 1998.
Web: www.colorline.com
Routes: Oslo – Kiel; Hirtshals – Kristiansand; Sandefjord – Stromstad; Hirtshals – Larvik (Express)

Name		Flag	Year	GT	Loa	Bm	Kts	Pass	Car	HGV	Type	Remarks
Bohus	(2)	Nor	1971	9,149	123.4	19.2	20	1520	230	40	P	ex Lion Princess-94, Europafarjan II-87, Europafarjan-85, Prinsessan Desiree-83
Color Fantasy	(2)	Nor	2004	75,027	223.7	35.0	22	2770	750	0	P	
Color Magic	(2)	Nor	2007	75,027	223.9	35.0	22	2750	750	0	P	
Color Viking	(2)	Nor	1985	19,763	134.0	24.0	16	2000	152	30	P	ex Stena Invicta-00, Peder Paars-91
SuperSpeed 1	(2)	Nor	2008	34,231	211.3	30.6	27	1929	764	0	P	

Cobelfret NV. Celandine. *Allan Ryszka Onions*

Cobelfret NV. Mazarine. *Hans Kraijenbosch*

Cobelfret NV. Serpentine. *Hans Kraijenbosch*

Name		Flag	Year	GT	Loa	Bm	Kts	Pass	Car	HGV	Type	Remarks
SuperSpeed 2	(2)	Nor	2008	34,231	212.8	30.6	27	1929	764	0	P	

Managed by subsidiary Color Line Marine AS.

Condor Ferries UK

Funnel: White with red above blue narrow bands.
Hull: Blue or white (fast ferries) with blue/red 'CONDOR Ferries' on white superstructure, red and blue bands above blue boot-topping
History: Founded 1964 jointly by Commodore Shipping Co Ltd and Holyman Ltd, becoming wholly owned by Commodore in 1998. In 2008 acquired by the Macquarie European Infrastructure Fund.
Web: www.condorferries.co.uk
Routes: Portsmouth – Channel Islands. Jersey – St. Malo; Poole – Jersey – St. Malo; Poole – Guernsey – Jersey; Jersey – Sark; Weymouth – Jersey and Guernsey

Name		Flag	Year	GT	Loa	Bm	Kts	Pass	Car	HGV	Type	Remarks
Commodore Clipper	(2)	Bhs	1999	14,000	129.1	23.4	18	500	279	94	P	
Commodore Goodwill	(2)	Bhs	1996	11,166	126.4	21.0	17	12	0	94	F	
Condor 10	(4wj)	Bhs	1993	3,241	74.2	26.0	38	576	90	-	T	
Condor Express	(4wj)	Bhs	1996	5,005	86.6	26.0	40	754	185	-	T	
Condor Vitesse *	(4wj)	Bhs	1997	5,007	86.6	26.0	40	754	200	-	T	ex InCat 044-98

* operated as a joint venture with Brittany Ferries.
Managed by subsidiary Condor Marine Services Ltd.

Destination Gotland Sweden

Funnel: Red with large white 'G'.
Hull: White with black 'Destination Gotland' separated by two red or red/grey arrows, red boot-topping.
History: Rederi AB Gotland founded in 1865.
Web: www.destinationgotland.se
Routes: Nynashamn – Visby; Oskarshamn – Visby; Grankullavik – Visby;

Name		Flag	Year	GT	Loa	Bm	Kts	Pass	Car	HGV	Type	Remarks
Gotland	(2)	Swe	2003	29,746	195.8	25.0	28	1500	500	-	P	
Gotlandia	(4wj)	Swe	1999	5,632	112.5	15.7	35	700	110	8	P	ex HSC Gotlandia-06, HSC Gotland-99
Gotlandia II	(4wj)	Swe	2006	6,554	122.0	16.7	36	780	160	8	P	
Visby	(2)	Swe	2003	29,746	195.8	25.0	28	1500	520	-	P	

Formed jointly by Silja Line and Rederi AB Gotland..
Also see Baltic Scandinavian Lines As

DFDS A/S Denmark

DFDS Seaways
Funnel: White with white cross on dark blue disc and diagonal stripes in three shades of blue.
Hull: White with blue 'DFDS SEAWAYS' and three diagonal blue stripes, blue boot-topping.
History: Founded 1866 as Det Forenede Dampskibs-Selskab (The United Steamship Company), when the three largest Danish shipping companies were merged; Formed Nordana Line in 1957 and Mols Line in 1966. By 1964, J Lauritzen held more than 50% of Company. Began collaboration with Tor Line in early 1970's and acquired control in 1982. Parent name changed to DFDS in 1971 and passenger services as Scandinavian Seaways from 1988 changing to DFDS Seaways in 1999. Prior to the acquisition of Norfolk Line, Vesterhavet A/S (Lauritzen) and DSV Holdings controlled 56% of DFDS with a further 15% held by Clipper Group. After the acquisition, Vesterhavet/DSV will hold about 36% and AP Moller-Maersk about 31% of the enlarged Company.
Web: www.dfds.com; www.dfdsseaways.co.uk
Routes: Copenhagen – Oslo; Esbjerg – Harwich; Ijmuiden (Amsterdam) – North Shields (Newcastle);

Name		Flag	Year	GT	Loa	Bm	Kts	Pass	Car	HGV	Type	Remarks
Crown of Scandinavia	(2)	Dis	1994	35,498	169.4	27.6	18	2136	400	8	P	I/a Thomas Mann
Dana Sirena	(2)	Dis	2002	22,382	199.4	23.4	22	600	-	155	P	I/a Golfo del Delfini
King of Scandinavia	(2)	Dis	1987	31,788	161.0	27.6	20	2280	570	-	P	ex Val de Loire-06, Nils Holgersson-93
Pearl of Scandinavia	(2)	Dis	1989	40,039	178.4	29.6	20	2000	350	72	P	ex Aquarius-01, Langkapuri Star Aquarius-01, Star Aquarius-93, Athena-93
Princess of Norway	(2)	Dis	1986	31,356	161.5	27.6	18	1377	355	35	P	ex Fjord Norway-06, Spir-03, Spirit of Tasmania-02, Peter Pan-93

AB DFDS Lisco
Funnel: Dark blue with white cross inside white ring.
Hull: White with blue 'DFDS LISCO', red boot-topping.
History: Founded 2001 as AS LISCO Baltic Service following re-organisation of Lithuanian Shipping Co, almost immediately being acquired by DFDS Tor Line and being renamed in 2006.
Web: www.lisco.lt
Routes: Klaipeda – Kiel; Klaipeda – Karlshamn; Klaipeda – Sassnitz;

Name		Flag	Year	GT	Loa	Bm	Kts	Pass	Car	HGV	Type	Remarks
Kaunas	(2)	Ltu	1989	25,606	190.9	26.0	16	289	460	49r	R	(conv-Ro-94)
Lisco Gloria	(2)	Ltu	2001	20,140	199.0	23.4	23	302	316	166	P	ex Dana Gloria-03, Golfo dei Coralli-02
Lisco Maxima	(2)	Ltu	2009	25,518	199.1	27.0	25	515	-	190	P	
Lisco Optima	(2)	Ltu	1999	25,206	186.0	25.6	21	240	221	172	P	ex Svealand-06, Alyssa-01,
Lisco Patria	(2)	Ltu	1991	18,332	154.0	24.0	18	408	-	120	P	ex Stena Traveller-04, TT-Traveller-02, Stena Traveller-96, TT-Traveller-95, Stena Traveller-92

Condor Ferries. Commodore Clipper. *Tom Walker*

Condor Ferries. Condor Vitesse. *Tom Walker*

DFDS Seaways. Crown of Scandinavia. *Hans Kraijenbosch*

Name		Flag	Year	GT	Loa	Bm	Kts	Pass	Car	HGV	Type	Remarks
Vilnius	(2)	Ltu	1987	22,341	190.9	26.0	16	144	0	120	R	ex Vilnyus

DFDS Tor Line

Funnel: Dark blue with white cross inside white ring.
Hull: Blue with white 'DFDS TOR LINE', red boot-topping.
History: Commenced operations as Tor Line in 1966, a joint venture between Swedish Trans Oil Shipping and Rex Shipping. DFDS acquired the passenger services in 1981 and the freight services in 1982.
Web: www.dfdstorline.com
Routes: Gothenburg – Immingham; Gothenburg – Tilbury (AngloBridge); Esbjerg – Harwich and Esbjerg – Immingham (BritanniaBridge); Gothenburg – Ghent and Ghent – Brevik (EuroBridge); Cuxhaven – Immingham (ElbeBridge); Immingham – Brevik (NorBridge); Rotterdam – Immingham and Ijmuiden – Newcastle (ShortBridge); Fredericia/Copenhagen/Aarhus – Klaipeda (BalticBridge); Karlshamn – Kiel – St Petersburg (NevaBridge)

Name		Flag	Year	GT	Loa	Bm	Kts	Pass	Car	HGV	Type	Remarks
Aquae †		Gbr	1986	12,189	145.0	20.4	17	12	0	160	F	ex Tor Cimbria-06, Dana Cimbria-00, I/a Mercandian Express II
Ark Forwarder §	(2)	Gbr	1998	21,104	182.6	25.5	22	12	-	189	F	ex Stena Forwarder-07, Mont Ventoux-05, Sea Centurion-02, I/a Stena Ausonia
Envoy ‡	(2)	Nis	1979	18,653	150.0	20.7	17	70	0	133	F	ex European Envoy-04, Ibex-98, Norsky-95, Norsea-86, Ibex-80
Tor Baltica	(2)	Lva	1977	14,374	163.6	19.9	18	12	0	142	F	ex Elk-01 (len-86)
Tor Begonia		Swe	2004	32,289	199.8	26.5	22	12	0	258	F	
Tor Belgia *		Swe	1978	21,491	193.3	25.0	16	12	200	207	F	ex Tor Britannia-99, Maersk Kent-92, Kamina-90, Ville du Havre-87, Foss Havre-81, Ville du Havre-78 (len-94)
Tor Bellona ‡		Nis	1980	22,748	177.0	26.5	21	0	0	213	F	ex Massillia-05, Dart 10-03, Mont Ventoux-01, Dart 10-99, Zhang Jia Kou-99
Tor Botnia		Ltu	2000	11,530	162.6	20.6	20	12	0	120	F	ex Finnmaster-09
Tor Britannia	(2)	Dis	2000	24,196	197.5	25.9	21	12	0	198	F	
Tor Corona †	(2)	Gbr	2008	25,609	187.1	26.5	20	12	0	230	F	
Tor Dania †	(2)	Gbr	1978	21,850	193.6	25.0	19	12	200	207	F	ex Brit Dania-93, Tor Dania-93, Maersk Essex-92, Dana Hafnia-89, Railo-88, G and C Express-88, Ville de Dunkerque-86, Foss Dunkerque-81, Ville de Dunkerque-79 (len-95)
Tor Ficaria		Dis	2006	32,289	199.8	26.5	22	12	0	258	F	
Tor Finlandia		Ltu	2000	11,530	162.6	20.6	20	12	0	120	F	ex Finnreel-09, Finnmaid-00
Tor Fionia †	(2)	Gbr	2009	25,609	187.1	26.5	20	12	0	230	F	
Tor Freesia		Swe	2005	32,289	199.8	26.5	22	12	0	258	F	
Tor Futura		Dis	1996	18,725	183.3	25.2	19	12	0	156	F	ex Dana Futura-00
Tor Hafnia †	(2)	Gbr	2008	25,609	187.1	26.5	20	12	0	230	F	
Tor Humbria **		Nis	1978	20,165	178.1	24.0	16	12	0	180	F	ex Borac-99, Finneagle-87, Fosseagle-85, Abuja Express-83, Emirates Express-81
Tor Jutlandia	(2)	Gbr	2010	25,609	184.8	26.5	20	12	0	250	F	
Tor Magnolia		Dis	2003	32,289	199.8	26.5	22	12	0	258	F	
Tor Minerva **		Nis	1978	21,215	177.4	24.0	16	12	0	180	F	ex Dana Minerva-00, Boracay-98, Karawa-87, Saudi Express-86, Jolly Avorio-86, Saudi Express-83, Bandar Abbas Express-80
Tor Petunia		Dis	2004	32,289	199.8	26.5	22	12	0	258	F	
Tor Primula		Dis	2004	32,289	199.8	26.5	22	12	0	258	F	
Tor Selandia	(2)	Swe	1998	24,196	197.5	25.2	21	12	0	198	F	
Tor Suecia	(2)	Swe	1999	24,196	197.0	25.9	21	12	0	198	F	

Chartered from * Eidsiva Rederi ASA, Norway, ** from CS & Partners A/S, Denmark, † from companies managed by Norbulk Shipping UK Ltd, ‡ from Taubatkompaniet AS, Norway or § from Stena Group

Norfolk Line, Netherlands

Funnel: Black with white 7-pointed star on broad pale blue band.
Hull: Pale blue with black 'NORFOLK LINE'.
History: Founded 1961 as a logistics company, entering shipping in 1969. Company acquired in 1984 by AP Moller-Maersk from Unilever and in 2005 acquired Norse Merchant Ferries. Acquired by DFDS in 2009 with Maersk taking a 31% shareholding in DFDS.
Web: www.norfolkline.com
Routes: Dover – Dunkerque; Rosyth – Zeebrugge; Vlaardingen (Rotterdam) – Felixstowe and Killingholme; Dublin/Belfast – Heysham/Liverpool; Esbjerg – Immingham/Harwich.

Name		Flag	Year	GT	Loa	Bm	Kts	Pass	Car	HGV	Type	Remarks
Dublin Viking	(2)	Gbr	1997	21,856	186.0	25.6	24	340	100	164	P	ex Mersey Viking-05
Humber Viking	(2)	Gbr	2009	29,004	193.3	26.0	21	12	0	254	F	
Lagan Viking	(2)	Gbr	2005	27,510	186.0	25.6	23	980	160	180	P	
Liverpool Viking	(2)	Gbr	1997	21,856	186.0	25.6	24	340	100	164	P	ex Lagan Viking-05
Maas Viking	(2)	Gbr	2009	29,004	193.3	26.0	21	12	0	254	F	
Maersk Anglia	(2)	Nld	2000	13,073	142.5	23.2	18	12	0	121	F	
Maersk Delft	(2)	Gbr	2006	35,923	186.7	28.4	25	780	200	120	P	
Maersk Dover	(2)	Gbr	2006	35,923	186.7	28.4	25	780	200	120	P	

DFDS Tor Line. Tor Finlandia. *Hans Kraijenbosch*

DFDS Tor Line. Tor Hafnia. *Hans Kraijenbosch*

DFDS Tor Line. Tor Magnolia. *Allan Ryszka Onions*

Name		Flag	Year	GT	Loa	Bm	Kts	Pass	Car	HGV	Type	Remarks
Maersk Dunkerque	(2)	Gbr	2006	35,923	186.7	28.4	25	780	320	146	P	
Maersk Exporter	(2)	Nld	1996	13,017	142.5	23.2	18	12	0	120	F	
Maersk Flanders	(2)	Nld	2000	13,073	142.5	23.2	18	12	0	121	F	
Maersk Importer	(2)	Nld	1996	13,017	142.5	23.2	18	12	0	120	F	
Mersey Viking	(2)	Gbr	2005	27,510	186.6	25.6	23	980	160	180	P	
Scottish Viking	(2)	Ita	2009	27,700	186.5	25.6	24	528	-	120	P	

Rederij G Doeksen en Zonen BV
Netherlands

NV Terschellinger Stoomboot Maatschappij

Funnel: Blue, some with white vertical bands.
Hull: White with blue 'seal' and three blue angled bands.
History: Founded 1923 to take over NV Terschellinger Stoomboot Maatschappij.
Web: www.rederij-doeksen.nl
Routes: Harlingen – Terschelling-West; Harlingen – Vlieland;

Name		Flag	Year	GT	Loa	Bm	Kts	Pass	Car	HGV	Type	Remarks
Friesland		Nld	1989	3,583	69.0	15.5	13	1790	122	16	P	
Midsland	(2)	Nld	1974	1,812	77.9	12.0	15	1600	65	-	P	ex Rheinland-93 (len-80)
Vlieland	(4)	Nld	2005	2,726	67.8	17.0	15	1300	59	-	T	

Also operates two smaller passenger vessels and one freight catamaran.

Rederi AB Eckero
Finland

Funnel: White with yellow 'E' on blue disc, blue top.
Hull: White with blue 'ECKERO LINE' and 'E' symbol interrupting blue above yellow bands, blue boot-topping.
History: gained majority control of Birka Line in 2007.
Web: www.eckeroline.fi of www.eckeroline.ee
Routes: Tallinn – Helsinki;

Name		Flag	Year	GT	Loa	Bm	Kts	Pass	Car	HGV	Type	Remarks
Eckero	(2)	Swe	1979	12,358	121.2	21.5	17	1500	270	30	P	ex Jens Kofoed-05
Nordlandia	(2)	Fin	1981	21,473	153.4	24.2	20	2048	55	65	P	ex Nord Gotlandia-98, Olau Hollandia-89
Translandia	(2)	Fin	1976	13,867	135.5	21.7	17	126	-	-	F	ex Transparaden-04, Rosebay-01, Eurocruiser-98, Eurostar-97, Rosebay-97, Transgermania-93

Birka Line AB, Finland

Funnel: White with separated blue, yellow and red angled stripes.
Hull: White with narrow blue band and blue boot-topping.
History: Founder 1971 as Birka Line, forming Birka Cruises in 1986.
Web: www.birkaline.com
Routes: Baltic cruising;

Name		Flag	Year	GT	Loa	Bm	Kts	Pass	Car	HGV	Type	Remarks
Birka Paradise	(2)	Fin	2004	34,728	176.9	28.0	21	1800	0	0	P	

Also see vessels in Cargo Section.

AG Ems
Germany

Funnel: Buff with black top.
Hull: White with black boot-topping.
History: Founded 1890.
Web: www.ag-ems.de
Routes: Emden and Eemshaven – Borkum; Wilhelmshaven – Helgoland..

Name		Flag	Year	GT	Loa	Bm	Kts	Pass	Car	HGV	Type	Remarks
Groningerland	(2)	Deu	1991	1,070	44.4	12.2	12	621	30	0	P	ex Hilligenlei-06
Helgoland	(2)	Deu	1972	1,812	77.9	12.0	15	1600	65	0	P	ex Westfalen-06
Munsterland	(2)	Deu	1986	1,859	78.7	12.6	15	1200	75	0	P	
Ostfriesland	(2)	Deu	1985	1,859	78.7	12.6	15	1200	75	0	P	

Also operates smaller passenger vessel and a passenger-only catamaran

Fastnet Line
Ireland

Funnel: White with black top.
Hull: Blue with black boot-topping.
History: Newly founded service commencing operations in 2010.
Web: www.fastnetline.com
Routes: Cork-Swansea.

Name		Flag	Year	GT	Loa	Bm	Kts	Pass	Car	HGV	Type	Remarks
Julia	(2)	Bhs	1982	22,161	153.4	24.2	20	1860	440	30	P	ex Christian IV-08, Bayard-90, Olau Britannia-90

Finnlines Oy
Finland

Funnel: White or black with black 'F' on white disc interrupting narrow blue band on broad white band or blue 'BC' between narrow blue bands.
Hull: White or blue with contrasting 'Finnlines' or 'FINNCARRIERS', red or blue boot topping.
History: Founded 1947 as subsidiary of Merivienti Oy by partly state-owned companies. Formed Finncarriers jointly with Finland Steamship Co (later Effoa)

DFDS – Norfolk Line. Maas Viking. *Hans Kraijenbosch*

DFDS – Norfolk Line. Maersk Dunkerque. *Tom Walker*

DFDS – Norfolk Line. Maersk Flanders. *Hans Kraijenbosch*

Rederij G Doeksen. Vlieland. *Hans Kraijenbosch*

Finnlines Oy. Birka Exporter. *Allan Ryszka Onions*

Finnlines Oy. Finnhawk. *C. Lous*

Finnlines Oy. Finnlady. *Hans Kraijenbosch*

Finnlines Oy. Finnpartner. *Hans Kraijenbosch*

Foreland Shipping. Beachy Head (in Transfennica charter colours). *Hans Kraijenbosch*

Name		Flag	Year	GT	Loa	Bm	Kts	Pass	Car	HGV	Type	Remarks

in 1975. In 1982, Enso-Gutzeit sold their 75% share of Finnlines to other operators and their share of Finncarriers to Effoa. In 1990, after several mergers, Finnlines was re-born, acquiring Bore Line in 1992 and entering into joint venture with Poseidon Schiffahrt AG, until the Stinnes Group share was acquired in 1997 including Railship and 40% of Team Lines. Balance of Team Lines acquired in 2001 and in 2002 Nordo-Link became a subsidiary. In 2007, the Italian Grimadi Group acquired a minority interest, later reportedly increased to 50.7% control.

Web: www.finnlines.fi
Routes: Numerous North Sea and Baltic services.

Name		Flag	Year	GT	Loa	Bm	Kts	Pass	Car	HGV	Type	Remarks
Amber		Nis	1993	6,719	122.0	19.0	12	12	0	92	F	
Antares	(2)	Nis	1988	19,963	157.6	25.3	20	12	500	100	F	ex Finnforest-88
Baltica		Deu	1990	21,124	157.7	25.0	19	5	0	164	F	ex Transbaltica-03, Ahlers Baltic-95
Birka Carrier		Fin	1998	12,251	154.5	22.7	20	12	0	125	F	ex United Carrier-02
Birka Exporter		Fin	1991	6,620	122.0	19.0	16	0	0	90	F	ex Grano-02
Birka Express		Fin	1997	12,251	154.5	22.7	20	12	0	125	F	ex United Express-02
Birka Shipper		Fin	1992	6,620	122.0	19.0	16	0	0	90	F	ex Styrso-02
Birka Trader		Fin	1998	12,251	154.5	22.7	20	12	0	125	F	ex United Trader-02
Birka Transporter		Fin	1991	6,620	122.0	19.0	16	0	0	90	F	ex Hamno-02
Europalink	(2)	Swe	2007	45,923	218.8	30.5	25	500	-	300	P	l/a Finnlady
Finlandia	(2)	Deu	1981	19,524	157.8	24.6	19	24	0	171	F	ex Transfinlandia-04
Finnarrow *	(2)	Swe	1996	25,996	168.0	27.7	21	119	800	0	F	ex Gotland-97
Finnclipper	(2)	Swe	1999	29,841	188.1	28.7	22	440	0	176	P	l/a Stena Seapacer 1
Finneagle	(2)	Swe	1999	29,841	188.0	28.7	20	440	0	176	P	l/a Stena Seapacer 2
Finnfellow	(2)	Swe	2000	33,769	188.1	28.7	21	452	0	160	P	ex Stena Britannica-03
Finnforest **	(2)	Swe	1978	15,525	156.0	22.7	17	12	0	143	F	ex Bore Britannica-96, Stena Britannica-88, Stena Hispania-86, Kotka Violet-85, Stena Hispania-84, Merxario Hispania-83, Atlantic Project-81 (wid-79)
Finnhansa	(2)	Fin	1994	32,531	183.0	28.7	18	90	0	230	F	
Finnhawk		Gbr	2001	11,530	162.6	20.6	20	12	0	120	F	
Finnktaft		Gbr	2000	11,530	162.6	20.6	20	12	0	120	F	
Finnlady	(2)	Fin	2007	45,923	218.8	30.5	25	500	0	300	P	ex Europalink-07
Finnmaid	(2)	Fin	2006	45,923	218.8	30.5	25	500	0	300	P	
Finnmill	(2)	Swe	2002	25,654	184.8	26.5	20	12	0	200	F	
Finnpartner	(2)	Swe	1994	32,534	183.0	28.7	18	90	0	230	F	
Finnpulp	(2)	Swe	2002	25,654	184.8	26.5	20	12	0	200	F	l/a Finncarrier
Finnsailor	(2)	Swe	1987	20,783	158.4	25.0	20	119	0	112	F	
Finnstar	(2)	Fin	2006	45,923	218.8	30.5	25	500	0	300	P	
Finntrader	(2)	Fin	1995	32,534	183.0	28.7	18	90	0	230	F	
Inowroclaw †	(2)	Pol	1980	14,786	137.2	23.0	15	12	0	112	F	
Nordlink	(2)	Swe	2007	45,923	218.8	30.5	25	500	0	300	P	
Transeuropa	(2)	Deu	1995	32,534	183.0	28.7	18	90	0	230	F	
Translubeca	(2)	Deu	1990	24,727	157.6	25.3	20	84	200	146	F	

* chartered to Stena Group.
** owned by Stromma Turism & Sjofart AB, both Sweden
† chartered from Euroafrica Linie Sp z oo, Poland
See also Foreland Shipping Ltd, UK

Fjord Line AS   Norway

Funnel: Red with yellow 'f' inside yellow ring, black top.
Hull: Red with white 'fjordline.no' and yellow wave below dark blue over narrow yellow bands.
History: Formed 1995 and merged with Master Ferries in 2008.
Web: www.fjordline.com
Routes: Bergen – Stavanger – Hirtshals; Hirtshals – Kristiansand;

Name		Flag	Year	GT	Loa	Bm	Kts	Pass	Car	HGV	Type	Remarks
Bergensfjord	(2)	Dis	1993	16,784	134.5	24.0	18	882	350	0	P	ex Atlantic Traveller-08, Duchess of Scandinavia-05, Bergen-03
Fjord Cat	(4wj)	Dis	1998	5,619	91.3	26.0	43	800	240	0	T	ex Master Cat-08, Incat 049-06, Mads Mols-05, Cat-Link V-99

Foreland Shipping   UK

Funnel: Yellow with crest on broad green band, black top.
Hull: Green with red boot-topping.
History: Founded 2001 by Andrew Weir Shipping, Bibby Line Group, James Fisher & Sons PLC and The Hadley Shipping Co to operate ships for British Government military supplies.
Web: www.foreland-shipping.co.uk
Routes: UK to British armed forces overseas bases; two normally chartered-out commercially, but available for emergency recall.

Name		Flag	Year	GT	Loa	Bm	Kts	Pass	Car	HGV	Type	Remarks
Anvil Point	(2)	Gbr	2003	23,235	193.0	26.0	17	12	0	189	F	
Beachy Head *	(2)	Gbr	2003	23,235	193.0	26.0	17	12	0	189	F	
Eddystone	(2)	Gbr	2002	23,235	193.0	26.0	17	12	0	189	F	
Hartland Point	(2)	Gbr	2002	23,235	193.0	26.0	17	12	0	189	F	
Hurst Point	(2)	Gbr	2002	23,235	193.0	26.0	17	12	0	189	F	
Longstone *	(2)	Gbr	2003	23,235	193.0	26.0	17	12	0	189	F	

Hurtigruten ASA. Trollfjord (in former funnel colours) . *F. de Vries*

Irish Ferries. Ulysses. *Mike Lennon*

LD Lines. Norman Voyager. *Allan Ryszka Onions*

Name		Flag	Year	GT	Loa	Bm	Kts	Pass	Car	HGV	Type	Remarks

currently chartered to Finnlines qv
Managed by Andrew Weir Shipping Ltd, UK.

Hurtigruten ASA Norway

Funnel: Black with white 'H' above wave on red disc.
Hull: Black with broad red upper band and red boot-topping.
History: Established 'Norwegian Coastal Express' service, operated by several companies and more recently by Ofotens of Vesteraalens Dampskips and Troms Fylkes Dampskibs, who merged in 2006.
Web: www.hurtigruten.no; www.hurtigruten.co.uk
Routes: Daily coastal service from Bergen to Kirkenes with 32 intermediate calls, also cruises to Greenland and Spitzbergen.

Name		Flag	Year	GT	Loa	Bm	Kts	Pass	Car	HGV	Type	Remarks
Finnmarken	(2)	Nor	2002	15,690	135.8	21.5	18	1009	50	0	P	
Fram	(2me)	Nor	2007	11,647	113.9	20.2	15	500	0	0	P	
Kong Harald	(2)	Nor	1993	11,204	121.8	19.2	18	691	50	0	P	
Lofoten		Nor	1964	2,621	87.4	13.3	16	500	0	0	P	
Midnatsol	(2)	Nor	2003	16,151	135.8	21.5	18	822	50	0	P	
Nordkapp	(2)	Nor	1996	11,386	123.3	19.5	15	883	50	0	P	
Nordlys	(2)	Nor	1994	11,204	121.7	19.2	15	691	50	0	P	
Nordnorge	(2)	Nor	1997	11,384	123.3	19.2	18	690	40	0	P	
Nordstjernen		Nor	1956	2,191	80.8	12.6	15	435	0	0	P	
Polarlys	(2)	Nor	1996	11,341	123.0	19.5	15	737	50	0	P	
Richard With	(2)	Nor	1993	11,205	121.8	19.2	15	691	50	0	P	
Trollfjord	(2)	Nor	2002	16,140	133.0	21.5	16	982	50	0	P	
Vesteralen	(2)	Nor	1983	6,262	108.6	16.5	17	410	40	0	P	

Irish Ferries Ireland

Funnel: Green with white shamrock symbol on pale blue, green and dark blue angled square edged white.
Hull: White with dark blue 'IRISH FERRIES' and pale blue, green and dark blue wave symbol, green boot-topping.
History: Founded 1987 as Irish Continental Line, part owned by Irish Shipping and Lion Ferry.
Web: www.irishferries.com
Routes: Dublin – Holyhead; Rosslare – Pembroke; Rosslare – Cherbourg; Rosslare – Roscoff;

Name		Flag	Year	GT	Loa	Bm	Kts	Pass	Car	HGV	Type	Remarks
Isle of Inishmore	(2)	Cyp	1997	34,031	182.5	27.8	21	2200	800	122	P	
Jonathan Swift	(4wj)	Cyp	1999	5,989	86.6	24.0	37	800	200	0	T	
Oscar Wilde	(2)	Bhs	1987	31,914	166.3	28.4	22	1464	580	95	P	ex Kronprins Harald-07
Ulysses	(2)	Cyp	2001	50,938	209.1	31.2	22	1875	1342	300	P	

Isle of Man Steam Packet Co Ltd UK

Funnel: Red, some with white three legged symbol within white ring.
Hull: Dark blue with white 'STEAM-PACKET.COM', narrow white band above red boot-topping;
History: Founded 1830 and now owned by Australian investor-management Macquarie Bank Ltd, which acquired the company in 2005 from Montague Private Equity, who had earlier acquired ownership from Sea Containers.
Web: www.steam-packet.com
Routes: Douglas – Heysham; Douglas – Liverpool/Birkenhead; Douglas – Belfast; Douglas – Dublin;

Name		Flag	Year	GT	Loa	Bm	Kts	Pass	Car	HGV	Type	Remarks
Ben-My-Chree	(2)	Iom	1998	12,504	125.2	23.4	18	500	303	90	P	
Manannan	(4wj)	Iom	1998	6,360	96.0	26.0	42	600	240	0	T	ex Incat 050-09, Joint Venture-08, Incat 050-02
Snaefell	(4wj)	Gbr	1991	3,003	74.0	26.0	35	450	80	0	T	ex Sea Express I-07, Seacat Isle of Man-05, Seacat Norge-97, Seacat Isle of Man-96, Seacat Boulogne-94, Hoverspeed France-94, Sardegna Express-92, Hoverspeed France-92
Viking	(4wj)	Gbr	1997	4,462	100.0	17.1	38	782	175	0	P	ex Superseacat Two-08

Isles of Scilly Steamship Co Ltd UK

Funnel: Buff with white '+' on blue houseflag.
Hull: White with red boot-topping.
History: Founded 1920.
Web: www.islesofscilly-travel.co.uk
Routes: Scilly Isles – Penzance;

Name		Flag	Year	GT	Loa	Bm	Kts	Pass	Car	HGV	Type	Remarks
Scillonian III	(2)	Gbr	1977	1,346	68.0	11.3	15	600	0	0	P	

*Also operates small coaster **Gry Maritha** (81/590 gt)*

LD Lines France

Funnel: White with blue-edged houseflag having white 'LD' on red diamond.
Hull: Dark blue with white/red 'www.LDLines.com', red boot-topping.
History: Subsidiary of Louis Dreyfus Armateurs founded 1893.

Name		Flag	Year	GT	Loa	Bm	Kts	Pass	Car	HGV	Type	Remarks
Web:	www.ldlines.co.uk											
Routes:	Boulogne – Dover; Le Havre – Portsmouth; Ramsgate – Ostend (jointly with TransEuropa Ferries qv)											
Norman Arrow		Gbr	2009	10,841	112.6	30.5	40	1200	195	30	T	(alternatively up to 417 cars)
Norman Bridge	(2)	Gbr	1999	22,152	180.0	24.3	20	399	130	40	P	ex Ave Liepaja-10, Blanca del Mar-08, Brave Merchant-06
Norman Leader		Gbr	2010	25,000	161.0	25.6	19	1215	200	60	P	
Norman Voyager *		Gbr	2008	26,500	186.5	25.6	24	800	185	120	P	
Ostend Spirit	(2)	Gbr	1992	28,833	163.4	27.0	21	1850	550	100	P	ex Norman Spirit-10, Pride of Aquitaine-05, PO Aquitaine-03, P&OSL Aquitaine-02, Stena Royal-99, Prins Filip-98

* chartered out to Celtic Ferries qv

Transmanche Ferries

Funnel:	Yellow with blue 'T' symbol on white disc.											
Hull:	Yellow with blue 'T' symbol on white disc.											
History:	Subsidiary operating route on behalf of Dieppe Public Ownership grouping.											
Web:	www.transmancheferries.com											
Routes:	Dieppe – Newhaven;											
Cote d'Albatre	(2)	Fra	2006	18,425	142.5	24.2	22	600	300	62	P	
Seven Sisters	(2)	Fra	2006	18,425	142.5	24.2	22	600	300	62	P	

Mann Lines   Germany

Funnel:	Black with white 'E' on broad pale blue band edged with narrow white bands.											
Hull:	Green with yellow 'Mann Lines'.											
History:	Subsidiary of privately-owned Mann Group previously operating as Argomann Ferry Service from 1992 to 2001.											
Web:	www.mannlines.com											
Routes:	Cuxhaven – Paldiski – Turku – Bremerhaven – Harwich; Paldiski – Haraholmen – Sheerness – Flushing;											
Estraden	(2)	Fin	1999	18,205	162.7	25.2	19	12	0	140	F	ex Amazon-01, Estraden-99

Chartered from OY Rettig Group AB, Finland.

Mols-Linien A/S   Denmark

Funnel:	White with yellow 'ML' symbol over blue diamond.											
Hull:	White with blue 'Mols-Linien', blue boot-topping.											
History:	Founded 1966 by DFDS, acquired 1984 by J Lauritzen and 1988 by investment group Difko. In 1999, Scandlines acquired 40% interest, later reduced to 30%, which in 2007 was acquired by Clipper Group.											
Web:	www.mols-linien.dk											
Routes:	Odden – Ebeltoft; Oden – Arhus; Kalundborg – Arhus;											
Mai Mols	(gt/4wj)	Dmk	1996	3,971	76.1	23.4	43	450	120	0	T	
Maren Mols	(2)	Dmk	1996	14,379	136.4	24.0	19	600	344	82	P	
Max Mols	(4wj)	Dmk	1998	5,617	92.0	26.0	45	800	240	0	T	ex Cat-Link IV-99
Mette Mols	(2)	Dmk	1996	14,221	136.4	24.0	19	600	344	82	P	
Mie Mols	(gt/4wj)	Dmk	1996	3,971	78.0	23.4	43	450	120	0	T	

AG Reederei Norden-Frisia   Germany

Funnel:	Yellow 'F' on equal black over red over blue bands.											
Hull:	White with black boot-topping.											
History:	Founded 1881.											
Web:	www.reederei-frisia.de											
Routes:	Norddeich to German Frisian Islands and excursions.											
Frisia I	(3)	Deu	1970	1,020	63.6	12.0	11	800	52	0	P	(len-85)
Frisia II	(2)	Deu	1978	1,125	63.5	12.0	11	1,350	42	0	P	
Frisia IV	(4me)	Deu	2002	1,574	70.7	13.4	12	1,350	58	5	P	
Frisia V	(3)	Deu	1965	1,007	63.0	12.0	11	800	52	0	P	(len/deep-72, len-84)

Also operates five smaller ferries and excursion vessels.

Nordic Ferry Services A/S   Denmark

Funnel:	Turquoise with black top.											
Hull:	White upper hull with service name above dark blue lower hull, black boot-topping.											
History:	Owned jointly by Clipper Group and Bornholmstrafikken A/S.											
Web:	www.alstrafikken.dk; www.fanoetrafikken.dk; www.langelandstrafikken.dk; www.samsoetrafikken.dk;											
Routes:	Operates five domestic ferry services serving Esbjerg, Fyn, Langeland and Samoe.											
Frigg Sydfyen	(2)	Dmk	1984	1,676	70.0	12.0	12	335	50	14	P	
Kanhave	(2)	Dmk	2008	4,250	91.4		16	600	122	30	P	
Kyholm	(2)	Dmk	1998	3,380	69.2	14.8	14	550	91	9	P	
Odin Sydfyen	(2)	Dmk	1982	1,698	70.4	12.0	12	335	50	14	P	

Name		Flag	Year	GT	Loa	Bm	Kts	Pass	Car	HGV	Type	Remarks
Thor Sydfyen	(2)	Dmk	1978	1,479	70.4	11.6	12	292	50	15	P	
Vesborg	(2)	Dmk	1995	2,208	53.8	14.8	11	440	72	6	P	

Also four smaller ferries.

Orkney Ferries Ltd   UK

Funnel: *Red with red 'I' inside red 'O' on broad white band.*
Hull: *Black with narrow white band above red boot-topping.*
History: *Formerly Orkney Islands Shipping Co and now owned by the Orkney islands Council.*
Web: *www.orkneyferries.co.uk*
Routes: *Linking Orkney mainland to 13 smaller islands.*
Operates a fleet of about nine vessels under 50m, the largest being Earl Sigurd (90/771 gt 140 px), Earl Thorfinn (90/771 gt 140 px) and Varagen (88/928 gt 144 px).

P&O Ferries Ltd   UK

Funnel: *Dark blue with diagonally quartered (white over yellow with blue and red sides) houseflag.*
Hull: *Dark blue with white 'P&O' and web-address.*
History: *Original parent company founded in 1840. Acquired Townsend Thoresen in 1987 and formed P&O North Sea Ferries in 1994. Operated jointly with Stena from 1988 to 1992 as P&O Stena Line Ltd. After sale of P&O cruises to Carnival and P&O Containers/Nedlloyd joint venture to AP Moller-Maersk, the ferry company was sold to Dubai-based DP World.*
Web: *www.poferries.com*
Routes: *Dover – Calais; * Portsmouth – Bilbao; Cairnryan – Larne; Troon – Larne; Liverpool – Dublin; Tilbury – Zeebrugge; Hull – Rotterdam; Hull – Zeebrugge; Middlesbrough – Zeebrugge; Middlesbrough – Rotterdam*

Name		Flag	Year	GT	Loa	Bm	Kts	Pass	Car	HGV	Type	Remarks
Celtic Star **	(2)	Cyp	1991	11,086	136.0	20.5	20	12	0	86	F	ex Northern Star-06, Celtic Star-02, Loon-Plage-99, Ioalaos-98, Kosei Maru-98
European Causeway	(2)	Bhs	2000	20,646	159.5	23.4	22	410	375	107	P	
European Endeavour	(2)	Gbr	2000	22,152	180.0	24.3	22	252	0	120	P	ex El Greco-07, Midnight Merchant-06
European Highlander	(2)	Bhs	2002	21,188	162.7	23.4	22	410	375	107	P	
European Mariner	(2)	Bhs	1978	5,897	116.3	17.4	15	12	37	71	F	ex European Highlander-01, Lion-98, Merchant Valiant-95, Salahala-90
European Seaway	(2)	Gbr	1991	22,986	179.7	27.8	21	200	0	120	F	
European Trader	(2)	Nld	1978	17,068	176.2	20.4	17	12	-	194	F	ex Tor Maxima-08, Dana Maxima-01 (len-95)
Express	(4wj)	Bhs	1998	5,902	91.0	26.0	43	900	240	0	T	ex Catalonia-03, Express Fastcraft-03, Catalonia-03, Portsmouth Express-02, Catalonia-02, Portsmouth Express-01, Catalonia-01, Portsmouth Express-00, Catalonia L-00, Catalonia-99
Norbank	(2)	Nld	1993	17,464	166.8	23.4	22	114	0	156	F	
Norbay	(2)	Gbr	1994	17,464	166.8	23.4	22	114	0	156	F	
Norcape	(2)	Nld	1979	14,087	150.0	20.7	18	12	0	125	F	ex Tipperary-89, l/a Puma
Norking	(2)	Fin	1980	17,884	170.9	23.0	19	12	0	155	F	ex Bore King-91 (len-95)
Norqueen	(2)	Fin	1980	17,884	170.9	23.0	19	12	0	155	F	ex Bore Queen-91 (len-95)
Norsky ***	(2)	Fin	1999	20,296	180.0	25.2	21	12	0	210	F	
Norstream	(2)	Fin	1999	19,992	180.0	25.2	21	12	0	210	F	
Pride of Bilbao *	(2)	Gbr	1986	37,583	176.8	28.4	22	2500	600	62	P	ex Olympia-93
Pride of Bruges	(2)	Nld	1987	31,598	179.4	25.1	18	1290	850	180	P	ex Norsun-03
Pride of Burgandy	(2)	Gbr	1993	28,138	179.7	27.8	21	1420	465	120	P	ex PO Burgundy-03, P&OSL Burgundy-02, Pride of Burgundy-98, l/d European Causeway
Pride of Calais	(3)	Gbr	1987	26,433	169.6	27.8	22	2290	585	100	P	ex PO Calais-03, P&OSL Calais-02, Pride of Calais-99
Pride of Canterbury	(2)	Gbr	1992	30,835	179.7	27.8	21	2000	537	124	P	ex European Pathway-03 (rblt F-03)
Pride of Dover	(3)	Gbr	1987	26,433	169.6	27.8	22	2290	585	100	P	ex PO Dover-03, P&OSL Dover-02, Pride of Dover-99
Pride of Hull	(2)	Gbr	2001	59.925	215.4	31.5	22	1376	250	400	P	
Pride of Kent	(2)	Gbr	1992	30,635	179.7	27.8	21	2000	537	124	P	ex European Highway-03 (rblt F-03)
Pride of Rotterdam	(2)	Nld	2001	59.925	215.4	31.5	22	1376	250	400	P	
Pride of York	(2)	Gbr	1987	31,785	179.2	25.1	18	1258	850	180	P	ex Norsea-02

* on charter from Irish Ferries and to be withdrawn from service September 2010.
** on charter from Jay Management Corp, Greece or *** from Bore Shipowners BV, Netherlands.

Polferries   Poland

Funnel: *Blue with red 'PZB' on white shield interrupting red band edged with narrow white bands.*
Hull: *White with blue 'polferries', blue boot-topping.*
History: *Operated by Polish Baltic Shipping Co*
Web: *www.polferries.pl*
Routes: *Gdansk – Nynashamn; Swinoujscie – Ystad; Swinoujscie – Copenhagen; Swinoujscie – Ronne;*

Name		Flag	Year	GT	Loa	Bm	Kts	Pass	Car	HGV	Type	Remarks
Baltivia	(2)	Bhs	1981	17,672	146.0	24.0	18	250	96	117	P	ex Dieppe-06, Saga Star-02, Girolata-93,

LD Lines – Transmanche Ferries. Cote d'Albatre. *Mike Lennon*

P&O Ferries. European Seaway. *Allan Ryszka Onions*

P&O Ferries. European Trader. *Hans Kraijenbosch*

P&O Ferries. Pride of Burgundy. *Allan Ryszka Onions*

P&O Ferries. Pride of Hull. *Tom Walker*

P&O Ferries. Pride of Kent. *Allan Ryszka Onions*

Red Funnel. Red Falcon. *Phil Kempsey*

SCA Transforest. Ostrand. *Hans Kraijenbosch*

Name		Flag	Year	GT	Loa	Bm	Kts	Pass	Car	HGV	Type	Remarks
												Saga Star-89 (conv F-89
Pomerania	(2)	Bhs	1978	12,087	127.4	21.7	20	984	277	0	P	(wid-97)
Scandinavia	(2)	Bhs	1980	23,842	146.1	24.0	21	1872	515	38	P	ex Visborg-03, Visby-03, Stena Felicity-97, Visby-90
Wawel	(2)	Bhs	1980	25,318	163.5	23.0	18	1800	430	75	P	ex Alkmini A-04, PO Canterbury-04, P&OSL Canterbury-02, Stena Fantasia-99, Fantasia-90, Fiesta-90, Tzarevetz-88, Scandinavia-82 (rblt F-90)

Red Funnel Ferries   UK

Funnel: Red with black top.
Hull: Red with black 'RED FUNNEL' interrupting broad grey band between narrow red bands on white superstructure.
History: Founded 1861 as Southampton, Isle of Wight & South of England Royal Mail Steam Packet Company, at one time owned by Associated British Ports, sold in 2000 to JP Morgan International, then in 2004 to the management and in 2007 to a Prudential Group fund.
Web: www.redfunnel.co.uk
History: Southampton, Isle of Wight and South of England Royal Mail Steam Packet PLC, UK
Routes: Southampton – Cowes.

Red Eagle	(2)	Gbr	1996	3,953	93.2	17.5	13	895	200	16	P	(len/deep-05)
Red Falcon	(2)	Gbr	1994	3,953	93.2	17.5	13	895	200	16	P	(len/deep-04)
Red Osprey	(2)	Gbr	1994	3,953	93.2	17.5	13	895	200	16	P	(len/deep-03)

also high-speed catamarans Red Jet 3 (98/213 gt 190 px) Red Jet 4 (03/342 gt 277 px) and Red Jet 5 (99/209 gt 177 px)

OY RG Line AB   Finland

Funnel: Black.
Hull: Blue with yellow band below superstructure with red/blue 'RGLINE'.
History: Founded 2001.
Web: www.rgline.com
Routes: Umea – Vaasa;

RG I	(2)	Fin	1983	10,271	140.1	20.5	14	75	0	69	F	ex Kahleberg-05 (conv Ro-92)

AS Saaremaa Laevakompanii   Estonia

Funnel: White, some with Company badge interrupting broad blue band.
Hull: White with dark blue boot-topping;
History: Founded 1992
Web: www.laevakompanii.ee
Routes: Kuivastu – Virtsu; Heltermaa – Rohuküla; Triigi – Sõru; Ruhnu – Munalaid;

Harilaid	(2me)	Est	1985	1,028	49.9	12.2	12	120	35	-	P	
Korgelaid	(2me)	Est	1987	1,028	49.7	12.2	12	120	35	-	P	
Ofelia	(2)	Est	1968	3,638	74.4	16.5	14	800	80	-	P	
Regula	(2)	Est	1971	3,774	71.2	16.3	14	800	105	-	P	
Scania	(2)	Est	1972	3,474	74.2	16.5	14	800	80	-	P	
Viire	(4me)	Est	1988	4,101	95.8	15.0	14	253	36	30	P	ex Troll-99, Difko Korsor-99, Superflex Charlie-90

SCA Transforest   Sweden

Funnel: Yellow with blue 'TA' symbol within blue ring, narrow blue base and top.
Hull: White with blue 'SCA TRANSPORT' interrupting blue band, blue boot-topping.
History: Built for Gorthon Lines AB and now long-term chartered from Rederi AB Transatlantic qv
Web: www.sca.com/transforest
Routes: London – Rotterdam – Helsingborg – Umeli – Sundsvall

Orbola		Swe	1996	20,168	170.6	23.5	16	0	0	149	F	(len-01)
Ortviken		Swe	1997	20,154	170.4	23.5	16	0	0	149	F	(len-00)
Ostrand		Swe	1996	20,171	170.6	23.5	16	0	0	149	F	(len-01)

Scandlines GmbH   Germany

Funnel: Black with inverted triangle having red top, yellow and blue sides
Hull: White with black 'Scandlines' on white superstructure, black lower section above red boot-topping
History: Scandlines Deutschland GmbH was formed in 1993 (formerly DFO), when the former East and West German railway companies merged their ferry services as Deutsche Bahn AG. Co-operation with their Danish and Swedish partners, Scandlines Danmark A/S (DSB Rederi A/S to 1997) and Scandlines AB continued. Scandlines AG was formed in 1998, but in 2007, the Danish Government and Deutsche Bahn AG sold the Group to two investment funds (40% each) and Deutsche Seerederei GmbH (20%) when it was again renamed Scandlines GmbH. Earlier, in 2006, Scandlines AB had been sold to Stena, who continue to operate joint routes in co-operation.
Web: www.scandlines.com
Routes: Puttgarden – Rodby; Rostock – Gedser; Helsingor – Helsingborg; Sassnitz – Trelleborg; Rostock – Trelleborg; Travemunde – Ventspils; Nynashamn – Ventspils; Rostock – Hanko

Scandlines GmbH. Mecklenburg-Vorpommern. *Hans Kraijenbosch*

Scandlines GmbH. Prins Joachim. *Hans Kraijenbosch*

Scandlines GmbH. Skane. *Hans Kraijenbosch*

SeaFrance SA. Seafrance Moliere. *Hans Kraijenbosch*

SeaFrance SA. Seafrance Nord Pas-De-Calais. *Allan Ryszka Onions*

Name		Flag	Year	GT	Loa	Bm	Kts	Pass	Car	HGV	Type	Remarks
Ask **	(2)	Dis	1982	13,144	171.0	20.2	18	176	0	69	P	ex Arka Marine-91, Nordic Hunter-91, Serdica-90, Seafreight Freeway-88, Stena Driver-85, Lucky Rider-84 (len-00)
Aurora		Deu	1982	20,381	154.9	25.0	18	12	0	164	F	ex Arcturus-91
Aurora af Helsingborg ‡	(4me)	Swe	1992	10,918	111.2	27.6	13	1250	238	0	R	
Deutschland	(4me)	Deu	1998	15,187	142.0	24.8	15	1040	304	0	R	
Gotaland ‡	(2)	Swe	1973	18,060	183.1	21.6	18	548	35	18	R	(also 44 rail wagons)
Hamlet	(4)	Dis	1997	10,067	111.2	27.6	13	1000	240	0	P	
Holger Dansk	(2)	Dis	1976	2,779	86.8	12.9	11	600	60	0	R	
Kronprins Frederik	(2)	Dis	1981	16,071	152.0	22.8	19	1060	200	40	P	
Mecklenburg-Vorpommern	(2)	Deu	1996	36,185	200.0	28.2	18	590	445	230	P	
Merchant		Deu	1983	20,594	155.0	25.0	18	12	0	164	F	ex Finnmerchant-03 (conv Ro-06)
Prins Joachim	(2)	Dis	1980	16,071	152.0	22.8	18	2280	210	46	P	
Prins Richard	(4me)	Dis	1997	14,822	142.0	24.8	18	1140	286	0	R	
Prinsesse Benedikte	(4me)	Dis	1997	14,822	142.0	23.2	18	1140	286	0	R	
Rostock *	(2)	Deu	1981	17,098	140.8	22.3	18	2071	450	54	P	ex Thjelvar-07, Color Traveller-06, Thjelvar-04, Sally Star-97, Travemunde Link-88, Travemunde-87
Sassnitz	(2)	Deu	1989	21,154	171.5	23.7	17	875	50	20	R	(also 48 rail wagons)
Schleswig-Holstein	(4me)	Deu	1997	15,187	142.0	24.8	15	1040	304	0	R	
Skane ‡	(2)	Swe	1998	42,705	200.2	29.0	21	680	500	110	R	(also 55 rail wagons)
Trelleborg ‡	(2)	Swe	1982	20,028	170.2	23.8	17	950	108	75	R	(also 55 rail wagons)
Tycho Brahe	(4me)	Dis	1991	11,148	111.2	27.8	13	1250	238	0	R	
Urd **	(2)	Dis	1981	13,144	150.8	20.2	18	78	0	69	P	ex Aktiv Marine-91, Boyana-90, Seafreight Highway-89, Easy Rider-85

*chartered-in from Rederi Gotland AB ** managed by Blaesbjerg Marine A/S

‡ owned by Scandlines AB, Sweden (formerly SweFerry and since 2006 a subsidiary of Stena Line AB qv)

SeaFrance SA France

Funnel:	White with blue above red 'SF' symbol, narrow red band below broad blue top.
Hull:	White with blue above red 'SF' symbol and blue 'SEAFRANCE', narrow red band above blue boot-topping.
History:	Founded 1909 as subsidiary of state-owned rail operator Societe Nationale des Chemins de Fer Francais (SNCF), renamed Societe Nouvelle d'Armement Transmanche (SNAT) in 1990 and the current style in 1995 after joint operations with Sealink and Stena ceased.
Web:	www.seafrance.com
Routes:	Calais – Dover

Name		Flag	Year	GT	Loa	Bm	Kts	Pass	Car	HGV	Type	Remarks
Seafrance Berlioz	(2)	Fra	2005	33,940	186.0	27.7	25	1900	700	120	P	
Seafrance Cezanne	(2)	Fra	1980	25,122	163.5	23.0	18	1800	650	0	P	ex Fiesta-96, Channel Seaway-90, Fantasia-89, Trapezitza-89, Soca-82, Ariadne-80 (conv Ro-90)
Seafrance Moliere	(2)	Fra	2002	30,285	203.9	25.4	27	1200	480	110	P	ex Jean Nicoli-08, Superfast X-07
Seafrance Nord Pas-De-Calais	(2)	Fra	1987	7,264	160.1	22.4	21	80	0	90	F	ex Nord Pas-de-Calais-96 (conv R)
Seafrance Renoir	(2)	Fra	1981	15,612	130.0	22.5	18	1400	330	0	P	ex Cote d'Azur-96
Seafrance Rodin	(2)	Fra	2001	33,796	185.8	27.7	25	1900	700	-	P	

Shetland Islands Council UK

Funnel:	Red.
Hull:	Blue with black or blue boot-topping.
History:	Local Authority operated services.
Web:	www.shetland.gov.uk/ferries
Routes:	Nine separate services linking the various groups of Shetland islands.

Name		Flag	Year	GT	Loa	Bm	Kts	Pass	Car	HGV	Type	Remarks
Dagalien	(2)	Gbr	2004	1,891	65.4	13.8	12	144	31	0	P	
Daggri	(2)	Gbr	2004	1,861	65.4	13.8	12	145	31	0	P	

Also operates 10 smaller less than 50 m.

Smyril Line Faroes

Funnel:	Black with 'bird head' inside wide red ring inscribed with 'SMYRIL LINE'.
Hull:	White with black 'SMYRIL LINE', black boot-topping.
History:	Established 1982
Web:	www.smyril-line.com
Routes:	Seydisfjordur – Torshavn – Esbjerg/Hanstholm

Name		Flag	Year	GT	Loa	Bm	Kts	Pass	Car	HGV	Type	Remarks
Norrona	(2)	Fro	2003	35.966	165.7	30.0	21	1482	644	130	P	

Spliethhoff's Bevrachtingskantoor BV — Netherlands

Transfennica, Finland

Funnel: *White with diagonally quartered white/red/orange/blue houseflag*
Hull: *White with blue 'TRANSFENNICA' and 'T' symbol, blue boot-topping.*
History: *Founded 1976 by Finnish paper/timber producers. In 2000, the owners UPM-Kymmene Corp, Metsä-Serla Corp and Myllykoski Paper Oy sold their interest to Finnlines Ab. Majority share acquired by Spliethoff's Bevrachtingskantor BV, Netherlands in 2002, who later acquired 100% control.*
Web: *www.transfennica.com*
Routes: *Complex routes connecting Tilbury, Antwerp, Zeebrugge, Lubeck, Gdynia, Hanko, Hamina, Rauma, Paldiski, St. Petersburg and Bilbao.*

Name		Flag	Year	GT	Loa	Bm	Kts	Pass	Car	HGV	Type	Remarks
Genca	(2)	Nld	2007	28,289	205.0	25.5	22	12	0	188	F	
Kraftca	(2)	Nld	2006	28,289	205.0	25.5	22	12	0	188	F	
Plyca	(2)	Nld	2009	28,289	205.0	25.5	22	12	0	188	F	
Pulpca	(2)	Nld	2008	28,289	205.0	25.5	22	12	0	188	F	
Timca	(2)	Nld	2006	28,289	205.0	25.5	22	12	0	188	F	
Trica	(2)	Nld	2007	28,289	205.0	25.5	22	12	0	188	F	

Newbuildings: Two further sister-ships on order to be named Steelca and Woodca, but delayed by shipbuilders bankruptcy.
Also operates two vessels chartered from Stena Line AB (see Ferry Section), four vessels from Ernst Russ GmbH & Co and one from Oy Rettig AB Bore (see Cargo Section)

St. Peter Line — Russia

Funnel: *White with blue wave symbol.*
Hull: *White with blue 'ST. PETER LINE', wave symbols and red crown.*
History: *Founded 2010 by Inflot Cruise & Ferry, Russia.*
Web: *www.stpeterline.com*
Routes: *St. Petersburg – Helsinki.*

Name		Flag	Year	GT	Loa	Bm	Kts	Pass	Car	HGV	Type	Remarks
Princess Maria	(2)	Dis	1981	34,093	166.1	28.4	22	1638	395	86	P	ex Queen of Scandinavia-10, Finlandia-90

Chartered from DFDS AS.

Stena Line AB — Sweden

Funnel: *Red with large white 'S' symbol, narrow white and dark blue top and bottom bands or dark blue with joint houseflags (P&O Stena);*
Hull: *White with blue 'Stena Line' and red band above blue boot-topping (passenger) or blue with white 'STENA LINE' (freight).*
History: *Founded 1962 as Sten A Olssen Handels A/B, when Skagenlinjen taken over.. Acquired Sessan Line in 1981, Varberg-Grena Linjen in 1983 and Lion Ferry (founded 1954) in 1985. In 1989, SZM (Crown Line) was acquired, followed by Sealink British Ferries (from Sea Containers) in 1990. P&O Stena Line joint venture formed 1998 until P&O acquired Stena 40% share in 2002. Scandlines AB acquired 2000.*
Web: *www.stenaline.co.uk*
Routes: *Frederikshavn – Oslo; Frederikshavn – Gothenburg; Gothenburg – Kiel; Varberg – Grenaa; Karlskrona – Gdynia; Harwich – Hook of Holland; Fishguard – Rosslare; Holyhead – Dun Laoghaire; Holyhead – Dublin; Stranraer – Belfast; Fleetwood – Larne*

Name		Flag	Year	GT	Loa	Bm	Kts	Pass	Car	HGV	Type	Remarks
Stena Adventurer	(2)	Gbr	2003	43,532	210.8	29.3	22	1500	-	210	P	
Stena Baltica	(2)	Bhs	1986	31,910	161.8	27.6	21	2100	220	80	P	ex Koningen Beatrix-02
Stena Britannica	(2)	Nld	2003	55,050	240.1	29.2	22	1040	1311	-	P	ex Stena Britannica II-03
Stena Caledonia	(2)	Gbr	1981	12,619	132.0	21.0	19	1000	306	62	P	ex St. David-91
Stena Carisma	(gt2wj)	Swe	1997	8,631	89.8	30.0	38	900	208	0	T	
Stena Carrier	(2)	Swe	2004	21,089	182.8	25.5	20	12	0	189	F	ex Stena Carrier II-04, (l/d 1998)
Stena Danica	(2)	Swe	1983	28,727	154.9	28.0	21	2300	550	82	P	
Stena Europe	(2)	Gbr	1981	24,828	149.1	26.0	20	2076	450	60	P	ex Lion Europe-98, Stena Europe-97, Stena Saga-94, Kronsprinsessan Victoria-88
Stena Explorer	(gt4wj)	Gbr	1996	19,638	125.0	40.0	40	1520	375	50	T	
Stena Forecaster *	(2)	Swe	2003	24,688	195.3	25.5	23	0	0	205	F	
Stena Forerunner *	(2)	Swe	2003	24,688	195.3	25.6	22	0	0	205	F	
Stena Foreteller	(2)	Swe	2001	24,688	195.3	25.6	22	0	0	205	F	ex Cetam Massilia-03, Stena Foreteller-02
Stena Freighter	(2)	Swe	2004	21,104	182.8	25.5	22	12	0	189	F	ex Stena Seafrieghter-04, l/d Sea Chieftain (1998)
Stena Germanica	(2)	Swe	1987	38,178	175.4	30.5	20	2500	540	26	P	l/a Stena Scandinavica
Stena Hollandica	(2)	Nld	2001	44,372	240.1	28.7	22	1067	-	250	P	(len-07)
Stena Jutlandica	(2)	Swe	1996	29,691	182.4	27.8	22	1700	550	122	P	ex Stena Jutlandica III-96
Stena Leader	(2)	Bmu	1975	12,879	157.4	19.0	17	80	90	100	F	ex European Leader-04, Buffalo-98 (len/conv Ro—88 & len-98)
Stena Lynx III	(4wj)	Bhs	1996	4,113	80.6	26.0	45	782	151	0	T	ex Elite-04, Stena Lynx III-03, P&O Stena Elite-98, Elite-98, Stena Lynx III-98
Stena Nautica	(2)	Swe	1986	19,504	13.5	24.0	18	2000	152	30	P	ex Lion King II-96, Lion King-96, Isle of Inisfree-95, Stena Nautica-92, Niels Klim-91
Stena Navigator	(2)	Gbr	1984	15,093	130.0	22.5	20	1800	330	54	P	ex Seafrance Manet-09, Stena Parisien-96, Champs Elysees-92
Stena Nordica	(2)	Swe	2000	24,206	169.8	24.0	25	405	375	-	P	ex European Ambassador-04

Spliethoff's – Transfennica. Pulpca. *Oliver Sesemann*

Stena Line AB. Stena Britannica. *Hans Kraijenbosch*

Stena Line AB. Stena Freighter. *Hans Kraijenbosch*

Name		Flag	Year	GT	Loa	Bm	Kts	Pass	Car	HGV	Type	Remarks
Stena Partner	(2)	Gbr	1978	21,162	184.8	23.5	17	166	0	180	F	ex Freeway-03, European Freeway-02, Cerdic Ferry-91, Stena Transporter-86, Syria-83, Alpha Enterprise-79 (wid/conv Ro-79, len-81)
Stena Pioneer	(2)	Bmu	1975	14,426	141.8	22.0	16	60	0	108	F	ex European Pioneer-04, Bison-08 (len/conv Ro-81, wid-95)
Stena Saga	(2)	Swe	1981	33,750	166.1	28.4	22	2000	450	55	P	ex Stena Britannica-94, Silvia Regina-91
Stena Scandinavica	(2)	Swe	1988	39,169	175.4	30.5	18	2500	540	26	P	I/a Stena Germanica
Stena Scanrail	(2)	Swe	1973	7,504	142.3	16.0	19	36	0	64r	R	ex Stena Searider-87, Trucker-85, Stena Searider-84, Searider-84, Stena Searider-83, Bahjah-81, Seatrader-76, I/a Stena Seatrader (len-76, conv P-87)
Stena Seafarer	(2)	Bmu	1975	10,957	141.8	19.0	18	45	0	93	F	ex European Seafarer-04, Puma-98, Union Trader-80, Union Melbourne-80 (len-75, conv P-87)
Stena Trader	(2)	Nld	2006	26,663	212.0	26.7	22	300	-	200	P	
Stena Transfer	(2)	Gbr	1977	21,162	184.6	23.5	17	166	0	180	F	ex Ideway-02, European Tideway-02, Doric Ferry-92, Hellas-86, Alpha Progress-79, I/a Stena Runner (wid/conv Ro-79, len-82)
Stena Transporter	(2)	Gbr	1978	16,776	151.0	19.9	17	80	0	160	F	ex Flanders-02, Pride of Flanders-02, Nordic Ferry-92, Merzaria Hispaniia-79, Merzario Espania-78
Stena Traveller	(2)	Nld	2007	26,663	212.0	26.7	22	300	0	200	P	
Stena Voyager	(gt4wj)	Gbr	1996	19,638	126.6	40.0	40	1520	360	50	T	
Newbuildings												
Stena Hollandica	(2)	Nld	2010	62,000	240.0	32.0	22	1200	230	300	P	
Stena Britannica	(2)	Gbr	2010	62,000	240.0	32.0	22	1200	230	300	P	

* on charter to Transfennica Shipping – see Ferry Section.
Also see Scandlines AB

HH-Ferries, Sweden

Funnel: Silver stovepipes only.
Hull: Blue with red 'HH-Ferries' on white superstructure, red boot-topping.
History: Commenced operations in 1996 as 'Sundbroen' by Per Henriksen's Mercandia Shipping, but sold in 1997 and renamed H-H Ferries. Sold again in 2001 to the Stena Group.
Web: www.hhferries.se
Routes: Helsingor – Helsingborg

Name		Flag	Year	GT	Loa	Bm	Kts	Pass	Car	HGV	Type	Remarks
Mercandia IV	(4me)	Dmk	1989	4,296	95.8	15.0	12	300	85	16	P	I/a Superflex November
Mercandia VIII	(4me)	Dis	1987	4,296	95.8	15.0	12	300	85	16	P	ex Svea Scarlett-96, Superflex Bravo-93

AS Tallink Grupp
Estonia

Funnel: White with red 'V' shape at base and blue 'V' above.
Hull: White with black 'TALLINK' or blue with white 'TALLINK'; some decorative colour schemes; White with dark blue 'SILJA'
History: Silja Oy was originally founded 1904 as collaboration between Finska Ångfartygs (Finland Steamship Co) and Bore Steamship Co on routes between Finland and Sweden. Agreement extended in 1918 to include Rederi AB Svea. Finland Steamship renamed Effoa in 1976, Bore withdrew in 1980 and Svea acquired by Johnson Line in 1981, when joint company renamed Effjohn. Jointly acquired Rederi Ab Sally in 1987, but their Viking Line interest was sold to other Viking partners. In 1995 Effjohn was renamed Silja Oy AB, then Neptun Maritime in 1998 before being acquired by Sea Containers in 1999 and renamed Silja Oyj Abp in 2000. Company sold to Tallink in 2006 and renamed.
Tallink Grupp was founded 1989 as a joint venture between Russia and Finnish operators. Acquired in 1993 by Estonian Shipping Co (founded 1965, Merged with competitor Inreko Laeva AS in 1994 and bought out their share in 1996. Acquired Baltic services of Superfast Ferries in 2006 and later in 2006 Silja Oy AB (from Sea Containers).
Web: www.tallink.com (with links to other Group sites)
Routes: Ten passenger and two cargo routes including Helsinki – Stockholm; Helsinki – Tallinn; Turku – Mariehamn – Stockholm; Helsinki – Rostock – Tallinn; Helsinki – Travemunde; Stockholme – Tallinn; Stockholm – Riga

Name		Flag	Year	GT	Loa	Bm	Kts	Pass	Car	HGV	Type	Remarks
Baltic Princess	(2)	Est	2008	48,915	212.0	29.0	24	2800	300	82	P	
Baltic Queen	(2)	Est	2009	48,915	212.0	29.0	24	2800	300	82	P	
Galaxy	(2)	Est	2006	48,915	212.1	29.0	22	2800	300	82	P	
Kapella	(2)	Est	1974	7,564	110.1	20.1	18	50	0	43	F	ex Marine Evangeline-98, Spirit of Boulogne-95, Marine Evangeline-93, Duke of Yorkshire-78
Regal Star	(2)	Bhs	1999	15,281	155.9	23.8	18	80	120	110	P	(I-1993)
Regina Baltica	(2)	Lva	1980	18,345	145.2	25.2	21	2000	540	60	P	ex Anna K-96, Anna Karenina-96, Baltika-91, Braemar-91, Viking Song-85
Romantika	(2)	Est	2002	40,803	192.9	29.0	22	2178	300	82	P	
Silja Europa	(2)	Fin	1993	59,912	201.8	32.0	21	3746	350	60	P	I/a Europa
Silja Festival	(2)	Lva	1985	34,414	168.0	27.6	22	2000	350	60	P	ex Wellamo-91
Silja Serenade	(2)	Fin	1990	58,376	203.0	31.5	21	2841	450	60	P	
Silja Symphony	(2)	Swe	1991	58,377	203.0	31.5	21	2841	470	60	P	
Star	(2)	Est	2007	36,249	186.0	27.7	27	1900	300	70	P	

Stena Line AB. Stena Trader. *Hans Kraijenbosch*

AS Tallink Grupp. Baltic Queen. *Marko Stampehl*

AS Tallink Gruup. Galaxy. *Marko Stampehl*

AS Tallink Grupp. Silja Europa. *Marko Stampehl*

AS Tallink Gruup. Star. *Marko Stampehl*

Rederi AB Transatlantic. TransPine. *Oliver Sesemann*

Name		Flag	Year	GT	Loa	Bm	Kts	Pass	Car	HGV	Type	Remarks
Superfast VII	(2)	Est	2001	30,285	203.3	25.0	26	1422	482	110	P	
Superfast VIII	(2)	Est	2001	30,285	203.3	25.0	26	1422	482	110	P	
Superstar	(2)	Est	2008	36,000	185.0	27.6	27	2080	300	82	P	
Vana Tallinn	(2)	Est	1974	10,002	153.7	22.3	21	1065	300	48	P	ex Thor Heyerdahl-94, Nord Estonia-93, Dana Regina-90
Victoria I	(2)	Est	2004	40,975	192.9	29.0	22	2500	370	65	P	

SeaWind Line Oy Ab

Funnel: White with blue band.
Hull: Blue with blue 'SeaWind' on white superstructure, black boot-topping.
History: Founded 1988 as subsidiary of Silja.
Web: www.seawind.fi
Routes: Stockholm – Turku

Name		Flag	Year	GT	Loa	Bm	Kts	Pass	Car	HGV	Type	Remarks
Sea Wind	(2)	Swe	1972	15,879	154.4	21.0	18	300	60	100	F	ex Saga Wind-89, Svealand-84 (len/wid-84, conv R-89)

TESO   Netherlands

Funnel: Red and green.
Hull: White with red 'TESO', black boot-topping.
History: Founded 1907 as Texels Eigen Stoomboot Onderneming and mainly owned by Texel residents.
Web: www.teso.nl
Routes: Den Helder – Den Hoorn (Texel)

Name		Flag	Year	GT	Loa	Bm	Kts	Pass	Car	HGV	Type	Remarks
Dokter Wagemaker	(4me)	Nld	2005	13,256	130.4	22.2	15	1750	200	30	P	
Schulpengat	(4me)	Nld	1990	8,311	110.4	18.2	11	1750	156	25	P	

Rederi AB Transatlantic   Sweden

Funnel: White with blue 'TA' symbol within blue ring on broad yellow band between blue band and blue top.
Hull: Dark blue with yellow 'TRANSATLANTIC', red boot-topping.
History: Founded 1972 and current company emerged from 2005 amalgamation of Gorthon Lines AB (founded 1915 as Gorthons Rederi A/B to 1987, Gorthon Lines AB to 1995 and B&N Gorthon Lines AB to 1997) and B&N Nordsjofrakt AB (previously AB Nordsjofrakt to 1990 and B&N Bylock & Nordsjofrakt AB to 1998).
Web: www.rabt.se
Routes: Bottenviken – Gothenburg – Lubeck; Kotka – Gothenburg – Lubeck

Name		Flag	Year	GT	Loa	Bm	Kts	Pass	Car	HGV	Type	Remarks
Oak		Gib	1984	13,525	158.2	22.0	14	0	0	120	F	ex Transoak-09, Ada Gorthon-08
TransFighter		Swe	2001	20,851	178.6	25.6	17	0	0	-	F	ex Finnfighter-09 (len-06)
TransPaper		Swe	2006	23,128	190.5	26.0	16	12	0	155	F	
TransPine		Swe	2002	20,851	178.6	25.6	17	0	0	-	F	ex Finnpine-08 (len-06)
TransPulp		Swe	2006	23,128	190.7	26.0	16	12	0	155	F	
TransReel		Swe	1987	18,773	166.0	22.6	20	0	100	160	F	ex Viola Gorthon-09 (conv-95)
TransTimber		Swe	2007	23,128	190.5	26.0	16	12	0	155	F	
TransWood		Swe	2002	20,851	178.6	25.6	17	0	0	-	F	ex Finnwood-08 (len-06)

Also see SCA Transforest, Sweden and Cargo Section.

TransEuropa Ferries   Belgium

Funnel: Buff with red 'T' over black 'E', narrow black top.
Hull: White with black and red 'TransEuropaFerries', narrow red band above black boot-topping.
History: Commenced operations in 1997 as joint venture with Sally Line, which withdrew in 1998. Original freight service extended to include passengers in 2004. Operating company is a subsidiary of Slovenian owners.
Web: www.transeuropaferries.com
Routes: Ramsgate – Ostend (jointly with LD Lines qv)

Name		Flag	Year	GT	Loa	Bm	Kts	Pass	Car	HGV	Type	Remarks
Eurovoyager	(2)	Cyp	1978	12,110	118.4	20.7	22	1300	250	55	P	ex Prins Albert-98
Gardenia	(2)	Cyp	1978	8,097	117.9	19.9	18	105	30	76	F	ex European Endeavour-02, European Enterprise-88
Larkspur	(2)	Bhs	1976	14,458	143.8	19.9	17	1155	300	56	P	ex Eurotraveller-99, Sally Sky-97, Viking 2-88, Gedser-86 (len-90)
Oleander	(3)	Cyp	1980	13,728	131.9	22.7	22	1326	220	50	P	ex P&OSL Picardy-01, Pride of Bruges-99, Pride of Free Enterprise-88
Primrose	(2)	Cyp	1975	12,046	118.4	20.0	22	1400	420	52	P	ex Princesse Marie-Christine-98 (wid/rblt-85)
Wisteria	(2)	Cyp	1978	9,677	131.0	22.0	21	1500	354	78	P	ex Duc De Normandie-05, Prinses Beatrix-86

TT Line   Germany

Funnel: White with large yellow over blue rectangles, narrow black top.
Hull: White with blue 'TT-Line' or ' TT-Line Clipper' and yellow over blue rectangles interrupting blue band, blue boot-topping.
History: Founded 1962 by Aug. Boltens Wm Miller's Nachfolger as OHG TT-Linie GmbH.

Rederi AB Transatlantic. TransTimber. *Hans Kraijenbosch*

TransEuropa Ferries. Gardenia. *Phil Kempsey*

Name		Flag	Year	GT	Loa	Bm	Kts	Pass	Car	HGV	Type	Remarks
Web:	www.ttline.com											
Routes:	Travemunde – Trelleborg; Rostock – Trelleborg;											
Huckleberry Finn	(2)	Swe	1988	26,391	177.2	26.0	20	400	280	167	P	ex Peter Pan IV-02, Peter Pan-01, Nils Dacke-93 (conv-93 & 01)
Nils Dacke	(2me)	Swe	1995	26,790	179.3	27.2	18	308	0	150	F	
Nils Holgersson	(2me)	Deu	2001	36,468	190.0	29.5	18	740	0	174	P	
Peter Pan	(2me)	Swe	2001	36,468	190.0	29.5	18	740	0	174	P	
Robin Hood	(2me)	Deu	1995	26,800	179.3	27.2	18	308	0	150	F	
Tom Sawyer	(2)	Deu	1989	24,728	177.2	26.0	20	400	280	160	P	ex Nils Holgersson-01, Robin Hood-93 (conv-92 & 01)

Unity Line Co Ltd   Poland

Funnel: White with two diagonal light blue stripes or * buff and blue divided vertically with diamond of opposite colours.
Hull: White with 'UNITY LINE' (light blue 'l', otherwise dark blue) above dark blue band, blue boot-topping.
History: Formed in 1994 jointly by Polish Steamship Co. and by Polish privatised * Euroafrica Shipping Lines Co. Ltd.
Web: www.unityline.pl
Routes: Swinoujscie – Ystad; Swinoujscie – Trelleborg;

Name		Flag	Year	GT	Loa	Bm	Kts	Pass	Car	HGV	Type	Remarks
Galileusz *	(2)	Cyp	1992	14,398	150.4	23.4	18	127	0	141	F	ex Via Tirreno-06
Gryf	(2)	Bhs	1990	18.653	158.0	24.0	16	180	0	120	F	ex Kaptan Burhanettin Isim-04
Jan Sniadecki *	(2)	Cyp	1988	14,417	155.2	21.6	16	57	0	102	R	(also some rail wagons)
Kopernik *	(2)	Pol	1977	13,788	158.4	21.6	18	360	0	18	R	ex Vironia-07, Star Wind-05, Rostock-99 (also 49 rail wagons)
Polonia	(2)	Bhs	1995	29,875	169.9	28.0	17	918	220	110	R	(also some rail wagons)
Skania	(2)	Bhs	1995	23,933	173.7	24.0	23	1397	90	110	P	ex Eurostar Roma-08, Superfast I-04
Wolin	(2)	Bhs	1986	22,874	188.9	23.1	18	150	57	36	R	ex Sky Wind-07, Oresund-98 (also 50 rail wagons)

Viking Line Ab   Finland

Funnel: White lower half, red upper part with black 'V' at base of white edged yellow diamond, black top.
Hull: Red with white 'VIKING LINE', narrow white band above blue boot-topping.
History: Established 1966 as a joint marketing company by Rederi Ab Vikinglinjen (renamed Rederi Ab Solstad in 1966 and Rederi Ab Sally in 1977), Rederi AB Slite and Rederi Ab Ålandsfärjan (renamed SF Line in 1967) to compete with Silja. Sally sold to Effjohn/Silja in 1987 and Slite declared bankrupt in 1993. SF Line renamed Viking Line in 1995.
Web: www.vikingline.fi
Routes: Helsinki – Tallinn; Helsinki – Stockholm; Turku – Mariehamn – Stockholm; Mariehamn – Kapellskar;

Name		Flag	Year	GT	Loa	Bm	Kts	Pass	Car	HGV	Type	Remarks
Amorella	(2)	Fin	1988	34,384	158.0	27.6	21	2420	630	53	P	
Gabriella	(2)	Fin	1992	35,492	169.4	27.6	21	2400	400	68	P	ex Silja Scandinavia-97, Frans Suell-94
Isabella	(2)	Fin	1989	35,154	169.4	27.6	21	2208	630	53	P	
Mariella	(2)	Fin	1985	37,799	175.7	28.4	22	2500	580	0	P	
Rosella	(2)	Fin	1980	16,850	136.1	24.2	21	1700	145	43	P	
Viking Cinderella	(2)	Swe	1989	46,398	191.0	29.0	22	2810	480	60	P	ex Cinderella-03
Viking XPRS		Swe	2008	34,000	185.0	27.7	25	2500	230	63	P	

Wagenborg Passagiersdiensten BV   Netherlands

Funnel: Black with two white bands.
Hull: White
History: Part of the Royal Wagenborg Group – see cargo section.
Web: www.wpd.nl
Routes: Ameland – Holwerd; Lauwersoog – Schiermonnikoog;

Name		Flag	Year	GT	Loa	Bm	Kts	Pass	Car	HGV	Type	Remarks
Monnik	(2)	Nld	1985	1,121	58.0	13.0	10	1000	48	12	P	ex Oerd-03
Oerd	(4)	Nld	2003	2,286	73.2	15.1	10	1463	72	0	P	
Rottum	(2)	Nld	1985	1,121	58.0	13.0	10	1000	48	12	P	ex Sier-95
Sier	(4)	Nld	1995	2,286	73.2	15.1	10	1463	72	0	P	

Also operates the chartered catamaran **Esonborg**.

Wightlink Ltd   UK

Funnel: Blue with white wave symbol.
Hull: White with blue/red 'WIGHTLINK' logo and with narrow red band above broad blue waterline band.
History: Owned by the railways companies from 1880 until sold by Sealink to Sea Containers in 1984, then passing in 1995 to a venture capital company. A management buy-out took place in 2001, followed by a sale to the Macquarie Group in 2005.
Web: www.wightlink.co.uk
Routes: Portsmouth – Fishbourne; Lymington – Yarmouth; Portsmouth – Ryde;

Name		Flag	Year	GT	Loa	Bm	Kts	Pass	Car	HGV	Type	Remarks
St. Catherine	(3)	Gbr	1983	2,036	76.1	16.8	12	784	142	-	P	
St. Cecilia	(3)	Gbr	1987	2,968	76.9	16.8	12	784	142	-	P	
St. Clare	(4)	Gbr	2001	5,359	87.0	18.0	13	878	204	-	P	
St. Faith	(3)	Gbr	1990	3,009	76.1	17.2	12	784	142	-	P	

Name		Flag	Year	GT	Loa	Bm	Kts	Pass	Car	HGV	Type	Remarks
St. Helen	(3)	Gbr	1983	2,983	77.0	17.2	12	784	142	-	P	
Wight Light	(2)	Gbr	2008	2,546	62.4	16.4	12	360	65	-	P	
Wight Sun	(2)	Gbr	2008	2,546	62.4	16.4	12	360	65	-	P	
Wight Sky	(2)	Gbr	2008	2,546	62.4	16.4	12	360	65	-	P	

also high-speed passenger catamarans **Wight Ryder I** *and* **Wight Ryder II**.

TT Line. Peter Pan. *Hans Kraijenbosch*

TT Line. Tom Sawyer. *Hans Kraijenbosch*

Unity Line. Galileusz. *Hans Kraijenbosch*

Wightlink. St. Clare. *Allan Ryszka Onions*

PART TWO
Northern European Coastal Cargo Vessels

Sirius Rederi AB. Olympus. *N. Kemps*

Name		Flag	Year	GT	DWT	Loa	Bm	Drt	Kts	Type	Remarks

A & A Trading Ltd

Latvia

Funnel: *None.* **Hull:** *with red boot-topping.* **History:** *Founded 2007.* **Web:** *None found.*

Name	Flag	Year	GT	DWT	Loa	Bm	Drt	Kts	Type	Remarks
Est	Nld	1987	920	1,496	64.2	10.5	3.7	11	C	ex Reest-01, Laura II-94, Riha-87
Nord	Ant	1991	1,189	1,891	64.7	11.5	4.4	10	C	ex Nordfjord-04, Willy II-01

ABC Maritime AG

Switzerland

Funnel: *White with blue sail/wave symbol, narrow black top.* **Hull:** *Black with red boot-topping.* **History:** *Founded 1982.* **Web:** *www.abcmaritime.ch*

Name	Flag	Year	GT	DWT	Loa	Bm	Drt	Kts	Type	Remarks
CT Longford	Mlt	2009	6,764	10,097	117.0	21.0	7.6	12	T	
Rhone	Mlt	2007	3,006	4,581	99.5	15.6	4.8	10	Tch	
Saint Michel	Mlt	1998	4,346	6,964	108.6	16.8	7.0	13	T	
San Benedetto	Che	1997	4,386	4,780	105.0	18.0	5.0	13	Ta	ex PM Alpha-01
San Benjamino	Che	2003	4,064	4,500	106.0	15.8	6.3	14	Ta	ex Cap Farina-02, l/a Bitumen Star
San Bernardino	Che	2002	3,977	4,232	106.0	15.8	6.0	13	Ta	ex Artha-05
San Nicola	Mlt	1995	4,228	6,506	110.0	16.1	6.8	12	Tch	ex Orient Tiger-01
Troy	Mlt	2005	2,632	3,577	92.9	14.1	5.7	13	Tch	

Abis Shipping Co BV

Netherlands

Funnel: *Dark blue.* **Hull:** *Dark blue with white 'Abis', black boot-topping.* **History:** *Founded 2007.* **Web:** *www.abisshipping.nl*

Name	Flag	Year	GT	DWT	Loa	Bm	Drt	Kts	Type	Remarks
Abis Albufeira	Nld	2009	2,976	4,200	89.9	13.6	5.4	11	Cc	
Abis Antwerpen	Nld	2009	2,976	4,200	89.9	13.6	5.4	11	Cc	
Abis Belfast	Nld	2010	2,998	3,800	90.0	14.0	5.4	12	Cc	
Abis Bergen	Nld	2010	2,998	3,800	90.0	14.0	5.4	12	Cc	
Abis Bilbao	Nld	2010	2,998	3,800	90.0	14.0	5.4	12	Cc	
Abis Bordeaux	Nld	2011	2,998	3,800	90.0	14.0	5.4	12	Cc	
Abis Cadiz	Atg	2010	4,255	6,050	114.4	14.4		12	Cc	
Abis Calais	Atg	2010	4,255	6,050	114.4	14.4		12	Cc	
Abis Cardiff	Atg	2010	4,255	6,050	114.4	14.4		12	Cc	
Abis Cuxhaven	Atg	2011	4,255	6,050	114.4	14.4		12	Cc	

Adriana Shipping & Trading BV

Netherlands

Funnel: *White with narrow black top or charterers colours.* **Hull:** *Blue with black boot-topping.* **History:** *Founded 2000.* **Web:** *None found.*

Name	Flag	Year	GT	DWT	Loa	Bm	Drt	Kts	Type	Remarks
CFL Racer *	Ant	2005	1,554	2,460	82.5	10.9	4.7	12	C	ex Grace-08, Bohemia-05, Grace-05
CFL Ruler *	Ant	2005	1,550	2,500	82.5	10.9	4.7	12	C	ex Adriana-08, Pasadena-05, l/a Adriana
Mike	Cyp	1985	978	1,411	70.0	10.4	3.5	10	C	ex Orion Ariel-98, Vita Nova-92
Yuko	Ant	1986	920	1,469	64.2	10.5	3.8	10	C	ex Noordzee-03, Hera-99, Sayonara-99, Laura-93

* managed by Powdermill Navigation Inc, Greece and on charter to Canada Feeder Lines BV, Netherlands qv

Joint Stock Co Afalita Shipping

Lithuania

Funnel: *White with narrow black top.* **Hull:** *Red with black boot-topping.* **History:** *Founded 1998 as JSC Afalita to 2004 and JSC Afalita Ship Management to 2006.* **Web:** *www.afalita.com*

Name	Flag	Year	GT	DWT	Loa	Bm	Drt	Kts	Type	Remarks
Afalina	Lth	1989	3,826	4,402	104.8	16.0	5.8	15	Ccp	ex Aila-05
Arina	Lth	1989	3,826	4,402	104.8	16.0	5.9	15	Ccp	ex Sofia-06
Klaipeda	Cyp	1995	2,394	3,697	104.8	12.3	5.4	11	Cc	ex Krems-08, Lady Serena-99, Espero-96
Peikko	Cyp	1983	1,521	1,723	82.5	11.3	3.6	10	Cc	ex Sabine L-98, RMS Germania-95, Sabine L-92
Thamesteel 1	Mhl	1989	1,984	2,818	89.3	12.5	4.3	11	Cc	ex Boklum-08, Lea-02, Sonja B-99

Also see Baum & Co GmbH & Co KG and Rohden Bereederung GmbH & Co KG.

Ahlmark Lines AB

Sweden

Funnel: *Black with black 'A' on broad white band.* **Hull:** *White or blue with red or black boot-topping.* **History:** *Founded 1847 as O F Ahlmark & Co A/B to 1993.* **Web:** *www.ahlmark-lines.se*

Name	Flag	Year	GT	DWT	Loa	Bm	Drt	Kts	Type	Remarks
Alstern *	Swe	1984	4,451	6,021	105.9	17.6	7.0	13	Cc	ex Scol Trader-86, Friesland-85
Fryken	Nld	1989	4,059	6,260	99.5	17.0	6.5	12	Cc/T	ex Coldstream Shipper-96, Norrsundet-93
Noren *	Swe	1985	4,483	6,154	106.0	17.5	6.9	13	Cc	ex Scol Carrier-86, Nordland-85
Saxen	Nld	1989	4,059	6,275	99.6	17.0	6.5	12	Cc/T	ex Coldstream Merchant-96, Skutskar-93
Sommen *	Swe	1983	4,426	6,150	106.0	17.6	7.0	13	Cc	
Unden *	Nld	1984	2,577	3,171	87.0	13.2	6.0	14	Cc	
Visten	Nld	1990	4,059	6,275	99.6	17.0	6.5	12	Cc/T	ex Coldstream Trader-96, Aldabi-93

owned by subsidiaries Ahlmarco BV, Netherlands (formed 1963) or * by Barkey Corp. NV (formed 1995) and managed by Marin Ship Management BV, Netherlands (www.marinship.nl)

Christian F Ahrenkiel GmbH & Co

Germany

Funnel: *Buff or buff with houseflag (three fish, laurel wreath and castle motif) on blue band, or charterers colours such as white with green 'UCT'.* **Hull:** *Black, orange or grey with red boot-topping.* **History:** *Founded 1950.* **Web:** *www.ahrenkiel.net*

Name	Flag	Year	GT	DWT	Loa	Bm	Drt	Kts	Type	Remarks
Alstergas *	Lbr	1991	4,200	5,694	100.0	15.9	7.2	14	Lpg	
Multitank Badenia	Deu	1997	3,726	5,846	99.9	16.5	6.8	15	Tch	

Name	Flag	Year	GT	DWT	Loa	Bm	Drt	Kts	Type	Remarks
Multitank Britannia	Deu	1996	3,726	5,846	100.0	16.5	6.8	15	Tch	

managed by Ahrenkiel Shipmanagement GmbH & Co KG (founded 1991 as Constantia Schiffahrts GmbH to 1999)
* managed for Conti Reederei.
Also see Odfjell ASA, Norway

Gebruder Ahrens KG   Germany

Funnel: *White.* **Hull:** *Turquoise with red boot-topping.* **History:** *Founded 1996.* **Web:** *None found.*

Hanna	Cyp	2008	9,981	11,252	134.4	22.5	8.7	18	CC	ex WEC Van Ruysdael-08, Hanna-08
WEC Van Gogh	Cyp	2004	9,962	11,408	134.4	22.5	8.7	18	CC	ex Larissa-08, Judith Borchard-07, I/a Larissa

Alderney Shipping Ltd   UK

Funnel: *Red with white flying bird symbol.* **Hull:** *Blue with red boot-topping.* **History:** *Founded 1969.* **Web:** *www.aldshp.com*

Burhou I	Gbr	1978	674	953	57.5	10.1	3.4	11	C	ex Lancresse-97, Bressay Sound-94, Edgar Dorman-89
Isis	Iom	1978	674	953	57.5	10.1	3.4	11	C	ex Deer Sound-94, David Dorman-89
Mungo	Bhs	1980	664	1,020	59.6	9.2	3.2	10	C	ex Tarquence-01 (len-94)

Parent Company is Allied Coasters Ltd (founded 1979 – www.alliedcoasters.co.uk)

Skips AS Alexandra   Norway

Funnel: *Red with white 'H' on light blue disc inside white ring.* **Hull:** *Green with red boot-topping.* **History:** *Founded 1985* **Web:** *None found.*

Achiever	Gib	1992	5,025	6,545	116.8	17.9	6.9	16	CC	ex Katherine Borchard-05, Gracechurch Jupiter-02, Jupiter-99
Alexandra S	Cok	1972	1,431	1,440	76.9	11.9	3.6	12	Cc	ex Alexandra-97, Alexandra S-85
Anita	Cok	1975	2,767	3,739	93.2	13.6	5.6	13	C	ex Junior-95, Larissa Star-93, Pafic-92, Nova-90, Junior Lotte-84
Tri Star	Cok	1978	4,162	4,122	104.2	16.0	6.7	15	Cc	ex Rosy River-99, Atlantis-93, Alybello-87, Atlantis-86, Maria Catharina-86, Baltic Link-83, Maria Catharina-80

Owned or managed by subsidiary Alexandra Management AS, Norway

Alfamarine Shipping Co Ltd   Russia

Funnel: *Blue with blue triangle outline on broad white band.* **Hull:** *Black or grey with red boot-topping.* **History:** *Founded 2008.* **Web:** *None found.*

Olympic-A	Mlt	1973	1,519	2,178	76.2	11.9	4.8	13	Cc	ex Lucy Mar-04, Nordbulk-04, Jampi-03, Lotta-01, Chiemsea-85, Chiemsee-82
Ophelia	Nis	1981	4,270	6,400	115.0	15.9	7.2	14	Tch	ex Sioux-01
Orion A	Rus	1982	2,593	4,165	88.0	13.1	6.4	13	Tch	ex Alea Tony-08, Bro Tony-05, United Tony-00, Lecko av Lidkoping-91

Alpha Shipping Co SIA   Latvia

Funnel: *Blue with white 'A' on pale blue square, narrow black top.* **Hull:** *Green or red with white 'www.alpha.lv', red boot-topping.* **History:** *Founded 1994 as Alpha Shipping Agency Ltd to 2004.* **Web:** *www.alpha.lv*

Cassiopeia	Atg	1981	1,939	2,890	88.0	11.3	4.7	11	Cc	ex Bellatrix-09, Helm Voyager-05, Angelburg-04, Margaretha-96
Magdalena	Atg	1990	2,371	4,247	88.3	13.2	5.5	12	C	
Pearl Vita	Atg	2000	2,999	4,900	95.1	13.2	6.2	12	Cc	ex Marbella-08, Charlotte C-05
Sirius	Atg	2001	5,381	7,567	105.6	18.2	6.6	12	B	ex Auriga-09
Sky Vita	Atg	1991	2,497	4,195	88.3	13.2	5.5	11	C	ex Flevo-05, Waltraud-92, Kirsten-91
Sun Vita	Mlt	1991	3,585	4,150	98.8	16.3	5.4	14	C	ex Spirit of Foynes-08, Sun Vita-06, Iduna-05, CMB Iduna-95, Iduna-94
Vela	Atg	1982	1,939	2,890	88.0	11.3	4.7	11	Cc	ex Diadem-09, Helm Trader-05, Tramp-04, Breitenburg-04, Keitum-95, Jule-94, Balder-93, Jule-88
Vita	Atg	1990	2,497	4,161	88.3	13.2	5.5	12	Cc	ex Emja-04

Also owns larger bulk carriers and dredger/hoppers.

Altex Shipping Co Ltd   Russia

Funnel: *White with narrow grey band, black top.* **Hull:** *Black with red boot-topping.* **History:** *Founded 1995 and controlled by the Government of The Russian Federation.* **Web:** *None found.*

Alexandre	Khm	1965	2,726	3,579	102.3	14.0	6.0	13	C	ex Yanales-95

Aludra Scheepsvaartkontorneming   Netherlands

Funnel: *White.* **Hull:** *Green with red boot-topping.* **History:** *Operating for subsidiary of Arcelor Mittal.* **Web:** *None found.*

Sea Riss	Nld	1992	1,595	2,200	79.7	11.0	4.2	12	C	ex Solon-97

Ahlmark Lines AB . Saxen. *Allan Ryszka Onions*

Alderney Shipping Ltd. Isis. *Tom Walker*

Alpha Shipping Co SIA. Sky Vita. *M. Beckett*

Name		Flag	Year	GT	DWT	Loa	Bm	Drt	Kts	Type	Remarks

Amasus Shipping BV   Netherlands

Funnel: *White or individual owners markings.* **Hull:** *Black, light blue or dark blue with red or black boot-topping.* **History:** *Founded 1981 as Amasus Shipping BV to 1999 and Amasus Chartering BV to 2002. Merged with Royal Shipping BV in 1999.* **Web:** *www.amasus.nl*

Name	Flag	Year	GT	DWT	Loa	Bm	Drt	Kts	Type	Remarks
Bravery	Nld	2004	1,552	1,864	82.2	11.4	3.4	-	C	
Eems Carrier *	Nld	1996	1,546	2,346	85.8	10.8	4.8	10	C	ex Koerier-08
Eems Coast *	Nld	1985	998	1,490	78.0	10.6	3.2	10	C	ex Galatea-08, Galaxa-92
Eems Delfia	Nld	1985	1,132	1,528	79.3	10.4	3.2	10	C	ex Venntrans-08, Zwartewater-05, Marina-95, Veritas-92
Eems Dollard	Nld	2003	2,545	3,850	88.6	12.5	5.4	-	C	ex Artemis-08
Eems Transporter *	Nld	2006	2,186	2,900	90.0	13.8	4.4	-	C	
Gitana †	Nld	2003	3,169	5,000	95.3	13.4	5.8	12	C	ex Trinitas-07
Ideaal	Nld	2010	2,600	3,500	-	-	-	-	C	ex Eems Runner-10
Navigable ‡	Nld	2010	2,460	3,500	-	-	-	-	C	
Navigare ‡	Nld	2010	2,460	3,500	-	-	-	-	C	
Novatrans	Nld	1991	2,561	3,284	88.0	12.6	5.3	12	Cc	ex Helene-08
Prudence *	Nld	2003	1,556	1,780	81.7	11.4	3.5	-	C	
Rhodanus ‡	Nld	1998	2,056	2,953	89.5	12.4	4.3	10	Cc	ex Hansa Kampen-06
Rimini	Nld	2008	1,862	2,600	87.3	11.4	4.3	-	C	ex Eems Spirit-08, Maria-08
Schokland	Nld	2010	2,600	3,500	-	-	-	-	C	
Sea Charente *	Nld	1996	1,638	2,270	82.3	11.4	4.0	11	C	ex Fisker-97
Sea Shannon	Nld	1998	1,670	2,268	82.5	11.3	4.1	10	C	l/a Joriston
Wisdom *	Nld	2004	1,552	1,842	82.2	11.4	3.4	10	C	

* managed or owned by subsidiary Amasus Support BV (founded 2006 initially as Delta Fleet Support BV)
† managed for Bakotrans Shipping, Netherlands (founded 2006 – www.bakotrans.nl) or ‡ for Geuze Shipping BV, Netherlands (founded 2002)
Also see Rederij C Kornet & Zonen BV, Netherlands

Amisco Ltd   Estonia

Funnel: *Red with white band or charterers colours.* **Hull:** *Red with red boot-topping.* **History:** *Founded 1997.* **Web:** *www.amisco.ee*

Name	Flag	Year	GT	DWT	Loa	Bm	Drt	Kts	Type	Remarks
Merita	Cyp	1985	3,329	4,496	98.7	15.7	5.7	14	Cc	ex Cis Brovig-05, Gisela Bartels-96, Gracechurch Harp-89, l/a Gisela Bartels (len-86)
Navita	Vct	1984	3,329	4,115	98.7	15.5	5.4	14	Cc	ex Ketty Brovig-04, Rockabill-98, Hasselwerder-94, Gracechurch Crown-90, Hasselwerder-89, City of Manchester-85, Hasselwerder-84 (len-89)
Regina Magdalena	Nis	1981	3,593	4,153	99.9	15.7	5.1	12	Cc	ex Regulus-03, Carolin-99, Njord-92, Manchester Prince-89, Njord-86, City of Oporto-85, Njord-81
WEC Majorelle	Cyp	1995	6,326	7,946	129.8	20.0	7.3	17	CC	ex Pirita-09, Nova-06, OOCL Neva-01, Nova-99, Norasia Adria-97, Nova-96

Amons & Co   Netherlands

Funnel: *Blue with narrow red top.* **Hull:** *Blue with red boot-topping.* **History:** *Founded 1852.* **Web:** *None found.*

Name	Flag	Year	GT	DWT	Loa	Bm	Drt	Kts	Type	Remarks
Marathon	Ant	1976	1,655	2,575	78.7	12.4	5.0	11	C	ex Vrouwe Alida-90
Sander	Ant	1984	2,472	3,065	90.0	13.6	4.5	11	Cc	ex Lucas-05, Oriental Dragon-98, Sonja-95, Martini-94, Paul-92, Tiger Wave-90, Paul-89, Band Aid I-86, Paul-85

Amur Shipping Co   Russia

Funnel: *White with blue over red bands, black top.* **Hull:** *Various.* **History:** *Controlled by Government of The Russian Federation and formed 1987 as Amur River Shipping Co to 1993.* **Web:** *None found.*

Name		Flag	Year	GT	DWT	Loa	Bm	Drt	Kts	Type	Remarks
Baltiyskiy-71	(2)	Khm	1967	1,948	2,128	96.0	13.2	3.3	10	C	
Baltiyskiy-106	(2)	Rus	1979	1,926	2,554	95.0	13.2	4.0	12	Cc	
Ivan Zhdanov		Rus	1995	4,978	5,885	(140.0)	16.6	4.5	10	C	
Kapitan Boldyrev	(2)	Rus	1975	2,478	3,361	114.0	13.2	3.8	10	C	ex Amur Voyager-01, Kapitan Boldyrev-98, Sormovskiy-112-93
Kapitan Konshin	(2)	Rus	1978	2,478	3,208	114.0	13.2	3.8	10	C	ex Sormovskiy-58-06, XVIII Syezd VLKSM-02
Kapitan Sosenkov		Rus	1998	4,978	5,885	140.0	16.7	4.5	-	C	l/a Amur
Krasnoye Sormovo	(2)	Rus	1979	2,478	3,233	114.0	13.2	3.8	10	C	
Lenaneft-2066		Rus	1988	2,863	3,045	122.8	15.3	3.1	10	T	
Morskoy-14		Rus	1968	1,662	1,810	88.0	12.4	3.3	10	C	
Omskiy-114	(2)	Rus	1983	2,360	2,923	108.4	14.8	3.0	10	C	
Omskiy-115	(2)	Rus	1983	2,463	3,197	108.4	14.8	3.3	10	C	ex Rashimi-01, Omskiy-115-83
Omskiy-116	(2)	Rus	1984	2,360	3,197	108.4	14.8	3.0	10	C	
Omskiy-117	(2)	Rus	1983	2,463	3,197	108.4	14.8	3.3	10	C	ex Elena-01, Yelena-97, Omskiy-117-94
Omskiy-121	(2)	Rus	1984	2,463	3,197	108.4	14.8	3.3	10	C	ex Svetlana-01, Omskiy-121
Omskiy-122	(2)	Rus	1984	2,463	3,197	108.4	14.8	3.3	10	C	ex Margarita 1-01, Omskiy-122-94
Omskiy-130	(2)	Rus	1987	1,534	3,070	108.4	14.8	3.3	10	C	ex Olga-06, Omskiy-130-99
Omskiy-131	(2)	Rus	1987	1,534	2,150	108.4	14.8	3.2	10	C	
Professor Kerichev		Rus	1979	2,478	3,218	114.0	13.2	3.8	10	C	
Sormovskiy-40	(2)	Rus	1978	2,478	3,147	114.0	13.2	3.7	10	C	
Sormovskiy-117	(2)	Rus	1979	2,478	3,134	114.0	13.2	3.7	10	C	

Name		Flag	Year	GT	DWT	Loa	Bm	Drt	Kts	Type	Remarks
Volga-4011	(2)	Rus	1991	4,966	5,985	139.8	16.6	4.5	10	Cc	
Volgoneft-301	(2)	Rus	1982	4,134	4,987	125.1	16.6	4.2	11	T	

Janus Andersen & Co AS — Denmark

Funnel: *Blue with white 'JA'.* **Hull:** *Blue or red with red boot-topping.* **History:** *Formed 1918.* **Web:** *www.janus-a.dk*

Name		Flag	Year	GT	DWT	Loa	Bm	Drt	Kts	Type	Remarks
Malene		Dis	1984	845	922	53.9	9.6	3.7	11	Cc	ex Markland Saga-90

Owned by Peter Knudsen and managed by Nordane Shipping A/S (founded 1994 – www.nordane.dk)

Aquachart SIA — Latvia

Funnel: *Black with white anchor symbol on broad blue band edged with narrow white bands.* **Hull:** *Black with red boot-topping.* **History:** *Founded 1997 as Aquachart Inc and subsidiary Aquaship formed 2000.* **Web:** *www.aquachart.lv or www.ship.lv*

Name	Flag	Year	GT	DWT	Loa	Bm	Drt	Kts	Type	Remarks
Arctic Sea	Mlt	1992	3,988	4,706	97.8	17.3	6.0	12	Cc	ex Jogaila-05, Torm Senegal-00, Alrai-98, Zim Venezuela-98, Okhotskoe-96
Arctic Spirit	Mlt	1987	6,395	7,850	131.6	19.3	7.0	15	Cc	ex Balkan Trader-05, Thirza-04, B othnia Stone-03, Sea Trader-02, Pavin Vinogradov-97
Arctic Star	Lbr	1991	6,395	7,850	131.6	19.3	7.0	15	Cc	ex Tegra-02, Akademik Glushko-00
Solombala	Lbr	1990	6,395	7,850	131.6	19.3	7.0	15	Cc	ex Nord-08, Olma-02, Kapitan Ponomarev-99, Kapitan Ponomaryov-97

Also operates refrigerated and fish carriers

SIA Aquarius Shipmanagement Co — Latvia

Funnel: *White with black top.* **Hull:** *Dark blue with red boot-topping.* **History:** *Founded 2002 as Aquarius SMC LLC to 2005.* **Web:** *None found.*

Name		Flag	Year	GT	DWT	Loa	Bm	Drt	Kts	Type	Remarks
Anund		Cyp	1975	2,240	2,750	81.4	13.4	5.0	13	Cc	ex Odin-84, Eco Liz-83, Odin-81
Astra *		Atg	1993	2,416	3,570	85.0	13.0	4.5	12	Cc	ex Elbetal-08, Lys-Chris-07, Marie Chris-93
Balder *		Atg	1986	1,790	2,800	82.5	12.5	4.5	11	Cc	ex Handorf-06, Jacqueline-99, Jutta R-90, Jacqueline-86
Brigga *		Atg	1994	2,818	4,216	91.5	13.6	5.8	12	C	ex Ewald O-08, Arabella C-04
Dolfijn		Atg	1989	1,987	2,450	81.2	12.4	5.0		C	
Forseti *		Atg	1993	2,416	3,574	85.0	13.0	5.4	11	Cc	ex Nauta-08, Heljo-06, Hornsund-97, Heljo-96
Frigga *		Atg	1994	2,818	4,216	91.5	13.6	5.8	12	Cc	ex Hertha O-07, Claudia C-04
Ladoga-3	(2)	Blz	1973	1,511	1,968	81.0	11.9	4.0	12	C	
Ladoga-5	(2)	Blz	1973	1,511	1,968	81.0	11.9	4.0	12	C	
Ladoga-8	(2)	Blz	1974	1,511	1,885	81.0	12.0	4.5	12	C	ex Norppa-81, Ladoga-8-74
Ran *		Atg	1986	1,943	2,859	89.0	12.5	4.8	10	C	ex Bever-06, Duisburg-06, Liliana-04, Duisburg-99, Phini-99, Erika H-97, Wilma-92
Rig *		Mlt	1989	2,351	3,200	87.0	13.0	5.1	11	C	ex Borneiro-05, Lady Anna-00, Amrum-95, Port Sado-93
Roseburg		Atg	1991	1,999	3,005	82.0	12.6	4.9	12	Cc	ex Forseti-07, Ivy-05, Balticborg-03
Skadi		Dma	1976	2,239	2,560	81.4	13.4	5.0	13	Cc	ex Weserberg-04, Pico Grande-00, Gotland-87, Jacob Becker-86

* managed by Astramar Transport Ltd, Latvia

ARA Atlantis CV — Netherlands

Funnel: *White with narrow black top or charterers colours.* **Hull:** *Light grey with red boot-topping.* **History:** *Management company founded 2006 and ship-owning company 2008.* **Web:** *www.aragroup.com*

Name	Flag	Year	GT	DWT	Loa	Bm	Drt	Kts	Type	Remarks
Ara Felixstowe	Gib	1991	3,818	4,660	103.5	16.0	6.1	14	Cc	ex Tossens-07, Francop-03, Aquitaine Spirit-97, CMBT Cutter-96, Emma-96, Rhein Lagan-94, Francop-94, Manchester Trader-92, Francop-91
Ara Zeebrugge	Cyp	1991	3,815	4,155	103.5	16.3	6.1	14	Cc	ex Merkur-05
Emily Borchard	Gib	2007	9,962	11,435	134.4	22.5	8.7	18	CC	ex Ara Atlantis-09, Actuaria-08

Managed by ARA Ship Management BV, Netherlands.

Arg Shipping SIA — Latvia

Funnel: *None.* **Hull:** *Dark blue with red boot-topping.* **History:** *Founded 2002 as Aquarius SMC LLC to 2005.* **Web:** *None found.*

Name		Flag	Year	GT	DWT	Loa	Bm	Drt	Kts	Type	Remarks
Cabrana	(2)	Blz	1988	1,853	2,075	82.5	11.4	4.0	10	Cc	ex Yeya-1-09, Ladoga-102-08
Sagitta	(2)	Blz	1988	1,853	2,075	82.5	11.4	4.0	10	Cc	ex Yeya-2-09, Ladoga-103-08

Joint Stock Co 'Arkus' — Russia

Funnel: *Black.* **Hull:** *Black with red boot-topping.* **History:** *Founded 2002 and controlled by Government of The Russian Federation.* **Web:** *None found.*

Name		Flag	Year	GT	DWT	Loa	Bm	Drt	Kts	Type	Remarks
Volgo-Balt 102	(2)	Sle	1969	2,457	3,246	114.1	13.2	3.5	10	C	
Volgo-Balt 107	(2)	Geo	1969	2,457	3,172	114.1	13.2	3.6	10	C	

Operated by subsidiary Arcus Shipping Co Ltd

Arklow Shipping Ltd — Ireland

Funnel: *White with coat of arms on white shield.* **Hull:** *Light green with dark green waterline over red or black boot-topping.* **History:** *Formed 1966 and in 2000 acquired Hanno Shipping BV (formed 1900 as Heinrich Hanno & Co BV).* **Web:** *www.asl.ie*

Name	Flag	Year	GT	DWT	Loa	Bm	Drt	Kts	Type	Remarks
Arklow Faith	Irl	2006	2,998	4,480	90.0	14.4	5.8	11	C	

Amasus Shipping BV. Sea Shannon. *David Walker*

Arklow Shipping Ltd. Arklow Rally. *M. Beckett*

Arklow Shipping Ltd. Arklow Rock. *N. Kemps*

Name		Flag	Year	GT	DWT	Loa	Bm	Drt	Kts	Type	Remarks
Arklow Fame		Irl	2006	2,998	4,480	90.0	14.4	5.8	11	C	
Arklow Flair		Irl	2007	2,998	4,480	90.0	14.4	5.8	11	C	
Arklow Fortune		Irl	2007	2,998	4,480	90.0	14.4	5.8	11	C	
Arklow Freedom		Irl	2008	2,998	4,480	90.0	14.4	5.8	11	C	
Arklow Racer		Irl	2004	2,999	4,390	90.0	14.0	5.7	11	Cc	
Arklow Raider		Irl	2007	2,999	4,530	90.0	14.0	5.7	11	Cc	
Arklow Rainbow		Irl	2006	2,999	4,530	90.0	14.0	5.7	11	Cc	
Arklow Rally *		Irl	2002	2,999	4,400	90.0	14.4	5.8	11	C	
Arklow Rambler *		Irl	2002	2,999	4,400	90.0	14.4	5.8	11	C	
Arklow Ranger *		Irl	2002	2,999	4,400	90.0	14.4	5.8	11	C	
Arklow Raven		Irl	2007	2,999	4,530	90.0	14.0	5.7	11	Cc	
Arklow Rebel		Irl	2005	2,999	4,504	90.0	14.0	5.7	11	Cc	
Arklow Resolve		Irl	2004	2,999	4,504	90.0	14.0	5.7	11	Cc	
Arklow Rival		Irl	2006	2,999	4,530	90.0	14.0	5.7	11	Cc	
Arklow River		Irl	2003	2,999	4,530	90.0	14.0	5.7	11	Cc	
Arklow Rock		Irl	2004	2,999	4,504	90.0	14.0	5.7	11	Cc	
Arklow Rogue		Irl	2007	2,999	4,530	90.0	14.0	5.7	11	Cc	
Arklow Rose		Irl	2002	2,999	4,530	90.0	14.0	5.7	11	Cc	
Arklow Rover		Irl	2004	2,999	4,530	90.0	14.0	5.7	11	Cc	
Arklow Ruler		Irl	2006	2,999	4,530	90.0	14.0	5.7	11	Cc	
Arklow Sand **		Nld	1998	2,316	3,193	90.0	12.5	4.7	11	Cc	
Arklow Sea **		Nld	1998	2,316	3,193	90.0	12.5	4.7	11	Cc	
Arklow Sky **		Nld	2000	2,316	3,171	90.0	12.5	4.7	11	Cc	
Arklow Spirit **		Bhs	1995	2,271	3,211	90.0	12.5	4.7	11	Cc	
Arklow Spray **		Bhs	1996	2,300	3,193	90.0	12.5	4.7	12	Cc	
Arklow Star **		Nld	1998	2,316	3,193	90.0	12.5	4.7	11	Cc	
Arklow Surf **		Nld	2000	2,316	3,171	90.0	12.5	4.6	11	Cc	
Arklow Venture **		Nld	1999	2,829	4,966	89.8	13.6	6.4	11	Cc	ex Sider Venture-04
Arklow Venus **		Nld	2000	2,829	4,903	89.8	13.6	6.4	11	Cc	ex Sider Venus-05
Arklow Viking **		Nld	1999	2,829	4,934	89.8	13.6	6.4	11	Cc	ex MRS Sonja-05
Arklow Wave		Irl	2003	8,938	13,977	136.4	21.2	8.4	13	C	
Arklow Willow		Irl	2004	8,935	13,873	136.4	21.2	8.4	13	C	
Arklow Wind		Irl	2004	8,938	13,777	136.4	21.2	8.4	13	C	

Newbuildings: Eight 9,750g 14,450d ('M' class) and four further 2,998g 4,480d ('F' class) cargo on order for 2010-11 delivery.
* owned or ** managed by subsidiary Arklow Shipping Nederland BV (formerly Hanno Shipping BV)

Armac Marine Management Ltd UK

Funnel: Pale blue with white 'A' in circle. **Hull:** Black with red boot-topping. **History:** Founded 2000 as subsidiary of Octopus Investments Ltd.
Web: www.armacshipping.co.uk; www.armacmarine.co.uk

Name		Flag	Year	GT	DWT	Loa	Bm	Drt	Kts	Type	Remarks
Ardent	(2)	Gbr	1983	700	1,180	50.0	9.5	3.6	9	C	
Christine Y		Bhs	1986	851	1,281	64.2	10.5	3.3	10	C	ex Anna-04, Willy-01
Falcon	(2)	Gbr	1991	1,382	2,225	78.0	11.0	4.0	9	C	ex Hoo Falcon-06
Lark	(2)	Gbr	1984	794	1,394	58.3	9.5	3.9	8	C	ex Hoo Laurel-06
Martin	(2)	Gbr	1986	794	1,412	58.3	9.5	3.9	8	C	ex Hoo Marlin-06
Pipit	(2)	Gbr	1984	794	1,394	58.3	9.5	3.9	9	C	ex Hoopride-06
River Carrier	(2)	Gbr	1986	794	1,400	58.3	9.6	3.9	9	C	ex Curlew-09, Hoocrest-06
River Trader	(2)	Gbr	1989	794	1,399	58.3	9.5	3.6	9	C	ex Teal-09, Hoo Beech-06
Swallow	(2)	Gbr	1986	794	1,412	58.3	9.5	3.9	8	C	ex Hoo Swan-06
Swift	(2)	Gbr	1989	794	1,399	58.3	9.5	3.9	9	C	ex Hoo Swift-06

Operated by Armac Shipping Services Ltd, trading as Coastal Bulk Shipping Ltd (www.coastalbulkshipping.co.uk) and River Bulk Shipping Ltd (www.riverbulkshipping.co.uk)

Arnesen Shipbrokers AS Norway

Funnel: Buff. **Hull:** Blue or * light grey with red boot-topping. **History:** Founded 1989 as Roger Arnesens Rederi. **Web:** www.arnesenshipbrokers.no

Name	Flag	Year	GT	DWT	Loa	Bm	Drt	Kts	Type	Remarks
Hege	Nis	1975	3,004	4,106	96.7	14.5	6.3	14	Cc	ex Koningshaven-01, OPDR Rabat-98, Rabat-97, Diana II-88, Diana-83
Sandra *	Nis	1977	2,282	2,456	81.4	13.4	6.0	13	Cc	ex Gerlin-01, Susan Borchard-91, Orion-90

ATR Schiffahrt GmbH & Co KG Germany

Funnel: Blue with black 'T' over black ''H'' on broad red band edged with narrow white bands. **Hull:** Red with red boot-topping. **History:** Founded 2003 as a subsidiary of Arp Thordsen Rautenberg-Landhandel GmbH. **Web:** www.arp-thordsen.de

Name	Flag	Year	GT	DWT	Loa	Bm	Drt	Kts	Type	Remarks
Ilka	Deu	1985	1,366	1,300	71.8	11.3	3.2	10	C	
Maike	Deu	1989	1,599	1,908	82.0	11.3	3.7	10	C	

Arpa Shipping BV Netherlands

Funnel: White or dark green with red/blue eight-pointed compass rose, either inside blue ring or on white disc. **Hull:** Blue or dark green, some with white 'ARPA', red boot-topping. **History:** Founded 1987. **Web:** www.arpa-shipping.nl

Name	Flag	Year	GT	DWT	Loa	Bm	Drt	Kts	Type	Remarks
Aristote	Bhs	1983	1,426	1,821	84.8	11.4	3.5	10	C	ex Turbulence-02

Name		Flag	Year	GT	DWT	Loa	Bm	Drt	Kts	Type	Remarks
Frelon	(2)	Mlt	1990	1,354	1,699	77.0	11.4	3.2	10	Cc	ex Orade-07, Sea Orade-98, I/a Orade
Helen		Bhs	1981	1,425	1,842	84.8	11.4	3.4	10	C	ex Urgence-02
Laguepe		Mlt	1987	1,412	1,780	81.0	11.3	3.3	9	Cs	ex Widor-04
Tramontane		Bhs	1983	1,426	1,821	84.7	11.5	3.4	10	C	ex Muriel-08, Stridence-02

Managed by SMS-Ship Management Support BV, Netherlands.

Artic Shipping AS Norway

Funnel: *White with white 'A' inside white ring on dark blue flag.* **Hull:** *Blue with green 'EWOS EXPRESS' on white panel interrupting white band, red boot-topping.* **History:** *Founded 1995 as Artic Shipping & Finans ANS to 2003.* **Web:** *www.articship.no*

Name	Flag	Year	GT	DWT	Loa	Bm	Drt	Kts	Type	Remarks
Artic Fjord	Nor	2004	1,725	1,612	58.9	13.8	5.4	-	C	
Artic Lady	Nor	2006	1,678	1,350	59.3	13.8	5.0	12	C	

Ast Shipping Co Ltd Russia

Funnel: *Not confirmed.* **Hull:** *Not confirmed.* **History:** *Founded 2004 and controlled by Government of the Russian Federation.* **Web:** *None found.*

Name	Flag	Year	GT	DWT	Loa	Bm	Drt	Kts	Type	Remarks
Crystal	Cyp	1990	740	1,068	64.3	10.0	4.0	10	Tch	ex Woo Cheong-07, Seiwa Maru-01
Oberon	Vct	1976	3,464	6,072	80.2	16.1	8.0	11	Cc	ex Alcorn-07, Sandy-04, Vilsandi-00, Khudozhnik Koryn-92, Looiersgracht-86
Sealord	Khm	1976	3,422	3,648	80.3	16.0	8.5	12	Cc	ex Esco Virgo-00, Blue Aquamarinr-98, Realengracht-88

Astromare Bereederungs GmbH & Co KG Germany

Funnel: *White with charterers colours.* **Hull:** *Blue with red boot-topping.* **History:** *Founded 2006.* **Web:** *None found.*

Name	Flag	Year	GT	DWT	Loa	Bm	Drt	Kts	Type	Remarks
Transanuna	Cyp	2007	7,720	9,593	141.6	20.6	7.3	18	CC	I/a Astrosprinter
Transjorund	Cyp	2007	7,720	9,544	141.6	20.6	7.3	18	CC	I/a Astrorunner

Atlantic Horizon Group Netherlands

Oost Atlantic Lijn BV/Netherlands

Funnel: *Red with red 'OAL' on broad white over green bands.* **Hull:** *Light grey, black or blue with red boot-topping.* **History:** *Founded 1960 and now part of Atlantic Horizon Group founded 2002.* **Web:** *www.atlantic-horizon.nl*

Name	Flag	Year	GT	DWT	Loa	Bm	Drt	Kts	Type	Remarks
Atlantic Comet	Cyp	1995	3,999	5,214	100.6	18.5	6.6	15	Cc	ex Janra-05
Atlantic Horizon	Cyp	2006	3,990	6,000	110.8	14.0	6.3	13	Cc	ex Michel-08
Atlantic Island	Cyp	2002	3,164	5,000	95.5	13.4	5.8	12	Cc	ex Westerscheldeborg-07
Atlantic Moon	Cyp	2002	3,164	5,000	95.5	13.4	5.8	12	Cc	ex Oosterscheldeborg-07
Atlantic Sun	Cyp	1996	2,848	4,264	90.5	13.2	5.8	11	Cc	ex Osterland-06, Sweder-03

Atrica-Marine Ltd Estonia

Funnel: *Yellow.* **Hull:** *Red with black boot-topping.* **History:** *Founded 1993.* **Web:** *www.atrica.ee*

Name	Flag	Year	GT	DWT	Loa	Bm	Drt	Kts	Type	Remarks
Tera	Atg	1985	1,861	3,035	91.0	11.4	4.9	10	Cc	ex Mega-07, Baltic Sun-06, Atlantic Sun-05, Marrow Star-00, Waddenzee-99

Avedoere Shipping A/S Denmark

Funnel: *White.* **Hull:** *Black.* **History:** *Founded 1997.* **Web:** *www.avedoereshipping.dk*

Name		Flag	Year	GT	DWT	Loa	Bm	Drt	Kts	Type	Remarks
Alga		Vct	1976	1,858	2,480	83.6	11.8	4.7	12	Cc	ex Thor Heidi-01, Bolmen-97, Fenris-96, Marie Lehmann-86 (len-79)
Anton	(2)	Vct	1972	2,498	3,143	114.0	13.0	3.6	10	C	ex Enely-97, Central-97, Volgo-Balt 156-93
Sabine	(2)	Vct	1970	2,478	3,355	114.2	13.0	3.8	10	C	ex Sormovskiy-19-00

Operated by subsidiary Smythe Shipping Inc, Russia.

Reederei Karl-Heinz Baase Germany

Funnel: *Buff, white with white anchor on blue houseflag or charterers colours.* **Hull:** *Blue with red or black boot-topping.* **History:** *Founded 1988.* **Web:** *None found.*

Name	Flag	Year	GT	DWT	Loa	Bm	Drt	Kts	Type	Remarks
Westwind II	Pan	1985	3,539	3,177	101.0	16.0	5.0	13	Cc	ex Westwind-07, Tertia-95

Reederei M Bahr-Viemann Germany

Funnel: *White with green three-leaf clover.* **Hull:** *Dark green.* **History:** *Founded 2008.* **Web:** *None found.*

Name	Flag	Year	GT	DWT	Loa	Bm	Drt	Kts	Type	Remarks
Christa Kerstin	Blz	1977	1,768	2,416	81.4	11.9	4.8	11	C	ex Monika-08, Mona Rosa-04, Stepenitz-99, Noordland-89

Bakotrans Shipping Netherlands

Funnel: *White.* **Hull:** *Blue with black boot-topping.* **History:** *Founded 2006.* **Web:** *www.bakotrans.nl*

Name	Flag	Year	GT	DWT	Loa	Bm	Drt	Kts	Type	Remarks
Gitana	Nld	2003	3,169	5,000	95.3	13.4	5.8		C	ex Trinitas-07

Managed by Amasus Shipping BV

Atlantic Horizon/Oost Atlantic Lijn. Atlantic Comet. *C. Lous*

ATR Schiffahrt GmbH. Ilka. *C. Lous*

Baltnautic Shipping Ltd. Lyrika. *Hans Kraijenbosch*

Name		Flag	Year	GT	DWT	Loa	Bm	Drt	Kts	Type	Remarks

Balimar Marine Service Ou — Estonia

Funnel: *White.* **Hull:** *Blue with red boot-topping.* **History:** *Founded 2007.* **Web:** *None found.*

Name		Flag	Year	GT	DWT	Loa	Bm	Drt	Kts	Type	Remarks
Capella		Atg	1982	1,939	2,885	88.0	11.3	4.7	11	Cc	ex Steinburg-05, Comet-95

Baltex Transport Morski Sp z oo — Poland

Funnel: *White.* **Hull:** *Blue with red boot-topping.* **History:** *Not confirmed.* **Web:** *None found.*

Laila II	(2)	Pol	1989	1,853	2,075	82.5	11.4	4.0	10	Cc	ex Lechia-09, Ladoga-108-08

Baltic Maritime Service Ltd — Estonia

Funnel: *White.* **Hull:** *Blue with red or black boot-topping.* **History:** *Founded 1992.* **Web:** *None found.*

Elke		Atg	1985	1,473	2,127	79.0	10.9	4.0	10	Cc	ex Kirsten-03, Fast Wal-98, Kirsten-93, Sabine-93
Helga		Atg	1984	1,472	2,131	79.0	10.9	4.0	10	Cc	ex Fast Karel-98, Helga-94, Hanne-90

Baltic Scandinavian Lines AS — Estonia

Funnel: *White with circular eight pointed emblem, narrow red top or * white with narrow blue top.* **Hull:** *Blue with red boot-topping or * green with black boot-topping.* **History:** *Founded 2005.* **Web:** *www.bsl.ee*

Sisu Canopus		Atg	1998	2,599	3,480	92.8	15.9	4.9	15	Cc	ex Marc Mitchell-08, Keteldijk-04, Helen T-03, Arfell-00, Keteldijk-99
Sisu Capella		Atg	1998	2,599	3,600	92.8	15.9	4.9	15	CC	ex William Mitchell-08, Ijsseldijk-04, Batavier VI-00, l/a Ijsseldijk

Also see Ferry Section.

Baltic Tanker Co Ltd — Russia

Funnel: *Not confirmed.* **Hull:** *Brown with red boot-topping.* **History:** *Founded 2008.* **Web:** *None found.*

Vanino		Rus	1986	1,896	3,389	77.5	14.3	5.4	10	T	ex Nemunas-08, Vostok-92

Baltic TransService Ltd — Russia

Funnel: *Dark blue with black top.* **Hull:** *Black with red boot-topping.* **History:** *Not confirmed* **Web:** *None found.*

Volgo-Balt 190	(2)	Kna	1975	2,554	3,173	113.9	13.2	3.6	10	C	
Volgo-Balt 194	(2)	Kna	1976	2,516	3,180	114.0	13.2	3.6	10	C	

Managed for Albros Shipping & Trading Co.

Baltimar A/S Ltd — Denmark

Funnel: *Black with dark green 'B' outline on broad white band.* **Hull:** *Dark green with red boot-topping.* **History:** *Founded 1982.* **Web:** *www.baltimar.com*

Granat		Atg	1991	2,854	3,181	91.3	14.7	5.0	12	Cc	ex Baltimar Euros-10, Industrial Carrier-99, Baltimar Euros-94

Baltnautic Shipping Ltd — Lithuania

Funnel: *Blue.* **Hull:** *Blue or red with red or black boot-topping.* **History:** *Founded 1998.* **Web:** *www.baltnautic.lt*

Amadeus		Vct	2001	1,435	1,680	80.0	11.4	3.4	9	Cc	ex Zeeland-09, Hansa Lyon-05
Ancora		Vct	1981	1,010	1,448	69.9	11.3	3.4	11	C	ex Waterway-07, Union Venus-94
Aquarius *		Lth	1996	1,141	1,500	81.4	9.5	3.2	9	C	ex Warber-08
Clarity		Vct	1981	986	1,448	69.9	11.3	3.4	11	C	ex Union Mars-01
Diamant		Lth	1985	998	1,497	78.0	10.0	3.2	10	C	ex Watum-95
Diamonde		Vct	1985	1,487	2,284	79.5	11.3	4.4	10	C	ex Diamond-99
Eurika		Lth	1983	999	1,474	79.9	10.1	3.2	11	C	ex Willem Sr.-01, Willeke-06, Steady-92, Yvonne-89
Jongleur		Vct	1991	1,999	3,030	81.5	12.4	5.0	12	Cc	ex Crown Alizee-07, Zwartemeer-02
Lyrika		Lth	1994	1,909	2,350	89.2	11.4	4.1	12	Cc	ex Mithril-06, Harns-04
Mare		Nld	1985	998	1,490	78.8	10.6	3.1	10	C	ex Scott-06, Njord-02, Deo Juvante-95, Huibertje Jacoba-87
Nautica		Vct	1992	1,587	2,166	88.0	11.9	3.6	11	C	ex Meander-05, Vesting-00
Nina 1		Vct	1984	998	1,485	78.0	10.1	3.2	10	C	ex Nina-04, Vahalis-00, Vios-97
Perseus		Lth	1986	1,392	1,570	72.0	11.5	3.3	11	Cc	ex Walker-08, Petersberg-98, Echo Elke-91, Petersberg-89
Rubyn		Vct	1986	1,512	2,450	79.6	11.3	4.4	9	C	ex Ruby-99
Troubadour		Vct	1992	1,789	2,450	90.0	11.4	3.9	11	Cc	
Viscount		Pan	1976	1,044	1,558	65.8	10.9	4.3	11	C	ex Salmona-05, Star Anna-03, Lough Mask-96, Rockford-95, Canford-94, Viscount-88
Waterway		Vct	1996	1,143	1,490	81.4	9.5	3.1	8	Cc	ex Alissa-08

* currently operated by RMS Rhein Maas-und See-Schiffahrtskontor GmbH qv.

Baltramp Shipping SP Z oo — Poland

Funnel: *Various including blue, black with white ring between narrow white bands or white with pale blue diamond.* **Hull:** *Blue or black with red boot-topping.* **History:** *Founded 1992.* **Web:** *None found.*

Drawa		Pol	1978	1,575	1,870	84.3	10.8	3.8	10	Cc	ex Amstelborg-99, Rhein-89, Rheintal-88

Name	Flag	Year	GT	DWT	Loa	Bm	Drt	Kts	Type	Remarks
Ina	Pol	1978	1,589	1,670	84.2	10.8	3.7	10	Cc	ex Auriga-01, Algerak-90, German-86
Osa	Pol	1985	1,782	2,507	83.2	11.5	4.4	10	Cc	ex Marman-05
Poprad	Pol	1986	1,567	1,750	81.2	11.4	3.4	9	Cc	ex Xandrina-08
Raba	Pol	1984	1,843	2,325	80.5	12.7	4.2	10	Cc	ex Mareike-05, Lys Coast-98, Erkaburg-91, Lys-Coast-91, Erkaburg-91
Rega	Pol	1979	1,545	1,930	85.0	10.0	3.7	11	C	ex Elm-02, Hydra-00, Waalborg-93, Vera Rambow-89

Managed by Wind Shipping ApS qv

Baltrechflot Ltd   Russia

Funnel: *Blue with narrow black top.* **Hull:** *Blue with red boot-topping.* **History:** *Not confirmed.* **Web:** *None found.*

Name		Flag	Year	GT	DWT	Loa	Bm	Drt	Kts	Type	Remarks
Aressa	(2)	Rus	1978	1,926	2,649	95.0	13.2	4.1	10	C	ex Baltiyskiy-103-09
Glory	(2)	Rus	1979	1,639	1,855	81.0	11.9	4.0	12	C	ex Ladoga-17
Porhov	(2)	Rus	1979	1,926	2,558	95.0	13.2	4.0	10	C	ex Baltiyskiy-105-08

Banier Scheepvaart BV   Netherlands

Funnel: *None.* **Hull:** *Turquoise with black boot-topping.* **History:** *Not confirmed.* **Web:** *None found.*

Name	Flag	Year	GT	DWT	Loa	Bm	Drt	Kts	Type	Remarks
Tharsis	Nld	2003	1,435	1,850	80.0	10.4	3.4	9	C	ex Christine-07, I/a Hansa Marseille

Banner Shipping BV   Netherlands

Funnel: *White with narrow green vertical line and green sailing ship on black shield outline.* **Hull:** *Green with black boot-topping.* **History:** *Founded 2007.* **Web:** *None found.*

Name	Flag	Year	GT	DWT	Loa	Bm	Drt	Kts	Type	Remarks
Banier	Nld	2009	2,834	3,659	94.7	13.4	5.3	-	C	

Managed by Spliethhoff's Bevrachtingskantoor BV (Wijnne & Barends BV) qv

Reederei Bartels   Germany

Funnel: *Cream with black top.* **Hull:** *Black with green boot-topping.* **History:** *Founded 1966 as Walter Bartels to 1990.* **Web:** *None found.*

Name	Flag	Year	GT	DWT	Loa	Bm	Drt	Kts	Type	Remarks
Francop	Atg	2003	7,519	8,622	137.5	21.7	7.5	19	CC	ex Tavastland-06
Jessica B	Atg	2000	6,326	7,977	133.0	18.9	7.3	18	CC	ex Jessica-02, Lucy Borchard-02, I/a Jessica
OOCL Neva	Atg	2001	9,981	11,390	134.0	22.8	8.7	18	CC	

Also operates one larger container ship.

Baum & Co GmbH & Co KG   Germany

Funnel: *Blue with flag comprising dark and light blue bands on white diamond on light blue band.* **Hull:** *Blue with red boot-topping.* **History:** *Founded 1973 as Befrachtungskontor W Baum & Co to 1989.* **Web:** *www.baumco.de*

Name	Flag	Year	GT	DWT	Loa	Bm	Drt	Kts	Type	Remarks
Anna	Atg	1998	4,150	5,400	100.6	16.2	6.4	14	Cc	ex Funchalense-07, Caroline Schulte-98, Magdalena Schulte-98
Annamarie	Gbr	2003	7,519	8,720	137.5	21.7	7.5	19	CC	ex Maersk Falsterbo-08, I/a Avilia
Blexen	Atg	1996	3,821	4,695	100.6	16.5	5.9	15	Cc	ex Portlink Caravel-06, CMBT Caravel-98, Blexen-96, Heike-96
Carolina	Atg	1996	6,362	6,750	121.4	18.5	6.7	16	CC	ex BG Antwerp-09, HMS Rotterdam-06, BG Antwerp-06, Monika Ehler-05
Emma	Atg	1985	3,412	4,104	96.1	16.2	6.0	14	Cc	ex Einswarden-98, Rangitata-98, Christa Thielemann-92, Nedlloyd Shuttle-91, Christa Thielemann-89
Gotaland	Gbr	2003	7,519	8,707	137.5	21.7	7.5	19	CC	I/a Italia
Karin	Atg	1996	3,821	4,766	93.0	16.5	5.9	15	Cc	ex HMS Portugal-04, Karin-96, I/a Vera
Tina	Atg	1982	5,424	7,752	106.5	19.1	7.7	14	Cc	ex Dettifoss-00, Rachel Borchard-91, Ilse Wulff-87, Convoy Ranger-87, Ilse Wulff-86
UAFL Express *	Atg	1984	3,784	5,189	99.5	17.2	6.5	14	Cc	ex Waddens-02, Southern Man-01, Capitaine Bligh-00, Waddens-99, Rangiora-98, Nedlloyd Trindad-95, Weser Guide-94, Zim Kingston-88, Weser Guide-84
Volkers	Atg	1998	4,115	5,190	100.6	16.3	6.4	14	Cc	ex Nenufar Europe-01, Volkers-01, MSC Vigo-01, Volkers-98

*Owned or managed by subsidiary Nordenhamer Bereederungs GmbH except * managed by JSC Afalita Shipping, Lithuania.*

BBC–Burger Bereederungs Contor GmbH & Co KG   Germany

Funnel: *White with houseflag (black 'HD' an a white diamond interupting white band between blue and red bands), black top.* **Hull:** *Blue with red boot-topping.* **History:** *Founded 1995 and associated with DT-Bereederungs GmbH & Co KG as part of Danz & Tietjens Shipping Group.* **Web:** *www.danz-tietjens.de*Alemania

Name	Flag	Year	GT	DWT	Loa	Bm	Drt	Kts	Type	Remarks
	Atg	1995	8,633	9,200	133.0	22.9	7.6	17	CCex	Sea Gale-07, Sophie Rickmers-97
CMA CGM Tobruk	Atg	1994	9,601	12,310	149.5	22.3	8.3	17	CC	ex Arminia-08, MOL Elite-05, Arminia-04, MOL Loyalty-04
Fortunia	Atg	1996	5,996	6,885	121.0	18.6	7.0	16	CC	ex Mercosul Brasil-00, Sea Rover-99, Fortunia-96
Holandia	Atg	2000	8,737	9.161	133.3	22.9	7.6	18	CC	ex Cala Phoenicia-09, Holandia-05, Cala Ponente-02, Holandia-02, Cala Ponente-02, Holandia-00
India	Gbr	2003	7,519	8,732	137.5	21.3	7.5	18	CC	ex Velazquez-09, CMA CGM Tatiana-05
Oland *	Mlt	2003	7,519	8,621	137.5	21.3	7.5	18	CC	

* operated by DT-Bereederungs GmbH & Co KG
Also operates four larger container ships.

Baltramp Shipping SP Z oo. Rega. *David Walker*

Reederei Bartels. Francop. *Hans Kraijenbosch*

Beluga Shipping GmbH. Beluga Fiction. *Hans Kraijenbosch*

Name	Flag	Year	GT	DWT	Loa	Bm	Drt	Kts	Type	Remarks

BD-Shipsnavo GmbH & Co Reederei KG   Germany

Funnel: *Dark blue with narrow black top.* **Hull:** *Dark blue with red boot-topping.* **History:** *Founded 1992 as BD-Navis Bereederungs GmbH to 2000.*
Web: *www.shipsnavo.de*

Name	Flag	Year	GT	DWT	Loa	Bm	Drt	Kts	Type	Remarks
Christian D	Atg	2001	3,811	5,408	91.7	17.0	6.5	-	C	ex Lilac Roller-10, Christian D-08, Kaptan Aslan Fatoglu-05

Bernd Becker KG   Germany

Funnel: *Orange or charterers colours.* **Hull:** *Blue with red boot-topping.* **History:** *Founded 2005.* **Web:** *None found.*

Name	Flag	Year	GT	DWT	Loa	Bm	Drt	Kts	Type	Remarks
Jork Ranger	Cyp	2005	7,852	9,288	140.6	21.8	7.3	18	CC	ex Eucon Progress-09, Jork Ranger-08, Samland-07
Jork Reliance	Atg	2007	7,852	9,344	140.6	21.8	7.3	18	CC	
Jork Ruler	Cyp	2006	7,852	9,331	140.6	21.8	7.3	18	CC	ex Eucon Leader-09
Samskip Explorer	Atg	2006	7,852	9,342	140.6	21.8	7.3	18	CC	I/d Jork Rover
Samskip Pioneer	Atg	2006	7,852	9.340	140.6	21.8	7.3	18	CC	I/d Jork Rider

owned or managed by subsidiary Bernd Becker Shipmanagement GmbH & Co KG (founded 2005)
Also manages one larger container ship.

Bell Chartering   Estonia

Funnel: *Blue or white with blue top.* **Hull:** *Blue with red boot-topping.* **History:** *Not confirmed.* **Web:** *None found.*

Name	Flag	Year	GT	DWT	Loa	Bm	Drt	Kts	Type	Remarks
Kagu		Dma	1976	1,589	2,807	63.6	12.5	6.6	10	C	ex Anna Kem-98, Anna Drent-93, Frendo Dansea-77, I/a Frendo North
La Rochelle	(2)	Vct	1992	2,691	2,845	108.9	15.1	3.2	10	C	ex Rochel-07, AKN Pride-07, Cast Salmon-05, I/a Nevskiy-36
Rasill	(2)	Vct	1992	2,882	2,250	108.9	15.1	2.8	10	C	ex Bass-04, Cast Bass-00, Mirka-92, I/a Nevskiy 37

Beluga Shipping GmbH   Germany

Funnel: *White with rectangle containing white whale tail against blue sky and waves.* **Hull:** *Blue with white 'BELUGA PROJECTS', red boot-topping.*
History: *Founded 1998* **Web:** *www.beluga-group.com*

Name	Flag	Year	GT	DWT	Loa	Bm	Drt	Kts	Type	Remarks
Beluga Constellation	Lbr	2006	10,899	12,477	159.8	21.5	7.6	17	C/hl	I/a Beluga Constitution
Beluga Constitution	Atg	2006	10,899	12,479	159.8	21.5	7.6	17	C/hl	
Beluga Emotion	Atg	2004	9.611	12,798	138.1	21.0	8.0	15	C/hl	I/a BBC Alabama
Beluga Endeavour	Atg	2004	9.611	12,828	138.1	21.0	8.0	15	C/hl	
Beluga Eternity	Atg	2004	9.611	12,806	138.1	21.0	8.0	15	C/hl	ex Asian Voyage-05
Beluga Facility	Atg	2009	9.611	12,744	138.1	21.0	8.0	15	C/hl	
Beluga Faculty	Atg	2009	9.611	12,679	138.1	21.0	8.0	15	C/hl	
Beluga Fairy	Atg	2009	9.611	12,662	138.1	21.0	8.0	15	C/hl	
Beluga Faith	Atg	2010	9.611	12,744	138.1	21.0	8.0	15	C/hl	
Beluga Family	Atg	2007	9.611	12,744	138.1	21.0	8.0	15	C/hl	
Beluga Fanfare	Atg	2007	9.611	11,526	138.1	21.0	8.0	15	C/hl	
Beluga Fantastic	Atg	2007	9.611	11,526	138.1	21.0	8.0	15	C/hl	
Beluga Fantasy	Lbr	2009	9.611	12,669	138.1	21.0	8.0	15	C/hl	
Beluga Fascination	Atg	2006	9.611	11,526	138.1	21.0	8.0	15	C/hl	
Beluga Favourisation	Atg	2007	9.611	12,782	138.1	21.0	8.0	15	C/hl	
Beluga Fealty	Atg	2010	9.611	12,744	138.1	21.0	8.0	15	C/hl	
Beluga Feasibility	Atg	2011	9.611	12,744	138.1	21.0	8.0	15	C/hl	
Beluga Felicity	Atg	2008	9.611	12,782	138.1	21.0	8.0	15	C/hl	
Beluga Festival	Atg	2010	9.611	12,744	138.1	21.0	8.0	15	C/hl	
Beluga Fiction	Atg	2007	9.611	12,744	138.1	21.0	8.0	15	C/hl	
Beluga Fidelity	Atg	2009	9.611	12,744	138.1	21.0	8.0	15	C/hl	
Beluga Finesse	Atg	2008	9.611	12,782	138.1	21.0	8.0	15	C/hl	
Beluga Firmament	Atg	2010	9.611	12,744	138.1	21.0	8.0	15	C/hl	
Beluga Flashlight	Atg	2010	9.611	12,744	138.1	21.0	8.0	15	C/hl	
Beluga Flirtation	Atg	2007	9.611	11,380	138.1	21.0	8.0	15	C/hl	
Beluga Foresight	Atg	2008	9.611	12,782	138.1	21.0	8.0	15	C/hl	
Beluga Formation	Lbr	2007	9.611	12,705	138.1	21.0	8.0	15	C/hl	
Beluga Fortitude	Atg	2008	9.611	12,744	138.1	21.0	8.0	15	C/hl	
Beluga Fortune	Atg	2008	9.611	12,744	138.1	21.0	8.0	15	C/hl	
Beluga Fraternity	Atg	2008	9.611	11,526	138.1	21.0	8.0	15	C/hl	
Beluga Frequency	Atg	2009	9.611	12,628	138.1	21.0	8.0	15	C/hl	
Beluga Indication	Atg	2000	11,130	13,289	162.2	20.4	7.9	17	C/hl	ex Nirint Iberia-07, Beluga Indication-06, CEC Apollon-04 (len-07)
Beluga Intonation	Atg	2000	11,130	13,426	162.2	20.4	7.9	17	C/hl	ex Nirint Atlas-07, Beluga Intonation-05, Nirint Atlas-04, TMC Atlas-03, Atlas-02, Industrial Atlas-02, CEC Atlas-01 (len-07)
Beluga Majesty	Gib	2006	8,971	10,744	154.9	21.5	7.0	18	CC	
Beluga Majority	Gib	2010	8,971	10,700	154.9	21.5	7.0	18	CC	
Beluga Mastery	Gib	2006	8,971	10,744	154.9	21.5	7.0	18	CC	
Beluga Maturity	Gib	2010	8,971	10,700	154.9	21.5	7.0	18	CC	
Beluga Mobilisation	Atg	2009	8,971	10,600	154.9	21.5	7.0	18	CC	
Beluga Modification	Gib	2009	8,971	10,700	154.9	21.5	7.0	18	CC	
Beluga Motivation	Gib	2006	8,971	10,700	154.9	21.5	7.0	18	CC	

Name	Flag	Year	GT	DWT	Loa	Bm	Drt	Kts	Type	Remarks
Beluga Motion	Gib	2009	8,971	10,700	154.9	21.5	7.0	18	CC	
Beluga Navigation	Atg	2006	6,296	9,775	132.2	15.9	7.7	15	C/hl	ex BBC Trinidad-09, I/a Beluga Navigation
Beluga Nomination	Atg	2006	6,296	9,821	132.2	15.9	7.7	15	C/hl	
Beluga Notation	Atg	2011	6,296	9,821	132.2	15.9	7.7	15	C/hl	
Beluga Notification	Atg	2010	6,296	9,821	132.2	15.9	7.7	15	C/hl	
Beluga Notion	Atg	2009	6,296	9,775	132.2	15.9	7.7	15	C/hl	
Beluga Novation	Atg	2010	6,296	9,821	132.2	15.9	7.7	15	C/hl	
Beluga Recognition	Atg	2005	8,963	10,509	134.7	21.5	8.0	17	C/hl	
Beluga Recommendation	Deu	2005	8,963	10,538	134.7	21.5	8.0	17	C/hl	
Beluga Resolution	Atg	2005	8,963	10,536	134.7	21.5	8.0	17	C/hl	
Beluga Revolution	Deu	2005	8,963	10,581	134.7	21.5	8.0	17	C/hl	
Beluga Seduction	Gib	2003	7,660	9,137	134.7	21.5	7.1	18	CC	
Beluga Sensation	Gib	2004	7,660	9,163	134.7	21.5	7.1	18	CC	
Beluga SkySails	Atg	2007	6,312	9,821	132.2	15.9	7.7	15	C/hl	
Beluga Stimulation	Gib	2004	7,660	9,137	134.7	21.5	7.1	18	CC	ex OOCL Novogoeod-06, I/a Beluga Stimulation
SITC Express	Gib	2005	8,971	10,747	154.9	21.5	7.0	18	CC	ex Beluga Magician-05
SITC Moderation	Lbr	2009	8,971	10,700	154.9	21.5	7.0	18	CC	ex Beluga Moderation-09
Werder Bremen	Gib	1999	6,378	7,114	121.4	18.2	6.7	16	CC	

Newbuildings: twelve 19,100 - 20,000 dwt 'P' class heavy-lift/container ships under construction for 2010-11 delivery.
Managed by Beluga Fleet Management GmbH & Co KG (founded 2005 as Beluga Bereederungs GmbH & Co KG)
Additionally operates four 20,000 dwt 'P' class and three 17,500 dwt 'Green' suffix class.
Also see Reederei Elbe Shipping GmbH & Co KG, Reederei Heino Winter KG and Vega-Reederei Friedrich Dauber GmbH & Co KG

Berends, Teekman & Westerbeek — Netherlands

Funnel: Blue with yellow 'M' **Hull:** Blue with black boot-topping. **History:** Founded 1997. **Web:** www.samshipping.nl

Name	Flag	Year	GT	DWT	Loa	Bm	Drt	Kts	Type	Remarks
Marit	Nld	2008	6,046	7,240	122.1	16.5	7.2	-	C	
Myrte	Nld	2008	6,046	7,125	122.0	16.5	7.2	-	C	
Sylvia	Nld	1999	3,998	5,750	107.1	15.3	6.2	-	C	

Operated by subsidiary Sam Shipping Vof

Berge Rederei AS — Norway

Funnel: White with black 'B' inside black ring with four darts at cardinal points. **Hull:** Black with red boot-topping. **History:** Founded 2000 and amalgamated in 2008 with Sletringen Bulk AS. **Web:** www.bergerederi.no

Name	Flag	Year	GT	DWT	Loa	Bm	Drt	Kts	Type	Remarks
Froan	Vct	1985	2,367	3,810	87.9	12.9	4.5	9	Cc	ex Wachau-07, Ruhrtal-94
Jago	Vct	1988	1,524	2,166	73.8	11.5	4.4	10	Cc	ex Falknes-09, Arklow Mill-04
Selvaagsund	Vct	1993	1,576	2,246	81.7	11.1	4.1	12	C	ex Aurora-08, Michel-06, Sea Rhine-05, Michel-02
Sletringen	Vct	1992	1,576	2,500	81.7	11.0	4.1	11	Cc	ex Vega-06

Managed and operated by TransMar AS

Bergen Shipping AS — Norway

Funnel: White with narrow blue zig-zag band. **Hull:** Dark blue with red boot-topping. **History:** Founded 1985 and acquired Riga Shipping in 2006. **Web:** www.bergen-shipping.no

Name	Flag	Year	GT	DWT	Loa	Bm	Drt	Kts	Type	Remarks
Havblik	Nis	1969	840	925	61.5	10.6	3.9	11	Cu	ex Linito-00, Aastun-95, Tromsbulk-91, Aasland-85, Venlo-81 (conv C-85)
Havglott	Nor	1968	811	1,060	56.2	10.1	4.3	11	C	ex Cynthia-06, Langefoss-99, Sea West-94, Hilmo-89, East Coast-87, Gulf Countess-84, Gabriela-81, Ariadne-80, Gabriela-79
Havhelt *	Lva	1977	2,021	2,896	80.0	14.4	5.3	13	C	ex Rodsher-07, Havang-96, Cimbris-91, Mokstein-88, Fenix-88
Havstein *	Atg	1993	2,446	3,709	87.9	12.9	5.2	10	Cc	ex Wirdum-07, Saar Breda-96, Wirdum-93, Comet-93, I/a Preussen
Kegums *	Nis	1989	3,555	4,225	103.7	15.2	5.0	12	Cc	ex Kajen-04, I/a Edina
Nordic Chantal *	Nis	1994	2,854	3,895	89.7	13.8	5.7	12	Cc	ex Bremer Saturn-06
RMS Riga *	Blz	1984	1,296	1,380	79.6	10.0	3.1	10	Cs	ex RMS Homberg-06, Tudor-02, Kirsten-88

Owned or managed by subsidiaries BSHIP Management AS, Norway or * Riga Shipping Ltd, Latvia (founded 1940 as Riga Shipping Co to 1995 - www.rigashipping.lv) and managed by Clermont Services, Latvia

Bergen Tankers AS — Norway

Funnel: White with red tanker broadside over blue globe crossed by wavy white lines. **Hull:** Light blue with white 'BERGEN TANKERS', red boot-topping. **History:** Founded 1991. **Web:** www.bgta.no

Name	Flag	Year	GT	DWT	Loa	Bm	Drt	Kts	Type	Remarks
Bergen Faith	Nor	1997	1,400	1,870	75.6	12.1	4.8	12	T	ex Bergskald-09, Senja-01
Bergen Nordic	Nor	2003	2,490	3,535	95.9	14.4	5.8	14	T	
Bergen Star	Nor	2006	3,618	4,157	89.9	16.5	6.0	14	T	
Bergen Troll	Nor	1990	1,280	1,865	65.7	12.0	5.1	11	T	ex Trollskald-09, Trollshell-92

Also owns a small bunkering barge and two small newbuildings.

BG Freight Line BV   Netherlands

Funnel and **Hull:** *Owners colours.* **History:** *Subsidiary of Peel Ports Group since 2005.* **Web:** *www.bgfreightline.com*
Container feeder service currently operating ten chartered vessels.

BG Stone AS   Denmark

Funnel: *White with black top or * blue with white band.* **Hull:** *Blue or ** black with red boot-topping.* **History:** *Subsidiary of quarrying company.*
Web: *www.bgstone.dk*

Name	Flag	Year	GT	DWT	Loa	Bm	Drt	Kts	Type	Remarks
Bal Bulk		1990	1,523	2,165	73.9	11.8	4.4	11	Cu	ex Fjordbulk-08, Fehn Broker-06, Arklow Moor-04
BG Stone 1 *	Dmk	1972	369	610	40.0	9.3	3.4	-	Cu	ex Flintholm-09, Bodil Sten-03, Bodil Dammann-94

Bibby Line Ltd   UK

Funnel: *Buff.* **Hull:** *Green or * red with red or black boot-topping.* **History:** *Founded 1807 as Bibby Steamship Co Ltd to 1931.* **Web:** *www.bibbyline.co.uk*

Name	Flag	Year	GT	DWT	Loa	Bm	Drt	Kts	Type	Remarks
Devon *	Pan	1985	7,145	12,721	123.3	20.0	8.8	13	Tch	ex Stolt Devon-08, Herefordshire-00, Burns-91, Stainless Master-91, Shoun Tenacity-89
Hertfordshire	Gbr	1995	1,864	2,489	82.4	11.5	4.8	12	Cc	ex Mira-06, Atair-06, RMS Atair-98, Atair-96
Syn Mira **	Mlt	1990	4,066	4,283	97.5	14.8	6.8	13	Lpg	ex Valsesia-06
Syn Mizar **	Mlt	1989	4,066	4,286	97.5	14.8	6.8	14	Lpg	ex Val Fiorita-06
Syn Zube **	Ita	2008	3,827	4,027	86.6	15.5	6.5	-	Lpg	

** managed by Bibby Ship Management Ltd, UK (www.bibbyshipmanagement.com), ** for Synergas Srl, Italy.*

Bidsted & Co AS   Denmark

Funnel: *Blue.* **Hull:** *Black with red boot-topping.* **History:** *Founded 1940.* **Web:** *www.bidsted.dk*

Name	Flag	Year	GT	DWT	Loa	Bm	Drt	Kts	Type	Remarks
ID Trader	Pan	1996	6,264	8,679	100.6	18.8	8.2	-	C	ex Odelia-05, Balabac Starit-03
ID Tuxpan	Lbr	1994	6,297	7,850	121.9	20.4	7.1	16	CC	ex Melfi Tuxpan-09, Seaboard Caribbean-08, Arnarfell-05, Gertie-96, CGM St. Elie-96, Gertie-95

Also operates large fleet of panamax and handy bulk carriers.

Bischoff Schiffahrtsbeteiligung GmbH   Germany

Funnel: *White.* **Hull:** *Red with red boot-topping.* **History:** *Founded 2002.* **Web:** *www.schiffahrt-online.de*

Name	Flag	Year	GT	DWT	Loa	Bm	Drt	Kts	Type	Remarks
Sea Lion	Gib	1993	2,815	4,110	88.4	15.0	6.0	14	Cc	ex Industrial Faith-97, Sea Lion-95, IAL Premier-95, Sea Lion-93
Svendborg	Dis	1993	2,462	3,450	81.1	13.8	5.9	13	Cc	ex BBC Colombia-09, CEC Svendborg-08, NDS Kuito-04, CEC Svendborg-03, Vedr-02, CEC Svendborg-02, Svendborg Governor-02, IAL Governor-94, Svendborg Governor-93

JMB Bjerrum & Jensen ApS   Denmark

Funnel: *Blue base with broad white band below black top.* **Hull:** *Blue with red boot-topping.* **History:** *Founded 1979.* **Web:** *www.bjerrum-jensen.dk*

Name	Flag	Year	GT	DWT	Loa	Bm	Drt	Kts	Type	Remarks
Caroline S	Dmk	1959	159	249	33.5	6.5	3.0	10	C	ex Caroline Samso-02, Jane-94, Janto-65
Hera *	Deu	1975	1,202	1,300	75.0	10.2	3.3	10	C	ex Herm Kiepe-96
Monsunen	Dis	1965	383	564	48.1	8.7	3.0	10	C	ex Ota Riis-72
Uno	Dis	1986	1,473	2,111	79.0	10.9	4.0	10	Cc	ex Elke-03
Vermland	Cok	1970	608	386	50.0	9.0	3.2	11	C	ex Gerd Gaustadnes-74 (len-79, NE-95)
Volo	Dis	1957	326	469	44.9	8.3	2.9	9	C	ex Lars Bagger-09, Ulsnaes-89, Welf

* managed for Fritz & Falco Kohlken Kusten-und-Seeschiffahrt (founded 1996)

Flintholm Sten & Grus ApS, Denmark

Funnel: *White.* **Hull:** *Black with red boot-topping.* **History:** *Founded 2003.* **Web:** *www.flintholmaps.dk*

Name	Flag	Year	GT	DWT	Loa	Bm	Drt	Kts	Type	Remarks
Sandholm	Dmk	1968	349	550	44.5	8.7	3.4	9	Dss	ex Inger Sten-06, Aluk-06, Stevns Hoj-86, Rigger Stevns-84, Argonaut R-80, Bredgrund-76

Klaus Blanck   Germany

Funnel: *White with black 'B' outline between narrow red lines, narrow pale blue top.* **Hull:** *Grey with red boot-topping.* **History:** *Founded 1991.*
Web: *None found.*

Name	Flag	Year	GT	DWT	Loa	Bm	Drt	Kts	Type	Remarks
Hela	Deu	1966	861	1,065	61.8	10.0	4.0	10	C	ex Lore-93, Wotan-91

Blue Circle Industries Plc   UK

Funnel: *Managers colours.* **Hull:** *Grey with red boot-topping.* **History:** *Founded 1900 as Associated Portland Cement Manufacturers Ltd to 1965.*
Web: *www.cement.bluecircle.co.uk*

Name	Flag	Year	GT	DWT	Loa	Bm	Drt	Kts	Type	Remarks
Floria	Pan	1976	6,023	9,560	128.3	18.3	7.6	15	Ce	
Koralia	Pan	1995	5,929	8,811	119.5	19.0	7.0	14	Ce	

Owned by subsidiary Lafarge Shipping Services Ltd, UK and managed by John T Essberger GmbH, Germany
Also operates two larger cement bulk carriers.

Beluga Shipping GmbH. Werder Bremen. *N. Kemps*

Bibby Line Ltd. Hertfordshire. *Tom Walker*

Name	Flag	Year	GT	DWT	Loa	Bm	Drt	Kts	Type	Remarks

De Bock Maritiem BV   Netherlands

Funnel: *White with company symbol (ibex on bow of hull).* **Hull:** *Dark green with red boot-topping.* **History:** *Founded 1999 as Gilbery de Bock Holding BV to 2007.* **Web:** *www.debockmaritiem.nl*

Name	Flag	Year	GT	DWT	Loa	Bm	Drt	Kts	Type	Remarks
Saffier	Nld	2008	3,970	5,800	100.0	15.2	6.6	-	C	
Smaragd	Nld	2003	2,339	3,195	90.0	12.5	4.6	11	C	

W Bockstiegel Reederei GmbH & Co KG   Germany

Funnel: *White or white with black or blue 'WB' or 'B' on white disc at centre of diagonally quartered houseflag or lifebelt (yellow/ upper/lower, blue sides), black or yellow top.* **Hull:** *Blue with white 'BBC' and black or red boot-topping or red with red boot-topping.* **History:** *Founded 1983 as Bockstiegel Bereederungs GmbH.* **Web:** *www.reederei-bockstiegel.de*

Name	Flag	Year	GT	DWT	Loa	Bm	Drt	Kts	Type	Remarks
A.B.Bilbao	Atg	1997	2,844	4,212	89.8	13.2	5.7	12	Cc	I/a Saar Bilbao
A.B.Dublin	Atg	1997	2,844	4,211	89.9	13.2	5.7	12	Cc	I/a Saar Dublin
A.B.Liverpool	Atg	1996	2,844	4,224	89.9	13.2	5.7	12	Cc	ex Saar Liverpool-96
A.B.Valencia	Atg	1996	2,844	4,250	89.9	13.2	5.7	12	Cc	ex Saar Valencia-97
Asian Carrier	Atg	2003	4,450	5,565	100.0	18.8	6.7	15	Cc	ex Asian Favour-08
Asian Glory	Atg	2005	9,956	13,727	147.8	23.3	8.5	15	CC	ex Alianca Pampas-09,
Asian Star	Atg	2005	9,956	13,823	147.8	23.3	8.5	15	CC	
Asian Trader	Atg	2003	9,966	13,732	147.8	23.3	8.5	15	CC	ex MSC Frisia-09, TS Bangkok-08, Asian Trader-03
Atlantic Hawk	Atg	2003	4,450	5,577	100.0	18.8	6.7	15	Cc	ex Caribbean Sina-03, Asian Hawk-03
Baltic Carrier	Atg	2010	6,850	9,500	107.0	18.2	7.1	13	Cc	
Baltic Commander	Atg	2010	6,850	9,500	107.0	18.2	7.1	13	Cc	
Baltic Cruiser	Atg	2010	6,850	9,500	107.0	18.2	7.1	13	Cc	
Baltic Island	Atg	2010	6,850	9,500	107.0	18.2	7.1	13	Cc	
Baltic Liner	Atg	2010	6,850	9,500	107.0	18.2	7.1	13	Cc	
Baltic Steamer	Atg	2010	6,850	9,500	107.0	18.2	7.1	13	Cc	
Baltic Trader	Atg	2009	6,850	9,500	107.0	18.2	7.1	13	Cc	
Baltic Voyager	Atg	2010	6,850	9,500	107.0	18.2	7.1	13	Cc	
BBC Alabama	Atg	2007	9,618	12,780	138.5	21.0	8.0	15	Cc	I/a Western Voyager
BBC Alaska	Atg	2008	9,627	12,840	138.0	21.0	8.0	15	Cc	
BBC Antigua	Atg	2009	9,618	12,750	138.0	21.0	8.0	15	Cc	
BBC Barbuda	Atg	2010	9,618	12,750	138.0	21.0	8.0	15	Cc	
BBC Campania	Atg	2004	9,618	12,835	138.0	21.0	8.0	16	Cc	ex Asian Cruiser-04
BBC Colorado	Atg	2008	9,618	12,742	138.0	21.0	8.0	15	Cc	
BBC Delaware	Atg	2007	9,611	12,782	138.1	21.0	8.0	15	Cc	
BBC Florida	Atg	2009	9,611	12,776	138.0	21.0	8.0	15	Cc	
BBC Georgia	Atg	2008	9,625	12,796	138.0	21.0	8.0	15	Cc	
BBC Italy	Atg	2001	6,204	7,612	107.8	18.2	7.3	14	Cc	ex Buccaneer-03, BBC Italy-01
BBC Louisiana	Atg	2008	9,618	12,764	138.0	21.0	8.0	15	Cc	
BBC Maine	Atg	2007	9,625	12,793	138.1	21.0	8.0	15	Cc	
BBC Maryland	Atg	2009	9,611	12,776	138.0	21.0	8.0	15	Cc	
BBC Mexico	Atg	2001	3,895	5,100	101.2	16.4	6.7	15	Cc	I/a Deborah
BBC Michigan	Atg	2010	9,618	12,750	138.0	21.0	8.0	15	Cc	
BBC Montana	Atg	2009	9,627	12,771	138.0	21.0	8.0	15	Cc	
BBC Ohio	Atg	2009	9,618	12,708	138.0	21.0	8.0	15	Cc	
BBC Oregon	Atg	2010	9,618	12,750	138.0	21.0	8.0	15	Cc	
BBC Peru	Atg	2001	6,204	8,760	107.8	18.2	8.0	14	Cc	I/a Atlantic Carrier
BBC Plata	Atg	2005	9,618	12,837	138.6	21.0	8.0	14	Cc	ex Asian Voyager-05
BBC Portugal	Atg	2001	2,545	3,490	86.4	12.8	5.6	12	Cc	ex Mareike B-02
BBC Spain	Atg	2001	6,204	7,625	107.8	18.2	7.3	14	Cc	
BBC Vermont	Atg	2008	9,625	12,863	138.6	21.0	8.0	15	Cc	
BBC Virginia	Atg	2010	9,618	12,750	138.0	21.0	11.0	15	Cc	
BBC Zarate	Atg	2007	9,620	12,834	138.6	21.0	8.0	15	Cc	
European Hawk	Atg	2009	6,834	9,500	107.0	18.2	7.1	13	Cc	
European Trader	Atg	2009	6,834	9,500	107.0	18.2	7.1	13	Cc	
European Voyager	Atg	2009	6,834	9,500	107.0	18.2	7.1	13	Cc	
European Wave	Atg	2009	6,834	9,500	107.0	18.2	7.1	13	Cc	
Faaborg	Atg	1999	2,997	4,450	99.9	12.8	5.7	13	Cc	ex BBC Gotland-04, I/a Ibiza
Greetsiel	Atg	2000	4,450	5,607	100.6	18.8	6.7	15	Cc	
Ice Bird	Cyp	2007	7,545	8,210	129.6	20.6	7.4	17	CC	
Ice Moon	Gib	2008	7,545	8,214	129.7	20.6	7.4	17	CC	
Ice Runner	Atg	2008	7,545	8,138	129.6	20.6	7.4	17	CC	
Ice Sun	Gib	2007	7,545	8,199	129.6	20.6	7.4	17	CC	
Knock	Atg	1999	4,450	5,603	100.8	18.8	6.7	15	Cc	ex Rio Arauca-08, Delmas Casablanca-06, TLI Atsah-02, Knock-01, Medex Spirit-00, Knock-00
Malte B	Atg	1998	2,300	3,440	86.4	12.8	5.6	12	Cc	I/a Oldeoog
Mell Seletar	Gib	2008	7,545	8,143	129.6	20.6	7.4	17	CC	ex Ice Star-09
Mell Senang	Atg	2008	7,545	8,248	129.6	20.6	7.4	17	CC	ex Ice crystal-09, Frisian Cruiser-08, Polarico-08
Nils B	Atg	1998	2,528	3,440	86.4	12.8	5.6	12	Cc	I/a Boreas
Orso	Atg	1999	4,028	5,250	100.6	18.5	6.5	15	Cc	ex SCM Lia-03, Orso-02

Name	Flag	Year	GT	DWT	Loa	Bm	Drt	Kts	Type	Remarks
Sina B	Atg	1984	1,298	1,537	74.9	10.6	3.4	10	C	ex Heike-97, Neil B-96, Sea Tiber-91, Line-88,
										Webo-Liner-86, Neil B-86
Suurhusen	Atg	1996	2,805	4,256	89.9	13.2	5.7	11	Cc	ex Saar Roma-96
Uphusen	Atg	1996	2,846	4,334	89.0	13.7	5.9	11	Cc	ex Saar Bremen-96
Western Carrier	Atg	2009	6,850	8,000	107.0	18.2	7.1	13	Cc	
Western Cruiser	Atg	2009	6,834	9,500	107.0	18.2	7.1	13	Cc	
Western Island	Atg	2009	6,834	9,500	107.0	18.2	7.1	13	Cc	
Western Steamer	Atg	2009	6,834	9,500	107.0	18.2	7.1	13	Cc	
Wolthusen	Atg	1995	2,846	4,342	90.3	13.7	5.9	11	Cc	ex Saar Hamburg-96

Newbuildings: Fourteen 12,700 grt 966 teu container ships (North Sea .....) on order for 2010-12 delivery Also owns nine 13,700 dwt 1,118 teu general cargo/container ships.

Boeckmans Belgie NV   Belgium

Funnel: *None.* **Hull:** *with red boot-topping.* **History:** *Founded 1999.* **Web:** *www.boeckmans.be*

Name	Flag	Year	GT	DWT	Loa	Bm	Drt	Kts	Type	Remarks
Marcel *	Bel	1993	2,449	3,710	87.9	12.8	5.5	10	Cc	
Marschenland	Bel	1985	1,373	1,550	75.0	10.8	3.7	11	C	

* managed for Bugge Shipping BV (founded 2008)

Boele Dredging Contractors BV   Netherlands

Funnel: *Black with white seven-pointed star onbroad light blue band.* **Hull:** *Light blue with red boot-topping.* **History:** *Founded 1953 and acquired by Royal P&O Nedlloyd BV in 2004, which was acquired by AP Moller in 2005.* **Web:** *www.johboele.nl*

Name	Flag	Year	GT	DWT	Loa	Bm	Drt	Kts	Type	Remarks
Maersk Erimo	Nld	1997	6,114	8,160	126.5	19.8	6.4	16	Cc	ex Marcosul Uruguay-05, Johannes Boele-02,
										UAL Angola-99, Johannes Boele-98, Seaboard Atlantic-98,
										Johannes Boele-97

Managed by Maersk Ship Management BV, Netherlands

Kapitan Siegfried Bojen Schiffahrtsbetrieb EK   Germany

Funnel: *White with blue 'B' on yellow flag or charterers colours.* **Hull:** *Blue with red boot-topping.* **History:** *Commenced ship-owning in 1966 and present company founded in 1994.* **Web:** *www.reederei-bojen.de*

Name	Flag	Year	GT	DWT	Loa	Bm	Drt	Kts	Type	Remarks
Baccara	Mlt	1998	2,997	4,450	99.9	12.8	5.7	13	Cc	
Bosporus	Atg	1996	2,997	4,431	99.9	12.8	5.6	13	Cc	ex Saar Bosporus-96, I/a German Trader
Casablanca	Atg	1994	2,061	3,002	88.5	11.4	4.9	10	Cc	ex Saar Casablanca-97
Edzard Cirksena	Atg	2008	2,451	3,630	88.6	12.4	5.1	10	Cc	
Fokko Ukena	Mlt	2007	2,451	3,627	88.6	12.4	5.1	10	Cc	
Hagen	Atg	1998	2,810	4,218	89.8	13.2	5.7	12	Cc	ex Kopenhagen-01
Helsinki	Atg	1997	2,810	4,221	89.9	13.2	5.7	13	Cc	
Imel Abdena	Atg	2008	2,451	2,900	88.6	12.4	5.1	10	Cc	
Jacaranda	Atg	1998	2,997	4,450	99.9	12.8	5.7	13	Cc	
Korsika	Atg	2001	2,997	4,450	99.9	12.8	5.7	13	Cc	
Memel	Atg	1999	2,997	4,450	99.9	12.8	5.7	13	Cc	
Moormerland	Atg	2005	2,184	2,928	88.6	12.4	4.4	10	Cc	
Okko Tom Brook	Atg	2007	2,451	3,638	88.6	12.4	5.1	10	Cc	
Oslo	Atg	1996	2,805	4,245	89.9	13.2	5.7	11	Cc	
Riga	Atg	1997	2,810	4,220	89.9	13.2	5.7	11	Cc	
Rorichmoor	Atg	2006	2,184	2,930	88.6	12.4	4.4	10	Cc	
Sardinia	Atg	1998	2,997	4,450	99.9	12.8	5.7	13	Cc	
Stadt Hemmoor	Atg	2005	2,184	2,910	88.6	12.4	4.4	10	Cc	
Stapelmoor	Atg	2006	2,184	2,930	88.6	12.4	4.4	10	Cc	
Tallin	Atg	1997	2,810	4,221	89.9	13.2	5.7	13	Cc	
Taranto	Atg	1995	2,061	3,009	88.5	11.4	5.0	10	Cc	
Wilson Aberdeen	Mlt	2009	2,451	3,614	88.6	12.4	5.1	10	Cc	ex Stortebeker-09
Wilson Amsterdam	Atg	2009	2,451	3,602	88.6	12.4	5.1	10	Cc	I/dn Tanne Kankena
Wilson Antwerp	Mlt	2008	2,451	3,600	88.6	12.4	5.1	10	Cc	ex Sibet Attena-08
Wilson Aveiro	Mlt	2008	2,451	3,605	88.6	12.4	5.1	10	Cc	ex Folkmar Allena-08, Wilson Aveiro-08
Wilson Aviles	Mlt	2008	2,451	3,606	88.6	12.4	5.1	10	Cc	ex Hero Omken-08
Wilson Avonmouth	Atg	2010	1,600	2,620	-	-	-	-	Cc	
Wilson Ayr	Mlt	2009	2,451	2,760	88.6	12.4	5.1	10	Cc	

Aug Bolten Wm Miller's Nachfolger (GmbH & Co) KG   Germany

Funnel: *Black with black 'B' inside red rectangle outline and diagonal cross on white houseflag or (*) black 'L' on blue-edged white disc at centre of blue diagonal crossed and edged houseflag on broad white band.* **Hull:** *Black with red boot-topping.* **History:** *Parent originally founded 1801 and shipping company formed in 1906. Until 1988, joint owner of Eurasia Shipping & Management with B Schulte.* **Web:** *www.aug-bolten.de*

Name	Flag	Year	GT	DWT	Loa	Bm	Drt	Kts	Type	Remarks
Ines Bolten	Cyp	2009	8,273	10,950	139.6	22.2	7.4	18	CC	
Iris Bolten	Deu	2008	8.273	10.950	139.6	22.2	7.4	18	CC	

Also operates fleet of larger vessels.

Kapitan Siegfried Bojen. Okko Tom Brook. *David Walker*

Kapitan Siegfried Bojen. Stadt Hemmoor. *David Walker*

Boomsma Shipping BV. Frisian Summer. *Allan Ryszka Onions*

Briese Schiffahrts GmbH & Co KG. Antora. *David Walker*

Boomsma Shipping BV   Netherlands

Funnel: *White.* **Hull:** *Blue with red boot-topping.* **History:** *Founded 1991.* **Web:** *www.boomsmashipping.nl*

Name	Flag	Year	GT	DWT	Loa	Bm	Drt	Kts	Type	Remarks
Frisian Lady	Nld	2002	3,666	4,684	104.2	15.2	5.5	14	Cc	
Frisian Spring	Nld	2007	4,087	6,550	118.1	13.4	6.2	12	Cc	
Frisian Summer	Nld	2008	4,087	6,558	118.9	13.4	6.2	12	Cc	
Frisiana	Nld	2009	5,765	8,100	128.5	15.9	6.8	14	Cc	
Frisium	Nld	1992	1,786	2,355	87.0	12.4	3.7	10	C	ex Thalassa-98
Noest	Nld	1995	1,546	2,310	85.1	10.8	4.1	11	Cc	ex Laurina-Neeltje-02, Laurina-05, Stina-06

Hermann C Boye & Co   Denmark

Funnel: *White or * white with symbol on white shield interupting red band.* **Hull:** *Black or red with red or green boot-topping.* **History:** *Founded 1880.*
Web: *None found.*

Name	Flag	Year	GT	DWT	Loa	Bm	Drt	Kts	Type	Remarks
Amanda	Dis	1981	1,441	1,795	81.0	11.3	3.3	10	Ccs	ex Eldor-02
Barbara	Dis	1966	1,068	1,296	66.2	10.7	4.0	11	Cc	ex Lette Lill-00, Britta-91, Ortrud-89, Carina-84, Regine-75, City of Antwerp-71, Regine-66
Elisabeth Boye *	Dis	1990	1,652	2,650	76.7	11.2	5.3	13	Cc	
Industrial Leader *	Dis	1996	3,030	4,100	88.4	15.1	6.0	13	Cc	ex Hans Boye-96

* managed by Dano Sp z o o, Poland (www.dano.com.pl)

Bremer Lloyd GmbH & Co KG   Germany

Funnel: *White with grey 'H' on white disc on red flag.* **Hull:** *Blue with red boot-topping.* **History:** *Founded 2007.* **Web:** *www.bremer-lloyd.de*

Name	Flag	Year	GT	DWT	Loa	Bm	Drt	Kts	Type	Remarks
Anna von Bremen	Atg	2009	6,296	9,250	132.2	15.9	7.7	15	Cc	
BBC New York	Atg	2009	6,361	9,570	132.2	15.9	7.7	15	Cc	ex Beluga Nation-09, Dutch Carina-09, I/dn Johann von Bremen
BBC Niteroi	Atg	2009	6,296	9,821	132.2	15.9	7.7	15	C/hl	ex Beluga Negotiation-09, Dutch Maren-08
Hans Specht	Atg	2009	6,296	9,250	132.2	15.9	7.7	15	Cc	
Hanseatic Sailor *	Atg	1984	2,191	1,979	77.7	13.2	3.5	11	Cp	ex Bremer Reeder-00
Hanseatic Scout *	Atg	2002	2,896	4,338	89.3	13.3	5.7	12	Cc	
Hanseatic Sea *	Atg	1976	1,896	1,400	80.9	12.9	3.4	11	Cp	ex Bremer Norden-04, Capella-90
Hanseatic Spirit *	Atg	1994	2,650	4,200	89.6	13.2	5.7	12	Cc	ex Gerarda-04
Hanseatic Star *	Gib	1985	1,586	1,738	83.4	11.3	3.5	10	Cc	ex Pamela-01, Boberg-88
Hanseatic Swan *	Atg	1994	3,806	4,766	100.6	16.5	5.9	15	Cc	ex Regina J-06, Portlink Hunter-03, Regina J-02, Bremer Handel-99, Regina J-97
Hanseatic Trader *	Atg	2001	2,780	3,972	89.3	13.4	6.2	11	Cc	ex Jaco Trader-05, Polar Breeze-01
Johann Philipp Specht	Atg	2009	6,296	9,250	132.2	15.9	7.7	15	Cc	
Stella Maris	Atg	2008	1,867	2,850	81.4	13.2	4.7	11	C	
Stella Moon	Atg	2008	1,850	2,850	81.4	13.2	4.7	11	C	

* owned by subsidiary Hanseatic Schiffahrt GmbH & Co KG (founded 2000 as Hanseatic Schiffahrt und Schiffsmanagement GmbH to 2008 – www.hanseatic-bremen.de)

Reederei Jan Breuer EK   Germany

Funnel: *White with narrow black top or charterers colours.* **Hull:** *Blue with red boot-topping.* **History:** *Founded 1981 as Henry Breuer KG to 1998.*
Web: *None found.*

Name	Flag	Year	GT	DWT	Loa	Bm	Drt	Kts	Type	Remarks
Rachel Borchard	Atg	2004	9,962	11,376	134.4	22.5	8.7	18	CC	ex Stina-09, Charlotte Borchard-06, I/a Stina

Briese Schiffahrts GmbH & Co KG   Germany

Funnel: *White with black outlined 'b', black, red and blue horizontal striped centre and narrow blue top or buff with same symbol on white houseflag.* **Hull:** *Light grey or dark blue some with white 'BBC Chartering', red or black boot-topping.* **History:** *Founded 1983 and associated with BBC Chartering & Logistic GmbH.*
Web: *www.briese.de*

Name	Flag	Year	GT	DWT	Loa	Bm	Drt	Kts	Type	Remarks
Accum	Gib	2010	2,400	3,300	87.0	12.0	5.0	11	Cc	
Alta Mar	Pmd	1995	2,840	4,137	89.7	13.6	5.7	13	Cc	ex Senator-96
Ameland	Atg	2009	5,313	6,500	115.5	16.5	5.7	13	Cc	
Amke	Gib	2006	5,232	6,425	115.5	16.5	5.7	13	Cc	I/a Strandplate
Andante	Gib	2005	5,232	6,419	115.9	16.5	5.7	13	Cc	ex Hohe Plate-05
Anja	Atg	2002	4,454	5,560	100.8	18.8	6.7	15	Cc	ex Apolo-03, I/a Frisia
Anmare	Atg	2009	2,452	3,670	87.0	12.0	5.0	11	Cc	
Anmiro	Atg	2009	2,461	3,670	87.0	12.0	5.0	11	Cc	
Antabe	Gib	1997	2,446	3,702	87.9	12.9	5.5	10	Cc	ex Northern Lady-01
Antari	Atg	1998	2,446	3,680	87.9	12.9	5.5	10	Cc	ex Wani Cell-05, Antari-04, Northern Coast-02
Antora	Atg	1998	2,446	3,680	87.9	12.9	5.5	10	Cc	ex Anpero-07, Wani Tofte-05, Anpero-04, Northern Island-01
Apolo	Deu	2003	4,448	5,539	100.8	18.8	6.7	15	Cc	ex Hoogsand-03
Barbarossa	Gib	2000	2,301	3,200	82.5	12.4	5.3	12	Cc	ex Flinthorn-05
Bavaria	Atg	1996	2,550	3,800	88.0	12.8	5.5	11	Cc	
BBC Adriatic	Atg	2008	5,261	6,042	115.6	16.5	5.7	13	Cc	
BBC Africa	Atg	2005	7,002	7,531	119.8	20.2	7.6	16	Cc	ex Eider-06
BBC Asia	Atg	2003	7,014	7,541	119.8	20.2	7.6	16	Cc	
BBC Atlantic	Gib	2005	5,261	6,419	115.9	16.5	5.7	13	Cc	ex Westerriede-05

Name	Flag	Year	GT	DWT	Loa	Bm	Drt	Kts	Type	Remarks
BBC Australia	Atg	2005	7,002	7,492	119.4	20.2	7.6	16	Cc	
BBC Austria	Atg	2009	7,014	7,695	119.8	20.2	7.6	16	Cc	
BBC Baltic	Atg	2008	5,261	6,159	115.6	16.5	5.7	13	Cc	
BBC Bulgaria	Gib	2004	3,198	4,313	98.9	13.8	5.7	13	Cc	ex Ostland-04
BBC Canada	Gib	1999	4,086	4,798	100.6	16.6	6.4	15	Cc	ex Memmert-00
BBC Denmark	Ant	1999	4,086	4,806	100.6	16.6	6.4	15	Cc	I/a Wangerooge
BBC Europe	Atg	2003	7,014	7,409	119.4	20.2	7.6	16	Cc	
BBC France	Gib	2005	3,198	4,310	98.9	13.8	5.7	13	Cc	ex Ostersand-05
BBC Germany	Atg	2003	7,004	7,617	119.8	20.2	7.6	16	Cc	
BBC Gibraltar	Deu	1998	2,528	3,442	85.6	12.8	5.5	12	C	ex Bremer Forest-01, Leda-98, I/a Oster Till
BBC Greenland	Atg	2007	7,002	7.536	119.8	20.2	7.6	16	Cc	
BBC Holland	Gib	2002	3,194	4,326	98.9	13.8	5.7	12	Cc	
BBC Iceland ***	Atg	1999	4,086	4,806	100.6	16.6	6.4	15	Cc	ex Industrial Accord-02
BBC Jade	Atg	2008	8,999	12,000	143.0	18.9	8.1	15	Cc	
BBC Japan	Atg	2000	4,090	4,726	100.6	16.6	6.4	15	Cc	ex Juister Riff-01
BBC Langeland	Atg	1998	4,559	6,375	105.0	16.2	7.0	14	Cc	ex BBC Helgoland-07, SCS Anne-07, Kimberely-05, Helgoland-99
BBC Nordland	Gib	2000	6,204	7,598	107.8	18.3	7.5	14	Cc	ex Isabella G-03, BBC Nordland-01, Nordland-01
BBC Pacific	Atg	2007	5,261	6,500	115.5	16.5	5.7	13	Cc	I/a Norderloog
BBC Romania	Gib	2006	3,198	4,305	98.9	13.8	5.7	13	Cc	I/a Jadeplate
BBC Scandinavia	Atg	2007	7,002	7,534	119.8	20.2	7.6	16	Cc	I/a Rysum
BBC Scotland	Gib	2002	4,090	4,713	100.6	16.6	6.4	15	Cc	I/a Knock
BBC Shanghai	Atg	2001	4,090	4,900	100.6	16.6	6.4	15	Cc	ex TLI Aquila-03, BBC Shanghai-03, I/a Baltic Sea
BBC Sweden	Gib	2003	3,198	4,310	98.9	13.8	5.7	13	Cc	
BBC Switzerland	Deu	2008	6,967	7,725	119.8	20.2	7.6	16	Cc	
Berum	Atg	1999	4,115	5,199	100.6	16.2	6.4	15	Cc	ex OPDR Sevilla-08
Bremer Reeder	Gib	2000	2,868	3,792	89.3	13.4	5.7	12	Cc	ex Polar Sea-04
Cimbris	Gib	2003	3,173	4,525	98.9	13.8	5.8	13	Cc	I/a Osterriff
Ditzum	Gib	2005	3,173	4,525	98.9	13.8	5.7	13	Cc	I/a Martensplate
Dollart ***	Gib	1995	2,532	3,560	88.0	12.8	5.5	11	Cc	
Eiland	Atg	2009	2,778	3,571	89.0	13.0	5.9	12	Cc	ex Huelin Dispatch-09
Fletum	Atg	1998	4,115	5,184	100.5	16.2	6.4	14	Cc	ex OPDR Cartagena-08 (conv CC-08)
Frisian Sky	Gib	2001	2,868	3,792	89.3	13.4	5.7	12	Cc	ex Polar Sky-04
Frisian Sun	Gib	1999	2,625	3,740	89.3	13.4	5.7	12	Cc	ex Polar Sun-00
Geise	Gib	2006	3,198	4,299	98.9	14.1	5.7	13	Cc	
Hanoi	Gib	2009	1,900	2,625	87.5	11.3	4.2	11	Cc	
Hollum	Atg	2009	5,261	6,500	115.5	16.9	5.7	13	Cc	
Jansum	Atg	1998	4,115	4,650	100.6	16.2	6.4	15	Cc	ex OPDR Casablanca-08
Kukkelborg	Atg	2009	2,452	3,680	87.0	12.0	5.0	11	Cc	
Leybucht	Gib	2009	2,400	3,540	86.0	12.4	5.3	12	Cc	
Medum	Atg	1998	4,115	4,800	100.6	16.2	6.4	15	Cc	ex OPDR Porto-08
Mekong	Gib	2009	1,900	2,625	87.5	11.3	4.2	11	Cc	
Milady	Gib	2005	2,545	3,817	88.6	12.5	5.4	12	Cc	
Miramar	Gib	1996	2,840	4,135	89.7	13.7	5.7	13	Cc	ex Geestborg-96
Musketier	Gib	2006	2,545	3,850	88.6	12.5	5.4	12	Cc	
Nordersand	Gib	2004	3,173	4,525	98.9	13.8	5.7	13	Cc	
Ostermarsch	Atg	2008	5,313	6,408	115.5	16.5	5.7	13	Cc	
Peter Ronna	Gib	2002	3,194	4,326	98.9	13.8	5.7	12	Cc	ex Svend-06, Peter Ronna-03
Pride	Gib	2002	2,061	3,000	88.5	11.4	4.9	11	Cc	ex Wani Pride-05, Accumersiel-02
Randzel	Gib	2006	3,173	4,516	98.9	13.8	5.7	12	Cc	
Richelieu	Gib	2007	2,545	3,850	88.6	12.5	5.4	12	Cc	
S. Gabriel	Deu	2002	4,454	5,560	100.8	18.8	6.7	15	Cc	ex Sea Breeze-04
S. Rafael	Deu	2000	4,454	5,539	100.6	18.8	6.7	15	Cc	ex Amrum-01
Santiago	Atg	1997	2,528	3,525	85.6	12.8	5.5	12	Cc	I/a Janssand
Saxum	Gib	2003	2,301	3,177	82.5	12.4	5.3	11	Cc	I/a Gerhard G
Sjard	Atg	1989	5,753	8,224	107.4	19.3	8.3	15	C/hl	ex Sea Breeze-98, Antje-97
Skaftafell	Gib	1997	4,078	4,900	100.6	16.8	6.4	15	Cc	ex BBC Brazil-04, Brake-03, BBC Brazil-03, Industrial Harmony-00, I/a Torum
Stortebeker	Gib	2000	2,301	3,171	82.5	12.4	5.3	12	Cc	
Tornator	Pmd	1995	2,840	4,178	87.7	13.7	5.7	12	Cc	
Unimar **	Gib	1997	2,820	4,135	89.7	13.6	5.7	13	Cc	ex Musketier-05
Wilke	Gib	1994	2,901	4,223	91.2	13.8	5.7	13	Cc	ex Leknes-99

Newbuildings: About 30 ships on order, mainly coasters but including two 17,300 dwt general cargo and four 37,700 dwt bulk carriers.
* owned by subsidiary Briese Nederland BV, Netherlands.
** managed for Atobatic Shipping AB, Sweden or *** for associated BBC Chartering & Logistic GmbH & Co KG (formed 1998).
BBC project cargo ships operate in Asia Project Chartering Group (APC Group) joint venture with Clipper Projects qv

Brink & Wolffel
Germany

Christian Jurgensen, Brink & Wolffel Schiffahrt. GmbH & Co., Germany
Funnel: *White or light grey with black 'L' on white diamond on blue upper and red lower rectangle, narrow black top.* **Hull:** *Blue or red with red boot-topping.*
History: *Not confirmed.* **Web:** *None found*

Name	Flag	Year	GT	DWT	Loa	Bm	Drt	Kts	Type	Remarks
Barbara	Deu	1996	2,984	4,850	98.7	16.9	5.9	15	CC	
Bonnie Rois	Deu	1998	2,990	4,791	99.5	16.9	5.9	16	CC	
Coastal Deniz	Atg	1991	3,125	4,485	89.1	16.2	6.1	14	Cc	ex Sybille-05, Rhein Merchant-00, Sybille-95, Baltic Bridge-93, Sybille-93
Coastal Isle	Deu	1991	3,125	2,973	89.1	16.2	6.1	14	Cc	ex Johanna-97
Leona	Deu	1987	1,593	1,900	82.0	11.5	3.7	10	C	ex Scot Carrier-94, I/a Leona
Priwall	Cyp	1992	2,446	3,735	87.9	12.8	5.5	10	Cc	
Zeya	Deu	1995	2,984	4,850	96.6	17.1	5.9	15	Cc	ex Ute Johanna-09

Also manages for other owners, see under Otto A Muller Schiffahrt GmbH (OAM), Germany.

Brise Schiffahrts GmbH
Germany

Funnel: *Light blue * with broad white band.* **Hull:** *Grey or * blue with red boot-topping.* **History:** *Founded 1985.* **Web:** *www.brise.de*

Name	Flag	Year	GT	DWT	Loa	Bm	Drt	Kts	Type	Remarks
APL Bogota	Atg	2004	6,704	8,329	132.6	19.2	7.2	17	CC	ex CMA CMG Manzanillo-07, I/a Kappeln
Birk	Atg	2003	6,704	8,015	132.6	19.2	7.2	17	CC	
Cembay *	Cyp	1997	3,017	4,216	88.2	13.6	6.1	12	Ce	ex Borneo-05, Gutshof-99, Borneo-98 (conv C-05)
Cemfjord *	Cyp	1984	1,850	2,327	83.2	11.5	4.4	10	Ce	ex Margareta-05 (conv C-98)
Cemisle *	Atg	2000	5,133	5,183	120.0	16.6	6.7	15	Ce	ex Grimsnis-09, Topaz-07, Gdynia-05 (conv C)
Cemluna *	Cyp	1991	2,706	3,828	89.5	13.5	5.3	11	Ce	ex Lea-05, Anja II-02 (conv C-05)
Cemsea *	Cyp	1994	2,827	4,479	91.5	13.6	5.8	12	Ce	ex Flinterland-04 (conv C-04)
Cemsky *	Cyp	1990	2,975	4,566	88.2	13.7	6.1	11	Ce	ex Transportor-04 (conv C-04)
Cemsol *	Cyp	1998	3,239	4,803	95.9	13.7	6.1	12	Ce	ex Barten-07 (conv C-07)
Cemstar *	Deu	1989	2,670	3,180	88.0	13.0	4.9	11	Ce	ex Lisa Lehmann-01 (conv Cc-01)
Cemvale *	Cyp	1992	2,894	4,257	88.2	13.7	5.8	11	Ce	ex Arklow Valley-06 (conv Cc-06)
Kati L	Cyp	2001	3,925	4,633	99.9	16.0	5.1	-	C	ex Lisa Lehmann-08, Bornholm-07
Kollund	Cyp	1994	2,818	4,170	91.5	13.6	5.8	12	Cc	ex Flintermar-03
MCC Chalice	Atg	2003	6,704	8,015	132.6	19.2	7.2	17	CC	ex Maersk Edinburgh-07, Sandwig-03
MSC Longoni	Atg	2003	6,704	8,015	132.6	19.2	7.2	17	CC	ex Missunde-03, Maas Trader-03
Norrland	Atg	1990	5,562	4,355	107.8	17.3	6.1	-	Cr	ex Medstar-02, Martha Russ-99
Wilson Holm	Atg	1990	2,827	4,261	88.2	13.7	5.8	11	Cc	ex Forester-05, Arklow Viking-00
Wilson Horn	Deu	1990	2,827	4,261	88.2	13.6	5.8	11	Cc	ex Thruster-05, Arklow Venture-00

*Operated by subsidiaries Brise Bereederungs GmbH & Co KG (formed 2001) or * Baltrader Schiffahrt.*

Britannia Aggregates Ltd
UK

Funnel: *Buff base and deep dark green top, broad white band with 'BRITANNIA AGGREGATES' between two narrow rings divided by diagonal trident with 'Britannia' bust above and 'Union Jack' shield below all in dark green, rings interrupted by three buff waves on each side.* **Hull:** *Green with red boot-topping.*
History: *Founded 1990 as joint venture between Brett Group and Redland Westminster Aggregates.* **Web:** *www.brett.co.uk*

Name	Flag	Year	GT	DWT	Loa	Bm	Drt	Kts	Type	Remarks
Britannia Beaver	Gbr	1991	3,610	5,786	100.0	17.7	6.2	12	Dss	

British Nuclear Fuels Ltd
UK

Funnel: *Blue with white 'BNFL' beneath white ring containing yellow pattern.* **Hull:** *Blue with yellow band, pale blue boot-topping.* **History:** *Founded 1979 as Pacific Nuclear Transport Ltd.* **Web:** *www.bnfl.com*

Name		Flag	Year	GT	DWT	Loa	Bm	Drt	Kts	Type	Remarks
Atlantic Osprey *		Gbr	1986	3,793	2,201	88.6	14.3	5.1	13	Ro	ex Arneb-02, Alster Rapid-95
Pacific Egret		Gbr	2010	6,780	4,850	103.9	17.3	6.8	-	Cn	
Pacific Grebe		Gbr	2010	6,780	4,850	103.9	17.3	6.8	-	Cn	
Pacific Heron		Gbr	2008	6,776	4,916	103.9	17.3	6.8	-	Cn	
Pacific Pintail	(2)	Gbr	1987	5,087	3,865	103.9	16.6	6.0	13	Cn	
Pacific Sandpiper	(2)	Gbr	1985	5,050	3,775	103.9	16.7	6.0	13	Cn	

*Owned by Pacific Nuclear Transport Ltd or * Nuclear Decommissioning Authority and managed by James Fisher (Shipping Services) Ltd qv*

The British Petroleum Co PLC
UK

BP Oil UK Ltd
Funnel: *Red with narrow white and green bands.* **Hull:** *Black with red boot-topping.* **History:** *Parent founded in 1909 and operating subsidiary in 1947.*
Web: *www.bp.com*

Name	Flag	Year	GT	DWT	Loa	Bm	Drt	Kts	Type	Remarks
Border Heather	Iom	2004	2,159	3,185	75.0	14.2	5.8	12	T	
Border Tartan	Iom	2005	3,248	4,975	79.9	17.0	6.3	12	T	
Border Thistle	Iom	2005	3,248	4,975	79.9	17.0	6.3	12	T	

Managed by subsidiary BP Shipping Ltd.

Briese Schiffahrts GmbH & Co KG. Musketier. *David Walker*

Brovigs Rederi AS. Brovig Wind. *N. Kemps*

Hermann Buss GmbH. Medangara. *Allan Ryszka Onions*

Name	Flag	Year	GT	DWT	Loa	Bm	Drt	Kts	Type	Remarks

Y & B Brons — Germany

Funnel: *White.* **Hull:** *Blue with red boot-topping.* **History:** *Founded 2004.* **Web:** *www.brons.de*

Name	Flag	Year	GT	DWT	Loa	Bm	Drt	Kts	Type	Remarks
Imina	Gib	2009	3,500	4,836	90.0	15.6	5.8	-	C	
Theda	Gib	2009	3,500	4,750	90.0	15.6	5.8	-	C	ex Blue Carmel-09

Brovigs Rederi AS — Norway

Funnel: *Buff with black 'B' on white diamond on black edged red rectangle.* **Hull:** *Blue or red with red boot-topping.* **History:** *Founded 1889 as Th Brovig to 1992 and now part of Gezina AS.* **Web:** *www.brovig.no*

Name	Flag	Year	GT	DWT	Loa	Bm	Drt	Kts	Type	Remarks
Brovig Bora	Gib	2006	2,627	3,502	92.9	14.1	5.6	-	Tch	ex Vedrey Fram-08, Atlantis Acra-07
Brovig Breeze *	Nis	2006	2,885	4,296	96.8	13.8	6.2	11	Tch	I/a Oceamn Breeze
Brovig Fjord *	Gib	2008	5,445	8,151	114.7	17.3	7.4	-	Tch	
Brovig Marin	Gib	2005	2,262	3,450	88.4	13.0	6.0	-	Tch	ex Vedrey Heden-08, Serra D-06
Brovig Viento *	Gib	2004	3,189	4,500	99.8	15.0	6.0	14	Tch	ex Lider Kerem-08
Brovig Vindur *	Gib	2005	3,178	4,653	99.8	15.0	6.0	14	Tch	ex Lider Yaman-07
Brovig Wind *	Nis	2005	2,889	4,280	96.0	14.2	6.2	-	Tch	

* managed by Brovigtank AS (founded 1936)

Brust Schiffahrts GmbH — Germany

Funnel: *White.* **Hull:** *Red with white 'SAAR', red boot-topping.* **History:** *Founded 1996.* **Web:** *None found.*

Name	Flag	Year	GT	DWT	Loa	Bm	Drt	Kts	Type	Remarks
Mermaid	Deu	1985	1,856	2,302	80.7	12.7	4.2	10	Cc	

Guido Buck Schiffahrts KG — Germany

Funnel: *White.* **Hull:** *Blue with red boot-topping.* **History:** *Founded 1999.* **Web:** *www.buck-schiffahrt.de or www.gross-buck-bereederung.de*

Name	Flag	Year	GT	DWT	Loa	Bm	Drt	Kts	Type	Remarks
Antonia B	Atg	1983	3,780	4,646	97.0	17.6	6.0	14	Cc	ex Clontarf-08, Hajo-03, Takitimu-98, Ocean-94, Velazquez-91, Ocean-88, City of Salerno-87, Ocean-86, Akak Ocean-86, Ocean-84
Ernst Hagedorn	Atg	1989	3,826	4,402	104.8	16.3	5.6	15	Cc	ex Winden-04
Norrvik	Iom	1979	2,041	3,300	80.3	13.9	6.6	13	C	ex Lady Bos-02

Owned or managed by subsidiary Gross/Buck Bereederungs GmbH & Co KG, Germany (founded 2006)

Hermann Buss GmbH & Cie KG — Germany

Funnel: *White with white 'H' and blue 'B' symbol interrupting red-edged narrow blue band or white with symbol on superstructure.* **Hull:** *Light grey with green above red boot-topping or green with red or grey boot-topping.* **History:** *Founded 1967 as Reederei Hermann Buss to 1988.* **Web:** *www.buss-gruppe.de*

Name	Flag	Year	GT	DWT	Loa	Bm	Drt	Kts	Type	Remarks
Agnes Scan	Atg	2006	2,545	3,459	88.5	12.8	5.5	12	Cc	I/a Guernsey
Alsen *	Cyp	2002	3,925	4,633	99.9	16.0	5.1	12	Cc	
Amalie Scan	Atg	2004	2,545	3,490	88.5	12.8	5.5	12	Cc	ex Jersey-05
Amiya Scan **	Atg	2003	2,546	3,482	86.5	12.9	5.5	12	Cc	ex BBC Bornholm-07
Amrum Trader	Atg	1997	5,941	8,081	132.3	19.5	6.9	17	CC	ex Seaboard Unity-98, Amrum Trader-97
Amstel Trader **	Nld	2003	6,704	8,015	132.6	19.2	7.2	17	CC	
Asko	Atg	2005	3,183	4,518	90.0	15.2	5.3	-	C	
Baltic Trader **	Nld	1995	4,984	6,974	116.4	19.5	7.1	15	CC	ex Norasia Attica-99, Baltic Trader-98, Zim Napoli I-97, Baltic Trader-97, Armada Trader-96, Baltic Trader-95
Bornholm *	Cyp	2006	4,967	7,869	120.0	15.2	7.1	14	Cc	
Caribbean Trader	Deu	1999	4,246	6,275	100.0	17.0	7.3	15	Cc	ex S&J Century-01, Industrial Century-00, I/a Caribbean Trader
Caroline Scan	Atg	1999	4,246	6,265	100.0	17.0	7.3	15	Cc	ex Caribbean Trader-08, UAL Nigeria-06, Caribbean Trader-03, S&J Century-01, Industrial Century-00, I/a Caribbean Trader
Catherine Scan	Atg	1999	4,251	6,265	100.0	17.0	7.3	15	Cc	ex Industrial Horizon-08, Sun Bird-00, Mellum Trader-99
Christina Scan **	Nld	1999	4,251	6,246	100.0	17.0	7.3	16	CC	ex Rijn Trader-05, UAL Europe-05, Rhine Trader-04, Industrial Future-03, Rhine Trader-99
Dintel Trader **	Cyp	2006	6,701	8,200	132.6	19.2	7.2	17	CC	ex ACX Polaris-08, I/a Medgulf
Emscarrier	Atg	2007	4,102	5,486	106.9	15.2	5.3	12	Cc	
Emsrunner *	Cyp	2006	4,102	5,499	106.9	15.2	5.3	12	Cc	
Falster *	Cyp	2002	3,925	4,350	99.9	16.0	5.1	12	Cc	
Frisian Trader **	Nld	1994	4,984	7,014	116.4	19.5	7.1	16	CC	ex Norasia Adria-99, Frisian Trader-98, Ems Bay-96, Frisian Trader-95
Gotland **	Nld	2001	3,925	4,650	100.0	16.0	5.1	12	Cc	
Hansen Scan	Atg	2006	4,990	7,800	118.6	15.2	7.1	14	Cc	ex Onego River-09
Hartwig Scan	Atg	2006	4,990	7,778	118.6	15.2	7.1	14	Cc	I/a Lifter
Hermann Scan	Atg	2007	4,990	7,800	118.6	15.2	7.1	14	Cc	
Hunze Trader **	Cyp	2008	7,170	8,200	131.5	19.2	7.7	17	CC	ex O M Nubium-08
Islander **	Nld	2003	6,704	8,015	132.6	19.2	7.2	17	CC	ex Ijssel Trader-08, CMA CGM Samurai-06, Ijssel Trader-05
Linge Trader **	Nld	2006	9,981	11,834	139.1	22.6	8.8	18	CC	
Maas Trader **	Nld	2006	9,981	11,827	139.1	22.6	8.8	18	CC	
Maersk Fuji	Cyp	2005	9,981	11,798	139.1	22.6	8.8	18	CC	ex Iller Trader-05

Name	Flag	Year	GT	DWT	Loa	Bm	Drt	Kts	Type	Remarks
Maersk Fukuoka	Cyp	2005	9,981	11,815	139.1	22.6	8.8	18	CC	ex Isar Trader-05
Medaegean *	Cyp	2008	9,946	11,968	139.1	22.6	8.8	18	CC	
Medangara *	Cyp	2008	5,335	6,795	119.3	16.5	6.3	12	Cc	
Medarctic *	Cyp	2009	5,335	6,796	119.3	16.5	6.3	12	Cc	
Medbalkash *	Cyp	2009	5,335	6,777	119.3	16.5	6.3	12	Cc	
Medbaykal	Cyp	2007	9,946	12,001	139.1	22.6	8.8	18	CC	
Medbothnia *	Cyp	2008	9,981	11,900	139.1	22.6	8.8	18	CC	
Medcaspian *	Cyp	2009	5,335	6,801	119.3	16.5	6.3	12	Cc	
Medonega *	Cyp	2008	5,335	6,812	119.3	16.5	6.3	12	Cc	
Merwe Trader **	Nld	2006	9,981	11,842	139.1	22.6	8.8	18	CC	ex fairwind 308-08, YM Mawei-07, Merwe Trader-06
Northsea Trader **	Nld	1995	4,984	6,928	116.4	19.5	7.1	16	CC	ex MSC Krasnodar-01, Northsea Trader-00, Gracechurch Comet-99, Northsea Trader-97, Texel Bay-96, Northsea Trader-95
Princess Mary	Atg	2000	4,251	6,259	100.0	17.0	7.3	15	Cc	ex Finex Trader-05, Industrial Frontier-03, Finex Trader-00
Reykjafoss	Nld	1999	7,541	8,450	127.4	20.4	7.7	17	Cc	ex Westersingel-05, Western-05, MSC Bosphorus-04, Westersingel-03, X-Press Italia-01, Westersingel-00
Ruth	Atg	1991	2,873	4,566	88.2	13.7	6.1	12	Cc	
Schelde Trader **	Nld	2003	6,704	8,015	132.6	19.2	7.2	17	CC	ex Mekong Chaiyo-09, Schelde Trader-05
Seaboard Pride	Atg	1998	6,674	8,329	132.5	19.5	7.2	17	CC	ex APL Quetzal-07, Stor Trader-03, Seaboard Pride-03, Stor Trader-01, Seaboard Pride-00, I/a Stor Trader
Skarpoe	Cyp	2005	3,183	4,508	89.8	15.2	5.3	12	Cc	
Storoe	Cyp	2004	3,183	4,507	89.8	15.2	5.3	12	Cc	
Tini	Atg	2005	6,701	8,200	132.6	19.2	7.2	17	CC	
Varmido	Atg	2004	3,183	4,501	89.8	15.2	5.3	12	Cc	
Victoria Scan **	Atg	1993	5,782	8.115	107.4	19.6	8.3	15	C/hl	ex Oxl Victory-09, BBC Sealand-07, Steinkirchen-01, Regine-01, Steinkirchen-01, Wiebke-00
Vindoe	Atg	2004	3,183	4,516	89.8	15.2	5.3	12	Cc	
Waal Trader **	Nld	2003	6,704	8,015	132.6	19.2	7.2	17	CC	ex Mekong Cayenne-09, Waal Trader 05, MCL Moscow-04, Waal Trader-04
Warnow Carp *	Atg	2009	9,946	11,968	139.1	22.6	8.8	18	CC	
Warnow Perch *	Atg	2007	9,946	11,968	139.1	22.6	8.8	18	CC	
Warnow Trout *	Atg	2008	9,900	11,983	139.1	22.6	8.8	18	CC	
Westerhaven **	Nld	2000	7,541	8,450	127.0	20.5	7.7	17	Cc	ex CTE Barcelona-01, Westerhaven-00
Westerkade	Nld	2000	7,541	8,450	127.0	20.5	7.7	17	Cc	
Western Trader	Atg	1991	4,164	4,744	111.1	16.1	6.0	14	Cc	ex Gracechurch Meteor-97, Western Trader-91
Zaan Trader **	Cyp	2005	6,701	8,200	132.6	19.2	7.2	17	CC	

*owned by subsidiaries * Medstar Shipmanagement Ltd., Cyprus (founded 1996) or ** Reider Shipping BV, Netherlands (founded 1999 – www.reidershipping.com) Vessels with 'Scan' suffix on charter to Scan-Trans Shipping, Denmark qv*

Busser Shipping CV
Netherlands

Funnel: *White.* **Hull:** *Blue with black boot-topping.* **History:** *Not confirmed.* **Web:** *None found.*

Dok Bua	Nld	2010	2,999	4,650	90.0	14.4	-	-	Cc	
Lelie	Nld	2000	2,450	3,697	88.0	12.4	5.6	11	Cc	ex Filia Alette-08, Texel-06, Rifgat-06
Lotus	Nld	1993	1,596	2,510	82.0	11.1	3.3	11	Cc	ex Nescio-01

BW Shipping Group Ltd
Bermuda

Yara International ASA/Norway
Funnel: *Black.* **Hull:** *Grey with blue 'YARA' and viking ship symbol, red boot-topping.* **History:** *Founded 1949 as Hydros Tankships A/S to 1976, then Hydroship A/S subsidiary of Norsk Hydro A/S, demerged and renamed Hydroship Services A/S in 2004 and later acquired by BW Shipping.* **Web:** *www.yara.com*

Yara Gas I	Nis	1977	1,744	2,060	72.0	12.8	4.5	11	Lpg	ex Hydrogas-04, Este-89 (conv C-89)
Yara Gas II	Nis	1977	1,744	1,964	72.0	12.8	4.4	12	Lpg	ex Hydrogas II-04, Britta II-92, Britta I-87, American Cheyenne-79, Britta-77 (conv Cc-92)
Yara Gas III	Nis	1975	2,198	2,645	81.5	13.4	5.0	13	Lpg	ex Hydrogas III-04, Coburg-96, Nautilus-88, American Cherokee-79, I/a Nautilus (conv Cc-96)

Managed by Larvik Shipping AS, Norway (www.larvik-shipping.no)

C2C Shipping Lines NV
Belgium

Container feeder service *currently operating three chartered vessels.* **History:** *Joint venture between Cobelfret and European Containers NV (ECS). Subsidiary of Peel Ports Group since 2005.* **Web:** *www.c2clines.com*

C & H Heuvelman Shipping BV
Netherlands

Funnel: *Red with white band.* **Hull:** *Red with red boot-topping.* **History:** *Founded 1990 as C&H Heuvelman Shipping & Trading BV to 2006.* **Web:** *www.unifleet.nl or www.northseatankers.com*

Cappadocian *		Gib	2006	3,988	5,667	108.0	16.0	6.0	-	Tch
Global Earth	(2)	Gib	2009	3,168	4,387	93.0	15.2	5.8	-	Tch
Global Lake	(2)	Gib	2010	5,340	7,500	111.5	17.6	7.2	-	Tch

Name		Flag	Year	GT	DWT	Loa	Bm	Drt	Kts	Type	Remarks
Global Libra	(2)	Gib	2010	3,500	5,000	102.5	15.2	7.2	-	Tch	
Global Moon	(2)	Gib	2009	3,168	4,387	93.0	15.2	5.8	-	Tch	
Global Ocean	(2)	Gib	2010	5,340	7,500	111.5	17.6	7.2	-	Tch	
Global River	(2)	Gib	2010	5,340	7,500	111.5	17.6	7.2	-	Tch	
Global Sea	(2)	Gib	2010	5,340	7,500	111.5	17.6	7.2	-	Tch	
Global Star	(2)	Gib	2010	3,160	4,300	93.0	15.2	5.8	-	Tch	ex Galaxy-10
Global Sun	(2)	Gib	2010	3,160	4,300	93.0	15.2	5.8	-	Tch	
Global Taurus	(2)	Gib	2010	3,500	5,000	102.5	15.2	7.2	-	Tch	
NST Amalia		Gib	2007	3,933	6,863	103.0	16.0	7.0	-	Tch	
NST Leoni		Gib	2006	2,906	4,580	90.0	15.2	5.9	-	Tch	
NST Natasja *		Gib	2005	2,890	4,318	93.3	14.2	6.2	12	Tch	ex Natasja Theresa-09, Dora-05
Trans Alina *		Gib	2001	3,441	5,060	99.4	15.3	6.3	14	Tch	

Newbuildings: two further 5,000 dwt tankers due for 2011 delivery.
*Operated by subsidiary Unifleet BV trading as NorthSeaTankers BV or * managed by Bernhard Schulte Shipmanagement.*

Campbell Maritime Ltd   UK

Funnel: *White or black with black 'GPG' on white diamond on broad red band edged with narrow white bands.* **Hull:** *Light grey with black boot-topping or blue with red boot-topping.* **History:** *Founded 1984.* **Web:** *www.cammar.co.uk*

Name	Flag	Year	GT	DWT	Loa	Bm	Drt	Kts	Type	Remarks
Alice PG **	Bhs	1994	3,627	6,248	102.1	16.0	6.5	12	T	
Douwent	Gbr	1987	1,311	1,800	79.7	11.2	3.7	12	Cc	ex Douwe S-05, Torpe-93
Eliza PG *	Iom	1992	3,338	5,440	96.2	16.1	6.3	12	T	
Emily PG *	Iom	1997	3,627	6,249	102.1	16.1	6.5	12	T	
Evie PG **	Gbr	2007	6,688	9,990	127.0	19.7	6.5	-	T	
Georgina PG **	Iom	2008	6,688	10,711	127.0	19.7	6.5	-	T	
Lesley PG *	Iom	1998	3,630	6,249	102.1	16.1	6.5	12	T	
Lucy PG **	Iom	2001	6,688	10,005	127.0	19.6	6.8	13	T	
Panda PG *	Iom	2004	4,414	6,725	114.0	17.0	6.8	14	T	ex Crestar-05, Ecem Kalkavan-04
Tessa PG *	Iom	2005	4,666	7,010	119.6	16.9	6.7	14	T	

** managed for Havinvest AS, Norway or ** Pritchard Gordon Tankers Ltd (Giles W Pritchard-Gordon & Co Ltd)*

Canada Feeder Lines BV   Netherlands

Funnel: *White.* **Hull:** *White with green band and 'CANADAFEEDERLINE.COM', light grey boot-topping.* **History:** *Founded 2007.* **Web:** *www.canadafeederlines.eu*

Name	Flag	Year	GT	DWT	Loa	Bm	Drt	Kts	Type	Remarks
CFL Momentum	Nld	2010	6,525	8,000	-	-	-	-	C	
CFL Patron	Nld	2008	4,040	6,500	118.4	13.4	6.1	12	C	
CFL Penhar	Nld	2010	4,087	6,500	118.4	13.4	6.1	12	C	
CFL Perfect	Nld	2009	4,106	6,500	118.4	13.4	6.1	12	C	
CFL Performer	Nld	2007	4,040	6,500	118.4	13.4	6.1	12	C	
CFL Progress	Nld	2009	4,106	6,510	118.4	13.4	6.1	12	C	
CFL Promise	Nld	2008	4,106	6,500	118.4	13.4	6.1	12	C	
CFL Prospect	Nld	2007	4,106	6,500	118.4	13.4	6.1	12	C	
CFL Proud	Nld	2009	4,106	6,500	118.4	13.4	6.1	12	C	
CFL Prudence	Nld	2008	4,106	6,500	118.4	13.4	6.1	12	C	

Newbuildings: One further 8,000 dwt general cargo vessel (CFL Marvel) due for 2011 delivery.
Managed by CFL Management BV – see other operated vessels with CFL prefix.

Candler Schiffahrts GmbH   Germany

Funnel: *Black, white with black top or charterers colours.* **Hull:** *Black with red boot-topping.* **History:** *Founded 1991 as Rolf D Candler Schiffahrt to 1997.* **Web:** *www.candler.eu*

Name	Flag	Year	GT	DWT	Loa	Bm	Drt	Kts	Type	Remarks
Accurate	Atg	1999	7,918	12,974	128.0	21.2	8.3	14	B	
Alert	Atg	1999	7,918	12,974	128.0	21.2	8.3	14	B	
BBC Tahiti	Atg	2007	6,569	7,800	116.2	18.1	7.0	12	Cc	ex FCC Embolden-07
BBC Tasmania	Atg	2008	6,569	8,091	116.2	18.0	7.0	12	Cc	ex FCC Pioneer-08
BBC Togo	Atg	2007	6,569	7,800	116.2	18.0	7.0	12	Cc	ex FCC Wealthy-08
BBC Tunisia	Atg	2008	6,569	8,091	116.2	18.0	7.0	12	Cc	
Ela *	Atg	1997	2,377	3,462	89.0	12.4	5.0	10	Cc	ex Francisca-07, Soli Deo Gloria-05
Glory	Atg	2006	6,393	8,378	116.2	18.0	7.1	12	Cc	ex FCC Glory-06
Notos	Atg	2004	5,458	8,049	125.2	16.4	7.2	12	Cc	ex Azerbaycan-04
Wisdom	Atg	2006	6,494	8,334	116.2	18.0	7.0	12	Cc	ex BBC Thailand-08, Wisdom-06, I/a FCC Wisdom

* managed for Internaut Shipping Europe GmbH & Co KG, Germany (Founded 2007 – www.internaut-shipping.de)

Cargo Shipping SP z oo   Poland

Funnel: *White with light blue top.* **Hull:** *Light blue with red boot-topping.* **History:** *Founded 2006.* **Web:** *None found.*

Name	Flag	Year	GT	DWT	Loa	Bm	Drt	Kts	Type	Remarks
Paper Moon	Atg	1990	2,292	2,706	84.9	12.8	4.4	11	Cc	ex Assiduus-05, Lehship-90, Assiduus-90
Paper Star	Atg	1989	2,292	2,750	84.9	12.8	4.4	11	Cc	ex Antina-05

BW Shipping Group/Yara International. Yara Gas III. *Allan Ryszka Onions*

Cargo Shipping SP z oo. Paper Moon. *David Walker*

Carisbrooke Shipping Ltd. Jade C. *Hans Kraijenbosch*

Name	Flag	Year	GT	DWT	Loa	Bm	Drt	Kts	Type	Remarks

Cargohunters AS — Estonia

Funnel: *Black with red bow symbol.* **Hull:** *Green or blue with red boot-topping.* **History:** *Founded 2002.* **Web:** *www.cargohunters.ee*

Name	Flag	Year	GT	DWT	Loa	Bm	Drt	Kts	Type	Remarks
Erlanda *	Vct	1991	1,999	3,005	82.0	12.5	5.1	12	Cc	ex Scheldeborg-03
Faustina *	Vct	1990	1,999	3,015	82.0	12.5	5.1	12	Cc	ex Flinterborg-03
Isidor	Cyp	1993	2,735	4,266	89.6	13.2	5.7	12	Cc	ex Ikiena-05
Jolanta	Mlt	1999	3,621	4,520	98.3	15.4	5.7	14	Cc	ex Marnediep-07
Kergi	Mlt	1991	4,059	5,850	108.8	16.6	6.5	15	Cc	ex Vergi-08, Emil-Nolde-05, Mir-98, Admiraal-97, Sea Admiral-95, Admiraal-92
Lenglo *	Vct	1983	1,946	2,904	88.0	11.5	4.7	11	C	ex Celtic Pride-09, Normannia-05, Baursberg-97
Sylve *	Nld	1990	1,999	2,950	82.0	12.5	4.9	12	Cc	ex Vios-01, Morgenstond II-97

* managed by subsidiary Craftchart Ou, Estonia (founded 2003 - www.craftchart.ee)
Also see Seatrade ServicesOu, Estonia

Carisbrooke Shipping Ltd — UK

Funnel: *Buff with buff 'CS' on blue rectangle.* **Hull:** *Light grey with green waterline over red boot-topping.* **History:** *Founded 1969 and acquired Beck Scheepvaartkantor in 2003.* **Web:** *www.carisbrookeshipping.net*

Name	Flag	Year	GT	DWT	Loa	Bm	Drt	Kts	Type	Remarks
Amy C	Gbr	2006	9,177	13,528	136.4	21.2	8.4	14	Cc	
Andrea Anon	Gbr	2006	5,604	8,099	108.2	18.2	7.0	12	C	I/a Anja C
Anja C *	Gbr	2006	5,604	8,099	108.2	18.2	7.0	12	C	
Charlotte C	Iom	2009	9,177	13,400	136.4	21.2	8.4	14	Cc	
Christine C	Gbr	2008	5,629	8,063	108.2	18.2	7.1	12	C	
Eileen C	Gbr	2007	2,990	4,998	89.8	14.5	6.3	13	Cc	
Esther C	Gbr	2008	5,629	8,050	108.2	18.2	7.1	12	C	
Geja C **	Iom	2002	7,511	10,596	142.7	18.3	7.3	15	Cc	
Greta C	Iom	2009	9,177	13,400	136.4	21.2	8.4	14	Cc	
Hanna C *	Gbr	2002	7,752	10,526	145.6	18.3	7.4	14	Cc	ex Opal Ace-09, Hanna C-06, Corral-04, Hanna C-02, I/a Anna C
Heather C	Gbr	2006	5,629	8,047	108.2	18.2	7.1	12	C	ex Esther C-07
Heleen C	Gbr	2006	9,177	13,528	136.4	21.2	8.4	14	Cc	
Jade C **	Iom	2005	7,767	10,884	145.6	18.3	7.4	14	Cc	
Jannie C *	Iom	2002	7,511	10,517	142.7	18.3	7.3	15	Cc	
Johanna C	Gbr	2009	9,530	12,914	138.1	21.0	8.0	14	Cc	
Julie C	Gbr	2009	9,530	12,914	138.1	21.0	8.0	14	Cc	
Karen C	Gbr	2010	4,145	6,250	108.1	15.5	6.7	11	C	
Karina C	Gbr	2010	4,145	6,250	108.1	15.5	6.7	11	C	
Karla C	Gbr	2010	4,145	6,250	108.1	15.5	6.7	11	C	
Kate C	Gbr	2010	4,145	6,250	108.1	15.5	6.7	11	C	
Kathy C	Gbr	2010	4,145	6,250	108.1	15.5	6.7	11	C	
Kelly C	Gbr	2010	4,145	6,250	108.1	15.5	6.7	11	C	
Kikke C	Gbr	2010	4,145	6,250	108.1	15.5	6.7	11	C	
Klazina C	Gbr	2007	5,629	8,047	108.2	18.2	7.1	12	C	
Kristin C	Gbr	2010	4,145	6,250	108.1	15.5	6.7	11	C	
Lauren C	Gbr	2007	2,990	5,000	89.8	14.5	6.3	13	Cc	
Lijun C	Gbr	2010	5,608	7,600	108.2	18.2	7.1	12	C	
Lisa C	Gbr	2007	2,990	5,000	89.8	14.5	6.3	13	Cc	
Margrete C **	Iom	2002	7,511	10,596	142.7	18.3	7.3	15	Cc	ex Cordillera-09, Margrete C-03
Michelle C	Gbr	2010	9,530	12,946	138.1	21.0	8.0	14	Cc	I/d Gemmy C
Minka C	Gbr	2008	3,391	5,000	99.6	14.5	6.3	13	Cc	
Mirjam C *	Gbr	2008	5,629	8,063	108.2	18.2	7.1	12	C	
Monica C	Gbr	2009	5,629	8,047	108.2	18.2	7.1	12	C	
Natacha C *	Gbr	2003	7,752	10,438	145.6	18.3	7.4	14	Cc	
Nicole C	Gbr	2008	2,990	5,000	89.8	14.5	6.3	13	Cc	
Nomadic Bergen	Gbr	2009	5,629	8,063	108.2	18.2	7.1	12	C	
Nomadic Hjellestad	Iom	2010	9,530	12,914	138.1	21.0	8.0	14	Cc	I/d Jessica C
Nomadic Milde	Iom	2010	9,530	12,914	138.1	21.0	8.0	14	Cc	
Paula C	Gbr	2008	2,990	5,000	89.8	14.5	6.3	13	Cc	I/d Julia C
Sally Ann C	Gbr	2006	9,177	13,400	136.4	21.2	8.4	14	Cc	
Shirkan C	Atg	2007	5,608	8,047	108.2	18.2	7.1	12	C	
Sian C	Gbr	2006	9,177	13,479	136.4	21.2	8.4	14	Cc	
Sonja C	Gbr	2008	5,629	8,047	108.2	18.2	7.1	12	C	
Steffi C	Gbr	2010	5,608	7,600	108.2	18.2	7.1	12	C	
Tina C	Gbr	2008	3,391	5,000	99.6	14.5	6.3	13	Cc	
UAL America *	Gbr	2005	7,767	10,884	145.6	18.3	7.4	14	Cc	ex Emily C-06
UAL Antwerp *	Gbr	2006	7,767	10,568	145.6	18.3	7.4	14	Cc	ex Sally Ann C-06
UAL Capetown	Gbr	2009	9,530	12,914	138.1	21.0	8.0	14	Cc	ex Janet C-09
UAL Europe *	Gbr	2006	7,767	10,683	145.6	18.3	7.4	14	Cc	ex Jill C-06
UAL Gabon	Gbr	2009	9,530	12,914	138.1	21.0	8.0	14	Cc	ex Jacqueline C-09
Vanessa C *	Gbr	2003	7,752	10,500	145.6	18.3	7.4	14	Cc	
Victoria C	Gbr	2007	2,990	5,000	89.8	14.5	6.3	13	Cc	

Carisbrooke Shipping Ltd. Lauren C. *Allan Ryszka Onions*

Cemex UK Marine Ltd. Sand Weaver. *Phil Kempsey*

Chemgas Shipping BV. Zephyr. *Phil Kempsey*

Name		Flag	Year	GT	DWT	Loa	Bm	Drt	Kts	Type	Remarks

Newbuildings: Three further 12,900 dwt (un-named, Celine C and Megan C) and one further 6,250 dwt (Kimberley C) due in 2011
* managed by Carisbrooke Shipping (Management) GmbH, Germany including ** owned by HCI Hanseatische Capital Beratungs GmbH
Also owns 19,400 dwt bulk carrier (Mark C).
See chartered vessels under Rederij C Kornet & Zonen BV, Rohden Bereederung GmbH & Co KG and Vaage Ship Management AS.

Carsten Rehder Schiffsmakler und Reederei GmbH · Germany

Funnel: *White with white CR on black diamond between narrow red bands.* **Hull:** *Black, dark blue or red with red or black boot-topping.* **History:** *Founded 1903 as Carsten Rehder to 1982.* **Web:** *www.carstenrehder.de*

Name		Flag	Year	GT	DWT	Loa	Bm	Drt	Kts	Type	Remarks
Franklin Strait		Atg	2000	4,450	5,585	100.6	18.8	6.7	15	CC	I/a Herm J
Hamilton Strait *		Mhl	1999	9,030	10,974	136.5	22.5	8.6	18	CC	ex Ibn Hayyan-08, Cape Capricorn-01
Hudson Strait *		Mhl	1999	9,030	11,386	135.6	22.5	8.6	18	CC	ex Cape Cleveland-04

* managed for FHH Fonds Haus Hamburg GmbH & Co KG
Also owns or manages 14 other larger container ships.

Cebo International BV · Netherlands

Funnel: *White with white 'cb' on broad blue top.* **Hull:** *Light grey with black boot-topping or * blue with red boot-topping.* **History:** *Oil and gas industry supplier founded in 1970's.* **Web:** *www.cebo-uk.com*

Name		Flag	Year	GT	DWT	Loa	Bm	Drt	Kts	Type	Remarks
Noblesse C		Nld	1980	1.095	1,622	65.1	11.4	4.5	11	Ce	ex Noblesse-98 (conv C-98)
Ritske *		Nld	1990	1,508	1,688	79.7	10.9	3.5	10	Cc	ex Hanse-05, Hanse Contor-92, I/a Elena

Operated by subsidiary Cebo UK Ltd (founded 1973)

Celtic Link Ferries Ireland Ltd · Ireland

Funnel: *Black with red symbol between green bands.* **Hull:** *Blue with red boot-topping.* **History:** *Founded 2005.* **Web:** *www.celticlinkferries.com*

Name		Flag	Year	GT	DWT	Loa	Bm	Drt	Kts	Type	Remarks
Ballyhealy		Pan	1981	1,939	2,890	88.0	11.4	4.7	11	Cc	ex Hunter-07, Deike-98
Magnolia 1		Pan	1983	2,768	2,848	95.6	13.5	4.3	11	Cc	ex Magnolia-08, Dever-01, Magnus E-98, Veerhaven-91, Magnolia-90

Managed by subsidiary KQ Shipping, Ireland (founded 2007).
Also see Ferries Section.

Cemex UK Marine Ltd · UK

Funnel: *White with red and dark blue diagonal stripes and dark blue 'cemex' below black top.* **Hull:** *Black with red boot-topping.* **History:** *Founded 1912 as South Coast Shipping Co Ltd to 2001 when renamed RMC Marine Ltd until acquired by Cemex in 2005.* **Web:** *www.cemex.co.uk*

Name		Flag	Year	GT	DWT	Loa	Bm	Drt	Kts	Type	Remarks
Sand Falcon		Gbr	1998	6,534	9,154	117.7	19.5	7.8	12	Dss	(len-03)
Sand Fulmar *		Gbr	1998	5,307	9,153	99.9	19.5	7.8	12	Dss	
Sand Harrier		Gbr	1990	3,751	5,916	99.0	16.5	6.6	11	Dss	
Sand Heron		Gbr	1990	3,751	5,916	99.0	16.5	6.4	11	Dss	
Sand Serin		Gbr	1974	1,282	2,120	66.6	12.2	4.8	10	Dss	
Sand Swan **		Gbr	1970	1,164	1,944	66.6	12.5	4.4	10	Dss	
Sand Weaver		Gbr	1975	3,497	5,271	96.4	16.7	6.1	12	Dss	
Welsh Piper *		Gbr	1987	1,251	1,923	69.0	12.5	4.4	11	Dss	

* owned by Cemex subsidiaries British Dredging Ltd or ** Mersey Sand Supplies Ltd

Charterfrakt Baltic Carrier AB · Sweden

Funnel: *White with white 'N' on blue square.* **Hull:** *Yellow with black 'HOLMEN CARRIER', black waterline above red boot-topping.* **History:** *Founded 1971.* **Web:** *www.charterfrakt.se*

Name		Flag	Year	GT	DWT	Loa	Bm	Drt	Kts	Type	Remarks
Baltic Bright		Swe	1996	9,708	6,300	134.4	20.5	5.7	15	Ro	
Baltic Print		Swe	1979	6,415	4,623	135.4	16.8	4.6	13	Ro	(len-82)

Chemgas Shipping BV · Netherlands

Funnel: *Grey or white with red houseflag om blue panel.* **Hull:** *Blue with red boot-topping.* **History:** *Founded 1985 as Gastankvaartmaatschappij Chemgas BV by Vopak. Subsidiary founded 2000 and Group acquired 2003 by Reederei Jaegers GmbH.* **Web:** *www.chemgas.nl*

Name		Flag	Year	GT	DWT	Loa	Bm	Drt	Kts	Type	Remarks
Chiltern		Bhs	2007	3,607	3,942	96.0	16.2	5.5	12	Lpg	ex Chemgas Durian-03
Salmon		Nld	1987	1,605	1,294	92.8	11.4	2.9	10	Lpg	
Sturgeon		Nld	1988	1,605	1,294	92.5	11.4	2.9	11	Lpg	
Tempest		Nld	2008	2,294	1,809	99.9	11.5	3.7	12	Lpg	
Thresher	(2)	Nld	2007	2,294	1,814	99.9	11.4	3.7	12	Lpg	
Trout	(2)	Nld	1990	1,997	1,520	105.6	11.9	2.9	11	Lpg	
Twaite	(2)	Nld	1991	1,997	1,640	105.6	12.0	3.0	11	Lpg	
Twister		Nld	2010	2,300	2,000	99.9	11.5	3.7	12	Lpg	
Typhoon		Nld	2010	2,300	2,000	99.9	11.5	3.7	12	Lpg	
Zephyr *		Nld	1985	1,621	1,800	92.6	11.4	3.2	11	Lpg	

Newbiudlings: two 2,300 gt lpg tankers for 2010-11 delivery.
* managed by Bernhard Schulte Shipmanagement, Cyprus, which also owns other operated vessels qv

Name		Flag	Year	GT	DWT	Loa	Bm	Drt	Kts	Type	Remarks

Chemical Tankers Europe   Netherlands

Funnel: Yellow with white 'K' on white edged black disc, narrow black top. **Hull:** Red with red boot-topping. **History:** Founded 2009.
Web: www.ctemanagement.nl

Name	Flag	Year	GT	DWT	Loa	Bm	Drt	Kts	Type	Remarks
Loya	Nld	2010	2,800	3,800	93.0	14.6	5.6	-	Tch	
Nena	Nld	2009	4,218	6,480	109.0	16.8	6.7	-	Tch	ex Nena K-10
Nosi	Nld	2010	4,218	6,480	109.0	16.8	6.7	-	Tch	
Toli	Nld	2009	2,617	3,442	92.9	14.1	5.7	-	Tch	

Chemikalien Seetransport GmbH   Germany

Funnel: Blue with white 'ST' inside larger 'C' between two narrow white bands. **Hull:** Blue with white 'GasChem', red boot-topping. **History:** Founded 1969.
Web: www.cst-hamburg.de

Name	Flag	Year	GT	DWT	Loa	Bm	Drt	Kts	Type	Remarks
Chemtrans Christian	Lbr	1990	7,083	9,490	126.2	17.8	8.4	16	Lpg	ex Norgas Christian-96

Also operates numerous larger tankers.

Clearwater Group   Netherlands

Funnel: Blue with white 'C' on large red oval disc. **Hull:** Blue with red boot-topping. **History:** Founded 1997. **Web:** www.clearwatergroup.nl

Name	Flag	Year	GT	DWT	Loa	Bm	Drt	Kts	Type	Remarks
Capewater	Nld	2009	3,674	5,125	100.0	16.1	6.7	15	Tch	
Clearwater	Nld	1995	1,620	2,304	79.9	10.9	4.4	11	Tch	
Cliffwater	Nld	2002	2,144	3,500	91.3	12.0	5.3	11	Tch	
Coastalwater	Nld	2000	2,140	3,591	91.7	14.4	5.3	12	Tch	
Cobaltwater	Nld	2006	3,530	5,733	100.0	16.0	7.0	15	Tch	ex Milas-C-06
Coolwater	Nld	2008	3,674	5,125	100.0	16.0	6.7	15	Tch	
Coralwater	Nld	1998	1,895	3,357	93.4	10.9	5.0	10	Tch	l/a Jeanine Theresa (1992)
Crystalwater	Nld	1997	1,655	2,683	80.0	11.1	5.1	12	Tch	

Clipper Group (Management) Ltd   Denmark

Clipper Projects Ship Management A/S

Funnel: White with blue 'C' symbol. **Hull:** Blue with red boot-topping. **History:** Founded 1972 and parent now based in Bahamas. Acquired Crescent Shipping Ltd jointly with London & Wessex Ltd in 1997 and partners share in 2002. Subsidiary Clipper Elite Carriers acquired T&C Thor Chartering (Tonnevold & Clausen) in 2003. Acquired Wonsild & Son AS in 2005 (founded 1904) and established Clipper Wonsild Tankers in 2006. Tanker business sold early in 2010 to Nordic Tankers A/S. **Web:** www.clipper-group.com; www.clipper-elite.com; www.cecshipmanagement.com;

Name	Flag	Year	GT	DWT	Loa	Bm	Drt	Kts	Type	Remarks
CEC Accord	Iom	1998	3,838	5,200	100.7	16.0	6.2	14	CC	ex Danial Delmas-03, Delmas Matadi-03, Mint Accord-01
CEC Ace	Iom	1997	3,838	5,200	100.8	16.0	6.2	14	Cc	ex Mekong Bright-04, CEC Ace-00, Mint Ace-99
CEC Action	Iom	1997	3,838	5,151	100.8	16.0	6.2	14	Cc	ex Melfi Ecuador-02, Mint Action-99
CEC Century	Bhs	2002	6,714	8,729	100,5	20.4	8.2	16	C/hl	ex Sea Century-03, CEC Century-03
CEC Commander	Bhs	1998	6,714	8,702	100.5	20.4	6.3	16	C/hl	ex CEC Carmarthen-04, Katrine Delmas-99, Clipper Carmarthen-99
CEC Concord	Bhs	2000	6,714	8,474	100.5	20.4	8.2	15	C/hl	ex CEC Crusader-04
CEC Copenhagen	Bhs	2001	6,714	8,484	100.5	20.4	8.2	15	C/hl	
CEC Cristobal	Bhs	1999	6,714	8,719	100.5	20.4	8.2	16	C/hl	ex Sea Cristobal-04, CEC Cristobal-04, CEC Chepstow-03, Clipper Chepstow-02
CEC Daisy	Iom	1993	2,815	4,111	88.4	15.2	6.0	13	Cc	ex Forum Polynesia-07, Sofrana Pasifika-06, CEC Daisy-05, Arktis Ace-02, Industrial Ace-99, Arktis Ace-94, Elsborg-93, Arktis Ace-93
CEC Delta	Iom	1991	2,815	4,110	88.4	15.0	6.0	13	Cc	ex Forum Rarotonga II-08, CEC Delta-07, Sea Delta-05, CEC Delta-04, CEC Pride-02, Arktis Pride-99
CEC Faith	Bhs	1994	4,980	7,120	101.1	19.2	7.3	14	Cc	ex UAL America-06, CEC Faith-04, Signet Faith-00, Arktis Faith-00, Melfi Faith-99, Melbridge Faith-97, Arktis Faith-97
CEC Fantasy	Bhs	1994	4,980	7,147	101.1	19.2	7.3	14	CC	ex Arktis Fantasy-99
CEC Fighter *	Bhs	1994	4,980	7,132	101.1	19.2	7.3	14	CC	ex Arktis Fighter-02, CEC Fighter-01, Arktis Fighter-01, Ville de Rodae-96, Arktis Fighter-96
CEC Force *	Iom	1995	4,980	7,225	101.1	19.2	7.3	14	Cc	ex Delmas India-07, ATL Force-05, CEC Force-00, Arktis Force-99, Melfi Force-98, Melbridge Force-97, Arktis Force-96, Melbridge Force-96, Arktis Force-95
CEC Future *	Bhs	1994	4,980	7,121	101.1	19.2	7.3	16	Cc	ex CMA CGM Tunis-04, CEC Future-03, Arktis Future-02, CEC Future-01, Signet Spirit-00, CEC Future-00, Arktis Future-99, Melbridge Flash-96, Arktis Future 94
CEC Hunter *	Iom	1995	3,810	5,392	97.4	16.4	6.7	14	Cc	ex Arktis Hunter-00
CEC Meadow	Bhs	1995	6,285	8,970	100.8	20.2	8.2	15	Cc	ex Arktis Meadow-00, Melfi Azteca-97, Melbridge Main-97, Arktis Meadow-95
CEC Meridian *	Bhs	1996	6,285	8,973	100.8	20.5	8.2	15	Cc	ex Arktis Meridian-02, CEC Meridian-01, Haiphong Star-01, Arktis Meridian-00
CEC Mermaid *	Bhs	1995	6,216	8,943	100.8	20.2	7.3	15	Cc	ex Sea Mermaid-04, CEC Mermaid-04, UAL Angola-00, CEC Mermaid-99, Anette Delmas-99, Arktis Mermaid-99, Maersk Salvador-98, Arktis Mermaid-98, Nedlloyd Corfu-97, Arktis Mermaid-96
CEC Mirage *	Bhs	1999	6,285	8,943	100.8	20.5	8.2	16	Cc	ex Nancy Delmas-00, Arktis Mirage-99

Name		Flag	Year	GT	DWT	Loa	Bm	Drt	Kts	Type	Remarks
CEC Morning		Iom	1996	6,310	8,973	100.8	20.4	7.3	15	Cc	ex Angkor Star-01, CEC Morning-00, Helene Delmas-99, Arktis Morning-99, Maersk Luanda-99, Arktis Morning-98
CIC Belem		Bhs	1992	4,860	6,262	111.3	18.0	5.8	12	C	ex Socofi Lake-04
CIC Brasil		Bhs	1992	4,860	6,273	111.3	18.0	5.8	12	C	ex Socofi Pearl-04, I/a Putyatin
CIC Breves		Bhs	1992	4,860	6,266	111.3	18.0	5.8	12	C	ex Socofi Star-04, Starnes-02, Socofi Star-96
Clipper Mariner *		Bhs	1996	6,285	8,972	100.8	20.2	7.3	15	C	ex Seaboard Explorer II-09, CEC Mariner-02, P&O Nedlloyd Belem-00, Arktis Mariner-00, Melfi Halifax-98, Melbridge Major-97, Arktis Mariner-96
Clipper Mayflower		Bhs	1996	6,285	8,973	100.8	20.4	7.3	15	Cc	ex Caribbean Carrier-09, CEC Mayflower-07, Papuan Gulf-06, CEC Mayflower-06, Arktis Mayflower-01, Melfi Venezuela-98, Arktis Mayflower-96
Clipper Mistral		Bhs	1998	6,285	8,973	100.8	20.2	8.2	15	Cc	ex Caribbean Express-09, CEC Mistral-07, Arktis Mistral-02
UAL Congo		Bhs	1998	6,714	8,447	100.5	20.4	6.3	16	Cc	ex CEC Champion-07, Nirint Champion-07, CEC Champion-04, CEC Westoe-03, Industrial Confidence-00, Clipper Westoe-99, I/a Clipper Caldicot

* owned by Clipper Projects A/S
Project cargo ships operate in APC Group joint venture Pool with BBC.
Also owns and manages a numberous larger tankers, bulk carriers and feeder container ships.
See Seatruck Ferries in Ferry Section.

Reederei Heinz Corleis KG   Germany

Funnel: *White with green/yellow 'C' symbol rising from green/yellow band or charterers colours.* **Hull:** *Dark blue with red boot-topping.* **History:** *Founded 1966.*
Web: *None found.*

Name	Flag	Year	GT	DWT	Loa	Bm	Drt	Kts	Type	Remarks
Capella	Gib	1999	2,780	3,792	89.1	13.4	5.7	12	Cc	ex Transmare-05
Delfin	Gib	1998	2,780	3,700	89.3	13.4	5.7	12	Cc	ex Lumare-05
Polaris	Deu	1988	7,944	6,494	123.9	20.4	6.2	14	C/ro	I/a Odin
Uranus	Atg	1992	5,025	6,541	116.7	18.2	6.9	16	CC	ex Lucy Borchard-05, Gracechurch Sun-02, Uranus-97

Manages ships for other owners, see Pohl Shipping Schiffahrts GmbH & Co KG, Germany (Baltic Forest Line GmbH & Co KG)
Also one larger container ship.

Corral Line A/S   Denmark

Funnel: *Black with blue band on broad white band.* **Hull:** *White with blue 'CORRAL LINE', black boot-topping.* **History:** *Founded 1958 as successors to Soenderborg Rederiaktieselskab.* **Web:** *None found.*

Name	Flag	Year	GT	DWT	Loa	Bm	Drt	Kts	Type	Remarks
Falconia	Pan	1973	3,013	1,959	88.3	13.0	5.0	13	Lv	ex Falcon-04, Philomena Purcell-02, Esteflut-82 (len/conv C-82)

Bernhard Cramer Schiffahrts GmbH   Germany

Funnel: *White with company logo below narrow black top.* **Hull:** *Blue with white 'MTC', red boot-topping.* **History:** *Founded 2003.* **Web:** *www.reederei-cramer.de*

Name	Flag	Year	GT	DWT	Loa	Bm	Drt	Kts	Type	Remarks
Adele C	Atg	1994	3,992	5,331	100.0	18.4	6.6	15	CC	ex City of Lisbon-04, Carol Ann-02

Reederei Frank Dahl   Germany

Funnel: *White with houseflag (diagonally divided red/white with white 'F' and red 'D').* **Hull:** *Light grey with red boot-topping.* **History:** *Founded 1983 as Frank Dahl and renamed following takeover of Gerhard Ahrens.* **Web:** *www.dahl-shipping.com*

Name		Flag	Year	GT	DWT	Loa	Bm	Drt	Kts	Type	Remarks
Danio	(2)	Atg	2001	1,499	1,805	80.9	11.4	3.2	13	C	
Finex *		Deu	2001	6,378	9,857	132.2	15.9	7.8	15	Cc	ex Volmeborg-06
Kugelbake		Deu	2009	1,868	2,673	79.3	18.6	3.9	12	Ro	
Marlin	(2)	Atg	2000	1,499	1,805	80.3	11.4	3.3	10	C	
Remora	(2)	Atg	2000	1,499	1,805	80.3	11.4	3.3	11	C	
Veerseborg *		Atg	1998	6,130	8,737	132.2	15.9	7.1	15	Cc	ex Matfen-07, Veerseborg-04
Vossborg *		Atg	2000	6,154	8,737	132.2	15.9	7.1	15	Cc	ex Vossborg-04, Morpeth-07

Operated by Amasus Shipping BV or * by Schulte & Bruns
Associated with Reederei Kontor Cuxhaven GmbH

Dania Marine   Denmark

Funnel: *White with blue top.* **Hull:** *Blue with red boot-topping.* **History:** *Founded 2000.* **Web:** *www.daniamarime.dk*

Name	Flag	Year	GT	DWT	Loa	Bm	Drt	Kts	Type	Remarks
Carolyn	Dmk	1974	1,872	2,330	75.5	11.8	5.0	11	C	ex Dori Bres-06
Dania Kirsten	Dis	1976	1,882	3,100	80.1	13.8	5.3	12	C	ex Cygnus-02, Birkholm-00, Vibro Star-98, Alantes-88, Ragni-80
Thor Blue *	Mlt	1992	2,815	4,110	88.4	15.2	5.3	13	Cc	ex CEC Blue-08, Arktis Blue-99
Thor Leader	Iom	1994	3,810	5,400	97.4	16.4	6.7	14	Cc	ex CEC Leader-09, CEC Crystal-03, Arktis Crystal-02
Thor Liberty	Iom	1994	3,810	5,400	97.4	16.4	6.7	14	Cc	ex CEC Liberty-09, White Rhino-08, CEC Liberty-07, CEC Hope-02, CIC Hope-01, Arktis Hope-99
Thor Libra	Iom	1995	3,810	5,401	97.4	16.4	6.7	15	Cc	ex CEC Vision-09, Arktis Vision-99
Thor Light	Iom	1993	3,810	5,401	97.4	16.4	6.7	14	Cc	ex CEC Light-09, CIC Light Arktis Light-99
Thor Pacific *	Mlt	1992	2,815	4,117	88.4	15.2	6.0	13	Cc	ex CEC Pacific-08, Arktis Pacific-00, Industrial Caribe-99, Arktis Pacific-94, I/a Arktis Swan

Name	Flag	Year	GT	DWT	Loa	Bm	Drt	Kts	Type	Remarks
Thor Pioneer *	Mlt	1993	2,815	4,110	88.4	15.2	6.0	13	Cc	ex CEC Pioneer-08, Sofrana Bligh-03, Industrial Frontier-99, Arktis Pioneer-97, Industrial Pioneer-95, Arktis Pioneer-95
Thor Spirit	Mlt	1988	7,876	7,190	115.2	19.2	7.3	15	C/hl	ex Beluga Spirit-08, BBC Egypt-08, Beluga Spirit-07, Ariana-05
Thor Spring *	Mlt	1993	2,815	4,110	88.4	15.2	6.0	13	Cc	ex CEC Spring-08, Sofrana Bligh-04, CEC Spring-03, Anking-02, CEC Spring-01, Arktis Spring-01, Mekong Spring-95, Arktis Spring-94
Thor Venture	Mlt	1992	2,815	4,110	88.4	15.2	6.0	12	Cc	ex CEC Venture-08, Arktis Venture-00, Industrial Venture-96, Arktis Venture-92

* managed by Graig Ship Management Ltd, UK.
Also owns two larger chartered-out containers ships.

Dannebrog Invest Denmark

Funnel: Charterers colours. **Hull:** Charterers colours. **History:** Founded 2006 as CS & Partners A/S. **Web:** www.cspartners.dk

Name	Flag	Year	GT	DWT	Loa	Bm	Drt	Kts	Type	Remarks
Dagmar *	Atg	1993	5,684	7,416	120.0	19.6	6.2	14	Cc	ex MSC Camargue-08, Ville de Mijo-04
Ingrid	Atg	1995	7,465	7,733	134.6	19.6	8.1	15	CC	ex MSC Aures-08, Monte Verde-05, Imperial-04, Dong Yuan-96
Ingrid Jakobsen	Atg	2006	3,933	6,863	103.0	16.0	7.0	11	Tch	
Kasteelborg	Nld	1998	6,142	9,085	130.7	15.9	7.5	14	Cc	
Keizersborg	Nld	1996	6,142	9,085	130.7	15.9	7.5	15	Cc	

* managed by Hansen & Lange I/S, Denmark (www.hansen-lange.com)
Also see DFDS in Ferry Section and Herning Shipping AS

Reederei Friedhelm Dede GmbH & Co KG Germany

Funnel: Buff with narrow black black top. **Hull:** Dark blue with red boot-topping. **History:** Founded 1971 as F Dede KG to 2009. **Web:** None found.

Name	Flag	Year	GT	DWT	Loa	Bm	Drt	Kts	Type	Remarks
Anna Sophie Dede	Atg	2001	9,961	11,382	134.4	22.5	8.7	18	CC	ex Holland Maas Antilles-06, Joanna Borchard-04, I/a Anna Sophie Dede
Lucy Borchard	Atg	2005	9,962	11,404	134.4	22.5	8.7	18	CC	ex MSC Caraibes-07, Holland Maas Caraibes-06
Joanna Borchard	Atg	2007	9,962	11,433	134.4	22.5	8.7	18	CC	ex Max Linus Dede-09, Joanna Borchard-08, Max Linus Dede-07

Den Herder Netherlands

Funnel: Red with narrow white band below black top. **Hull:** Dark blue with red boot-topping. **History:** Not confirmed. **Web:** None found.

Name	Flag	Year	GT	DWT	Loa	Bm	Drt	Kts	Type	Remarks
Scelveringhe	Nld	2004	5,116	7,745	116.5	18.0	6.4	13	Dss	
Swalinge	Nld	1977	2,071	3,064	81.7	14.0	5.3	12	Dss	ex Tina H-96, Funda-88, Tina Holwerda-87, Fenja-86, Tina Holwerda-77 (conv C-95)

Dennis Maritime Oy Finland

Funnel: White with narrow black top. **Hull:** Blue with red boot-topping. **History:** Not confirmed. **Web:** None found.

Name	Flag	Year	GT	DWT	Loa	Bm	Drt	Kts	Type	Remarks
Annika	Fin	1946	624	850	57.2	9.3	3.6	10	C	ex Sandstorm-97, Sangard-79, Underas Sandtag V-78, Bardal-65, Wolfram-64, Lucerne-56, Bardal-51 (NE-67, len-72)
Josefine	Fin	1986	852	1,280	64.3	10.6	3.3	9	C	ex Schokland-03, Buizerd-96
Nathalie	Fin	1989	852	1,300	64.2	10.6	3.4	11	C	ex Urkerland-05, Panda-01, Waran-93

Managed by OY Baltic Commerce International Ltd

DFDS Lys-Line Rederi AS Norway

Funnel: Dark blue with white 'Maltese Cross'. **Hull:** Dark blue with white 'DFDS LYS-LINE', red boot-topping. **History:** Founded 1970 as Simonsen & Slang A/S to 1997 and as Lys-Line ASA to 2005. Danish DFDS acquired 66% in 2002 and remainder in 2005. **Web:** www.lysline.no

Name	Flag	Year	GT	DWT	Loa	Bm	Drt	Kts	Type	Remarks
Lysblink	Nis	2000	7,409	7,500	129.0	18.0	6.6	16	Ccp	(len-04)
Lysbris	Nis	1999	7,409	7,500	129.0	18.0	6.6	16	Ccp	(len-04)
Lysfoss	Nis	1989	4,471	3,600	101.7	17.0	5.9	14	Ccp	(len-99)
Lystind	Nis	1990	4,471	3,728	94.4	17.0	5.9	14	Ccp	
Lysvik	Nis	1998	7,409	5,175	129.0	18.0	6.5	16	Ccp	(len-04)
Skog	Nis	1991	4,471	3,728	99.4	17.0	5.9	14	Ccp	ex Lys-Skog-09 (len-99)

Also operates chartered-in vessels.
See Ferry Section for ferries and roll-on, roll-off vessels.

Peter Dohle Schiffahrts-KG Germany

Funnel: Black with black 'PD' on white diamond on white edged red band or § white with houseflag. **Hull:** Dark grey with red boot-topping or § light grey with white 'FEEDERLINK' and red boot-topping. **History:** Founded 1956 as Robert Bornhofen KG to 1962. **Web:** www.doehle.de

Name	Flag	Year	GT	DWT	Loa	Bm	Drt	Kts	Type	Remarks
Agatha	Atg	1998	5,381	6,750	107.6	18.3	6.2	12	B	
Alina	Atg	1998	5,381	6,790	107.6	18.2	6.2	12	B	
Analena	Gbr	2006	9,990	11,206	134.4	22.5	8.7	18	CC	ex MSC Portugal-08, Analena-06
Annabella	Gbr	2006	9,981	11,273	134.4	22.5	8.7	18	CC	

Peter Dohle Schiffahrts-KG. Alina. *N. Kemps*

Peter Dohle Schiffahrts-KG. Annabella. *Oliver Sesemann*

Name	Flag	Year	GT	DWT	Loa	Bm	Drt	Kts	Type	Remarks
Attika	Atg	2001	5,381	7,511	107.6	18.3	6.6	12	B	
Aurelia	Atg	1998	5,381	7,567	107.6	18.3	6.6	12	B	
Auriga	Atg	2001	5,381	7,567	107.6	18.3	6.6	12	B	
Beatrice	Atg	1994	4,927	6,918	107.1	18.3	6.2	12	Cc	ex Alexandria-07
Belina	Atg	1997	4,927	6,918	107.0	18.4	6.2	12	Cc	ex Aida-07
Benita	Atg	1995	4,927	6,918	107.1	18.4	6.2	12	Cc	ex Anglia-07, Arabia-96
Carla	Atg	2005	5,581	7,616	108.4	18.2	6.7	12	C	
Cassandra	Atg	2005	5,581	7,634	108.4	18.2	6.7	12	C	
Catalina	Atg	2007	5,581	7,578	108.4	18.2	6.7	12	C	
Cecilia	Atg	2005	5,581	7,488	108.4	18.2	6.7	12	C	
Celina	Atg	2005	5,581	7,580	108.4	18.2	6.7	12	C	
Centa	Atg	2006	5,581	7,561	108.4	18.2	6.7	12	C	
Chyra	Atg	2007	5,581	7,601	108.4	18.2	6.7	12	C	
Cimbria	Atg	2006	5,581	7,618	108.4	18.2	6.7	12	C	
Cindia	Atg	2005	5,581	7,594	108.4	18.2	6.7	12	C	
Clara	Atg	2006	5,581	7,600	108.4	18.2	6.7	12	C	
Corsa *	Deu	1998	3,999	5,356	101.1	18.5	6.5	15	CC	ex Corsar08
Cremona	Atg	2005	5,581	7,601	108.4	18.2	6.7	12	C	
Creola	Atg	2006	5,581	7,609	108.4	18.2	6.7	12	C	
Diana	Atg	2007	9,556	13,450	138.1	21.0	8.0	14	Cc	
Doris T ‡	Atg	1977	1,973	2,150	79.0	12.4	4.8	12	Cc	ex Libra II-97, Libra-85
Hajo **	Atg	1991	3,818	4,650	103.5	16.2	6.1	15	Cc	ex Portlink Sprinter-04, Nincop-02, OPDR Tejo-99, Nincop-95, Norasia Alexandria-95, Nincop-93, City of Valletta-92, Nincop-91
Impala	Atg	2008	9,556	13,425	138.1	21.0	8.0	14	Cc	
Katherine Borchard	Gbr	2005	9,962	11,416	134.4	22.5	8.7	18	CC	ex MSC Yorkshire-07, Holland Maas Habana-05, I/a Aquila
Komet III §	Atg	1990	4,169	4,752	111.1	16.1	6.0	15	Cc	ex Portugal Bridge-97, Komet III-96, Gracechurch Comet-96, Komet III-91
Liberta	Atg	2007	9,556	13,447	138.1	21.0	8.0	14	Cc	
Planet V §	Deu	1994	4,964	7,014	116.4	19.5	7.1	16	Cc	ex Gracechurch Planet-97, Planet V-96
Sagitta	Atg	2008	9,556	13,464	138.1	21.0	8.0	14	Cc	
Tinka *	Atg	1992	5,006	6,580	116.7	18.2	6.9	16	Cc	ex Inka Dede-06, Judith Borchard-03, Gracechurch Comet-02, Inka Dede-01, Armada Sprinter-96, Inka Dede-95, Rhein Liffey-94, Inka Dede-93

* owned by subsidiaries Dohle (IOM) Ltd (founded 1994 as Midocean Maritime Ltd to 2001 – www.doehle-iom.com) or ** by Globehelier Maritime Co Ltd
‡ managed by Interscan Schiffs GmbH, Germany.
§ managed for Henry Gerdau KG GmbH & Co (founded 1952)
Also owns and operates numerous larger vessels, including container ships up to 75,500 gt

Hammonia Reederei GmbH & Co KG
Funnel: *Charterers colours.* **Hull:** *Dark grey with red boot-topping.* **History:** *Founded 2003.* **Web:** *www.hammonia-reederei.de*

Name	Flag	Year	GT	DWT	Loa	Bm	Drt	Kts	Type	Remarks
Alexia	Lbr	2004	9,957	13,872	147.9	23.3	8.5	19	CC	ex Islandia-08, SYMS Taishan-06, Islandia-05, Alexia-04
OOCL Narva	Deu	3004	9,981	11,424	134.4	22.5	8.7	18	CC	I/a Finnlandia

Formed jointly with HCI Capital AG (founded 2003 – www.hammonia-reederi.de)
Also operates 27 large container ships and has four very large bulk carriers on order.

Mezeron Ltd., Isle of Man (UK)
Funnel: *Black with houseflag (blue with red 'M' on white disc) on broad white band.* **Hull:** *Blue with red boot-topping.* **History:** *Acquired by Dohle in 2008.* **Web:** *None found.*

Name	Flag	Year	GT	DWT	Loa	Bm	Drt	Kts	Type	Remarks
Silver River	Iom	1968	277	373	44.7	7.4	2.7	10	C	ex Nathurn-86, Sea Trent-82, Seacon-71

Dr Peters GmbH & Co KG   Germany

DS Schiffahrt GmbH & Co KG
Funnel: *White with white 'DS' logo on turquoise square between narrow turquoise bands.* **Hull:** *Green with red boot-topping.* **History:** *Founded 2001 as subsidiary of parent company founded 1960.* **Web:** *www.ds-schiffahrt.de*

Name	Flag	Year	GT	DWT	Loa	Bm	Drt	Kts	Type	Remarks
Cape Brett	Mhl	1992	8,940	10,481	140.0	23.0	7.6	16	CC	ex Susan Borchard-02, Cape Brett-01, Melbridge Brett-00, Cape Brett-99, Eagle Commitment-98
Cape Campbell	Mhl	1998	9,038	11,031	135.7	22.5	8.6	18	CC	ex Tiger Pearl-99, I/a Cape Campbell
Cape Charles	Mhl	1998	9,038	11,031	135.7	22.5	8.6	18	CC	ex YM Doha-09, Cape Charles-08, Tiger Sea-00, I/a Cape Charles
Cape Cook	Mhl	1998	9,038	11,400	135.6	22.5	8.6	18	CC	ex SITC Philippines-09, Cape Cook-07, MOL Accuracy-06
DS Ability	Lbr	2007	9,940	13,835	147.9	23.5	8.5	19	CC	ex SITC Ability-08, DS Ability-07
DS Accuracy	Lbr	2007	9,940	13,751	147.9	23.5	8.5	19	CC	ex SITC Accuracy-08, DS Accuracy-07
DS Activity	Lbr	2008	9,940	13,809	147.9	23.5	8.5	19	CC	
DS Agility	Lbr	2008	9,940	13,856	147.9	23.5	8.5	19	CC	
DS Blue Ocean	Gbr	2007	7,545	8,201	129.6	29.6	7.4	16	CC	ex RBD Constantia-07
DS Blue Wave	Gbr	2007	7,545	8,166	129.6	29.6	7.4	16	CC	ex JRS Canopus-07

Also owns eight feeder container ships over 10,000 gt and numerous very large container ships, bulk carriers and tankers.
Also see Stolt-Nielsen Group.

Peter Dohle Schiffahrts-KG. Clara. *M. Beckett*

Peter Dohle - Mezeron Ltd. Silver River. *Tom Walker*

Name		Flag	Year	GT	DWT	Loa	Bm	Drt	Kts	Type	Remarks

Drabert Schiffahrts GmbH — Germany

Funnel: *Dark green with white 'D'.* **Hull:** *Dark grey with red boot-topping.* **History:** *Founded 1997.* **Web:** *None found.*

Name		Flag	Year	GT	DWT	Loa	Bm	Drt	Kts	Type	Remarks
Elke D		Atg	1988	1,307	1,529	74.9	10.6	3.4	10	C	ex Berit L-06
Jan D		Atg	1991	1,981	3,260	90.0	11.9	4.9	11	C	ex Fri River-08, Empire-04
Lisa D		Atg	1984	1,162	1,685	73.7	11.7	3.7	10	C	ex Rachel-03, Sunergon-94
Magda D		Atg	1984	1,298	1,537	74.9	10.6	3.3	10	C	ex Richard C-05, RMS Anglia-99, Richard C-98
Wiebke D		Atg	1980	1,441	1,795	81.0	11.3	3.3	10	Cs	ex Pandor-97

Kapitan Manfred Draxl Schiffahrts GmbH & Co KG — Germany

Funnel: *White with light blue top, or with black 'D' between two pairs of narrow blue bands.* **Hull:** *Blue with black or red boot-topping.* **History:** *Founded 1984.* **Web:** *www.reederei-draxl.com*

Name		Flag	Year	GT	DWT	Loa	Bm	Drt	Kts	Type	Remarks
Aegir		Atg	1997	6,393	8,350	132.3	19.4	7.3	17	CC	
Aja		Atg	2008	4,255	6,050	114.4	14.5	6.0	13	Cc	
Alwis		Atg	2009	4,255	6,050	114.4	14.5	6.0	13	Cc	
Artus		Atg	2000	6,386	8,745	132.4	19.4	7.3	17	CC	
Blue Lion		Atg	2009	4,255	6,050	114.4	14.5	6.0	13	Cc	
Blue Lotus		Atg	2009	4,255	6,050	114.4	14.5	6.0	13	Cc	
Blue Stream		Atg	2001	2,829	4,850	89.8	13.6	6.4	12	Cc	ex River Aln-09
Daniel		Atg	2006	9,990	11,208	134.4	22.8	8.7	18	CC	
Doerte		Atg	1994	3,957	5,388	102.0	16.4	6.0	16	CC	ex Mathilda-03, Dorte-94
Elisabeth		Atg	1993	3,958	5,350	108.0	16.4	6.0	16	CC	
Gertrud		Atg	1995	4,628	5,660	113.0	16.4	6.1	16	CC	ex Emma-07, Gertrud-96
Gudrun		Atg	1995	4,628	5,660	113.1	16.4	6.1	16	CC	ex City of Oporto-04, Pelayo-01, City of Oporto-98, Jane-98, Gudrun-95
Kirsten		Lux	1996	5,522	6,850	118.0	19.4	7.3	17	CC	
Manfred		Atg	2008	7,464	8,125	129.6	20.6	7.4	17	CC	
Miriam		Atg	1998	4,163	5,055	100.0	16.2	6.4	15	Cc	
North Express		Atg	1997	5,549	7,061	118.0	19.4	7.5	17	CC	ex Ingrid-06, CTE Valencia-01, Ingrid-01, Maersk Mombasa-98, Ingrid-97
Oberon		Atg	1996	8,633	9,200	132.9	23.1	7.7	17	CC	ex Sea Cloud-07, FAS Odessa-97, Alida-96
River Blythe		Atg	2000	2,858	4,850	89.8	13.6	6.4	12	Cc	I/a Baldur
River Tyne		Atg	1999	2,858	4,935	89.8	13.6	6.4	12	Cc	I/a Thor
Sophia		Atg	2008	7,464	8,166	129.6	20.6	7.4	17	CC	

Drevin Reedereiverwaltung Rainer — Germany

Funnel: *Buff with narrow black top.* **Hull:** *Light grey with red boot-topping.* **History:** *Founded 1983 as Rainer Fred August Drevin.* **Web:** *www.reederei-drevin.de*

Name		Flag	Year	GT	DWT	Loa	Bm	Drt	Kts	Type	Remarks
Maike D		Gbr	2000	6,326	7,944	133.0	18.9	7.3	18	CC	ex Katherine Borchard-02, I/a Maike

Also owns one larger container ship.

Reederei Bernd Drewitz GmbH & Co KG — Germany

Funnel: *Black with black 'RBD' interrupting three narrow red bands on broad white band edged with narrow red bands.* **Hull:** *Black with red boot-topping.* **History:** *Founded 2006.* **Web:** *none found.*

Name		Flag	Year	GT	DWT	Loa	Bm	Drt	Kts	Type	Remarks
CCL Ningbo		Cyp	2009	7,464	8,157	129.6	20.6	7.4	17	CC	
RBD Borea		Cyp	2007	7,545	8,226	129.6	20.6	7.4	17	CC	
RBD Esperanza		Cyp	2008	7,545	8,210	129.6	20.6	7.4	17	CC	
RBD Jutlandia		Cyp	2009	7,464	8,165	129.6	20.6	7.4	17	CC	

Managed by S & D Shipmanagement GmbH & Co KG, Germany (www.sdship.de)

Duglas Ltd — Russia

Funnel: *White with narrow blue above red bands.* **Hull:** *Grey with red boot-topping.* **History:** *Founded 1996 and controlled by Government of the Russian Federation.* **Web:** *None found.*

Name		Flag	Year	GT	DWT	Loa	Bm	Drt	Kts	Type	Remarks
Aivita		Bhs	1977	2,019	2,899	82.3	13.9	5.3	12	C	ex Lizrix -02, Yorksee-96, Katharina-90, Karlsvik-86, I/a Eriesee
Baltiyskiy-108	(2)	Rus	1979	1,926	2,600	95.0	13.2	4.0	12	Cc	
Baltiyskiy-109	(2)	Rus	1979	1,926	2,600	95.0	13.2	4.0	12	Cc	
Natali		Atg	1983	2,837	2,352	91.0	13.5	4.5	10	Ro	ex Laila-04
Svyataya Elena	(2)	Geo	1972	3,946	3,822	138.8	16.5	3.8	10	C	ex Fosa-02, Volgo-Don 5035-99
V. Ushakov		Cyp	1985	2,295	2,591	95.9	14.2	4.1	10	C/ro	ex Rolf Buck-05

East Shipping Co Ltd — Russia

Funnel: *White with narrow black top.* **Hull:** *Black with red boot-toppin.* **History:** *Founded 2004 and controlled by Government of The Russian Federation.* **Web:** *www.east-trans.ru*

Name		Flag	Year	GT	DWT	Loa	Bm	Drt	Kts	Type	Remarks
Antlia	(2)	Rus	1980	2,470	2,960	108.4	15.0	3.1	9	Cc	ex Omskiy-106-93
Piligrim 2	(2)	Rus	1988	1,556	1,849	82.0	11.6	3.6	11	Cc	ex Tavriya-2-00, TK-2-88
Piligrim 3	(2)	Rus	1988	1,557	1,849	82.0	11.6	3.6	11	Cc	ex Tavriya-4-01, TK-4-88

Reederei Eckhoff GmbH & Co KG   Germany

Funnel: *Yellow with blue 'H' and 'E' on white side panels of blue/white diagonally quartered houseflag.* **Hull:** *Blue with red boot-toppin.* **History:** *Family commenced ship-owning in 1896, later trading as Reederei Eckhoff KG from 1991 and Reederei Hans-Peter Eckhoff GmbH & Co KG from 1994, the present company founded in 2001 as JSM-Shipping GmbH & Co KG to 2008.* **Web:** *www.reederei-eckhoff.de*

Name	Flag	Year	GT	DWT	Loa	Bm	Drt	Kts	Type	Remarks
Ann-Sofie Scan	Atg	1999	2,545	3,490	86.4	13.0	5.5	12	Cc	ex Forum Avarua-10, Ann-Sofie Scan-09, Skagen-05, I/a Ile de France
BBC Brazil **	Mhl	2002	7,576	10,380	142.7	18.3	7.3	14	Cc	ex Ursula-05, Ile de Re-02
BBC England **	Mhl	2003	7,576	10,380	142.7	18.3	7.3	14	Cc	ex Frida-04, I/a Ile de Reunion
BBC Thailand *	Atg	2008	6,478	7,966	116.2	18.0	7.0	-	C	ex Sansibar-08, Heng Yuan 7-08
Capri	Atg	2002	6,808	9,600	132.2	15.9	7.7	15	Cc	ex Onego Capri-09, Sider Capri-09, I/a Sider Alie
Joy	Atg	2004	3,289	5,745	104.6	13.6	6.2	12	C	ex Sider Joy-09, Ile de Elbe-04
List	Atg	2000	4,028	5,099	100.6	18.5	6.5	16	Cc	ex Delmas Mauritius-06, Jolly Arancione-03, Marcape-02
Monte	Deu	2003	3,289	5,751	104.6	13.6	6.2	12	C	ex Sider Montediprocida-08, Ile de Yeu-03
Onego Ponza	Atg	2002	6,806	8,700	138.9	15.9	7.7	15	Cc	ex Sider Ponza-09, I/a Sider Monique
S. Fighter	Atg	2001	8,861	11,957	134.2	20.4	7.0	17	Cc	ex Beluga Inspiration-06, CEC Anax-02
S. Pacific **	Mhl	2004	7,813	10,385	145.6	18.3	7.3	14	Cc	ex Ile de Malene-04
S. Partner **	Mhl	2004	7,813	10,385	145.6	18.3	7.3	14	Cc	ex UAL Gabon-08, S. Partner-04
Stinnes Passat	Atg	2001	8,861	12,007	134.2	20.4	8.4	17	C/hl	ex Obsession-09, Nirint Force-09, Beluga Independence-07, CEC Arctic-01
Westerland	Atg	2000	4,028	5,085	100.6	18.5	6.5	16	Cc	ex Marcliff-05

** managed for Bluewater Capital GmbH or ** for HCI Capital AG qv*

Echoship ApS   Denmark

Funnel: *Owners colours.* **Hull:** *Owners colours, often with white web address.* **History:** *Founded 1990.* **Web:** *www.echoship.dk*
Currently acts as chartering manager for individual owners in respect of about 27 vessels between 1,730 – 7,100 dwt.

EE Shipping AB   Sweden

Funnel: *White with blue/red 'EE' symbol.* **Hull:** *Blue with red boot-topping.* **History:** *Founded 1998 as Nordic Forest Terminals AB to 2006.* **Web:** *www.eeshipping.com*

Name	Flag	Year	GT	DWT	Loa	Bm	Drt	Kts	Type	Remarks
EE Endeavour	Gib	2001	3,784	4,625	93.3	16.5	6.3	14	Cc	ex CEC Endeavour-08, Endeavour 1-06, CEC Endeavour 1-05, Endeavour 1-05, CEC Endeavour-04, Pannon Star-04
EE Enterprise	Gib	2002	3,784	4,525	93.3	16.5	6.3	14	Cc	ex CEC Enterprise-08, Pannon Sun-04

Also manages three large ro-ro vessels operated by DFDS – see Ferry Section.

Eestinova OU   Estonia

Funnel: *White with blue symbol.* **Hull:** *Dark blue with red boot-topping.* **History:** *Founded 2002.* **Web:** *www.eestinova.ee*

Name	Flag	Year	GT	DWT	Loa	Bm	Drt	Kts	Type	Remarks
Emi Leader	Mlt	2009	2,997	4,498	89.9	14.0	5.8	-	C	
Emi Proud	Mlt	2008	2,997	4,502	89.9	14.0	5.8	-	C	
Siderfly	Vct	1985	2,881	4,190	99.8	14.6	5.2	11	Cc	ex Borgfeld-01, Eemsea-99, Borgfeld-99 (len-90)
Sun Leader	Mlt	1990	2,292	2,690	84.9	12.9	4.4	11	Cc	ex Fairdeal-09, Christopher-05

Reederei Ehler KG   Germany

Funnel: *Cream with white 'HE' on dark blue flag.* **Hull:** *Green with red boot-topping.* **History:** *Founded 1978 as Heinz Ehle KG.* **Web:** *None found.*

Name	Flag	Year	GT	DWT	Loa	Bm	Drt	Kts	Type	Remarks
Andrea	Gib	2005	9,981	11,416	134.4	22.8	8.7	18	CC	
Anke Ehler	Deu	2000	5,067	6,840	117.9	18.2	7.9	17	CC	
Nathalie Ehler	Gbr	2002	9,981	11,390	134.4	22.5	8.7	18	CC	ex Rachel Borchard-04, I/a Nathalie Ehler

Also owns one larger container ship.

Eicke Schiffahrts KG   Germany

Funnel: *Red/brown.* **Hull:** *Red/brown with red boot-topping.* **History:** *Founded 1990.* **Web:** *None found.*

Name	Flag	Year	GT	DWT	Loa	Bm	Drt	Kts	Type	Remarks
Allegretto	Atg	2006	3,128	4,568	90.0	15.2	5.3	12	Cc	
Charlotte Borchard	Atg	2004	9,962	11,434	134.4	22.5	8.7	18	CC	ex Allegro-09, Ruth Borchard-09, Allegro-08, Ruth Borchard-06, Allegro-04
Kornett *	Atg	2007	9,962	11,434	134.4	22.5	8.7	18	CC	
Laura Ann *	Gbr	2002	9,981	11,368	134.4	22.5	8.7	18	CC	ex Holland Maas Caraibes-05, Ruth Borchard-04, I/a Laura Ann
Tiwala *	Atg	2008	4,102	5,484	106.8	15.2	5.3	12	Cc	ex Emstransporter-08

Newbuildings: Two 4,500 gt 5,500 dwt coasters due for 2010-11 delivery
Managed or * owned by subsidiary Winfried Eicke Bereederungs GmbH & Co (formed 2005)

Eide Shipping AS   Norway

Funnel: *White with black 'E' inside red ring, black top fin.* **Hull:** *Black with red boot-topping.* **History:** *Founded 1984.* **Web:** *www.eide-shipping.no*

Name	Flag	Year	GT	DWT	Loa	Bm	Drt	Kts	Type	Remarks
Eide Junior	Nor	1978	1,552	1,626	70.8	12.8	3.9	11	Cc	ex Urania-00, Ulsnis-89

Operated by subsidiary Eide Maritim AS (founded 2006)

Drabert Schiffahrts GmbH. Lisa D. *Oliver Sesemann*

East Shipping Co Ltd. Piligrim 3. *David Walker*

Name	Flag	Year	GT	DWT	Loa	Bm	Drt	Kts	Type	Remarks

Eidsvaag AS — Norway

Funnel: *Dark blue with dark blue 'E' on broad white band.* **Hull:** *Dark blue with red boot-topping.* **History:** *Founded 1995 as Per Eidsvaag, later Knud O Eidsvaag to 1998.* **Web:** *www.eidsvaag-rederi.no*

Name	Flag	Year	GT	DWT	Loa	Bm	Drt	Kts	Type	Remarks
Eidsvaag	Nor	1996	498	1,000	37.5	8.5	4.0	12	C	
Eidsvaag Junior	Nor	2001	1,163	1,050	50.0	12.0	5.0	-	Cp	
Eidsvaag Marin	Nor	1995	1,121	1,305	58.6	11.1	4,5	10	C	ex Schokland-06, Aaltje-Jacoba-03
Eidsvaag Orion	Nor	1993	1,596	2,511	81.7	11.1	4.5	11	C	ex Cito-05
Eidsvaag Polaris	Nor	1999	1,768	2,440	82.3	11.3	4.3	10	C	ex Brielle-08, Sea-Lily-05
Eidsvaag Sirius	Nor	2006	2,409	3,200	82.5	12.5	4.9	11	Cc	ex Marietje Benita-09

Reederei Eilbrecht GmbH & Co KG — Germany

Funnel: *White with black 'E' inside black edged diamond, narrow black top.* **Hull:** *Blue with black boot-topping.* **History:** *Founded 1985 as Eilbrecht & Janssen KG being renamed in 1990 when the partnership was dissolved.* **Web:** *www.eilbrecht.net*

Name	Flag	Year	GT	DWT	Loa	Bm	Drt	Kts	Type	Remarks
Caribbean Sina	Atg	2004	4,462	5,100	100.0	18.8	6.7	15	Cc	ex Colca-09, Caribbean Sina-08, CMA CGM Maroni-06, Caribbean Sina-05, I/a Atlantic Voyager
Donau	Atg	2005	3,995	5,752	111.4	13.4	5.7	12	C	ex Hanna-08, Navitas-07
Ems	Atg	2005	3,995	6,051	111.4	13.4	5.7	12	C	ex Cito-07
Osterems	Gib	1999	2,780	3,715	89.3	13.3	5.7	12	Cc	ex Merwekreek-06, Baltic Shamrock-05, Polar Star-02
Rio Para	Atg	2004	4,462	5,608	100.0	18.8	6.7	15	Cc	ex CMA CGM Rio Para-06, Asian Wave-04
Tomke	Gib	2000	2,301	3,171	82.5	12.4	5.3	12	Cc	

Eimskip EHF (The Iceland Steamship Co Ltd) — Iceland

Funnel: *White with broad blue band, some with blue 'E' below black top.* **Hull:** *Black with white 'EIMSKIP', red boot-topping.* **History:** *Founded 1914 as hf Eimskipafelag Islands to 1985. Merged with P/FSkipafelagid Foroyar (Faroe Ship Ltd) in 2005. Acquired by Avion Group in 2005 and in 2006, formed a 65% owned joint venture with Finnish-owned Containerships Ltd Oy (founded 1995 as Ships-Cont Ltd Oy) and after Eimskip acquired 50% interest in Lithuanian-owned Kirsiu Linija (founded 1995), later increased to 70%, Kirsiu was merged into Containerships Group.* **Web:** *www.eimskip.com*

Name	Flag	Year	GT	DWT	Loa	Bm	Drt	Kts	Type	Remarks
Bruarfoss	Atg	1992	7,676	8,627	126.6	20.8	6.3	15	CC	ex Maersk Euro Quarto-01, I/a Maersk Forto
Holmfoss	Atg	2007	3,538	2,500	81.6	16.0	6.1	14	Rp	
Irafoss	Atg	1991	1,574	1,890	81.2	11.3	3.6	10	Cc	ex Trinket-05, Nessand-94, Hanse Controller-91
Laxfoss	Atg	1995	1,682	2,500	81.7	11.0	4.5	10	C	ex Stroombank-05, Futura-03, Sea Maas-99, Futura-96
Norland	Fro	1976	2,655	1,700	86.8	14.5	4.6	14	Cp	ex Nordland-05 (len-82)
Polfos	Atg	2008	3,538	2,500	81.6	16.0	6.1	14	Rp	
Selfoss	Atg	1991	7,676	8,627	126.6	20.7	6.3	15	CC	ex Hanne Sif-99, Vento di Ponente-96, Elisabeth Delmas-96, Hanne Sif-95, Maersk Euro Tertio-94, I/a Hanne Sif
Storfoss	Atg	2006	2,990	2,713	80.0	16.0	6.0	16	R	
Svartfoss	Atg	2005	2,990	2,737	80.0	16.0	6.0	16	R	I/a Kristian With

Also owns two larger container ships.

Containerships Group, Finland

Funnel: *White with blue disc inside red square outline.* **Hull:** *Red with white 'CONTAINERSHIPS', red boot-topping.* **History:** *See above.* **Web:** *www.containerships.fi*

Name	Flag	Year	GT	DWT	Loa	Bm	Drt	Kts	Type	Remarks
Containerships VI *	Deu	1999	9,953	13,645	154.5	21.8	9.0	20	CC	
Containerships VII	Fin	2002	10,288	13,965	158.8	21.8	8.9	21	CC	
Containerships VIII *	Deu	2006	9,902	13,400	155.2	21.8	8.9	20	CC	I/a Mira

* chartered from Reederei Hans-Peter Wegener, Germany.

Eitzen Group — Norway

Funnel: *Black with white 'E' symbol inside blue ring on broad red band.* **Hull:** *Brown with white 'EITZEN CHEMICAL', red boot-topping.* **History:** *Founded 1883 as Camillo Eitzen & Co to 1936 and formerly trading to 1984 as Tschudi & Eitzen and as Tschudi & Eitzen AS to 2003, when the partnership was dissolved.* **Web:** *www.eitzen-group.com*

Name	Flag	Year	GT	DWT	Loa	Bm	Drt	Kts	Type	Remarks
Sichem Anne	Mhl	1997	5,818	9,202	115.4	18.6	7.7	12	Tch	ex Songa Anne-06, Anne-05, Golden Michi-04
Sichem Castel	Mlt	1992	3,224	4,216	87.5	15.2	6.2	14	Tch	ex Pointe du Castel-08
Sichem Colibri	Mlt	2001	2,764	3,591	91.7	14.4	5.8	13	Tch	ex Colibri-05
Sichem Cormoran	Mlt	1987	3,446	5,453	100.5	15.9	6.4	14	Tch	ex Pointe du Cormoran-08, Domenico Ievoli-96
Sichem Croisic	Mlt	2001	5,214	7,721	112.0	17.0	7.3	14	Tch	ex Pointe de Croisic-08
Sichem Fenol	Mlt	1985	4,441	7,158	107.0	18.2	6.8	12	Tch	ex Fenol-05, Sunrise Fair-97, Unix Fair-94, Southern Fair-90, Kyokuho Iris-87
Sichem Iris	Mlt	2008	5,744	8,139	115.0	18.2	7.5	-	Tch	
Sichem Lily	Mlt	2009	5,744	8,110	115.3	18.2	7.5	-	Tch	
Sichem Marbella	Mlt	1991	4,954	7,715	114.1	18.2	6.8	12	Tch	ex J.M.S. Emerald-04, Sun Emerald-03, Stolt Otome-00
Sichem Orchid	Mlt	2008	5,744	8,139	115.0	18.2	7.5	-	Tch	
Sichem Palace	Sgp	2004	5,451	8,807	112.0	19.0	7.6	14	Tch	
Sichem Pearl	Sgp	1994	5,965	10,331	125.0	18.7	7.8	13	Tch	ex Perla-04, Panam Perla-02
Sichem Princess Marie-Chantal	Mlt	2003	5,364	8,016	113.0	18.2	7.4	-	Tch	
Sichem Provence	Mlt	1996	5,367	8,758	112.0	19.0	7.5	13	Tch	ex FS Provence-07, Golden Kay-00
Sichem Sablon	Mlt	1991	2,910	4,470	86.5	15.2	6.5	12	Tch	ex Pointe du Sablon-08, Matagrifone-97
Sichem Sparrow	Mlt	2001	2,764	3,591	92.9	14.4	5.8	13	Tch	ex Sparrow-05

Eimskip EHF. Holmfoss. *C. Lous*

Eitzen Group/Sigas Kosan A/S. Sigas Centurion. *Allan Ryszka Onions*

Name	Flag	Year	GT	DWT	Loa	Bm	Drt	Kts	Type	Remarks
Sigas Ettrick	Mlt	1991	3,023	3,621	88.0	14.8	6.0	13	Lpg	ex Ettrick-05
Sigas Lanrick	Mlt	1992	3,023	3,620	88.0	14.9	6.0	14	Lpg	ex Lanrick-05
Sigas Master	Mlt	1985	1,692	1,929	70.9	12.9	5.4	13	Lpg	ex Jakob Kosan-06, Jakob Tholstrup-90, Markland-87
Tour Margaux	Atf	1992	5,499	9,063	112.0	17.7	8.0	13	Tch	
Tour Pomerol	Atf	1998	7,274	10,379	120.0	19.3	8.3	15	Tch	

Newbuildings: Twelve 28-61,000 dwt bulk carriers on order for 2010-12 delivery.
In addition to the above, the Company operates 21 chemical tankers between 13-25,000 dwt and 9 chemical tankers over 40,000 dwt, also six larger LPG tankers and several large tankers and bulk carriers.

Sigas Kosan A/S, Denmark

Funnel: *As above.* **Hull:** *Brown with white 'EITZEN GAS', red boot-topping.* **History:** *Founded 2001 as a joint venture with J Lauritzen, their share being acquired in 2006.* **Web:** *www.sigas-kosan.com*

Name	Flag	Year	GT	DWT	Loa	Bm	Drt	Kts	Type	Remarks
Sigas Centurion **	Sgp	1984	2,169	1,872	81.1	13.8	4.9	12	Lpg	ex Kilgas Centurion-01, Tarihiko-99
Sigas Champion **	Sgp	1995	2,458	2,347	74.0	14.1	4.8	11	Lpg	ex Kilgas Champion-01
Sigas Commander	Sgp	1996	2,458	2,347	74.0	14.1	4.8	11	Lpg	ex Kilgas Commander-01
Sigas Crusader **	Sgp	1996	2,458	2,284	74.0	14.0	4.8	12	Lpg	ex Kilgas Crusader-01
Sigas Duke	Mlt	1982	2,252	2,950	76.7	14.0	6.8	12	Lpg	ex Knud Kosan-06, Knud Tholstrup-91, Traenafjord-82
Sigas Laura	Sgp	1992	2,223	2,004	73.6	14.0	5.0	12	Lpg	ex Laura Kosan-06
Sigas Linda	Sgp	1992	2,223	2,003	74.6	14.0	5.0	12	Lpg	ex Linda Kosan-06
Sigas Lotta **	Sgp	1992	2,223	2,004	73.6	14.0	5.0	12	Lpg	ex Lotta Kosan-06
Sigas Lydia	Sgp	1993	2,224	2,004	74.0	14.0	5.0	12	Lpg	ex Lydia Kosan-06
Sigloo Crystal	Sgp	1991	7,949	12,240	131.4	20.0	9.4	16	Lpg	ex Polar Belgica-06, Eurogas Terza-95, Polar Belgica-95, Eurogas Terza-93
Sigloo Discovery	Sgp	1989	7,954	12,310	131.4	20.0	9.4	16	Lpg	ex Polar Discovery-06, Eurogas -93
Sigloo Endurance	Sgp	1990	7,946	12,178	131.4	20.0	9.4	16	Lpg	ex Polar Endurance-07, Eurogas Seconda-93

*All owned by subsidiaries of J Lauritzen A/S and managed by Eitzen Gas AS or Eitzen subsidiary EMS Ship Management, except * managed by Thome Ship Management, Singapore or ** V. Ships Ltd, Monaco.*
Also operates some larger Lpg tankers.

Reederei Elbe Shipping GmbH & Co KG   Germany

Funnel: *White with black 'H' on white disc on red/dark blue eight-pointed star, narrow black top.* **Hull:** *Dark blue with red boot-topping.* **History:** *Founded 1986 as Reederei Wolfgang Hammann KG to 2003.* **Web:** *www.reederei-elbe-shipping.de*

Name	Flag	Year	GT	DWT	Loa	Bm	Drt	Kts	Type	Remarks
Baumwall	Gib	1995	3,999	4,650	100.2	15.5	6.5	14	Ccp	ex Lehmann Loader-09, Baumwall-08
Beluga Function	Lbr	2007	9.611	12,744	138.1	21.0	8.0	15	C/hl	
Beluga Fusion	Lbr	2006	9.611	12,744	138.1	21.0	8.0	15	C/hl	
Tistedal	Gib	1996	4,464	4,600	116.0	16.6	5.1	15	Ccp	ex Lyspol-99, Tistedal-98

Also operates larger heavy-lift vessels chartered to Beluga.

Rederiaktiebolaget Gustaf Erikson   Finland

Funnel: *Black with black 'GE' on broad white band or charterers colours.* **Hull:** *White with red boot-topping.* **History:** *Founded 1913 as Mariehamns Rederi AB to 1974. Part of family holding sold 1987 to Odfjell and Uni-Trans, but repurchased in 1992. Company taken-over in 2006 by OCT Shipping Ab.* **Web:** *www.geson.ax*

Name	Flag	Year	GT	DWT	Loa	Bm	Drt	Kts	Type	Remarks
Ahtela	Fin	1991	8,610	6,700	139.5	19.0	6.2	16	Rop	ex Finnoak-08, Ahtela-97 (len-98)
Amore	Cyp	1988	851	1,280	64.3	10.5	3.4	11	C	ex Amaret-04, Mare-03, Sagitta-00, Turan-93, Nescio-93
OCT Challenger	Fin	1980	863	1,195	62.8	10.7	4.0	12	C	ex Sabina-05, Ash-98, Atol-97, Urkerland-94, Autol-90, Punta Motela-87
Tingo	Gib	1991	3,828	4,452	103.5	16.2	6.7	15	Cc	ex Christina-07

Erria A/S   Denmark

Funnel: *White with dark blue 'ERRIA' and ships bow in colours of Danish flag, above two narrow dark blue wavy lines.* **Hull:** *Red with red or black boot-topping.* **History:** *Founded 2007 as merger between BR Shipmanagement (founded 1990) and Fabricius Marine AS (founded 2005 by merger of Redereit Fabricius A/S (founded 1992) and BR Marine A/S).* **Web:** *www.erria.dk*

Name	Flag	Year	GT	DWT	Loa	Bm	Drt	Kts	Type	Remarks
Erria Anne	Mlt	2007	3,269	4,709	99.0	15.0	6.1	14	Tch	ex Duzgit Progress-07
Erria Dorthe	Mlt	2007	3,219	4,671	99.0	15.0	6.1	14	Tch	ex Duzgit Prosperity-07
Erria Helen	Mlt	2006	7,257	11,336	129.8	19.6	8.1	10	Tch	ex Alaattin Bey-07
Erria Ida	Mlt	2006	7,257	11,347	129.8	19.6	8.0	13	Tch	ex M. Can Bey-08
Erria Julie	Mlt	2007	3,300	4,696	99.9	15.0	6.0	14	Tch	
Erria Maria	Dis	2001	4,336	6,744	113.5	16.9	6.8	14	Tch	ex Maria Jakobsen-07
Erria Mie	Mlt	2007	7,232	11,336	129.8	19.6	8.0	12	Tch	ex Hamza Sfe Bey-08
Erria Nimmer	Mlt	2008	3,300	4,692	99.9	15.0	6.0	14	Tch	
Erria Vietnam	Atg	2008	1,850	2,900	81.3	13.2	4.5	-	C	

Newbuildings: Three 6,500 dwt chemical tankers.
Also operates two larger feeder container ships and a joint venture in Vietnam with two coasters.
See also CS & Partners A/S

A/S Ersco   Norway

Funnel: *Red with black top.* **Hull:** *Red with red boot-topping.* **History:** *Founded 1984 as Speed Bulk Shipping to 1988.* **Web:** *www.continental ship.no*

Name	Flag	Year	GT	DWT	Loa	Bm	Drt	Kts	Type	Remarks
Vivara	Mhl	2000	5,659	6,847	108.7	17.8	7.0	12	Cc	ex OMG Kolpino-09, Moksheim-08

Reederei Elbe Shipping GmbH. Baumwall. *N. Kemps*

John T Essberger GmbH & Co KG. Georg Essberger. *C. Lous*

Name	Flag	Year	GT	DWT	Loa	Bm	Drt	Kts	Type	Remarks
Wani Logger	Brb	1976	2,602	3,092	87.9	14.6	5.4	14	Cc	ex Logger-96, Norrbotten-92, Well Martin-89, Westerdiek-86, Gastrikland-80, Westerdiek-77
Wani Point	Brb	1979	2,062	2,525	88.0	12.7	4.6	13	Cc	ex Gardpoint-03, Lys-Point-97, Gardpoint-96, Lys-Point-95 (len-87)
Wani Will	Brb	1978	2,020	2,250	88.0	12.7	5.3	13	Cc	ex Gardwill-03, Lys-Wind-96, Gardwill-96, Ullero-92, Lys-Tind-88 (len-93)

Managed by subsidiary Continental Ship Management AS, Norway (founded 1989).
Also see Union Transport and Wilson

Esmeralda Schiffahrts GmbH   Germany

Funnel: *Charterers colours.* **Hull:** *Charterers colours.* **History:** *Founded 1988 as Gisela Waller Bereederung to 2000.* **Web:** *None found.*

Name	Flag	Year	GT	DWT	Loa	Bm	Drt	Kts	Type	Remarks
Gaastborg *	Ant	1996	2,820	4,200	89.7	13.7	5.7	13	Cc	
Geulborg *	Ant	1994	2,769	4,200	90.2	13.6	5.7	12	Cc	
Giessenborg *	Ant	1997	2,820	4,123	89.8	13.7	5.7	14	Cc	ex Baltic Erin-03, Giessenborg-99
Gooteborg *	Ant	1998	2,820	4,128	89.7	13.7	5.7	13	Cc	
Gouweborg *	Ant	1994	2,769	4,182	90.2	13.6	6.0	12	Cc	
Griftborg *	Ant	1995	2,771	4,149	87.7	13.7	5.7	13	Cc	
Grachtborg *	Ant	1997	2,820	4,105	89.7	13.7	5.7	13	Cc	
Kroonborg *	Nld	1995	6,142	9,085	130.7	15.9	7.5	14	Cc	
Markborg	Ant	1997	6,540	9,400	134.6	16.5	7.1	16	Cc	ex MSC Suomi-04, Markborg-02
MCL Tunis	Atg	1996	4,489	6,054	100.7	17.8	6.6	14	Cc	ex Kas Commander-09, Nirint Commander-08, Sloman Commander-07, Delmas Commander-00, Comma-00, Sloman Commander-99
Medemborg	Ant	1997	6,540	9,200	134.5	16.5	7.1	16	Cc	ex Arion-03
Merweborg	Ant	1997	6,540	9,400	134.6	16.5	7.1	16	Cc	ex MSC Bothnia-02, Merweborg-00
Osteborg *	Ant	1992	1,999	3,030	82.0	12.5	4.9	12	Cc	ex Zeus-99
Remsborg	Ant	1990	1,999	3,015	82.0	12.6	4.9	12	Cc	ex Eemsborg-09
Rhinborg *	Ant	1991	1,999	2,952	82.1	12.5	4.9	11	Cc	ex Rijnborg-06
SITC Dalian	Atg	2000	9,413	12,649	144.8	22.4	8.2	17	CC	
SITC Qingdao	Atg	2000	9,413	12,649	144.8	22.4	8.2	17	CC	
Vechtborg	Nld	1998	6,130	8,664	132.2	15.9	7.1	15	Cc	
Vlistborg	Atg	1999	6,130	8,664	132.2	15.9	7.1	15	Cc	

* managed for W Waller KG, Germany and operated by Wagenborg Shipping BV, Netherlands

John T Essberger GmbH & Co KG   Germany

Funnel: *Black with large blue 'E' on broad white band.* **Hull:** *Orange with red or black boot-topping.* **History:** *Founded 1924 as John T Essberger GmbH to 1986. Dutch subsidiary founded 1940 as Gebr Broere BV to 1994, renamed Broere Shipping BV to 2000, then Vopak Chemical Tankers BV to 2004 and Broere Shipping BV to 2009. Vopak Chemical Tankers acquired in 2004 (amalgamation of van Ommeren and Pakhoed in 1999) and amalgamated with Transocean Shipmanagement GmbH (founded 1990) in 2005.* **Web:** *www.rantzau.de*

Name	Flag	Year	GT	DWT	Loa	Bm	Drt	Kts	Type	Remarks
Alcedo	Nld	1999	1,813	2,731	90.0	12.0	4.3	11	Tch	
Annette Essberger	Pmd	1992	2,634	3,743	90.0	14.5	6.2	14	Tch	ex Alcoa Chemist-08, Annette Essberger-97
Ardea	Nld	2000	1,813	2,750	90.0	12.0	4.3	12	Tch	
Bastiaan Broere *	Nld	1988	3,693	5,098	104.3	17.0	6.2	15	Tch	
Caroline Essberger	Nld	2009	5,642	8,400	124.3	17.2	7.5	-	Tch	
Christian Essberger	Deu	2000	3,557	4,705	99.9	15.4	6.6	15	Tch	
Dutch Aquamarine *	Nld	2000	4,671	6,430	118.0	17.0	6.5	15	Tch	
Dutch Emerald *	Nld	2000	4,500	6,500	118.0	17.0	6.5	15	Tch	
Dutch Engineer *	Nld	1986	2,183	2,570	80.9	14.5	5.1	14	Tch	
Dutch Faith *	Nld	1996	3,419	4,442	99.9	17.1	5.5	14	Tch	
Dutch Mariner *	Nld	1986	2,183	2,570	81.0	14.5	5.2	14	Tch	
Dutch Mate *	Nld	1989	4,297	6,250	118.0	17.1	6.2	15	Tch	
Dutch Navigator *	Nld	1991	3,693	5,098	104.3	17.1	6.2	15	Tch	
Dutch Pilot *	Nld	1984	2,137	3,052	91.1	13.7	5.1	12	Tch	ex Neeltje Broere-93 (new forepart-93)
Dutch Spirit *	Nld	1996	3,419	4,442	99.9	17.1	5.5	14	Tch	
Eberhart Essberger	Pmd	1986	2,238	2,898	81.0	14.0	5.5	12	Tch	ex Ebro-08, Eberhart Essberger-95
Georg Essberger	Pmd	2004	3,790	5,771	100.0	16.5	6.8	15	Tch	
Heinrich Essberger	Pmd	1986	2,238	2,898	81.0	13.8	5.5	13	Tch	ex Reno-08, Heinrich Essberger-94
Jacobus Broere *	Nld	1989	3,693	5,098	104.3	17.0	6.2	15	Tch	
John Augustus Essberger	Pmd	1992	2,634	3,750	90.0	14.5	6.2	13	Tch	ex Tejo Chemist-08, John Augustus Essberger-97
Liselotte Essberger	Deu	1992	2,634	3,687	90.0	14.5	6.2	14	Tch	ex Lima Chemist-08, Liselotte Essberger-97
Patricia Essberger	Deu	2000	3,557	4,711	99.9	15.4	6.6	15	Tch	
Philipp Essberger	Pmd	2003	3,785	5,700	100.0	16.5	6.8	15	Tch	
Roland Essberger	Pmd	1992	2,634	3,741	90.0	14.5	6.1	14	Tch	ex Douro Chemist-08, Roland Essberger-97
Valbell	Lbr	1992	5,286	9,146	113.5	17.8	7.7	14	Ce	ex Halla No.5-04
Vedrey Freene **	Nis	2010	3,040	3,400	-	-	-	-	Tch	

* owned by subsidiary John T Essberger BV, Netherlands.
** acquired from Svithoid Tankers AB, Sweden (in liquidation)

Name	Flag	Year	GT	DWT	Loa	Bm	Drt	Kts	Type	Remarks

Euroafrica Line Zeglugowe Sp z oo — Poland

Funnel: Blue with yellow diagonal wedge interrupted by yellow/blue diamond. Hull: Grey with blue 'EuroAfrica', red boot-topping. History: Founded 1991 as Polskie Linie Euroafrica Co Ltd following privatisation and restructuring of Polish Ocean Lines. Web: www.euroafrica.com.pl

Name	Flag	Year	GT	DWT	Loa	Bm	Drt	Kts	Type	Remarks
Amber	Nis	1993	6,719	5,387	122.0	19.0	6.2	16	Rop	
Azuryt	Cyp	1988	6,030	9,590	113.1	18.9	8.5	14	Cc	ex Onego Voyager-08, Jaco Stove-03, Mekhanik Kurako-03, Solomon Chief-00, Capitaine Tasman-99, Mekhanik Kurako-97, Tiger Star-95, Mekhanik Kurako-94, Back Bay-94, Mekhanik Kurako-92, Printca-89
Malachit	Cyp	1989	6,030	9,595	113.1	18.9	8.5	14	Cc	ex Aleksandrov-07, Tasman Chief-04, Aleksandrov-03, Aleksandr Ovchinnikov-93, Steelca-89
Opal	Cyp	1981	6,742	9,408	130.8	19.0	8.0	14	Cc	ex Favorit-97, Carolyn-93, Beeco America-93, Columbus Niugini-89, Beeco America-88, Bernardo de Zamacola-86, Isla Jambeli-83, Maria Ines-82, Bernardo de Zamacola-81
Rubin	Cyp	1981	6,742	9,291	130.8	19.0	8.0	14	Cc	ex Marine Star-95, Beeco Asia-88, Blas de Lezo-86, Maria Francisca-82, Blas de Lezo-81

Euroceanica (UK) Ltd — UK

Funnel: White with light/dark blue cystal symbol. Hull: Orange with white 'CRYSTAL POOL', red boot-topping. History: Founded 2004 and associated with Rimorchiatori Riuniti SpA. Web: www.euroceanica.com

Name	Flag	Year	GT	DWT	Loa	Bm	Drt	Kts	Type	Remarks
Crystal Amaranto	Gbr	1999	6,785	9,887	126.8	19.7	7.7	-	Tch	ex Euro Amaranto-08, Isola Amaranto-05
Crystal Amethyst	Lux	1993	5,677	8,143	112.0	18.2	7.5	14	Tch	
Crystal Diamond	Lux	2006	7,903	11,340	126.2	19.0	8.3	13	Tch	
Crystal Emerald	Lux	1993	5,677	8,143	112.0	18.2	7.5	14	Tch	
Crystal Pearl	Lux	1994	5,677	8,143	112.0	18.2	7.5	14	Tch	
Crystal Syke	Gbr	1998	6,572	9,554	112.0	18.2	7.5	14	Tch	
Crystal Topaz	Lux	2006	7,903	11,340	126.2	19.0	7.6	13	T	

Newbuildings: two 9,000 dwt tankers on order.
Managed by Crystal Pool Ltd (www.crystal.fi)

European Containers Service NV — Belgium

Funnel: White with narrow black top. Hull: Blue with red boot-topping. History: Founded 1995 as joint venture between Cobelfret NV and European Containers Services NV. Web: www.ecs.be

Name	Flag	Year	GT	DWT	Loa	Bm	Drt	Kts	Type	Remarks
C2C Astralis	Bel	2005	6,901	9,217	129.9	19.4	7.3	17	CC	ex C2C Lupus-07, Lupus J-05

Operated with other chartered-in vessels by subsidiary C2C Shipping Lines Ltd, Ireland (formed 2002 – www.c2clines.com)

Exmar Marine NV — Belgium

Funnel: Black with red 'E' on broad white band. Hull: Orange with red boot-topping. History: Founded 1981 by the Saverys family, which acquired CMB in 1992 and demerged in 2003. Web: www.exmar.be

Name	Flag	Year	GT	DWT	Loa	Bm	Drt	Kts	Type	Remarks
Angela	Hkg	2009	3,493	3,996	97.2	16.5	5.4	-	Lpg	
Anne	Hkg	2010	3,493	3,996	97.2	16.5	5.4	-	Lpg	
Debbie	Hkg	2009	3,419	3,828	97.7	16.0	5.4	-	Lpg	
Elisabeth	Hkg	2009	3,493	3,990	97.2	16.5	5.4	-	Lpg	
Helane	Hkg	2008	4,484	5,366	106.0	17.6	6.0	-	Lpg	
Joan	Hkg	2009	3,493	4,001	97.2	16.5	5.4	-	Lpg	
Marianne	Hkg	2009	3,493	4,001	97.2	16.5	5.4	-	Lpg	
Magdalena	Hkg	2008	3,493	3,996	97.2	16.5	5.4	-	Lpg	
Sabrina	Hkg	2008	4,484	5,359	106.0	17.6	6.0	-	Lpg	

Operated by joint venture with Wah Kwong Shipping Co Ltd, Hong Kong.
Also owns larger Lpg and Lng tankers.

Fahrdorfer Schiffahrts GmbH & Co KG — Germany

*Funnel: Black with red 'S' link symbol on broad white band. Hull: Dark blue with red boot-topping or * red with black boot-topping. History: Founded 1989 as Wolfgang Schmidt to 2000. Web: None found.*

Name	Flag	Year	GT	DWT	Loa	Bm	Drt	Kts	Type	Remarks
Merit *	Gib	2000	2,301	3,171	82.5	12.4	5.3	12	Cc	
Merle	Atg	1994	2,456	3,706	87.5	12.9	5.5	12	Cc	ex Lys Clipper-06, Apollo-95

Fast Lines Belgium NV — Belgium

Funnel: Red. Hull: Blue with red boot-topping or red with white 'FAST-LINES' or full web address and black boot-topping. History: Founded 1995. Web: www.fast-lines.com

Name	Flag	Year	GT	DWT	Loa	Bm	Drt	Kts	Type	Remarks
Fast Ann *	Vut	1980	1,740	1,990	85.9	11.4	3.0	10	Cc	ex Saphir-92
Fast Filip *	Vut	1980	1,740	1,990	85.9	11.4	3.5	10	Cc	ex Smaragd-92
Fast Jef	Bel	1996	2,066	3,180	88.0	12.5	4.6	12	Cc	ex Breehorn-97
Fast Julia	Bel	1984	1,391	2,284	79.8	11.1	4.1	10	Cc	ex Silmaril-05, Jehan-98
Fast Sam	Bel	1994	1,983	3,204	90.4	12.5	4.6	11	Cc	ex Sprinter-99
Fast Sus	Bel	1996	2,055	3,234	90.0	12.5	4.6	11	Cc	ex Aletis-99
Fast Wil *	Vut	1985	1,391	2,285	80.0	11.1	4.1	10	Cc	ex Christina-97

*Managed or * owned by Fast Baltic Sp z oo, Poland.*

Euroafrica Line Zeglugowe Sp z oo. Malachit. *C. Lous*

Faversham Ships Ltd. Verity. *Tom Walker*

James Fisher and Sons Plc. Audacity. *Phil Kempsey*

Faversham Ships Ltd   UK

Funnel: Light blue with narrow white band below black top. **Hull:** *Dark blue or light grey with red boot-topping.* **History:** *Founded 1994.*
Web: *www.favershamships.co.uk*

Name		Flag	Year	GT	DWT	Loa	Bm	Drt	Kts	Type	Remarks
Beaumont		Gbr	2005	2,545	3,820	88.6	12.5	5.4	12	Cc	
Islay Trader	(2)	Brb	1992	1,512	2,386	74.9	11.4	4.4	10	C	ex Lass Moon-07, Moon-92
Nordstrand		Brb	1991	1,960	2,800	88.3	12.5	4.4	11	Cc	ex Nicole-93
Shetland Trader	(2)	Brb	1992	1,515	2,386	74.9	11.4	4.4	11	C	ex Lass Mars-07, I/a Mars
Valiant	(2)	Brb	1993	1,512	2,366	74.9	11.4	4.4	11	C	ex Lass Neptun-08, Wolgast-94, Lass Neptun-93, I/a Neptun
Vedette		Iom	1990	2,033	3,502	86.0	14.2	5.3	10	Cc	
Velox		Iom	1992	2,033	3,502	86.0	14.2	5.3	10	Cc	
Verity		Iom	2001	2,601	3,360	91.3	14.0	4.9	14	Cc	ex Union Mercury-09, Estime-04
Victress	(2)	Brb	1992	1,515	2,386	74.9	11.4	4.3	11	C	ex Lass Uranus-08, I/a Uranus
Viscount	(2)	Brb	1993	1,513	2,366	74.9	11.4	4.4	10	C	ex Lass Saturn-08, Greifswald-94, Lass Saturn-93

Fehn Bereederubgs GmbH & Co KG   Germany

Funnel: White with narrow black top. **Hull:** *Blue, red, green or yellow with red boot-topping.* **History:** *Founded 2003.* **Web:** *www.fehnship.de*

Name	Flag	Year	GT	DWT	Loa	Bm	Drt	Kts	Type	Remarks
BBC Anglia *	Atg	1997	4,078	4,900	100.6	16.6	6.4	15	Cc	ex Industrial Alliance-99, Bremer Forest-97, Wilgum-97
Ceg Cosmos	Gib	1983	1,139	1,102	63.0	11.3	3.3	10	Cc	ex Elisabeth-07
Ceg Galaxy	Atg	1983	1,035	1,063	74.6	9.5	2.9	10	Cc	ex Scout Marin-08, Wilke-93, Sea Dart-89, Wilke-88
Ems Majestic	Atg	1996	1,999	3,420	91.2	11.9	5.1	11	Cc	ex Holland-08, Daniel-06
Ems Trader	Atg	1999	2,056	2,953	89.5	12.4	4.3	10	Cc	ex Hansa Lubeck-06
Fehn Antares	Atg	2008	2,984	4,450	90.0	14.4	5.9	-	Cc	ex Vechtdijk-08
Fehn Calais	Atg	1997	1,675	2,270	82.5	11.4	4.0	9	C	ex Aldebaran-07, Margaretha-06, Aldebaran-06
Fehn Caledonia	Atg	2010	1,942	2,600	87.9	11.4	4.1	-	C	
Fehn Capella	Atg	1996	1,682	2,503	81.9	11.1	4.5	10	C	ex Elise-07, Flevoborg-96
Fehn Captain	Atg	2010	1,942	2,600	87.9	11.4	4.1	-	C	
Fehn Cartagena	Gib	1984	1,372	1,550	75.0	10.8	3.7	11	C	ex Sylvia-07, Heimatland-03, Athos-97, Heimatland-96
Fehn Castor	Atg	1991	1,282	1,750	75.0	10.8	3.7	10	C	ex Priscilla-07, Adriana-03, Flardinga-98
Fehn Challenge	Atg	2010	1,942	2,600	87.9	11.4	4.1	-	C	
Fehn Chelsea	Atg	2010	1,942	2,600	87.9	11.4	4.1	-	C	
Fehn Chief	Atg	2010	1,942	2,600	87.9	11.4	4.1	-	C	
Fehn Coast	Atg	1989	910	1,086	69.1	9.5	2.8	9	Cc	ex Noortland-08, Noort-08
Fehn Coral	Atg	1991	1,559	1,800	79.7	11.1	3.7	10	Cc	ex Aqua-07, Jaguar-06, Vera-96, Vera Rambow-96
Fehn Courage	Atg	2009	1,942	2,600	87.9	11.4	4.1	-	C	
Fehn Heaven	Atg	1997	2,844	4,250	89.9	13.2	5.7	12	Cc	ex A.B.Amsterdam-07, Saar Amsterdam-97
Fehn Leader	Nld	2010	5,735	8,800	-	-	-	-	Cc	
Fehn Liberty	Cyp	2010	6,200	8,000	-	-	-	-	Cc	
Fehn Light	Cyp	2010	6,200	8,000	-	-	-	-	Cc	
Fehn Mirage	Gib	2002	2,061	2,974	88.5	11.4	4.9	10	Cc	ex Harleriff-06, Wani River-05
Fehn Mistral	Gib	1993	2,478	3,834	85.4	13.3	4.8	13	Cc	ex Bremer Uranus-06
Fehn Sirius	Atg	2001	2,891	4,228	89.9	13.4	5.7	12	Cc	ex Dependent-08, I/d Polar Snow
Fehn Sky	Gib	1997	2,844	4,212	89.9	13.2	5.7	12	Cc	ex A.B.Lubeck-07, I/a Saar Lubeck
Fingal **	Ant	1984	1,409	1,545	79.0	10.9	3.3	10	Cc	ex Kirsten-05, Anastasia-04, Kirsten-03, Anastasia-03, Nadja-01, Mari Claire-98, Kirsten-94
Sanna	Ant	1984	1,410	1,562	79.0	10.9	3.3	10	Cc	ex Sonja-04, Desiree-01, Mari Line-98, Sea Ems-96
Sea Ems	Nld	1996	1,682	2,503	81.7	11.1	4.5	10	C	ex Holland-06, Ladon-05
Sea Thames	Atg	2001	1,723	2,250	86.9	11.4	3.7	-	C	ex Fehn Castle-07, Anke-06
Simone	Ant	1986	1,416	1,550	79.0	11.6	3.3	10	Cc	ex Norder Till-04, Triton-98, Mari France-96, Simone-94

Newbuildings:
* managed by Briese Schiffahrts GmbH & Co KG or ** by Lee Shippig Co Ltd, Ireland.

Uwe Fischer KG   Germany

Funnel: Yellow. **Hull:** *Blue with red boot-topping.* **History:** *Not confirmed.* **Web:** *None found.*

Name	Flag	Year	GT	DWT	Loa	Bm	Drt	Kts	Type	Remarks
Andrina F	Atg	1990	1,568	1,890	81.2	11.3	3.7	9	Cc	ex Simone-92
Petra F	Atg	1985	1,567	1,976	81.2	11.5	3.7	9	Cc	

James Fisher and Sons Plc   UK

Funnel: Dark blue with yellow 'Fisher' (some below flying sea-bird). **Hull:** *Light grey, dark blue or black with red boot-topping.* **History:** *Founded 1847, acquired P&O Tankships in 1996 (previously Rowbotham to 1970, Ingram Corp (US) to 1985, Marine Transport Lines (US) to 1990 when P&O acquired 50% and balance in 1993. FT Everard & Sons Ltd acquired in 2006.* **Web:** *www.james-fisher.co.uk*

Name	Flag	Year	GT	DWT	Loa	Bm	Drt	Kts	Type	Remarks
Asperity *	Gbr	1997	2,965	3,778	88.8	16.5	5.6	13	T	
Audacity	Gbr	1997	2,965	3,778	88.8	16.5	5.6	13	T	
Chartsman	Lbr	1993	4,842	6,397	101.6	17.5	6.9	12	T	
Clyde Fisher **	Bhs	2005	8,424	12,984	127.1	20.4	8.7	12	T	
Cumbrian Fisher **	Bhs	2004	8,446	12,921	127.1	20.4	8.7	12	T	
Forth Fisher *	Gbr	1997	3,368	4,972	91.0	15.6	6.2	12	T	I/a Quarterman
Galway Fisher *	Gbr	1997	3,368	4,967	91.0	15.6	6.2	12	T	I/a Wheelsman

James Fisher and Sons Plc. Cumbrian Fisher. *Allan Ryszka Onions*

Fjord Shipping A/S. Frigg. *F. de Vries*

Flinter Groep. Flinterlinge. *N. Kemps.*

Name	Flag	Year	GT	DWT	Loa	Bm	Drt	Kts	Type	Remarks
Humber Fisher	Gbr	1998	2,760	4,765	91.4	15.5	6.0	12	T	
Mersey Fisher *	Gib	1998	2,760	4,765	91.4	15.5	6.0	12	T	
Milford Fisher *	Gbr	1998	3,368	4,973	91.0	15.6	6.2	12	T	
Pembroke Fisher	Bhs	1997	9,356	14,204	135.2	20.4	8.1	12	Tch	ex Monte Bello-02
Sarnia Liberty	Gib	2008	3,017	3,392	79.9	15.7	5.5	12	T	ex Vedrey Thor-09
Sarnia Cherie	Gib	2007	3,043	3,392	79.9	15.7	5.5	11	T	ex Vedrey Tora-09
Seniority **	Bhs	2006	3,860	4,426	95.1	17.0	5.9	11	T	I/a Superiority
Shannon Fisher **	Bhs	2005	3,514	5,420	85.3	17.0	6.3	-	T	
Solent Fisher *	Bhs	1997	3,368	4,970	91.0	15.6	6.2	12	T	I/a Bridgeman
Solway Fisher **	Bhs	2006	3,501	5,422	85.3	17.0	6.3	-	T	
Speciality **	Bhs	2006	3,859	4,426	95.1	17.0	5.9	11	T	
Stability	Gbr	2004	2,603	3,517	92.9	14.1	5.7	13	Tch	ex Atlantis Armona-05
Steersman	Lbr	1994	4,842	6,403	101.6	17.5	6.9	12	T	
Summity	Gbr	2005	2,627	3,503	92.9	14.1	5.7	13	Tch	I/a Atlantis Aldabra
Superiority **	Bhs	2007	3,860	4,430	95.1	17.0	5.9	11	T	ex Seniority-07
Supremity	Gbr	2007	3,860	4,430	95.1	17.1	5.9	11	Tch	
Thames Fisher	Gbr	1997	2,760	4,765	91.4	15.5	6.0	12	T	

All managed by James Fisher (Shipping Services) Ltd, UK
* owned by subsidiary James Fisher Everard Ltd or ** by First Ship Lease Pte Ltd, Bermuda

KG Fisser & van Doornum Gmbh & Co   Germany

Funnel: *Black with three red vertical markings within red ring on white disc on white edged broad dark green band.* **Hull:** *Dark grey or black with red boot-topping.* **History:** *Founded 1879 and associated with Österreichischer Lloyd/Krohn Shipping Group.* **Web:** *www.fissership.com*

Name	Flag	Year	GT	DWT	Loa	Bm	Drt	Kts	Type	Remarks
Camira	Irl	1997	4,107	3,960	100.0	16.2	6.4	15	Cc	
Corona	Cyp	1998	4,150	4,800	100.0	16.2	6.4	14	Cc	
Cosa	Atg	1972	4,255	6,329	101.5	16.0	7.2	13	Cc	ex Ventus-85, Erika Fisser-79 (len/rblt-90)
Frontier Challenger	Cyp	1998	4,128	4,800	100.0	16.2	5.9	14	Cc	ex Seaboard Freedom-07, Kronoborg-01
Innes	Cyp	1976	4,372	6,300	106.6	16.6	6.8	12	Cc	ex Conticarib-96, Innes-94, Inn-92, Ventus-79, Josun-78
MSC Bahamas	Irl	1997	4,095	4,800	100.0	16.2	6.4	15	Cc	ex Connemara-07
Okapi	Ant	1972	4,255	6,348	101.5	16.0	7.2	13	Bc	ex Tabla-86, Boca Tabla-82, Imela Fisser-73 (len/rblt-90)
Pyrgos	Atg	1972	4,255	6,364	101.5	16.0	7.2	13	Bc	ex Villiers-86, Elisabeth Fisser-79 (len/rblt-91)
Wasaborg	Cyp	1997	4,128	5,400	100.5	16.2	6.4	15	Cc	ex P&O Nedlloyd Belem-98, Wasaborg-98

Fjord Shipping A/S   Norway

Funnel: *White with white 'F' on blue square.* **Hull:** *Red with dark red boot-topping.* **History:** *Founded 1995.* **Web:** *None found.*

Name	Flag	Year	GT	DWT	Loa	Bm	Drt	Kts	Type	Remarks
Fjordtank	Pan	1986	729	1,245	64.5	10.0	4.2	10	Tch	ex Triton IV-99, Yamabishi Maru No.21-99
Freyja	Mlt	1974	1,665	2,200	77.1	12.5	4.8	12	Tch	ex Hordafor Pilot-99, Essberger Pilot-97, Tom Lima-92, Solvent Explorer-87, Essberger Pilot-77
Frigg	Mlt	1982	1,876	2,959	80.9	13.0	5.2	12	Tch	ex Kyndill-02, Torafjord-85
Vestland	Pan	1984	1,023	1,330	67.2	10.8	3.8	11	C	ex Sevald-95, Barbanza-94
West Carrier	Bhs	1992	1,425	1,830	74.0	11.5	4.4	10	C	ex Vliehors-05, Almenum-04

Also operates 10 small refrigerated vessels.

Flekkefjord Shipping AS   Norway

Funnel: *Yellow, some with houseflag.* **Hull:** *Dark blue or green with red boot-topping.* **History:** *Founded 1995.* **Web:** *None found.*

Name	Flag	Year	GT	DWT	Loa	Bm	Drt	Kts	Type	Remarks
Anette	Nis	1979	1,713	1,600	79.7	12.8	3.5	11	Cc	ex Antares-97
Arundo *	Vct	1985	1,957	2,892	88.0	11.5	4.7	11	Cc	ex Heidberg-06
Defender	Vct	1980	1,512	2,190	82.5	11.4	4.2	10	Cc	ex Dredger-04, Falko-01, Marne-95, Sea Elbe-94, I/a Christa Schutt
Ingeborg Pilot	Nis	1981	1,196	1,053	63.0	11.4	3.3	10	Cc	ex Tora-96

Managed by Inter-Marine AS, Norway or * owned by subsidiary Lighthouse Shipping AS

Flinter Groep   Netherlands

Funnel: *White with red 'Flinter' and red/white dots/dashs forming 'F' on broad blue/grey band.* **Hull:** *Light grey with red boot-topping.* **History:** *Founded 1989 as Flinter Groningen BV to 2007. Flinter Management BV formed 1997, acquiring Ancora Shipping BV in 2002. Merged with Finnish-based Nordic Chartering late in 2009.* **Web:** *www.flinter.nl*

Name	Flag	Year	GT	DWT	Loa	Bm	Drt	Kts	Type	Remarks
Citadel	Nld	2008	3,990	6,000	110.8	14.0	6.1	12	C	
Dependent	Nld	2006	2,999	4,536	89.8	14.0	6.0	12	Cc	
Flinteramerica	Nld	2010	6,600	11,047	132.6	15.9	7.8	14	Cc	
Flinterarctic	Nld	2010	6,600	11,047	132.6	15.9	7.8	14	Cc	
Flinteratlantic	Nld	2010	6,600	11,047	132.6	15.9	7.8	14	Cc	
Flinterbaltica	Nld	2004	2,474	3,400	82.5	12.5	5.3	12	Cc	
Flinterbay	Nld	2004	2,474	3,483	82.5	12.5	5.3	12	Cc	ex Flinterbjorn-08
Flinterbelt	Nld	2005	2,474	3,480	82.5	12.5	5.3	12	Cc	
Flinterbirka	Nld	2006	2,474	3,480	82.5	12.5	5.3	12	Cc	
Flinterboreas	Nld	2005	2,474	3,486	82.5	12.5	5.3	12	Cc	
Flinterborg	Nld	2008	3,990	6,059	110.8	14.0	6.1	12	C	

Name	Flag	Year	GT	DWT	Loa	Bm	Drt	Kts	Type	Remarks
Flinterbothnia	Nld	2003	2,474	3,400	82.5	12.5	5.3	12	Cc	
Flinterbright	Nld	2004	2,474	3,475	82.5	12.5	5.3	12	Cc	ex Flinterborg-08
Flinterbrise	Nld	2006	2,474	3,480	82.5	12.5	5.3	12	Cc	
Flintercape	Nld	2009	7,702	9,140	141.7	20.6	7.3	19	CC	
Flintercarrier	Nld	2008	7,702	9,140	141.7	20.6	7.3	19	CC	
Flinterclear	Nld	2009	7,720	9,140	141.7	20.6	7.3	19	CC	
Flintercoast	Nld	2008	7,702	9,140	141.7	20.6	7.3	19	CC	
Flintercoral	Nld	2009	7,720	9,140	141.6	20.6	7.3	19	CC	
Flintercrown	Nld	2009	7,700	9,140	141.7	20.6	7.3	19	CC	
Flinterdijk	Nld	2000	4,503	6,359	111.8	15.0	6.4	13	Cc	
Flinterduin	Nld	2000	4,503	6,359	111.8	15.0	6.4	14	Cc	
Flintereems *	Nld	1999	4,503	6,359	111.8	14.6	6.3	13	Cc	
Flinterforest	Nld	2004	2,999	4,537	89.8	14.0	6.0	12	Cc	
Flinterfortune	Nld	2008	2,999	4,537	89.8	14.0	6.0	12	Cc	
Flinterfury	Nld	2007	2,999	4,537	89.8	14.0	6.0	12	Cc	
Flinterhaven *	Nld	1997	4,368	6,067	111.8	14.6	6.3	13	Cc	
Flinterhunze	Nld	2001	2,548	3,300	91.3	13.8	4.7	13	Cc	ex Hunzedijk-05
Flinterjute	Nld	2008	2,999	4,537	89.8	14.0	6.0	12	Cc	
Flinterland	Nld	2007	5,057	7,705	120.0	15.2	7.1	14	Cc	
Flinterlinge	Nld	2000	2,548	3,300	91.3	13.8	4.9	13	Cc	ex Lingedijk-05
Flintermaas *	Nld	1999	4,503	6,200	111.8	14.6	6.3	13	Cc	
Flintermar	Nld	2006	5,057	7,750	120.0	15.2	7.1	14	Cc	ex UAL Malabo-09, Flintermar-06
Flinterrachel	Nld	2009	3,442	5,622	98.8	14.0	6.1	11	C	
Flinterrebecca	Nld	2008	3,442	5,622	98.8	14.0	6.1	11	C	
Flinterschelde	Nld	2009	6,577	9,120	129.4	17.3	7.2	15	Cc	
Flinterspace	Nld	2010	6,577	9,120	129.4	17.3	7.2	15	C	
Flinterspirit	Nld	2001	4,503	6,358	111.8	15.0	6.4	13	Cc	
Flinterspring	Nld	2009	6,577	9,120	129.4	17.3	7.2	15	Cc	
Flinterstream	Nld	2009	6,577	8,850	129.4	17.3	7.2	15	Cc	
Flintersuomi	Nld	2010	6,577	9,120	129.4	17.3	7.2	15	Cc	
Flintersurf	Nld	2010	6,577	9,120	129.4	17.3	7.2	15	Cc	
Flinterwave	Nld	2004	2,999	4,537	89.8	14.0	6.0	12	Cc	
Flinterzee *	Nld	1997	4,368	6,075	111.8	14.6	6.3	13	Cc	
Gerarda	Nld	2006	2,999	4,537	89.8	14.0	6.0	12	Cc	
Henny	Nld	1982	1,241	1,791	65.5	11.4	4.6	11	C	ex Liamare-04, Dependent-00
Jorvik	Nld	2000	2,450	3,900	88.0	12.3	5.6	10	Cc	ex Tasman-06
Linda Marijke	Nld	1992	1,359	1,850	75.3	10.8	4.0	12	C	
Noorderkroon	Nld	2008	2,999	4,500	89.8	14.0	6.0	12	Cc	
Nordic Diana †	Nld	1996	2,774	4,180	89.8	13.6	5.7	13	Cc	ex Doggersbank-08
Nordic Erika †	Nld	2009	2,663	3,724	87.9	12.6	5.3	-	C	
Orcana	Nld	2006	2,999	4,530	89.8	14.0	6.0	12	Cc	
Pioneer	Nld	2010	6,621	11,048	132.6	15.9	7.8	14	Cc	
Tasman	Nld	2007	2,999	4,537	89.8	14.0	6.0	12	Cc	
UAL Aberdeen	Nld	2002	6,577	9,120	129.4	16.9	7.2	15	Cc	ex Flintersky-05
UAL Africa	Nld	2002	6,577	9,122	129.4	17.0	7.1	15	Cc	ex Flinterstar-02
UAL Lobito	Nld	2003	3,153	4,371	90.0	15.2	5.4	12	Cc	
UAL Texas	Nld	2002	6,577	9,073	129.4	16.9	7.2	15	Cc	ex Flintersun-02
UAL Trader **	(2) Ant	2006	1,668	2,346	78.1	16.0	3.5	-	C	l/a Danum
Zeus *	Nld	2000	6,142	9,100	130.2	15.9	7.5	14	Cc	

Newbuildings: Four further 7,400 dwt and three further 11,000 dwt general cargo ships for 2010-11 delivery.
* managed for Bergen Banking Shipping AS, Norway or ** for Universal Africa Lines, Netherlands (www.universalafricalines.com)
† operated by Nordic Chartering Ltd, Finland
Also see Wagenborg Shipping BV

H Folmer & Co   Denmark

Funnel: *Red with white 'D' or white with white 'F' on broad red band.* **Hull:** *Black with red boot-topping.* **History:** *Founded 1968.* **Web:** *www.folmer.dk*

Name	Flag	Year	GT	DWT	Loa	Bm	Drt	Kts	Type	Remarks
Danalith	Dis	1976	1,440	1,300	72.0	13.1	3.9	12	C	
Danica Brown	Dis	1986	997	1,563	61.6	10.3	3.4	9	Cc	
Danica Four	Dis	1984	997	1,563	61.6	10.3	3.3	9	Cc	
Danica Green	Dis	1981	902	1,130	60.0	9.6	3.4	11	Cc	
Danica Rainbow	Dis	1987	1,087	1,718	66.8	10.2	3.7	11	Cc	
Danica Red	Dis	1983	902	1,130	60.0	9.7	3.4	11	Cc	
Danica Sunbeam	Dis	1988	1,087	1,787	66.8	10.2	3.5	10	Cc	
Danica Sunrise	Dis	1989	1,087	1,778	66.8	10.2	3.5	11	Cc	
Danica Violet	Dis	1986	1,087	1,718	66.8	10.2	5.6	9	Cc	
Danica White	Dis	1985	997	1,563	61.6	10.3	3.4	10	Cc	
Hanne Danica	Dis	1992	1,409	2,191	71.8	11.7	4.9	12	Cc	
Karina Danica	Dis	1991	1,352	2,130	69.4	11.6	4.9	13	Cc	
Marianne Danica	Dis	1993	1,409	2,200	71.8	11.7	4.9	11	C	

Fonnes Shipping AS — Norway

Funnel: *White with white 'F' on red square.* **Hull:** *Black with black boot-topping.* **History:** *Founded 1997.* **Web:** *www.fonnesshipping.no*

Name	Flag	Year	GT	DWT	Loa	Bm	Drt	Kts	Type	Remarks
Bergfjord	Nld	2000	2,451	3,697	88.0	12.3	5.6	10	Cc	ex Storm-06, Robbengat-05
Fensfjord *	Nld	2006	4,035	6,050	111.4	13.4	5.7	12	Cc	
Nordfjord *	Nld	2006	3,990	6,000	110.8	14.0	6.1	-	Cc	ex Jan Van Gent-09

* managed by Wagenborg Shipping BV

Reederei Bijan Foroohari KG — Germany

Funnel: *White with white 'BF' above wavy line on blue band below narrow black top or charterers colours.* **Hull:** *Light grey with green boot-topping.* **History:** *Founded 1995.* **Web:** *www.foroohari.com*

Name	Flag	Year	GT	DWT	Loa	Bm	Drt	Kts	Type	Remarks
BF Catania	Atg	1995	3,999	5,314	101.1	18.5	6.6	15	Cc	ex Catania-09, Rita-06
BF Esperanza	Atg	2003	9,990	11,170	134.4	22.5	8.7	18	CC	ex Maersk Freeport-09, Esperanza-03, I/a Pioneer Sea
BF Leticia	Atg	2003	9,990	11,204	134.4	22.5	8.7	18	CC	ex Maersk Fortaleza-09, Maria-03
BF Maryam	Atg	1993	3,992	5,335	100.0	18.4	6.6	15	Cc	ex Katharina Ehler-08
Cartagena	Atg	1995	3,999	5,218	101.1	18.5	6.6	15	Cc	ex Constanza-05, Annegret-05
Maersk Ferrol	Atg	2004	9,990	11,202	134.4	22.5	8.7	18	CC	I/a Frieda
Melody	Gib	1993	3,992	5,336	100.0	18.4	6.5	15	Cc	ex Euro Melody-04, Melody-03, Frieda-02, Scandinavian Bridge-99, Frieda-92
Valencia	Atg	1996	3,999	5,215	101.1	18.5	6.6	15	Cc	ex Hanna-07
Victoria	Atg	1998	3,999	5,215	101.1	18.5	6.5	15	Cc	ex Rija-07
WEC Rubens	Cyp	1996	6,362	7,225	121.4	18.5	6.7	16	Cc	ex Carla-09, City of Lisbon-05, Partnership-96
WEC Van Eyck	Atg	2006	9,962	11,432	134.4	22.5	8.7	18	CC	ex Euphonia-09
WEC Vermeer	Atg	2004	9,962	11,424	134.4	22.5	8.7	18	CC	ex Confianza-09, Miriam Borchard-07, Confianza-04

Several managed or operated by subsidiary BF Shipmanagement GmbH & Co KG, Germany
Also owns two larger container ships.

Fortmarine Ou — Estonia

Funnel: *White with black top.* **Hull:** *Dark blue or * orange with red boot-topping.* **History:** *Founded 2002.* **Web:** *www.fortmarine.ee*

Name		Flag	Year	GT	DWT	Loa	Bm	Drt	Kts	Type	Remarks
Fort Azov	(2)	Khm	1970	2,457	3,261	114.0	13.0	3.6	10	C	ex Novaya Ladoga-09, Leniskaya Iskra-92, Volgo-Balt 125
Fort Knox		Nld	1985	3,913	6,446	96.8	15.5	7.1	12	Cc	ex Shemut-09, Ijsselborg-05, Ijsselland-96
Fort Ross		Vct	1977	2,234	3,300	84.0	15.7	5.3	13	C/ro	ex Dutch Liner-04, North Empress-00, Express-87, ScanDutch Iberia-86, Osteexpress-86, Elma Ocho-82, Zim Caribe-81, Osteexpress-79, Ghazi II-78, Osteepress-78
Lemo *		Vct	1980	2,052	2,730	82.5	12.8	5.1	12	Cc	ex Delta B-02, Eemnorge-00, Delta B-98, Westgard-97, Laura-92, Lavola-84
Volgo-Balt 179	(2)	Sle	1973	2,357	3,506	114.0	13.0	3.9	10	C	

Frakt A/S — Norway

Funnel: *Buff.* **Hull:** *Bright blue with red boot-topping.* **History:** *Founded 1985.* **Web:** *None found.*

Name	Flag	Year	GT	DWT	Loa	Bm	Drt	Kts	Type	Remarks
Myras	Nor	1991	1,999	3,005	82.0	12.5	4.9	12	Cc	ex Maple-08, Westerborg-06, Bothniaborg-04

Freese Shipping GmbH — Germany

Funnel: *Blue with blue disc and fish symbols on broad white band or charterers colours.* **Hull:** *Blue with red boot-topping or charterers colours.* **History:** *Founded 1964.* **Web:** *www.freeseship.com*

Name	Flag	Year	GT	DWT	Loa	Bm	Drt	Kts	Type	Remarks
Beluga Efficiency	Atg	2004	9.611	12,806	138.1	21.0	8.0	15	C/hl	ex BBC Carolina-07, Beluga Efficiency-06
Beluga Elegance	Atg	2004	9.611	12,806	138.1	21.0	8.0	15	C/hl	ex BBC Maryland-04, I/a Nordwind
Beluga Federation	Atg	2006	9.611	12,744	138.1	21.0	8.0	15	C/hl	I/a Jasper
Beluga Foundation	Atg	2006	9.611	12,744	138.1	21.0	8.0	15	C/hl	I/a Amber
El Bravo	Atg	2006	9,931	13,760	147.8	23.3	8.5	19	CC	ex TS Moji-07, Magnus F-06
Ulrike F	Atg	2005	9,931	13,879	147.8	23.3	8.5	19	CC	ex TS Singapore-07, Ulrike F-05

Newbuildings: Two 28,000 dwt multi-purpose/container ships on order for 2011 delivery.
Also owns one 20,500 gt bulk carrier and two 17,300 dwt multi-purpose/container ships.

Gdansk Sea Lines Co Ltd — Poland

Funnel: *Blue with blue outlined white 'GSL' above red line on broad white band or charterers colours.* **Hull:** *Bright blue with red boot-topping.* **History:** *Founded 2007 as a subsidiary of Gdansk Remontowa shipyard.* **Web:** *www.gslines.pl*

Name	Flag	Year	GT	DWT	Loa	Bm	Drt	Kts	Type	Remarks
BBC Gdansk	Atg	2010	6,155	7,500	122.5	18.2	7.2	15	C/hl	
BBC Kwiatowski	Atg	2008	6,155	7,500	122.5	18.2	7.2	15	C/hl	ex Eugeniusz Kwiatowski-08

Also owns one 27,000 dwt bulk carrier.

Gdanska Zegluga Sp z oo — Poland

Funnel: *None.* **Hull:** *Blue with red boot-topping.* **History:** *Founded 1946.* **Web:** *www.zegluga.pl*

Name		Flag	Year	GT	DWT	Loa	Bm	Drt	Kts	Type	Remarks
Laila 5	(2)	Pol	1988	1,853	2,075	82.5	11.4	4.0	10	Cc	ex Ladoga-105-08

Also operates fleet of eight small coastal passenger ships.

H Folmer & Co. Danica Four. *Hans Kraijenbosch.*

Reimer Glusing Transport GmbH. Finja. *F. de Vries*

Godby Shipping AB. Miranda. *F. de Vries*

Name	Flag	Year	GT	DWT	Loa	Bm	Drt	Kts	Type	Remarks

Gefo Gesellschaft fur Oeltransporte mbH & Co — Germany

Funnel: Black with black 'GEFO' on yellow band between narrow blue bands. *Hull:* Red with red boot-topping. **History:** Founded 1968. **Web:** www.gefo.com

Name	Flag	Year	GT	DWT	Loa	Bm	Drt	Kts	Type	Remarks
Bellini	Deu	1999	2,195	2,750	93.6	12.3	4.4	12	Tch	
Donizetti	Deu	1999	2,195	2,750	93.6	12.3	4.4	12	Tch	
Mozart	Deu	1999	2,195	2,750	93.6	12.3	4.4	12	Tch	
Puccini	Deu	1998	2,195	3,052	93.6	12.5	4.7	13	Tch	
Rossini	Deu	1998	2,195	2,750	93.6	12.5	4.7	12	Tch	
Verdi	Deu	1998	2,195	2,750	93.6	12.3	4.4	12	Tch	

Kaptain Josef Gerdes Schiffahts GmbH & Co KG — Germany

Funnel: White with dark blue 'G' on light blue diamond, narrow blue top. *Hull:* Blue with red boot-topping. **History:** Founded 1993. **Web:** www.reederei-gerdes.de

Name	Flag	Year	GT	DWT	Loa	Bm	Drt	Kts	Type	Remarks
Ajos G	Atg	1996	2,061	3,000	88.5	11.4	5.0	10	Cc	
Anna G	Deu	1994	3,992	5,350	100.0	18.4	6.5	15	Cc	ex Rhein Partner-05, Berolin-98, UB Jaguar-97, Iberian Bridge-96, Berolin-94
Brigit G	Atg	2010	2,545	3,800	88.6	12.5	5.4	12	Cc	
Carolin G	Atg	2008	2,545	3,813	88.6	12.5	5.4	12	Cc	
Christina G	Atg	2008	2,545	3,813	88.6	12.5	5.4	12	Cc	
Dette G	Atg	1995	3,999	5,315	101.1	18.2	6.6	15	CC	ex Jacob Becker-06, UB Tiger-97, Jacob Becker-95
Gerhard G	Atg	2010	4,309	6,050	114.4	14.4	8.1	13	Cc	
Gerhein G	Atg	1988	910	1,085	69.1	9.5	3.0	9	Cc	ex Karina G-98, Sea Douro-96, I/a Leda
Gertrud G	Atg	2009	4,309	6,050	114.4	14.4	8.1	13	Cc	
Heinrich G	Atg	1997	2,446	3,695	87.9	12.9	5.5	10	Cc	ex Northern Land-01
Helene G	Gib	2001	2,301	3,171	82.5	12.4	5.3	11	Cc	
Karina G	Atg	2007	2,545	3,813	88.6	12.5	5.4	12	Cc	
Nikar G	Atg	2000	2,301	3,171	82.5	12.4	5.3	11	Cc	
Niklas G	Atg	2010	4,309	6,050	114.4	14.4	8.1	13	Cc	
Ulrike G	Atg	2002	2,994	4,419	99.8	12.8	5.7	13	Cc	

Get2Sea A/S — Denmark

Funnel: White or * red. *Hull:* Blue with red boot-topping. **History:** Founded 2005. **Web:** None found.

Name	Flag	Year	GT	DWT	Loa	Bm	Drt	Kts	Type	Remarks
Sea Runner	Dmk	1983	2,649	3,525	90.4	14.0	5.9	14	Cc	ex Andra-07, Enno B-03, Torm Assinie-98, Enno B-98, Karin B-98, Marina Heeren-96

Managed by subsidiary Get2Land ApS, Denmark

Geuze Shipping BV — Netherlands

Funnel: Blue. *Hull:* Blue with red boot-topping. **History:** Founded 2002. **Web:** None found.

Name	Flag	Year	GT	DWT	Loa	Bm	Drt	Kts	Type	Remarks
Irene V	Vct	1979	1,694	2,040	72.3	12.8	4.5	12	Cc	ex Heimly-05, Hajo-99, Nicholas-90, Osterheide-87
Sirius	Tgo	1972	823	941	60.7	9.5	3.8	9	C	ex Anne Sofie-00, Bremer Roland-84

Hans-Peter Gewandt — Germany

Funnel: Buff. *Hull:* Pale turquoise with black boot-topping. **History:** Founded 1993. **Web:** None found.

Name	Flag	Year	GT	DWT	Loa	Bm	Drt	Kts	Type	Remarks
Ingrid	Cyp	1990	1,960	2,803	89.3	12.5	4.3	10	Cc	

Global Hanseatic Shipping GmbH & Co KG — Germany

Funnel: White or charterers colours. *Hull:* Black with red boot-topping. **History:** Founded 2001 as subsidiary of GHF Gesellschaft fur Handel und Finanz (founded 1985). **Web:** www.global-hanseatic.de

Name	Flag	Year	GT	DWT	Loa	Bm	Drt	Kts	Type	Remarks
Euro Adventure	Gbr	2009	8,032	9,023	138.2	21.7	7.7	18	CC	
Euro Discovery	Gbr	2008	8,032	9,002	138.2	21.7	7.7	18	CC	ex WEC Dali-09, Euro Discovery-08
Euro Snow	Gbr	2002	6,191	7,997	132.5	19.2	7.0	18	CC	
Euro Solid	Gbr	2006	7,112	8,800	125.8	21.7	7.8	18	CC	
Euro Squall	Gbr	2002	6,191	7,979	132.5	19.2	6.9	18	CC	
Euro Storm	Gbr	2001	6,191	7,992	132.5	19.2	7.0	18	CC	
Global Hebe	Atg	2005	5,029	7,486	119.6	16.8	6.3	12	B	ex Leonore-08, Sider Sky-05
Global Hekate	Atg	2008	5,164	7,448	120.0	16.8	6.3	12	B	
Global Helena	Atg	2009	5,164	7,448	120.0	16.8	6.3	12	B	
Global Helios	Atg	2006	5.184	7,448	120.0	16.8	6.3	12	C	ex Ostedijk-07, Fly-06, Sider Fly-06
Global Hemera	Atg	2008	5,164	7,448	120.0	16.8	6.3	12	B	ex Sider Cat-08
Global Hera	Atg	2006	5.184	7,448	120.0	16.8	6.3	12	C	ex Geestedijk-07, Sky-07, Sider Sky-06
Global Hermes	Atg	2006	5.184	7,448	120.0	16.8	6.3	12	C	ex Estedijk-07, Sea-06, Sider Sea-06
Global Hestia	Atg	2007	5.184	7,448	120.0	16.8	6.3	12	C	ex Tide-07, Sider Tide-07

Global Marine Shipping Services BV   Belgium

Funnel: *White with yellow symbol or grey with black 'WSCo' on black edged white diamond at centre of red/white diagonally quartered band.* **Hull:** *Light grey with black or pink boot-topping.* **History:** *Founded 2007.* **Web:** *None found.*

Name	Flag	Year	GT	DWT	Loa	Bm	Drt	Kts	Type	Remarks
Aladin	Mda	1982	1,499	1,768	82.5	11.4	3.5	10	Cc	
Sesam	Mda	1981	1,499	1,768	82.5	11.3	3.5	10	Cc	

Globia Shipping Co Ltd   Germany

Funnel: *Buff with white disc at centre of red/blue diagonally quartered houseflag.* **Hull:** *Blue with red boot-topping.* **History:** *Not confirmed.* **Web:** *None found.*

Name	Flag	Year	GT	DWT	Loa	Bm	Drt	Kts	Type	Remarks
Globia	Vct	1979	1,095	1,622	66.2	11.5	4.5	11	C	ex Clonlee-03, Rockfleet-00, Globe-93

Managed by RMS Lubeck Schiffahrts GmbH

Reimer Glusing Transport GmbH   Germany

Funnel: *Black with white 'GT' on yellow above blue bands or * 'C' on red above blue bands.* **Hull:** *Black with red boot-topping.* **History:** *Founded 1992.* **Web:** *www.gluesing-transport.de*

Name	Flag	Year	GT	DWT	Loa	Bm	Drt	Kts	Type	Remarks
Finja *	Deu	2000	1,102	1,335	67.3	11.7	3.7	10	T	
Jana	Deu	2005	1,164	1,324	69.4	11.7	3.7	10	T	

* operated by subsidiary Cuxhavener Mineral Ol GmbH, which operates several smaller tankers.

Godby Shipping AB   Finland

Funnel: *White with white 'S' on large green 'G', narrow green or black top.* **Hull:** *Green or white with black boot-topping.* **History:** *Founded 1972.* **Web:** *www.godbyshipping.fi*

Name	Flag	Year	GT	DWT	Loa	Bm	Drt	Kts	Type	Remarks
Link Star	Fin	1989	5,627	4,453	106.5	17.2	6.1	15	Rop	
Midas	Fin	1990	5,873	4,234	108.4	17.5	5.8	15	Rop	ex Bore Sea
Mimer	Fin	1990	5,873	4,232	108.4	17.5	5.8	15	Rop	ex Bore Star-93
Miranda *	Fin	1999	10,471	7,250	153.5	20.9	7.3	20	Rop	
Misana *	Fin	2007	15,586	11,407	165.8	23.4	7.3	20	Rop	
Misida *	Fin	2007	15,586	11,407	165.8	23.4	7.3	20	Rop	
Mistral *	Fin	1998	10,471	7,438	153.5	20.9	7.0	20	Rop	

* on charter to UPM-Kymmene Seaways, Finland.

Golo Shipping GmbH & Co KG   Germany

Funnel: *White.* **Hull:** *Blue with black boot-topping.* **History:** *Founded 2002.* **Web:** *www.golo-shipping.de*

Name	Flag	Year	GT	DWT	Loa	Bm	Drt	Kts	Type	Remarks
Golo River	Ant	1991	1,256	1,820	76.1	10.8	3.6	-	C	ex Frisiana-05
Jamina	Atg	1997	4,015	6,250	99.4	17.0	6.4	15	Cc	ex Regina-09, Gracechurch Crown-07, Regina-02, Monarch-02, Celtic Monarch-02, Emily Borchard-99, Gracechurch Meteor-97, I/a Celtic Monarch

Reederei Gerd Gorke GmbH & Co KG   Germany

Funnel: *White or charterers colours.* **Hull:** *Blue with red boot-topping.* **History:** *Founded 1985.* **Web:** *www.r-gg.de*

Name	Flag	Year	GT	DWT	Loa	Bm	Drt	Kts	Type	Remarks
BBC Ecuador *	Atg	2001	5,548	6,450	122.2	18.2	6.5	16	C/hl	ex Beluga Satisfaction-02
Beluga Evaluation	Atg	2006	9.611	12,705	138.1	21.0	8.0	15	C/hl	

* managed by Beluga Shipping GmbH qv

Rederi AB Gotland   Sweden

Funnel: *Red with black symbol on broad white band below black top.* **Hull:** *Red with red boot-topping.* **History:** *Founded 1865.* **Web:** *www.gotlandsbolaget.sw*

Name	Flag	Year	GT	DWT	Loa	Bm	Drt	Kts	Type	Remarks
Red Teal	Lbr	2007	4,859	6,874	119.1	16.9	6.7	14	Tch	
Red Wing	Lbr	2005	4,859	6,843	119.1	16.9	6.7	14	Tch	

Graig Shipping plc   UK

Funnel: *White with blue 'C' and diamond, narrow black top.* **Hull:** *Blue with red boot-topping.* **History:** *Founded 1919.* **Web:** *www.graig.com*

Name	Flag	Year	GT	DWT	Loa	Bm	Drt	Kts	Type	Remarks
Fanja	Pan	2000	6,714	8,480	100.5	20.4	8.2	16	C/hl	ex CEC Courage-08, Shanghai Star-01, CEC Courage-00
Hamra	Pan	2001	6,714	8,729	100.5	20.4	8.2	16	C/hl	ex CEC Caledonia-08

Managed by Graig Ship Management Ltd, who also manage vessels for Clipper Projects A/S and Thor Rederi A/S.
Associated with Idwal Williams & Co Ltd.

Green Reefers ASA   Norway

Funnel: *Green with white 'GR'.* **Hull:** *Dark green with white 'Green Reefers', grey boot-topping.* **History:** *Founded 1989 as Camar A/S, almost immediately being renamed Nomadic Shipping ASA to 2003.* **Web:** *www.greenreefers.no*

Name	Flag	Year	GT	DWT	Loa	Bm	Drt	Kts	Type	Remarks
Green Bergen	Bhs	1998	3,817	4,000	97.6	15.7	6.0	15	Rc	ex Frio Pusan-05, I/a Persey
Green Cooler	Bhs	1990	5,084	6,123	109.0	18.0	7.4	16	Rc	ex Erikson Cooler-96
Green Explorer	Bhs	1991	3,999	5,129	109.9	16.3	7.3	16	Rc	ex Northern Explorer-08
Green Freezer	Bhs	1991	5,084	6,120	109.0	18.0	7.4	16	Rc	ex Erikson Freezer-96

Reederei Gerd Gorke GmbH. BBC Ecuador. *Hans Kraijenbosch*

Green Reefers ASA. Green Bergen. *C. Lous*

Name	Flag	Year	GT	DWT	Loa	Bm	Drt	Kts	Type	Remarks
Green Frost	Bhs	1985	3,398	2,979	85.9	16.0	6.0	15	R	ex Nidaros-93, Olavur Gregersen-88
Green Ice	Bhs	1985	3,398	2,900	84.6	16.2	5.9	15	Rc	ex Tinganes-93, Svanur-88
Green Iceland	Bhs	1993	4,683	6,697	113.8	16.3	8.3	18	R	ex Caribic-06
Green Karmoy	Bhs	1989	5,084	6,120	109.0	18.0	7.4	16	Rc	ex Arctic Ice-01, Wisida Arctic-00, Belinda-96, Erikson Arctic-94
Green Klipper	Bhs	1991	4,091	5,416	108.2	16.2	7.9	17	R	ex Orange Klipper-06
Green Neptunic	Phl	1989	3,998	5,165	109.9	16.3	7.4	16	Rc	ex Neptunic-07
Green Nova	Bhs	1992	5,225	6,454	115.0	17.8	6.7	16	R	ex Nova Klipper-07
Green Ocean	hs	1992	4,091	5,416	108.2	16.2	7.9	17	R	ex Oceaan Klipper-07
Green Spring *	Mlt	1989	4,970	6,522	124.7	17.8	7.3	17	R	ex Frio Naruto-96
Green Summer *	Mlt	1988	4,970	6,489	124.7	17.8	7.3	17	R	ex Frio Hellenic-96
Green Tromso	Bhs	1997	3,817	4,000	97.6	15.7	6.0	15	Rc	ex Silver Fjord-06, Frio Hamburg-05, Venera-99
Green Winter *	Mlt	1989	4,970	6,526	124.7	17.8	7.3	17	R	ex Frio Canarias-96
Wilson Express	Nis	1983	6,182	4,200	128.1	18.0	5.6	20	Rc	ex Green Bergen-04, Bentago-98

*Managed by Green Management AS (founded 1996) or * by Norbilk Shipping UK Ltd (www.norbulkshipping.com)*
Currebtly operates a total of about 44 ships, including larger refrigerated ships and fish carriers.

Wolfgand Grimpe Marine   Germany

Funnel: *White with blue/green symbol.* **Hull:** *Dark blue with red boot-topping.* **History:** *Founded 1991.* **Web:** *www.wgmc.de*

Name	Flag	Year	GT	DWT	Loa	Bm	Drt	Kts	Type	Remarks
Blue Dragon	Atg	2007	2,545	3,696	88.6	12.5	5.4	11	Cc	
Clare Christine	Atg	2009	2,545	3,850	88.6	12.5	5.4	11	Cc	
Johanna Desiree	Atg	2009	2,400	3,850	88.6	12.5	5.4	11	Cc	

Grona Shipping GmbH & Co KG   Germany

Funnel: *White with blue band.* **Hull:** *Blue with red boot-topping.* **History:** *Founded 2006.* **Web:** *www.grona-shipping.com*

Name	Flag	Year	GT	DWT	Loa	Bm	Drt	Kts	Type	Remarks
Emsmoon	Atg	2000	4,563	6,359	111.8	15.0	6.4	13	Cc	ex Morgenstond III-05

Newbuildings: Eleven 5,200 dwt and six 6,250 dwt general cargo vessels on order for 2010-11 delivery.

Ditmar Grothmann   Germany

Funnel: *White with dark green/white diagonally quartered houseflag, narrow black top.* **Hull:** *Dark green with red boot-topping.* **History:** *Founded 1987.* **Web:** *None found.*

Name	Flag	Year	GT	DWT	Loa	Bm	Drt	Kts	Type	Remarks
Merlin	Atg	1981	1,939	2,890	88.0	11.3	4.7	11	Cc	ex Andrea-07, Lania-98, Carola-94

Hagland Shipping AS   Norway

Funnel: *White.* **Hull:** *Blue with white 'HAGLAND', red boot-topping.* **History:** *Founded 1983 as R G Hagland Shipping A/S to 1987.* **Web:** *www.hagland.com*

Name	Flag	Year	GT	DWT	Loa	Bm	Drt	Kts	Type	Remarks
Hagland Bona	Mlt	1996	2,456	3,715	87.9	12.9	5.5	11	Cc	ex Auriga-07, Wani Auriga-01, Auriga-00, RMS Auriga-99, Auriga-96
Hagland Borg	Mlt	1996	2,456	3,703	88.0	12.9	5.5	11	Cc	ex Aries-07, RMS Aries-01, I/a Aries
Hagland Boss	Mlt	1996	2,456	3,694	87.9	12.9	5.5	10	C	ex Ansiro-07, Wani Wind-05, Ansiro-04, Northern Wind-01
Michelle	Mlt	1975	3,123	4,240	94.2	15.4	6.0	12	Cc	ex Amulet-94
Minerva	Bhs	1992	2,446	3,735	87.9	12.8	5.5	10	Cc	ex Julia Isabel-05, Saar Berlin-96, Julia Isabel-95

Harald Halvorsen AS   Norway

Funnel: *White.* **Hull:** *Dark blue with red boot-topping.* **History:** *Founded 1945.* **Web:** *None found.*

Name	Flag	Year	GT	DWT	Loa	Bm	Drt	Kts	Type	Remarks
Kongsvaag	Nor	1971	1,732	2,665	90.9	11.8	4.7	-	Cc	ex Rytind-07, Pike-87, Alandsea-85, Alandzee-83, Alandsee-82 (len-94)

Hammann & Prahm Reederei   Germany

Funnel: *Black 'HP' separated by green diamond on white band between upper green and lower red bands.* **Hull:** *Blue with red or black boot-topping.* **History:** *Founded 1985.* **Web:** *www.leafeandhawkes.co.uk*

Name	Flag	Year	GT	DWT	Loa	Bm	Drt	Kts	Type	Remarks
Eric Hammann	Deu	1991	1,156	1,323	58.8	11.7	3.6	9	Cc	
Evert Prahm	Deu	1996	1,598	2,390	78.3	11.7	4.5	11	C	
Lore Prahm	Deu	1989	1,156	1,323	58.0	11.8	3.6	9	Cc	
Rebecca Hammann	Deu	1995	1,595	2,420	76.4	11.7	4.5	10	C	
Selene Prahm	Deu	1994	1,584	2,422	75.1	11.7	4.5	10	C	
Walter Hammann	Deu	1988	1,156	1,323	58.8	11.7	3.5	9	Cc	
Wilhelmine Steffens	Deu	1981	1,022	1,092	74.3	9.5	2.9	10	C	ex RMS Scotia-96, Wilhelmine Steffens-92, Lucky Star-91

Operated since 1987 by Leafe & Hawkes Ltd., UK

M Hannestad AS   Norway

Funnel: *White or charterers colours.* **Hull:** *Light grey with red boot-topping.* **History:** *Not confirmed.* **Web:** *www.hannestad.as*

Name	Flag	Year	GT	DWT	Loa	Bm	Drt	Kts	Type	Remarks
Ability	Nis	1978	2,822	4,245	91.1	14.3	6.4	12	Cc	ex Stability-00
Anicia	Nis	1983	4,426	6,021	106.0	17.5	7.0	13	Cc	ex Skagern-07, Icecrystal-95, Skagern-85
Dalhem	Pan	1977	2,581	2,937	88.4	15.5	4.8	13	Cc	ex Vento do Ponente-08, Dalhem-06, Sabine D-96, Gustav Behmann-89, Contship Two-79, Gustav Behmann-77

Hammann & Prahm Reederei. Lore Prahm. *David Walker*

Hanson Aggregates Marine Ltd. Arco Humber. *F. de Vries*

Name	Flag	Year	GT	DWT	Loa	Bm	Drt	Kts	Type	Remarks
Debora *	Nis	1965	2,331	2,390	94.0	13.2	4.7	13	C	ex Porrino-90, Lill-Nina-88, Conti Liban-83, Cremon-75
Nina	Mlt	1984	4,489	6,158	106.0	17.5	7.0	13	Cc	ex Libra-08, Free Spirit-04, Ahlers Belgica-99, Cam Bubinga-97, Ahlers Belgica-96, Kent Trader-93, Ahlers Belgica-92, ScanDutch Levant-91, Insulano-89, Shetland-86, Scol Broker-86, Shetland-84
Sally	Nis	1977	1,678	1,964	72.0	12.8	4.5	12	Cc	ex Annika-M-01, Loga-90, Anja-88
Sirte Star	Vct	1986	6,819	7,705	121.2	20.1	8.0	14	CC	ex Wan Ning He-98, Neustadt-92

* managed for AB Debora (Hastshipping AB), Sweden.
Several currentlyon charter to Jonsson Nova Logistics qv

Hansa Hamburg Shipping International GmbH — Germany

Funnel: Red/brown with black symbol on white square. **Hull:** Dark blue with red boot-topping. **History:** Founded 1999. **Web:** www.hansahamburg.de

Name	Flag	Year	GT	DWT	Loa	Bm	Drt	Kts	Type	Remarks
Wappen von Augsburg	Gbr	2009	5,145	8,132	116.9	18.0	7.4	15	Tch	
Wappen von Bayern	Gbr	2003	5,145	8,252	116.4	18.0	7.4	15	Tch	
Wappen von Berlin	Gbr	2003	5,145	8,254	116.4	18.0	7.4	15	Tch	
Wappen von Bremen	Gbr	2003	5,145	8,211	116.4	18.0	7.4	15	Tch	
Wappen von Dresden	Gbr	2007	5,145	8,157	116.9	18.0	7.4	15	Tch	
Wappen von Flensburg	Gbr	2008	5,200	8,154	116.9	18.0	7.4	15	Tch	
Wappen von Frankfurt	Gbr	2005	5,145	8,250	116.9	18.0	7.4	15	Tch	
Wappen von Hamburg	Gbr	2002	5,145	8,241	116.9	18.0	7.4	15	Tch	
Wappen von Leipzig	Gbr	2004	5,145	8,230	116.4	18.0	7.4	15	Tch	
Wappen von Munchen	Gbr	2003	5,145	8,266	116.4	18.0	7.4	15	Tch	
Wappen von Nurnberg	Gbr	2007	5,200	8,154	116.9	18.0	7.4	15	Tch	
Wappen von Stuttgart	Gbr	2006	5,145	8,184	116.9	18.0	7.4	15	Tch	

Managed by Wappen Reederei GmbH & Co KG (founded 2002 - www.wappen-reederei.de)
Also owns fleet of larger container ships and tankers

Hanse Capital Gruppe — Germany

Funnel: Charterers colours. **Hull:** Red with red boot-topping. **History:** Founded 1987. **Web:** www.hanse-capital.de

Name	Flag	Year	GT	DWT	Loa	Bm	Drt	Kts	Type	Remarks
SCL Marie-Jeanne	Lbr	2008	5,599	7,739	108.1	18.2	6.8	-	Cc	
SCL Thun	Lbr	2005	9,990	12,578	140.0	21.5	8.4	17	Cc	

Managed by Team Ship Management GmbH & Co KG, Germany qv

Hanse Shipping GmbH — Germany

UCT United Chemical Transport GmbH

Funnel: White with green 'UCT' above green line, black top. **Hull:** Red with red boot-topping. **History:** Founded 1986 and UCT subsidiary formed 2005. **Web:** www.ucete.com

Name	Flag	Year	GT	DWT	Loa	Bm	Drt	Kts	Type	Remarks
UCT Elizabeth	Mhl	2004	5,955	8,563	118.1	18.8	7.4	14	Tch	ex Cape Elizabeth-08
UCT Ellis	Mhl	2005	5,815	8,657	115.0	18.8	7.4	14	Tch	ex Cape Ellis-08
UCT Elwood	Mhl	2005	5,955	8,544	118.1	18.8	7.4	14	Tch	ex Cape Elwood-08
UCT Engle	Mhl	2005	5,815	8,643	115.0	18.8	7.4	14	Tch	ex Cape Engle-08
UCT Espen	Mhl	2005	5,815	8,674	115.0	18.8	7.4	14	Tch	ex Cape Espen-08
UCT Everad	Mhl	2004	5,955	8,571	118.1	18.8	7.4	14	Tch	ex Cape Everad-08

Managed by Columbia Shipmanagement (Deutschland) GmbH (www.csm-d.com)

Hansel Schiffahrts-und-Bereed GmbH & Co KG — Germany

Funnel: White. **Hull:** Light grey with red boot-topping. **History:** Founded 1995 as Peter Hansel to 1997 and Reederei Peter Hansel to 1999. Subsidiary founded 2005. **Web:** www.werse.eu

Name	Flag	Year	GT	DWT	Loa	Bm	Drt	Kts	Type	Remarks
Ems	Atg	2007	3,766	5,408	91,7	17.0	6.6	14	Cc	ex Rhone-07
Hudson	Atg	2002	6,354	9,804	108.3	18.6	8.3	13	Cc	ex Hispanica-08, Apollo Lion-05, Onego Sailor-05, Apollo Lion-04
Jade	Bhs	1989	2,881	2,742	91.3	14.7	4.6	12	Cc	ex Baltimar Boreas-10, Boreas Scan-09, Industrial Bridge-09, Baltimar Boreas-06, Superseven-98, Perla-95, Superseven-92
Mauritz	Atg	2000	6,354	9,861	108.5	18.5	8.3	13	Cc	ex Nickolaos-08, Langefoss-02, Kegostrov-01
MCL Alger	Atg	2002	3,660	5,762	105.1	15.6	6.1	12	C	ex Aasee-08, Sider Anna-07, Anna C-05 (len/wid-02)
MCL Antwerpen	Atg	1996	6,114	7,761	126.6	20.0	6.4	16	CC	ex Hannes C-09, Normed Istanbul-08, Hannes C-08, Aries-04, P&O Nedlloyd Corsica-02, Nedlloyd Corsica-98, Aries-96
Nephrit	Atg	1988	2,854	3,168	91.3	14.7	5.0	12	Cc	ex Jon Sanders-10, Baltimar Notos-09, Notos Scan-09, Baltimar Notos-06, Industrial Spirit-01, Baltimar Notos-01, Industrial Navigator-97, Baltimar Notos-96, Permint Suria-94, Baltimar Venus-91, Jon Sanders-91, Baltimar Venus-88
Opal	Bhs	1991	2,854	2,700	91.2	14.7	5.0	12	Cc	ex Baltimar Saturn-10, Orient Vision-96, Baltimar Comdiflate-95, Aotea Link II-92, Baltimar Comdiflate-92
Rubin	Bhs	1990	2,854	2,700	91.3	14.7	5.0	12	Cc	ex Baltimar Venus-10, Venus Scan-09, Baltimar Venus-05, Lae Chief-98, Mekong Venus-98, Baltimar Venus-98, Superten-94

Name		Flag	Year	GT	DWT	Loa	Bm	Drt	Kts	Type	Remarks
Saphir		Atg	1991	2,854	3,181	91.2	14.7	5.0	13	Cc	ex Baltimar Sirius-10, Moresby Chief-98, Baltimar Sirius-98, Mekong Sirius-98, IAL President-97, Baltimar Sirius-94, Kirk Pride-92, Baltimar Sirius-91
Shiva		Atg	1990	2,854	3,168	91.2	14.7	5.0	12	Cc	ex Baltimar Orion-10
Southern Pasifika		Atg	2003	5,234	5,650	109.4	18.2	6.7	-	CC	ex Indic-10, Southern Pasifika-09, Caledonie Express-07, Pac Sunda-05
Topas		Atg	1988	2,854	2,742	91.3	14.7	4.6	13	Cc	ex Baltimar Neptune-10, Neptune Scan-07, Baltimar Neptune-05, Saigon Neptune-92, Mary Durack-91, Baltimar Neptune-88

Operated by subsidiary Werse Bereederungs GmbH & Co KG, Germany

Hanson Aggregates Marine Ltd   UK

Funnel: *Orange/brown with seven white and two orange/brown small squares forming 'H' on broad blue band, black top.* **Hull:** *Blue with red boot-topping.*
History: *Formed 1999 by merger of Hanson Aggregates and ARC Marine Ltd, founded 1951 as Seaborne Aggregates renamed Amey Marine in 1968 and ARC in 1973, later acquiring Sand Supplies (Western) Ltd in 1989, Civil & Marine Ltd in 1999 and The Holms Sand & Gravel Co in 1996.* **Web:** *www.hanson.co.uk*

Name		Flag	Year	GT	DWT	Loa	Bm	Drt	Kts	Type	Remarks
Arco Adur		Gbr	1988	3,498	5,360	98.3	17.7	6.3	12	Dss	
Arco Arun		Gbr	1987	3,476	5,360	98.3	17.5	6.3	12	Dss	
Arco Avon		Gbr	1986	3,474	5,360	98.3	17.5	6.3	12	Dss	
Arco Axe		Gbr	1989	3,498	5,348	98.3	17.7	6.3	12	Dss	
Arco Beck	(2)	Gbr	1989	3,325	4,745	99.6	17.0	6.3	12	Dss	ex Cambeck-97
Arco Dart	(2)	Gbr	1990	1,309	1,700	67.7	13.0	4.1	10	Dss	
Arco Dee	(2)	Gbr	1990	1,309	1,812	67.7	13.0	4.1	10	Dss	
Arco Dijk	(2)	Gbr	1992	4,960	9,823	113.2	19.6	7.7	12	Dss	ex Camdijk-97
Arco Humber		Gbr	1972	5,487	8,962	107.0	20.0	7.4	14	Dss	ex Deepstone-86

Reederei Alnwick Harmstorf & Co GmbH KG   Germany

Funnel: *Yellow with white 'H' on broad blue band edged with narrow white bands, narrow black top.* **Hull:** *Blue with red boot-topping.* **History:** *Family shipping activities started in 19th century and present company founded in 1950 as A.F. Harmstorf & Co GmbH to 2000. One-time owners of Schlichting-Werft, Busumer and Flensburger shipyards.* **Web:** *www.harmstorf-co.com*

Name	Flag	Year	GT	DWT	Loa	Bm	Drt	Kts	Type	Remarks
Florence	Atg	1995	7,869	10,740	129.8	22.0	8.3	16	CC	ex Lagarfoss-05, Florence-04, APL Belem-04, APL Rose-01, Sea Explorer II-99, Shansi-98
Ines *	Deu	1997	9,602	12,340	149.6	22.3	8.3	17	CC	ex Alianca Andes-06, MB Europe-04, Meteor-03
Irene *	Deu	1996	9,650	12,400	149.5	22.3	8.3	17	CC	ex Alianca Patagonia-06, MB Canada-04
Jacqueline	Atg	1995	7,869	10,730	129.8	22.0	8.3	17	CC	ex Delmas Kaveri-08, Jacqueline-06, Safmarine Warri-02, Jacqueline-01, Maersk Zanzibar-01, Malaysia Star-99, Shantung-99, Melanesian Chief-98, Shantung-97
Madeleine	Atg	2000	4,454	5,537	100.6	18.8	6.7	15	Cc	l/a Borkum
Marguerite *	Atg	1995	8,633	9,319	132.9	23.1	7.7	17	CC	ex Aurora-04, Kent Merchant-98, Miriam Borchard-96, Aurora-95
Sitc Passion *	Atg	2005	9,590	12,827	142.7	22.6	8.2	18	CC	ex Alice-08
Sitc Progress *	Atg	2006	9,590	12,814	142.7	22.6	8.2	18	CC	ex Sara-08
Sofrana Tourville	Atg	1995	7,869	10.734	129.8	22.0	8.3	17	CC	ex Tiger Stream-08, Sylvette-08, Szechuen-04, Maersk Nairobi-01, Thailand Star-99, Szechuen-99, Tasman Chief-99, Kokopo Chief-98, Szechuen-96
Suzanne	Atg	1994	7,869	10.747	129.8	22.0	8.3	17	CC	ex Maersk Asia Decimo-07, Soochow-96, Micronesian Chief-95, Soochow-94

* managed for Premium Capital Emissionshaus GmbH & Co KG (founded 2004)
Also operates larger ships.

Harren & Partner Reederei GmbH & Co KG   Germany

Funnel: *White with black 'H&P' below light/dark turquoise dart symbols, * white or charterers colours.* **Hull:** *Blue, green or * black with red or black boot-topping.* **History:** *Founded 1989 as Harren & Partner Schiffahrts GmbH to 2002.* **Web:** *www.harren-partner.de*

Name		Flag	Year	GT	DWT	Loa	Bm	Drt	Kts	Type	Remarks
CFS Pacora		Jam	2008	7,464	8,124	129.6	20.6	7.4	18	CC	
CFS Pafilia		Jam	2006	7,578	8,450	127.9	20.4	7.8	18	CC	
CFS Palamedes		Jam	2005	7,578	8,393	126.6	20.4	7.7	18	CC	
CFS Palencia		Atg	2000	5,691	6,872	121.9	19.0	6.9	17	CC	ex Zim Kingston IV-04, Palencia-00
CFS Pamplona		Atg	2004	6,434	8,692	133.6	19.4	7.4	18	CC	l/a Parnavera
CFS Panavera		Jam	2005	7,578	8,508	127.0	20.4	7.8	18	CC	
CFS Paradero		Jam	2007	8,246	11,194	139.6	22.2	7.4	18	CC	
Condock IV **	(2)	Gib	1984	6,786	4,490	106.0	19.6	3.7	13	C/bg	ex Submerger II-93, Este Submerger II-92
Condock V **	(2)	Deu	1984	6,763	4,762	106.0	19.6	5.0	13	C/bg	ex Submerger I-93, Este Submerger I-92
Emstal *		Atg	1994	3,791	4,766	100.6	16.5	5.9	15	Cc	ex Portlink Runner-04, Emstal-02, OPDR Douro-99, Emstal-95
Lys Point		Atg	2005	6,901	9,236	139.8	19.4	7.3	18	CC	l/d as Pachuca
Odertal		Atg	2007	3,183	4,507	90.0	15.2	5.3	12	Cc	
Paimpol		Atg	1996	5,752	5,100	100.9	18.6	6.6	16	Ro	ex La Paimpolaise-07, Palamos-04, Fret Mame-03, Palamos-02, Scan Pacific-01
Palessa		Atg	2001	6,274	7,069	118.0	19.7	7.3	17	C/hl	ex Fret Moselle-04, l/a Pantaleon

Name	Flag	Year	GT	DWT	Loa	Bm	Drt	Kts	Type	Remarks
Pampero	Atg	1995	4,628	5,660	113.4	16.4	6.1	16	Cc	ex Cari Sun-97, Pampero-96, Cari Sun-96, Pampero-95
Panagia	Atg	2004	7,002	7,846	119.8	20.2	7.6	15	C/hl	
Pancaldo	Atg	2000	6,272	7,071	118.0	19.4	7.3	16	C/hl	
Pantanal	Atg	2004	7,002	7,837	119.8	20.2	7.6	16	C/hl	
Panthera	Atg	2001	6,274	7,069	118.0	19.7	7.3	17	C/hl	
Paramar	Cyp	1999	2,820	4,023	89.7	13.6	5.7	13	Cc	
Paranga	Jam	1994	3,790	4,766	100.6	16.5	5.9	12	Cc	ex Rhein Master-01, Rhein Lagan-96, Paranga-95
Patria	Atg	1999	5,825	5,795	100.9	18.6	6.9	15	Ro	ex Fret Savoie-01, Patria-99
Paz Colombia	Atg	2000	4,863	7,840	118.6	15.2	7.0	15	Cc	l/a Palmares
Rheintal *	Deu	1996	3,830	4,766	100.5	16.5	5.9	12	Cc	ex Calderon-97, Rheintal-96
Solymar	Cyp	1998	2,820	4,023	89.7	13.6	5.7	13	Cc	
Sun Bird **	Gib	2009	3,199	4,409	90.0	15.2	5.3	12	C	l/a Vechtetal
Transmar	Atg	1998	2,820	4,138	89.7	13.6	5.7	13	Cc	
Ultramar	Pmd	1997	2,820	4,128	89.7	13.6	5.7	13	Cc	l/a Papagena

* owned by subsidiary Ems-Fracht Schiffahrts GmbH & Co KG
** managed for H & P Dockschiff Verwaltungs GmbH, Germany
Also owns and manages larger ships

Hartman Shipping BV   Netherlands
Funnel: White. **Hull:** Blue with black boot-topping. **History:** Not confirmed. **Web:** None found.

Barentszzee	Nld	1973	1,045	1,536	71.2	9.8	3.8	10	C	ex Gersom-95, Realta-87

Hartman Seatrade CV   Netherlands
Funnel: Dark blue with blue 'H' on white square. **Hull:** Dark blue with lighter blue boot-topping. **History:** Founded 1999. **Web:** www.hartmanseatrade.nl

Deo Volente	Nld	2007	2,961	3,750	104.8	15.6	5.8	18	C/hl	
Eendracht *	Nld	2009	2,961	3,750	105.0	15.6	5.8	18	C/hl	
Pacific Dawn	Nld	2010	2,999	3,750	105.0	15.6	5.8	18	C/hl	

* owned by subsidiary Global Seatrade CV (formed 2007 – www.globalseatrade.com)

Hartmann Schiffahrts GmbH & Co KG   Germany
Funnel: White with blue 'h' symbol above narrow blue band, black top. **Hull:** Blue with white 'FEEDERLINES' or 'MTL', red boot-topping. **History:** Parent company founded 1981, Cypriot management subsidiary Intership Navigation Co Ltd formed 1988, GasChem Services in 1990, Dutch subsidiary Feederlines formed 1995. Holding company formed 2001, renamed Hartmann AG in 2008. **Web:** www.hartmann-reederei.de; www.feederlines.nl; www.intership-cyprus.com; www.unitedbulkcarriers.com

Antares I	Lbr	1996	6,114	8,160	125.5	19.8	6.4	16	Cc	ex P&O Nedlloyd Capri-03, Antares-97
Frisia Aller	Lbr	2007	9,948	13,700	147.8	23.3	8.5	19	CC	
Frisia Inn	Lbr	2008	9,948	13,720	148.0	23.3	8.3	19	CC	ex Mell Senoko-09, Frisia Inn-08
Frisia Lahn	Lbr	2008	9,948	13,739	147.9	23.3	8.3	19	CC	
Frisia Spree	Lbr	2008	9,948	13,850	147.9	23.3	8.3	19	CC	
Germania	Lbr	1993	8,721	8,890	125.2	19.0	8.0	16	C/ro	
Mell Saraca	Lbr	2009	9,948	13,765	147.9	23.3	8.5	19	CC	ex Frisia Rhein-09
Mell Sembawang	Lbr	2007	9,948	13,758	147.9	23.3	8.3	19	CC	ex Cape Lambert-09, l/a Frisia Alster
Mell Sentosa	Lbr	2007	9,948	13,699	148.0	23.3	8.3	19	CC	ex SITC Power-07, l/a Frisia Iller
Neptun	Lbr	1996	6,114	7,761	126.6	20.2	6.4	16	Cc	ex P&O Nedlloyd Corinth-03, TMM Jalisco-97, Neptun-96

Newbuildings: Several on order including seven further 6,500 dwt general cargo vessels for 2011-12 delivery.
Also owns 13 larger container ships, two 79,000 gt/150,000 dwt tankers and six 31,000 gt/53,500 dwt bulk carriers.
Apart from the main subsidiaries listed, the various operating subsidiaries also include MCP–Mini Container Pool (Cyprus), MTL–Maritime Transport+Logistik GmbH & Co KG (Germany), UBC–United Bulk Carriers (Germany), UCC–United Container Carriers (Germany) and UPT-United Product Tankers (Germany).

GasChem Services GmbH & Co KG, Germany

Danubegas	Deu	1998	4,201	4,197	98.5	15.4	6.5	14	Lpg	
Gaschem Atlantic	Lbr	2009	7,208	9,127	129.0	17.8	9.1	16	Lpg	
Gaschem Baltic	Lbr	2004	7,208	9,157	129.0	17.8	8.6	16	Lpg	l/a Balticgas
Gaschem Caribic	Lbr	2009	7,208	9,150	129.0	17.8	8.6	16	Lpg	
Gaschem Dollart	Lbr	1990	4,200	5,688	99.9	15.9	7.2	14	Lpg	ex Dollart Gas-06
Gaschem Hunte	Lbr	2000	5,725	5,777	118.3	17.2	6.8	14	Lpg	ex Huntegas-05
Gaschem Isar	Lbr	1991	4,200	5,688	100.0	15.9	7.2	14	Lpg	ex Isargas-05
Gaschem Jade	Lbr	1992	4,822	6,240	113.0	15.9	7.0	14	Lpg	ex Jadegas-06
Gaschem Jumme	Lbr	1993	4,822	6,292	113.7	15.9	7.0	14	Lpg	ex Jummegas-05
Gaschem Mosel	Lbr	2007	5,945	7,407	114.9	18.8	8.1	16	Lpg	
Gaschem Pacific	Lbr	2009	7,208	9,150	129.0	17.8	8.6	16	Lpg	
Gaschem Phoenix	Lbr	1993	4,484	5,500	99.9	16.2	6.8	14	Lpg	ex Phoenix Gas-05
Gaschem Rhone	Deu	2008	5,970	7,415	114.9	16.8	8.1	16	Lpg	
Gaschem Shinano	Lbr	2007	5,945	7,413	114.9	16.8	8.1	16	Lpg	
Gaschem Weser	Lbr	1999	5,725	5,807	116.3	17.2	5.8	14	Lpg	
Maido	Atf	1999	4,201	4,200	96.5	15.2	6.4	14	Lpg	l/a Travegas
Maingas	Lbr	2001	3,932	3,467	96.9	15.6	5.5	13	Lpg	
Max Planck	Lbr	1992	4,429	5,560	99.9	16.2	7.2	14	Lpg	l/a Oriongas
Odergas	Lbr	1999	4,201	4,197	98.5	15.2	6.4	14	Lpg	
Rio Gas	Lbr	1986	7,581	7,840	136.3	19.0	6.8	15	Lpg	

Hartmann Schiffahrts/Feederlines BV. Sloterdiep. *N. Kemps*

Hartmann Schiffahrts/GasChem. Gaschem Isar. *Allan Ryszka Onions*

Name	Flag	Year	GT	DWT	Loa	Bm	Drt	Kts	Type	Remarks
Saargas	Lbr	2001	3,932	3,600	96.9	15.6	5.5	13	Lpg	
Santa Clara	Lbr	1985	7,581	7,850	136.3	19.1	6.8	15	Lpg	

Feederlines BV, Netherlands

Name	Flag	Year	GT	DWT	Loa	Bm	Drt	Kts	Type	Remarks
Amsteldiep	Nld	1996	4,099	5,916	110.4	15.9	6.1	15	CC	ex Tyne Bridge-98, Amsteldiep-97, Emily Borchard-97, I/a Amsteldiep
Balticdiep	Prt	2007	4,102	5,490	106.9	15.2	5.3	12	Cc	
Barentsdiep	Nld	2010	4,102	5,490	106.9	15.2	5.3	12	Cc	
Beltdiep	Nld	2009	4,102	5,499	106.9	15.2	5.3	12	Cc	
Borndiep	Nld	1998	3,454	5,020	106.6	13.8	5.6	12	Cc	
Bosporusdiep	Nld	2008	4,102	5,490	106.9	15.2	5.3	12	Cc	
Boterdiep	Nld	1999	5,638	8,300	121.3	15.9	7.4	14	Cc	
Castor	Nld	1996	4,178	5,905	110.4	15.9	6.1	15	CC	ex Iberian Bridge-98, Castor-97
Eemsdiep	Nld	1996	3,170	4,680	98.8	13.8	5.7	14	Cc	
Ijsseldiep	Nld	1998	3,600	5,000	106.6	13.8	5.6	12	Cc	
Leuvediep	Nld	2008	5,598	8,101	108.2	18.2	7.0	11	C	
Lingediep	Nld	2008	5,598	8,112	108.2	18.2	7.0	11	C	
Loenerdiep	Nld	2008	5,598	8,100	108.2	18.2	7.0	11	C	
Loodiep	Nld	2008	5,598	8,113	108.2	18.2	7.0	11	C	
Lunamar	Nld	2000	3,170	4,675	98.9	13.8	5.7	14	Cc	ex Scheldediep-07
Maasdiep	Nld	1997	5,296	6,853	118.2	18.8	6.5	16	Cc	ex UAL Mexico-09, Maasdiep-08, UAL Africa-00, Cielo del Brasile-98, I/a Maasdiep
MCP Amsterdam	Nld	2007	5,272	8,023	117.0	19.7	6.4	15	Cc	
MCP Bilbao	Nld	2007	5,272	8,025	117.0	19.7	6.5	15	Cc	
MCP Kopenhagen	Nld	2007	5,272	8,024	117.0	19.7	6.4	15	Cc	
MCP London	Nld	2007	5,272	7,881	117.0	19.7	6.4	15	Cc	
MCP Rotterdam	Nld	2008	5,272	7,853	117.0	19.7	6.4	15	Cc	
Nordland	Nld	2002	5,052	7,750	118.6	15.2	7.0	12	Cc	I/d Voornediep
Novomar	Nld	1999	3,170	4,750	98.9	13.8	5.7	12	Cc	ex Slochterdiep-07, Elara-02
Onego Merchant	Nld	2004	5,057	7,750	120.0	15.2	7.1	14	Cc	I/a Vriesendiep
Onego Traveller	Nld	2004	5,057	7,750	120.0	15.2	7.1	14	Cc	I/d Vennendiep
OSC Rotterdam	Nld	2004	5,057	7,762	120.0	15.2	7.1	14	Cc	ex UAL Rotterdam-09, Veelerdiep-04
OSC Victoriadiep	Nld	2007	5,057	7,750	120.0	15.2	7.1	14	Cc	I/a Victoriadiep
OSC Vlistdiep	Nld	2007	4,990	7,800	118.6	15.2	7.1	14	Cc	I/a Vlistdiep
Schuitendiep	Nld	2000	3,170	4,646	98.9	13.8	5.8	14	Cc	
Singeldiep	Nld	2000	3,170	4,750	98.8	13.8	5.7	12	Cc	ex Europa-02
Sloterdiep	Ant	2000	3,170	4,556	98.9	13.8	5.8	12	Cc	ex Sinope-02
Sneekerdiep	Nld	2000	3,170	4,750	98.9	13.8	5.7	13	Cc	ex Callisto-02
Spaarnediep	Nld	2000	3,170	4,650	98.9	13.8	5.7	12	Cc	
UAL Angola	Cyp	2000	7,111	7,868	124.0	19.4	7.0	16	Cc	ex Damsterdiep-01
UAL Coburg	Nld	2005	5,057	7,763	120.0	15.2	7.1	14	Cc	
UAL Cyprus	Nld	2008	4,990	7,756	118.6	15.2	7.1	14	Cc	
UAL Rodach	Cyp	2001	7,111	8,141	126.4	19.4	7.0	16	C	ex Dinteldiep-01
UBC Manzanillo	Atg	2010	5,624	7,800	108.0	18.0	7.0	14	C	
UBC Maracaibo	Atg	2010	5,624	7,800	108.0	18.0	7.0	14	C	
UBC Mariel	Atg	2009	5,624	7,816	108.0	18.0	7.0	14	C	
UBC Miami	Nld	2009	5,630	7,811	108.0	18.0	7.0	14	C	
UBC Mobile	Nld	2010	5,630	7,815	108.0	18.0	7.0	14	C	
UBC Moin	Atg	2009	5,630	7,807	108.0	18.0	7.0	14	C	
UBC Montego Bay	Nld	2009	5,630	7,811	108.0	18.0	7.0	14	C	
UBC Montreal	Nld	2009	5,630	7,801	108.0	18.0	7.0	14	C	
UBC Moon	Atg	2009	5,630	7,807	108.0	18.0	7.0	14	C	
Varnadiep	Nld	2002	4,938	7,250	118.6	15.2	7.1	12	Cc	I/a Scan Leader
Vasadiep	Nld	2002	4,941	7,875	118.6	15.2	7.1	12	Cc	I/a Scan Runner
Vechtdiep	Nld	2000	4,938	7,200	118.6	15.2	6.7	15	Cc	
Veersediep	Nld	2001	4,938	7,250	118.6	15.2	6.7	15	Cc	
Velserdiep	Nld	2003	5,057	7,750	120.0	15.2	7.1	14	Cc	ex Onego Trader-10, Velserdiep-04
Vikingdiep	Nld	2008	5,040	7,750	120.0	15.2	7.1	12	Cc	
Vliediep	Nld	2001	4,941	7,200	118.6	15.2	6.7	15	Cc	
Vossdiep	Nld	2003	4,967	7,250	118.6	15.2	7.1	15	Cc	
Wisaforest	Nld	2002	5,052	7,750	118.6	15.2	7.0	12	Cc	
Zuiderdiep	Nld	1998	5,638	8,302	121.4	15.9	7.3	14	Cc	

Intership Navigation Co Ltd, Cyprus

Name	Flag	Year	GT	DWT	Loa	Bm	Drt	Kts	Type	Remarks
Allerdiep	Cyp	2008	2,954	4,191	90.0	15.2	4.3	12	C	
Almadiep	Cyp	2002	2,954	4,200	90.0	15.2	4.3	12	C	ex MTL Kouris-02
Alsterdiep	Cyp	2008	2,954	4,191	90.0	15.2	4.3	12	C	
Amazondiep	Cyp	2008	2,984	4,180	90.0	15.2	4.3	12	C	
Amurdiep	Cyp	2009	2,950	4,200	90.0	15.2	4.3	12	C	
Annerdiep	Cyp	2003	2,983	4,323	90.0	15.2	4.3	12	C	
Araldiep	Cyp	2009	2,954	4,191	90.0	15.2	4.3	12	C	
Capitaine Tasman	Ton	2002	7,091	8,127	126.4	19.4	8.3	16	Cc	ex Fua Kavenga II-02

Name	Flag	Year	GT	DWT	Loa	Bm	Drt	Kts	Type	Remarks
Dinkeldiep	Cyp	2010	4,000	6,500	105.2	15.2	6.2	12	Cc	
Doloresdiep	Cyp	2010	4,000	6,500	105.2	15.2	6.2	12	Cc	
Dondiep	Cyp	2010	4,000	6,500	105.2	15.2	6.2	12	Cc	
Doradiep	Cyp	2010	4,000	6,500	105.2	15.2	6.2	12	Cc	
Dourodiep	Cyp	2010	4,000	6,500	105.2	15.2	6.2	12	Cc	
Drentediep	Cyp	2010	4,000	6,500	105.2	15.2	6.2	12	Cc	
MCP Alstertal	Cyp	2007	5,272	8,023	117.0	19.7	6.5	14	Cc	
MCP Altona	Lbr	2007	5,272	7,853	117.0	19.7	6.4	15	Cc	
MCP Blankenese	Lbr	2008	5,272	7,853	117.0	19.7	6.5	15	Cc	
MCP Famagusta	Cyp	2008	5,315	7,709	117.0	19.7	6.4	15	Cc	
MCP Goteborg	Cyp	2008	5,272	7,852	117.0	19.7	6.5	15	Cc	
MCP Hamburg	Lbr	2007	5,272	7,853	117.0	19.7	6.4	15	Cc	
MCP Harburg	Lbr	2008	5,272	7,853	117.0	19.7	6.4	15	Cc	
MCP Nicosia	Cyp	2007	5,315	7,709	117.0	19.7	6.4	15	Cc	
MCP Pachna	Cyp	2009	5,338	7,734	117.0	19.7	6.4	15	Cc	
MCP Paphos	Cyp	2009	5,315	7,673	117.0	19.7	6.4	15	Cc	
Onego Mistral	Cyp	2007	5,315	7,708	117.0	19.7	6.4	15	Cc	ex OSC Mistral-08, MCP Limassol-07
Onego Monsoon	Cyp	2008	5,315	7,709	117.0	19.7	6.4	15	Cc	ex MCP Falkenberg-09
Onego Passat	Cyp	2007	5,315	7,708	117.0	19.7	6.4	15	Cc	ex OSC Passat-08, MCP Larnaca-07
Onego Zonda	Cyp	2008	5,315	7,709	117.0	19.7	6.4	15	Cc	ex MCP Kyrenia-08
UBC Cartagena	Cyp	2009	5,794	8,380	117.0	19.7	8.4	15	Ce	
UBC Cebu	Cyp	2009	5,794	8,380	117.0	19.7	8.4	15	Ce	
UBC Cork	Cyp	2009	5,794	8,380	117.0	19.7	8.4	15	Ce	

Newbuildings: Four further 6,500 dwt general cargo and four larger vessels for 2011-12 delivery.
The company also owns 8 larger vessels.

Hav Ship Management AS   Norway

Funnel: Black with houseflag (white 'HAV' on red, black, red vertical panels) on broad white band. **Hull:** Dark blue, green or light grey with red boot-topping.
History: Founded 1999 as Hav Shipping AS to 2008. **Web:** www.havshipmanagement.no; www.hav.no

Name	Flag	Year	GT	DWT	Loa	Bm	Drt	Kts	Type	Remarks
Arctica Hav	Bhs	1984	1,532	2,324	82.5	11.4	4.2	10	Cc	ex Union Venus-03, Pinguin-95, Hansa-89
Atlantica Hav	Bhs	1982	1,514	1,721	82.5	11.4	3.5	10	Cc	ex Pernille W-01, Pionier-89
Baltica Hav	Bhs	1983	1,528	1,761	82.5	11.4	3.6	10	Cc	ex Dioli-99, Baltica-94
Britannica Hav	Mlt	1985	1,521	1,740	82.5	11.3	3.5	10	Cc	ex Acer-07, Oblix-05, Dominique Trader-04, Provence-98, Pero-96
Celtica Hav	Bhs	1984	1,537	1,720	82.5	11.3	3.5	10	Cc	ex Astrix-05, Georgette Trader-04, Steel Trader-00, Pirat-98, Haithabu-94
Danica Hav	Bhs	1984	1,536	1,720	82.5	11.4	3.5	10	Cc	ex Union Arbo-01, Birka-94
Germanica Hav	Vct	1984	1,566	1,717	82.5	11.4	3.7	10	Cc	ex Saxo-09, Poseidon-98
Hav Dolphin	Bhs	1994	2,075	3,010	88.3	12.5	4.6	12	Cc	ex Canum-07, Saar Rouen-96, Canum-95
Hav Marlin	Bhs	1994	1,990	3,041	88.3	12.5	4.6	12	Cc	ex Freepsum-08, Saar Genoa-96, I/a Freepsum
Hav Snapper	Bhs	1991	1,961	2,767	88.3	12.5	4.4	11	Cc	ex Walzberg-09, Groothusen-02, Saar London-96, Rex-91
Hav Zander	Bhs	1990	1,960	2,999	89.0	12.5	4.4	11	Cc	ex Jumper-09, Karibu-97, Petra-95
Icelandica Hav	Bhs	1982	1,513	1,721	82.5	11.4	3.5	10	Cc	ex Mike-05, Patria-94
Nordica Hav	Bhs	1982	1,514	1,900	82.5	11.4	3.5	10	Cc	ex Alizee-00, Bingum-95, Echo Carrier-90, Bungsberg-90
Swedica Hav	Bhs	1986	1,616	1,920	82.5	11.3	3.8	10	Cc	ex Ophir-06, Sea Weser-01, Jan Meeder-97

HCI Capital AG   Germany

Funnel: Charterers colours. **Hull:** Grey with red boot-topping. **History:** Founded 1985. **Web:** www.hci.de

Name	Flag	Year	GT	DWT	Loa	Bm	Drt	Kts	Type	Remarks
Gaschem Ice *	Lbr	1996	7,955	12,217	131.4	20.0	9.4	16	Lpg	ex Northern Ice-05, Eurogas Quinta-96
Islandia	Lbr	2004	9,957	13,872	147.9	23.3	8.5	19	CC	ex SYMS Taishan-06, Islandia-05, Alexia-04

* managed by Harpain Shipping GmbH, Germany
See also Carisbrooke Shipping and Reederei Eckhoff GmbH & Co KG. Also owns numerous larger vessels.

KG Paul Heinrich GmbH & Co   Germany

Funnel: Buff with red flag containing red 'PH' on white diamond, narrow black top. **Hull:** Light grey with white 'SAL', green above red boot-topping.
History: Founded 1949. **Web:** www.sal-shipping.com

Name	Flag	Year	GT	DWT	Loa	Bm	Drt	Kts	Type	Remarks
Annegret *	Atg	2000	8,397	9,359	151.6	20.7	7.8	20	C/hl	
Annemieke	Atg	1998	8,388	9,544	151.6	20.7	7.9	20	C/hl	
Annette	Atg	2003	8,383	9,147	151.6	20.4	7.8	18	C/hl	
Gloria	Atg	1997	8,388	9,531	151.5	20.7	7.8	20	C/hl	
Grietje *	Atg	2000	8,397	9,360	151.6	20.4	7.9	19	C/hl	
Lena	Atg	1998	8,388	9,534	151.6	20.6	7.8	20	C/hl	
Maria	Atg	2004	8,383	9,422	151.6	20.4	7.9	18	C/hl	
Paula	Atg	2000	8,397	8,967	151.6	20.4	7.9	18	C/hl	
Wiebke	Atg	2000	8,397	9,531	151.7	20.7	7.9	18	C/hl	
Wilma	Atg	1997	8,388	9,549	151.6	20.6	7.9	20	C/hl	

Operated by SAL-Schiffahrtskontor Altes Land GmbH & Co and * managed by Luhe Engineering GmbH
Also owns three larger heavy-lift vessels.

Hav Ship Management AS. Britannica Hav. *M. Beckett*

KG Paul Heinrich GmbH & Co. Gloria. *Allan Ryszka Onions*

Name	Flag	Year	GT	DWT	Loa	Bm	Drt	Kts	Type	Remarks

Reederei Hans Heinrich KG Germany

Funnel: *White.* **Hull:** *Blue with red boot-topping.* **History:** *Founded 1992 as Petra Heinrich KG.* **Web:** *None found.*

Name	Flag	Year	GT	DWT	Loa	Bm	Drt	Kts	Type	Remarks
Anna Sirkka	Deu	2006	9,981	11,271	134.4	22.5	8.7	18	CC	ex Annaland-09, l/a Anna Sirkka
Helgaland	Gbr	2003	7,519	8,622	137.5	21.3	7.5	19	CC	ex Helga-03
Lappland	Deu	1998	5,058	6,650	117.9	18.2	7.1	17	CC	

Managed by HH Shipping GmbH & Co.

Reederei Held Germany

Funnel: *Buff with black 'H' divided by white wavy line on white square.* **Hull:** *Light grey with red boot-topping.* **History:** *Founded 1910.* **Web:** *www.reederei-held.de or www.shipmanagement.net*

Name	Flag	Year	GT	DWT	Loa	Bm	Drt	Kts	Type	Remarks
Anne Scan	Atg	1997	2,528	3,526	88.6	12.8	5.5	12	Cc	ex Herford-07, Moldavia-07, Lebasee-06, Sao Vicemte-97, l/a Lebasee
Catharina	Atg	1999	2,999	5,057	94.9	13.2	6.2	12	C	ex Catharina C-09
Isartal	Atg	1989	2,369	3,782	87.9	12.9	4.5	11	Cc	
Janet	Mlt	1998	2,748	4,570	89.9	13.2	6.0	11	Cc	ex Janet C-08
Johanne	Mlt	1998	2,748	4,570	89.9	13.2	5.6	11	Cc	ex Johanna C-08

Newbuilding: 4,500 gt 5,500 dwt coaster for 2010 delivery.
Managed by Held Bereederungs GmbH & Co KG (formed 2007)

Reederei Uwe Helms KG Germany

Funnel: *Blue.* **Hull:** *Blue with red boot-topping.* **History:** *Founded 1985.* **Web:** *None found.*

Name	Flag	Year	GT	DWT	Loa	Bm	Drt	Kts	Type	Remarks
Jerome H	Atg	1985	1,297	1,525	74.9	10.6	3.4	10	C	

Helmsing & Grimm GmbH & Co Germany

Funnel: *White with black toothed top.* **Hull:** *Black with red boot-topping.* **History:** *Founded 1836 as Helmsing & Grimm to 1983.* **Web:** *None found.*

Name	Flag	Year	GT	DWT	Loa	Bm	Drt	Kts	Type	Remarks
Adelaide	Cyp	1972	5,202	7,470	124.5	16.4	7.1	15	C	ex Leo Schroder-83
Daniel	Pan	1979	8,547	11,121	146.4	19.6	7.9	16	Cc	ex Aries-98, Fossum-85, Sudan Crown-83, Fossum-82
Senya	Cyp	1973	5,202	7,470	124.5	16.4	7.1	15	C	ex Lutz Schroder-86

C J Helt & Co Denmark

Funnel: *Blue.* **Hull:** *Blue with red boot-topping.* **History:** *Founded 1972, but filed for bankruptcy late in 2009.* **Web:** *www.cjhelt.dk*

Name	Flag	Year	GT	DWT	Loa	Bm	Drt	Kts	Type	Remarks
Dantic	Vct	1981	1,139	1,102	63.0	11.3	3.3	10	Cc	ex Irmgard-07
Lis Weber	Vct	1980	1,751	2,422	85.9	11.3	4.0	10	Cc	ex Alliance-09, Heimglimt-05, Stephanie S-04, RMS Lettia-96, Stephanie Siemer-93
Nortic	Dis	1969	1,109	1,036	64.6	11.0	3.5	11	C	ex Supidana-08, Finla-97, Dinah-85, Stefanie-76
Skantic	Vct	1974	1.081	1,094	64.6	10.1	3.6	11	C	ex Skanlill-99, Skanlith-83

Herning Shipping AS Denmark

Funnel: *Red with shield (white seagull on grey tool against blue sky and red brick wall above green/white land).* **Hull:** *Red with red boot-topping.*
History: *Founded 1963 as Tankskibsrederiet Herning A/S to 2008.* **Web:** *www.herning-shipping.com*

Name	Flag	Year	GT	DWT	Loa	Bm	Drt	Kts	Type	Remarks
Anette Theresa ‡	Iom	2006	8,455	12,940	127.2	20.4	8.7	-	Tch	
Annelise Theresa	Dis	2009	5,706	7,885	101.4	19.1	7.6	14	Tch	
Birthe Theresa *	Cyp	1995	2,094	3,403	87.6	12.4	5.5	12	Tch	ex Anna Theresa-02
Bitten Theresa	Dis	1998	3,356	5,527	106.3	16.0	5.7	12	Tch	ex Emilia Theresa-02
Caroline Theresa	Dis	2009	5,706	8,241	101.4	19.1	7.6	14	Tch	
Charlotte Theresa	Dis	2008	7,728	11,372	129.6	19.2	8.5	15	Tch	
Dagmar Theresa	Dis	2001	2,654	4,454	92.3	13.8	5.4	12	Tch	
Ditte Theresa †	Mlt	2008	5,713	8,025	101.4	19.1	7.6	14	Tch	
Else Maria Theresa	Dis	2001	2,788	4,307	96.3	14.2	6.1	13	Tch	
Hanne Theresa	Dis	2002	2,682	4,282	92.3	13.6	8.1	12	Tch	ex Laila Theresa-05
Ida Theresa §	Mhl	2009	8,278	12,713	121.8	20.4	8.7	13	Tch	
Irene Theresa §	Mhl	2009	8,278	12,713	121.8	20.4	8.7	13	Tch	
Jette Theresa	Dis	2009	7,728	11,372	129.6	19.2	8.5	15	Tch	
Karina Theresa	Dis	2009	5,695	7,871	101.4	19.1	7.6	14	Tch	
Kristina Theresa ‡	Iom	2006	8,455	12,972	127.2	20.4	8.7	-	Tch	
Malou Theresa ‡	Mlt	2008	5,289	7,842	122.7	17.2	6.7	-	Tch	
Maria Theresa	Dis	2002	2,659	4,473	92.3	13.6	6.2	11	T	
Rikke Theresa	Dis	2007	2,666	3,456	92.9	14.1	5.7	13	T	
Ruth Theresa **	Mlt	2008	5,713	8,025	101.4	19.1	7.6	14	Tch	
Sara Theresa *	Sgp	2003	2,490	2,954	87.5	14.4	5.3	12	T	
Serra Theresa *	Sgp	2003	1,074	1,520	70.1	10.5	4.2	10	Tch	
Sofie Theresa	Dis	2004	2,660	3,418	92.9	14.1	5.7	13	T	
Susanne Theresa	Dis	2006	2,611	3,464	92.9	14.1	5.7	13	Tch	
Tina Theresa	Dis	2009	5,706	7,963	92.9	14.1	5.7	13	Tch	
Trine Theresa ‡	Mlt	2007	5,236	7,915	122.7	17.2	6.7	-	Tch	

Name	Flag	Year	GT	DWT	Loa	Bm	Drt	Kts	Type	Remarks
Vitta Theresa *	Sgp	1991	1,892	2,925	97.5	10.9	4.4	10	Tch	(len-97)

Newbuildings: Four further 5,700 grt tankers for 2010-11 delivery.
* owned by subsidiary Herning Shipping Asia Pte Ltd, Singapore or † by Dannebrog Invest, Denmark
** managed by CS & P Skibe A/S, ‡ by Bernhard Schulte Shipmanagement or § by Columbia Shipmanagement (Deutschland) GmbH
Also operates about 14 other chartered tankers.

Reederei Hesse GmbH & Co KG   Germany

Funnel: *Cream or charterers colours.* **Hull:** *Green or * blue with white 'MTL', red boot-topping.* **History:** *Founded 1992 as Reederei Klaus Hesse to 2001.*
Web: *www.reederei-hesse.de*

Name	Flag	Year	GT	DWT	Loa	Bm	Drt	Kts	Type	Remarks
Bothniadiep *	Prt	2006	4,102	5,457	106.7	15.2	5.3	11	C	
Laakdiep *	Prt	2007	5,598	7,778	108.2	18.2	6.8	11	C	
Larensediep *	Prt	2007	5,598	7,778	108.2	18.2	6.8	11	C	
Magdalena	Atg	2008	7,519	9,907	124.5	20.8	7.4	-	CC	
Reymar	Gib	1995	2,901	4,196	91.2	13.8	5.8	12	Cc	ex Reitdiep-08, Mercator-98, Reitdiep-95

* chartered-out to Maritime Transport + Logistik (Hartmann Schiffahrts GmbH & Co KG) qv
Shares offices and staff with Moormerland Schiffahrts GmbH qv

A/B Broderna Hoglund   Sweden

Funnel: *White with deep black top.* **Hull:** *Dark blue with red boot-topping.* **History:** *Founded 1936.* **Web:** *www.lsshipping.se*

Name	Flag	Year	GT	DWT	Loa	Bm	Drt	Kts	Type	Remarks
Sydfart	Swe	1879	176	280	31.7	6.5	3.2	8	C	ex Ann-77, Stigfjord-72, Hamnfjord-69, Olof Tratalja-65 (NE-53)
Via *	Swe	1967	1,219	1,115	68.2	10.9	3.8	11	C	ex Key-03, Bremer Saturn-84
Vidi	Swe	1969	1,335	2,030	74.0	10.8	5.1	12	C	ex Swe-Trader-09, Rauk-01, Klinte-92, Larus-84, Bergvik-77, Larus-76, Actuaria-76, City of Dublin-71
Vina *	Swe	1969	1,303	2,226	76.3	11.9	4.4	13	C	ex Windia-06, Flensia-95, Eystein-95, Iris I-94, Iris-93, Tor Baltic-76, Iris-75
Vinga *	Swe	1971	1,097	1,042	64.6	11.0	3.7	10	C	ex Acamar-84, I.W.Winck-80, Jytte Bres-80, Wrath-74, Jytte Bres-72

* owned by subsidiary LS Shipping AB (Ljustero Sjo AB), Sweden

Geir Hokland AS   Norway

Funnel: *Dark blue, white or cream.* **Hull:** *Blue with red or black boot-topping.* **History:** *Not confirmed.* **Web:** *None found.*

Name	Flag	Year	GT	DWT	Loa	Bm	Drt	Kts	Type	Remarks
Bulk Viking	Nor	1972	874	945	60.7	9.5	3.5	9	Bu	ex Thunbox 2-85, Viking Sigvald-79 (conv C-98)
Helene H	Nor	1978	1,925	2,262	79.8	12.8	4.4	12	Cc	ex Christine O-06, John Bluhm-98
Sveabulk	Nor	1979	1,016	1,465	72.3	11.2	3.4	10	Bu	ex Euro Bulk-00, Quiescence-98
Sveanord	Nor	1976	834	1,068	59.7	10.3	3.9	12	Bu	ex Nordnes-96, Finnport I-94, Andramari-93

Operated by Seaworks AS qv

Holwerda Shipmanagement BV   Netherlands

Funnel: *Blue with white 'H' symbol crossed by two blue wavy arrows.* **Hull:** *Blue with red boot-topping.* **History:** *Founded 1955 as Scheepvaartkantoor Holwerda to 1983 and Holwerda Scheepvaart BV to 1987.* **Web:** *www.holwerdaship.com*

Name	Flag	Year	GT	DWT	Loa	Bm	Drt	Kts	Type	Remarks
Anja	Nld	1995	2,996	4,622	100.0	16.7	6.0	15	Cc	ex Nyland-09, I/a Helene
Aura	Nld	2003	7,519	8,658	137.5	21.3	7.5	18	CC	
Elisabeth	Nld	2000	5,067	6,850	117.9	18.2	7.1	17	CC	
Freya	Nld	2000	5,067	6,850	117.9	17.9	7.1	17	CC	ex Dalsland-07, Frederika-00
Gotland	Nld	2003	7,519	8,709	137.5	21.3	7.5	19	CC	ex Tina-03
Marja	Nld	1995	3,999	5,216	100.6	18.5	6.6	15	CC	ex Magda-04
Tanja	Nld	1986	3,801	4,636	103.5	16.0	5.6	14	Cc	ex Kate-96, Containerships II-90, I/a Kate
Vanquish	Nld	1995	2,997	4,624	100.0	16.5	6.0	15	CC	ex Varmland-05, I/a Wilhelm

HS Schiffahrts GmbH & Co KG   Germany

Funnel: *White with houseflag (blue above yellow with black 'S' on white diamond).* **Hull:** *Blue with red boot-topping.* **History:** *Founded 2003 as subsidiary of HS Bereederungs GmbH & Co KG (founded 2000).* **Web:** *www.hs-schiffahrts.de*

Name	Flag	Year	GT	DWT	Loa	Bm	Drt	Kts	Type	Remarks
Christina	Lbr	2009	4,255	6,050	114.4	14.4	6.0	13	Cc	
Doris Schepers	Deu	2007	7,852	9,400	140.6	21.8	7.3	18	CC	
Heinz Schepers	Atg	1993	3,992	5,350	100.0	18.4	6.6	15	Cc	ex Margret-03, Mediterraneo-03, Margret-99
Henrike Schepers	Atg	2008	7,852	9,231	140.6	21.8	7.3	18	CC	
Johann	Atg	2010	4,300	6,050	114.4	14.4	6.0	13	Cc	
Johanna Schepers	Atg	2009	7,987	9,400	140.6	21.8	7.3	18	CC	
Karin Schepers	Atg	2007	7,852	9,400	140.6	21.8	7.3	18	CC	
Kaspar Schepers	Atg	2010	7,987	9,400	140.6	21.8	7.3	18	CC	
Kristin Schepers	Cyp	2008	7,852	9,400	140.6	21.8	7.3	18	CC	
Margaretha	Atg	1994	2,446	3,726	87.9	12.9	5.5	11	C	ex Lys Clipper-09, Lys Carrier-08, Nunki-94
Maria Elise	Atg	2009	4,255	6,050	114.4	14.4	6.0	13	Cc	
Maria Schepers	Atg	1989	2,749	3,144	94.5	15.9	5.0	14	Cc	ex Otto Becker-01
Neptun	Atg	1998	2,039	3,210	89.4	12.5	4.8	11	Cc	ex Emmaplein-04

Reederei Uwe Helms KG. Jerome H. *M. Beckett*

Herning Shipping AS. Maria Theresa. *Phil Kempsey*

Name	Flag	Year	GT	DWT	Loa	Bm	Drt	Kts	Type	Remarks

Huelin-Renouf Shipping Ltd

Channel Islands (UK)

Funnel: *Dark blue with houseflag on staff (white with red diagonal cross and light blue 'H' on yellow diamond at centre).* **Hull:** *Dark blue with red boot-topping.* **History:** *Founded 1935 and subsidiary of Channel Islands Services Ltd.* **Web:** *www.huelin-renouf.co.uk*

Name	Flag	Year	GT	DWT	Loa	Bm	Drt	Kts	Type	Remarks
Huelin Dispatch	Gib	1999	2,532	3,390	86.4	12.8	5.5	12	Cc	ex Bremer Forest-09, Paapsand-01
Huelin Endeavour	Irl	1983	2,046	1,874	78.0	13.8	5.0	13	CC	ex Coastal Wave-09, Pellworm-98, Neptunus-95, Craigantlet-88
Ronez *	Gbr	1982	870	1,117	64.7	10.1	3.5	10	Ce	

* managed by World Self Unloaders Ltd, UK

Ice Reefers Group

Estonia

Funnel: *Blue.* **Hull:** *White with red boot-topping.* **History:** *Founded 2004.* **Web:** *www.icereefers.ee*

Name	Flag	Year	GT	DWT	Loa	Bm	Drt	Kts	Type	Remarks
Normandic	Blz	1983	3,960	5,220	108.3	16.3	7.4	16	Rc	

INOK NV

Belgium

Funnel: *White with dark blue 'C' on pale blue square.* **Hull:** *Dark blue or green with red boot-topping.* **History:** *Founded 2000.* **Web:** *www.inok-nv.com*

Name		Flag	Year	GT	DWT	Loa	Bm	Drt	Kts	Type	Remarks
Dune-2	(2)	Vct	1983	2,516	3,472	113.9	13.2	3.9	10	C	
Helle		Mlt	1991	1,716	3,294	83.5	13.7	5.5	11	Tch	ex Clipper Helle-09, Helle Wonsild-07, Helle Terkol-95
Komarno		Cyp	1993	2,446	3,701	87.9	12.8	5.5	10	Cc	
Kuban	(2)	Vct	1980	1,578	1,850	81.0	12.0	4.0	12	C	ex Ladoga-18-05
Onda	(2)	Vct	1989	3,086	3,332	116.1	13.0	4.1	10	Cc	ex Amur 2531-08
Rusich-2	(2)	Rus	2004	4,970	5,485	128.2	16.5	4.3	11	C	
Rusich-3	(2)	Rus	2004	4,970	5,485	128.2	16.5	4.3	11	Cc	
Rusich-4	(2)	Rus	2004	4,970	5,485	128.2	16.5	4.3	11	Cc	
Rusich-5	(2)	Rus	2005	4,970	5,485	128.2	16.5	4.3	11	Cc	
Rusich-6	(2)	Mlt	2005	4,970	5,485	128.2	16.5	4.3	11	Cc	
Sandra-II	(2)	Kna	1976	2,478	3,134	114.0	13.0	3.7	10	C	ex Professor I. I. Krakovskiy-04
Sv. Apostol Andrey	(2)	Mlt	2002	4,974	5,435	128.2	16.5	4.3	11	Cc	
Sv. Georgiy Pobedonosets	(2)	Mlt	2003	4,974	5,440	128.2	16.5	4.3	11	Cc	
Sv. Knyaz Vladimir	(2)	Mlt	2003	4,974	5,440	128.2	16.5	4.3	11	Cc	
Svyatitel Aleksiy	(2)	Mlt	2003	4,974	5,435	128.2	16.5	4.3	11	Cc	
Ugra	(2)	Vct	1979	1,639	2,155	81.0	11.8	4.3	12	Cc	ex Ladoga-15-05
Virma-2	(2)	Vct	1981	2,516	3,510	113.9	13.2	3.9	10	C	ex Volgo-Balt 234-06
Vodla	(2)	Khm	1975	2,557	3,506	114.0	13.2	3.9	10	C	ex Volgo-Balt 187-05
Volkhov	(2)	Vct	1978	1,639	2,085	81.0	11.8	4.4	12	Cc	ex Ladoga-12-07

Also manages vessels for various Russian owners.

Interorient Navigation Co Ltd

Cyprus

Funnel: *Buff with blue 'IN' symbol inside blue ring.* **Hull:** *Black or light grey with red boot-topping.* **History:** *Formed 1977 in Germany.* **Web:** *www.interorient.com*

Name	Flag	Year	GT	DWT	Loa	Bm	Drt	Kts	Type	Remarks
Antares	Lbr	1993	4,842	6,417	101.6	17.5	6.9	12	T	ex Anchorman-02
Rudderman	Lbr	1994	4,842	6,419	101.6	17.5	6.9	12	T	
Sea Pioneer	Mlt	2005	9,910	14,003	148.0	23.3	8.5	19	CC	ex Olympian Racer-09, Sinotrans Tokyo-08, Olympian Racer-05

Also owns and operates a very large fleet of larger product tankers and bulk carriers.

Interscan Schiffahrts GmbH

Germany

Funnel: *White with black 'IS' between narrow red Bands.* **Hull:** *Dark green with red boot-topping.* **History:** *Founded 1978.* **Web:** *www.interscan.net*

Name	Flag	Year	GT	DWT	Loa	Bm	Drt	Kts	Type	Remarks
Doris T	Atg	1977	1,972	2,150	79.0	12.4	4.8	12	C	ex Libra II-97, Libra-85
Ida	Cyp	1986	1,616	2,019	82.5	11.3	3.9	10	Cc	ex Sooneck-05
Karin	Deu	1998	4,246	6,288	100.0	17.0	7.3	15	Cc	ex UAL Houston-06, Proteus-03, Karin-02, Industrial Millenium-02, I/a Karin
Paivi	Cyp	2008	2,474	3,450	82.5	12.6	5.3	12	Cc	
Pandora *	Cyp	2004	6,701	8,238	132.6	19.2	7.2	17	CC	
Patria	Cyp	1996	2,210	3,519	82.5	12.5	5.7	13	Cc	
Patriot	Cyp	1994	2,163	3,086	82.4	12.6	5.2	12	Cc	
Pernille	Cyp	2009	2,474	3,492	82.5	12.6	5.3	12	Cc	
Phantom	Gib	2000	2,329	3,220	82.5	12.5	5.4	12	Cc	
Pinta	Gib	1993	2,190	2,795	82.5	12.6	4.9	11	Ccp	
Pioneer *	Cyp	2004	6,701	8,238	132.6	19.2	7.2	17	CC	
SITC Friendship *	Atg	2005	6,701	8,200	132.6	19.2	7.2	17	CC	ex Paphos-05
Tim	Cyp	2008	2,474	3,450	82.5	12.6	5.3	12	Cc	
Widor	Deu	1987	1,412	1,780	81.0	11.4	3.3	10	Cs	

* managed by Marlow Ship Management Deutschland GmbH & Co KG

Interorient Navigation Co Ltd. Rudderman. *N. Kemps*

AS Kristian Jebsens Rederi. Tinnes. *F. de Vries*

Name	Flag	Year	GT	DWT	Loa	Bm	Drt	Kts	Type	Remarks

Intersee Schiffahrts GmbH & Co KG   Germany

Funnel: *Cream with narrow white band on broad dark blue band, narrow black top or ** white.* **Hull:** *Light grey with red boot-topping or ** blue with black boot-topping.* **History:** *Founded 1976.* **Web:** *www.intersee.de*

Name	Flag	Year	GT	DWT	Loa	Bm	Drt	Kts	Type	Remarks
Aachen	Atg	2004	3,870	5,780	108.1	14.4	6.1	13	Cc	I/a Lea
Alana	Atg	1999	2,999	5,049	95.2	13.2	6.0	12	Cc	
Alexia *	Ant	2008	7,878	11,149	145.6	18.2	7.4	14	Cc	
Amalia *	Ant	2006	3,870	5,780	106.1	14.4	6.1	14	Cc	ex Francesca-06
Amanda	Ant	2005	3,870	5,780	106.1	14.4	6.1	14	Cc	
Angelika	Atg	2004	7,769	10,500	145.5	18.2	7.4	14	Cc	ex Akrafell-08, Angelika-05
Anja	Atg	2000	5,968	9,219	127.9	15.9	7.4	14	Cc	ex TMC Brazil-02, Anja-01, I/a Sabina
Annalisa	Atg	2000	6,154	8,737	132.2	15.9	7.1	15	Cc	ex Malte Rambow-03
Aurora *	Ant	2005	3,870	5,780	106.1	14.4	6.1	14	Cc	ex Farina-06
Barbara **	Atg	1997	4,015	6,250	100.0	17.2	6.4	15	Cc	ex Louise Borchard-06, Euro Phoenix-04, Princess I-02, Celtic Princess-02, Louise Borchard-01, Celtic Princess-97
Berta	Atg	2004	6,264	7,400	113.1	18.4	6.4	16	CC	
Carola	Atg	2000	6,382	8,600	129.5	15.9	7.4	14	Cc	I/a Beatrice
Celia	Atg	2005	6,264	8,250	118.4	18.4	8.2	16	Cc	
Christina	Atg	1998	2,834	4,743	89.8	13.2	6.2	12	Cc	
Cliff	Mhl	2000	7,970	9,865	133.2	20.8	7.8	18	CC	ex Tiger Cliff-07, Box Oslo-
Dania	Atg	2000	2,997	4,956	95.0	13.2	6.2	12	C	
Emilia	Atg	2006	6,264	8,348	118.4	18.4	8.2	16	Cc	
Esmeralda *	Atg	1998	2,834	4,614	89.9	13.2	6.1	12	Cc	
Greta	Ant	1999	2,999	5,000	95.0	13.2	6.2	12	Cc	
Isabella	Atg	1998	2,844	4,230	89.9	13.2	5.7	12	Cc	ex Isabella 1-01, I/a Isabella
Jana	Atg	2002	6,301	8,700	132.2	15.9	7.1	15	Cc	I/a Chandra Kirana
Julia *	Ant	2006	3,870	5,780	106.1	14.4	6.1	14	Cc	I/a Emma
Julietta	Atg	2002	7,406	10,610	142.7	18.2	7.4	14	Cc	
Katharina	Atg	2008	7,878	11,105	145.6	18.2	7.4	14	Cc	
Katja	Atg	2000	6,382	9,000	129.4	15.9	7.4	15	Cc	ex MSC Apapa-02, Katja-01
Lara *	Nld	1998	3,954	5,500	100.9	14.5	6.5	14	C	
Lavina	Atg	1995	4,015	6,250	100.0	17.1	6.4	15	Cc	ex Patricia S-08, Joanna Borchard-07, Patricia S-07, Susan Borchard-04, Patricia S-03, Prince I-02, Celtic Prince-02, Judith Borchard-01, Gracechurch Sun-97, Celtic Prince-96
Leandra	Atg	2008	7,878	11,105	145.6	18.2	7.4	14	Cc	
Maxima *	Ant	2008	7,878	10,500	145.6	18.2	7.4	14	Cc	
Nadja	Atg	2004	7,769	10,500	145.6	18.2	7.4	14	Cc	ex Hvassafell-08, Nadja-05
Nicola *	Ant	2000	2,999	5,050	95.2	13.2	6.2	12	C	
Nina *	Nld	1998	3,954	5,727	101.9	15.0	6.3	14	C	ex Melody-02, Nina-98
Olesya	Mhl	2009	6,153	9,152	117.6	19.0	7.5	12	T	
Olivia	Atg	1996	4,015	6,250	100.8	17.2	6.4	15	Cc	ex Gracechurch Harp-07, Olivia-02, Sovereign-02, Celtic Sovereign-02, Ruth Borchard-01, Gracechurch Comet-97, Celtic Sovereign-96
Orestina	Mhl	2009	6,153	9,133	117.6	19.0	7.5	12	T	
Petra	Ant	2000	2,545	3,850	88.6	12.5	5.4	13	Cc	
Rebecca	Atg	2001	7,406	10,500	142.7	18.2	7.4	14	Cc	
Rosa	Atg	2000	2,998	5,050	95.2	13.2	6.3	12	C	
Sabrina	Atg	2002	7,406	10,500	142.7	18.2	7.4	14	Cc	ex SCM Olympic-05, Sabrina-04, MSC Rades-04, Sabrina-02
Sandra	Ant	2000	2,545	3,850	88.6	12.5	5.4	13	Cc	
Serena	Atg	2004	7,767	10,534	145.6	18.2	7.4	14	Cc	
Sofia	Ant	2005	3,870	5,780	106.1	14.4	6.1	13	Cc	
Tatjana	Atg	2000	6,382	9,000	129.4	15.9	7.4	15	Cc	ex TMC Brazil-02, Tatjana-02
Thekla	Atg	2003	6,301	8,567	132.2	15.9	7.2	14	Cc	ex Suryawati-03
Uta	Atg	2007	7,878	10,500	145.6	18.2	7.4	14	Cc	
Victoria	Atg	2004	7,767	10,500	145.6	18.2	7.4	14	Cc	
Winona	Atg	2004	6,361	9,857	132.2	15.9	7.8	15	Cc	I/a Vermontborg
Xenia	Atg	2002	7,406	10,610	142.7	18.2	7.4	14	Cc	
Zara	Ant	2000	2,999	5,050	95.2	13.2	6.3	14	Cc	

Newbuildings: two 7,800 grt feeder container and six 8,044 gt 9,000 dwt tankers on order, also six large bulk carriers.
* owned by subsidiary Transship Management CV, Netherlands (formed 1999)
** managed by Olivia Schiffahrts GmbH, Germany

JSC Irtysh Shipping Co   Russia

Funnel: *White with blue crescent, small blue and red squares beneath narrow blue band.* **Hull:** *Blue with red boot-topping.* **History:** *Founded 1995 and controlled by the Government of The Russian Federation.* **Web:** *www.irsc.ru*

Name	Flag	Year	GT	DWT	Loa	Bm	Drt	Kts	Type	Remarks
Irtysh 1	Rus	1996	2,086	2,913	88.4	12.3	4.5	10	Cc	I/a Ataman Golovatiy
Irtysh 2	Rus	1996	2,086	2,913	88.4	12.3	4.4	11	C	

Name	Flag	Year	GT	DWT	Loa	Bm	Drt	Kts	Type	Remarks

Jacobsen Shipping A/S — Norway

Funnel: *White.* **Hull:** *Blue with red boot-topping.* **History:** *Founded 1995.* **Web:** *None found.*

Name	Flag	Year	GT	DWT	Loa	Bm	Drt	Kts	Type	Remarks
Hein	Bhs	1971	1,276	1,049	72.9	11.0	4.6	11	Cc	ex Inge Meyn-95, Gerda Freese-83, Magula-79

Managed by Colchester Dock Transit Co Ltd, UK

Kristian Gerhard Jebsen Skipsrederi AS — Norway

Funnel: *Black with blue wedge within white eclipse burgee flag on broad red band or * black with large white 'G'.* **Hull:** *Light grey with red boot-topping or * black with red boot-topping.* **History:** *Founded 1967.* **Web:** *www.kgjs.no; www.kgjcement.com*

Name	Flag	Year	GT	DWT	Loa	Bm	Drt	Kts	Type	Remarks
Bornholm Cement	Bhs	1976	3,227	4,323	98.3	15.8	6.3	15	Ce	
Capri Cement	Bhs	1985	7,602	13,180	121.8	20.0	8.3	13	Ce	ex El Mexicano-08, Tarjun-03, Gefion-02
Cembalo	Bhs	1973	2,583	3,252	84.9	14.7	6.7	14	Ce	ex Cembulk-93, Cembalo-90, Cembulk-89 (deep-86)
Cembay	Bhs	1997	5,997	10,103	113.3	19.4	8.0	13	Ce	(conv C-)
Cemcon	Bhs	1981	3,875	6,243	106.8	15.8	6.8	11	Ce	ex Galizano-96
Cemtrans	Bhs	1981	4,668	7,359	119.2	15.8	6.8	11	Ce	ex Universe Star-99, Cal Uno-94, Los Molin-86, Los Molinucos-86
Cyprus Cement	Bhs	2002	3,701	4,555	97.0	17.3	6.1	12	Ce	ex Chan 2-05, Bati Em-04, Prokoply Galushin-02
Falkland Cement	Bhs	1973	3,067	4,156	98.7	17.1	5.5	14	Ce	ex Cemfeed-04, Cem Feeder-04, Terceirense-97, Cement King-89
Fayal Cement	Bhs	1978	3,525	4,270	97.6	14.0	6.0	14	Ceu	ex Cem Freight-05, Cem Freighter-04, Goliath II-96, Goliath-93
Ibiza Cement	Bhs	1975	4,454	6,436	118.0	16.0	6.9	13	Ce	ex Cen Tico-04, Cem Atlantico-04, Malena-01, Carina 2-98, Koei Maru No.3-95
Iceland Cement	Bhs	1978	2,865	3,655	98.6	14.4	5.3	13	C	ex Cem Crusher-04, Kapall-97, Otter-85, Zurs-84, Agate-81, Solklint-80 (len-81, conv C-97)
Malta Cement	Bhs	1991	2,429	3,961	88.3	13.2	5.7	12	Ceu	ex Lidan-05, l/d Lidanes
Rathboyne *	Nis	1997	4,406	6,649	113.4	15.8	6.7	14	Tab	
Rathrowan *	Nis	1991	2,920	4,059	96.0	14.5	5.9	12	Tab	
Shetland Cement	Bhs	1978	1,094	1,180	62.7	11.2	3.6	10	Ceu	ex Cem Press-04, Cem Express-04, Frima Star-01, Avebe Star-97, Star-85 (conv C-86)

* managed for subsidiary Gearbulk Shipowning Ltd (founded 1991)
KJG Cement subsidiary operates 26 cement carriers up to 29,000 dwt with four newbuildings on order.
Gearbulk also operates the largest fleet of open-hatch gantry-craned bulk carriers.

AS Kristian Jebsens Rederi — Norway

Funnel: *Blue with blue 'herring-bone' band on broad white band.* **Hull:** *Dark grey or black with white 'JEBSENS', red boot-topping.* **History:** *Founded 1929.* **Web:** *www.jebsens.com*

Name	Flag	Year	GT	DWT	Loa	Bm	Drt	Kts	Type	Remarks
Clydenes	Mlt	1996	4,783	7,184	99.9	17.1	6.8	12	C	ex Arklow Bridge-05
Steines **	Atg	1978	6,355	8,139	121.0	18.0	7.6	14	Cc	ex Millennium N-05, Millennium-04, Aquatius 2-98, Aquarius-97, Boxy-89
Telnes	Mlt	1982	6,944	10,110	117.7	20.6	8.5	14	Bu	
Tertnes *	Nld	1985	7,845	11,546	129.0	20.5	8.7	13	Bu	(len/conv B-92)
Tinnes	Atg	1983	6,944	10,110	117.7	20.6	8.5	14	Bu	ex General Bonifacio-88, Tinnes-86
Tornes	Pan	1984	6,389	8,721	113.0	20.2	8.3	15	Bu	
Tradenes	Mlt	1985	6,389	8,709	113.0	20.2	8.3	15	Bu	ex Enterprise-08, Torgnes-96
Trollnes	Pan	1985	6,398	8,909	112.0	20.5	8.2	14	Bu	
Trones	Pan	1986	7,556	11,339	121.8	20.5	8.3	-	Bu	

Managed by subsidiary AJ Shipmanagement GmbH, Germany or * managed for Van Oord Groep NV, Netherlands.
** managed by HJH Shipmanagement GmbH & Co KG, Germany
Also owns or manages three larger bulk carriers with eleven other bulk carriers (24,500-33,500 dwt) on order.

Jens & Meyer Schiffahrts KG — Germany

Funnel: *Blue with white band beneath narrow black top.* **Hull:** *Blue with red boot-topping.* **History:** *Founded 1990.* **Web:** *None found.*

Name	Flag	Year	GT	DWT	Loa	Bm	Drt	Kts	Type	Remarks
Alteland	Deu	1990	5,999	4,300	114.0	17.2	5.9	15	Rop	ex Lehmann Paper-10, Alteland-08, Ortviken-96, Alteland-90
Ness	Gib	1996	3,998	3,881	100.2	15.5	5.5	14	Ccp	ex Lehmann Lifter-09, Ness-08

Jens & Waller KG — Germany

Funnel: *White with narrow black top or charterers colours.* **Hull:** *Red with red boot-topping.* **History:** *Founded 1994 as Jens & Waller GmbH & Co KG to 2008.* **Web:** *www.reederei-jenswaller.de*

Name	Flag	Year	GT	DWT	Loa	Bm	Drt	Kts	Type	Remarks
Helmut	Cyp	2006	9,961	11,202	134.4	22.5	8.7	18	CC	ex Livland-09, Helmut-06
Ruth	Cyp	2008	9,961	11,253	134.4	22.5	8.7	18	CC	
WEC Goya	Cyp	2008	9,961	11,405	134.4	22.5	8.7	18	CC	ex Wilhelm-08

Name		Flag	Year	GT	DWT	Loa	Bm	Drt	Kts	Type	Remarks

JFK Advies   Netherlands

Funnel: *White.* **Hull:** *Blue with black boot-topping.* **History:** *Founded 1993.* **Web:** *www.jfkadvies.nl*

Name	Flag	Year	GT	DWT	Loa	Bm	Drt	Kts	Type	Remarks
Lifana	Nld	1983	1,116	1,424	79.3	10.3	3.2	10	C	ex Thalassa-91

Jonsson Nova Logistics   Sweden

Funnel: *Owners colours.* **Hull:** *Blue or red with yellow or white 'JonssonNova', red boot-topping.* **History:** *Founded 1933.* **Web:** *www.jnab.se*
Operator only currently with about eight coasters on charter from various owners

JR Shipping BV   Netherlands

Funnel: *White with company symbol (red 'J' and blue 'R' separated by white seabird in flight).* **Hull:** *Blue with red boot-topping.* **History:** *Founded 1993.*
Web: *www.jrshipping.nl*

Name	Flag	Year	GT	DWT	Loa	Bm	Drt	Kts	Type	Remarks
Bermuda Islander	Nld	2001	2,937	3,725	100.0	15.9	4.9	15	CC	ex Geest Externo-07, l/a Externo
Echo	Nld	1999	10,384	12,310	149.0	22.7	7.8	19	CC	ex Selma Kalkavan-07
Eclips	Nld	1997	10,384	12,123	149.0	22.7	7.8	19	CC	ex Mukaddes Kalkavan-07
Elation	Nld	1994	5,026	6,449	117.0	18.2	6.9	16	CC	ex Conceiver-09, Gerdia-05, Gracechurch Star-02, Gerdia-96, Alum Bay-96, Gerdia-94
Electra	Nld	1995	6,326	8,002	133.0	18.9	7.3	18	CC	ex Arctic Fox-07, OOCL Narva-04, OOCL Nevskiy-01, Arctic Fox-98
Electron	Nld	1998	5,056	6,896	117.9	18.2	7.1	17	CC	ex Ingrid-07
Elevation	Nld	1994	5,026	6,449	117.0	18.2	6.9	16	Cc	ex Perceiver-09, Cervantes-05, Regia-97, Portland Bay-96, Regia-94
Elite	Nld	2005	11,662	13,382	149.1	22.5	8.7	18	CC	ex MSC Batave-07, Holland Maas Batave-05, l/a Elite (len-07)
Elusive	Nld	1995	6,326	8,001	133.0	18.9	7.3	18	CC	ex Arctic Ocean-07, Norasia Arabia-97, Arctic Ocean-96
Encounter	Nld	2004	7,642	9,335	134.7	21.5	7.1	18	CC	ex Enforcer-09
Endeavor	Nld	2005	7,642	9,168	134.7	21.5	7.1	17	CC	
Energizer	Nld	2004	7,642	9,500	134.7	21.5	7.0	18	CC	
Evidence	Nld	1997	9,191	13,100	145.6	23.3	8.8	18	CC	ex Maersk Rauma-09, Sea Nordica-05
Evolution	Nld	1996	9,191	13,100	145.6	23.3	8.8	19	CC	ex Maersk Roscoff-08, Sea Baltica-05
Expansa	Nld	2001	2,936	3,820	100.0	15.9	4.9	14	CC	ex Vento di Ponente-09, Expansa-08
OOCL St. Petersburg	Nld	2005	11,662	13,740	149.1	22.5	8.7	18	CC	l/a Elan (len-07)
Somers Isles	Atg	1991	3,815	4,654	103.5	16.2	6.1	14	Cc	ex Eldorado-06, Corvette-05, Portlink Corvette-01, CMBT Corvette-00, Corvette-94, Lloyd Scandinavia-92, Dana Corvette-91, l/a Corvette
X-Press Matterhorn	Nld	2004	7,642	9,450	134.7	21.5	7.1	18	CC	ex Enforcer-09
X-Press Monte Bianco	Nld	2005	7,642	9,146	134.7	21.5	7.1	18	CC	ex Ensemble-09
X-Press Monte Rosa	Nld	2005	7,642	9,146	134.7	21.5	7.1	18	CC	ex Endurance-09, Uppland-08, Endurance-05

Newbuildings: Two 2,998 gt, 4,450 dwt vessels on order for 2011 delivery (to be named Esprit and Estime)
Managed by JR Ship Management BV, Netherlands
Also three larger container ships

Jumbo Shipping Co SA   Switzerland

Funnel: *White with red elephant and red/blue eight-pointed star within green key outline.* **Hull:** *Blue with white 'JUMBO SHIPPING' or 'www.jumboship.nl', red boot-topping.* **History:** *Founded 1968.* **Web:** *www.jumboship.nl*

Name	Flag	Year	GT	DWT	Loa	Bm	Drt	Kts	Type	Remarks
Daniella *	Nld	1989	5,818	7,600	98.4	20.9	7.1	-	C/hl	ex Stellaprima-90
Fairlane	Nld	2001	7,971	7,051	110.5	20.5	7.7	15	C/hl	
Fairlift *	Nld	1990	6,953	7,780	100.3	21.0	7.4	13	C/hl	
Fairload *	Nld	1995	4,962	7,500	95.7	17.8	6.8	14	C/hl	
Fairmast *	Nld	1983	6,792	6,833	110.0	20.4	7.3	12	C/hl	(conv Ro/hl-86)
Jumbo Challenger *	Nld	1983	6,555	6,375	109.9	19.2	7.3	13	C/hl	(conv Ro/hl-86)
Jumbo Spirit *	Nld	1995	4,962	5,200	95.7	18.4	6.8	14	C/hl	
Jumbo Vision	Nld	2000	7,966	6,993	110.1	20.9	7.7	15	C/hl	
Stellanova *	Nld	1996	4,962	5,198	99.8	18.0	6.4	14	C/hl	
Stellaprima *	Nld	1991	6,902	7,600	100.3	21.0	7.4	13	C/hl	

* owned by subsidiary Kahn Scheepvaart BV, Netherlands (formed 1956 as Kahn's Scheepvaart en Handelsmaats NV to 1974)
Also operates four larger heavy-lift ships capable of lifting up to 1,800 tonnes.

Jungerhans Maritime Services GmbH & Co KG   Germany

Funnel: *White with narrow black top or charterers colours.* **Hull:** *Blue with red boot-topping.* **History:** *Founded 1983 as Reederei Heinrich Jungerhans to 1995 and Jungerhans & Co Reedereiverwaltung OHG to 2003.* **Web:** *www.juengerhans.de*

Name	Flag	Year	GT	DWT	Loa	Bm	Drt	Kts	Type	Remarks
Andromeda J	Deu	2006	8,273	11,052	139.6	22.2	7.4	18	CC	
Aquarius J	Atg	2004	6,454	8,508	133.6	19.4	7.4	18	CC	ex C2C Aquarius-07, l/a Aquarius J
Atair J	Gbr	2004	6,454	8,500	133.6	19.4	7.4	17	CC	
BG Felixstowe	Atg	2006	8,246	11,005	139.6	22.2	7.4	18	CC	ex Gracechurch Star-09, Katherine Borchard-07, Diana J-06
Canopus J	Atg	2004	6,901	9,238	139.9	19.4	7.3	17	CC	ex Lys Box-07, Canopus J-04
Castor J	Atg	2009	8,445	10,000	139.0	20.0	7.7	16	C/hl	

JFK Advies. Lifana. *Oliver Sesemann*

JR Shipping BV. Elusive. *Oliver Sesemann*

Name	Flag	Year	GT	DWT	Loa	Bm	Drt	Kts	Type	Remarks
Cepheus J	Gbr	2003	6,454	8,500	133.6	19.4	7.4	17	CC	
C2C Spica	Atg	2007	8,246	11,186	139.6	22.2	7.4	18	CC	l/a Spica J
Dana Gothia	Deu	2003	6,370	8,372	133.6	19.4	7.2	17	CC	ex Maersk Westland-06, l/a Corvus J
Dana Hollandia	Deu	2002	6,370	8,372	133.6	19.4	7.2	17	CC	ex Maersk Waterford-06, l/a Cetus J
Delphinus J	Atg	2009	8,445	10,000	139.0	20.0	7.7	16	C/hl	
Deneb J	Atg	2006	8,246	11,059	139.6	22.2	7.4	18	CC	ex Gracechurch Crown-09, Rachel Borchard-07, Deneb J-06
Furnas *	Prt	1998	4,450	5,555	100.6	18.8	6.7	15	CC	ex Hydra J-07, Mekong Star-02, Hydra J-00
Gracechurch Jupiter	Atg	2006	8,273	10,977	139.6	22.2	7.4	18	CC	ex Ruth Borchard-07, l/a Aldebaran J
Heinrich J	Atg	1998	5,850	6,800	119.8	20.0	6.5	17	CC	ex P&O Nedlloyd Belem-00, Heinrich J-99
Herm J	Cyp	2005	6,454	8,495	133.6	19.4	7.3	17	CC	
Industrial Cape	Atg	2001	7,252	8,034	119.8	20.0	7.1	16	C/hl	ex Industrial Comet-05, l/a Lyra J
Industrial Century	Atg	2001	7,252	8,077	119.8	20.0	7.7	16	C/hl	ex Luna J
Industrial Champ	Atg	2000	7,252	8,034	119.9	20.0	7.7	16	C/hl	ex Ursa J-01
Industrial Crescent	Atg	2002	7,252	8,097	119.8	20.0	7.7	16	C/hl	l/a Pollux J
Industrial Dart	Atg	2008	7,223	7,969	119.8	20.0	7.7	16	C/hl	ex Johann J-08
Industrial Dawn	Atg	2008	7,223	7,947	119.8	20.0	7.7	16	C/hl	l/a Orion J
Industrial Destiny	Atg	2006	7,223	8,004	119.8	20.0	7.7	16	C/hl	l/a Drago J
Industrial Diamond	Atg	2006	7,223	7,968	119.8	20.0	7.7	16	C/hl	l/a Aquila J
Industrial Dolphin	Atg	2007	7,223	7,996	119.8	20.0	7.7	16	C/hl	ex Henricus J-07
Industrial Dream	Atg	2007	7,223	7,973	119.8	20.0	7.7	16	C/hl	l/a Vela J
Industrial Eagle	Atg	2008	8,750	10,340	139.0	20.0	7.7	16	C/hl	l/d Apus J
Industrial Egret	Atg	2009	8,750	10,293	139.0	20.0	7.7	16	C/hl	l/d Bellatrix J
Michael J	Deu	1998	4,900	6,770	119.8	20.0	6.6	17	CC	ex APL Miami-07, P&O Nedlloyd Manaus-00, Michael J-99
Norma J	Atg	2007	8,246	11,178	139.6	22.2	7.4	18	CC	
Pavo J	Atg	2007	8,246	11,182	139.6	22.2	7.4	18	CC	ex Gracechurch Harp-09, Sebas-08, Pavo J-07
Pegasus J	Atg	2006	8,273	11,025	139.6	22.2	7.4	18	CC	ex Gracechurch Planet-08, Lucy Borchard-07, l/a Pegasus J
Perseus J	Cyp	2008	10,965	12,558	139.3	22.8	8.7	19	CC	ex WEC Van Eyck-09, HMS Van Eyck-08, Perseus J-08
Pictor J	Deu	2009	10,965	12,640	139.3	22.8	8.7	19	CC	
Sea Explorer **	Atg	1997	3,850	4,766	100.6	16.5	5.9	15	Cc	ex Tim-01, Cagema St. Vincent-99, l/a Tim
Stella J	Atg	2000	4,419	5,730	99.9	18.8	6.7	15	CC	ex Ibn Zuhr-04, l/a Stella J
Tucana J	Atg	2007	8,273	11,153	139.6	22.2	7.4	18	CC	

Newbuildings: About 20 container ships on order for 2010-11 delivery.
* managed by Mutualista Acoreana de Transportes Maritimos SA, Azores or ** by Sirius Schiffahrts GmbH, Germany
Also operates ten larger container ships up to 51,000 dwt.

'K' Line European Sea Highway Services GmbH — Germany

Funnel: *Red with white 'K'.* **Hull:** *Red with white 'KESS', red boot-topping.* **History:** *Parent company Kawasaki Kisen KK founded 1919. KESS 100% subsidiary formed 2003 to succeed 1990 joint venture with E.H.Harms GmbH & Co. Car Feeder Service, Germany.* **Web:** *www.klineurope.com*

Name		Flag	Year	GT	DWT	Loa	Bm	Drt	Kts	Type	Remarks
Elbe Highway		Bhs	2005	23,498	7,750	147.9	25.0	7.9	18	V	
Ems Highway	(2)	Cyp	1999	9,233	3,414	99.9	19.7	5.5	15	V	ex Feederbaltic-04
Isar Highway	(2)	Cyp	2000	9,233	3,414	99.9	19.7	5.5	16	V	ex Feederscandic-04
Main Highway *	(2)	Cyp	1998	9,233	3,347	99.9	19.5	5.5	15	V	ex Feedermate-01
Neckar Highway *	(2)	Cyp	1999	9,233	3,387	99.9	19.5	5.5	15	V	ex Feederpilot-05
Schelde Highway		Pan	1993	8,659	3,222	99.9	20.5	5.6	14	V	ex Feederchief-04
Seine Highway		Bhs	2007	23,498	8,100	147.9	25.0	7.9	18	V	
Thames Highway		Bhs	2005	23,498	7,750	147.9	25.0	7.9	18	V	
Weser Highway		Mlt	1993	8,659	3,222	99.9	20.5	5.6	14	V	ex Feedercaptain-04

managed by subsidiary Stargate Shipmanagement GmbH, Germany (founded 1999) or * managed for P D Gram & Co AS, Sweden

Rederij K&T Holland CV — Netherlands

Funnel: *White with green 7-leaf symbol between narrow green bands, narrow black top.* **Hull:** *Blue with red boot-topping.* **History:** *Founded 2001.* **Web:** *www.flagship.nl*

Name	Flag	Year	GT	DWT	Loa	Bm	Drt	Kts	Type	Remarks
Alserbach	Nld	1997	2,905	4,490	88.2	13.7	6.1	12	Cc	ex Claudia-Isabell-00
Antje K	Nld	2002	3,037	4,250	90.3	15.2	5.6	12	Cc	
Berthold K *	Nld	2008	2,967	4,442	89.9	14.4	5.8	-	C	ex Union Ruby-09
Bettina K	Nld	1994	2,449	3,713	88.0	12.8	5.5	10	Cc	
Clara K *	Nld	2007	3,057	4,285	89.9	15.2	5.6	12	Cc	
Daniel K *	Nld	2002	3,037	4,247	90.3	15.2	5.6	12	Cc	
Elisabeth K	Nld	1994	2,499	3,710	87.9	12.8	5.5	12	Cc	
Elke K	Nld	1993	2,440	3,712	87.9	12.8	5.5	11	Cc	
Geert K	Nld	2001	2,545	3,783	88.6	12.5	5.4	11	Cc	ex HC Hanna-07, Oosterstraat-04
John-Paul K	Nld	2002	3,037	4,250	90.3	15.2	5.6	13	Cc	
Juergen K *	Nld	2001	2,545	3,850	88.6	12.5	5.4	11	Cc	ex HC Ida-07, Oosterpoort-04
Karl-Jakob K	Nld	2006	3,037	4,247	90.3	15.2	5.6	12	Cc	
Klostertal	Nld	1996	5,622	7,000	108.8	17.8	7.2	12	Cc	
Marianne K	Nld	1994	2,450	3,717	88.0	12.8	5.5	10	Cc	ex Corona-00
Pitztal	Nld	1995	5,624	6,920	109.7	17.8	7.2	12	Cc	
Stefan K	Nld	1995	2,449	3,710	88.0	12.8	5.5	12	Cc	
Yvonne K *	Nld	2002	2,545	3,783	88.6	12.5	5.4	11	Cc	ex HC Freya-07, Oosterbrug-04

Rederij K&T Holland CV. Clara K. *Tom Walker*

Rederij K&T Holland CV. Klostertal. *Hans Kraijenbosch*

Konig & Cie GmbH & Co KG. Cape Egmont. *C. Lous*

Name		Flag	Year	GT	DWT	Loa	Bm	Drt	Kts	Type	Remarks
Zillertal		Nld	1996	5,602	7,142	109.7	17.8	7.2	12	Cc	

* owned by subsidiary Rufinia Beheer BV, Netherlands
All managed by Flagship Management Co BV, Netherlands or by Alstership, Hamburg.

J Kahrs Bereederungs GmbH & Co KG — Germany

Funnel: *Buff with houseflag (white with white 'K' on dark blue diamond over two dark blue bands).* **Hull:** *Blue with red boot-topping.* **History:** *Founded 2004.*
Web: *None found.*

Name	Flag	Year	GT	DWT	Loa	Bm	Drt	Kts	Type	Remarks
BG Dublin	Atg	2007	7,852	9,322	140.6	21.8	7.3	18	CC	I/a Slidur
Samskip Courier	Atg	2006	7,852	9.340	140.6	21.8	7.3	18	CC	ex Swipall-06
Samskip Express	Atg	2006	7,852	9,313	140.6	21.8	7.3	18	CC	I/d Syyndir
Skirner	Cyp	2006	7,852	9,322	140.6	21.8	7.3	18	CC	
Sleipner	Cyp	2005	7,852	9,322	140.6	21.8	7.3	18	CC	ex Halland-07

'Kevin S' GmbH & Co KG — Germany

Funnel: *White.* **Hull:** *Blue with red boot-topping.* **History:** *Founded 2000.* **Web:** *None found.*

Name	Flag	Year	GT	DWT	Loa	Bm	Drt	Kts	Type	Remarks
Kevin S	Atg	1984	1,857	2,200	80.2	12.7	4.2	10	Cc	ex Emsland-08

Klaveness Maritime Logistics AS — Norway

Funnel: *Yellow with blue 'K' on white disc and blue edged narrow white band.* **Hull:** *Grey or orange with red boot-topping.* **History:** *Founded 1946 as Gorrissen & Klaveness A/S to 1958 and as Torvald Klaveness & Co AS to 2005.* **Web:** www.klaveness.com

Name	Flag	Year	GT	DWT	Loa	Bm	Drt	Kts	Type	Remarks
Allegro *	Gib	2002	4,185	5,916	109.2	15.0	6.2	12	Cc	ex Alliance-06, Normed Gemlik-03, Alliance-02
Cemstar	Mhl	1977	4,082	6,088	113.7	15.6	6.0	14	Ce	(len-85)
Conberria	Mhl	1981	4,101	6,157	106.8	15.8	6.8	11	Ce	ex Berria-86
Euphony *	Gib	1983	3,075	3,219	92.4	15.2	4.4	12	Cc	ex Smaland-02, Anita Maria-97, Gerd Schepers-94
KCL Ballerina	Fin	1983	3,686	3,683	95.8	16.5	5.5	12	Ce	ex Envik-04
KCL Banshee	Mhl	1983	3,615	5,667	103.6	15.5	6.4	12	Ce	ex Cem Jin-04, Kurohime Maru-03
Ostanvik	Swe	1974	4,013	4,940	107.1	16.1	6.0	14	Ce	
Sunnanvik	Swe	1978	7,454	9,060	124.0	18.0	7.7	14	Ce	
Vastanvik	Swe	1966	2,256	3,282	90.5	13.0	5.8	-	Ce	

* owned for Scandinavian Bulkers KS formed jointly with RS Platou Finans AS and managed by Q-Shipping BV qv.
Also larger cement carriers and panamax bulk carriers.

Klingenberg Bereederungs & Befrachtungs OHG — Germany

Funnel: *White with houseflag (green 'A' and black 'K').* **Hull:** *Dark blue with red boot-topping.* **History:** *Founded 1906 as Albert Hauschild GmbH & Co and acquired 1966 as Armin Klingenberg Schiffahrts KG to 1997.* **Web:** www.klicon.com

Name	Flag	Year	GT	DWT	Loa	Bm	Drt	Kts	Type	Remarks
Catalina	Atg	2009	6,450	8,600	123.2	20.8	7.1	17	Cc	
Celina	Atg	2002	6,409	8,350	123.1	20.8	6.9	17	Cc	ex CMA CGM Caucase-09, CMA CGM Alger-06, Celina-02
FAS Dammam	Atg	1997	9,068	11,116	131.3	22.8	8.7	17	Cc	ex Jessilena-00
Gina	Atg	2008	6,450	8,600	123.2	20.8	7.1	17	Cc	
Janina	Atg	2002	6,409	8,350	123.1	20.8	6.9	17	Cc	
Karina	Atg	1997	9,068	11,116	131.5	22.8	8.7	17	Cc	ex Dania Carina-01, Karina-01
Kiara	Atg	2009	6,450	8,600	123.2	20.8	7.1	17	Cc	
Marina	Atg	2003	6,409	8,192	123.1	20.8	6.9	17	Cc	
Nadja	Atg	2003	6,409	8,198	123.1	20.8	6.9	17	Cc	
Nicola	Atg	1999	9,068	11,030	131.4	22.8	8.7	17	Cc	ex Sinar Medan-02, Nicola-99
Viola	Atg	2008	6,479	8,152	123.2	20.8	7.1	17	Cc	

Klip Marine Shipmanagement Ltd — Estonia

Funnel: *Blue with broad white band or white with narrow pale blue top.* **Hull:** *Blue, green or red with red or black boot-topping.* **History:** *Founded 1990 as Baltic Group International Shipping Ltd to 2003 and as Klip Marine Ltd to 2007.* **Web:** www.klipmarine.ee

Name	Flag	Year	GT	DWT	Loa	Bm	Drt	Kts	Type	Remarks
Adele	Atg	1991	2,481	3,269	87.5	13.0	5.0	12	Cc	ex Adele J-05, MF Mare-99, Intermodal Mare-96, Trident Star-95, Adele J-93, Medeur Secondo-93, Adele J-92
Belland	Mlt	1986	2,673	2,973	88.0	13.0	4.4	11	Cc	ex Belgrad-09, Atria-04, Arosita-02, Kea-00, Emsbroker-00, Atria-99
Carina	Atg	1990	2,463	3,200	87.4	13.0	5.1	12	Cc	ex Carina J-05, Coastal Breeze-00, Hanni J-98, Herm J-97, Cari-Star-94, Primo-92, Medeur Primo-92, Rhein Carrier-91, Herm J-90
Cool Aster	Mlt	1984	3,955	5,250	108.5	16.3	7.4	16	R	ex Nyantic-03
Eeland	Mlt	1985	2,932	3,050	95.7	14.4	4.3	12	Cc	ex Eeva-09, Midgard-05, Artemis-98, Marlen-L-92
Kadri	Mlt	1995	3,117	4,506	99.9	13.6	5.6	13	C	ex Flinterdam-06, I/a Flinterzijl
Kaie	Mlt	1990	2,374	4,161	88.3	13.2	5.7	12	C	ex Eversmeer-05, Cady-97, Skagern-93
Kaili	Mlt	1996	3,117	4,512	99.4	13.6	5.2	13	Cc	ex Flinterzijl-06
Kaja	Mlt	1981	3,149	4,500	93.3	15.5	5.8	-	Cc	ex Frey-08, Egypt Star-04, Phoenix-00, Prime Venture II-00, Concord-93, ECL Concord-92, Concord-91, Australian Eagle II-83, Concord-83, Eastmed Queen-82, Concord-81
Katre	Mlt	1991	2,497	4,173	88.3	13.2	5.4	12	Cc	ex Apollo Bear-07, Lydia B-04, Venlo-97

Name	Flag	Year	GT	DWT	Loa	Bm	Drt	Kts	Type	Remarks
Mosvik	Atg	1987	2,236	2,850	82.3	12.6	4.9	11	Cc	ex Star Vita-07, Pia-05
Nedland	Mlt	1987	2,673	3,004	88.0	13.0	4.7	11	Cc	ex Nedgard-09, Dyggve-01, Domaide-95, Petuja-94
Sydland	Atg	1981	2,225	2,574	80.8	13.4	5.1	13	Cc	ex Sydgard-04, Verena-93, Ina Lehmann-89,
Univoyager	Mlt	2008	2,979	4,500	90.0	15.3	5.5	-	C	ex Ozcan Atasoy-08
Uniwind	Mlt	1990	3,125	3,070	89.1	16.2	4.8	14	Cc	ex Ranfoss-08, Effort-04, Jana-04, Somers Isles-02, Jana-99

Knuppel Schiffahrts GmbH & Co KG   Germany

Funnel: *White or charterers colours.* **Hull:** *Blue or * red with red boot-topping.* **History:** *Founded 1971 as Hans-Hermann Knuppel to 1997.* **Web:** *www.kk.ship.de*

K-Breeze	Atg	2008	8,246	11,182	139.6	22.2	7.4	-	CC	
K-Ocean	Gbr	1998	6,362	7,223	121.4	18.5	6.7	16	CC	ex City of Oporto-08, K-Ocean-04, Alk-03
K-River	Atg	1997	6,362	7,225	121.4	18.5	6.7	16	CC	ex Mary Ann-07, CTE Valencia-98
K-Stream	Gbr	1997	6,362	7,223	121.4	18.5	6.7	16	CC	ex Jane-06, Karin-98
K-Water	Atg	2007	6,930	8,200	131.5	19.2	7.5	-	CC	
K-Wave	Gbr	2007	7,170	8,200	131.5	19.2	7.5	-	CC	
Seaboard Caribe	Atg	2008	8,246	11,190	139.6	22.2	7.4	-	CC	ex K-Storm-09

Operated by subsidiary K & K Schiffahrts GmbH & Co KG, Germany formed jointly with Hans Kruger GmbH.
Also owns one larger container ship.

Knutsen OAS Shipping AS   Norway

Molo Sun AS
Funnel: *White with white 'M' on red square.* **Hull:** *Blue with red boot-topping.* **History:** *Parent founded 1896 as Knut Knutsen OAS to 1982 and subsidiary formed in 2007.* **Web:** www.knutsenoas.com

Molo Sun	Nor	1985	1,477	1,770	77.4	11.4	3.8	11	C	ex Anja Anna-90, Butjadingen-88 (len-92)
Molo Trader	Nor	1987	1,392	1,570	72.0	11.5	3.6	11	Cc	ex Myrtind-08, Performer-05, Piano-99, Sullberg-88

Managed by subsidiary Knutsen Management AS, Norway (formed 2006)

Reederei Ernst Komrowski   Germany

Funnel: *White with white diamond at centre of dark blue/red diagonally quartered flag or charterers colours.* **Hull:** *Black with red boot-topping or charterers colours.* **History:** *Founded 1953 as Ernst Komrowski Reederei GmbH to 1938.* **Web:** www.komrowski.net

BBC Karan	Gbr	1998	8,811	7,331	126.5	20.3	6.7	14	Ro	ex BBC Arctic-07, Scan Arctic-07, Rickmers Arctic-06, Scan Arctic-06
BBC Kelan	Gbr	1998	8,811	7,493	126.5	20.3	6.7	14	Ro	ex Rio Kelan-07, Scan Bothnia-07
BBC Konan	Gbr	2000	8,831	7,184	126.8	20.0	6.7	14	Ro	ex BBC Finlandia-07, Rickmers Finlandia-06, Scan Finlandia-05
BBC Kusan	Gbr	2000	8,831	7,195	126.9	20.0	6.7	14	Ro	ex BBC Germania-07, Rickmers Germania-06, Scan Germania-05
Mangan	Ant	2005	6,474	8,494	133.6	19.4	7.4	17	CC	ex Rogaland-09, Mangan-05, I/a Aries J
Taipan	Deu	2007	10,965	12,612	140.6	22.8	8.7	19	CC	
Tetuan	Gbr	2003	6,434	8,496	133.6	19.4	7.4	17	CC	ex Varmland-09, Tetuan-05, Columba J-04
Tongan	Deu	2007	10,965	12,612	140.6	22.8	8.7	19	CC	

Also owns ten larger container ships and nine large bulk carriers.

Konig & Cie GmbH & Co KG   Germany

Funnel: *Charterers colours.* **Hull:** *Red with red boot-topping.* **History:** *Founded 1999.* **Web:** www.emissionshaus.com

Agaman *	Lbr	1999	4,450	5,562	100.6	18.8	6.7	15	CC	ex Sea Cherokee-02, Agaman-02
Cape Egmont	Mhl	2003	8,351	12,761	127.2	20.4	8.5	13	Tch	I/a Samho Family
Cape Esmeralda	Mhl	2004	8,351	12,842	127.2	20.4	8.5	13	Tch	

*managed by Columbia Shipmanagement Ltd or * by Komrowski Befrachtungskontor GmbH & Co*

Reederei Konig GmbH   Germany

Funnel: *Green with ship symbol on white disc.* **Hull:** *Dark grey with red boot-topping.* **History:** *Founded 2008.* **Web:** *None found.*

Marion K	Atg	1981	1,127	1,663	69.4	10.8	4.3	11	C	ex Lore D-08, Niquel-01, Angelique V-94
Solveig K	Atg	1978	1,678	2,775	72.3	12.8	4.4	12	Cc	ex Minchen D-08, Schulau-99

C Koole Tanktransport BV   Netherlands

Funnel: *Yellow/orange or white with white 'KOOLE' above red symbol/band on yellow/orange square.* **Hull:** *Light grey with red boot-topping.* **History:** *Founded 1992.* **Web:** www.koole.com

Star Aruba	Nld	1972	1,151	1,531	71.0	10.4	3.7	12	T	ex Kropelin-92 (conv C-93)
Star Bonaire	Nld	1997	2,257	3,420	90.1	12.0	5.1	12	T	
Star Curacao	Nld	2008	3,578	4,400	109.6	13.6	5.5	-	T	

Name	Flag	Year	GT	DWT	Loa	Bm	Drt	Kts	Type	Remarks

Kopervik Shipping AS   Norway

Funnel: *White with black 'K'.* **Hull:** *Black, dark blue or * red with red boot-topping.* **History:** *Founded 1994.* **Web:** *www.kopervikshipping.no*

Name	Flag	Year	GT	DWT	Loa	Bm	Drt	Kts	Type	Remarks
Fri Lake	Bhs	1999	2,218	3,640	89.4	12.5	5.2	12	Cc	ex Helena-06
Fri Moon *	Ant	2001	1,599	2,300	88.0	11.4	3.7	10	C	ex Reest-07, I/a Lennard
Fri Ocean	Bhs	2000	2,218	3,400	89.4	12.5	5.2	12	Cc	ex Vera-06
Fri Sea	Bhs	2001	2,601	3,330	91.3	14.0	4.9	13	Cc	ex Union Mars-09, Esprit-04
Fri Sky	Bhs	1981	1,511	1,766	82.5	11.3	3.7	10	Cc	ex Hester-02, Javazee-98, Anga-96, Vineta-94
Fri Star	Bhs	1981	1,499	1,773	82.5	11.4	3.5	10	Cc	ex Pax-01
Fri Stream	Bhs	1995	2,051	3,270	90.0	12.5	4.6	11	Cc	ex Storm-05, Tertius-01
Fri Sun	Ant	1980	1,513	1,551	82.5	11.4	4.2	10	Cc	ex Fensfjord-05, Deo Volente-99, Elbstrand-95
Fri Tide	Bhs	2000	2,218	3,400	89.4	12.5	5.2	12	Cc	ex Claudia-06
Fri Wave *	Ant	1990	2,190	3,283	82.5	12.6	5.3	10	Cc	ex Emily-07
Frifjord	Bhs	1986	1,212	1,131	63.0	11.3	3.4	10	Cc	ex Eros-97

Gerd Koppelmann   Germany

Funnel: *White with narrow black top.* **Hull:** *White with with red boot-topping.* **History:** *Founded 1955.* **Web:** *None found.*

Name	Flag	Year	GT	DWT	Loa	Bm	Drt	Kts	Type	Remarks
Tiznit	Deu	1997	7,981	11,401	138.1	21.8	8.4	19	CC	ex Concordia-07, Chiquita Las Americas-00, I/a Concordia

Reederei Jorg Kopping   Germany

Funnel: *Dark blue.* **Hull:** *Dark blue with red boot-topping.* **History:** *Founded 1984 as Jorg Kopping to 1996, then Jorg Kopping Shipping Co to 1997.*
Web: *www.kship.de*

Name	Flag	Year	GT	DWT	Loa	Bm	Drt	Kts	Type	Remarks
Geest Trader	Atg	1995	2,899	3,950	99.2	16.4	4.9	14	CC	ex Limburg-95
JSV Yaiza	Atg	2005	7,852	9,322	140.6	21.8	7.3	18	CC	ex Vohburg-09, Geestdijk-08
Lantau Bay	Atg	2007	9,610	12,829	142.7	22.6	8.2	18	CC	
Lantau Beach	Atg	2007	9,610	12,829	142.7	22.6	8.2	18	CC	
Lantau Bee	Atg	2008	9,610	12,829	142.7	22.6	8.2	18	CC	
Lantau Breeze	Atg	2008	9,610	12,780	142.7	22.6	8.2	18	CC	
Lantau Bride	Atg	2008	9,610	12,821	142.7	22.6	8.2	18	CC	
Lantau Bridge	Atg	2008	9,610	12,774	142.7	22.6	8.2	18	CC	
Neuburg	Cyp	2004	7,852	9,322	140.6	21.8	7.3	18	CC	ex Geeststroom-08

Also manages two larger container ships.

Rederij C Kornet & Zonen BV   Netherlands

Funnel: *Yellow with red 'K' inside green 'C'.* **Hull:** *Dark blue or green with red or black boot-topping.* **History:** *Founded 1938.* **Web:** *www.rederijkornet.nl*

Name	Flag	Year	GT	DWT	Loa	Bm	Drt	Kts	Type	Remarks
Albertus F **	Nld	2007	1,862	2,600	87.3	11.4	4.3	-	C	ex Eems Stream-08
DC Merwestone	Nld	1974	2,373	5,011	90.7	13.6	6.3	10	C	ex Sereen-06, Scorpio-01, Proton-98, Swallow-80 (rblt/len-01)
Eems River *	Nld	2010	2,600	3,500	-	-	-	-	C	
Eems Rover *	Nld	2009	2,600	3,500	-	-	-	-	C	
Eems Servant	Nld	2009	1,862	2,600	87.3	11.4	4.3	10	C	
Eems Sky *	Nld	2008	1,862	2,600	87.3	11.4	4.3	10	C	
Eems Solar *	Nld	2009	1,862	2,600	87.3	11.4	4.3	10	C	
Eems Spirit *	Nld	2010	1,862	2,600	87.3	11.4	4.3	10	C	I/a Maria
Eems Space *	Nld	2009	1,862	2,600	87.3	11.4	4.3	10	C	
Eems Spring *	Nld	2010	1,862	2,600	87.3	11.4	4.3	10	C	
Eems Sprinter *	Nld	2007	1,862	2,620	87.3	11.4	4.3	10	C	ex Christiaan-07
Eems Star *	Nld	2008	1,862	2,600	87.3	11.4	4.3	10	C	
Eems Stream	Nld	2010	1,862	2,600	87.3	11.4	4.3	10	C	I/a Gersom
Eems Sun	Nld	2009	1,862	2,600	87.3	11.4	4.3	10	C	
Eemslift Christiaan	Nld	1998	3,862	4,979	100.7	16.4	6.3	16	Cc	ex BBC Islander-08, Islander-07, Seaboard Endeavour-05, Delta-99
Ingunn †	Nld	2001	2,999	5,004	95.2	13.2	6.2	12	C	ex Merwezoon-07
Jetstream	Nld	2010	2,999	4,500	-	-	-	-	C	
Sereno	Nld	1991	3,828	4,452	103.5	16.0	6.1	15	Cc	ex Passaden-07, ECL Captain-92, Passaden-91
Soave	Nld	1991	3,828	4,452	103.5	16.0	6.1	15	Cc	ex Smaragden-07

* managed by Amasus Shipping BV or ** by Wagenborg Shipping BV qv
† on charter to Carisbrooke Shipping Ltd qv

Krabbeskars Rederi AB   Sweden

Funnel: *Dark blue with red/white shield emblem on broad white band.* **Hull:** *dark blue with red boot-topping.* **History:** *Founded 1997.* **Web:** *None found.*

Name	Flag	Year	GT	DWT	Loa	Bm	Drt	Kts	Type	Remarks
Onyx	Atg	1996	1,476	2,542	76.7	12.2	5.1	12	T	ex Jette Theresa-07, Ilona Theresa-02, Densa Gundem

OY Kraftline AB   Finland

Funnel: *Dark blue with broad white band.* **Hull:** *Green with black boot-topping.* **History:** *Not confirmed.* **Web:** *None found.*

Name	Flag	Year	GT	DWT	Loa	Bm	Drt	Kts	Type	Remarks
Alholmen	Fin	1984	2,580	3,171	87.0	13.2	6.0	14	Cc	ex Ahlholmen-07, Mangen-07

Name	Flag	Year	GT	DWT	Loa	Bm	Drt	Kts	Type	Remarks

Krey Schiffahrts GmbH   Germany

Funnel: *Cream with black top or charterers colours.* **Hull:** *Blue or dark green with red boot-topping.* **History:** *Founded 1990.* **Web:** *www.krey-schiffahrt.de*

Name	Flag	Year	GT	DWT	Loa	Bm	Drt	Kts	Type	Remarks
Addi L	Gib	1995	2,876	4,557	88.2	13.6	6.1	11	Cc	ex Blinke-97, Apis-96
BBC Ontario	Cyp	2004	9,611	12,711	138.1	21.0	8.0	15	C/hl	
Countess Anna	Atg	1994	1,589	2,684	82.5	11.6	4.8	10	Cc	ex Wiebke K-05
Graf Uko	Atg	1991	2,481	2,900	87.5	13.0	5.1	12	Cc	ex Nordstrand-05, MF Malta-01, Intermodal Malta-96, Wannsee-94, Zelo-94, Wannsee-94, Medeur Terzo-92, Wannsee-92
Nordkap	Gib	2000	6,204	8,275	107.8	18.2	7.8	14	Cc	ex Normed Hamburg-08, Flinternoord-05, Nordkap-04
SCM Athina	Atg	2000	6,170	7,734	107.8	18.2	7.8	14	Cc	ex BBC Atlantic-03, Sudkap-01
SCM Elpida	Atg	2000	6,170	7,725	107.8	18.2	7.8	14	Cc	ex BBC Pacific-05, Westkap-02

Uwe Horst Kruse   Germany

Funnel: *White.* **Hull:** *Blue with red boot-topping.* **History:** *Founded 1989.* **Web:** *None found.*

Name	Flag	Year	GT	DWT	Loa	Bm	Drt	Kts	Type	Remarks
Tista	Gib	1979	2,096	2,240	83.8	12.8	4.4	12	Cc	ex Lys Vista-00, Tista-98

KTM Shipping AS   Norway

Funnel: *White.* **Hull:** *Blue with red boot-topping.* **History:** *Founded 1981 as Karmoy AS.* **Web:** *www.ktm.no*

Name	Flag	Year	GT	DWT	Loa	Bm	Drt	Kts	Type	Remarks
Carten Elina	Pan	1981	2,876	3,319	94.7	13.8	5.1	12	C	ex Lysholmen-03 (len-94)
Carten Maria	Pan	1985	3,176	3,040	85.0	16.0	5.9	14	Ccp	ex Lyshav-09

Kystfrakt AS   Norway

Funnel: *Buff.* **Hull:** *Black with red boot-topping.* **History:** *Not confirmed.* **Web:** *None found.*

Name	Flag	Year	GT	DWT	Loa	Bm	Drt	Kts	Type	Remarks
Baroy	Vct	1974	1,926	1,118	76.0	13.5	3.5	13	Cp	ex Lena-01, Nour Han-95, Katia-93, Burfell-93, Hekla-92, Vela-84, I/a Polstraum

Oy Langh Ship AB   Finland

Funnel: *White with white triangle on red square.* **Hull:** *Red with black boot-topping.* **History:** *Founded 1983.* **Web:** *www.langh.fi*

Name	Flag	Year	GT	DWT	Loa	Bm	Drt	Kts	Type	Remarks
Aila	Fin	2007	9,131	11,497	141.2	21.3	8.6	17	CC	
Hjordis	Fin	1996	5,239	6,526	119.9	18.1	6.8	17	Cc	
Laura	Fin	1996	5,239	6,535	119.9	18.1	6.8	17	Cc	
Linda	Fin	2007	9,131	11,487	141.2	21.3	8.6	17	CC	
Marjatta	Fin	1996	5,239	6,410	119.9	18.2	6.8	17	Cc	

Lauranne Shipping BV   Netherlands

Funnel: *White with red square.* **Hull:** *Dark blue with black boot-topping.* **History:** *Founded 1996.* **Web:** *www.lauranne-shipping.com*

Name	Flag	Year	GT	DWT	Loa	Bm	Drt	Kts	Type	Remarks
Laura-H		Gib	2002	2,962	5,413	109.9	14.0	5.7	13	T	
LS Anne *		Gib	2008	3,992	5,757	105.5	16.8	6.3	-	T	
LS Christine	(2)	Gib	2007	5,729	8,400	125.4	18.0	7.1	14	Tch	
LS Concorde		Gib	2003	3,057	4,692	99.9	15.0	6.0	14	Tch	ex Concorde-06, I/a Haci Habib Baynak
LS Eva		Gib	2007	3,264	4,726	99.9	15.0	6.1	14	Tch	
LS Jamie		Gib	2009	3,992	5,756	105.5	16.8	6.3	-	T	

* managed for TTS - Tanker Transport Services BV, Netherlands (founded 1965 – www.ttstankers.com)
Also owns one larger product tanker.

J Lauritzen A/S   Denmark

Lauritzen Kosan A/S

Funnel: *Yellow with blue 'K' on yellow diamond on broad blue band.* **Hull:** *Yellow with blue 'KOSAN' or white 'LPG', red boot-topping or † red, black or red boot-topping.* **History:** *Parent founded 1884 and subsidiary formed 1953 as Tholstrup Brodene & Co, amalgamating with Trans-Kosan AS in 1976 and acquired in 1989 as Lauritzen Kosan Tankers AS to 1999.* **Web:** *www.lauritzenkosan.com*

Name	Flag	Year	GT	DWT	Loa	Bm	Drt	Kts	Type	Remarks
Alexandra Kosan	Iom	2008	7,465	8,500	115.0	18.6	8.7	-	Lpg	
Anette Kosan †	Pan	2001	3,435	3,844	97.7	16.0	5.4	13	Lpg	ex Qem Star-04
Bente Kosan †	Sgp	1998	3,540	2,854	99.9	16.2	4.8	13	Lpg	ex Treasure Gas-05
Brit Kosan †	Sgp	1999	3,433	3,359	95.7	16.0	5.0	13	Lpg	ex Antares Gas-04
Charlotte Kosan †	Pan	2003	3,435	3,857	97.7	16.0	5.4	13	Lpg	ex Luna Gas-04
Ellen Kosan †	Sgp	1996	3,050	3,163	96.6	15.0	5.1	13	Lpg	ex Lady Anne-06, Pegasus Gas-04
Gitta Kosan #	Dis	1990	4,086	4,828	98.3	16.2	6.7	14	Lpg	
Greta Kosan #	Dis	1990	4,086	4,811	98.3	16.2	6.7	14	Lpg	
Helena Kosan	Iom	2007	7,465	8,500	115.0	18.6	8.7	-	Lpg	
Isabella Kosan	Iom	2007	7,465	8,500	115.0	18.6	8.7	-	Lpg	
Lady Mathilde **	Pan	2001	3,435	3,856	97.7	16.0	5.4	13	Lpg	ex Lynx Gas-04
Leonora Kosan	Iom	2009	7,465	8,545	115.0	18.5	8.7	-	Lpg	
Lizzie Kosan †	Sgp	1996	3,540	3,695	99.9	16.2	5.5	13	Lpg	ex Lady Fatime-06, Hanjin Yingkou-04

Uwe Horst Kruse. Tista. *David Walker*

Oy Langh Ship AB. Aila. *Hans Kraijenbosch*

Lauranne Shipping BV. LS Eva. *Allan Ryszka Onions*

Reederei Lehmann. Karin Lehmann. *N. Kemps*

Name	Flag	Year	GT	DWT	Loa	Bm	Drt	Kts	Type	Remarks
Marianna Kosan	Iom	2008	7,465	8,500	115.0	18.6	8.7	-	Lpg	
Ocean Primero ‡	Gbr	1993	3,096	3,567	101.5	14.0	5.1	12	Lpg	ex Coral Acropora-06 (len-96)
Ocean Primus ‡	Gbr	1992	3,693	4,444	99.4	15.0	6.4	15	Lpg	ex Gerda Kosan-06, Tarquin Mariner-02
Ocean Prism ‡	Gbr	2007	7,465	8,500	115.0	18.9	8.7	-	Lpg	
Ocean Prize ‡	Iom	2008	7,465	8,500	115.0	18.6	8.7	-	Lpg	
Sophia Kosan *	Sgp	2008	9,175	10,343	120.4	19.8	8.8	-	Lpg	
Stella Kosan *	Sgp	2008	9,175	10,316	120.4	19.8	8.8	-	Lpg	
Stina Kosan *	Sgp	2008	9,175	10,348	120.4	19.8	8.8	-	Lpg	
Tanja Kosan	Iom	2004	4,693	5,950	107.9	15.8	7.3	15	Lpg	ex Tarquin Vale-02
Telma Kosan	Lbr	1994	4,317	5,771	105.4	15.7	7.0	15	Lpg	ex Tarquin Ranger-02
Tenna Kosan	Iom	1998	5,103	6,130	112.6	16.4	7.2	16	Lpg	
Tessa Kosan	Iom	1999	5,103	6,130	112.6	16.0	8.3	16	Lpg	
Tilda Kosan	Iom	1999	4,693	5,992	107.9	15.7	7.3	16	Lpg	ex Tarquin Dell-02
Victoria Kosan	Iom	2009	7,465	8,556	115.0	18.5	8.7	-	Lpg	

Newbuildings: six 4,000dwt Lpg tankers due for 2010-11 delivery
* owned by LKT Gas Carriers, Singapore (formed 2008 jointly with Tailwind AS)
** owned by Unigas Kosan Ltd, Hong Kong (formed 2002 jointly with CMB subsidiary Exmar NV as Exmar Kosan Ltd to 2005)
† managed by Star Management Associates, Japan
‡ managed for Allocean Ltd, UK or # for Viken Marine AS subsidiary of Viken Shipping AS, Norway.

Gasnaval SA, Spain

Funnel: *Black with large red 'G' on red-edged large white disc.* **Hull:** *Black with white 'GASNAVAL', red boot-topping.* **History:** *Founded 1981.* **Web:** *As above.*

Name	Flag	Year	GT	DWT	Loa	Bm	Drt	Kts	Type
Becquer	Esp	1987	2,796	3,659	84.6	14.5	6.6	14	Lpg
Berceo	Pmd	1991	4,691	4,380	105.0	15.1	6.1	13	Lpg
Gongora	Esp	1987	2,796	3,659	84.6	14.5	6.6	14	Lpg
Cervantes	Pmd	1992	3,669	4,630	97.6	15.3	6.8	15	Lpg

Managed by Lauritzen Kosan A/S, Denmark.
Also see Eitzen Group

Reederei M Lauterjung GmbH — Germany

Funnel: *Blue with yellow half sun above narrow pale wavy line.* **Hull:** *Blue with red boot-topping.* **History:** *Founded 1983.* **Web:** *www.sunship.de*

Name	Flag	Year	GT	DWT	Loa	Bm	Drt	Kts	Type
Aarhus	Atg	2010	4,600	5,670	107.0	16.6	6.6	14	Cc
Arion	Atg	1999	1,846	2,500	89.7	11.7	4.5	12	Cc
Borkum	Atg	2010	4,600	5,670	107.0	16.6	6.6	14	Cc
Copenhagen	Atg	2010	4,600	5,670	107.0	16.6	6.6	14	Cc
Delia	Atg	2000	1,846	2,500	89.7	11.7	4.5	12	Cc
Ebeltoft	Atg	2010	4,600	5,670	107.0	16.6	6.6	14	Cc
Esjberg	Atg	2010	4,600	5,670	107.0	16.6	6.6	14	Cc
Hestia	Atg	2000	1,846	2,500	89.7	11.7	4.5	12	Cc
Nestor	Atg	2000	1,846	2,500	89.7	11.7	4.5	12	Cc
Thebe	Atg	2000	1,846	2,500	89.7	11.7	4.5	12	Cc
Theseus	Atg	2000	1,846	2,500	89.7	11.7	4.5	12	Cc
Zeus	Atg	2000	1,846	2,500	89.7	11.7	4.5	12	Cc

Newbuilkdings: Four further 5,670 dwt vessels on order for 2011 delivery.
Owned or managed by subsidiary Sunship Schiffahrtskontor KG (founded 1979)
Also manages three 'Great Lakes' bulk carriers, two large open-hatch bulk carriers, seven 2500 teu container ships and two car carriers.

Reederei Lehmann — Germany

Funnel: *Yellow with red castle on blue edged white disc.* **Hull:** *Blue or grey with red or black boot-topping.* **History:** *Parent founded 1926 and ship-owners since 1950s.* **Web:** *www.hans-lehmann.de*

Name	Flag	Year	GT	DWT	Loa	Bm	Drt	Kts	Type	Remarks
Anna Lehmann	Atg	2000	2,820	4,111	89.7	13.6	5.7	13	Cc	
Botnia *	Atg	2008	5,285	8,300	120.8	17.6	6.3	-	C	ex Lehmann Timber-09
Edgar Lehmann	Gib	2007	8,491	12,000	140.3	20.0	7.8	13	Cc	
Hans Lehmann	Atg	2007	8,555	12,000	140.3	20.0	7.8	13	Cc	
Heike Lehmann	Atg	1985	2,564	3,070	87.9	12.8	4.5	11	C	
Karin Lehmann	Atg	2000	2,820	4,071	89.7	13.6	5.7	13	Cc	
Marie Lehmann	Deu	1987	2,642	3,017	88.0	13.0	4.4	11	Cc	
Siegfried Lehmann *	Mmr	1980	2,225	2,570	80.8	13.4	5.0	13	Cc	

*managed by KW-Bereederungs GmbH (www.kw-shipping.com) or * by Uniteam Marine Ltd, Cyprus (www.uniteammarine.com)*

Liepajas Juras Birojs — Latvia

Funnel: *Black or * white with dark blue band.* **Hull:** *Dark blue with red boot-topping.* **History:** *Founded 2000.* **Web:** *www.ljbirojs.lv*

Name	Flag	Year	GT	DWT	Loa	Bm	Drt	Kts	Type	Remarks
Bluebird	Vct	1982	1,115	1,688	67.4	11.3	4.1	10	Cc	ex Alice-95, Alila-92, Peacock Venture-88
Liepajas *	Vct	1990	2,030	3,080	74.7	12.7	6.0	12	Cu	
Sava Ocean *	Vct	1993	2,026	3,080	74.7	12.7	6.0	11	Cc	

* operated by subsidiary Liepajas Shipping Co SIA (formed 2006)

Rederi Ab Lillgaard   Finland

Funnel: *White with overlapping blue and red diamond outlines on yellow diamond interrupting blue band, blue top.* **Hull:** *Dark blue, green or white with red boot-topping.* **History:** *Founded 1974.* **Web:** *www.lillgaard.aland.fi*

Name		Flag	Year	GT	DWT	Loa	Bm	Drt	Kts	Type	Remarks
Breant		Fin	1979	5,197	3,328	110.5	16.5	4.6	12	Ro	(NE-88)
Christa		Fin	1983	2,795	2,852	95.6	13.5	4.4	11	Cc	
Explorer *		Nld	1986	7,580	7,875	123.4	20.0	7.4	14	Ccp	ex Kent Explorer-09, Normed Istanbul-03, Weser-Harbour-03, Abitibi Orinoco-01, Weser-Harbour-88, Scol Venture-87, Weser-Harbour-86
Fjardvagen	(2)	Fin	1972	6,040	2,607	109.5	20.4	4.9	17	Ro	ex Norman Commodore-95, Pride of Portsmouth-91, Mads Mols-89, Mols Trader-87, Merchant Trader-87, Sir Lamorak-86, Lakespan Ontario-83, Lady Catherine-81, Lune Bridge-80, Anu-80, Norcliff-74, Anu-73
Forte *		Nld	1989	3,998	4,001	90.8	15.9	6.4	15	Rop	
Hoburgen	(2)	Bhs	1985	9,080	4,818	121.5	21.0	5.3	14	Ro	ex Dart 5-00, Perseus-96, Bazias 5-95, I/a Balder Ra
Largo *		Nld	1989	3,998	4,001	90.8	15.9	6.4	15	Rop	
Tanja **		Nld	1986	3,801	4,636	103.5	16.2	5.6	14	CC	ex Kate-96, Containerships II-90, I/a Kate
Trader *		Nld	1986	7,580	7,879	123.0	20.0	7.4	14	Ccp	ex Kent Trader-09, Normed Antwerp-03, Abitibi Claiborne-01, Weser-Importer-88, Scol Enterprise-87, Weser-Importer-86

* managed by BV Kustvaartbedrijf Moermann or ** by Holwerda Shipmanagement BV, both Netherlands.

Limarita UAB   Lithuania

Funnel: *Dark blue.* **Hull:** *Dark blue with red boot-topping.* **History:** *Founded 2005.* **Web:** *www.forsa.lt*

Name	Flag	Year	GT	DWT	Loa	Bm	Drt	Kts	Type	Remarks
Tanja	Atg	1989	2,190	2,735	82.5	12.6	4.7	11	Cc	
Verona	Atg	1988	2,184	2,735	82.0	12.7	4.7	11	Cc	ex Martyna-05, Marjesco-04, Unitas H-96

Managed by UAB Juru Agentura 'Forsa', Lithuania (founded 1993)

Lithuanian Shipping Co   Lithuania

Funnel: *White with yellow 'L' on red-edged dark green band below black top.* **Hull:** *Black or blue with red or green boot-topping.* **History:** *Founded 1991, reorganised 2001 and currently 56% government owned.* **Web:** *www.ljl.lt*

Name	Flag	Year	GT	DWT	Loa	Bm	Drt	Kts	Type	Remarks
Akvile	Ltu	1997	3,893	5,600	102.8	15.9	6.1	13	Cc	
Alka	Ltu	1994	7,085	7,365	132.8	19.9	6.9	15	Cc	ex Onego Breeze-05, Sea Spirit-04, Good Most-98, Zeya-94
Asta	Ltu	1996	3,891	5,805	102.8	15.9	6.6	13	Cc	
Audre	Ltu	1997	3,893	6,085	102.8	15.9	6.6	13	Cc	
Daina	Ltu	1998	3,893	5,836	102.8	15.9	6.6	13	Cc	
Skalva	Ltu	1985	5,974	9,498	113.0	19.0	8.4	14	Cc	ex Paleisgracht-04
Staris	Ltu	1985	6,994	9,650	123.4	20.0	8.0	16	Ccp	ex Concord-02, Abitibi Concord-96, Concord-94, Abitibi Concord-92
Svilas	Ltu	1985	6,996	9,650	123.4	20.0	8.0	16	Ccp	ex Macado-02, Abitibi Macado-96

Hermann Lohmann Bereederungen GmbH & Co KG   Germany

Funnel: *White.* **Hull:** *Blue with red boot-topping.* **History:** *Founded 1985.* **Web:** *www.lohmann-shipping.de*

Name	Flag	Year	GT	DWT	Loa	Bm	Drt	Kts	Type	Remarks
Helas	Cyp	2001	2,545	3,850	89.0	12.5	5.4	13	Cc	ex Oostersingel-05
Lia-C	Mlt	2001	2,999	4,928	94.9	13.2	6.2	12	Cc	
Magda	Ant	2006	1,945	2,443	87.6	11.4	4.2	12	C	ex Paula-09, Friendship-07
Scout	Atg	1999	2,615	3,480	92.8	15.9	4.9	15	Cc	ex OXL Scout-09, AS Africa-08, Arnarnes-06, Radeplein-04

Newbuildings: four 4,900 gt general cargo vessels on order for 2011 delivery.

Gido Luhrs Schiffahrts KG   Germany

Funnel: *Black with yellow 'LL inside yellow diamond outline on blue square.* **Hull:** *Dark grey with white 'APOLLO', red black boot-topping.* **History:** *Founded 1986 as Gido Luhrs to 1999.* **Web:** *None found.*

Name	Flag	Year	GT	DWT	Loa	Bm	Drt	Kts	Type	Remarks
Apollo Condor	Atg	1972	4,255	6,341	101.0	16.0	7.2	13	Bc	ex Rosali-01, Linda II-93, Endurance-89, Baucis-88, Alice Bolten-73 (len/rblt-92)
Apollo Eagle	Atg	1972	4,225	6,341	101.2	16.1	7.2	12	Bc	ex Christiane Schulte-98, Christa-92, Christiane Schulte-87 (len/rblt-92)
Apollo Falcon	Atg	1972	4,255	6,336	101.4	16.0	7.2	13	Bc	ex Artemis I-99, Artemis-82, Susan Miller-78 (len/rblt-91)
Apollo Hawk	Atg	1972	4,255	6,329	101.5	16.1	7.2	13	Bc	ex Esther-98, Esther Bolten-74 (len/rblt-91)
Apollo Lupus	Atg	2002	2,914	4,294	96.3	13.6	5.6	10	Cc	
Apollo Lynx	Atg	2002	2,914	4,294	96.3	13.6	5.6	10	Cc	

Operated by subsidiary L&L Shipping GmbH, Germany (founded 1999)

Lund, Mohr & Giaever-Enger AS (LMG Marin)   Norway

Funnel: *Black with broad blue band edged with narrow yellow bands or * blue with white 'FT' inside white diamond outline.* **Hull:** *Pale blue or black with red boot-topping.* **History:** *Ship managers since 1945 and owners since 1990.* **Web:** *www.sunbay.no*

Name	Flag	Year	GT	DWT	Loa	Bm	Drt	Kts	Type	Remarks
Bewa *	Nis	1975	1,920	3,220	79.9	13.0	5.6	10	C	ex Havso-93, Karin Bewa-76 (len-79)
Danubia **	Nis	1984	1,781	2,550	83.2	11.5	4.3	10	Cc	ex Albis-03, Danubia-97

Name	Flag	Year	GT	DWT	Loa	Bm	Drt	Kts	Type	Remarks
Indian *	Nis	1975	1,920	3,220	79.9	13.0	5.7	12	C	ex Tina-93, Indian Coast-79 (len-80)
Remo	Nis	1976	5,312	8,650	120.1	16.6	7.7	14	C	ex Bremon-03 (deep-82, len-79)

*Owned by subsidiary Sunbay Management AS, Norway (founded 1998) or * managed by Sunbay for Farley Trading.*
*** managed for Wind Shipping AS, Norway (founded 1990 and subsidiary of Erling H Samuelsens Rederi A/S - founded 1929).*
Also see Torso Rederi AB, Sweden

Lupin Shipping Ltd Sweden

Funnel: *Black.* **Hull:** *Dark blue with red boot-topping.* **History:** *Founded 1989 by Alvar Olsson.* **Web:** *None found.*

Name	Flag	Year	GT	DWT	Loa	Bm	Drt	Kts	Type	Remarks
Laguna	Vct	1977	1,689	1,600	71.4	12.9	3.8	10	Cc	ex Nordcarrier-09, Kiekeberg-89
Lamaro	Vct	1972	1,282	1,769	70.9	11.0	4.5	12	C	ex Lamar-97, Antares-94, Sandrea-93, Lamaro-92, Tamara-85
Landia	Vct	1969	1,208	1,964	74.0	10.8	5.1	12	Cc	ex Irlo-03, Anta-94, Simone-89, Tina-76
Lavinia	Vct	1972	2,497	2,400	93.2	13.4	7.5	14	Cc	ex Nordtimber-09, Gyle-01, Rhein Merchant-95, Frisia 1-91, Duneck-86
Lian	Vct	1975	1,547	2,723	73.4	11.5	5.5	-	C	ex Sian-04, Ilse-00, Sian-97, Irina-91
Livia	Vct	1976	2,279	2,560	81.4	13.4	5.2	13	Cc	ex Stina-05, Stefanie-96, Canopus-95
Lona	Vct	1972	1,861	2,958	84.2	13.6	5.3	12	C	ex Loyal Trader-03, Bulk Master-95, Soknatun-93

O E Maeland Shipping Norway

Funnel: *White with red houseflag.* **Hull:** *Blue with red boot-topping.* **History:** *Founded 1986.* **Web:** *None found.*

Name	Flag	Year	GT	DWT	Loa	Bm	Drt	Kts	Type	Remarks
Hako	Nor	1971	1,593	1,645	76.3	11.9	4.0	13	Cc	ex Sea Girl-94, I/a Fortuna

Manx Car Carriers Ltd UK

Funnel: *White with white 'NMC' on pale blue disc interrupting dark blue band, narrow red top.* **Hull:** *Blue with red boot-topping.* **History:** *Founded 1993.*
Web: *www.hoegh.com; www.nissancarrier.co.jp*

Name	Flag	Year	GT	DWT	Loa	Bm	Drt	Kts	Type	Remarks
City of Amsterdam	Lbr	1999	9,960	2,779	99.9	20.6	5.3	15	V	
City of Barcelona	Iom	1993	9,576	2,402	99.9	20.6	5.0	15	V	
City of Paris **	Lbr	1999	9,950	2,793	99.9	20.6	5.3	15	V	
City of Rome *	Lbr	1999	9,960	2,794	99.9	20.6	5.3	15	V	
City of Sunderland	Iom	1993	9,576	2,417	99.9	20.6	5.0	16	V	

*Subsidiary of Nissan Motor Car Carrier Co Ltd, managed by Anglo-Eastern (UK) Ltd or * by MOL Ship Management (Europe) BV*
*** owned by Hoegh Autoliners and managed by MOL Ship Management (Europe) BV.*

MarConsult Gesellschaft fur Reedereiberatung mbH Germany

Funnel: *Dark blue with red 'MC' on white diamond or charterers colours.* **Hull:** *Grey with red boot-topping.* **History:** *Founded 2003 following end of merger between Marconsult Gesellschaft (formed 1991) and Johs Thode GmbH (founded 1890).* **Web:** *www.mc-schiffahrt.de*

Name	Flag	Year	GT	DWT	Loa	Bm	Drt	Kts	Type	Remarks
Marchaser	Atg	1999	8,737	9,113	133.4	22.9	7.7	18	CC	ex Angela Jurgens-04
Marfeeder	Deu	1996	4,986	6,506	116.4	19.5	7.1	17	CC	ex Antje Jurgens-04, Portugal Bridge-99, Antje Jurgens-97
Rubin	Deu	1998	4,028	5,092	100.6	18.5	6.5	15	CC	ex MOL Forerunner-08, Rubin-07, SCM Guri-03, Rubin-01, ATL Pride-00, Signet Pride-00, Rubin-99, Seafreight Pride-99, Rubin-99
SITC Prestige	Atg	2007	9,610	12,779	142.7	22.6	8.2	18	CC	ex Marcliff-09
SITC Prospect	Atg	2007	9,610	12,780	142.7	22.6	8.2	18	CC	ex Marcloud-08
Smaragd	Deu	1998	4,028	5,250	100.6	18.5	6.5	15	CC	ex MTC Jaguar-03, Smaragd-02, SJ Glory-01, Signet Glory-00, Seafreight Glory-99, Smaragd-98
Topas	Mlt	1999	4,028	5,092	100.5	18.5	6.5	15	Cc	

Compagnie Maritime Marfret France

Funnel: *Blue with red 'MF', black top.* **Hull:** *Black or light grey with red or pink boot-topping.* **History:** *Formed 1957 as Armement Marseille-Fret SA until 1989.* **Web:** *www.marfret.fr*

Name	Flag	Year	GT	DWT	Loa	Bm	Drt	Kts	Type	Remarks
Marfret Mejean	Lux	1998	3,862	4,974	100.7	16.4	6.2	16	Cc	ex CMA CGM Amazonia-08, Dorado-02, Echo Trader-00, Seaboard Enterprise-00, Echo Trader-99
Marfret Niolon	Lux	1991	7,395	5,283	123.0	19.0	6.6	16	Ro	ex Nordia-08, Bore Nordia-05, Finnseal-03, Bore Nordia-97
Marin	Lux	1991	5,972	4,750	114.4	18.0	6.2	16	Rop	ex Bore Mari-05, Finnbeaver-02,Ann-Mari-97

Maritime Management AS Norway

Funnel: *White.* **Hull:** *Blue with red boot-topping.* **History:** *Founded 2005 as Jensen Shipping AS to 2005.* **Web:** *www.marman.no*

Name	Flag	Year	GT	DWT	Loa	Bm	Drt	Kts	Type	Remarks
Artic Senior	Nor	1982	830	610	47.6	11.2	3.2	11	Rop	ex Terningen 2-08, Sanco Captain-03, Aukaskjaer-97, Blue Marlin-94, Corline-92
Calypso III	Pan	1984	3,120	4,145	88.6	15.5	6.5	13	C	ex Thor Amalie-08, Maritime Bay-07, Amalie-06, Thor Amalie-04, Helga-98, Mulafoss-97, Helga-93, Calypso-92, Band Aid Hope-86, Calypso-85
Henriette	Fro	1971	2,900	3,700	88.5	13.8	6.5	13	Cc	ex Denise-90, Frauden-85, Frauke-81, Comar II-74, Frauke-72
Nina	Atg	1979	1,713	1,640	79.5	12.8	3.5	11	Cc	ex Eberstein-99

Name		Flag	Year	GT	DWT	Loa	Bm	Drt	Kts	Type	Remarks
Solanjo *		Nis	1981	1,533	1,900	67.8	13.8	3.1	12	Bu	ex Stako-06

* owned by Salina AS, Norway

Falkeid Shipping AS, Norway

Funnel: White with pale blue top. **Hull:** Blue with red boot-topping. **History:** Founded 1998. **Web:** None found.

Name		Flag	Year	GT	DWT	Loa	Bm	Drt	Kts	Type	Remarks
Falkland		Mlt	1986	2,367	3,812	87.9	12.8	4.5	9	Cc	ex Durnstein-07, Visurgis-95
Falksund		Nor	1985	1,297	1,738	74.9	10.6	-	10	C	ex Breklum-05, Osterhusen-02, Jessica S-94
Falkvaag		Nor	1958	568	447	44.6	8.2	3.2	9	C	ex Feistein-01, Morefjord-95, Mary Lou-93, Osheim-72 (len-89)
Falkvik		Nor	1965	499	615	50.6	8.7	3.2	11	C	ex Nyfjord-07, Renate-05, Sylvia-92, Eksor-88, Bulkfart-86, Eldaroy-85, Pokal-80, Svennor-74, Bios-74, Ferro-70

Marship (Marine Shipping Co Ltd) Russia

Funnel: White with small blue 'C', narrow black top. **Hull:** Blue with white 'MARSHIP MOSCOW', red boot-topping. **History:** Founded 1990 and controlled by Government of The Russian Federation. **Web:** www.marship.ru

Name		Flag	Year	GT	DWT	Loa	Bm	Drt	Kts	Type	Remarks
Bratsk	(2)	Rus	1981	2,441	3,031	108.4	14.8	3.1	10	C	
Kalitva	(2)	Rus	1974	2,463	3,174	108.1	14.2	3.3	10	C	
Little Ann	(2)	Rus	1972	2,573	2,907	114.0	13.2	3.5	10	C	ex Reliance-00, Andrey Petrikov-97
Naruksovo	(2)	Rus	1969	2,478	2,925	114.2	13.2	3.4	10	C	ex Nadezhda-09, Sormovskiy-6-95
Nakhodka	(2)	Rus	1978	2,441	3,031	108.4	14.8	3.1	10	C	
Nikolay Psomiadi	(2)	Blz	1986	2,426	3,174	108.4	15.0	3.3	10	C	ex Omskiy-35-91
Omskiy-14	(2)	Rus	1980	2,463	3,174	108.4	15.0	3.3	10	C	
Omskiy-105	(2)	Rus	1980	2,441	3,248	108.4	15.0	3.3	10	C	ex Captain Podoljan-06, Omskiy-105-02
Omskiy-107	(2)	Rus	1981	2,441	2,905	108.4	15.0	3.1	10	C	ex Argo I-07, Argo-05, Omskiy-107-01
Omskiy-125	(2)	Rus	1985	2,441	3,248	108.4	14.8	3.3	10	C	ex Nadja-06, Omskiy-125-00
Omskiy-205	(2)	Rus	1993	2,958	3,476	113.3	14.8	3.6	10	C	ex Berill-06, Carat-05, Skif-99
Omskiy-207	(2)	Rus	1995	2,992	2,828	114.0	14.8	3.2	10	C	ex Aktion-08, Action-03, Nataly S-98, Favorit A-97

Reederei O Marten GmbH & Co KG Germany

Funnel: White with white 'M' between narrow white wavy bands on broad dark blue band. **Hull:** Black with red boot-topping. **History:** Founded 2005. **Web:** www.reederei-marten.de

Name	Flag	Year	GT	DWT	Loa	Bm	Drt	Kts	Type	Remarks
O M Aestatis	Lbr	2006	7,170	8,200	131.5	19.2	7.9	-	CC	
O M Autumni	Lbr	2007	7,170	8,200	131.5	19.2	7.9	-	CC	
O M Humorum	Lbr	2008	7,170	8,200	131.5	19.2	7.9	-	CC	
O M Imbrium	Lbr	2008	7,170	8,200	131.5	19.2	7.9	-	CC	
Undarum	Cyp	2009	7,170	8,200	132.7	19.2	7.7	-	CC	l/a O M Undarum

Also operates larger container ships

Master Shipping Joint Stock Co Russia

Funnel: White with narrow black top. **Hull:** Brown with red boot-topping. **History:** Founded 1998 and controlled by Government of The Russian Federation. **Web:** None found.

Name	Flag	Year	GT	DWT	Loa	Bm	Drt	Kts	Type	Remarks
Altership	Rus	1991	3,466	4,236	95.0	15.8	6.3	15	Cc	ex Fiddler-98, Kirzhach-97
MCL Trader	Rus	1990	3,466	4,236	95.0	15.8	6.3	15	C	ex Drummer-97, Pizhma-97

Maxxl Shipping BV Netherlands

Funnel: Charterers colours. **Hull:** Red with black boot-topping. **History:** Formed 2007. **Web**: www.maxxlshipping.nl

Name	Flag	Year	GT	DWT	Loa	Bm	Drt	Kts	Type	Remarks
Orarikke	Cyp	2008	4,030	6,886	103.0	16.0	7.0	12	T	ex Britta Theresa-10, Borealis-08
Orarose	Cyp	2008	3,952	6,450	103.0	16.0	7.0	12	T	ex Zodiacal-09
Vedrey Barfodh *	Nis	2010	3,040	3,400	-	-	-	-	T	

Newbuildings: Two further 6,800 dwt tankers on order for 2010 delivery.
* acquired from Svithoid Tankers AB, Sweden (in liquidation)

MC Shipping Inc Monaco/UK

Funnel: White with white 'M' and 'C' on red/blue disc vertically halved by yellow anchor, black top. **Hull:** Orange or black with red boot-topping. **History:** Founded 1989 and acquired 2007 by private equity group Bear Stearns from Navalmar and Weco-rederi. **Web:** www.mcshipping.com

Name	Flag	Year	GT	DWT	Loa	Bm	Drt	Kts	Type	Remarks
Auteuil *	Bhs	1995	3,617	2,588	93.0	17.6	4.2	13	Lpg	ex Spica Gas-98
Blackfriars Bridge	Iom	1981	4,884	6,118	110.9	15.5	7.5	14	Lpg	ex Dorothea Schulte-06
Cheltenham *	Bhs	1990	3,376	4,318	99.6	15.8	5.8	12	Lpg	
Coniston *	Bhs	1991	3,847	4,801	99.9	17.2	6.0	14	Lpg	
Deauville *	Bhs	1995	3,617	2,601	93.0	17.6	4.2	13	Lpg	ex Taurus Gas-98
Grasmere	Bhs	1997	5,961	7,638	121.0	19.0	6.8	15	Lpg	
Kendal	Bhs	2003	7,893	8,709	120.0	20.0	7.4	15	Lpg	
Keswick	Bhs	2003	7,884	8,692	120.0	20.0	7.4	15	Lpg	
London Bridge	Iom	1980	4,884	6,137	110.9	15.5	7.5	14	Lpg	ex Hermann Schulte-06
Longchamp *	Bhs	1990	3,415	4,316	99.6	15.7	5.8	13	Lpg	ex Leo Gas-00
Malvern *	Bhs	1990	3,368	4,148	99.1	15.8	5.7	12	Lpg	

* managed for MPC–Munchmeyer Petersen & Co GmbH, Germany
Also see Schulte Group

Meerpahl & Meyer Bereederungs GmbH & Co KG   Germany

Funnel: *White with houseflag comprising black 'M' on white diamond, black top.* **Hull:** *Blue with red boot-topping.* **History:** *Founded 1986.*
Web: *www.mumbux.de*

Name		Flag	Year	GT	DWT	Loa	Bm	Drt	Kts	Type	Remarks
Cranz		Atg	1977	2,089	2,461	86.5	12.8	4.9	13	Cc	ex Christian-07, Alita-95 (len-87)
Jork		Cyp	2001	9,981	11,385	134.4	22.5	8.7	18	CC	ex Margaretha-07
Leeswig		Atg	1996	2,901	4,515	88.0	13.7	6.1	10	Cc	ex Frieda-07
Sara Borchard		Atg	2006	9,962	11,431	134.4	22.5	8.7	18	CC	ex Buxtehude-09, Rita-07

Owned or managed by subsidiary Hans-Uwe Meyer Bereederereung GmbH & Co KG

Karl Meyer Reederei GmbH & Co KG   Germany

Funnel: *White with turquoise 'M' symbol interwoven with horizontal orange arrow.* **Hull:** *Dark blue or * white with red boot-topping.* **History:** *Formed 1956 as shipping subsidiary of waste-management company and owning coasters since 1976.* **Web:** *www.karl-meyer.de*

Name		Flag	Year	GT	DWT	Loa	Bm	Drt	Kts	Type	Remarks
Bjorn M		Deu	1955	328	480	47.6	8.5	2.7	9	C	ex Traute-86
Gotland *		Deu	1984	1,860	3,035	91.1	11.4	4.9	11	Cc	ex Euklid-07, Sena-94, Maelo-92, Zuiderzee-88
Halland *		Deu	1986	1,899	2,295	82.1	12.6	4.2	11	Cc	ex Guadalupe II-08, Lys Corona-97, Sprante-96, I/a Emma
Helgoland		Deu	1955	492	632	54.1	8.0	2.9	8	C	ex Kaja H-98, Gauensiek-86, Witte Kliff-71, Marschenland-65 (len/deep-78)
Jutland *		Deu	1978	1,495	1,548	76.8	11.5	3.4	12	Cc	ex Denika-04, Sea Merlan-97, I/a Merlan
Langeland *		Deu	1985	1,832	2,287	80.7	12.7	4.2	11	Cc	ex Martha Hammann-06
Lolland *		Deu	1981	1,811	2,668	78.6	12.8	4.6	10	Cc	ex Navigator-06

* managed by Wilhelm EF Schmid GmbH qv

Bernd Meyering Schiffahrts KG   Germany

Funnel: *White with white ring overlapping blue over yellow bands.* **Hull:** *Light blue or black with red or black boot-topping.* **History:** *Founded 1987.*
Web: *None found.*

Name		Flag	Year	GT	DWT	Loa	Bm	Drt	Kts	Type	Remarks
Baltic Sea		Cyp	2005	2,978	4,716	99.6	16.9	5.9	15	Cc	
Blue Note		Atg	2010	3,845	4,750	-	-	-	-	C	
Blue Tune		Atg	2010	3,845	4,750	-	-	-	-	C	
Jens M		Atg	2010	3,845	4,750	-	-	-	-	C	
Marita M		Atg	2010	3,845	4,750	-	-	-	-	C	
Rhein Carrier		Atg	1991	3,818	4,650	103.5	16.2	6.1	14	Cc	ex Churruca-98, Cimbria-93, Lloyd Iberia-92, Dana Sirena-91, I/a Cimbria

Operated by subsidiary Bernd Meyering Verwaltungs GmbH (formed 2006)

Millwood Shipping Inc   UK

Funnel: *Buff with broad white band below black top.* **Hull:** *Green with red boot-topping.* **History:** *Not confirmed.* **Web:** *None found.*

Name	Flag	Year	GT	DWT	Loa	Bm	Drt	Kts	Type	Remarks
Jonsen	Gbr	1977	1,987	2,210	79.0	12.5	4.8	11	Cc	ex Jonrix-07, Langeland II-94, Langeland-83

Mirfak Scheepvaart BV   Netherlands

Funnel: *Not confirmed.* **Hull:** *Red with red boot-topping.* **History:** *Not confirmed.* **Web:** *None found.*

Name	Flag	Year	GT	DWT	Loa	Bm	Drt	Kts	Type	Remarks
Labici B		1978	2,697	3,636	82.2	15.0	6.1	13	Cc	ex Herman Bodewes-99, Herman Danielsen-86, Herman Bodewes-84

Kare Misje & Co Rederi A/S   Norway

Funnel: *Yellow with red 'M' inside white ring.* **Hull:** *Green or blue with white 'MISJE BULK' with red or black boot-topping.* **History:** *Founded 1998.*
Web: *www.misje.no*

Name		Flag	Year	GT	DWT	Loa	Bm	Drt	Kts	Type	Remarks
Anmi		Bhs	1992	2,373	4,245	88.3	13.2	5.5	12	Cc	ex Arklow Freedom-05, MB Clyde-97
Bimi		Bhs	1992	2,373	4,250	88.3	13.2	5.5	12	Cc	ex Arklow Fortune-05, MB Humber-97
Cemi		Bhs	1991	2,370	4,270	88.3	13.2	5.7	12	C	ex Cemile-04
Imi		Bhs	1993	2,715	4,293	89.8	13.2	5.5	12	C	ex Marja-06
Jomi		Bhs	1991	2,827	4,258	88.2	13.7	5.8	11	Cc	ex Arklow View-04
Kaami		Bhs	1994	2,715	4,293	89.8	13.2	5.6	12	C	ex Marjolein-06
Nordfjell	(2)	Nor	1978	4,578	3,043	108.8	16.6	5.5	14	Rop	ex Fast One-87 (len-80)
Nordskott	(2)	Nor	1979	4,578	2,600	108.8	16.6	5.5	14	Rop	ex Fast Two-87 (len-81)
Romi		Bhs	1992	2,370	4,250	88.3	13.2	5.5	11	Cc	ex Arklow Faith-05, MB Thames-97
Strami		Bhs	2002	2,373	4,220	88.3	13.2	5.5	12	Cc	ex Arklow Fame-05, MB Avon-97
Sunmi		Bhs	1993	2,825	4,148	90.5	13.4	5.6	11	C	ex Fehn Sun-07, Apollo Fox-06, Nesserland-03, Swift-00
Swami		Bhs	1995	2,839	4,304	90.5	13.2	5.7	12	Cc	ex Arklow Swan-07, Swan-04

Kustvaartbedrijf Moerman BV   Netherlands

Funnel: *Yellow with green 'M' on white disc interrupting green/white/green bands.* **Hull:** *Red with black, red or green boot-topping.* **History:** *Founded 1949 and commenced shipowning in 1953. Acquired by Bylock & Nordsjofrakt, Sweden in 1994, but became independent again in 2005.* **Web:** *www.kvbmoerman.nl*

Name	Flag	Year	GT	DWT	Loa	Bm	Drt	Kts	Type	Remarks
Capricorn	Nld	2000	4,871	6,600	117.8	15.2	6.3	14	Cc	
Roelof	Nld	1992	5,780	8,224	107.4	19.3	8.3	14	C/hl	ex BBC Frisia-07, Calypso-00, Annegret-99
Transandromeda	Nld	1999	4,871	6,663	118.6	15.2	6.3	14	Cc	ex Andromeda-09

Name	Flag	Year	GT	DWT	Loa	Bm	Drt	Kts	Type	Remarks
Transwing	Nld	1999	2,774	4,135	90.4	13.6	5.7	12	C	ex Swing-09

Also manages vessels for other owners, see under Rederi AB Lillgaard, Finland.
Also owns one larger general cargo vessel.

Reederei Heinz Moje KG   Germany

Funnel: *White with narrow black top or charterers colours.* **Hull:** *Blue with red boot-topping.* **History:** *Founded 1947 and now subsidiary of USC-Barnkrug Gbr (formed 2004).* **Web:** *www.reederei-moje.de*

CMA CGM Casablanca	Gib	2005	9,990	11,209	125.1	22.5	8.7	18	CC	ex Maersk Fawley-09, I/a Passat
Dinah Borchard	Atg	2008	7,532	8,733	127.0	20.4	7.8	18	CC	ex Monsun-09
Maris	Deu	1995	3,999	5,325	100.6	18.2	6.6	15	Cc	
Mistral	Gib	2008	9,961	11,254	135.0	22.7	8.7	18	CC	

Also see Elbdeich Reederei GmbH founded jointly by Heinz Moje with other partners.

Walther Moller & Co   Germany

Funnel: *Black.* **Hull:** *Blue with red boot-topping.* **History:** *Founded 1941 and operating subsidiary formed 1985.* **Web:** *www.wmco.de*

Coneste	Atg	2003	9,990	11,153	134.4	22.5	8.8	18	CC	ex Maersk Fremantle-09, I/a Coneste
WEC Velaquez	Cyp	2007	9,962	11.433	134.4	22.5	8.8	18	CC	ex Conelbe-08

Operated by subsidiary Bernd Bartels GmbH.

Moscow River Shipping Co   Russia

Funnel: *White with light blue over red bands, narrow black top.* **Hull:** *Grey or black with red boot-topping.* **History:** *Founded 1994 and controlled by the Governement of The Russian Federation. In 2002, took over Western Shipping Co (founded 1956 as Western River Shipping Co to 1994).* **Web:** *None found.*

Amur-2512	(2)	Rus	1986	3,086	3,159	115.7	13.4	4.0	10	Cc	
Amur-2513	(2)	Rus	1986	3,086	3,159	115.7	13.4	4.0	10	Cc	
Amur-2524	(2)	Rus	1988	3,086	3,148	116.0	13.4	4.0	10	Cc	
Amur-2532	(2)	Rus	1989	3,086	3,148	116.1	13.4	4.0	10	Cc	
Sormovskiy-41	(2)	Rus	1980	2,478	3,134	114.0	13.2	3.7	10	C	
Sormovskiy-42	(2)	Rus	1980	2,478	3,134	114.0	13.2	3.7	10	C	
Sormovskiy-49	(2)	Rus	1984	2,478	3,135	114.0	13.2	3.7	10	C	
Sormovskiy-53	(2)	Rus	1986	2,466	3,135	114.0	13.2	3.7	10	C	
Sormovskiy-3060	(2)	Rus	1988	3,048	3,391	118.7	13.2	3.9	10	Cc	
Vera	(2)	Rus	1976	2,457	3,183	114.0	13.0	3.6	10	C	ex Volgo-Balt 192-06
Volgo-Balt 225	(2)	Rus	1980	2,457	2,893	114.0	13.0	3.6	10	C	
Volgo-Balt 243	(2)	Rus	1983	2,554	2,893	114.0	13.0	3.6	10	C	
Volgo-Balt 244	(2)	Rus	1983	2,457	2,893	114.0	13.0	3.6	10	C	

Operated by subsidiary Western Shipping Co.

Ewald Muller & Co GmbH   Germany

Funnel: *White.* **Hull:** *Green or blue with red boot-topping.* **History:** *Founded 1986.* **Web:** *www.ewald-mueller.de*

Elizabeth F *	Nld	1991	1,276	1,686	79.1	10.5	3.7	10	C	ex Derk-05, Skylge-01, Sea Loire-99, Skylge-97, I/a Terschelling
Ewald	Atg	1999	1,599	2,262	87.9	11.3	3.7	10	C	
Little Jane *	Nld	1988	851	1,276	64.3	10.6	3.4	11	C	ex Coral-03, Sirocco-98, Boeran-91

* owned by Dutch subsidiary Foppen Maritiem and managed by Wagenborg Shipping BV Netherlands.

Otto A Muller Schiffahrt GmbH (OAM)   Germany

Funnel: *White.* **Hull:** *Blue with black boot-topping.* **History:** *Founded 1889 as Otto A Muller GmbH to 1998.* **Web:** *www.oam.de*

Eva Maria Muller	Atg	1998	2,446	3,722	88.0	13.0	5.5	10	Cc	
Monika Muller	Atg	1998	2,446	3,723	88.0	13.0	5.5	10	Cc	

Managed by Christian Jurgensen, Blink & Wolffel Schiffahrt GmbH qv

Mikkal Myklebusthaug Rederi AS   Norway

Funnel: *Various including charterers colours.* **Hull:** *Dark blue, green or grey with red, green or black boot-topping.* **History:** *Founded 1967.* **Web:** *www.mmred.no*

Angela	Gib	2005	9,962	11,403	134.4	22.5	8.7	18	CC	
Believer	Mlt	1992	5,006	6,620	116.8	18.2	6.9	16	Cc	ex Sven Oltmann-04, Emily Borchard-03, Gracechurch Planet-02, Sven Oltmann-99
Dina Trader	Gib	2007	9,981	11,267	134.4	22.5	8.7	18	CC	ex Jan-Fabian-08
Edmy	Nis	1980	2,768	4,700	85.9	14.3	6.1	14	Cu	ex Austvik-04
Fonnland	Nis	1992	2,416	3,601	85.0	13.0	5.4	12	Cc	ex Aura-07, Lyme Bay-98, Jens-93
Green Fast	Gib	1996	5,522	7,000	118.0	19.4	7.5	17	CC	ex Zim Venezuela V-06, Nenufar Atlantico-02, Pan Tau-98, Medfeeder Malta-98, Pan Tau-97
Grinna	Nis	1972	1,562	1,306	76.6	12.3	3.5	12	Cc	ex Freida-95, Dilshan-91, Jenna-90, Dilshan-90, Meriem-89, Eco Sado-81, Merc Asia-73

Name		Flag	Year	GT	DWT	Loa	Bm	Drt	Kts	Type	Remarks
Jan D		Gib	1982	5,404	6,580	113.7	19.0	6.5	14	CC	ex Maersk Canarias-99, Dania-94, Nedlloyd Daisy-94, Dania-93, Alcyone-92, Kastamonu-88, Contship Lugano-85, Kastamonu-85, I/a Alcyone
Langenes		Nis	1983	4,043	6,231	95.0	17.6	7.4	14	Cc	ex Timbus-00, I/a Hans-Gunther Bulow

Nagel Reederei
Germany

Funnel: *White.* **Hull:** *Blue with black boot-topping.* **History:** *Founded 1989.* **Web:** *None found.*

Name		Flag	Year	GT	DWT	Loa	Bm	Drt	Kts	Type	Remarks
Grimm		Deu	1992	3,564	4,175	104.8	15.4	4.1	12	Ccp	
Kalina		Cyp	1996	6,362	7,225	121.4	18.5	6.7	16	CC	ex Rachel Borchard-01, Sound-97, Kalina-96

Navalis Shipping GmbH & Co KG
Germany

Funnel: *Yellow with red 'tw' on side panels of blue/white diagonally quartered houseflag, narrow black top.* **Hull:** *Dark grey or green with white 'NAVALIS', red boot-topping.* **History:** *Founded 1972.* **Web:** *www.navalis-ship.com*

Name		Flag	Year	GT	DWT	Loa	Bm	Drt	Kts	Type	Remarks
Aland		Iom	2007	5,257	7,056	117.0	16.5	5.7	12	Cc	
Angermanland		Atg	1989	3,845	4,334	104.9	16.0	5.4	14	Cc	
Dalarna		Iom	1997	3,796	4,400	100.7	16.2	4.8	11	Cc	ex Aurico 1-97
Estland		Iom	2002	3,978	5,040	100.0	16.5	5.2	11	Cc	
Fembria		Iom	2006	5,257	7,400	117.3	16.5	5.7	12	Cc	
Finnland		Iom	2006	5,257	7,099	117.0	16.5	6.0	12	Cc	
Lettland		Gib	2001	3,978	4,400	100.0	16.5	5.2	11	Cc	
Livland		Gib	2001	3,978	4,400	100.0	16.5	5.2	12	Cc	
Majala		Atg	1999	7,970	10,000	133.2	20.8	7.8	18	CC	ex MSC Prony-09, Sezela-08, Box Hamburg-04, Cagema St. Lucia-02, Maersk Nouadhibou-00, Box Hamburg-99
Meriwa		Vct	1996	5,006	6,807	116.4	19.5	7.1	16	CC	ex Arklow Castle-05
Mondena		Atg	1999	9,978	12,048	149.0	22.7	7.8	18	CC	ex CMA CGM Victoria-09, Maersk Rawson-06, Mondena-03, Yuksel Guler-03
Osterbotten		Iom	2002	4,185	5,880	109.2	15.0	6.2	13	Cc	ex Balticon Antwerp-09, Osterbotten-07, Normed Izmir-05, Lekstroom-02
Seeland		Iom	2006	5,257	7,064	117.3	16.5	5.7	14	Cc	
Silva		Iom	2001	3,978	4,400	100.0	16.5	5.2	11	Cc	
Sofrana Surville		Atg	2007	9,939	12,400	136.8	23.2	8.7	18	CC	ex Monia-07
Tornedalen		Iom	2000	4,211	5,572	99.9	16.5	6.1	14	Cc	

Newbuildings: two 5,140 gt coasters for 2010 delivery.
Managed by subsidiary Schiffahrtskontor Tom Worden GmbH & Co KG, Germany (founded 1911)
Also operates larger container ships.

Naviglobe NV
Belgium

Funnel: *White.* **Hull:** *Light grey with black boot-topping.* **History:** *Founded 2002.* **Web:** *None found.*

Name		Flag	Year	GT	DWT	Loa	Bm	Drt	Kts	Type	Remarks
Prince Henri		Lux	1990	2,522	4,686	110.0	12.5	5.5	12	Tch	
Regina		Lux	1987	1,731	2,680	110.0	11.4	2.2	11	T	

Operated by subsidiary Navimer SA, Luxembourg.

Rederi AS Nedjan
Sweden

Funnel: *White with white 'Ö' on blue square.* **Hull:** *Blue with red boot-topping.* **History:** *Founded 2002.* **Web:** *None found.*

Name		Flag	Year	GT	DWT	Loa	Bm	Drt	Kts	Type	Remarks
Forte		Swe	2004	5,225	6,419	115.9	16.5	5.7	13	Cc	ex Volna-05

Managed by Osterstroms Rederi AB, Sweden (www.osterstroms.se)

Nes HF
Iceland

Funnel: *Blue with broad white band.* **Hull:** *Blue with red boot-topping.* **History:** *Founded 1974.* **Web:** *www.nes.is*

Name		Flag	Year	GT	DWT	Loa	Bm	Drt	Kts	Type	Remarks
Haukur		Nis	1990	2,030	3,050	74.7	12.7	6.0	12	Cc	ex Sava River-00
Lomur		Nis	1983	1,516	1,570	72.5	11.3	3.6	10	Cc	ex Ocelot-94, Captain Most-90, Karen Dania-87
Svanur		Nis	1983	1,516	2,600	72.5	11.7	3.6	10	Cc	ex Svanur II-95, Louise-95, Lynx-94, Jette Dania-92, Skipper Most-92, Jette Dania-87

Neva-Balt Co Ltd
Russia

Funnel: *Black with white symbol on red disc.* **Hull:** *Black with red boot-topping.* **History:** *Founded 2004 and controlled by the Government of The Russian Federation.* **Web:** *None found.*

Name		Flag	Year	GT	DWT	Loa	Bm	Drt	Kts	Type	Remarks
Volgo-Balt 136	(2)	Rus	1971	2,457	3,294	113.8	13.0	3.6	10	C	
Volgo-Balt 195	(2)	Rus	1976	2,516	3,180	114.0	13.0	3.6	10	C	

Rederiet Nielsen Og Bresling A/S
Denmark

Funnel: *Green with narrow black top.* **Hull:** *Red with red/brown boot-topping.* **History:** *Founded 1960.* **Web:** *www.bresline.dk*

Name		Flag	Year	GT	DWT	Loa	Bm	Drt	Kts	Type	Remarks
Birthe Bres		Dis	2007	2,658	3,740	87.9	12.5	5.3	12	C	
Jytte Bres		Dis	1999	2,876	4,748	89.0	13.3	6.3	12	C	

Nagel Reederei. Grimm. *Oliver Sesemann*

Nordic Tankers A/S. Clipper Nadja. *Allan Ryszka Onions*

Name	Flag	Year	GT	DWT	Loa	Bm	Drt	Kts	Type	Remarks
Lone Bres	Dis	2000	2,876	4,748	89.0	13.3	6.3	12	C	
Nina Bres	Dis	2007	2,658	3,740	87.9	12.5	5.3	12	C	
Sine Bres	Dis	2006	2,658	3,750	87.9	12.5	5.3	12	C	

Newbuilding: One further 3,740 dwt coaster due for 2010 delivery.

Ove R Nielsen ApS   Denmark

Funnel: *White.* **Hull:** *Blue with red boot-topping.* **History:** *Founded 1997.* **Web:** *None found.*

Adriane	Dis	1970	1,371	1,307	69.8	11.5	3.6	12	Cc	ex Cito-97, Adria-90, Adriana-86

Reederei Nimmrich & Prahm GmbH   Germany

Funnel: *White with dark blue 'NP'.* **Hull:** *Dark blue with red boot-topping.* **History:** *Founded 1998.* **Web:** *www.nimmrich.de*

Anna	Atg	2005	3,618	4,811	100.7	15.2	5.6	12	Cc	
Celia	Atg	2007	3,610	4,800	100.7	15.2	5.6	12	Cc	
Emilie K	Atg	2008	3,642	4,450	100.7	15.2	5.6	13	Cc	ex Martha-08
Emma	Atg	2009	6,155	7,761					Cc	
Frida	Atg	2005	3,610	4,800	100.7	15.2	5.6	12	Cc	
Kirsten K	Atg	2008	3,642	4,442	100.7	15.2	5.6	13	Cc	ex Ida-08
Maria K	Atg	2007	3,642	4,800	100.7	15.2	5.6	13	Cc	ex Greta-07
Susan K	Atg	2007	3,642	4,464	100.7	15.2	5.6	13	Cc	ex Sonja-07

Newbuildings: Two 4,400 gt feeder container ships and five 4,800 dwt general cargo vessels for 2010 delivery.
Managed by subsidiary Nimmrich & Prahm Bereederungs GmbH & Co KG, Germany (founded 1998)

Noordriver Shipping BV   Netherlands

Funnel: *White.* **Hull:** *Dark blue with black boot-topping.* **History:** *Founded 2007.* **Web:** *www.noordriver.com*

Bente	Nld	2008	2,991	4,000	89.6	14.5	5.7	-	C	ex Bornrif-09
Ephesus	Ant	1983	1,316	2,175	73.3	11.3	4.5	-	C	ex Orka-07, Ork-06, Orka-05
Ilse	Mlt	1993	2,449	3,729	88.0	12.8	5.5	11	Cc	ex Esteilse-07, Ilse K-07, Scorpius-00, Ursa-98
Lieke	Nld	2010	7,476	9,000	122.2	19.8	7.2	-	C	

Newbuildings: One further 9,000 dwt vessel on order for 2010 delivery.

Norbar Minerals AS   Norway

Funnel: *White.* **Hull:** *Green with red boot-topping.* **History:** *Founded 1994.* **Web:** *None found.*

Comabar	Nis	1985	1,211	1,117	63.0	11.5	3.4	10	Cc	ex Ingrid Maria-05, Gesche-97
Norbar II	Nor	1995	1,685	2,500	81.7	11.1	4.5	10	C	ex Yvonne-08, Stern-04

Nor Lines AS   Norway

Funnel: *Black with white 'N' symbol on white-edged broad red band.* **Hull:** *Black with white 'NOR LINES', red boot-topping.* **History:** *Founded 2000 as Nor-Cargo Shipping A/S to 2004.* **Web:** *www.norlines.no*

Karmsund	Brb	1979	2,728	1,250	89.4	14.5	4.6	13	Ccp	(len-87)
Nordhav ‡	Nis	1980	2,865	4,469	103.0	19.7	6.6	16	Ro	ex Cres-98
Nordjarl	Nor	1985	3,968	2,607	95.5	17.6	5.2	15	Rc	ex Ice Pearl-95
Nordkyn	Nor	1979	2,503	1,600	77.6	14.5	5.1	14	Cp	
Nordvaag *	Dmk	1979	2,854	1,460	88.8	14.5	4.5	12	Ccp	ex Blikur-08 (len-84)
Nordvaer	Nor	1986	2,731	2,050	79.9	15.0	5.0	13	Cp	ex Victoriahamn-93
Nordvik *	Dis	1978	2,854	1,450	88.8	14.5	4.5	14	Ccp	ex Lomur-08
Sunnmore	Nor	1985	2,706	2,000	79.9	15.0	5.0	-	Cp	
Tananger	Fro	1980	4,636	4,380	102.5	16.5	6.1	14	Ro	ex Forest Swan-95, Jerome B-93, Canis-91

Newbuildings: Two 6,470 gt roll-on, roll-off vessels on order for 2010 delivery.
*Owned by Harald Saetre AS, * by Norresundby Shipping A/S, Denmark or ‡ by Troms Fylkes Dampskibs.*
Also see Sea-Cargo Skips AS, Norway (under Seatrans DA)

Nordane Shipping A/S   Denmark

Funnel: *Black with green 'S' inside green ring on broad white band.* **Hull:** *Green with red boot-topping.* **History:** *Founded 1965 as Stevns Charter and Towage A/S.* **Web:** *www.nordane.dk*

Moresby Express	Atg	1991	3,113	3,658	92.7	15.1	5.3	12	Cc	ex Island Express-09, Capitaine Fearn-05, Beacon Strait-04, Industrial Beacon-03, Dora-Maar-99, Industrial Beacon-99, Bremer Makler-96, Gordon Reid-95
Leopard	Dis	1989	1,093	1,771	67.0	10.3	4.5	11	Cc	ex Skanlith-96
Lynx	Dis	1994	1,395	2,120	73.5	11.4	4.5	11	Cc	ex Southern Havannah-98, Lynx-97, Thor Rikke-97
Puma	Dis	1994	1,395	2,120	73.5	11.4	4.5	11	Cc	ex Thor Lisbeth-97

Also see Janus Andersen & Co AS, Denmark

Nordic Tankers A/S. Clipper Sola. *Phil Kempsey*

Norresundby Shipping A/S. Saturn. *Oliver Sesemann*

Nordcapital Holding GmbH & Cie KG Germany

ER Schiffahrt GmbH & Cie KG

Funnel: *Black with white 'ER' on broad blue band edged with narrow white bands or charterers colours.* **Hull:** *Dark blue with pink boot-topping or charterers colours.* **History:** *Both companies formed 1998.* **Web:** *www.nordcapital.com or www.er-ship.com*

Name		Flag	Year	GT	DWT	Loa	Bm	Drt	Kts	Type	Remarks
E.R.Helsinki		Deu	2010	9,965	12,400	-	-	-	-	CC	
E.R.Riga		Lbr	2010	9,965	12,400	-	-	-	-	CC	
E.R.Tallin		Lbr	2010	9,965	12,400	-	-	-	-	CC	
E.R.Visby		Lbr	2010	9,965	12,400	-	-	-	-	CC	

Nordgrens Rederi AB Sweden

Funnel: *Cream.* **Hull:** *Red with red boot-topping.* **History:** *Founded 1984.* **Web:** *www.nordgrensrederi.se*

Name		Flag	Year	GT	DWT	Loa	Bm	Drt	Kts	Type	Remarks
Landy		Cyp	1992	4,090	4,450	111.1	16.1	6.0	14	Cc	ex Gastrikland-06, Sea Voyager-98, Gastrikland-96

Nordic Tankers A/S Denmark

Funnel: *Black with dark blue teardrop below light blue block on broad white band or former Clipper Wonsild colours white with blue 'C' symbol or ‡ dark green with black 'EM' on white edged light blue disc.* **Hull:** *Red (Nordic) dark blue or ‡ dark green with red boot-topping.* **History:** *Founded 2004 and early in 2010 acquired the tanker business of Clipper Group, who will now have a 31% interest in Nordic.* **Web:** *www.nordictankers.dk*

Name		Flag	Year	GT	DWT	Loa	Bm	Drt	Kts	Type	Remarks
Anna Johanne †		Dis	1994	1,716	3,294	85.0	13.8	5.5	11	Tch	
Caroline Wonsild ‡		Ita	1994	2,349	2,693	89.6	14.0	5.2	13	Tch	
Clipper Barbera	(2)	Bhs	2006	3,021	3,548	90.5	14.6	5.4	11	Tch	
Clipper Bardolino	(2)	Bhs	2007	2,999	3,569	90.5	14.6	5.4	11	Tch	
Clipper Barolo	(2)	Bhs	2005	3,021	3,522	90.5	14.6	5.4	11	Tch	ex Crescent Barolo-05
Clipper Beaune	(2)	Gbr	2005	2,865	3,491	88.1	14.6	5.4	11	T	ex Crescent Beaune-07 (conv Tch-06)
Clipper Bordeaux	(2)	Gbr	2006	2,865	3,543	88.1	14.6	5.4	11	Tch	I/a Crescent Bordeaux
Clipper Bourgogne	(2)	Gbr	2008	2,865	3,544	88.1	14.6	5.4	11	Tch	
Clipper Bricco	(2)	Bhs	2008	2,999	3,541	90.5	14.6	5.4	11	Tch	
Clipper Brunello	(2)	Bhs	2008	2,999	3,532	90.5	14.6	5.4	11	Tch	
Clipper Burgundy	(2)	Gbr	2007	2,865	3,557	88.1	14.6	5.4	11	Tch	
Clipper Cuillin		Bhs	2005	2,616	3,424	95.9	14.4	5.8	12	Tch	ex Crescent Cuillin-07, I/a Naslipi
Clipper Daisy		Mhl	1998	7,092	12,756	124.0	22.2	8.8	13	Tch	ex Panam Sol-08, Opal Sun-02
Clipper Highlander		Gbr	2003	1,300	1,862	78.9	10.5	4.3	-	T	ex Crescent Highlander-06, Montipora-04, Kerem D-03 (conv Tch-08)
Clipper Inge		Dis	2005	4,473	6,203	100.0	17.2	7.0	14	Tch	ex Inge Wonsild-07
Clipper Karen		Ita	2006	7,687	11,290	116.5	20.0	8.1	13	Tch	
Clipper Karina		Ita	2006	7,687	11,420	116.5	20.0	8.4	13	Tch	
Clipper Kate		Ita	2006	7,687	11,259	116.5	20.0	8.1	13	Tch	
Clipper Katja		Bhs	2007	7,687	11,255	116.5	20.0	8.4	13	Tch	
Clipper Kira		Bhs	2007	7,687	11,299	116.5	20.0	8.4	13	Tch	
Clipper Kitty		Bhs	2007	7,687	11,322	116.5	20.0	8.4	13	Tch	
Clipper Klara		Bhs	2007	7,687	11,283	116.5	20.0	8.4	13	Tch	
Clipper Kristin		Bhs	2006	7,687	11,316	116.5	20.0	8.4	13	Tch	
Clipper Krystal		Bhs	2007	7,687	11,420	116.5	20.0	8.4	13	Tch	
Clipper Kylie		Bhs	2007	7,687	11,260	116.5	20.0	8.4	13	Tch	
Clipper Lancer		Bhs	2006	6,522	9,971	118.4	19.0	8.2	14	Tch	
Clipper Leader		Bhs	2004	6,522	10,126	118.4	19.0	8.2	13	Tch	ex Panam Trinity-06, Clipper Leader-04
Clipper Leander		Bhs	2004	6,522	10,098	118.4	19.0	8.2	14	Tch	
Clipper Legacy		Bhs	2004	6,522	10,048	118.4	19.0	8.2	14	Tch	
Clipper Legend		Bhs	2004	6,522	10,048	118.4	19.0	8.2	13	Tch	
Clipper Loyalty		Bhs	2007	6,522	10,000	118.4	19.0	8.2	13	Tch	
Clipper Marianne		Dis	2005	4,473	6,228	100.0	17.2	7.0	12	Tch	ex Marianne Wonsild-07
Clipper Nadja		Dis	1996	4,128	5,752	99.8	16.4	6.7	12	Tch	ex Nadja Wonsild-06, Bro Nadja-03, United Nadja-00
Clipper Nelly		Dis	1997	4,137	5,767	99.8	16.4	6.7	12	Tch	ex Nelly Wonsild-07, Bro Nelly-03, United Nelly-00
Clipper Nora		Dis	1997	4,137	5,811	99.8	16.4	6.7	13	Tch	ex Nora Wonsild-07, Bro Nora-03, United Nora-00
Clipper Saga **		Nis	2007	2,613	4,053	89.0	13.3	5.7	12	Tch	
Clipper Sira		Nis	2006	2,613	4,053	89.0	13.3	5.7	11	Tch	
Clipper Sola **		Nis	2008	2,613	4,054	89.0	13.3	5.7	12	Tch	
Clipper Sund **		Nis	2008	2,613	4,054	89.0	13.3	5.7	12	Tch	
Clipper Tobago		Bhs	1999	5,483	8,834	112.5	18.8	7.8	14	Tch	ex Botany Treasure-06
Clipper Trinidad		Bhs	1998	5,483	8,823	113.0	18.8	7.8	13	Tch	ex Botany Trust-06
Costanza Wonsild ‡		Ita	1994	2,349	2,698	89.6	14.0	5.2	13	Tch	
Frances Wonsild ‡		Ita	1994	2,349	2,697	89.6	14.0	5.2	13	Tch	
Janne Wonsild ‡		Ita	1993	2,349	2,694	89.6	14.0	5.2	13	Tch	
Mary Wonsild ‡		Ita	1994	2,349	2,698	89.6	14.0	5.2	13	Tch	
Nordic Copenhagen *		Sgp	2005	8,448	12,959	127.2	20.4	8.7	13	Tch	ex Sichem Copenhagen—07
Nordic Helsinki *		Nis	2007	8,539	13,034	128.6	20.4	8.7	13	Tch	ex Spectator-07
Nordic Oslo *		Sgp	2005	8,448	12,975	127.2	20.4	8.7	13	Tch	ex Sichem Oslo-07
Nordic Stockholm *		Nis	2007	8,452	12,885	127.2	20.4	8.7	13	Tch	ex New Trader-07

Name	Flag	Year	GT	DWT	Loa	Bm	Drt	Kts	Type	Remarks
Sarah Wonsild ‡	Ita	1993	2,349	2,702	89.6	14.0	5.2	13	Tch	

Newbuildings: Several 7,665 gt 9,600 dwt chemical tankers tankers (Clipper S class) for 2010/1 delivery
* managed by EMS Ship Management (Denmark) A/S
** owned by Brodrene Klovning Shipping AS, Norway
† managed for A/S Danena, Denmark or ‡ for Marittima Etnea Srl (Amoretti Armatori Group), Italy
Also owns and manages a large number of larger tankers and bulk carriers.

Normed International BV   Netherlands

Funnel: *Owners colours.* **Hull:** *Owners colours with white 'NORMED' on hull.* **History:** *Founded 1990.* **Web:** *www.normed.com.tr*
Newbuildings: Two 8,400 gt vessels on order for 2010 delivery.
Currently charters about 10 vessels, some with 'NORMED' prefix.

Norresundby Shipping A/S   Denmark

Funnel: *Blue.* **Hull:** *Blue with red boot-topping.* **History:** *Not confirmed.* **Web:** *www.nrsbshipping.dk*

Name	Flag	Year	GT	DWT	Loa	Bm	Drt	Kts	Type	Remarks
Danstar	Dis	1976	1,440	1,389	72.0	13.1	3.9	12	C	ex Satelith-86
Klevstrand	Dis	1970	1,194	996	71.2	13.2	3.0	12	Cp	
Livarden	Dis	1973	1,449	1,626	78.5	11.5	4.4	10	Cp	(len-75)
Mina	Dis	1979	2,065	1,251	76.7	14.0	4.9	12	Cp	ex Scan Mina-06, Jaxlinn-05, Nordvag-04, Trans Vag-01
Saturn	Dis	1966	627	772	53.6	9.4	3.4	10	C	ex Dorca-89, Douro Star-79, Wilma Frank-72
Scan Fjell *	Nor	1978	2,195	1,900	77.0	14.0	5.4	12	Cp	ex Trans Fjell-02

* owned by Scan Carrier A/S, Denmark and managed by Norwegian Ship Assistance Consulting AS, Norway.
Also see Nor Lines AS

North Atlantic Shipping Ltd   Ireland

Funnel: *Green with broad white band beneath black top.* **Hull:** *Dark blue with white 'FEEDERLINK', red boott-topping.* **History:** *Founded 2003 as Nolan Shipping Ltd.* **Web:** *www.northatlanticshipping.com*

Name	Flag	Year	GT	DWT	Loa	Bm	Drt	Kts	Type	Remarks
Clonlee	Iom	1996	3,999	5,210	100.6	18.2	6.6	15	CC	ex Vera-07, P&O Nedlloyd Finland-05, Vera-02
Clonmore	Irl	1993	5,299	7,485	126.8	16.6	6.9	15	CC	ex Banjaard-04, Texel Bay-95, Banjaard-94

Joint-Stock Co Northern River Shipping Lines   Russia

Funnel: *White or black with blue 'NRSL' beneath white sail and hull symbol on blue square below white over blue over red bands, narrow black top.*
Hull: *Blue with red boot-topping.* **History:** *Founded 1923 as Northern River Shipping Co to 1995 and controlled by the Government of The Russian Federation.*
Web: *None found.*

Name		Flag	Year	GT	DWT	Loa	Bm	Drt	Kts	Type	Remarks
Amur-2518	(2)	Rus	1987	3,086	3,159	117.7	13.4	4.0	10	Cc	
Amur-2526	(2)	Rus	1988	3,086	3,159	116.0	13.4	4.0	10	Cc	
Amur-2537	(2)	Rus	1991	3,086	3,159	116.0	13.4	4.0	10	Cc	
Kolguev	(2)	Rus	1971	2,478	3,225	114.0	13.2	3.7	10	C	ex XXIV Syezd KPSS-92
Sormovskiy-3063	(2)	Rus	1989	3,048	3,391	119.2	13.4	3.9	10	Cc	
Sormovskiy-3068	(2)	Rus	1990	3,048	3,391	118.7	13.4	4.1	10	Cc	
STK-1005	(2)	Rus	1984	1,573	1,663	82.0	11.6	2.8	11	Cc	
STK-1020	(2)	Rus	1986	1,573	1,663	82.0	11.6	2.8	10	Cc	
STK-1026	(2)	Rus	1986	1,573	1,663	82.0	11.6	2.5	10	Cc	
STK-1029	(2)	Rus	1987	1,573	1,660	82.0	11.6	2.5	10	Cc	
Volgo-Balt 246	(2)	Rus	1984	2,516	3,150	113.0	13.0	3.7	10	C	

Also operates five coasters with 'Dubai' prefix managed by Dubai-based ship manager.

Joint Stock Northern Shipping Co   Russia

Funnel: *White with red 'N' and blue 'NSC' interrupting three narrow blue bands or with narrow blue over red bands and light blue polar bear symbol, black top.*
Hull: *Grey, blue or black with red-boot-topping.* **History:** *Founded 1870 and controlled by the Government of The Russian Federation.* **Web:** *www.ansc.ru*

Name	Flag	Year	GT	DWT	Loa	Bm	Drt	Kts	Type	Remarks
Aleksandr Sibiryakov	Mlt	1989	6,395	7,075	131.4	19.9	7.0	14	Cc	ex A. Sibiryakov-95
Inzhener Plavinskiy	Mlt	1988	8,026	9,382	156.1	19.3	7.0	13	Cc	
Iogann Makhmastal	Rus	1990	6,395	7,075	131.6	19.3	7.0	14	Cc	
Ivan Ryabov	Rus	1979	5,370	6,070	130.3	17.4	6.9	16	Cc	ex Heidenau-93
Jupiter I	Mlt	1985	1,839	2,167	78.6	12.6	4.3	12	Cc	ex Jupiter-04, Dirk-86
Kapitan Kuroptev	Mlt	1998	4,998	4,618	98.2	17.6	6.7	12	Cc	
Kapitan Lus	Mlt	1994	4,998	4,678	93.6	17.6	7.0	12	C	
Kapitan Mironov	Mlt	1995	4,998	4,678	98.2	17.6	6.7	12	C	
Kapitan Ryntsyn	Rus	1988	2,610	2,925	86.2	13.0	4.6	11	Cc	ex Carola-02, Tricolor Star II-96, Coringle Bay-91, Tiger Sea-90, Carola R-89
Kapitan Yakovlev	Mlt	1996	4,998	4,678	98.2	17.6	6.7	12	C	
Kholmogory	Rus	1995	2,986	4,830	98.4	16.9	5.9	15	Cc	ex Jenna Catherine-08
Mekhanik Brilin	Rus	1991	2,489	2,636	85.2	14.5	5.1	12	C	
Mekhanik Fomin	Rus	1991	2,489	2,650	85.4	14.5	5.1	12	C	
Mekhanik Kottsov	Rus	1991	2,489	2,650	85.4	14.5	5.1	12	C	
Mekhanik Kraskovskiy	Rus	1992	2,489	2,650	85.4	14.5	5.1	12	C	
Mekhanik Makarin	Rus	1991	2,489	2,650	85.4	14.5	5.1	12	C	
Mekhanik Pustoshnyy	Rus	1992	2,489	2,650	85.4	14.5	5.1	12	C	

Name	Flag		Year	GT	DWT	Loa	Bm	Drt	Kts	Type	Remarks
Mekhanik Pyatin	Rus		1992	2,489	2,650	85.4	14.5	5.1	12	C	
Mekhanik Semakov	Rus		1991	2,489	2,650	85.4	14.5	5.1	12	C	
Mekhanik Tyulenev	Rus		1992	2,489	2,650	85.4	14.5	5.1	12	C	
Mekhanik Yartsev	Rus		1990	2,489	2,650	85.2	14.5	5.1	12	C	
Mikhail Cheremnykh	Rus		1973	3,527	4,054	97.3	16.2	6.4	14	C	
Mikhail Lomonosov	Rus		2000	2,990	4,805	99.6	16.9	5.9	15	Cc	ex Validus-07, Vento I Garbi-03, Validus-03, Millennium-01
Pavel Korchagin	Rus		1980	5,370	6,017	130.3	17.4	6.9	15	C	
Pioner Belorussii	Rus		1978	5,370	6,070	130.3	17.4	6.9	15	C	
Pioner Estonii	Rus		1976	5,370	6,070	130.3	17.3	7.3	15	C	
Pioner Karelil	Rus		1978	5,370	6,070	130.3	17.4	6.9	15	C	
Pioner Kazakhstana	Rus		1979	5,370	6,070	130.3	17.4	6.9	15	C	
Pioner Litvy	Rus		1977	4,814	6,070	130.3	17.4	6.9	15	C	
Pioner Moldavii	Rus		1979	4,814	6,070	130.3	17.4	6.9	15	C	
Pioner Severodvinska	Rus		1975	5,370	6,070	130.3	17.3	6.9	15	C	
Pioner Yakutii	Rus		1977	5,370	6,070	130.3	17.3	6.9	15	C	
Sergey Kuznetsov	Rus		1987	2,610	2,871	87.0	13.0	4.6	11	Cc	ex Mekong Fortune-02, Saigon Fortune-93, Fortune Bay-92, Markham Bay-91, Magdalena R-88
Tekhnolog Konyukhov	Rus		1979	5,370	6,095	130.0	17.4	6.9	16	Cc	ex Rabenau-93
Zamoscvorechye	Mlt		1997	4,998	4,678	98.2	17.6	6.7	-	C	l/a Kapitan Ryntsyn

Also owns larger vessels.

NorthSeaTankers BV   Netherlands

See under C & H Heuvelman Shipping BV

North-Western Shipping Joint Stock Co   Russia

Funnel: White with narrow blue over red bands or with black anchor and 'N' narrow black top or orange/brown with blue 'n', anchor and rope on white square. **Hull:** Light grey, blue or black with red boot-topping. **History:** Founded 1923 as North-Western River Shipping Co to 1992 and controlled by the Government of The Russian Federation. **Web:** www.nwsc.spb.ru

Name		Flag	Year	GT	DWT	Loa	Bm	Drt	Kts	Type	Remarks
Alexander Kuprin **		Mlt	1996	2,319	3,030	89.5	13.4	4.5	11	Cc	
Alexander Tvardovskiy **		Mlt	1995	2,319	3,030	89.5	13.4	4.5	11	Cc	
Aleksandr Grin **		Mlt	1997	2,319	3,030	89.5	13.4	4.5	11	Cc	
Amur-2507	(2)	Rus	1985	3,086	3,152	115.7	13.4	4.0	10	Cc	ex Volgo-Balt 255-85
Amur-2510	(2)	Rus	1986	3,086	3,159	115.7	13.4	4.0	10	Cc	
Amur-2514 *	(2)	Rus	1986	3,086	3,159	115.7	13.4	4.0	10	Cc	
Amur-2520	(2)	Rus	1987	3,086	3,148	115.7	13.4	4.0	10	Cc	
Amur-2521	(2)	Rus	1987	3,086	3,148	115.7	13.4	4.0	10	Cc	
Amur-2525	(2)	Rus	1988	3,086	3,148	116.0	13.4	4.0	10	Cc	
Amur-2527	(2)	Rus	1988	3,086	3,148	116.0	13.4	4.0	10	Cc	
Aviakonstruktor Polikarpov	(2)	Rus	1983	2,466	3,353	114.0	13.0	3.6	10	C	
Baltiyskiy-102 *	(2)	Rus	1978	1,926	2,554	95.0	13.2	4.0	12	Cc	
Baltiyskiy-107 *	(2)	Rus	1979	1,926	2,554	95.0	13.2	4.0	12	Cc	
Baltiyskiy-110 *	(2)	Rus	1980	1,926	2,554	95.0	13.2	4.0	12	Cc	
Baltiyskiy-201 **		Mlt	1994	2,264	2,803	89.5	13.4	4.3	11	Cc	
Baltiyskiy-202 **		Mlt	1994	2,264	2,803	89.5	13.4	4.3	12	Cc	
Khudozhnik Vetrogonskiy	(2)	Rus	1987	4,911	6,277	139.8	16.6	4.5	10	C	ex Volga-4003-04
Konstantin Paustovskiy **		Mlt	1996	2,319	3,030	89.5	13.4	4.5	11	Cc	
Leonid Leonov **		Mlt	1994	2,264	2,800	89.5	13.4	4.3	11	Cc	
Mikhail Dudin **		Mlt	1996	2,319	3,030	89.5	13.4	4.5	11	Cc	
Nevskiy-22	(2)	Rus	1983	2,196	3,000	110.7	14.8	3.0	10	C	
Omskiy-98	(2)	Rus	1978	2,550	3,152	108.4	15.0	3.3	10	C	
Omskiy-99	(2)	Rus	1979	2,447	3,108	108.4	15.0	3.3	10	C	
Omskiy-100 *	(2)	Rus	1979	2,550	3,060	108.4	15.0	3.0	10	C	
Omskiy-141 *	(2)	Rus	1979	2,550	3,070	108.4	15.0	3.0	10	C	
Omskiy-132	(2)	Rus	1988	2,551	2,853	108.4	15.0	3.1	10	C	
Omskiy-133	(2)	Rus	1988	2,551	2,853	102.0	15.0	3.1	10	C	
Omskiy-134	(2)	Rus	1988	2,550	2,853	108.4	14.8	3.1	10	C	
Omskiy-135	(2)	Rus	1988	2,550	2,853	108.4	14.8	3.1	10	C	
Omskiy-137	(2)	Rus	1989	2,498	2,667	108.4	15.0	3.0	10	C	
Omskiy-140	(2)	Rus	1989	2,470	2,886	108.4	15.0	3.1	10	Cc	
Omskiy-141 *	(2)	Rus	1989	2,460	2,760	108.4	15.0	3.1	10	C	
Rusich-7 *	(2)	Mlt	2006	4,970	5,485	128.2	16.5	4.3	11	Cc	
Sheksna *		Rus	1994	2,052	2,769	82.4	12.5	5.0	12	Cc	
Sibirskiy-2128	(2)	Rus	1982	3,409	3,480	127.7	15.4	3.2	10	Cc	
Sibirskiy 2131	(2)	Rus	1982	3,978	3,507	129.5	15.8	3.6	10	Cc	
Sibirskiy 2132	(2)	Rus	1983	3,978	4,137	129.5	15.8	3.6	10	C	

Joint Stock Northern Shipping Co. Jupiter I. *F. de Vries*

Joint Stock Northern Shipping Co. Mekhanik Fomin. *C. Lous*

North-Western Shipping Joint Stock Co. Baltiyskiy-110. *C. Lous*

Name		Flag	Year	GT	DWT	Loa	Bm	Drt	Kts	Type	Remarks
Sibirskiy 2133	(2)	Rus	1983	3,978	4,137	129.5	15.8	3.7	10	C	
Skulptor Anikushin	(2)	Rus	1989	4,966	6,277	139.8	16.4	6.4	10	C	ex Volga-4008-01
Sormovskiy-3001	(2)	Rus	1981	2,491	3,100	114.1	13.2	3.7	10	C	
Sormovskiy-3003	(2)	Rus	1981	2,491	3,100	114.1	13.2	3.7	10	C	
Sormovskiy-3055 *	(2)	Rus	1986	3,041	3,134	119.2	13.4	3.7	10	Cc	
Sormovskiy-3056	(2)	Rus	1986	3,041	3,134	119.2	13.2	3.7	10	Cc	
Sormovskiy-3057	(2)	Rus	1987	3,041	3,134	119.2	13.4	3.7	10	Cc	
Sormovskiy-3058	(2)	Rus	1987	3,041	3,134	119.2	13.4	3.7	10	Cc	
Sormovskiy-3064 *	(2)	Rus	1989	3,048	3,391	118.7	13.4	4.8	10	Cc	
Sormovskiy-3067	(2)	Rus	1990	3,048	3,391	119.2	13.4	4.8	10	Cc	
Stas ***		Pan	2008	2,765	3,177	102.6	12.8	5.0	-	C	
STK-1003	(2)	Rus	1983	1,408	1,260	82.0	11.6	2.5	10	C	
STK-1004 *	(2)	Rus	1983	1,573	1,669	82.0	11.6	2.5	10	C	
STK-1009 *	(2)	Rus	1984	1,408	1,669	82.0	11.6	2.8	10	C	
STK-1012 *	(2)	Rus	1985	1,573	1,669	82.0	11.9	2.8	10	C	
STK-1028	(2)	Rus	1987	1,575	1,669	82.0	11.6	2.5	10	C	
STK-1031	(2)	Rus	1987	1,408	1,669	82.0	11.6	2.8	10	C	
STK-1036	(2)	Rus	1988	1,408	1,706	82.0	11.9	2.8	11	C	
Svir	(2)	Rus	1980	2,794	3,345	105.9	16.7	3.4	10	C	ex Volgo-Don 5078-92
Valentin Pikul **		Mlt	1994	2,264	2,917	89.5	13.4	4.3	11	Cc	
Vasiliy Malov *	(2)	Rus	1978	1,926	2,554	95.0	13.2	4.0	12	Cc	ex Baltiyskiy-104-81
Vasiliy Shukshin **		Mlt	1995	2,264	2,792	89.5	13.4	4.4	11	Cc	
Volgo-Balt 201	(2)	Rus	1977	2,457	2,893	113.9	13.0	3.6	10	C	
Volgo-Balt 204	(2)	Rus	1977	2,457	3,191	114.0	13.0	3.6	10	C	
Volgo-Balt 211	(2)	Rus	1978	2,457	3,180	114.0	13.0	3.6	10	C	
Volgo-Balt 215	(2)	Rus	1978	2,457	2,893	114.0	13.0	3.6	10	C	
Volgo-Balt 238	(2)	Rus	1982	2,457	3,150	114.0	13.0	3.6	10	C	
Volgo-Don 5065	(2)	Rus	1977	3,394	3,775	138.8	16.7	3.5	10	C	
Volgo-Don 5076	(2)	Rus	1980	3,958	3,962	138.8	16.7	2.9	10	C	
Volgo-Don 5077	(2)	Rus	1980	3,958	3,962	138.8	16.7	2.9	10	C	
Volgo-Don 5080	(2)	Rus	1981	3,958	3,962	138.8	16.7	2.9	10	C	
Volgo-Don 5084	(2)	Rus	1982	3,958	3,962	138.8	16.7	2.9	10	C	
Volgo-Don 5088	(2)	Rus	1984	3,958	3,962	138.8	16.7	2.9	10	C	
Volgo-Don 5091 *	(2)	Rus	1986	3,978	3,352	138.8	16.7	2.9	10	C	
Volgo-Don 5105	(2)	Rus	1989	3,973	3,352	138.8	16.7	2.9	10	C	
Volzhskiy-40	(2)	Rus	1991	4,045	4,178	138.0	16.0	3.1	11	C	
Volzhskiy-44	(2)	Rus	1991	4,197	4,178	138.5	16.0	3.1	11	C	
Volzhskiy-47	(2)	Rus	1991	4,045	5,017	138.5	16.5	3.5	10	C	
Volzhskiy-50	(2)	Rus	1991	4,045	4,178	138.4	16.0	3.1	11	C	

*managed by Volga-Neva Ltd, Russia, ** by INOK NV, Belgium (www.inok-nv.com) or *** by Russochart GmbH, Germany (www.russochart.de)*

Northwood (Fareham) Ltd UK

Funnel: *Black with two white bands.* **Hull:** *Black with red boot-topping.* **History:** *Founded in 1920's under current name since 1960, being acquired in 1997 as a joint venture by Westminster Gravels (Bos Kalis) and Redland (now Lafarge).* **Web:** *None found.*

Name	Flag	Year	GT	DWT	Loa	Bm	Drt	Kts	Type	Remarks
Donald Redford	Gbr	1981	681	964	53.5	10.7	3.4	9	Dss	(len/conv C-90)
Norstone	Gbr	1971	1,143	1,803	67.2	12.5	4.5	10	Dss	ex Sand Skua-97

Owned jointly by Redland Ltd. and Lafarge.

Norwegian Ship Assistance Consulting AS Norway

Funnel: *Black with red 'N' over 'S', narrow black top.* **Hull:** *Blue or black with white 'SCAN SHIPPING' or 'BALTIC LINE', red boot-topping.* **History:** *Not confirmed.* **Web:** *www.nsac.no*

Name	Flag	Year	GT	DWT	Loa	Bm	Drt	Kts	Type	Remarks
Baltic Trader	Pan	1975	1,739	1,664	82.5	12.7	3.7	12	C	ex Tinto-02, Lysfoss-83 (len-87)
Fykan	Pan	1970	1,395	1,016	71.2	13.2	3.0	12	Cp	ex Palo-96, Trans Sun-90, Fykan-87
Ulriken	Pan	1972	1,470	1,626	78.5	11.5	4.4	11	Cp	

Also see Janus Andersen & Co AS, Denmark

Nye Sulevaer Norway

Funnel: *White with large black 'S' between narrow black band and narrow black top.* **Hull:** *Blue with black boot-topping.* **History:** *Founded 1994.* **Web:** *None found.*

Name	Flag	Year	GT	DWT	Loa	Bm	Drt	Kts	Type	Remarks
Sule Viking	Nor	1987	1,599	2,262	80.3	11.3	4.4	11	Cc	ex Gudrun II-07, Gudrun-90 (len-94)
Suledrott	Nor	1984	1,520	1,837	76.5	11.5	3.9	10	C	ex Ute-04 (len-94)
Sulevaer	Nor	1977	1,242	1,258	67.0	11.7	4.5	11	Bu	ex Nordstar-94

Nyki Shipping BV Netherlands

Funnel: *Buff with white 'NS' on blue square.* **Hull:** *Blue with red or black boot-topping.* **History:** *Founded 2005 to merge interests of Anglo Dutch Management Services Ltd, UK and VW Nyki Shipping BV.* **Web:** *www.vwnyki.nl*

Name	Flag	Year	GT	DWT	Loa	Bm	Drt	Kts	Type	Remarks
Amny Dollard	Gib	2002	2,545	3,725	88.6	12.5	5.4	10	Cc	ex Esperance-07

North-Western Shipping Joint Stock Co. Valentin Pikul. *David Walker*

Nye Sulevaer. Sule Viking. *Allan Ryszka Onions*

Nyki Shipping BV. Amny Dollard. *N. Kemps*

Name	Flag	Year	GT	DWT	Loa	Bm	Drt	Kts	Type	Remarks
Amny Ems	Gib	2003	2,545	3,850	88.6	12.5	5.4	10	Cc	ex Espoire-07, Steel Queen-06, Espoire-04
Aspen	Atg	1999	1,989	3,037	82.0	12.6	5.0	12	Cc	ex Amy-06
Birch	Atg	1990	1,552	2,412	79.6	11.3	4.4	10	Cc	ex Sea Mersey-05, Remmer-00
Cedar	Atg	1981	1,499	1,766	82.5	11.3	4.1	10	Cc	ex Aqua Pioneer-05
Elm	Atg	1982	1,939	2,890	88.0	11.3	4.7	11	Cc	ex Christina Kerstin-07, Esteburg-90, Bilbao-89, Sea Este-88, Esteburg-83
Ivy	Cyp	1985	2,061	3,030	88.0	11.3	4.9	11	CC	ex Coimbra-05, Gerda Rambow-95
Larch	Atg	1984	2,119	3,500	92.1	11.5	5.2	10	Cc	ex Joiner-05, Ruth-W-02
Maple	Gib	1985	2,590	3,053	88.0	12.8	5.3	11	Cc	ex Simon B-08, Paula-06
May	Vct	1985	2,472	3,055	90.0	13.7	4.4	11	Cc	ex Sodade-08, Ina Lehmann-00, Werner-91, Sea Louise-87, Werner-86
Merle	Gib	1991	1,548	2,412	79.6	11.3	4.4	10	CC	ex Freya-07, Birch-05, Freya-05
Oak	Bhs	1983	1,560	2,401	87.8	11.1	4.1	11	Cc	ex Breezand-05
Oostzee	Nld	1978	815	1,150	63.0	9.4	3.4	10	C	ex Zwartewater-95, Almenum I-92, Almenum-92
Salix	Atg	1986	2,120	3,020	92.1	11.3	5.2	9	Cc	ex Viseu-06, Bargstedt-96

Managed by VW Nyki Shipping BV

Odfjell ASA   Norway

Funnel: *White with blue diagonal chain link symbol, black top.* **Hull:** *Orange with blue 'ODFJELL SEACHEM', red or black boot-topping.* **History:** *Formed 1914 as Storli ASA to 1998; Seachem merged 1989 and Ceres Hellenic merged 2000. Acquired 50% of Flumar Brazil in 1999 and remainder in 2008 from Kristian Gerhard Jebsen Skips.* **Web:** *www.odfjell.com*

Name	Flag	Year	GT	DWT	Loa	Bm	Drt	Kts	Type	Remarks
Bow Asia	Sgp	2004	6,219	9,888	114.8	19.4	8.2	13	Tch	
Bow Balearia *	Lbr	1998	3,726	5,846	99.9	16.5	6.8	15	Tch	ex Multitank Balearia-05
Bow Bracaria *	Lbr	1997	3,726	5,846	99.9	16.5	6.8	15	Tch	ex Multitank Bracaria-05
Bow Brasilia *	Lbr	1997	3,726	5,846	99.9	16.5	6.8	15	Tch	ex Multitank Brasilia-05
Bow Master	Sgp	1999	4,667	6,046	103.6	16.6	7.1	13	Tch	
Bow Mate	Sgp	1999	4,667	6,001	103.6	16.6	7.1	13	Tch	
Bow Pilot	Sgp	1999	4,667	6,005	103.6	16.6	7.1	13	Tch	
Bow Querida	Sgp	1996	6,737	10,115	126.7	19.0	7.8	13	Tch	ex Giada D-06, Jo Giada D-05, Giada D-00
Bow Sailor	Sgp	1999	4,667	6,008	103.6	16.6	7.1	13	Tch	
Bow Singapore	Sgp	2004	6,219	9,888	114.8	19.4	8.2	13	Tch	

* managed by Ahrenkiel Shipmanagement GmbH & Co KG, Germany qv
Also owns and operates numerous larger product/chemical tankers.

J O Odfjell A/S   Norway

Funnel: *Blue with white interlinked 'JO' symbol.* **Hull:** *Orange some with blue 'JO TANKERS', red boot-topping.* **History:** *Parent founded 1977, Dutch subsidiary JO Tankers BV in 1981 as Winterport Tankers to 1990 and JO Management BV to 1996, Norwegian subsidiary JO Tankers AS founded in 1989 as JO Management A/S to 1996.* **Web:** *www.jotankers.com*

Name	Flag	Year	GT	DWT	Loa	Bm	Drt	Kts	Type	Remarks
Jo Spirit	Lbr	1998	4,425	6,248	107.4	15.9	7.0	13	Tch	l/a Proof Spirit

managed by JO Tankers AS

Reederei Jurgen Ohle KG   Germany

Funnel: *White with broad turquoise band below narrow black top.* **Hull:** *Turquiose with red boot-topping.* **History:** *Founded 1983.* **Web:** *None found.*

Name	Flag	Year	GT	DWT	Loa	Bm	Drt	Kts	Type	Remarks
Dornbusch	Deu	1996	3,999	5,220	101.1	18.5	6.6	15	Cc	ex Norrland-08, l/a Dornbusch
Finja	Cok	1978	1,925	2,271	79.8	12.8	4.4	12	C	ex Rika-09, Hanni-98, G.H.Ehler-90
Hanni	Deu	1998	5,056	6,867	117.9	18.2	7.1	17	CC	ex Svealand-07
Jana	Deu	2009	8,273	11,007	139.6	22.2	7.4	-	CC	
Mare	Deu	2009	8,273	10,700	139.6	22.2	7.4	-	CC	
Ragna	Deu	1998	3,999	5,215	101.1	18.5	6.6	15	CC	ex Baumwall-06, l/a Ragna

Onarheim Management AS   Norway

Funnel: *White with black 'O' on red band, narrow black top.* **Hull:** *Red with black boot-topping.* **History:** *Founded 2008.* **Web:** *None found.*

Name	Flag	Year	GT	DWT	Loa	Bm	Drt	Kts	Type	Remarks
Onarfjell	Pan	1980	2,783	3,726	90.2	14.0	6.2	13	Tch	ex Anglo-08, Queen Tredaer-06, Proof Gallant-98
Onarfjord	Pan	1875	1,640	2,321	79.9	12.1	5.4	13	Tch	ex Avant-08, West Avant-03, Glory-01, Dutch Glory-00

Onego Shipping & Chartering BV   Netherlands

Funnel and **Hull:** *Not confirmed.* **History:** *Founded 2004.* **Web:** *www.onega.nl*

Name	Flag	Year	GT	DWT	Loa	Bm	Drt	Kts	Type	Remarks
Onego Spirit	Blz	1991	3,936	4,725	97.8	17.3	6.0	12	C	ex Rybno-08, Rybnovsk-03, Myanmar Progress-93, Rybnovsk-92

Orion VoF   Netherlands

Funnel: *White with red stars between blue diagonal stripes, narrow black top.* **Hull:** *Turquiose with red boot-topping.* **History:** *Not confirmed.* **Web:** *None found.*

Name	Flag	Year	GT	DWT	Loa	Bm	Drt	Kts	Type	Remarks
Orion	Nld	1998	2,985	4,852	98.4	16.9	5.9	15	CC	ex Europe Orion-08, Condor-06, Uppland-04, Admiral Star-01, Bremer Zukunft-00

Nyki Shipping BV. Elm. *David Walker*

Nyki Shipping BV. Oak. *David Walker*

Odfjell ASA. Bow Brasilia. *Allan Ryszka Onions*

Reederei Jurgen Ohle KG. Hanni. *Oliver Sesemann*

Orion Shipping Co

Russia

Funnel: *Pale green with white 'JS' symbol on red disc above black 'VOLGA' or white with blue over red bands, narrow black top.* **Hull:** *Black, blue or various other colours.* **History:** *Founded 1940 as White Sea & Onega River Shipping Co to 1992 and merged with Neva Shipping in 2007.* **Web:** *www.bop.onego.ru*

Name		Flag	Year	GT	DWT	Loa	Bm	Drt	Kts	Type	Remarks
Aleksandr Shotman	(2)	Rus	1987	3,041	3,265	119.2	13.4	3.8	10	Cc	ex Sormovskiy 3059-89
Aleksey Novoselov		Rus	1989	4,997	5,446	138.3	16.5	3.8	10	C	ex Volzhskiy-29-02
Amur-2509 **	(2)	Rus	1985	3,086	3,152	115.7	13.4	4.0	10	Cc	
Amur-2515 **	(2)	Rus	1986	3,086	3,152	113.9	13.4	4.0	10	Cc	
Amur-2517 **	(2)	Rus	1987	3,086	3,152	115.7	13.4	4.0	10	Cc	
Amur-2522	(2)	Rus	1987	3,086	3,152	116.0	13.4	4.0	10	Cc	
Amur-2528	(2)	Rus	1989	3,086	3,148	116.0	13.4	4.0	10	Cc	
Amur-2540	(2)	Rus	1991	3,086	3,152	116.0	13.4	4.0	10	C	
Baltiyskiy-56 †	(2)	Rus	1966	1,865	2,140	95.6	13.2	3.4	10	C	
Baltiyskiy-101 *	(2)	Rus	1978	1,926	2,555	95.0	13.2	4.2	10	Cc	
Belorus	(2)	Rus	2005	4,182	5,489	108.3	16.5	4.8	10	C	
Boris Pevkin	(2)	Rus	1990	4,997	5,375	138.3	16.5	3.8	10	C	ex Volzhskiy-28-02
Evgeniy Sokolnitskiy	(2)	Rus	1989	5,076	5,375	138.3	16.5	3.8	10	C	ex Volzhskiy-30-01
Girvas **	(2)	Rus	1981	2,776	3,292	105.9	16.7	3.4	10	C	ex Volgo-Don 5081-93 (short-94)
Kalevala	(2)	Rus	1986	2,829	3,220	105.3	16.7	3.4	10	C	ex Volgo-Don 5092-94 (short-94)
Kapitan Abakumov	(2)	Rus	2007	4,182	5,464	108.3	16.7	4.8	10	Cc	
Kapitan Konkin	(2)	Rus	2008	4,182	5,468	108.3	16.7	4.8	10	Cc	
Kapitan Kozhevnikov †	(2)	Rus	2009	4,182	5,467	108.3	16.7	4.8	10	Cc	
Karel	(2)	Rus	2006	4,182	5,495	108.3	16.7	4.8	10	Cc	
Kazakh	(2)	Rus	2006	4,182	5,509	108.3	16.7	4.8	10	Cc	
Kelarvi		Rus	1995	1,596	2,300	81.4	11.3	4.2	11	Cc	
Kento		Rus	1994	1,596	2,300	81.4	11.5	4.2	9	Cc	
Keret		Rus	1994	1,596	2,300	81.4	11.5	4.2	10	Cc	
Kivach **	(2)	Rus	1985	2,829	3,220	105.3	16.7	3.4	10	C	ex Volgo-Don 5090-95 (short-93)
Kizhi	(2)	Rus	1986	2,829	3,220	105.3	16.7	3.4	10	C	ex Volgo-Don 5093 (short-93)
Koriangi		Rus	1993	1,596	2,300	81.4	11.5	4.2	9	Cc	
Kovera		Rus	1995	1,596	2,300	81.4	11.5	4.2	11	Cc	
Leonid Khotkin	(2)	Rus	1989	5,076	5,446	138.5	16.5	3.8	10	C	ex Volzhskiy-27-02
Lezhevo		Rus	1995	1,596	2,300	81.4	11.5	4.3	10	C	
Meg		Rus	1993	1,596	2,300	81.4	11.5	4.2	10	Cc	
Nadvoitsy	(2)	Rus	1988	2,829	3,220	105.3	16.7	3.4	10	C	ex Volgo-Don 5099-94 (short-94)
Onego *		Rus	1991	1,574	1,890	81.2	11.3	3.6	9	Cc	
Petrozavodsk	(2)	Rus	1990	4,282	4,178	138.9	16.5	3.2	10	C	ex Volzhskiy-39-99
Pyalma	(2)	Rus	1988	2,829	3,220	105.3	16.7	3.4	10	C	ex Volgo-Don 5097-94 (short-94)
Pyotr Anokhin	(2)	Rus	1989	3,048	3,503	119.2	13.4	4.1	10	Cc	l/a Sormovskiy-3065
Pyotr Strelkov	(2)	Rus	1990	5,076	5,375	138.3	16.5	3.8	11	C	ex Volzhskiy-36-01 (len-01)
Rossiyanin	(2)	Rus	2005	4,182	5,454	108.3	16.5	4.8	10	Cc	
Samur 12 **	(2)	Rus	1984	1,846	2,755	86.7	12.0	2.5	10	C	ex Kapitan Napitukhin-04, ST-1309
Sandal		Rus	1993	1,596	2,300	81.2	11.4	4.3	11	Cc	
Seg		Rus	1993	1,596	2,300	81.4	11.5	4.2	9	Cc	
Shala	(2)	Rus	1986	2,829	3,220	105.3	16.7	3.4	10	C	ex Volgo-Don 5094-94 (short-94)
Shizhnya **	(2)	Rus	1987	2,829	3,220	105.3	16.7	3.5	10	C	ex Volgo-Don 5098-94 (short-94)
Shuya		Rus	1994	2,889	3,148	96.0	13.4	4.3	11	Cc	
Sormovskiy-45	(2)	Rus	1982	2,478	3,135	114.0	13.2	3.7	10	C	
Sormovskiy-48	(2)	Rus	1983	2,466	3,134	114.0	13.2	3.7	10	C	
Sormovskiy-50	(2)	Rus	1983	2,466	3,135	114.0	13.2	3.7	10	C	
Suna		Rus	1994	2,889	3,148	96.0	13.4	4.3	11	Cc	
Suoyarvi		Rus	1994	1,596	2,300	81.4	11.5	4.2	10	Cc	
Syam		Rus	1993	1,596	2,300	81.4	11.5	4.2	9	Cc	
Tulos		Rus	1995	1,596	2,300	81.4	11.5	4.2	11	C	
Toyvo Vyakhya	(2)	Rus	1985	2,466	3,135	114.0	13.2	3.7	10	C	
Ukrainets	(2)	Rus	2005	4,182	5,499	108.3	16.5	4.8	10	Cc	
Ulusland 1 **		Rus	1982	1,988	2,864	87.6	11.3	4.5	11	C	ex Susa-03, Lumar-01, Eleonore-00, Altamira-95, Bottensee-95
Vasiliy Klimov	(2)	Rus	2007	4,182	5,471	108.3	16.5	4.8	10	C	
Viktor Taratin	(2)	Rus	1989	5,076	5,415	138.3	16.7	3.8	10	C	
Vladimir Noskov †		Rus	2009	4,182	5,467	108.3	16.5	4.8	10	C	
Volga	(2)	Rus	1991	4,966	6,277	139.8	16.6	4.5	10	Cc	
Volga-4002	(2)	Rus	1987	4,911	5,845	139.8	16.6	4.3	10	Cc	
Volga-4004	(2)	Rus	1988	4,911	5,845	139.8	16.6	4.5	10	Cc	
Volga-4006	(2)	Rus	1988	4,911	5,845	139.8	16.6	4.5	10	Cc	
Volga-4007	(2)	Rus	1989	4,911	5,845	139.8	16.6	4.5	10	Cc	
Volga-4009	(2)	Rus	1990	4,966	5,985	139.8	16.6	4.5	10	Cc	
Volgo-Balt 220 *	(2)	Rus	1979	2,516	2,893	114.0	13.2	3.6	10	C	
Volgo-Balt 223 *	(2)	Rus	1979	2,516	3,180	114.0	13.2	3.6	10	C	
Volgo-Balt 226 *	(2)	Rus	1980	2,516	2,893	114.0	13.2	3.6	10	C	
Volgo-Balt 227 *	(2)	Rus	1980	2,516	3,180	113.9	13.2	3.6	10	C	

Name		Flag	Year	GT	DWT	Loa	Bm	Drt	Kts	Type	Remarks
Volgo-Balt 228 *	(2)	Rus	1980	2,516	3,180	114.0	13.2	3.6	10	C	
Volgo-Balt 229	(2)	Rus	1981	2,516	3,180	113.9	13.2	3.6	10	C	
Volgo-Balt 230 *	(2)	Rus	1981	2,516	3,180	114.0	13.2	3.6	10	C	
Volgo-Balt 231 *	(2)	Rus	1981	2,516	3,180	114.0	13.2	3.6	10	C	
Volgo-Balt 232 *	(2)	Rus	1981	2,516	3,180	114.0	13.2	3.6	10	C	
Volgo-Balt 235 *	(2)	Rus	1981	2,516	3,180	114.0	13.2	3.6	10	C	
Volgo-Balt 236 *	(2)	Rus	1982	2,516	3,180	114.0	13.3	3.6	10	C	
Volgo-Balt 237 *	(2)	Rus	1983	2,516	3,180	114.0	13.2	3.6	10	C	
Volgo-Balt 239 *	(2)	Rus	1982	2,516	3,180	114.0	13.2	3.6	10	C	
Volgo-Balt 240 *	(2)	Rus	1982	2,516	3,180	114.0	13.2	3.6	10	C	
Volgo-Balt 245 *	(2)	Rus	1983	2,516	3,180	114.0	13.2	3.6	10	C	
Volzhskiy-33	(2)	Rus	1990	5,076	5,375	138.3	16.7	3.8	10	C	ex Dmitriy Varvarin-09
Vyg		Rus	1992	1,598	2,300	81.2	11.3	3.7	11	Cc	

managed for Onego-Balt Shipping Co LLC, Russia (founded 1999)
** managed by Albatros-Petersburg Shipping Co.*
† owned by White Sea-Onega Shipping Co, Russia*

Osterreichischer Lloyd Seereederei   Austria

Funnel: *White with white 'O' on blue square , narrow blue top or * dark blue with black top.* **Hull:** *Light grey or * black with red boot-topping or charterers colours.* **History:** *Originally founded in 1836, but ceased to exist in 1918. Reformed in 1951 and from 1978 as Osterreichischer Lloyd Bereederungs GmbH to 1988, operating as ship management company in partnership with Krohn GmbH & Co KG until 2008, when again renamed.* **Web:** *www.oelsm.com*

Name	Flag	Year	GT	DWT	Loa	Bm	Drt	Kts	Type	Remarks
Amurdiep	Cyp	2009	2,984	4,250	89.9	15.2	5.1	12	C	
Anna Elisabeth	Aut	1999	4,930	5,969	113.1	16.4	6.7	16	Cc	l/a Oltet
Anna Gabriele	Aut	2000	4,930	5,969	113.1	16.4	6.7	16	Cc	l/a Ostrov
Kalliope *	Mlt	1994	5,624	6,920	108.8	17.8	7.2	13	C	ex Donbass-98
MCP Graz	Cyp	2009	5,272	8,024	117.0	19.7	6.5	15	CC	
MCP Linz	Cyp	2008	5,272	7,852	117.0	19.7	6.5	14	CC	
MCP Salzburg	Cyp	2008	5,272	8,024	117.0	19.7	6.5	15	CC	
MCP Vienna	Cyp	2008	5,272	8,024	117.0	19.7	6.5	15	CC	
MCP Villach	Cyp	2008	5,272	8,024	117.0	19.7	6.5	15	CC	
Vans Queen	Lbr	1978	11,861	7,892	121.0	20.0	7.7	16	Ro	ex Seki Cedar-99
Wilson Hook	Cyp	2003	2,993	4,280	89.9	15.2	5.6	12	Cc	
Wilson Hull	Cyp	2001	3,037	4,247	89.9	15.2	5.6	12	Cc	
Wilson Sky	Cyp	2001	3,037	4,281	89.9	15.2	5.6	13	C	ex Weissenkirchen-01, Marble Fjord-01

Pallas Shipping AB   Sweden

Funnel: *White with lettering on black eclipse burgee flag.* **Hull:** *Green with white 'PALLAS BULK', black boot-topping.* **History:** *Founded 2008 as subsidiary of Pallas Oil AB.* **Web:** *www.pallasoljor.se*

Name	Flag	Year	GT	DWT	Loa	Bm	Drt	Kts	Type	Remarks
Pallas Ocean	Brb	1986	1,999	3,960	88.0	13.2	5.3	12	C	ex Olivier-08

Passat Joint Stock Co (UAB Passat)   Lithuania

Funnel: *Yellow or * dark blue.* **Hull:** *Red with red or black boot-topping.* **History:** *Founded 1991.* **Web:** *www.passat.lt*

Name		Flag	Year	GT	DWT	Loa	Bm	Drt	Kts	Type	Remarks
Lokys		Atg	1982	1,934	2,890	88.0	11.5	4.7	11	Cc	ex Lucky-04, Poetenitz-99, Diogo do Couto-95, Svenja-86
Stropus *	(2)	Ltu	1990	4,966	6,277	139.8	16.5	4.5	10	C	ex Freedom III-07, Geo Prelude-98, Fruzhi-93
Vigo		Atg	1983	1,945	2,904	88.0	11.3	4.7	11	Cc	ex Polterberg-04

Olaf Pedersen's Rederi A/S   Norway

Funnel: *White with broad black band and narrow black top.* **Hull:** *Blue or red with red or black boot-topping.* **History:** *Founded 1936 as Olaf Pedersen.* **Web:** *www.nordic-maritime.no*

Name	Flag	Year	GT	DWT	Loa	Bm	Drt	Kts	Type	Remarks
Bustein	Dma	1972	1,591	2,450	76.1	11.8	5.2	10	C	ex Aasvaer-05, Muhlenberg-85
Leistein	Bhs	1996	2,744	4,775	89.0	13.2	6.1	11	Cc	ex Lukas-06, Emily C-04
Mostein	Bhs	1996	2,744	4,775	89.0	13.2	6.1	11	Cc	ex Moritz-07, Mark C-04

Operated by subsidiary Nordic Maritime Services AS (founded 1998
Associated with United Gas Carriers BV (Unigas International), also operates Red Sea Marine Services jointly with Bakri Navigation.

Carl F Peters GmbH & Co   Germany

Funnel: *Cream with red 'E' or 'L' inside black ring interrupting black diagonal stripe on white square, black top.* **Hull:** *Light grey with red boot-topping.* **History:** *Founded 1989.* **Web:** *None found.*

Name	Flag	Year	GT	DWT	Loa	Bm	Drt	Kts	Type	Remarks
Claus	Gib	2004	4,973	7,402	106.1	16.5	7.4	12	Tch	
Eberhard *	Atg	1983	3,075	5,238	105.8	15.1	5.6	12	Tch	(len-85)
Heinrich	Gib	2002	4,401	6.711	114.0	16.9	6.8	15	Tch	
Paul E	Gib	2006	4,677	6,975	119.6	16.9	-	-	Tch	
Regina Eberhardt	Atg	1984	8,902	8,968	136.3	21.5	7.0	16	Cc	ex Sea Regina-98, Kent Merchant-94, Regina Eberhardt-93, Merkur Africa-93, Capricomus-90, Independent Endeavour-90, Cape Byron-88, Capricomus-87, Tabuco-86, Capricomus-86, Husa-85, Capricomus-85, Capri Eagle-85, Contship Alpha-85, Capricomus-84

Orion VoF. Orion. *Allan Ryszka Onions*

Phoenix Reederei. ACX Demonstrator. *N. Kemps*

Name	Flag	Year	GT	DWT	Loa	Bm	Drt	Kts	Type	Remarks
Willy	Gib	2003	4,973	7,415	106.1	16.5	7.5	13	Tch	

* managed for Leth & Co, Germany

A/O Petroflot Russia

Funnel: *White with narrow black top.* **Hull:** *Green or red with red boot-topping.* **History:** *Founded 2002 and controlled by Government of The Russian Federation.*
Web: *None found.*

Name	Flag	Year	GT	DWT	Loa	Bm	Drt	Kts	Type	Remarks
Aqua Fruit	Kna	1983	3,955	5,250	108.5	15.9	7.4	16	R	ex Nautic-07, Roko-07, Nautic-03
Beronike	Blz	1985	2,007	2,470	78.4	12.8	4.5	10	Cc	ex Brandaris-07
Fastrex	Kna	1992	1,946	2,060	75.9	12.8	4.5	10	Cc	ex Baltrader-09, Fortuna 1-08, Goplana II-94
Yamburg	Geo	1977	1,801	2,623	81.2	11.8	5.1	11	Cc	ex Alk-04, Talea-00, Anna H-94, Parnass-88

Managed by SIA Baltmar Shipmanagement, Latvia

Phoenix Reederei Bereederungs GmbH & Co KG Germany

Funnel: *Cream with black top or charterers colours.* **Hull:** *Blue or dark green with red boot-topping.* **History:** *Founded 1994 as Phoenix Reederei GmbH to 2006.*
Web: *www.phoenix-reederei.de*

Name	Flag	Year	GT	DWT	Loa	Bm	Drt	Kts	Type	Remarks
ACX Demonstrator *	Deu	1975	2,134	2,570	81.5	13.4	5.0	13	Cc	ex Hemo-07, Dunkerque Express II-02, Svealand-99, Ulla-89, Osteclipper-86, Nic-Clipper-79, Osteclipper-78
BBC Greece	Atg	1997	4,559	6,375	105.0	16.2	7.4	14	Cc	ex Hilde K-04
BBC Reydarfjordur	Gib	1998	5,025	5,450	116.1	16.6	6.1	16	Cc	ex Boltentor-07, CMA CGM Skikda-06, CMA CGM Alger-01, Boltentor-01, Diamante-00, Boltentor-99
BBC Svendborg	Atg	1995	3,572	5,027	96.7	15.8	6.2	14	Cc	ex Falderntor-06, Huon Gulf-03, Falderntor-02, Boyne River-02, Falderntor-01, Delmas Mahury-99, Ivaran Primero-97, Falderntor-96
BBC Venezuela	Atg	1999	3,821	5,240	100.0	15.8	6.3	14	Cc	ex Global Africa-01, Fockeburg-00
Emsbroker	Deu	2002	4,183	5,917	109.2	15.0	6.2	13	Cc	ex Alexander-06, Normed Bremen-05, I/a Lingestroom
Emstor	Gib	1996	4,180	4,953	107.7	16.4	6.3	16	Cc	ex EWL Tinidad-06, Emstor-04, Torm Cameroun-03, Emstor-01, Maersk Castries-00, Maersk Maracaibo-98, Emstor-97
Forum Fiji II	Deu	1999	4,620	5,650	116.1	16.6	6.1	16	Cc	ex Ratstor-08, Forum Fiji II-06, Ratstor-03
Hafentor	Prt	1998	5,025	5,450	116.1	16.6	6.2	16	Cc	ex Maersk Kingston-99, Hafentor-98
Haneburg	Atg	1998	8,530	11,108	136.2	21.0	8.5	17	CC	ex Safmarine Tana-02, Haneburg-01
Herrentor	Gib	1998	4,620	5,650	116.1	16.6	6.1	16	Cc	ex MOL Caribe-02, Herrentor-01
Jummetor	Prt	1997	4,180	4,950	107.7	16.4	6.3	16	CC	ex Torm Cote d'Ivoire-03, Jummetor-01, Delmas Manoka-01, Jummetor-00, Maersk Bridgetown-00, Maersk Cartagena-98, Jummetor-97
Neutor	Prt	1997	5,025	5,450	116.1	16.6	6.2	16	Cc	ex APL San Juan-09, CMA CGM Caribbean-05, Neutor-02, P&O Nedlloyd Manaus-99, Neutor-98
Nordertor	Atg	1998	5,025	5,449	116.1	16.6	6.2	16	Cc	
Sudertor	Atg	1999	4,620	5,450	116.1	16.6	6.1	16	Cc	ex Delmas Seychelles-05, Papuan Gulf-03, Sudertor-02, Ibn Bajjah-01, Sudertor-00
Tuxpan Reef	Atg	1995	3,458	5,215	96.7	15.8	6.2	14	Cc	ex Ledator-01, Delmas Kourou-99, Delphine-97, Ledator-95
Wesertor	Deu	1997	4,180	4,985	108.6	16.4	6.3	15	Cc	ex SCM Tepuy-04, Wesertor-02, Evenburg-02, Maersk Coral-00, I/a Evenburg

Newbuildings: Five 8,550 gt 11,500 dwt general cargo ships for 2010-11 delivery.
* managed for DK Group Netherlands BV

Pohl Shipping Schiffahrts GmbH & Co KG Germany

Baltic Forest Line GmbH & Co KG

Funnel: *White with broad red band having black 'BFL' on three white fir tree shapes.* **Hull:** *Dark blue with black or red boot-topping.* **History:** *Founded 1982 and operating subsidiary formed 1997.* **Web:** *www.pohlgruppe.de*

Name	Flag	Year	GT	DWT	Loa	Bm	Drt	Kts	Type	Remarks
Baltic Carrier	Gib	1997	2,280	3,130	82.5	12.3	5.0	11	Cc	
Baltic Merchant	Gib	1997	2,280	3,110	82.5	12.3	5.0	11	Cc	
Baltic Sailor	Gib	1997	2,280	3,110	82.5	12.3	5.0	11	Cc	
Baltic Skipper	Gib	1998	2,280	3,110	82.5	12.3	5.0	11	Cc	

Managed by Reederei Heinz Corleis KG and chartered to Pool-Carriers – see below.

Pool-Carriers Schiffahrts GmbH & Co KG Germany

Funnel: *Owners colours.* **Hull:** *Owners colours with white 'P+C'.* **History:** *Pool operator founded 2004.* **Web:** *www.pool-carriers.de*
Currently operates 12 coasters on charter with six newbuildings due for delivery during 2010.

Pot Scheepvaart BV Netherlands

Funnel: *Green base with black 'P' and green 'S' on broad white band below black top.* **Hull:** *Light grey with black boot-topping.* **History:** *Founded 1973 as Pot Scheepvaart BV to 1986 then Pot Scheepvaartbedrijf CV.* **Web:** *www.pot-scheepvaart.nl*

Name	Flag	Year	GT	DWT	Loa	Bm	Drt	Kts	Type	Remarks
Doggersbank	Nld	2006	3,990	6,000	110.8	14.8	6.2	13	C	ex Jaguar-08
Drogdenbank	Nld	2009	3,990	6,000	110.8	14.8	6.2	13	C	
Kwintebank	Nld	2002	6,378	9,600	132.2	15.9	7.8	15	Cc	
Scheldebank	Nld	2007	2,999	4,500	89.8	14.0	6.0	13	Cc	

Name	Flag	Year	GT	DWT	Loa	Bm	Drt	Kts	Type	Remarks
Schouwenbank	Nld	1998	2,774	4,140	89.9	13.6	5.7	13	Cc	
Skagenbank	Nld	2005	2,999	4,500	89.8	14.0	6.0	13	Cc	
Steenbank	Nld	2005	2,999	4,500	89.8	14.0	6.0	12	Cc	
Stroombank	Nld	2009	2,999	4,550	89.8	14.0	6.0	13	Cc	
Varnebank	Nld	2000	6,130	8,727	132.2	15.9	7.1	15	Cc	
Vissersbank	Nld	1994	1,682	2,503	81.7	11.0	4.5	11	C	

J Poulsen — Denmark

Funnel: Black with broad red band or red with black 'D' at centre of white horizontal/vertical cross, black top. **Hull:** Black with red boot-topping. **History:** Founded 1930. **Web:** www.jpship.dk

Name	Flag	Year	GT	DWT	Loa	Bm	Drt	Kts	Type	Remarks
Marsus	Dis	1986	1,091	1,122	67.9	10.1	3.4	10	Cc	
Ocean Bird	Dis	1991	3,320	4,222	94.4	15.5	5.6	13	Cc	
Pangani **	Gib	2004	7,002	7,920	119.8	20.2	7.6	15	Cc	
Pegasus	Dis	1981	1,161	1,275	62.9	11.2	3.9	11	Cc	
Sea Bird	Dis	1990	3,273	4,270	94.4	15.5	5.6	13	Cc	
Star Bird	Dis	1993	3,351	5,215	96.7	15.8	6.3	15	Cc	ex Felston-94
Thor Athos	Dis	1987	3,132	4,143	88.6	15.7	6.6	13	Cc	ex Thor Kis-87, Thor Eagle-01, Steinkirchen-97, Svenja-92

Operated by subsidiary J Poulsen Shipping A/S (founded 1981 as J Poulsen Chartering A/S to 1987)
* managed by Inter-Marine AS, Norway or ** by Harren & Partner Ship Management GmbH & Co KG, Germany.
Also partner with Harren & Partner Schiffahrts GmbH, Germany in K/S Combi Lift owning one large heavy-lift ship.

Prakse Sia — Latvia

Funnel: White. **Hull:** Blue with red boot-topping. **History:** Not confirmed. **Web:** Not found.

Name	Flag	Year	GT	DWT	Loa	Bm	Drt	Kts	Type	Remarks
Gerda	Lva	1989	852	1,279	64.3	10.5	3.4	10	C	ex Dan Provider-07, Sandettie-04, Voran 93
Liva Greta	Lva	1988	851	1,280	64.2	10.5	3.4	8	C	ex Elstar-08, Varnebank-96

Pregel Chartering GmbH — Germany

Funnel: Buff with houseflag (white diagonal cross with blue upper and red lower segments) or white with black top. **Hull:** Green or blue with red boot-topping. **History:** Founded 2001 and management subsidiary in 2002. **Web:** www.pregel-chartering.de

Name	Flag	Year	GT	DWT	Loa	Bm	Drt	Kts	Type	Remarks
Anda	Mlt	1981	2,723	2,860	95.6	13.5	4.3	12	Cc	ex Odin-03, Stadt Papenburg-02, Odin-97, Vela-91
Helma	Mlt	1990	3,845	3,936	104.9	16.3	5.9	14	Cc	ex Halsingland-08
Laima	Cyp	1989	2,554	3,020	108.4	15.0	3.1	-	C	ex Daugavpils-01
Selga	Atg	1984	3,093	3,185	95.5	15.2	4.4	12	Cc	ex Uppland-07, Karin-92
Valda	Atg	1985	2,696	2,934	92.5	13.9	4.5	11	Cc	ex Medelpad-05, Merlin-97

Managed by Pregel Management GmbH

Prima Shipping Oy AB — Finland

Funnel: White with blue 'G' on white diamond on broad blue band. **Hull:** Blue with red boot-topping. **History:** Founded 1987 and associated with Rederei AB Gronqvist. **Web:** www.primashipping.fi

Name	Flag	Year	GT	DWT	Loa	Bm	Drt	Kts	Type	Remarks
Carisma	Fin	1985	1,473	2,100	79.0	10.9	3.9	10	Cc	ex Beetpulp Trader-07, Hella-03, Hel-92
Carissa	Fin	1988	1,986	2,618	82.5	12.5	4.6	11	Cc	ex Marta-06, Karin-05
Casandra	Fin	1970	1,197	1,900	74.0	10.9	5.1	12	Cc	ex Anne-94, Frank-92, Frank Nibbe-85, Ostestern-77, Owen Kersten-73, I/a Ostestern
Celia	Fin	1986	851	1,276	64.3	10.6	3.4	11	C	ex Heron-06, Regina-98, Nes-95, Lingedijk-92
Celina	Fin	1992	1,599	2,250	81.7	11.0	4.1	12	C	ex Elwin-07, Marietje Andrea-05
Cleopatra	Fin	1982	1,999	2,954	83.3	12.6	5.4	13	C	ex Nora-01 (len-86)

J J Prior Transport Ltd — UK

Funnel: Red with black top. **Hull:** Black with red boot-topping. **History:** Founded 1934. **Web:** www.jjprior.co.uk

Name	Flag	Year	GT	DWT	Loa	Bm	Drt	Kts	Type	Remarks
Bert Prior	Gbr	1961	175	289	32.9	6.8	2.5	-	C	(len-63)
Brenda Prior	Gbr	1968	198	279	32.3	6.9	2.7	7	C	ex Cherly M-87, Kiption-84
James Prior	Gbr	1963	191	300	34.1	6.8	2.6	-	C	ex James P-95
Lodella	Gbr	1970	181	315	31.7	6.8	2.6	7	C	
Mark Prior	Gbr	1969	191	295	31.7	6.7	2.6	6	C	ex Lobe-94
Nigel Prior	Gbr	1966	172	264	29.4	6.7	-	7	C	ex Roina-01
Peter Prior	Gbr	1969	392	609	44.4	7.8	3.2	9	C	ex Holm Sound-98, Gore-87, Eloquence-85

Q-Shipping BV — Netherlands

Funnel: Blue with black top or charterers colours. **Hull:** Dark blue or red (tankers) with black boot-topping. **History:** Founded 1990 by Scheepvaartsbedrijf K De Groot (founded 1982) as Euro Marine Services BV to 1997. **Web:** www.q-shipping.nl

Name	Flag	Year	GT	DWT	Loa	Bm	Drt	Kts	Type	Remarks
Ammon **	Nld	2005	2,545	3,800	88.6	12.5	5.4	-	Cc	
Australis	Cyp	2008	1,921	2,959	83.0	12.6	4.8	10	Tch	
Brilliante	Gib	1997	3,782	5,557	100.9	14.5	6.3	14	Cc	ex Baltic Prestige-06, AKN Prestige-05, Morgenstond II-05
Distinto *	Gib	2000	3,244	4,131	100.0	18.3	4.6	13	Cc	ex Grachtdiep-07
Festivo	Gib	1979	6,413	4,600	135.9	16.8	4.6	13	Ro	ex Baltic Press-08 (len-82)

Name	Flag	Year	GT	DWT	Loa	Bm	Drt	Kts	Type	Remarks
Forza	Nld	2000	3,244	4,031	100.0	18.3	4.6	13	Cc	ex Gouwediep-06
Harmony	Nld	1977	3,785	4,150	97.5	16.0	5.7	14	Cc	ex Zim Espana-01, West Moor-95, Westermoor-86, Essex Courage-83, Westermoor-83
Hathor **	Nld	2007	2,545	3,850	88.6	12.5	5.4	-	Cc	
Lontano *	Deu	2000	3,244	4,130	100.0	16.3	4.6	13	Cc	ex Grootdiep-07
Metallica	Gib	1989	3,826	4,402	104.8	16.2	5.6	14	Cc	ex Linda-05
Nekton	Nld	1996	1,996	3,246	84.8	12.6	4.8	10	Cc	ex Aquarius-04
Oralake	Cyp	2004	1,860	2,813	82.3	12.5	4.8	11	T	ex Baltic Swan-06, Oralake-05, I/a Elka-S
Priority	Cyp	2009	4,030	6,450	103.0	16.0	7.0		Tch	
Sonoro	Gib	2000	3,244	4,130	100.0	16.3	4.6	13	Cc	ex Gaastdiep-06
Sunergon	Nld	2006	2,241	3,121	88.7	12.5	5.0	12	Cc	
Vantage ***	Nld	2007	3,971	3,650	93.2	15.9	5.0	15	CC	
Volente	Gib	1999	3,244	4,131	100.0	16.3	4.6	12	Cc	ex Geuldiep-06

owned by subsidiary Short Sea Bulkers AS, Norway
*** managed for Hunze Lloyd BV or *** for Vantage CV, both Netherlands*
Also see Klaveness Maritime Logistics.

Quadrant Bereederungs GmbH & Co KG   Germany

Funnel: *White with black top or charterers colours.* **Hull:** *Blue with red boot-topping.* **History:** *Founded 1997 as subsidiary of Magellan Chartering Services GmbH (founded 1992) and part of DS Schiffahrt GmbH & Co KG.* **Web:** *www.quadrant-ship.de*

Name	Flag	Year	GT	DWT	Loa	Bm	Drt	Kts	Type	Remarks
Husky Racer	Gbr	1997	9.991	12,950	139.1	24.2	9.2	19	CC	ex Maersk Rijeka-08, Maersk Jarry-04, Husky Racer-00, Maersk Jarry-99, Aachen-99, Maersk Jarry-99, Husky Racer-98, Aachen-98
Husky Runner	Gbr	1997	9,962	13,455	139.1	23.9	9.2	19	CC	ex Maersk Helsinki-02, I/a Husky Runner
Maersk Flensburg	Gbr	2002	9,990	11,135	134.4	22.5	8.7	18	CC	ex Pioneer Ocean-02
Maersk Funchal	Atg	2004	9,990	11,181	134.4	22.5	8.7	18	CC	I/a Pioneer Sea
Magellan Planet	Atg	2002	6,277	7,973	133.0	18.7	7.2	18	CC	ex Charlotte Borchard-09, Gracechurch Planet-07, Pioneer Hawk-02
Magellan Star	Atg	2002	6,277	7,968	133.0	18.7	7.2	18	CC	ex Judith Borchard-09, Gracechurch Star-08, I/a Pioneer Albatros
Miriam Borchard	Atg	2002	6,277	7,977	133.4	18.7	7.2	18	CC	ex Gracechurch Jupiter-08, Pioneer Falcon-02
Pioneer Bay	Atg	1999	4,450	5,400	100.8	18.8	6.7	15	Cc	ex Amisia J-05
Pioneer Buzzard	Atg	2002	6,277	7,957	133.4	18.7	7.2	18	CC	ex Gracechurch Meteor-09, Pioneer Buzzard-02
Susan Borchard	Atg	2002	6,277	7,970	133.4	18.7	7.2	18	CC	ex Gracechurch Comet-09, I/a Pioneer Eagle
Taroudant	Gbr	2003	9,990	11,188	134.4	22.5	8.7	18	CC	ex Pioneer Lake-09, Maersk Florence-09, I/a Pioneer Lake

Reederei Rambow KG   Germany

Funnel: *White with houseflag (re/white diagonally quartered with blue 'R' on white disc at centre, narrow black top or charterers colours.* **Hull:** *Cream with red boot-topping.* **History:** *Founded 1890.* **Web:** *www.reedereirambow.de*

Name	Flag	Year	GT	DWT	Loa	Bm	Drt	Kts	Type	Remarks
Gerda	Deu	1995	3,999	5,212	101.1	18.5	6.6	15	CC	ex P&O Nedlloyd Russia-05, Gerda-02
Helmuth Rambow	Atg	2005	9,957	13,779	147.8	23.3	8.5	19	CC	ex SYMS Songshan-08, Helmuth Rambow-05
Henneke Rambow	Deu	2007	9,981	11,274	134.4	22.5	8.7	18	CC	
Karin Rambow	Atg	2005	9,957	13,807	147.9	23.3	8.5	19	CC	ex ANL Yarrunga-09, Karin Rambow-05
Malte Rambow	Atg	2005	9,957	13,827	147.9	23.3	8.5	19	CC	ex SYMS Hengshan-08, Malte Rambow-05
Safmarine Saloum	Atg	2006	9,957	13,734	147.9	23.3	8.5	19	CC	ex Katsina-06, Safmarine Santos-06, Benedikt Rambow-06
Sven	Deu	1996	6,362	7,223	121.4	18.5	6.7	16	CC	ex Lucy Borchard-00, Solid-97, Sven-96

Also owns two larger container ships.

The Ramsey Steamship Co Ltd   Isle of Man (UK)

Funnel: *Black with white Maltese cross on broad red band.* **Hull:** *Light grey with black boot-topping.* **History:** *Ship-owners since 1914.* **Web:** *www.ramsey-steamship.com*

Name	Flag	Year	GT	DWT	Loa	Bm	Drt	Kts	Type	Remarks
Ben Ellan	Iom	1981	538	824	50.0	9.3	3.4	9	C	ex River Tamar-90
Ben Maye	Iom	1979	548	805	48.8	9.1	3.6	10	C	ex Vendome-95, Peroto-94
Ben Varrey	Iom	1986	997	1,544	63.8	11.7	3.9	10	C	ex Triumph-99

Rass Schiffahrt GmbH & Co   Germany

Funnel: *Buff with black 'R' in gateway interrupting two narrow blue bands on broad white band or charterers colours.* **Hull:** *Dark blue or light grey with red boot-topping.* **History:** *Current company founded 1995.* **Web:** *www.rass-shipping.com*

Name	Flag	Year	GT	DWT	Loa	Bm	Drt	Kts	Type	Remarks
CMA CGM Agadir	Atg	2007	9,996	11,814	139.1	22.6	8.8	18	CC	ex Hoheweg-08
CMA CGM Meknes	Atg	2008	9,996	11,800	138.1	22.6	8.8	18	CC	ex Hohefels-09
Hohebank	Atg	2007	9,996	11,828	139.1	22.6	8.8	18	CC	
Hoheplate	Atg	2007	9,996	11,800	139.1	22.6	8.8	19	CC	
Hoheriff	Atg	2007	9,996	11,846	139.1	22.6	8.8	19	CC	ex MCC Sulo-09, Hoheriff-08
Hohesand	Gbr	1996	6,362	7,223	121.4	18.2	6.7	16	CC	ex Hohebank-03
Inga Lena	Gbr	1997	6,362	7,225	121.4	18.2	6.7	16	CC	ex Charlotte Borchard-01, Inga Lena-98, I/a Hoheriff

Name		Flag	Year	GT	DWT	Loa	Bm	Drt	Kts	Type	Remarks

Reskom Tyumen Ltd — Russia

Funnel: White with white over blue over red bands below black top. **Hull:** Blue with red boot-topping. **History:** Founded 2003 and controlled by the Government of The Russian Federation. **Web:** None found.

Name		Flag	Year	GT	DWT	Loa	Bm	Drt	Kts	Type	Remarks
Tyumen-1	(2)	Rus	1988	3,086	3,329	116.0	13.4	4.0	10	Cc	ex Amur-2523-07
Tyumen-2	(2)	Rus	1989	3,086	3,148	116.1	13.4	4.0	10	Cc	ex Amur-2529-07
Tyumen-3	(2)	Rus	1990	3,086	3,152	116.1	13.4	4.0	10	Cc	ex Midland-101-07, Kegums-02

Oy Rettig AB Bore — Finland

Funnel: Buff with white cross on broad blue band or * cream. **Hull:** White with green boot-topping or * red with black boot-topping. **History:** Founded 1897 as Hoyrylaiva Bore Oy, later O/Y Bore Line A/B merging in 1987 with Oy Rettig AB. Acquired Rederi AB Engship (founded 1973) in 2006 and Bror Husell Chartering AB Ltd (founded 1966 as Bro Hussels Rederier to 1983) in 2007. **Web:** www.boregroup.com

Name		Flag	Year	GT	DWT	Loa	Bm	Drt	Kts	Type	Remarks
Borden	(2)	Fin	1977	10,100	6,615	142.2	19.3	7.2	17	Ro	ex Cetam Victoriae-04, Borden-02, Blue Sky-92, Bore Sky-91
Fingard		Fin	2000	2,997	4,956	94.9	13.2	6.2	12	Cc	ex Transitorius-07
Klenoden		Fin	1991	3,828	4,455	103.5	16.2	6.7	15	Cc	
Najaden		Fin	1989	3,826	4,402	104.8	16.3	5.6	14	Ccp	
Nordgard *		Nld	1999	2,780	3,740	89.3	13.4	5.7	12	Cc	ex Liamare-06, Thalassa-06
Ostgard *		Nld	2001	2,868	3,792	89.1	13.3	5.7	12	Cc	ex Rufinia-06
Seagard **		Fin	1999	10,488	7,226	153.5	20.6	7.0	22	Ro	
Swegard		Fin	2001	2,997	4,956	95.0	13.2	6.2	12	Cc	ex Merwedelta-07
Sydgard *		Nld	2000	2,868	3,780	89.3	13.3	5.7	12	Cc	ex Griend-06, Polar Snow-03
Trenden		Fin	1989	3,826	4,402	104.8	16.3	5.8	15	Ccp	
Westgard *		Nld	2000	2,868	3,780	89.3	13.3	5.7	12	Cc	ex Sabinia-06

* owned by subsidiary Bore Shipowners BV, Netherlands.
** chartered to Spliethoff's Bevrachtingskantoor BV, Netherlands (Transfennica)
Also see vessels chartered out to United European Car Carriers in Ferry section.

Rhein Maas-und See-Schiffahrtskontor GmbH — Germany

Funnel: White with blue 'RMS' inside blue diamond, * orange with black 'H' betweem narrow black bands. **Hull:** Blue, light grey, green or brown with white 'RMS' and red or black boot-topping. **History:** Founded 1966 and acquired 2007 by Rhenus Group. **Web:** www.rheinmaas.de

Name		Flag	Year	GT	DWT	Loa	Bm	Drt	Kts	Type	Remarks
Brake **		Tuv	1957	603	817	57.5	8.5	3.4	9	C	ex Marlies-90 (len-78)
Pride of Braila	(2)	Nld	1998	2,077	3,200	110.0	11.4	3.6	13	CC	
Pride of Veere	(2)	Nld	1998	2,034	3,200	110.0	11.4	3.6	13	CC	
RMS Baerl *		Atg	1999	2,136	2,879	99.9	11.5	3.9	10	Cc	ex Kirsten-06, Rhonediep-99
RMS Beeck *		Atg	1995	1,996	3,246	84.8	12.4	4.8	10	C	ex Seabreeze-04
RMS Buchholz *		Atg	1997	2,375	3,471	89.1	12.5	4.9	11	Cc	ex Regulus-04
RMS Duisburg		Atg	1999	2,042	2,230	99.9	11.5	3.4	10	Cc	ex Cpt. L'Alexandre-06, Moseldiep-99
RMS Goole		Atg	2005	2,069	2,620	80.1	12.4	4.5	10	C	
RMS Jurmala †		Blz	1981	2,363	2,700	80.8	13.0	4.7	11	Cc	ex RMS Rheinhausen-06, Roma-02
RMS Laar		Atg	1985	1,570	2,304	82.5	11.3	4.2	10	Cc	ex Georg Luhrs-03
RMS Libava †		Blz	1983	1,281	1,566	74.9	10.6	3.4	10	C	ex RMS Ruhrort-07, Amisia-98
RMS Neudorf		Atg	1990	1,985	2,620	82.5	12.5	4.5	11	Cc	ex Sagitta-07, I/a Rosemarie
RMS Rahm		Atg	1995	1,682	2,500	81.7	11.1	4.5	10	Cc	ex Kelt-08, Nes-06, Boeran-95
RMS Ratingen		Atg	2002	1,898	2,688	88.0	11.4	4.1	11	Cc	
RMS Ruhrort		Atg	1993	1,681	2,503	81.7	11.1	4.5	10	C	ex Panta Rhei-08, Talos-06, Jason-00
RMS Saimaa		Atg	2005	2,069	2,634	80.1	12.4	4.5	10	C	
RMS Twisteden		Atg	2002	1,898	2,530	88.0	11.4	4.1	11	Cc	
RMS Vindava †		Blz	1989	1,307	1,739	74.9	10.6	3.7	10	C	ex RMS Rahm-07, Henning S-05
RMS Voerde		Atg	1999	1,846	2,460	89.6	11.7	4.5	13	Cc	
RMS Wanheim		Atg	1990	1,985	2,620	82.5	12.5	4.5	11	Cc	ex Cosmea-07
RMS Wedau		Atg	1985	1,546	1,708	82.5	11.4	3.5	10	Cc	ex Moldavia-03, Dania Carina-96

* managed for BWK Schiffinvest GmbH (founded 2004) or ** RMS Schiffahrtskontor Bremen GmbH (founded 1988 as RMS Bremen Schiffahrtskontor GmbH).
† managed by Clermont Services, Latvia for various owners.

Rhoon Scheepvaart CV — Netherlands

Funnel: White with black top. **Hull:** Dark blue with red boot-topping. **History:** Not confirmed. **Web:** None found.

Name		Flag	Year	GT	DWT	Loa	Bm	Drt	Kts	Type	Remarks
Rhoon		Nld	2000	1,780	2,432	82.5	11.4	4.3	10	C	ex Rana-05

Managed by Hudig & Veder Chartering BV

Rickmers Reederei GmbH & Cie KG — Germany

Funnel: Black with houseflag (white 'R' on red over green) on broad white band. **Hull:** Green with white 'RICKMERS', black boot-topping. **History:** Founded 1889 as Rickmers Reismuhlen Rhederei & Schiffbau AG, became Reederei Bertram Rickmers GmbH to 1992 and . Rickmers Linie sold to Hapag Lloyd in 1988 and re-acquired 2000. Acquired CCNI (Deutschland) GmbH (formed 1999) from Compania Chilena de Navegacion Interoceanica in 2004. **Web:** www.rickmers.com or www.rickmers-linie.de

Name		Flag	Year	GT	DWT	Loa	Bm	Drt	Kts	Type	Remarks
Berulan		Atg	1995	8,633	9,200	133.0	22.9	7.7	17	CC	ex Magdalena-98, Berulan—97, Louise Borchard-96, I/a Berulan
Daniela		Lbr	2003	5,593	7,107	124.2	18.2	6.5	16	CC	ex PAC Makassar-07
Inga H		Lbr	2003	5,593	7,055	124.2	18.2	6.5	16	CC	ex PAC Palawan-07

Pohl Shipping Schiffahrts GmbH. Baltic Merchant. *F. de Vries*

Pot Scheepvaart BV. Steenbank. *N. Kemps*

Oy Rettig AB Bore. Najaden. *N. Kemps*

Rhein Maas-und See-Schiffs GmbH. RMS Wedau. *N. Kemps*

Rhein Maas-und See-Schiffs. Pride of Veere. *Hans Kraijenbosch*

Name		Flag	Year	GT	DWT	Loa	Bm	Drt	Kts	Type	Remarks
Peter		Lbr	1999	5,025	5,650	116.1	16.6	6.1	16	CC	ex MOL Foresight-09, Sieltor-07
Siefke		Lbr	2002	5,234	5,700	109.4	18.2	6.7	-	CC	ex PAC Sulu-07
Umgeni		Deu	1992	9,601	12,576	149.7	22.3	8.3	17	CC	ex Delmas Portugal-09, CMA CGM Karibu-05, Delmas Marula-05, New Orient-04, R.C.Rickmers-99, Nedlloyd Caldera-98, Sea-Land Mexico-95, TSL Bold-94, R.C.Rickmers-92

Owns over 40 other larger container ships with over 50 large newbuildings on order for 2010-12 delivery.
* Managed for Hamburger Emissionshaus GmbH & Co KG (founded 2007 - www.hen-fonds.de)

GC Rieber & Co AS   Norway

Funnel: *Blue with red 'O' on white top.* **Hull:** *Blue with red boot-topping.* **History:** *Founded 1879.* **Web:** *www.rieber-shipping.no*

Name		Flag	Year	GT	DWT	Loa	Bm	Drt	Kts	Type	Remarks
Polar Explorer	(2)	Bhs	1992	2,881	3,300	91.6	16.2	4.5	14	Cr	ex Sophie-07, NDS Benguela-05, Sophie-04, Pacific Chile-98, Sophie-93
Polar Pearl	(2)	Bhs	1993	2,881	3,280	91.5	16.2	4.5	14	Cr	ex Karin B-07, Pacific Ecuador-98, Karin B-94
Polar Sea	(2)	Bhs	1993	2,881	3,288	91.6	16.2	4.5	14	Cr	ex Lisbeth C-07, Santa Paula-03, Lisbeth C-01, Pacific Peru-98, Lisbeth C-94

Operated by subsidiary GC Rieber Shipping AS (founded 1930); also operates numerous research ships.

J R Rix & Sons Ltd   UK

Funnel: *Blue with white 'J' over 'R' on red diamond.* **Hull:** *Black or dark green with red boot-topping.* **History:** *Founded 1947.* **Web:** *www.rix.co.uk*

Name		Flag	Year	GT	DWT	Loa	Bm	Drt	Kts	Type	Remarks
Lizrix		Gbr	2008	1,343	1,942	77.5	10.6	4.5	-	T	
Rix Harrier	(2)	Gbr	1979	572	1,046	45.7	9.5	3.9	8	T	ex Breydon Enterprise-97, Wib-87 (conv C-97)
Rix Hawk	(2)	Gbr	1976	562	1,036	45.9	10.0	3.9	9	T	ex Breydon Venture-99, Wis-86 (conv C-99)
Rix Kestrel		Gbr	1957	206	300	50.9	5.4	2.3	8	T	ex Burdale H-93
Rix Merlin		Gbr	2005	496	750	53.0	7.9	3.1	8	T	
Rix Osprey		Gbr	1959	207	300	50.9	5.2	2.3	8	T	ex Beldale H-96 (rblt-79)
Rix Owl		Gbr	2003	316	500	60.8	6.0	2.4	8	T	
Rix Phoenix		Gbr	2006	268	500	59.0	6.0	2.2	8	T	(pt ex Rix Falcon – blt-90)
Ronrix		Irl	1978	2,563	2,908	96.3	12.4	4.8	12	Cc	ex Killarney-02, Anholt-86, Neuwerk-81 (len-78)
Salrix		Irl	1977	2,563	2,908	96.3	12.4	4.7	10	Cc	ex Kylemore-02, Borssum-95, Bregenz-92, Bornholm-86, Neukloster-81 (len-77)

Dry cargo ships managed by Rix Shipping Co Ltd
also operates smaller tank barges

RMS Lubeck Schiffahrts GmbH   Germany

Funnel: *Yellow with white disc at centre of blue/red diagonally quartered flag.* **Hull:** *Blue or light grey with black or red boot-topping.* **History:** *Founded 1988.*
Web: *None found.*

Name	Flag	Year	GT	DWT	Loa	Bm	Drt	Kts	Type	Remarks
Jolanda	Atg	1956	499	964	57.8	9.0	3.5	10	C	ex Svend Dammann-89, Robox-69
Largona	Vct	1978	866	1,195	63.7	10.6	4.0	12	C	ex Biscay Spirit-95, Irimo-87
Salona	Hnd	1973	939	1,443	60.9	9.6	4.3	11	C	ex Atlantic Fosna-90, Frei Mignon-90, Kimare-88, Arklow Dawn-87, I/a Annemor
Largo II	Hnd	1973	531	680	49.7	8.3	3.5	11	C	ex Jannie-89, Sterno-84, Saralil-79
Lisa S *	Atg	1968	872	1,400	59.7	10.0	4.6	11	Cc	ex Kevin-S-06, Hemo-00, Antje B-96, Claus-86
Mistral *	Atg	1966	1,064	1,196	68.4	10.6	4.0	11	C	ex Nadine-98, Ragna-90, Tillia-83, Suderelv-78, Frieda Graebe-73
San Remo	Vct	1965	1,283	1,225	72.1	11.3	3.7	12	C	ex Saxen-89

* managed for other owners.

Rohden Bereederung GmbH & Co KG   Germany

Funnel: *White with green houseflag having green 6-pointed star on white diamond or charterers colours.* **Hull:** *Dark green or black with black or red boot-topping.* **History:** *Founded 1959 as Rohden Schiffsbetriebs GmbH & Co KG to 1996.* **Web:** *www.rohden.de*

Name	Flag	Year	GT	DWT	Loa	Bm	Drt	Kts	Type	Remarks
Baghira	Atg	1998	6,246	7,232	121.9	18.6	7.3	17	CC	ex APL San Jose-09, Baghira-07, Anibal-04, SCM Olympos-04, Anibal-03, Asia Feeder-99
Balu C *	Atg	2008	5,629	8,045	108.2	18.2	7.1	12	Cc	
Coronel **	Atg	1978	2,089	2,461	86.6	12.8	4.9	13	Cc	ex Lys Coronel-00, Coronel-97, Christel-85 (len-86)
Cygnus	Atg	2000	2,528	3,380	86.4	12.8	5.5	11	Cc	ex Aquila-01, Offshore I-00, I/a Eemnes
Delphinus	Atg	1997	5,730	6,870	121.9	19.0	6.9	17	CC	ex Rio Zulia-09, CMA CGM Barbados-08, Delphinus-04, Anna-Lina-99, Lauritzen Peru-99, Anna-Lina-98, I/a Greil
Shirkan C *	Atg	2007	5,608	8,045	108.2	18.2	7.1	12	Cc	
UAL Malongo	Atg	1998	2,528	3.414	86.4	12.8	5.5	11	Cc	ex Agena-08, I/a Offshore II

* operated by Carisbrooke Shipping Ltd qv
** managed by JSC Afalita Shipping, Lithuania.
Also owns four larger container ships.

RMS Lubeck Schiffahrts GmbH. Largona. *Oliver Sesemann*

Ab Ronja Marin. Ramona. *Oliver Sesemann*

Name		Flag	Year	GT	DWT	Loa	Bm	Drt	Kts	Type	Remarks

Rolldock NV — Netherlands

Funnel: *Blue with narrow white band on broad grey band.* **Hull:** *Light grey with red boot-topping.* **History:** *Founded 2006 to take over shipping interests of Zadeko Shipping NV, Belgium.* **Web:** *www.rolldock.com*

Name		Flag	Year	GT	DWT	Loa	Bm	Drt	Kts	Type	Remarks
NileDutch Cabinda	(2)	Ant	1983	4,998	4,250	104.9	18.0	4.6	12	C/ro	ex Norlandia-07, Barber Norlandia-85, Norlandia-84
NileDutch Nordica	(2)	Atg	1984	4,999	4,250	104.8	18.2	4.5	12	C/ro	ex Nordica-07, Berulan-91, ScanDutch Liguria-91, Berulan-89, Hans Behrens-88
Rolldock Sea	(2)	Nld	2009	12,802	6,902	140.6	24.0	5.6	18	HLs	
Rolldock Shore	(2)	Nld	2010	12,802	6,902	140.6	24.0	5.6	18	HLs	
Rolldock Sky	(2)	Nld	2010	12,802	6,902	140.6	24.0	5.6	18	HLs	
Rolldock Spring	(2)	Nld	2010	12,802	6,902	140.6	24.0	5.6	18	HLs	
Rolldock Star	(2)	Nld	2009	12,802	6,902	140.6	24.0	5.6	18	HLs	
Rolldock Sun	(2)	Nld	2009	12,802	6,902	140.6	24.0	5.6	18	HLs	

Newbuildings: Two further 6,900 dwt ro-ro, semi-submersible, heavy-lift carriers on order for 2011-12 delivery.

Ab Ronja Marin Ltd — Finland

Funnel: *Blue with yellow symbol on white disc.* **Hull:** *Blue with red or black boot-topping.* **History:** *Founded 1999.* **Web:** *www.ronjamarin.fi*

Name	Flag	Year	GT	DWT	Loa	Bm	Drt	Kts	Type	Remarks
Ramona	Fin	1985	1,297	1,450	74.9	10.6	3.4	10	C	ex Maria H-08
Riona	Fin	1988	910	1,083	69.1	9.5	3.0	9	C	ex Triton Elbe-07, Howden-99, Sea Danube-96

Rord Braren Bereederungs GmbH & Co KG — Germany

Funnel: *Yellow with red device on white band.* **Hull:** *Dark blue or * green with charterers name, red boot-topping.* **History:** *Founded 1990.* **Web:** *www.reedereibraren.de*

Name	Flag	Year	GT	DWT	Loa	Bm	Drt	Kts	Type	Remarks
Bremer Anna	Gib	2003	3,152	4,352	90.0	15.2	5.3	12	Cc	ex Anna Braren-03
Bremer Elena	Gib	2007	3,172	4,316	90.0	15.2	5.3	12	Cc	ex Elena Braren-03
Bremer Johanna	Gib	2008	3,172	4,350	90.0	15.2	5.3	12	Cc	
Bremer Victoria	Gib	2000	1,782	2,440	82.5	11.3	4.3	11	C	ex Aegir-05
Cellus *	Deu	1998	4,231	6,350	100.0	17.0	7.3	14	Cc	I/a Heike Braren
Forester *	Deu	1995	4,110	6,471	100.0	17.2	7.3	14	Cc	I/a Ute Braren
Timbus *	Deu	1999	4,230	6,350	100.0	17.0	7.3	14	Cc	ex Brar Braren-99

Rederiet C Rousing A/S — Denmark

Funnel: *White with blue edged white shield having red 'CR' and black anchor, narrow pale blue top.* **Hull:** *Light blue with red boot-topping.* **History:** *Founded 1979 as Carsten Rousing to 1995.* **Web:** *www.rousing.net*

Name	Flag	Year	GT	DWT	Loa	Bm	Drt	Kts	Type	Remarks
Anders Rousing	Dis	1979	1,324	1,565	69.0	11.4	3.5	10	C	ex Norbox-95, Heljo-89
Ann Rousing	Dmk	1991	2,326	2,752	84.9	12.9	4.3	11	Cc	ex Balmung-08, Panda II-99, Edith-91
Faxborg *	Dmk	1968	924	1,190	59.3	10.6	4.0	11	C	ex Lone Baand-08, Miquelon-90, Prince of Gotland-87, Birgit T-83, Miquelon-82, Pep Miquelon-79, Miquelon-76, Karelli Coast-74, Jytte Bewa-73, Merc Jytte-70
Rebecca Rousing	Dmk	1983	1,645	1,768	82.5	11.4	3.6	10	Cc	ex Ali Baba-05
Sarah Rousing *	Dis	1979	1,456	1,578	81.9	10.0	3.5	10	C	ex Alexander-94
Volo *	Dmk	1957	326	469	44.9	8.3	2.9	9	C	ex Lars Bagger-09, Ulsnaes-89, Welf

* managed by Baltic Shipping Co A/S, Denmark (www.balticshipping.dk)

Rova Shipping GmbH & Co KG — Germany

Funnel: *White.* **Hull:** *Blue with black boot-topping.* **History:** *Shipping subsidiary of established building products company.* **Web:** *None found.*

Name	Flag	Year	GT	DWT	Loa	Bm	Drt	Kts	Type	Remarks
Rova	Atg	1986	1,986	2,798	76.8	12.0	4.7	-	Cc	ex Lammy-09, Salvinia-02, Alblas-94

Ernst Russ GmbH & Co — Germany

Funnel: *Black with red 'ER' bordered by narrow red bands.* **Hull:** *Black or grey with red boot-topping.* **History:** *Founded 1893 as Ernst Russ to 1992.* **Web:** *www.ernst-russ-de*

Name		Flag	Year	GT	DWT	Loa	Bm	Drt	Kts	Type	Remarks
Antje Russ		Deu	1998	5,056	6,858	118.5	18.2	7.1	17	CC	ex Antje-08, I/a Antje Russ
Caroline Russ *	(2)	Atg	1999	11,500	7,250	153.5	23.6	7.0	20	Rop	
Christian Russ		Ant	1994	7,167	8,858	134.1	19.7	8.0	16	CC	ex Ivaran Sexto-99, Christian Russ-98, Nedlloyd Crete-98, Christian Russ-96
Elisabeth Russ *	(2)	Atg	1999	11,500	7,250	153.5	23.6	7.0	20	Rop	
Friedrich Russ *	(2)	Atg	1999	11,500	7,250	153.5	23.6	7.0	20	Rop	
Johanna Russ		Atg	2006	9,956	13,784	147.9	23.3	8.5	19	CC	
Martha Russ		Atg	1990	5,562	4,415	107.8	17.3	6.8	15	Rop	
Pauline Russ *	(2)	Atg	1999	11,500	7,250	153.5	23.6	7.0	20	Rop	

* on charter to Transfennica Shipping – see Ferry Section under Spliethoff's Bevrachtingskantour BV.

Team Lines GmbH & Co KG

Funnel: *White with dolphin symbol on funnel or superstructure.* **Hull:** *Owners colours.* **History:** *Founded 1991 jointly with Mathies Reederei GmbH and Finnlines Deutschland AG (later renamed Poseidon Schiffahrts AG). Finnlines share sold to Belgium-based Delphis NV in 2006.* **Web:** *www.teamlines.de*

Name	Flag	Year	GT	DWT	Loa	Bm	Drt	Kts	Type	Remarks
El Toro *	Lbr	2006	9,957	13,633	147.8	23.3	8.5	19	CC	I/a Maya 2

Name		Flag	Year	GT	DWT	Loa	Bm	Drt	Kts	Type	Remarks

* managed by Anglo-Eastern (Germany) GmbH
Currently operates 17 feeder container ships, five being greater than 1000 TEU.

Knut Saetre & Sonner · Norway

Funnel: *Dark blue with grey 'S' on broad white band below black top.* **Hull:** *Blue with black or red boot-topping.* **History:** *Founded 1967.* **Web:** *www.ksaetre.no*

Name		Flag	Year	GT	DWT	Loa	Bm	Drt	Kts	Type	Remarks
Frakt		Vct	1988	1,523	2,181	73.9	11.8	4.4	10	Cc	ex Arklow Bay-04, I/d Arklow Mansion
Frakto		Vct	1990	1,524	2,160	73.8	11.5	4.4	11	Cc	ex Arklow Meadow-00
Rana Frakt		Nor	1987	1,156	1,323	58.0	11.7	3.5	10	Cc	ex Heyo Prahm-97
Tri Frakt		Nor	1973	2,677	3,777	84.3	14.4	6.3	14	C	ex Frakt-94, Kiri-94, Makiri-92, Makiri Smits-84

Saimaa Trade Wind · Russia

Funnel: *White with narrow red band below black top.* **Hull:** *Blue with black boot-topping.* **History:** *Founded 2006 and controlled by Government of The Russian Federation.* **Web:** *None found.*

Name		Flag	Year	GT	DWT	Loa	Bm	Drt	Kts	Type	Remarks
STK-1007	(2)	Rus	1984	1,572	1,347	82.0	11.6	2.9	10	C	
STK-1008	(2)	Rus	1984	1,572	1,347	82.0	11.6	2.9	10	C	

Saime-K SIA · Latvia

Funnel: *White lower part, upper part blue with two narrow white bands.* **Hull:** *Light grey with red boot-topping.* **History:** *Founded 1992.* **Web:** *None found.*

Name	Flag	Year	GT	DWT	Loa	Bm	Drt	Kts	Type	Remarks
Angela	Atg	1995	3,806	4,766	99.8	16.5	5.8	14	Cc	ex Angela J-06, CMBT Cruiser-96, I/a Angela J
Apia	Vct	1983	3,435	5,221	98.7	15.5	5.5	14	Cc	ex Robert-05, CTE Istanbul-01, Robert-00, Rhein Partner-93, Robert-92, ECL Commander-92, Robert-91, Gracechurch Crown-86, Akak Success-84, Robert-84 (len-91)
Vanguard	Atg	1994	3,806	4,766	100.6	16.5	5.9	15	Cc	ex Cari Sea-95, Angela J-94

Samskip HF · Iceland

Funnel: *White with black 'samskip' and narrow black top or * white with turquoise 'B'.* **Hull:** *Dark blue or * dark grey with white 'SAMSKIP', red boot-topping.* **History:** *Founded 1946, acquiring Bruno Bischoff Reederei GmbH & Co in 1998 and Geest North Sea Line and Seawheel in 2005.* **Web:** *www.samskip.com*

Name	Flag	Year	GT	DWT	Loa	Bm	Drt	Kts	Type	Remarks
Arnarfell	Fro	2005	8,830	11,143	137.5	21.3	8.5	18	CC	
Bremer Roland *	Gib	1985	1,610	1,230	71.2	11.6	3.2	10	Cp	
Helgafell	Fro	2005	8,830	10,900	137.5	21.3	8.5	18	CC	

* owned by subsidiary Bruno Bischoff Reederei GmbH, Germany (founded 1959)
Operates chartered feeder container ships including four with 'Samskip' prefix.
Also owns Ost-West-Handel und Schiffahrt GmbH, Germany operating 8 large refrigerated vessels.

Sandfrakt Rederi AS · Norway

Funnel: *White with white/red 'S' symbol on blue disc or blue with symbol inside white wheel or ** blue with two narrow white bands.* **Hull:** *Blue with black boot-topping or ** light grey with green boot-topping.* **History:** *Founded 1972.* **Web:** *www.sandfrakt.no*

Name	Flag	Year	GT	DWT	Loa	Bm	Drt	Kts	Type	Remarks
Faktor	Nor	1971	793	823	55.3	10.5	3.3	11	C	ex Rytind-87, Scanblue-77, Bente Steen-77
Mercator I *	Nor	1971	1,406	1,370	76.3	11.9	3.9	13	Cc	ex Mercator-00, Lautonia-89, Heinrich Knuppel-85
Nor Feeder **	Gib	1998	3,999	5,202	101.8	18.5	6.5	16	Cc	ex Jan Fabian-06
Nor Viking	Nis	1977	2,133	3,048	80.1	14.4	5.6	13	C	ex Norro-92, Norrviken-88
Norholm	Gib	1995	3,443	4,708	93.5	15.1	6.3	12	Cc	ex Njord-05, Birgit-02
Norne	Gib	1996	3,443	4,927	93.5	15.1	6.1	11	Cc	ex Torne-96
Norsund	Bhs	1991	2,705	3,982	89.5	13.6	5.3	12	Cc	ex Sarah-01, MSC Larisa-98, Sarah-97, Cortes-96, Sarah-96

* owned by Sama Shipping formed jointly by Sandfrakt (40%), Trond Mannes Holding (40%) and Karmoy Skipsconsult (20%)
** managed by Karmoy Skipsconsult Management AS, Norway.

Scan-Trans Shipping · Denmark

Funnel: *White or owners colours.* **Hull:** *Green or blue with white web address and red boot-topping.* **History:** *Parent founded 1975 and shipping subsidiary in 2002.* **Web:** *www.scan-trans.com*

Name	Flag	Year	GT	DWT	Loa	Bm	Drt	Kts	Type	Remarks
Henan Scan	Lka	2009	4,990	7,750	118.6	15.2	7.1	-	Chl	ex Mercs Uhana-09
Haugaard Scan	Lka	2009	4,990	7,800	118.6	15.2	7.1	-	Chl	ex Mercs Uva-09
Mercs Mihintale	Lka	1983	8,975	14,279	141.0	20.5	8.9	15	Cc	ex Safmarine Namibe-08, Manaslu-04, Fu Shan-96, Integrity-94, Renata-94
Safmarine Lualaba	Lka	2009	9,772	12,343	140.0	21.8	8.2	-	C	ex Sarah Friedrich-09

Newbuildings: Four 8,445 gt 10,000 dwt heavy-lift general cargo vessels on order for 2010-11 delivery.
Managed by Reederei Eugen Friederich GmbH & Co KG, Germany.
Currently charters about 15 vessels under 10,000 dwt all capable of carrying project cargo, including several with 'Scan' suffix charter names.

Scanscot Shipping Services (Deutschland) GmbH · Germany

Funnel: *Black, broad dark green top with white 'S' over two narrow black bands.* **Hull:** *Dark green with white 'SCANSCOT', red boot-topping.* **History:** *Originally founded in 1967 by Scottish and Scandinavian owners, operating under current name since 1995.* **Web:** *www.scanscot-shipping.com*

Name	Flag	Year	GT	DWT	Loa	Bm	Drt	Kts	Type	Remarks
Hyundai Britania	Iom	2009	12,679	9,391	142.0	23.0	-	-	Ro	ex Scan Britania-10
Hyundai Buffalo	Deu	2003	8,831	6,785	126.8	20.0	6.7	14	Ro	ex Scan Brasil-08
Nirint Pride	Iom	2000	8,861	12,007	134.2	20.4	8.4	17	Cc	ex CEC Atlantic-03

Name	Flag	Year	GT	DWT	Loa	Bm	Drt	Kts	Type	Remarks
Scan Atlantic	Iom	1999	8,821	7,100	126.9	20.0	6.7	14	Ro	
Scan Hansa	Iom	1999	8,821	7,228	126.9	20.0	6.7	14	Ro	
Scan Oceanic	Gbr	1997	5,752	5,100	100.9	18.6	6.6	16	Ro	

Newbuildings: three further 12,600 gt vessels due for 2010 delivery.
Also operates several chartered vessels with 'Scan' or 'S.' prefixes.

Reederi Schepers GBR   Germany

Funnel: *Buff, some with white 'S' and red 'K' on green houseflag or charterers colours.* **Hull:** *Light grey with red boot-topping.* **History:** *Founded 1984.*
Web: *www.schepers.de*

Name	Flag	Year	GT	DWT	Loa	Bm	Drt	Kts	Type	Remarks
Annette	Atg	1991	3,815	4,155	103.5	16.2	6.1	14	Cc	ex Portlink Tracer-03, Rhein Trader-02, Rhein Lee-93, Rhein Trader-93
Helene *	Atg	2001	9,981	11,500	139.0	22.6	8.8	18	CC	
Herm Kiepe *	Atg	1997	9,991	13,059	139.1	23.9	9.2	19	CC	
Oostvoorne **	Atg	1996	2,036	2,800	90.6	13.8	4.6	13	CC	ex Happy Hopper-04, Oostvoorne-04, Heereweg-04, Lys Viking-00, Heereweg-96
Rockanje **	Atg	1999	2,035	2,780	90.6	13.8	4.3	13	CC	ex Seawheel Merchant-08, Heerebrug-04, Vento di Garbi-03, Herrebrug-00
Westvoorne **	Atg	1996	2,035	2,850	90.6	13.8	4.2	13	CC	ex Heeresingel-04, Lys Rover-00, Heeresingel-96

Newbuildings: Four 8,000 dwt general cargo due for 2010 delivery (Brielle, MCL Bremen, MCL Tunis and Rhoon)
** owned by subsidiaries Kiepe Schepers Containerschiff KG (founded 2005) or ** by Schepers Navigamus Trans GmbH & Co KG, Germany (founded 2004 and managed by Hartel Shipping & Chartering BV, Netherlands – www.hartel.nl)*

Reederei Rudolf Schepers KG   Germany

Funnel: *Pale blue with narrow black top or * yellow with 'RS' and two white angled lines on blue panel below narrow black top.* **Hull:** *Blue with pale blue waterline and superstructure or * black with yellow waterline band above red boot-topping and yellow superstructure.* **History:** *Founded 1990.*
Web: *www.reederei-rudolf-schepers-haren.de*

Name	Flag	Year	GT	DWT	Loa	Bm	Drt	Kts	Type	Remarks
Aurora	Cyp	2001	9,981	11,386	134.4	22.5	8.7	18	CC	
Borussia Dortmund *	Cyp	1996	6,378	7,147	121.4	18.5	6.7	16	CC	

Also owns two larger container ships with two other 32,000 gt container ships on order.

Reederei Thekla Schepers GmbH & Co KG   Germany

Funnel: *Blue with black top.* **Hull:** *Blue with black boot-topping.* **History:** *Founded 1969.* **Web:** *www.reederei-ts.de*

Name	Flag	Year	GT	DWT	Loa	Bm	Drt	Kts	Type	Remarks
Katharina B	Atg	1997	3,999	5,865	100.0	18.2	6.6	16	CC	
Margareta B	Atg	1998	3,999	5,397	100.0	18.2	6.6	16	CC	
Marus	Deu	1996	2,906	3,950	99.5	16.4	5.0	15	CC	ex Geest Atlas-05, Bell Atlas-97
Thea B	Atg	1995	2,899	3,950	99.3	16.2	4.9	14	Cc	ex Bell Astron-97, I/a Thea B

owned by subsidiary Tesch Bereederungs Gmbh & Co. KG (founded 1989)
Also owns several larger container ships with newbuildings on order.

Reederei Karl Schluter GmbH & Co KG   Germany

Funnel: *White with narrow black top.* **Hull:** *Blue or black with red boot-topping.* **History:** *Founded 1986.* **Web:** *www.rks-rd.de*

Name	Flag	Year	GT	DWT	Loa	Bm	Drt	Kts	Type	Remarks
Pride of Sneek	Deu	1999	2,988	4,810	99.6	16.9	5.9	15	Cc	ex Ute S-09, Ute-04

Also owns fleet of larger container ships and some bulk carriers.

Wilhelm EF Schmid GmbH   Germany

Funnel: *Black with device on broad white band.* **Hull:** *Dark blue with black or red boot-topping or * light green with dark green boot-topping.*
History: *Founded 1984.* **Web:** *www.seeschmid.de*

Name	Flag	Year	GT	DWT	Loa	Bm	Drt	Kts	Type	Remarks
Hogeland	Deu	1950	475	681	58.8	7.5	3.2	8	C	ex Natalie-07, Margot Schlichting-01, Elli Ahrens 71 (len/deep-78, len-92)
Nordland I	Deu	1962	269	389	41.9	7.5	2.4	8	C	ex Helena K-89, Braker Wappen-78, Nordhelm-75
Steenborg *	Deu	1967	718	781	55.0	9.6	3.4	8	C	ex Berta Morgenroth-81

Also manages some vessels for Karl Meyer Reederei GmbH & Co KG qv

Rudolf Schoening GmbH   Germany

Funnel: *White with charterers colours.* **Hull:** *Grey, red or black with red or black boot-topping.* **History:** *Founded 1999.* **Web:** *www.sdship.de*

Name	Flag	Year	GT	DWT	Loa	Bm	Drt	Kts	Type	Remarks
CCL Osaka	Cyp	2008	7,545	8,205	129.6	20.6	7.4	16	CC	I/d JRS Corvus
JRS Canis *	Cyp	2006	7,545	8,241	129.2	20.6	7.4	16	CC	
JRS Capella *	Cyp	2004	7,464	8,262	129.5	20.6	7.4	16	CC	
JRS Carina *	Cyp	2008	7,545	8,300	129.6	20.6	7.4	15	CC	
JRS Castor	Mlt	2010	6,600	9,300	107.0	18.2	8.0	-	Cc	
JRS Merkur	Mlt	2010	6,668	9,386	107.0	18.2	8.0	-	Cc	
JRS Pegassus	Mlt	2010	6,600	9,300	107.0	18.2	8.0	-	Cc	
RBD Alexa *	Cyp	2006	7,545	8,184	129.6	20.6	7.4	16	CC	
Thule	Deu	1996	2,842	4,123	89.4	13.6	5.7	13	Cc	

* managed by S & D Shipmanagement GmbH & Co KG

Rudolf Schoening GmbH/Navigia BV. Spaarnedijk. *Oliver Sesemann*

The Schulte Group. Happy Harrier. *Allan Ryszka Onions*

Name	Flag	Year	GT	DWT	Loa	Bm	Drt	Kts	Type	Remarks

Navigia Shipmanagement BV/Netherlands

Funnel: *White with green 'NAVIGIA' under blue wave symbol or charterers colours.* **Hull:** *Red with red boot-topping.* **History:** *Founded 1996.* **Web:** *www.navigia.nl*

Name	Flag	Year	GT	DWT	Loa	Bm	Drt	Kts	Type	Remarks
Amsteldijk	Cyp	2005	2,978	4,711	99.6	16.9	5.9	15	Cc	
Damsterdijk	Nld	2007	2,984	4,450	90.0	14.4	5.9	11	C	
Dinteldijk	Nld	2007	2,984	4,450	90.0	14.4	5.9	11	C	
Eemsdijk *	Cyp	2007	9,935	9,934	140.7	23.2	8.7	18	CC	
Flevodijk	Cyp	2010	9,960	12,400	140.7	23.2	8.7	18	CC	
Friesedijk	Cyp	2010	9,960	12,400	140.7	23.2	8.7	18	CC	
Hunzedijk	Nld	2009	2,984	4,450	90.0	14.4	5.9	11	C	
Ijsseldijk	Nld	2009	2,984	4,450	90.0	14.4	5.9	11	C	
Lingedijk	Nld	2009	2,984	4,450	90.0	14.4	5.9	11	C	
Marnedijk	Cyp	2006	7,545	8,185	129.6	20.6	7.4	15	CC	
Merwedijk	Nld	2001	6,420	8,298	132.2	19.4	7.3	17	CC	
RBD Gabriela	Cyp	2010	9,000	11,000	164.5	21.4	7.3	19	CC	
RBD Holsatia	Cyp	2010	9,000	11,000	164.5	21.4	7.3	19	CC	
Reggedijk	Nld	2009	2,984	4,450	90.0	14.4	5.9	11	C	
Rhonedijk	Cyp	2010	6,200	8,000	107.0	18.2	-	13	C	
Scheldedijk	Nld	2009	2,984	4,450	90.0	14.4	5.9	11	C	
Siegedijk	Cyp	2010	6,200	8,000	107.0	18.2	-	13	Cc	I/a Weserdijk
Sirrah	Nld	2002	6,386	8,446	132.3	19.4	7.3	17	CC	
Spaarnedijk	Cyp	2005	2,978	4,810	99.6	16.9	5.9	15	Cc	
Veendijk	Nld	2009	2,998	4,450	90.0	14.4	5.9	11	C	
Veersedijk	Nld	2001	6,420	8,441	132.2	19.4	7.3	18	CC	
Velserdijk	Nld	2008	2,984	4,450	90.0	14.4	5.9	11	C	
Voornedijk	Nld	2009	2,984	4,450	90.0	14.4	5.9	11	C	
Waaldijk	Nld	2009	2,984	4,450	90.0	14.4	5.9	11	C	
Weserdijk	Cyp	2010	6,200	8,000	107.0	18.2	-	13	Cc	
WMS Amsterdam *	Cyp	2005	7,464	8,213	129.6	20.6	7.4	15	CC	
WMS Groningen *	Cyp	2006	7,545	8,173	129.6	20.6	7.4	15	CC	
WMS Harlingen *	Cyp	2006	7,545	8,173	129.6	20.6	7.4	15	CC	
WMS Rotterdam *	Cyp	2005	7,464	8,218	129.6	20.6	7.4	15	CC	
WMS Vlissingen *	Cyp	2005	7,464	8,282	129.6	20.6	7.4	15	CC	

Newbuildings: Two further 8,000 dwt vessels on order for 2010 delivery.
* managed for Schoening subsidiary Mare Shipmanagement BV, Netherlands (founded 2004)

Schroeder & Co   Germany

Funnel: *Black or charterers colours.* **Hull:** *Green with red boot-topping.* **History:** *Founded 2001.* **Web:** *www.schroeder-co.de*

Name	Flag	Year	GT	DWT	Loa	Bm	Drt	Kts	Type	Remarks
Matua II	Mhl	1996	7,565	7,733	134.7	19.6	8.0	15	CC	ex Muirfield-08, Gemartrans Pioneer-06, Orient Artemis-04, MSC Malawi-03, Artemis-98, MSC Acapulco-99, Artemis-98, Bei Yuan-96
Susanne	Lbr	1992	9,151	9,868	133.7	23.0	7.6	18	CC	ex Thor Susanne-99, Maersk Basse Terre-99, Thor Susanne-98, Susanne Sif-98, Norasia Adria-96, Susanne Sif-92

Managed by Uniteam Marine Shipping GmbH
Also owns two larger feeder container ships.

The Schulte Group   Germany

Funnel: *Black with white 'S' on red disc on broad green band or charterers colours or blue with blue 'U' on broad red band ('Unigas' pool).* **Hull:** *Dark grey with red boot-topping.* **History:** *Founded 1955, the Schulte family having originally been in partnership as Schulte & Bruns from 1883* **Web:** *www.beschulte.de or www.bs-shipmanagement.com*

Name	Flag	Year	GT	DWT	Loa	Bm	Drt	Kts	Type	Remarks
Christoph Schulte	Sgp	2007	9,110	10,309	120.4	19.8	8.8	16	Lpg	
Clamor Schulte	Sgp	2007	8,234	9,192	128.67	18.6	8.4	16	Lpg	
Franz Schulte	Iom	2006	8,455	12,900	127.2	20.4	8.7	13	Tch	I/a Cederberg
Gas Pioneer	Cyp	1992	1,173	1,400	76.1	11.4	3.3	10	Lpg	ex Kilgas Pioneer-97, Annagas-92
Gas Renovatio	Mhl	1997	3,603	3,940	99.0	16.2	5.5	12	Lpg	ex Cheviot-07, Chemgas Mango-03
Gaschem Atrice **	Lbr	1984	6,755	8,711	126.1	18.6	8.1	15	Lpg	ex Atrice-05, Beatrice-94, Norgas Explorer-93, Beatrice-88
Gaschem Ben Flor	Lbr	1985	6,867	9,129	127.4	18.6	8.3	11	Lpg	ex Ben Flor-04
Happy Bee	Pan	1997	5,420	7,246	113.6	16.5	7.6	15	Lpg	
Happy Bird	Iom	1999	6,051	6,020	118.9	17.2	7.8	16	Lpg	ex Tarquin Crest-02
Happy Bride	Iom	1999	4,693	4,626	106.3	15.8	6.3	15	Lpg	ex Tarquin Loch-02
Happy Eagle	Phl	1993	3,733	4,512	98.6	15.0	6.5	15	Lpg	
Happy Fellow	Phl	1992	3,703	4,444	99.4	15.0	6.5	15	Lpg	ex Sunny Fellow-95
Happy Girl	Phl	1989	3,643	4,247	98.3	15.4	6.3	15	Lpg	ex Sunny Girl-95
Happy Harrier	Iom	1988	3,595	4,320	98.3	15.0	6.6	15	Lpg	ex Tarquin Trader-02
Lady Elena	Lbr	1998	3,465	4,288	99.6	15.5	5.8	13	Lpg	ex Elena-98
Lady Hilde	Lbr	1999	2,998	3,183	96.0	15.5	5.6	13	Lpg	
Lady Kathleen	Lbr	1998	3,465	4,288	99.6	15.5	5.8	13	Lpg	
Lady Margaux	Sgp	2000	3,435	3,856	97.7	16.0	5.4	13	Lpg	ex Canopus Gas-04
Lady Martine	Lbr	1998	2,998	3,183	96.0	15.0	5.5	13	Lpg	

The Schulte Group – OPDR. OPDR Lisboa. *Hans Kraijenbosch*

Scotline Ltd. Scot Venture. *Hans Kraijenbosch*

Name	Flag	Year	GT	DWT	Loa	Bm	Drt	Kts	Type	Remarks
Lady Stephanie **	Lbr	1991	3,415	4,240	(92.0)	15.8	5.8	13	Lpg	
Mistral ‡	Cyp	1990	3,494	4,428	99.8	15.8	5.9	12	Lpg	ex Derwent-04
Monsoon ‡	Cyp	1989	3,219	3,814	99.1	16.0	5.3	12	Lpg	ex Ben Nevis-04
Moritz Schulte	Iom	2002	8,234	9,174	128.7	18.6	8.4	16	Lpg	
NST Amalia **	Gib	2007	3,933	6,863	103.0	16.0	7.0	11	Tch	ex Amalia Theresa-09
Philine Schulte	Iom	1998	6,051	7,950	118.5	17.2	7.8	16	Lpg	ex Tarquin Pride-02
Pretty Lady	Mhl	1994	6,107	7,598	112.2	17.6	8.5	15	Lpg	ex Happy Lady-09, Pugliola-00, I/a Jade Star
Seagas General	Cyp	1982	4,605	4,596	105.6	17.6	5.9	13	Lpg	ex Sigas General-05, Kilgas General-01, Balder Phenix-98
Seagas Governor	Cyp	1983	4,658	4,563	105.6	17.6	5.9	13	Lpg	ex Sigas Governor-06, Kilgas Governor-01, Gaz Polaris-97, Polaris Gas-95, Gas Crest-91
Sichem Amethyst	Pan	2006	5,303	8,817	115.0	18.2	7.8	-	Tch	ex Songa Amethyst-07
Ullswater †	Bhs	1996	5,945	7,678	121.0	19.3	6.8	14	Lpg	
Windermere †	Bhs	1995	5,752	7,046	119.0	18.8	6.7	14	Lpg	

* owned by subsidiary Bernhard Schulte Shipmanagement (Cyprus) Ltd (founded 1972 as Hanseatic Shipmanagement Ltd to 1976 and Hanseatic Shipping Co Ltd to 2008 – www.bs-shipmanagement.com) and ‡ managed by Chemgas Shipping BV, Netherlands.
** owned by subsidiary Bernhard Schulte Shipmanagement (Deutschland) GmbH & Co KG (founded 2000 as Reimarus Schiffahrtskantor GmbH to 2006, Hanseatic Shipping (Deutschland) GmbH and Vorsetzen Schiffs GmbH (formed 2000) to 2008) - www.bs-shipmanagement.com)
† managed by MC Shipping SAM, Monaco qv
Also owns and manages very large fleet of larger vessels, mainly of container ships and bulk carriers.

Oldenburg-Portugiesische Dampfschiffs-Rhederei GmbH & Co KG/Germany
Funnel: Yellow with blue over red bands. Hull: Yellow with blue 'OPDR', red boot-topping. History: Founded 1882 as Oldenburg-Portugiesische Dampfschiffs-Rhederei Kusen, Heitmann & Co KG to 1983 and acquired by Schulte Group in 1996. Web: www.opdr.de

OPDR Cadiz	Esp	2003	7,360	8,394	128.0	20.6	7.4	16	CC	
OPDR Las Palmas`	Esp	2002	7,360	8,407	128.0	20.6	7.4	16	CC	
OPDR Lisboa	Cyp	2007	7,545	8,150	129.6	20.6	7.4	16	CC	ex OPDR Sankt Petersburg-07
OPDR Tanger	Cyp	2008	7,545	8,394	128.0	20.6	7.4	16	CC	I/a OPDR Rotterdam
OPDR Tenerife	Esp	2002	7,360	8,394	128.0	20.6	7.4	16	CC	ex FOCS Tenerife-08, OPDR Tenerife-02

Reederei Thomas Schulte   Germany
Funnel: Black with white 'TS' on red diamond on broad green band. Hull: Dark green with red boot-topping. History: Founded 1987 by son of Bernhard Schulte – see above. Web: www.reederei-t-schulte.de

Carolin Schulte	Cyp	1999	9,030	10,935	135.6	22.5	8.6	18	CC	ex Cape Canet-10, YM Faha-09
Emilia Schulte	Cyp	1999	9,030	11,031	135.7	22.7	8.6	19	CC	ex Cape Canaveral-08, Tiger Sea-01, Cape Canaveral-01
Henry Schulte	Cyp	2000	9,030	11,031	135.6	22.5	8.6	18	CC	ex Cape Creus-10, MSC Caledonien-08, Cape Creus-06

Newbuildings: Three further 9,000 gt container ships on order.
Also owns about 24 larger container ships up to 40,000 gt.

SCL Reederei AG   Switzerland
Funnel: Buff with blue 5-petal flowerhead on white diamond or charterers colours. Hull: Light grey or green with red boot-topping or blue with black boot-topping. History: Founded 2005. Web: www.enzian-shipping.com

Celine	Che	2001	6,382	8,600	129.5	15.9	7.4	14	Cc	
Sabina	Che	2000	5,968	9,231	127.9	15.9	7.5	14	Cc	
Safmarine Akwaba	Che	2008	9,938	12,576	139.9	21.8	8.4	16	Cc	
Safmarine Andisa	Che	2008	9,938	12,633	139.9	21.8	8.4	16	Cc	ex Safmarine Anita-08
Safmarine Angela	Che	2007	9,938	12,605	139.9	21.8	8.4	16	Cc	ex Safmarine Akwaba-07
Safmarine Anita	Che	2008	9,938	12,560	139.9	21.8	8.4	16	Cc	
Safmarine Basilea	Che	2005	9,990	12,500	140.0	21.5	8.4	17	Cc	
Safmarine Leman	Che	2005	9,990	12,579	140.0	21.5	8.4	17	Cc	
SCL Bern	Che	2005	9,990	12,578	140.0	21.5	8.4	17	Cc	ex SITC Bern-06, SCL Bern-05
SCL Elise	Lbr	2009	5,599	7,694	108.2	18.2	6.8	12	Cc	ex Transitorius-09
SCL Margrit	Lbr	2009	5,599	7,776	108.2	18.2	6.8	12	Cc	
SCL Nicole	Lbr	2009	5,599	7,678	108.2	18.2	6.8	12	Cc	ex Merwedelta-09

Newbuildings: Four 18,000 dwt general cargo vessels on order
managed by Enzian Ship Management AG, Switzerland, smaller vessels operating in Pool with other owners.

Scotline Ltd   UK
Funnel: Blue with white 'X', narrow black top. Hull: Light grey with red boot-topping. History: Founded 1979. Web: www.scotline.co.uk

Scot Carrier	Gbr	1997	1,882	2,495	81.9	12.5	4.3	11	Cc	ex Dependia-04
Scot Explorer	Gbr	1996	1,882	2,600	81.6	12.5	4.3	11	Cc	ex Bornrif-04
Scot Isles	Gbr	2001	2,594	3,179	90.0	13.8	4.9	14	C	
Scot Mariner	Gbr	2001	2,594	3,300	90.0	13.8	4.9	13	Cc	
Scot Pioneer	Gbr	2006	2,528	3,638	90.0	12.5	5.4	13	Cc	ex Harns-08
Scot Ranger	Gbr	1997	2,260	3,418	84.9	12.7	5.1	11	C	
Scot Venture	Gbr	2002	2,594	3,300	90.0	13.8	4.9	13	Cc	

Managed by Intrada Ships Management Ltd, UK.

Name	Flag	Year	GT	DWT	Loa	Bm	Drt	Kts	Type	Remarks

Seabess Ltd — UK

Funnel: Light blue with dark green 'U' on white disc inside dark green ring. **Hull:** Light blue with white 'SEABESS', red boot-topping. **History:** Not confirmed. **Web:** None found.

Name	Flag	Year	GT	DWT	Loa	Bm	Drt	Kts	Type	Remarks
Saline	Nld	1993	1,990	3,604	89.9	13.0	5.0	12	C	I/a Salt Trader

Managed by HC Shipping & Chartering Ltd, UK

Seatrade Groningen BV — Netherlands

Funnel: Dark blue with white 'S' attached to blue 'G' on orange square. **Hull:** White with dark blue 'SEATRADE', red boot-topping. **History:** Founded 1951 as NV Scheepvaarts Groningen to 1973. **Web:** www.seatrade.com; www.seatrade.nl

Name	Flag	Year	GT	DWT	Loa	Bm	Drt	Kts	Type	Remarks
Antigua	Ant	1991	4,190	4,468	105.4	16.0	6.8	15	Rc	ex Soria-96, Escambray-96
Antilla	Ant	1990	4,190	4,487	105.4	16.0	6.8	15	Rc	ex Salamanca-96, Yumuri-96
Aruba	Nld	1990	4,190	4,468	105.4	16.0	6.8	15	R	ex Segovia-96, Vinales-95
Asiatic	Bhs	1986	3,757	4,988	106.0	16.3	7.0	16	R	ex Sanuki Reefer-91
Breiz Klipper **	Ant	1991	3,563	5,900	110.9	16.2	7.8	17	Rc	
Coppename	Ant	1990	4,666	4,433	108.8	16.4	6.5	16	Rc	ex Sierra Nafria-08, Coppename-01
Fiona	Ant	1986	3,978	5,232	109.1	16.3	7.3	16	R	ex Cape Blanc-97, Nayadic-95
Goyen	Vct	1987	3,999	5,450	107.4	16.2	7.6	15	Rc	ex Aven-02, Royal Klipper-97
Holland Klipper	Nld	1989	3,999	5,363	107.7	16.2	7.6	18	R	
Jarikaba	Ant	1986	4,238	4,277	107.5	16.0	6.2	16	R	ex Sierra Nieves-08, Jarikaba-01
New Hayatsuki	Mhl	1990	4,287	4,900	116.2	16.2	6.9	16	R	
New Hirotsuki	Pan	1990	4,288	5,178	116.2	16.2	6.9	16	R	
New Takatsuki	Pan	1991	4,446	5,248	120.7	16.6	6.9	15	R	ex Reefer Queen-01
Nickerie	Nld	1985	4,202	4,278	108.0	18.0	6.2	16	R	I/a Americ
Nostalgic	Bhs	1986	3,978	5,175	109.1	16.3	7.3	16	Rc	ex Green Nostalgic-07, Nostalgic-06, Northern Express-00
Nova Bretagne	Bhs	1990	4,482	5,109	120.7	16.6	6.8	15	R	ex Sun Sophia-06, Gracious-99, Azur Grace-93
Nova Caledonia	Mlt	1986	4,964	6,544	124.7	17.8	7.3	17	R	ex Melone-00, Nice Approach-97, Cygnus-92, Pegasus-89
Nova Flandria	Lbr	1990	4,574	5,517	120.2	16.4	7.2	16	R	ex Sohya Star-05, Sohya-97
Nova Terra *	Bhs	1985	4,361	5,475	109.0	16.4	7.7	16	R	ex Adriatic Universal-90
Nova Zeelandia	Ant	1986	4,440	5,508	115.0	16.8	7.3	18	R	ex Mashu Reefer-92, Mashu Maru-88
Polestar	Pan	1990	4,574	5,470	120.2	16.4	7.2	16	R	
Sierra Cazorla	Pan	1984	2,618	2,725	91.9	14.2	5.1	13	R	

* owned by subsidiary Dammers Shipmanagement NV
** managed for Jaczon BV, Netherlands (founded 1955 – www.jaczon.nl)
Also owns, manages or operates numerous larger reefers listed in **Ocean Ships**

Seatrade Services Ou — Estonia

Funnel: Black with white diamond on white-edged broad red band or red. **Hull:** Red with black boot-topping. **History:** Founded 2005 and associated with Euro-Baltic Shipping Services Ou. **Web:** www.seatrade.ee

Name	Flag	Year	GT	DWT	Loa	Bm	Drt	Kts	Type	Remarks
Karsnes	Est	1997	3,833	4,766	100.6	16.5	5.9	15	Cc	ex Gerd J-06, P&O Nedlloyd Obock-05, Gerd J-00, Cagema St. Lucia-99, I/a Gerd J
Opus *	Atg	1979	2,862	3,279	98.7	15.9	4.2	12	Cc	ex Nadine-02, Canopus I-00, Canopus-94

* managed by Craftchart Ou, Estonia (see under Cargohunters AS)

Seatrans DA — Norway

Funnel: Orange with overlapping black 'ST' symbol inside black diamond outline or blue with white 'S' between narrow white bands or white with white 'S' on broad blue band between narrow blue bands. **Hull:** Orange with black 'SEATRANS', * yellow with black 'HOLMEN CARRIER', red boot-topping. **History:** Founded 1970 as I/S Seatrans to 1988. **Web:** www.seatrans.no

Name	Flag	Year	GT	DWT	Loa	Bm	Drt	Kts	Type	Remarks
Baltic Guide	Nis	1982	7,307	5,500	115.6	19.0	6.1	15	Cp	ex Trans Fennia-02
Baltic News *	Nis	1990	5,603	4,944	115.9	17.8	4.3	15	Cp	ex Nornews Supplier-98, Gold River-95
Copernicus	Lbr	1987	1,525	2,181	73.8	11.5	4.4	11	Tch	ex Arklow Manor-00 (conv Cc-00)
Trans Arctic	Nis	1991	4,712	6,930	116.8	17.5	7.7	15	Tch	
Trans Dania	Nis	1989	5,167	5,353	113.4	17.8	6.7	15	Cp	
Trans Emerald	Nis	2005	5,815	8,650	115.0	18.8	7.4	14	Tch	
Trans Fjell	Nis	2007	3,033	3,402	88.8	13.4	5.9	13	Tch	
Trans Fjord	Sgp	1994	5,401	9,108	113.6	17.7	8.0	13	Tch	ex Leman IV-03
Trans Holm	Nis	1981	4,259	3,666	96.5	17.5	5.3	13	Tch	ex Estrella-93 (conv Cp-93)
Trans Scandic	Nis	1992	4,716	6,927	116.8	17.8	7.7	15	Tch	
Trans Sea	Nis	1992	4,433	6,783	106.8	17.7	6.7	13	Tch	ex Geneve-02
Trans Sund	Bhs	1991	3,206	4,794	96.4	15.3	6.2	14	Tch	ex Lis Terkol-96, Stolt Lis Terkol-94
Trans Vik	Nis	1991	3,206	4,794	96.4	15.3	6.2	14	Tch	ex Bente Terkol-96, Stolt Bente Terkol-94

Sea-Cargo Skips AS/Norway

Funnel: White with white 'S' on broad blue band between narrow blue bands or white with white 'N' on blue band. **Hull:** Blue, * black or ** red with white 'SEA-CARGO' red boot-topping. **History:** Formed 2001 by merger of Seatrans DA (60%) and Nor-Cargo (40%). **Web:** www.sea-cargo.no

Name	Flag	Year	GT	DWT	Loa	Bm	Drt	Kts	Type	Remarks
Cometa **	Nis	1981	4,610	4,450	102.5	16.5	6.2	13	Rop	
SC Aberdeen	(2) Bhs	1979	4,234	3,041	109.0	16.5	4.8	15	Ro	ex Tungenes-01, Astrea-92, I/a Erik Jarl
SC Baltic	Bhs	1975	3,382	3,994	94.6	15.0	5.7	13	Cp	ex Trans Baltic-01 (len-85)
SC Nordic *	Nor	1986	4,876	4,020	110.5	17.6	6.3	15	Cp	ex Trans Nordia-01

Sea-Cargo Skips AS. SC Baltic. *N. Kemps*

Seatrans DA. Baltic News. *F. de Vries*

Name	Flag	Year	GT	DWT	Loa	Bm	Drt	Kts	Type	Remarks
Trans Carrier	Nis	1994	8,407	6,266	125.0	19.7	6.2	14	Rop	ex Swan Hunter-99, Parchim-07, Swan Hunter-96, Korsnas Link-94

*owned by Nordic Carriers AS and managed by Norresundby Shipping A/S or ** by Nor Lines AS qv*

Seatrend Shipping NV — Belgium

Funnel: *Blue with narrow white band below narrow black top.* **Hull:** *Blue with red boot-topping.* **History:** *Founded 1982 as Sea River Line NV to 1989 then Seatrade Shipping NV to 1994. Ownership transferred to Netherlands in 1997, but reformed in 2002.* **Web:** *www.seatrendshipping.com*

Name	Flag	Year	GT	DWT	Loa	Bm	Drt	Kts	Type	Remarks
Orabelt	Cyp	2009	2,918	4,139	90.9	15.3	5.6		Tch	ex Prospero-09

Newbuildings: Two tankers under construction for 2010 delivery.

Seavoss Schiffahrt GmbH & Co KG — Germany

Funnel: *Red five-pointed star within black 'V' on inverted white triangle above blue (fwd) and red (aft) lower sections, each with white five-pointed star.* **Hull:** *Black with red boot-topping.* **History:** *Founded 1974.* **Web:** *www.seavoss.de*

Name	Flag	Year	GT	DWT	Loa	Bm	Drt	Kts	Type	Remarks
Ardesco	Svk	1995	2,061	3,004	88.5	11.4	5.0	11	Cc	ex Annlen-G-08, Duisburg-96, Annlen G-95
Baltic Sea	Atg	1992	2,449	3,713	87.9	12.8	5.5	12	Cc	ex RMS Sonsbek-09, Baltic Sea-06, Uranus-05
Black Sea	Atg	1992	2,449	3,710	88.0	12.8	5.5	10	Cc	ex Sunrise-05, Stadt Wilhelmshaven-92, I/a Castor
Idannus	Atg	1995	2,050	3,370	88.0	12.8	4.9	12	Cc	ex Zeelandia-07, Liamare-05, Tendo-04
Short Sea	Svk	1991	2,450	3,710	87.8	12.9	5.5	10	Cc	ex Irish Sea-08, Red Sea-06, Jupiter-05, MSC Bahamas-02, Jupiter-00

Seaworks AS — Norway

Funnel: *Cream.* **Hull:** *Blue, black or red with red boot-topping.* **History:** *Founded 1997* **Web:** *www.seaworks.no*

Name	Flag	Year	GT	DWT	Loa	Bm	Drt	Kts	Type	Remarks
Bogtind	Nor	1953	548	518	52.2	8.5	3.7	11	Bu	ex Hidrafjord-76, Moholmen-73, Audtun-72, Marilene-70, Iris-67
Nidaroe	Nor	1965	551	610	48.7	9.7	3.5	11	Bu	ex Brit Mari-84, Normannes-74, Balka-74, Brigitta Coast-72, Jeffmine-72 (conv C-89)
Sveatind **	Nor	1975	707	847	57.6	9.3	3.4	11	Bu	ex Kalve-85, Sunstad-83 (conv C-85)

*managed by Geir Hokland AS or ** by Norbulk AS, both Norway.*
Also operates cable ships and landing craft.

See-Transit Bereederungs GmbH — Germany

Funnel: *White with dark blue houseflag.* **Hull:** *Dark green with white 'SEE-TRANSIT, black boot-topping.* **History:** *Founded 1989 as See-Transit Schiffahrts und Speditions GmbH.* **Web:** *www.seetransit.de*

Name		Flag	Year	GT	DWT	Loa	Bm	Drt	Kts	Type	Remarks
Conro Trader	(2)	Atg	1978	6,051	4,550	110.0	18.0	4.2	12	Ro	ex Helena Husmann-86, Areucon Caroline-78 (len-82)
Petersburg		Atg	1985	1,838	2,285	80.6	12.6	4.2	11	Cc	ex Peter S-93
See-Stern *		Atg	2005	1,552	1,863	82.2	11.3	3.4	11	Cc	

managed by BW-Bereederungs GmbH & Co KG

Morten Seines Rederi — Norway

Funnel: *White with black 'S'.* **Hull:** *Blue with red boot-topping.* **History:** *Founded 1998.* **Web:** *None found.*

Name	Flag	Year	GT	DWT	Loa	Bm	Drt	Kts	Type	Remarks
Rana Express	Nor	2000	2,532	3,604	86.4	12.8	5.5	11	Cc	ex Adelheid Sibum-07, Neuwerk-03, Eemcarib-00

Royal Dutch Shell Plc — UK

Shell Transport & Trading Plc

Funnel: *Cream with narrow black top.* **Hull:** *Red with red boot-topping.* **History:** *Founded 1907 on 60:40 basis by Royal Dutch Petroleum Co (founded 1890) and Shell Transport & Trading Co Ltd (founded 1897). Took control of Mexican Eagle Petroleum Co in 1919 and formed Shell-Mex Ltd in 1921, which in 1932 merged with BP to form Shell-Mex & BP Ltd until separated in 1975.* **Web:** *www.shell.com*

Name	Flag	Year	GT	DWT	Loa	Bm	Drt	Kts	Type	Remarks
Acavus	Iom	2005	8,351	12,400	127.2	20.4	8.5	14	Tch	ex Cape Eden-05
Achatina	Iom	2005	8,351	12,887	127.2	20.4	8.5	14	Tch	ex Cape Essvik-05

Owned by Viken Shipping AS, Norway and managed by Shell Transport & Trading Plc subsidiary Stasco Ship Management, UK (founded 1994 as Shell International Shipping Ltd to 1995).

Shipchart Co Ltd — Russia

Funnel: *White with black top.* **Hull:** *Black with red boot-topping.* **History:** *Founded 2000 as Rio Maritime Management to 2005.* **Web:** *None found.*

Name		Flag	Year	GT	DWT	Loa	Bm	Drt	Kts	Type	Remarks
Alena	(2)	Mlt	1991	4,057	4,540	138.4	16.5	3.2	10	C	ex Leonid Bykov-01, Volzhskiy-41-93
Alexandra	(2)	Mlt	1991	4,096	4,540	138.5	16.5	3.1	10	C	ex Vladimir Filkov-03, Volzhskiy-46-94
Kate	(2)	Mlt	1990	3,082	3,709	107.4	16.5	3.7	11	C	ex Volzhskiy-37-03 (short-93)
Lana	(2)	Mlt	1990	3,082	3,377	107.4	16.5	3.7	11	C	ex Volzhskiy-35-00 (short-93)
Lana II	(2)	Mlt	1990	3,082	3,977	107.4	16.5	3.5	11	C	ex Volzhskiy-38-01 (short-93)
Nataly I	(2)	Mlt	1990	3,082	3,977	107.4	16.5	3.5	11	C	ex Grigoriy Nosov-06, Volzhskiy-32-02 (short-93)

Name		Flag	Year	GT	DWT	Loa	Bm	Drt	Kts	Type	Remarks

ShipCom Bereederungs GmbH & Co KG Germany

Funnel: *Black with white 'Ö' on dark blue band.* **Hull:** *Green.* **History:** *Founded 2000.* **Web:** *www.shipcom-management.de*

Name		Flag	Year	GT	DWT	Loa	Bm	Drt	Kts	Type	Remarks
Adrana *		Gib	1997	4,320	6,366	100.0	17.2	7.3	15	Cc	ex Christina-07, Kanilai-03, Christina-02, Christina Star-02, Christina-97, I/a Papagena
Albis		Gib	2011	2,998	4,250	90.0	14.4	5.8	11	C	
Amisia		Gib	2010	2,998	4,400	90.0	14.4	5.8	11	C	
Danubia		Gib	2011	2,998	4,250	90.0	14.4	5.8	11	C	
Furioso		Gib	1997	4,244	5,450	99.9	16.5	6.1	13	Cc	ex Sequana-07, I/a Kar Oguzhan
Nemuna		Atg	1998	2,863	4,156	89.7	13.6	5.7	13	Cc	
Risoluto		Gib	1997	2,848	4,168	89.7	13.6	5.7	13	Cc	ex Thamesis-06
RMS Lagona		Atg	2000	1,894	2,668	88.0	11.4	4.1	11	Cc	ex Crescent Seine-03
RMS Rhenus		Atg	2000	1,898	2,688	88.0	11.4	4.1	11	Cc	ex Crescent Rhine-03
Vigoroso		Gib	2007	4,244	5,580	99.9	16.5	6.1	13	Cc	I/a Kar Cengizhan
Visurgis		Deu	1997	2,853	4,167	90.0	13.6	5.7	13	Cc	

* managed by Boese Bereederungs GmbH & Co KG
Also operates chartered vessels.

Reederei Bernd Sibum GmbH & Co KG Germany

Funnel: *White with blue flag having blue 'S' on yellow diamond.* **Hull:** *Blue with red boot-topping.* **History:** *Founded 1996.* **Web:** *www.sibum.de*

Name		Flag	Year	GT	DWT	Loa	Bm	Drt	Kts	Type	Remarks
Alexander Sibum		Atg	2006	9,981	11,814	139.1	22.6	8.8	18	CC	
Anna-Maria Sibum		Atg	2005	2,997	4,435	99.8	12.8	5.7	12	CC	ex Hermann Wessels-05
Anne Sibum		Cyp	2007	10,585	13,172	151.7	23.4	8.0	18	CC	
BCL Iwona		Atg	2006	6,701	8,200	132.6	19.2	7.2	17	CC	ex Katharina Sibum-06
Bernhard Sibum		Atg	2006	9,981	11,846	139.1	22.6	8.8	18	CC	
Delta Hamburg		Cyp	2008	10,542	13,172	151.7	23.4	8.0	18	CC	ex Grete Sibum-08
Gerd Sibum		Atg	1998	3,999	5,400	100.0	17.9	6.6	16	CC	ex Maersk Salerno-99, Gerd Sibum-98
Heinrich Sibum		Atg	2007	9,981	11,822	139.2	22.6	8.8	18	CC	
Helena Sibum		Atg	2006	6,701	8,238	132.6	19.2	7.2	17	CC	ex Asia Star-08
Maria Sibum		Atg	2004	6,701	8,223	132.6	19.2	7.2	17	CC	ex Susan Borchard-09, Maria Sibum-06
Rita Sibum		Atg	2005	6,701	8,300	132.6	19.2	7.2	17	CC	ex Vento Di Maestrale-08, Euro Star-07
Stefan Sibum		Deu	2008	10,585	13,172	151.7	23.4	8.0	18	CC	

Also owns three larger feeder container ships.

Kurt Siemer Germany

Funnel: *Red base with black 'S' on white top.* **Hull:** *Blue with red boot-topping.* **History:** *Founded 1969.* **Web:** *None found.*

Name		Flag	Year	GT	DWT	Loa	Bm	Drt	Kts	Type	Remarks
Katharina Siemer		Cyp	1985	2,061	3,357	88.0	11.5	5.2	11	Cc	ex Katharina S-99, RMS Hispania-95, Katharina Siemer-93

Sierra Maritime Ltd Estonia

Funnel: *White or * blue with red 'V' on white disc.* **Hull:** *Blue with red boot-topping.* **History:** *Founded 2004.* **Web:** *www.sierramaritime.ee*

Name		Flag	Year	GT	DWT	Loa	Bm	Drt	Kts	Type	Remarks
Fortes		Vct	1986	3,219	4,257	100.6	14.3	5.3	12	Cc	ex CEC Weser-05, Weser-00, Industrial Grace-98, Amke-97, Norbrit Weser-87
Virtus *		Vct	1985	3,307	4,800	92.2	15.9	6.6	14	Cc	ex Lee Frances-05

Oy Sillanpaa Trading Ltd Finland

Funnel: *White.* **Hull:** *Blue with red boot-topping.* **History:** *Formed 1997 as subsidiary of sea defence material supplier founded 1984.* **Web:** *www.sillanpaa.com*

Name		Flag	Year	GT	DWT	Loa	Bm	Drt	Kts	Type	Remarks
Anja		Hnd	1974	3,287	4,020	106.6	14.5	6.0	14	Cu	ex Thames Star-01, Janne Wehr-95, Containerships I-87, Janne Wehr-85, Roxanne Kersten-83, Janne Wehr-81, Roxanne Kersten-81, Janne Wehr-80
Jopi	(2)	Fin	1985	473	555	51.2	9.8	2.1	7	Cst	ex Volna 4-01 (conv hopper-92)
Mari		Nld	1978	1,925	2,265	79.8	12.8	4.5	12	Cu	ex Anne-98, Pentland-95, Mara-93, Trabant-91
Rakel		Nld	1977	1,660	2,060	67.3	12.8	4.5	12	Cu	ex Baltic Champ-02, Pico Ruivo-95, Nordlicht II-83
Topi	(2)	Fin	1985	473	530	51.2	9.8	2.2	7	Cst	ex Volna 3-04 (conv hopper-92)
Ville	(2)	Fin	1985	473	563	51.5	9.8	2.2	7	Cst	ex Aalto 5-96, Volna 5-92 (conv hopper-92)

Rederiet M H Simonsen ApS Denmark

Funnel: *Light blue with white 'S', blue top.* **Hull:** *Dark red with red or black boot-topping.* **History:** *Founded 1931.* **Web:** *www.mhsimonsen.com*

Name		Flag	Year	GT	DWT	Loa	Bm	Drt	Kts	Type	Remarks
Oradana	(2)	Dis	1971	1,639	2,495	76.0	11.5	4.8	10	Tch	ex Scarlino Primo-89
Oraholm		Dis	2006	3,709	4,598	106.2	15.6	5.8	15	Tch	
Orahope		Dis	2002	2,631	3,514	92.9	14.1	5.6	13	Tch	
Orakota		Dis	1981	1,755	2,578	85.0	13.0	4.7	12	T	ex Dakota I-94, Dakota-94, Doris-86
Oraness		Dis	1985	1,804	2,440	78.0	12.7	4.3	11	T	ex Inisheer-02, Dunkerque Express-99, Inisheer-95, Lia Venture-88, Flagship 1-86, Elisa von Barssel-85 (conv Cc-02)
Orasila		Dis	2006	2,194	1,700	77.2	13.4	4.5	14	Tch	
Orasund		Dis	2008	3,691	4,598	106.2	15.6	5.8	15	Tch	

Seavoss Schiffahrt GmbH. Short Sea. *David Walker*

Reederei Bernd Sibum GmbH. Gerd Sibum. *Hans Kraijenbosch.*

Smith BV. Maasborg (in Wagenborg colours). *Hans Kraijenbosch*

Name	Flag	Year	GT	DWT	Loa	Bm	Drt	Kts	Type	Remarks
Oratank	Dis	2008	3.691	4,483	106.2	15.6	5.8	15	Tch	
Orateca	Dis	1982	1,756	2,650	84.8	13.0	4.7	11	T	ex Tecumseh-95

Sirius Rederi AB   Sweden

Funnel: White with white outlined 'S' at centre of 4-pointed blue star on raised white disc on broad white band between blue bands. **Hull:** Blue with white band above black boot-topping. **History:** Founded 1994 and acquired Rederi AB Brevik in 2006. **Web:** www.sirius-rederi.com

Name	Flag	Year	GT	DWT	Loa	Bm	Drt	Kts	Type	Remarks
Angon *	Swe	1997	1,627	2,490	85.3	12.3	5.1	12	T	ex Alvtank-05, Bjarkoy-02
Lexus **	Swe	2005	2,947	4,320	87.8	13.4	6.6	12	T	ex Stoc Regina-08
Lotus **	Swe	2004	2,956	4,479	87.8	13.4	6.6	12	T	ex Stoc Petrea-08
Marinus	Swe	2003	4,823	7,082	119.1	16.9	6.8	15	Tch	ex Norvik-08, I/a Aksoy Saros
Neptunus	Swe	1991	4,609	7,035	99.6	17.0	6.5	12	Tch	ex Dalcor-01, Talcor-96, Alcor-91 (conv C/T-02)
Nimbus	Swe	1991	4,614	7,070	99.6	17.0	6.5	12	Tch	ex Dalnati-01, Talnati-96, Alnati-91 (conv C/T-01)
Olympus	Swe	2006	7,515	9,189	124.5	18.0	7.6	15	Tch	ex Scanvik-06
Saturnus	Swe	1990	5,774	8,490	120.3	17.8	7.8	14	Tch	ex Furevik-05
Scorpius	Swe	2006	7,636	11,249	129.8	19.6	8.0	13	Tch	I/a Besiktas Ireland
Tellus	Swe	2006	7,515	8,300	123.8	18.0	7.6	15	Tch	ex Kungsvik-06

* managed for Goteborg Bunker AB or ** part owned by Stoc Tankers AB qv

I M Skaugen SE   Norway

Norgas Carriers AS/Norway

Funnel: Blue with blue 'Norgas' at base of oval ring on broad white band. **Hull:** Orange with black boot-topping. **History:** Parent founded 1916 as I M Skaugen & Co to 1978 and I M Skaugen A/S to 1990, when it merged with A/S Laboremus (founded 1910) and Kosmos Shipping A/S (founded 1912) becoming I M Skaugen ASA to 2007. Subsidiary founded 1982, as Norwegian Gas Carriers AS to 2001 to manage five-owner Pool of lpg-tankers, two of the other owners subsequently being taken-over. **Web:** www.norgas.org

Name	Flag	Year	GT	DWT	Loa	Bm	Drt	Kts	Type	Remarks
Norgas Alameda	Hkg	2003	8,720	9,265	124.9	19.8	8.3	16	Lpg	
Norgas Camilla	Sgp	2010	8,350	10,200	109.5	21.0	8.0	-	Lpg	
Norgas Carine *	Sgp	1989	7,260	9,259	132.2	18.0	8.6	17	Lpg	ex Norgas Teviot-98, Teviot-96
Norgas Cathinka	Sgp	2009	8,350	10,200	109.5	21.0	8.0	-	Lpg	
Norgas Challenger *	Sgp	1984	5,739	7,492	115.1	17.5	7.9	14	Lpg	ex San Francisco-89
Norgas Chief	Hkg	1983	7,791	8,379	119.6	19.0	8.3	14	Lpg	ex Einar Tambarskjelve-88
Norgas Energy	Hkg	1979	6,521	9,095	116.6	19.5	8.6	-	Lpg	ex Chem Energy-90, Helice-88
Norgas Napa	Hkg	2003	9,691	10,762	137.1	19.8	6.7	-	Lpg	
Norgas Orinda	Hkg	2003	8,720	9,260	124.9	19.8	8.3	16	Lpg	
Norgas Pan *	Sgp	2009	8,331	10,200	109.5	21.0	6.7	-	Lpg	
Norgas Patricia *	Sgp	1991	7,095	9,470	126.2	17.9	8.6	16	Lpg	
Norgas Petaluma	Hkg	2003	8,720	9,352	124.9	19.8	8.3	16	Lpg	
Norgas Shasta	Hkg	2003	9,691	10,770	137.1	19.8	8.3	-	Lpg	
Norgas Sonoma	Hkg	2003	8,720	9,352	124.8	19.8	8.3	16	Lpg	
Norgas Trader *	Sgp	1981	7,000	8,493	118.7	18.5	8.8	16	Lpg	ex Coral Temse-87
Norgas Traveller *	Sgp	1980	6,711	7,187	130.1	17.6	7.6	14	Lpg	ex Chem Olefine-91, Olefine Gas-90, Crusader Point-87, Beate-80 (len/conv C-87)
Norgas Voyager	Hkg	1972	7,173	8,700	125.3	19.1	8.6	16	Lpg	ex Hardanger-88
Princess of Yosu **		1970	1,673	2,545	86.4	12.1	5.2	12	Tch	ex Stainless Lady-96, Ametist-89, Kimia Jaya-86, Chemical Distributor-83

* owned by subsidiaries I M Skaugen Marine Services Pte Ltd, Singapore (formed 2004 as Norgas Carriers Pte Ltd to 2006) or ** by Princess Carriers AS, Norway (founded 1996)

Sloman Neptun Schiffahrts-Aktiengesellschaft   Germany

Funnel: Black with light green band or blue over yellow bands, or blue with blue 'U' on broad red band ('Unigas'). **Hull:** Dark grey with white 'SLOMAN NEPTUN', red boot-topping or dark red with grey boot-topping. **History:** Founded 1873 as Dampfschiffahrts-Gesellschaft Neptun to 1974. **Web:** www.sloman-neptun.com

Name	Flag	Year	GT	DWT	Loa	Bm	Drt	Kts	Type	Remarks
Alphagas	Atg	1996	4,924	6,360	114.6	15.7	7.3	16	Lpg	
Betagas	Atg	1997	4,924	6,375	114.6	15.8	7.3	16	Lpg	
Deltagas	Atg	1992	3,011	3,700	88.4	14.2	6.2	14	Lpg	
Epsilongas	Atg	2000	5,278	6,175	107.9	17.1	7.5	16	Lpg	
Etagas	Ant	1988	7,314	9,384	134.7	18.6	8.3	16	Lpg	
Gammagas	Atg	1992	3,703	4,447	99.4	15.0	6.5	14	Lpg	
Jotagas	Atg	1997	5,420	7,241	113.5	16.5	7.6	15	Lpg	ex Tarquin Moor-02
Kappagas	Atg	2001	5,278	6,211	108.0	16.8	7.5	16	Lpg	
Lady Elena *	Atg	1998	3,465	4,294	99.6	15.5	5.8	13	Lpg	ex Elena-98
Omegagas	Atg	1999	3,366	3,890	95.5	14.4	6.3	15	Lpg	
Sigmagas	Atg	1998	6,051	7,876	118.9	17.2	7.7	16	Lpg	ex Tarquin Forth-02
Sloman Producer	Atg	2004	7,260	7,630	120.9	18.7	6.9	15	Ro
Sloman Provider	Atg	2000	7,260	7,630	120.9	18.7	6.9	15	Ro
Sloman Trader	Deu	1983	7,947	9,989	128.8	20.5	8.2	14	Ro	ex Tropic Quest-00, Ellensborg-98, Tropic Quest-93, St. Aquarius-88, Aquarius-87
Sloman Traveller	Deu	1984	7,947	9,950	128.8	20.5	8.2	14	Ro	ex Tropic Reign-00, Elsborg-98, Tropic Reign-94, Tropic Reef-88, Sagittarius-88
Thetagas	Atg	2008	9,110	10,309	119.0	19.8	8.8	16	Lpg	

Name		Flag	Year	GT	DWT	Loa	Bm	Drt	Kts	Type	Remarks

* managed by Bernhard Schulte Shipmanagement (Deutschland) GmbH
LPG tankers operate in United Gas Carriers Pool (Unigas International). Also see Olaf Pedersen's Rederi, Schulte Group and Anthony Veder Rederijzaken BV

Smith BV — Netherlands

Funnel: *Managers colours.* **Hull:** *Managers colours.* **History:** *Founded 1986 as Rederij H J Smith to 2006.* **Web:** *None found.*

Name	Flag	Year	GT	DWT	Loa	Bm	Drt	Kts	Type	Remarks
Delfborg	Nld	2007	3,990	6,000	110.8	14.0	6.1	14	C	
Koningsborg	Nld	1997	6,142	9,067	130.7	15.9	7.5	14	Cc	
Maasborg	Nld	2005	3,990	6,000	110.8	14.0	6.1	14	C	

Managed by Wagenborg Shipping BV

SMS - Ship Management Support — Netherlands

Funnel: *None.* **Hull:** *Blue with red boot-topping or * yellow with black boot-topping.* **History:** *Not confirmed.* **Web:** *None found.*

Name		Flag	Year	GT	DWT	Loa	Bm	Drt	Kts	Type	Remarks
Andre-Michel 1		Mlt	1986	1,318	1,613	79.1	11.4	3.3	10	C	ex Marianne-04, Harns-94
Aristote		Bhs	1983	1,426	1,821	84.8	11.4	3.5	10	C	ex Turbulance-02
Laguepe *		Mlt	1987	1,412	1,780	81.0	11.3	3.3	10	Cs	ex Widor-04
Finola	(2)	Dis	1988	3,228	1,974	85.4	14.0	3.5	13	Lv	ex Christina C-97 (conv Cc/Ro-97, len-91)

Also manages vessels for other owners, see under Arpa Shipping BV

Reederei Speck Gbr — Germany

Funnel: *Black with black symbol on broad white band.* **Hull:** *Black.* **History:** *Founded 1970 as Schiffahrtskontor Claus Speck GmbH to 2000.* **Web:** *None found.*

Name	Flag	Year	GT	DWT	Loa	Bm	Drt	Kts	Type	Remarks
Trans Agila	Atg	1995	2,997	4,550	97.3	15.9	5.9	14	Cc	ex Agila-06, l/a Alessandra Lehmann
Trans Alrek *	Atg	2006	2,978	4,790	99.6	16.9	5.9	15	Cc	
Trans Frej	Atg	1994	2,997	4,470	97.3	15.9	5.9	14	Cc	ex Frej-06
Trans Odin	Atg	1994	2,997	4,530	97.3	15.9	5.9	14	Cc	ex Odin-06

* managed for subsidiary of Rederi AB Transatlantic, Sweden.

SIA Spectrum Shipping — Latvia

Funnel: *White with multi-coloured semi-circle, black top.* **Hull:** *Blue with red boot-topping.* **History:** *Founded 2004.* **Web:** *None found.*

Name	Flag	Year	GT	DWT	Loa	Bm	Drt	Kts	Type	Remarks
East Express	Mlt	1983	3,504	3,126	97.5	16.0	5.0	13	Cc	ex Taurus-02, Hirsholm-00, Nordia-96, Anna-89
Soul Sound	Mlt	1983	2,046	1,876	78.0	13.8	5.0	13	Cc	ex Coastal Sound-04, Kirsten-98, Christopher Caribe-93, Saturnus-92, Craigavad-88

Spliethhoff's Bevrachtingskantoor BV — Netherlands

Funnel: *Orange wiith black 'S' on diagonally quartered houseflag.* **Hull:** *Brown with green over red boot-topping.* **History:** *Founded 1921.* **Web:** *www.spliethoff.nl*

Name	Flag	Year	GT	DWT	Loa	Bm	Drt	Kts	Type	Remarks
Aalsmeergracht	Nld	1992	7,949	12,900	129.8	18.9	8.6	15	Cc	
Achtergracht	Nld	1990	7,949	12,900	129.8	18.9	8.6	14	Cc	
Admiralengracht	Nld	1992	7,949	12,900	129.8	18.9	8.6	14	Cc	
Alblasgracht	Nld	1991	7,949	12,900	129.8	18.9	8.6	14	Cc	
Alexandergracht	Nld	1992	7,949	12,900	129.8	18.9	8.6	14	Cc	
Amstelgracht	Nld	1992	7,949	12,900	129.8	18.9	8.6	14	Cc	
Anjeliersgracht	Nld	1990	7,949	12,900	129.8	18.9	8.6	14	Cc	
Ankergracht	Nld	1991	7,949	12,900	129.8	18.9	8.6	14	Cc	
Apollogracht	Nld	1991	7,949	12,900	129.8	18.9	8.6	14	Cc	
Archangelgracht	Nld	1992	7,949	12,900	129.8	18.9	8.6	14	Cc	
Artisgracht	Nld	1992	7,949	12,900	129.8	18.9	8.6	14	Cc	
Atlasgracht	Nld	1991	7,949	12,900	129.8	18.9	8.6	14	Cc	
Avataq †	Nld	1989	6,037	9,682	113.2	19.2	8.5	14	Cc	ex Lootsgracht-07, Mekhanik Volkosh-92, Tiger Speed-92, Mekhanik Volkosh-91, Poleca-89
Beluga Legislation **	Nld	2006	8,999	12,000	143.0	18.9	7.9	12	C/hl	ex Kent Legislation-09, Beluga Legislation-07, Morgenstond II-07
Morgenstond I **	Nld	2007	8,999	12,000	143.0	18.9	7.9	12	C/hl	ex Beluga Locomotion-09, Kent Locomotion-08, Beluga Locomotion-08, Morgenstond I-07
Edamgracht	Nld	1995	8,448	12,754	136.3	18.9	8.5	15	Cc	
Edisongracht	Nld	1995	8,448	12,754	136.3	18.9	8.5	15	Cc	
Eemsgracht	Nld	1995	8,448	12,754	136.3	18.9	8.5	15	Cc	
Eglantiersgracht	Nld	1994	8,448	12,760	136.3	18.9	8.5	15	Cc	
Egmondgracht	Nld	1994	8,448	12,760	136.3	18.9	8.5	15	Cc	
Elandsgracht	Nld	1995	8,448	12,754	136.3	18.9	8.5	15	Cc	
Emmagracht	Nld	1995	8,448	12,760	136.3	18.9	8.5	15	Cc	
Erasmusgracht	Nld	1995	8,448	12,754	136.3	18.9	8.5	15	Cc	
Eurogracht	Nld	1995	8,448	12,754	136.3	18.9	8.5	15	Cc	
Faunagracht	Nld	2010	8,448	13,400	137.0	18.9	8.8	14	Cc	
Fleurgracht	Nld	2010	8,448	13,400	137.0	18.9	8.8	14	Cc	
Floretgracht	Nld	2010	8,448	13,400	137.0	18.9	8.8	14	Cc	
Fagelgracht	Nld	2009	8,448	13,400	137.0	18.9	8.8	14	Cc	

Spliethhoff's Bevrachtingskantoor BV. Alexandergracht. *F. de Vries*

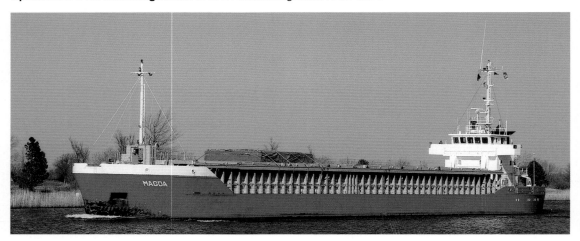

Spliethhoff's/Wijnne & Barends. Magda (prior to renaming). *Oliver Sesemann*

Stephenson Clarke Shipping Ltd. Durrington. *Oliver Sesemann*

Name	Flag	Year	GT	DWT	Loa	Bm	Drt	Kts	Type	Remarks
Flevogracht	Nld	2009	8,448	13,400	137.0	18.9	8.8	14	Cc	
Floragracht	Nld	2009	8,448	13,400	137.0	18.9	8.8	14	Cc	
Floretgracht	Nld	2010	8,448	13,400	137.0	18.9	8.8	14	Cc	
Fortunagracht	Nld	2009	8,448	13,400	137.0	18.9	8.8	14	Cc	
Oleander *	Mhl	1990	6,299	6,538	118.6	19.8	6.3	15	CC	
Umiavut †	Nld	1988	6,039	9,682	113.1	19.2	8.5	14	Cc	ex Lindengracht-00, Kapitan Silin-92, I/a Newca

Newbuildings: Two further 13,400 dwt vessels on order for 2010 delivery.
* owned by subsidiaries Bermuda Container Line Nederland BV (formed 1986 as Holland Ship Management BV to 1991) or ** C T Drent Beheer BV (formed 1983 as Rederij C T Drent & Zn to 1990).
† managed by Spliethoff Agency for Umialarik Transportation, Netherlands
Also operates larger general cargo/heavy lift vessels, including sixteen 'S' class up to 23,700 dwt and eight 18,143 dwt 'D' class
See Ferry Section for Transfennica vessels.

BigLift Shipping BV
Funnel: Yellow with narrow black top. Hull: Yellow with blue 'BIGLIFT', red boot-topping. History: Founded 1973 as Mammoet-Hansa Shipping BV to 1990, then Mammoet Shipping BV to 2000, Spliethoff acquiring a majority share in 1995 and full control in 2000, when the company was renamed..
Web: www.bigliftshipping.com

Tracer	Nld	1999	6,714	8,734	100.7	20.4	8.2	16	C/hl	
Transporter	Nld	1999	6,714	8,469	100.7	20.4	8.2	16	C/hl	
Traveller	Nld	2000	6,714	8,729	100.7	20.4	8.2	16	C/hl	

Also owns and operates a number of larger heavy-lift vessels, including newbuildings under construction.

Wijnne & Barends Cargadoors-en-Agentuurkantoren BV
Funnel: Black with black 'W&B' on white band, white with white 'BW' on blue 8-pointed star or owners markings including white with red 'M' inside blue diamond outline. Hull: Blue or orange with black boot-topping, or grey with red boot-topping. History: Founded 1855, Spliethoff acquired share in 2001 and took full control in 2003. Web: www.wijnne-barends.nl

Aldebaran	Nld	2001	2,337	3,193	90.0	12.5	4.6	11	Cc	ex Emuna-07
Amadeus	Nld	2003	1,719	2,250	87.0	11.4	3.8	-	C	ex Geminus-09
Belterwiede *	Nld	2005	3,990	6,080	110.8	14.0	6.1	-	Cc	ex Pioneer-07
Douwe-S **	Nld	2009	2,850	3,500	94.7	13.4	5.3	-	Cc	
Fiducia **	Nld	2009	2,850	3,500	94.7	13.4	5.3	-	Cc	
Helene	Nld	2010	2,850	3,500	94.7	13.4	5.3	-	Cc	
Hendrika Margaretha †	Nld	1993	2,058	3,250	81.1	12.4	5.2	11	Cc	ex Donau-04
Lady Carina	Nld	2001	4,235	5,438	108.5	15.9	5.9	14	Cc	ex Carina-10
Lady Christina	Nld	2000	4,235	5,438	108.5	15.9	5.9	14	Cc	ex Christina-10
Lady Clarissa	Nld	2000	4,235	5,438	108.5	15.9	5.9	14	Cc	ex Clarissa-09
Lady Claudia	Nld	1999	4,235	5,438	108.5	15.9	5.9	14	Cc	ex Claudia-10
Lady Helene	Nld	2010	2,850	3,500	94.7	13.4	5.3	-	C	
Lady Inger	Nld	1996	3,323	4,182	88.1	14.4	5.9	13	Cc	ex Inger-09
Lady Irina	Nld	1997	3,322	4,161	88.1	14.4	5.9	13	Cc	ex Irina-10
Lady Isabel	Nld	1997	3,225	4,250	88.1	14.5	5.9	13	Cc	ex Isabel-10
Lady Kirsten	Nld	1995	2,561	3,290	88.0	12.6	5.3	12	Cc	ex Kirsten-10, Aros News-96, I/a Kirsten
Lady Marie Christine	Nld	2010	2,850	3,500	94.7	13.4	5.3	-	C	
Lady Magda	Nld	1993	2,561	3,284	88.0	12.6	5.3	12	Cc	ex Magda-10
Lady Mathilde	Nld	1995	2,561	3,332	88.0	12.6	5.3	11	Cc	ex Mathilde-09
Lady Menna	Nld	1996	2,561	3,332	88.0	12.5	5.3	12	C	ex Menna-09
Lady Nola	Nld	2002	1,978	2,117	80.0	12.1	4.0	12	C	ex Nola-09
Lady Nona	Nld	2002	1,978	2,117	80.0	12.1	4.0	12	C	ex Nona-09
Lady Nora	Nld	2001	1,978	2,117	80.0	12.1	4.0	12	C	ex Nora-10
Lady Nova	Nld	2002	1,978	2,117	80.0	12.1	4.0	12	C	ex Nova-10
Lady Olga	Nld	1994	2,561	3,290	88.0	12.6	5.3	12	Cc	ex Olga-09
Lammy **	Nld	2009	2,850	3,500	94.7	13.4	5.3	-	Cc	
Mare	Nld	2004	2,080	2,933	89.0	12.4	4.4	-	Cc	
Marie Christine	Nld	2010	2,850	3,500	94.7	13.4	5.3	-	Cc	
Meridiaan	Nld	2009	5,887	8,130	128.5	15.9	6.8	-	Cc	
Najade **	Nld	2009	2,850	3,500	94.7	13.4	5.3	-	Cc	
Passaat	Nld	1994	1,937	3,150	82.4	12.4	4.8	12	C	ex Sardijn-07, Vlieree-05, Vlieland-02
Ramspol *	Nld	2009	5,887	8,130	128.5	15.9	6.8	-	Cc	
Warber **	Nld	2010	2,850	3,500	94.7	13.4	5.3	-	Cc	

* managed by Ramspol vof, Netherlands.
† managed for Rederij de Koning Gans CV (formed 2004) or ** for other owners
Also see Banner Shipping BV

Sprante Schiffahrts Kontor GmbH   Germany
Funnel: Black with black 'S' over blue over white over red bands. Hull: Red with red boot-topping. History: Founded 1985. Web: None found.

Eider	Svn	1978	1,934	2,495	91.8	13.5	4.0	12	C	ex Coastal Breeze-07, Eider-02 (len-94)
Futura Carrier	Svn	2007	2,569	3,363	97.5	13.6	4.2	12	Cc	ex RMS Kiel-08
Gina R *	Geo	1971	1,773	1,426	76.6	12.8	4.1	12	Cc	ex Unika-01, Arnis-85
Maja	Svn	1979	1,624	1,638	79.2	13.5	3.5	12	Cc	ex Maja-M-02
Susann	Vct	1979	1,507	1,341	67.8	11.7	4.2	12	Cc	ex Aqua Star-04, Susanne L-99, Bremer Mercur-95, Susanne L-89, Bremer Mercur-85, Susanne L-84

* managed by NC Schiffahrtsburo GmbH & Co KG

Name	Flag	Year	GT	DWT	Loa	Bm	Drt	Kts	Type	Remarks

Stabben Junior AS
Norway

Funnel: *Black.* **Hull:** *Black with red boot-topping.* **History:** *Not confirmed.* **Web:** *None found.*

Name	Flag	Year	GT	DWT	Loa	Bm	Drt	Kts	Type	Remarks
Stabben Junior	Vct	1983	1,939	2,888	88.0	11.5	4.7	11	Cc	ex Treuburg-04, Sea Weser-99, I/a Jenika

Srab Shipping AS
Sweden

Funnel: *White with red 'SRAB' above two blue waves on yellow square.* **Hull:** *Red with dark red boot-topping.* **History:** *Founded 1993 as Soderkopings Rederi AB to 1997.* **Web:** *www.srab.se*

Name	Flag	Year	GT	DWT	Loa	Bm	Drt	Kts	Type	Remarks
Nordic Glory	Pmd	2007	4,861	6,954	119.1	16.9	7.1	14	Tch	ex Pakri Glory-08
Nordic Victory	Pmd	2006	4,861	6,954	119.1	16.9	7.1	14	Tch	ex Pakri Victory-08
Prima	Prt	2008	4,870	6,954	119.1	16.9	7.1	14	Tch	

Newbuildings: Four 5,600 gt 8,400 dwt chemical tankers on order for delivery delayed from 2009 to 2010/11.

Reederei Jurgen Stahmer KG
Germany

Funnel: *White with dark blue anchor and red 'S' above narrow dark blue band.* **Hull:** *Blue with black boot-topping.* **History:** *Founded 1979.* **Web:** *None found.*

Name	Flag	Year	GT	DWT	Loa	Bm	Drt	Kts	Type	Remarks
Anna Marie	Atg	1996	2,345	3,992	82.5	12.7	5.3	11	Cc	ex Norderfeld-02, Oyat-98

Rederij H Steenstra BV
Netherlands

Funnel: *White.* **Hull:** *Blue with red or black red boot-topping.* **History:** *Founded 1972.* **Web:** *None found.*

Name	Flag	Year	GT	DWT	Loa	Bm	Drt	Kts	Type	Remarks
Anmar-S	Nld	1993	1,666	1,590	82.0	12.4	3.9	11	C	ex Fast Sim-05, Veritas-01
Anne-S	Nld	1997	2,375	3,471	89.0	12.4	4.9	11	C	ex Elan-04
Hendrik-S	Nld	2001	2,311	3,200	82.5	12.4	5.3	11	C	ex Aquatique-05

Also see Union Transport Group

Stephenson Clarke Shipping Ltd
UK

Funnel: *Black with broad silver band.* **Hull:** *Black with white 'SCS Bulk', red boot-topping.* **History:** *Commenced ship-owning in 1730 – the oldest British shipping company - and formed in 1865 as Stephenson Clarke & Co to 1922, became subsidiary of Powell Duffren in 1986, part sold in 1992 and acquired wholly by Isle of Man based International Maritime Group in 1997.* **Web:** *www.scsbulk.com*

Name	Flag	Year	GT	DWT	Loa	Bm	Drt	Kts	Type	Remarks
Dallington	Iom	1975	7,788	12,140	137.6	18.6	7.9	14	C	
Durrington	Iom	1981	7,788	11,990	137.6	18.6	7.9	14	C	
Newcastle	Mlt	2001	4,211	5,571	99.9	16.5	6.1	14	Cc	ex Sandy-08, Norbotten-07, I/a Gotland
Storrington	Iom	1982	7,788	11,990	137.6	18.6	7.9	14	C	

All managed by Stephenson Clarke Shipmanagement Ltd.

Jan Stepniewski I S-ka Sp z oo
Poland

Funnel: *Blue or red with white 'S' inside large 'J'.* **Hull:** *Blue with red red boot-topping.* **History:** *Founded 1993.* **Web:** *www.seatowage.com.pl*

Name	Flag	Year	GT	DWT	Loa	Bm	Drt	Kts	Type	Remarks
Iris 1	Mlt	1980	1,532	1,478	81.9	10.0	3.6	10	C	ex Fast Sim-97, Opal-92, Larissasee-88
Janina	Vct	1988	910	1,258	69.1	9.5	3.3	9	Cc	ex Sola-01, Natascha-91
Johanna	Vct	1980	1,525	2,320	78.6	12.1	4.1	11	C	ex Union Robin-03, Elisabeth S-95
Liliana	Vct	1980	910	1,263	69.1	9.5	5.4	9	Cc	ex Ner-01, Monika-90
Max	Svk	1980	1,084	1,173	74.2	9.9	2.9	10	Cc	ex Otter-06, RMS Westfalia-02, Karin E-92, Atoll-92
Zuzanna	Svk	1982	1,059	1,150	74.2	9.9	2.9	10	Cc	ex Beaver-06, RMS Lagune-02, RMS Normandia-93, Lagune-93

Operated by Wind Shipping ApS qv

Stoc Tankers AB
Sweden

Funnel: *White with white 'STOC' on blue/grey band.* **Hull:** *Green with red or black red boot-topping.* **History:** *Founded 2003.* **Web:** *www.stoctank.com*

Name	Flag	Year	GT	DWT	Loa	Bm	Drt	Kts	Type	Remarks
Stoc Marcia	Cyp	2007	3,219	4,634	100.0	15.0	6.1	12	Tch	

Also owns one 20,000 dwt product tanker and is part-owner of two tankers under Sirius Rederi AB qv

Stolt-Nielsen SA
Norway

Stolt Tankers BV/Netherlands

Funnel: *White with white 'S' on large red square, black top.* **Hull:** *Black with red boot-topping.* **History:** *Parent founded 1891 and subsidiary founded 1886 as B Stolt-Nielsen & Co to 1930, then B Stolt-Nielsen & Sonner A/S to 1922, Jacob Stolt-Nielsen A/S to 1970, Stolt-Nielsens Rederi A/S to 1999 and Stolt-Nielsen Transportation Group BV to 2007.* **Web:** *www.stolt-nielsen.com*

Name		Flag	Year	GT	DWT	Loa	Bm	Drt	Kts	Type	Remarks
Stolt Acacia *		Cym	1986	6,895	9,939	119.6	19.0	8.3	13	Tch	ex Stolt Australia-06
Stolt Aguila		Cym	2009	6,703	12,260	123.9	20.0	8.9	13	Tch	ex Sichem Yangtze-09
Stolt Avocet		Cym	1992	3,853	5,758	99.9	16.8	6.8	12	Tch	
Stolt Ayame *		Hkg	1991	4,987	9,070	111.6	18.8	7.6	13	Tch	ex Sampet Hope-97, Stellar Hope-95
Stolt Azalea *		Lbr	1988	4,740	7,582	108.0	18.2	7.1	12	Tch	
Stolt Azami *		Hkg	1997	6,356	11,564	117.3	20.0	8.8	13	Tch	
Stolt Botan *		Lbr	1998	6,415	11,553	117.3	20.0	8.8	13	Tch	
Stolt Cormorant †	(me)	Cym	1999	3,818	5,498	96.2	16.2	6.5	12	Tch	
Stolt Dipper		Cym	1992	3,206	4,738	96.3	15.1	6.2	13	Tch	ex Margit Terkol-96, Stolt Margit Terkol-94

Stolt-Nielsen SA. Stolt Cormorant. *Phil Kempsey*

Stolt-Nielsen SA. Stolt Skua. *N. Kemps*

Name	Flag		Year	GT	DWT	Loa	Bm	Drt	Kts	Type	Remarks
Stolt Egret †	Cym		1992	3,853	5,758	99.9	17.1	6.8	12	Tch	
Stolt Fulmar †	(me)	Cym	2000	3,818	5,498	96.2	16.2	6.5	13	Tch	
Stolt Gannet	Cym		1992	4,950	7,949	112.2	18.0	7.5	14	Tch	ex Marinor-05
Stolt Guillemot	Gbr		1993	3,204	4,698	96.4	15.3	6.2	13	Tch	ex Sasi Terkol-96
Stolt Hikawa	Cym		1992	4,529	8,080	108.0	18.2	7.2	13	Tch	
Stolt Jasmine *	Pan		2005	6,868	12,430	123.2	20.0	8.8	13	Tch	
Stolt Kestrel	Cym		1992	3,853	5,741	99.9	17.1	6.8	12	Tch	
Stolt Kikyo *	Lbr		1998	6,426	11,545	117.2	20.8	8.8	13	Tch	
Stolt Kite	Cym		1992	3,206	4,735	96.4	15.3	6.2	13	Tch	ex Randi Terkol-96
Stolt Kittiwake	Gbr		1993	3,204	4,710	96.4	15.3	6.2	13	Tch	ex Astrid Terkol-96
Stolt Lily *	Hkg		1988	4,740	7,582	108.0	18.2	7.1	12	Tch	
Stolt Pelican	Cym		1996	3,711	5,797	99.9	16.5	6.7	15	Tch	ex Isebek-08, Multitank Saxonia-97
Stolt Petrel	Gbr		1992	3,206	4,761	96.4	15.3	2.5	11	Tch	ex Edny Terkol-96
Stolt Puffin	Cym		1993	3,853	5,758	99.9	17.1	6.8	12	Tch	
Stolt Quetzal	Cym		2009	7,603	12,260	123.9	20.0	8.9	13	Tch	
Stolt Razorbill	Gbr		1995	3,716	5,797	100.0	16.5	6.7	15	Tch	ex Multitank Iberia-07
Stolt Shearwater †	(me)	Cym	1998	3,550	5,300	96.0	16.2	6.4	12	Tch	
Stolt Skua	Cym		1999	5,342	8,594	112.0	19.0	7.5	13	Tch	ex Bow Wave-06, Yao Ru-00
Stolt Suisen *	Hkg		1998	6,426	11,553	117.3	20.8	8.7	12	Tch	
Stolt Teal	Cym		1999	5,342	8,588	112.0	19.0	7.5	13	Tch	ex Bow Wind-06, Gui Zhen-00
Stolt Tern	Cym		1991	3,206	4,759	96.4	15.1	6.2	13	Tch	ex Jytte Terkol-96, Stolt Jytte Terkol-92

Newbuildings: Two 5,900 dwt chemical tankers for 2010 delivery.
* managed for NYK Stolt Shipholding Inc formed 1994 jointly with Nippon Yusen Kaisha (NYK Line), Japan.
† managed for DS Rendite-Fonds, Germany
Subsidiaries also own large tank barges operating in the European inland system and coastal tankers operating in China and the Far East

Rederi Stornes AS   Norway

Funnel: Blue with white ships wheel and red top. **Hull:** Blue with black boot-topping. **History:** Founded 2006. **Web:** None found.

Borgenfjord	Nld	1996	1,682	2,500	81.7	11.1	4.5	-	C	ex Leonie-06, Fivelborg-98

Storesletten Rederi AS   Norway

Funnel: Yellow. **Hull:** Blue or * red with black boot-topping. **History:** Founder commenced shipowing in 1961 and limited company founded 2001. **Web:** www.storesletten.no

Name	Flag	Year	GT	DWT	Loa	Bm	Drt	Kts	Type	Remarks
Heidi	Fro	1979	4,126	5,672	104.8	16.1	6.6	14	Cc	ex Eco Jasmin-04, Sea Tiger-04, MSC Ecuador-02, Dania Suhr-01, Nedlloyd Antilles-98, ScanDutch Sicilia-92, Hansedamm-86, Ville du Zenith-85, Karaman-85, I/a Hansedamm
Helene	Fro	1980	5,938	7,958	126.3	20.1	6.6	15	CC	ex Saturn-01, Monagas-99, Saturn-98, FAS Trieste-96, EWL Rotterdam-96, Saturn-95, Zim Caribe III-94, Gothia-91, Medipas Sky-88, Nicolo Gazzolo-88, Gothia-87, Jumna Pioneer-86, Gothia-85, Concorde Antilles-85, CCNI Andino-84, Gothia-82, European Eagle-80, Gothia-80
Ingvild	Nis	1977	3,694	4,418	98.7	16.1	5.7	14	Cc	ex Ole-01, Maersk Euro Decimo-94, Maersk Turbo-91, Pegasus-88, Planet I-85, Ville du Levant-83, Planet-79
Tone *	Nis	1979	5,378	7,283	126.3	18.1	6.5	15	CC	ex Dania-Carina-07, Katherine Borchard-00, Concordia-86, Katherine Borchard-86, Concordia-85, Zim Australia-82, I/a Concordia

Reederei Erwin Strahlmann   Germany

Funnel: Black with black 'ES' on black edged white diamond on blue over white over red bands. **Hull:** Blue or green some with white 'ECHOSHIP', red boot-topping. **History:** Founded 1988. **Web:** www.reederei-strahlmann.de

Name	Flag	Year	GT	DWT	Loa	Bm	Drt	Kts	Type	Remarks
Alesia	Atg	2008	4,726	7,574	116.1	15.9	6.4	13	C	
Arlau	Atg	2004	2,461	3,701	87.9	12.8	5.5	11	C	
Bekau	Atg	2005	2,461	3,701	87.9	12.8	5.5	11	C	
Belizia	Atg	2008	4,723	7,560	116.1	15.9	6.4	13	C	
Bondenau	Atg	2007	2,461	3,704	87.9	12.8	5.5	11	C	
Bounder	Atg	1989	1,984	3,202	89.3	12.5	4.7	11	Cc	ex Borsteler Berg-97, Hetlo-94, Borsteler Berg-92
Bramau	Atg	2005	2,461	3,704	87.9	12.8	5.5	11	C	
Burgtor	Atg	1989	2,351	3,414	87.0	13.0	5.1	11	Cc	ex Lady Linda-04, Mellum-94, Port Lima-93
Carrier	Atg	1985	1,584	2,379	82.0	11.3	3.5	10	C	ex Inga-02
Cecilia	Atg	2009	4,723	7,400	116.1	15.9	6.4	13	C	
Connorth	Atg	1998	7,171	8,965	126.9	20.0	7.9	17	CC	ex Access D-08, Access F-06, Steamers Power-04, Tiger Power-03
Consouth	Atg	1998	7,171	8,937	126.9	20.0	7.9	17	CC	ex Amazing D-08, Amazing F-06, Steamers Progress-04
Conwest	Atg	1998	7,171	8,937	126.9	20.0	7.9	17	CC	ex Ambitious D-08, Ambitious F-06, Steamers Prosperity-04, Mekong Progress-01, Steamers Prosperity-00, Mariners Prosperity-00
Damina	Atg	2010	4,726	7,575	116.1	15.9	6.4	13	C	

Reederei Erwin Strahlmann. Arlau. *N. Kemps*

Reederei Erwin Strahlmann. Eider. *M. Beckett*

Name	Flag	Year	GT	DWT	Loa	Bm	Drt	Kts	Type	Remarks
Dealer	Atg	1982	1,692	2,322	80.3	11.4	4.3	10	C	ex Lena S-01
Dornum	Atg	1993	1,662	2,388	81.8	11.5	3.8	10	Cc	ex Saar Madrid-96
Eider	Atg	2003	2,461	3,672	87.9	12.8	5.5	11	C	ex Gretchen Muller-03
Eilsum	Atg	1991	1,662	2,376	81.8	11.4	4.4	10	Cc	ex Saar Lisboa-96, I/a Eilsum
Elbetor	Atg	1990	2,351	3,398	87.0	13.0	5.1	11	Cc	ex Lady Clara-05 Baltrum-95, Port Faro-93
Elsebeth	Atg	1986	1,636	2,267	82.5	11.3	4.2	10	Cc	ex Sea Elbe-01, Silke-95
Helse	Atg	1992	1,582	2,378	81.2	11.4	3.6	10	Cc	I/a Hansa Carrier
Holstentor	Atg	1989	2,351	3,393	87.0	13.0	5.1	11	Cc	ex Lady Greta-04, Borkum-95, Port Vouga-93
Jamtland	Gib	1992	4,071	5,697	104.4	16.2	6.4	14	Cc	ex Chopin-10, Jamtland-06, Chopin-03, Jamtland-02, Chopin-97, Ville d'Autan-93, Chopin-92, Stella Adriatic-92, I/a Christina
Jevenau	Atg	2007	2,461	3,702	87.9	12.9	5.5	11	Cc	
Joker	Atg	1984	1,559	2,315	82.5	11.4	4.2	10	Cc	ex Elisia-02
Kossau	Atg	2007	2,461	3,701	87.9	12.9	5.5	11	Cc	
Krempertor	Atg	1990	2,351	3,432	87.0	13.2	5.1	11	Cc	ex Lady Lisa-04, Rottum-94, Port Foz-93
Kruckau	Atg	2003	2,461	3,683	87.9	12.8	5.5	11	Cc	ex Reti Muller-03
Lancer	Atg	1997	4,276	5,055	100.6	16.2	6.4	15	Cc	ex Carl C-09, Athlete F-05, Steamers Fortune-04
Lifter	Atg	2007	4,990	7,778	118.6	15.2	7.1	14	Chl	ex Hartwig Scan-07, Lifter-07
Linnau	Atg	2006	2,461	3,698	87.9	12.9	5.5	11	Cc	
Luhnau	Atg	2007	2,461	3,720	87.8	12.8	5.5	10	Cc	
Malena	Atg	2007	2,588	3,342	86.5	12.8	5.5	12	Cc	ex Asha Scan-08, Malena-07
Marne	Atg	2005	2,530	3,410	86.6	12.8	5.6	12	Cc	
Melfi Caribe	Atg	1998	7,171	8,937	126.9	20.0	7.9	17	CC	ex Accord D-08, Cook Strait-06, Steamers Prospect-04
Muhlenau	Atg	2004	2,461	3,670	87.9	12.9	5.5	11	Cc	
Nanuk	Atg	2007	2,588	3,350	86.5	12.8	5.5	12	Cc	ex Atima Scan-09, Nanuk-07
Norderau	Atg	2005	2,461	3,711	87.9	12.9	5.5	11	Cc	
Ohlau	Atg	2007	2,461	3,689	87.9	12.9	5.5	11	Cc	
Ostenau	Atg	2005	2,461	3,710	87.9	12.9	5.5	11	Cc	
Pewsum	Atg	1990	1,960	3,025	88.3	12.5	4.6	11	Cc	ex Jens R-02
Pilsum	Atg	1993	1,662	2,371	81.8	11.4	4.3	10	Cc	ex Heiko B-02, Pilsum-98, Saar Rotterdam-96, I/a Pilsum
Pinnau	Atg	2003	2,461	3,686	87.9	12.8	5.5	12	Cc	ex Gertrud Muller-03
Piper	Atg	1982	1,710	2,316	80.3	11.4	4.3	11	C	ex Simone-04
Provider	Atg	1981	1,834	2,623	78.6	12.8	4.6	10	Cc	ex Ruthensand-99, Echo Trader-90, Ruthensand-87
Rantum	Atg	1989	1,984	3,217	89.3	12.5	4.7	11	Cc	ex Waldtraut B-02
Rodau	Atg	2004	2,461	3,712	87.9	12.9	5.5	11	Cc	
Roger	Atg	1984	1,520	2,171	82.5	11.4	4.0	10	Cc	ex Gudrun-92, Aros Anglia-92, Gudrun-90
Rysum	Atg	1991	1,662	2,380	81.8	11.4	4.4	10	Cc	ex Saar Emden-96, Rysum-92
Southern Phoenix	Atg	2006	2,588	3,345	86.5	12.8	5.5	12	Cc	ex Tuperna-09, Anette Scan-09, Tuperna-07
Stadum	Atg	1989	1,984	3,223	89.3	12.5	4.3	11	Cc	ex Westerhusen-02, Alpha-99, Barbel-93
Steinau	Atg	2006	2,461	3,712	87.9	12.9	5.5	11	Cc	
Suderau	Atg	2005	2,461	3,670	87.9	12.9	5.5	11	Cc	
Thunder	Atg	1984	1,559	1,735	82.5	11.3	3.5	10	Cc	ex Sandfeld-04, Paloma I-97, Paloma-96, Landkirchen-93
Trader	Atg	1980	1,527	2,290	82.5	11.4	4.0	10	Cc	ex Cranz II-01, Cranz-98, Matthias-93, Vouksi-91, Matthias-91, Echo Matthias-90, Elbe-89
Uttum	Atg	1993	1,662	2,368	81.8	11.5	4.4	10	Cc	ex Saar Antwerp-97

Strand Shipping A/S   Norway

Funnel: *White wth white 'R' on red rectangle or * black with broad white band.* **Hull:** *Red with red or black boot-topping.* **History:** *Founded 1988 and management subsidiary formed in 1997.* **Web:** *www.strand-shipping.no; www.rana-ship.no*

Name	Flag	Year	GT	DWT	Loa	Bm	Drt	Kts	Type	Remarks
Ranosen	Mlt	1986	3,300	4,107	92.4	15.7	6.0	13	Cc	ex Pavo-07, Pride of Foynes-06, Pavo-06, Normed Istanbul-01, Pavo-00, Seevetal-98
Varangerfjord *	Nor	1975	1,656	2,130	75.8	11.9	4.7	11	Cc	ex Varanger-09, Ranafjord-07, Hilros-93, Ume-85

Operated by subsidiary Rana Ship Management AS, Norway

Svensk Karnbranslehantering AB   Sweden

Funnel: *White with white 'G' on broad red band.* **Hull:** *Red with red boot-topping.* **History:** *Not confirmed.* **Web:** *www.skb.se*

Name	Flag	Year	GT	DWT	Loa	Bm	Drt	Kts	Type	Remarks
Sigyn	(2) Swe	1982	4,166	2,044	90.3	18.0	4.0	11	Cn	

Managed by Destination Gotland AB

Edvin Svenson Skeppsmakleri AB   Sweden

Funnel: *Yellow with white 'E' on blue disc on white band or * white 'E' on green disc, narrow black top.* **Hull:** *Blue with black boot-topping.* **History:** *Founded 1994.* **Web:** *www.edvin-svenson.se*

Name	Flag	Year	GT	DWT	Loa	Bm	Drt	Kts	Type	Remarks
Ala	Pan	1968	1,064	1,203	68.4	10.6	4.0	12	C	ex Gala-95, Tor Normandia-77, Gala-76
Alva *	Pan	1968	1,037	1,335	68.4	10.5	4.3	12	C	ex Hannes D-04, Windo-98, Mjovik-91, Windo-90, Nincop-88

Reederei Erwin Strahlmann. Holstentor. *M. Beckett*

Reederei Erwin Strahlmann. Steinau. *M. Beckett*

Edvin Svenson Skeppsmakleri AB. Alva. *N. Kemps*

Tarbit Shipping AB. Bitflower. *Allan Ryszka Onions*

Name		Flag	Year	GT	DWT	Loa	Bm	Drt	Kts	Type	Remarks

Rederi Swedia AB
Sweden

Funnel: Pale blue with three yellow diagonal lines on dark blue disc. **Hull:** Dark blue or orange with red boot-topping. **History:** Founded 1978 as Vingatank Rederi AB to 1988. **Web:** www.swedia.se

Name		Flag	Year	GT	DWT	Loa	Bm	Drt	Kts	Type	Remarks
Charisma av Goteborg *		Swe	1962	329	599	44.9	6.9	3.6	9	T	ex Charisma-06, Charisma av Goteborg-04, Triton av Goteborg-97, Lion King-97, Triton-96, Alvtank-93, Furenas-79
Smaragd ***		Swe	1980	1,276	1,714	69.5	11.8	4.3	11	T	ex Amity-00, Christian-88
Vinga Helena *		Swe	1985	4,320	6,400	115.0	15.8	7.2	14	Tch	ex Ottoman-98, Manitou-94
Vinga Safir		Swe	2000	1,685	2,653	79.9	12.8	5.2	-	T	ex Yaren-05
Vingatank		Swe	2002	2,834	4,298	96.3	14.2	6.2	11	Tch	

* operated by Nordtank Shipping, Denmark or by Swedia for ** Fjordtank Rederi AB or *** Krabbeskars Rederi AB, both Sweden.

Rederi Swedish Bulk AB
Sweden

Funnel: Black with black 'SB' on large yellow panel. **Hull:** Blue with red boot-topping. **History:** Founded 2001. **Web:** www.swedishbulk.se

Name		Flag	Year	GT	DWT	Loa	Bm	Drt	Kts	Type	Remarks
Resolute		Vct	1967	2,659	4,475	99.9	13.9	6.1	13	C	ex Total Impression X-08, Vikanes-05, Tofton-95, Rugia-76
Swe-Bulk		Cyp	1991	2,480	3,237	87.4	13.0	4.7	12	Cc	ex Severnaya Dvina-08, Ingo J-05, MF Levant-99, Intermodal Levant-96, Diana J-93, Queensee-93

S Switynk
Netherlands

Funnel: Grey with large white 'S'. **Hull:** Grey with red boot-topping. **History:** Founded 2003. **Web:** www.amelandshipping.nl; www.skylgeshipping.nl

Name		Flag	Year	GT	DWT	Loa	Bm	Drt	Kts	Type	Remarks
Ameland		Nld	2009	6,046	7,610	122.1	16.6	7.2	14	C	
Skylge		Nld	2009	6,046	7,610	122.1	16.6	7.2	14	C	

Tanto AS
Norway

Funnel: White with deep black top. **Hull:** Black with red boot-topping. **History:** Not confirmed. **Web:** None found.

Name		Flag	Year	GT	DWT	Loa	Bm	Drt	Kts	Type	Remarks
Aunborg		Cok	1976	1,086	1,564	65.8	10.8	4.3	10	C	ex Jamie-98, Marico-95, Gina P-93, Kwintebank-92, Els Teekman-84

Tarbit Shipping AB
Sweden

Funnel: Blue with white 'TBS' between narrow white bands. **Hull:** Light grey or blue with red boot-topping. **History:** Founded 1953 and commenced ship-owning in 1962 as Knut Holger Hermansson to 1995. **Web:** www.tarbit.se

Name		Flag	Year	GT	DWT	Loa	Bm	Drt	Kts	Type	Remarks
Bit Oktania		Swe	2004	9,490	13,602	134.8	21.6	9.0	14	Tch	
Bitfjord		Swe	1971	1,573	1,986	85.2	12.3	3.5	12	Tch	ex Esso Valloy-95 (len-97)
Bitflower		Swe	2003	4,936	6,314	114.6	16.5	6.7	15	Tch	
Bithav		Swe	2000	4,980	6,440	114.6	16.5	6.7	15	Tch	
Margita *		Swe	1971	1,924	3,296	86.2	13.5	5.1	12	Tch	ex Deniz-A-90, Alchimist Flensburg-84, Chemathene-80, Alchimist Flensburg-79

* owned by subsidiary TSA Tanker Shipping AB (founded 1992 – www.tsatanker.se)
Also owns two 24,800 dwt tankers.
Associated with Theodora Tankers BV qv

Tarntank Rederi AB
Sweden

Funnel: Cream with white bird on dark blue disc, narrow dark blue top. **Hull:** Light grey with red boot-topping. **History:** Founded 1958. **Web:** www.tarntank.se

Name		Flag	Year	GT	DWT	Loa	Bm	Drt	Kts	Type	Remarks
Tarnbris		Nis	2007	7,315	10,250	129.5	19.8	8.0	15	Tch	
Tarndal		Nis	1998	5,685	8,269	115.1	18.3	7.2	13	Tch	ex Dicksi-05
Tarnfors	(me)	Nis	1998	5,698	8,245	115.1	18.3	7.2	15	Tch	I/a Guervik
Tarnhav		Dmk	2002	9,980	14,796	141.2	21.6	9.0	14	Tch	
Tarnholm		Dmk	2005	9,993	14,825	141.2	21.6	9.0	14	Tch	
Tarnsjo		Nis	1993	6,534	9,960	129.1	18.3	7.6	12	T	
Tarnvag		Swe	2003	9,993	14,803	141.2	21.6	9.0	14	Tch	
Tarnvik		Dmk	2001	9,980	14,796	141.2	21.6	9.0	14	Tch	
Ternland		Dmk	1996	6,534	10,877	129.2	18.4	8.1	14	T	

Taylor & Taylor
UK

Funnel: Red. **Hull:** Red with red boot-topping. **History:** Not confirmed. **Web:** None found.

Name		Flag	Year	GT	DWT	Loa	Bm	Drt	Kts	Type	Remarks
Red Baroness		Gbr	1979	964	1,450	65.1	10.7	4.0	10	C	ex Harma-00
Red Duchess *		Gbr	1969	1,285	1,298	75.7	11.0	3.5	11	Cc	ex Aasland-05, Minitrans-86, Bell Cavalier-78, Valdes-75, Bell Cavalier-74, Valdes-73, I/a Geertien Bos

* managed by Coast Lines Shipping Ltd, Ireland.

Team Lines Deutschland GmbH & Co KG
Germany

Container feeder service currently operating fourteen chartered vessels. **History:** Subsidiary of UK-based Peel Ports Group since 2005. **Web:** www.teamlines.de

Tarntank Rederi AB. Tarnvik. *F. de Vries*

Team Ship Management GmbH. Normed Bremen. *Hans Kraijenbosch*

Name		Flag	Year	GT	DWT	Loa	Bm	Drt	Kts	Type	Remarks

Team Ship A/S   Denmark

Funnel: *Dark blue.* **Hull:** *Dark blue with white 'TEAMSHIP.COM', red boot-topping.* **History:** *Founded 1996.* **Web:** *www.teamship.dk*

Name		Flag	Year	GT	DWT	Loa	Bm	Drt	Kts	Type	Remarks
Ocean Team	(2)	Vct	1976	3,285	2,758	81.8	15.5	5.6	11	C/hl	ex Lilleborg-09, Perge-05, Strong Texan-03, Dock Express Texas-89, Happy Runner-84

Also operates other chartererd vessels.

Team Ship Management GmbH & Co KG   Germany

Funnel: *Charterers colours.* **Hull:** *Blue with black boot-topping.* **History:** *Founded 2005.* **Web:** *www.teamship.de*

Name	Flag	Year	GT	DWT	Loa	Bm	Drt	Kts	Type	Remarks
Bente	Mlt	2010	3,556	4,455	90.0	15.4	5.6	11	C	
Berit	Nld	2010	3,500	4,500	90.0	15.4	5.6	11	C	
Christoph M	Mlt	2010	3,500	4,500	90.0	15.4	5.6	11	C	
Hermann W	Mlt	2010	3,500	4,500	90.0	15.4	5.6	11	C	
Joerg N	Mlt	2010	3,500	4,500	90.0	15.4	5.6	11	C	
Marlene	Mlt	2010	3,500	4,500	90.0	15.4	5.6	11	C	
Merle	Mlt	2010	3,500	4,500	90.0	15.4	5.6	11	C	
Normed Amsterdam	Mlt	2007	8,407	11,201	129.4	19.0	8.7	16	Cc	
Normed Bremen	Mlt	2006	8,407	11,143	129.3	19.0	8.7	16	Cc	I/a Team Spirit
OXL Lotus	Deu	1997	5,752	5,104	101.3	18.9	6.6	16	C/ro	ex Palawan-08, Fret Meuse-03, Palawan-02, Scan Partner-01
OXL Nomad	Bhs	1997	6,714	8,874	100.5	20.4	8.2	16	Cc	ex UAL Nigeria-07, CEC Conway-07, Clipper Conway-02, Maersk Takoradi-99, Clipper Conway-98
OXL Samurai	Bhs	1998	6,714	8,874	100.5	20.4	8.2	16	Cc	ex OXL Sultan-09, Challenge-08, CEC Challenge-07, CEC Cowbridge-05, Seaboard Patriot-02, Clipper Cowbridge-01
Tim B	Mlt	2010	3,500	4,500	90.0	15.4	5.6	11	C	
TPC Classic	Mhl	2010	8,407	11,150	129.4	19.0	8.7	16	Cc	
TPC Dream	Mhl	2010	8,407	11,150	129.4	19.0	8.7	16	Cc	
TPC Eagle	Mhl	2010	8,407	11,150	129.4	19.0	8.7	16	Cc	

Also see Hanse Capital Gruppe, Germany

Thames Shipping Services   UK

Funnel: *Green or black.* **Hull:** *Green.* **History:** *Founded 1893 as C Crawley Ltd and formed by Metcalf Motor Coasters Ltd in early 1900's.* **Web:** *None found.*

Name	Flag	Year	GT	DWT	Loa	Bm	Drt	Kts	Type	Remarks
Aquatic	Gbr	1963	199	315	35.1	7.5	2.3	-	T	ex Busby-85
Aqueduct	Gbr	1964	594	908	62.3	10.2	3.0	10	T	ex Charcrest-91
Tommy	Gbr	1963	217	315	35.1	7.5	2.3	8	T	ex Batsman-87

Also operates other smaller ships

Theodora Tankers BV   Netherlands

Funnel: *Blue with white 'TBS' between narrow white bands.* **Hull:** *Blue with red boot-topping.* **History:** *Founded 1947 as Rederij Theodora BV to 1999, Furness acquired majority interest in 1966 merging with Pakhoed in 1990 and Van Ommeren in 1999 as Vopak Theodora Tankers BV to 2001, when bought-out.* **Web:** *www.theodora.nl*

Name	Flag	Year	GT	DWT	Loa	Bm	Drt	Kts	Type	Remarks
Bitland	Nld	1995	4,025	4,450	105.0	15.8	5.8	14	Ta	ex Tasco 2-98
Stella Lyra	Nld	1989	2,874	3,480	95.8	14.5	5.7	12	Ta	
Stella Maris	Nld	2004	4,064	4,531	106.0	15.8	6.3	14	Ta	ex Scipion-05
Stella Orion	Nld	2004	4,074	4,999	104.6	15.2	6.3	13	Ta	ex Etoile Lava-06
Stella Polaris	Nld	1999	5,396	8,297	117.2	17.0	7.6	14	Ta	
Stella Virgo	Nld	2003	4,074	4,999	104.0	15.2	6.3	13	Ta	ex Horizon Lava-07
Stella Wega	Nld	1996	3,983	4,350	105.6	15.9	6.0	15	Ta	
Theodora	Nld	1991	4,098	6,616	110.6	17.0	7.1	14	Ta	

Associated with Tarbit Shipping AB qv

Rederij Ter Stege   Netherlands

Funnel: *Black with grey shield (two vertical black lines and three black birds) on broad white band.* **Hull:** *Dark blue with pale blue band over red boot-topping.* **History:** *Founded 2007.* **Web:** *None found.*

Name	Flag	Year	GT	DWT	Loa	Bm	Drt	Kts	Type	Remarks
Ambassadeur	Nld	2007	3,990	6,000	110.8	14.0	5.3	13	C	

THH Shipping ApS   Denmark

Funnel: *Black with white 'HTH' on red shield.* **Hull:** *Red with red boot-topping.* **History:** *Founded 1998 as Tomchart ApS to 2005.* **Web:** *www.thhshipping.dk*

Name	Flag	Year	GT	DWT	Loa	Bm	Drt	Kts	Type	Remarks
Anna Stevns	Pan	1975	1,889	2,215	75.4	11.8	5.0	11	Cc	ex Silke Polax-04
Buse Stevns	Atg	1984	1,892	2,887	79.0	12.6	5.1	10	Cc	ex Celtic Carrier-06, Pamela Everard-01
Niels Stevns	Atg	1086	1,892	2,887	79.0	12.6	5.1	10	Cc	ex Siuita-07, Sociality-00, Stevonia-87
Nural Stevns	Atg	1984	1,892	2,887	79.0	12.7	5.1	10	Cc	ex Celtic Pioneer-06, Selectivity-01
Olivier Stevns	Atg	1984	1,892	2,887	79.0	12.7	5.1	10	Cc	ex Pia Stevns-09, Celtic Forester-06, Sanguity-01, Willonia-88
Stevns Pearl	Atg	1984	4,366	5,907	99.9	17.8	6.9	13	Cc	ex Diana Scan-09, Stevns Pearl-05, CPC Holandia-95, Conti Holandia-87

Name		Flag	Year	GT	DWT	Loa	Bm	Drt	Kts	Type	Remarks

Thien & Heyenga Bedreederungs-und Bef. GmbH Germany

Funnel: *Buff with white 'T&H' on red band between black and blue bands or charteres colours.* **Hull:** *Black or * blue with red boot-topping.*
History: *Founded 1977* **Web:** *www.tuh.de*

Name	Flag	Year	GT	DWT	Loa	Bm	Drt	Kts	Type	Remarks
Appen Charlotte *	Lbr	2008	9,610	12,400	142.7	22.6	8.2	18	CC	
Appen Paula *	Mhl	2006	9,954	13,710	148.0	23.3	8.5	19	CC	ex CSAV Atlas-09, Fa Mei Shan-08, I/a Maersk Recife
Mell Saujana *	Lbr	2008	9,610	12,400	142.7	22.6	8.2	18	CC	ex Appen Anita-09
Neerlandic	Atg	1985	3,955	5,386	108.8	16.3	7.3	16	Rc	
Nova Galicia	Ant	1983	6,149	6,730	137.8	18.6	7.5	18	R	ex Sun Princess-96, Sun Field-94
Shamrock	Brb	2000	4,654	4,850	120.0	18.0	5.4	16	Ro	
Stadt Berlin	Atg	1998	9,528	12,920	146.4	22.7	8.3	20	CC	ex Mekong Sapphire-01, Stadt Berlin-01, Sea-Land Mexico-99, I/a Stadt Berlin
Stadt Bremen	Atg	2003	9,528	12,895	146.4	22.7	8.3	20	CC	ex Tharos-08, EWL Rotterdam-03, Stadt Bremen-03
Stadt Celle	Atg	2005	9,957	13,710	147.9	23.3	8.5	19	CC	ex Delmas Tamboti-07
Stadt Dusseldorf	Deu	1998	9,528	12,850	146.5	22.7	8.3	20	CC	ex EWL Curacao-08, Stadt Dusseldorf-03, Sea-Land Guatemala-99, Stadt Dusseldorf-99
Stadt Emden	Deu	2002	9,528	12,760	147.8	22.7	8.3	19	CC	ex EWL Hispania-08, Stadt Emden-06, P&O Nedlloyd Araucania-05, MOL Rainbow-03, I/a Lania
Stadt Flensburg	Atg	2003	9,528	12,920	146.5	22.7	8.3	19	CC	ex EWL Canada-08, Melfi Havana-06, I/a Alassa
Stadt Goslar	Atg	2006	9,957	13,715	147.9	23.3	8.5	19	CC	ex Delmas Karee-07
Stadt Hamburg	Gib	1998	9,528	12,850	146.5	22.7	8.3	20	CC	ex CMA CGM Ivory-07, Fas Gulf-06, Stadt Hamburg-03, Pelor-02, Stadt Hamburg-01, Cala Pilar-01, Stadt Hamburg-00
Stadt Hameln	Atg	2007	9,957	13,749	148.0	23.3	8.5	19	CC	ex APL Galapagos-07, Stadt Hameln-07
Stadt Hannover	Cyp	1994	3,978	5,273	104.8	16.6	6.6	16	Cc	ex Arcadian Faith-01, FLS Colombia-97, Arcadian Faith-94
Stadt Lauenburg	Atg	2007	9,610	12,788	143.6	22.6	8.2	18	CC	
Stadt Luneburg	Cyp	2004	9,528	12,920	146.5	23.3	8.5	19	CC	I/a Doros
Stadt Munchen	Atg	1999	9,528	12,918	146.5	22.7	8.3	19	CC	ex P&O Nedlloyd Muisca-05, Stadt Munchen-03
Stadt Ratzeburg	Atg	2007	9,610	12,774	142.7	22.6	8.2	18	CC	
Stadt Rendsburg	Cyp	2004	9,528	12,920	146.5	22.7	8.3	19	CC	
Stadt Rotenburg	Atg	2003	9,528	12,920	146.5	22.7	8.3	19	CC	ex EWL Central America-08, Pirsos-07, Melfi Italia II-03
Ulla Scan *	Atg	1999	4,086	4,806	100.6	16.6	6.4	15	Cc	ex Balticon Hamburg-09, BBC America-07, Karsnes-05, BBC America-05, Bingum-99

* managed for Appencapital GmbH & Co KG, Germany (Founded 2005 – www.appencapital.com)
Also owns or manages about 19 larger container ships (including 3 newbuildings) and five larger refrigerated cargo ships.

Johs Thode GmbH & Co KG Germany

Funnel: *Various.* **Hull:** *Blue or dark green with red or black boot-topping or red with green boot-topping.* **History:** *Founded 1890 as Johs Thode GmbH & Co, merging in 2000 with MarConsult Schiffahrtskontor until separating in 2003.* **Web:** *www.johs-thode.de*

Name	Flag	Year	GT	DWT	Loa	Bm	Drt	Kts	Type	Remarks
Altona *	Atg	1980	5,307	6,660	113.2	19.1	6.5	14	CC	ex Nedlloyd Lotus-95, Altona-93, Manchester Trader-91, Karyatein-89, I/a Altona
Astrid	Atg	1985	5,608	7,120	116.5	20.3	6.2	13	C/ro	ex Vento di Tramontana-03, Astrid-03, Vento di Tramontana-03, FAS Gemlik-02, BBC Germany-01, FAS Gemlik-01, Cam Ayous Express-96, Nedlloyd Tulip-95, Ville d'Orient-92, Kathe Husmann-88, Bacol Vitoria-87, I/a Kathe Husmann
Hanse Confidence	Atg	2004	9,701	11,050	140.5	22.8	8.7	18	CC	ex X-Press Fuji-09, Christine-07, TS Yokohama-07
Hanse Courage	Atg	2005	9,701	11,023	140.5	22.8	8.7	18	CC	ex X-Press Elbrus-09, Gabriella-07, TS Pusan-07, TS Nagoya-05
Hanse Spirit	Cyp	2005	7,713	9,655	141.7	20.6	7.3	18	CC	ex Merwedestroom-07
Hanse Vision	Cyp	2005	7,713	9,604	141.6	20.6	7.3	18	CC	ex Maasstroom-07
Hanseduo	Atg	1984	6,670	8,350	117.5	20.4	7.5	16	CC	ex Sea Mariner-98, Kent Explorer-96, Joanna Borchard-95, Emcol Carrier-89, Caravelle88, Holcan Elbe-86, Kahira-86, Caravelle-84
Hansewall	Atg	1985	6,659	8,340	117.5	20.5	7.5	16	CC	ex MCC Clipper-09, Hansewall-05, Joanna Borchard-97, Levant Lesum-96, Levant Neva-96, Lucy Borchard-94, Miriam Borchard-92, Kalymnos-90, I/a Hansewall

* owned by Walter Meyer Schiffahrts KG.

Thor Rederi A/S Denmark

Funnel: *White.* **Hull:** *Red with green boot-topping.* **History:** *Founded 1998 as subsidiary of Sydfyenske Holding Group.* **Web:** *www.t-red.dk*

Name		Flag	Year	GT	DWT	Loa	Bm	Drt	Kts	Type	Remarks
Arafura Endeavour		Dis	1992	2,815	4,110	88.4	15.2	5.3	13	Cc	ex Arktis Atlantic-02, Mekong Sentosa-95, Arktis Atlantic-94, Vigour Atlantic-94, Arktis Atlantic-93
Celica		Vct	1979	813	1,191	63.0	9.5	3.4	10	C	ex Tim-01, St. Michael-94, Jeanette B-90, St. Michael-89
Thor Elisabeth		Atg	1991	2,815	4,110	88.4	15.2	6.0	13	Cc	ex Roxanne-06, CEC Dawn-05, Industrial Pioneer-99, Arktis Dawn-96
Thor Falcon		Dis	1992	1,964	2,784	83.2	13.0	5.4	14	Cc	ex Scan Falcon-02
Thor Gitte		Dis	1997	4,078	4,900	101.3	16.8	6.4	15	Cc	ex BBC Singapore-08, Bremer Timber-04, Ranzel-97
Thor Hanne	(2)	Atg	2004	1,967	3,235	69.8	17.6	4.5	-	C	ex Kimtrans Mega Virgo-05
Thor Hawk		Dis	1992	1,964	2,784	83.2	13.0	5.4	14	Cc	ex Nine Hawk-03, Scan Hawk-01

Johs Thode GmbH & Co. Hanse Spirit. *Hans Kraijenbosch*

Erik Thun AB. Bro Globe. *F. de Vries*

Name		Flag	Year	GT	DWT	Loa	Bm	Drt	Kts	Type	Remarks
Thor Ingeborg		Dis	1997	4,050	4,900	100.6	16.8	6.4	15	Cc	ex BBC Argentina-07, S. Gabriel-04, Industrial Unity-99, Odin-99, Industrial Unity-98, Odin-98
Thor Inger		Dis	1988	1,187	1,210	67.4	11.5	3.5	11	Cc	ex Southern Havannah-97, Thor Inger-95, Inger Riis-94
Thor Irene		Atg	1993	2,815	4,110	88.4	15.2	6.0	13	Cc	ex Sea Dream-05, CEC Dream-04, Moana-01, Arktis Dream-00, Mekong Dream-95, Arktis Dream-94, Vigour Penang-93, ex Arktis Dream-93
Thor Swan		Dis	1991	1,964	2,600	83.2	13.0	5.4	13	Cc	ex Scan Swan-02

Owned or managed by subsidiary T-Red A/S (formed 2004)

Erik Thun AB Sweden

Funnel: *White with yellow 'ETAB' on yellow edged blue swallowtail flag, black top or ‡ white with narrow black top.* **Hull:** *Blue or green with red boot-topping.*
History: *Founded 1926.* **Web:** *www.thun.se*

Name		Flag	Year	GT	DWT	Loa	Bm	Drt	Kts	Type	Remarks
Bro Galaxy *		Nld	2001	4,107	7,559	114.7	15.0	6.8	13	Tch	
Bro Garland *		Nld	2009	4,212	7,559	116.4	15.0	6.8	-	Tch	
Bro Gazelle		Nld	2009	4,212	7,515	116.4	15.0	6.8	-	Tch	
Bro Gemini *		Nld	2003	4,107	7,559	115.0	15.3	6.8	13	Tch	
Bro Genius *		Nld	2003	4,107	7,559	115.0	15.3	6.8	13	Tch	
Bro Globe *		Nld	2001	4,107	7,559	115.0	15.3	6.8	13	Tch	
Bro Glory *		Nld	2000	3,653	6,535	103.5	15.0	7.1	13	Tch	ex United Glory-00
Bro Goliath *		Nld	2004	4,745	7,108	119.1	16.9	6.8	14	Tch	ex Mareld-07
Bro Gothia *		Nld	2003	4,814	7,157	119.1	16.9	6.8	11	Tch	
Bro Grace *		Nld	1999	3,653	6,535	103.5	15.0	6.8	13	Tch	ex United Grace-00
Bro Granite *		Nld	2004	4,107	7,559	115.0	15.3	6.8	12	Tch	
Bro Gratitude *		Nld	2003	4,107	7,559	115.0	15.3	6.8	12	Tch	
Eken		Swe	2003	2,556	4,775	89.0	13.4	5.9	11	C	
Eos †	(2)	Nis	1976	3,963	6,198	102.0	15.4	6.7	12	Bu	ex Eemsborg-84 (len-84)
Ice Star		Nld	1997	2,904	5,390	89.0	13.4	7.0	13	C	
Kalkvik		Nis	2007	5,325	9,402	113.5	15.9	7.9	13	Cu	
Kinne *		Nld	2004	2,810	4,775	89.0	13.4	5.9	11	C	
Lecko		Nld	2003	2,556	4,775	89.0	13.4	5.9	11	C	
Luro		Nld	2003	2,556	4,919	89.0	13.4	5.9	11	C	
Malmnes		Nis	1993	5,883	9,891	126.7	15.9	7.7	13	Bu	
Mornes		Nis	1991	5,385	9,125	116.6	15.8	7.9	-	Bu	
Naven		Nis	1991	2,497	4,175	88.3	13.2	5.5	-	C	ex Anna Buck-98
Nordanhav		Swe	1992	5,953	9,891	126.7	15.9	7.7	13	Bu	ex Moxnes-96
Nordic Amanda ‡		Nld	1991	1,999	3,015	82.2	12.5	4.9	11	Cc	ex Bergfjorg-04, Panta Rei-03, Skagenbank-99
Nossan		Swe	1990	2,248	4,250	88.3	13.2	5.5	12	C	
Ostanhav		Swe	1983	3,800	5,748	108.4	13.1	6.9	12	Cu	
Snow Star *		Nld	1996	2,904	5,398	89.0	13.4	7.0	12	C	
Sunnanhav		Nis	2006	5,325	9,402	110.0	15.9	7.9	13	Bu	
Tidan		Swe	1990	2,250	4,250	88.3	13.2	5.5	12	C	
Tuna		Nld	2004	2,810	4,775	89.0	13.4	5.9	11	C	

* managed by Marin Ship Management BV, Netherlands (www.mfmarinedivision.nl)
† managed for Emmaboda Shipping AB, Sweden
‡ operated by Nordic Chartering (see under Flinter Group)
Also owns larger tankers managed by Marin Ship Management.

Wilhelm Tietjen Befrachtungs GmbH Germany

Funnel: *Buff with blue shield.* **Hull:** *Light grey with black boot-topping.* **History:** *Not confirmed.* **Web:** *www.tietjen-online.de*

Name	Flag	Year	GT	DWT	Loa	Bm	Drt	Kts	Type	Remarks
Hannelore	Deu	1965	658	719	55.1	9.3	3.2	10	C	ex Karina W-06, Adele Hagenah-89

TL Shipping GmbH & Co KG Germany

Funnel: *White with narrow black top.* **Hull:** *Black with red boot-topping.* **History:** *Founded 2003 emerging from TSB Trans Baltic Schiffahrt formed in 1987.*
Web: *www.tl-shipping.de*

Name	Flag	Year	GT	DWT	Loa	Bm	Drt	Kts	Type	Remarks
Bluestar	Lbr	1997	6,459	8,865	121.2	17.7	8.1	17	Cc	ex Onego Tramper-09, Bluestar-08, CMA CGM Venezuela-06, CSAV Andino-05, CMA CGM Mahgreb-04, Kont Miriam-03, Seafreight Star-99, Ivaran Quinto-98, Kont Miriam-97, I/a Remo IV
Eaststar	Lbr	1997	6,459	8,865	121.2	17.7	8.1	17	Cc	ex Aynur Urkmez-05, Seaboard Columbia-01, Aynur Urkmez-00, UFS Tauro-99, Aynur Urkmez-99, Kont Plaus-98
Nordstar	Lbr	1997	6,459	8,865	121.2	17.7	8.1	17	Cc	ex Remo II-08, MSC Apollonia-03, Remo II-03, Melfi Totonto-00, TMM Cozumel-99, Remo II-97
Oceanstar	Lbr	1997	6,459	8,865	121.2	17.7	8.1	17	Cc	ex Onego Tracer-09, Oceanstar-08, Beliz Urkmez-05, P&O Nedlloyd Panama-02, Beliz Urkmez-01, Seaboard Commerce-01, Beliz Urkmez-00, Zim Venezuela II-99, Beliz Urkmez-99, Kont Ileyac-97

Managed by Phoenix Reederei Bereederungs GmbH & Co KG, Germany.

Erik Thun AB. Nordic Amanda. *C. Lous*

Torbulk Ltd. Independent. *David Walker*

TMS Ship Management GmbH & Co KG   Germany

Funnel: White with narrow black top. *Hull:* Black with red boot-topping. *History:* Not confirmed. *Web:* www.tmsships.com

Name	Flag	Year	GT	DWT	Loa	Bm	Drt	Kts	Type	Remarks
Onego Breeze	Cyp	1990	3,186	4,139	93.0	15.0	6.3	12	Cc	ex Northern Navigator-05, Nesse-02, Wila Buck-98, FAS Colombo-97, Wila Buck-94

Torbulk Ltd   UK

Funnel: Blue with raised blue diamond having white diagonal 'TOR' above red, white, red diagonal lines. *Hull:* Black or grey with red boot-topping. *History:* Founded 1986 as ship managers and ship-owners in 1989 as Torbulk Shipping (UK) Ltd to 1991. *Web:* www.torbulk.co.uk

Name		Flag	Year	GT	DWT	Loa	Bm	Drt	Kts	Type	Remarks
Cementina ***		Com	1960	1,096	1,205	76.1	10.8	4.2	12	Ce	ex Cemking-99, Kabedi-91, Curlew-90, Halliburton 602-88, Cementina-78 (len-04)
Independent ***		Brb	1982	2,113	2,671	91.9	12.4	5.5	12	C	ex Duobulk-04, Fjellvang-98, Marpol Gyda II-94, Eide Rescue V-94, Monchgut-91 (conv-94, len-98)
Sea Hawk *		Brb	1989	1,959	3,015	87.7	12.5	4.6	11	Cc	ex Christa K-06, Mindful-99, I/a Christian
Sea Hunter *		Brb	1990	2,443	3,181	87.5	13.0	4.8	12	Cc	ex Sirius P-07, Highland-99, Sirrah-95
Sea Kestrel *	(2)	Gbr	1993	1,382	2,225	77.8	11.1	4.0	10	C	ex Union Sapphire-04, Hoo Kestrel-03
Sea Mithril *	(2)	Gbr	1992	1,382	2,220	77.8	11.1	4.0	9	C	ex Bowcliffe-05, Fast Ken-99, Bowcliffe-94
Sea Ruby *	(2)	Gbr	1992	1,382	2,225	78.0	11.1	4.0	10	C	ex Union Ruby-04, Hoo Larch-03
Shoreham ***		Brb	1987	1,785	2,535	77.1	13.2	5.0	12	C	ex Sea Eagle-09, Hope-00, Shoreham-93, Ballygarvey-90
Swan Diana		Cym	1983	2,113	2,859	90.0	12.4	5.5	12	Bu	ex Priority-05, Triobulk-04, Allvag-98, Eide Rescue III-95, Werdau-91 (conv-95, len-98)
Swanland **		Brb	1977	1,978	3,150	81.0	13.9	5.4	12	C	ex Elsborg-96, Artemis-94, Elsborg-88, Carebeka IX-83
Thames ***		Pan	1974	2,929	4,357	98.5	15.5	5.4	12	Dss	ex Pelicano-08, Arco Thames-01
Torrent ***	(2)	Brb	1991	999	1,733	63.6	11.0	4.1	9	C	

* managed for GT Gillie & Blair Ltd (founded 1911 as GT Gillie Ltd to 1925 – www.gillieblair.com) or ** for Swanland Shipping Ltd (founded 1996) or *** for Independent Shipping Ltd, UK (part of Dudman Group).

Hans Martin Torkelsen   Norway

A/S Aasen Shipping

Funnel: White with underlined white 'a' on light blue square, narrow black top. *Hull:* Black with redor black boot-topping. *History:* Parent founded 1981 and ship-owning subsidiary 1985 as KS AS Aasen Shipping to 1995. *Web:* www.aasenchar.com

Name	Flag	Year	GT	DWT	Loa	Bm	Drt	Kts	Type	Remarks
Aasfjord	Nis	1978	3,086	3,960	94.2	15.4	5.8	13	Cc	ex Irafoss-97, Keflavik-89, Charm-82
Aasheim	Nis	2001	4,112	5,826	107.1	15.0	6.2	12	Cc	ex Montana-05
Aasli	Nis	1994	3,968	6,630	100.7	16.0	7.0	11	C	ex Globe-04, Comtesse-00
Aasnes	Nis	1981	3,136	4,015	94.2	15.4	5.9	13	Cc	ex Medallion-02
Aasvik	Nis	1986	3,088	4,319	94.4	15.5	6.1	12	Cc	ex Hydrobulk-00 (conv Bu-00)

Torso Rederi AB   Sweden

Funnel: Black with white 'T' on broad red band. *Hull:* Blue with white web address, red boot-topping. *History:* Subsidiary of G P Svenssons Skeppsmakleri AB founded 1985. *Web:* www.torsorederi.se

Name	Flag	Year	GT	DWT	Loa	Bm	Drt	Kts	Type	Remarks
Windena	Swe	1979	1,772	2,822	75.1	12.6	5.4	12	C	ex Erna-02, Menna-95
Windstar *	Nis	1991	2,237	3,272	82.5	12.6	5.3	11	Cc	ex Athene-06, Wani Star-05, Star-02, Huberna-91

* managed by Sunbay Management AS qv

Rederi AB Transatlantic   Sweden

Funnel: White with blue 'TA' symbol within blue ring on broad yellow band between blue band and blue top. *Hull:* Dark blue with yellow 'TRANSATLANTIC', red boot-topping. *History:* Founded 1972 and current company emerged from 2005 amalgamation of Gorthon Lines AB (founded 1915 as Gorthons Rederi A/B to 1987, Gorthon Lines AB to 1995 and B&N Gorthon Lines AB to 1997) and B&N Nordsjofrakt AB (previously AB Nordsjofrakt to 1990 and B&N Bylock & Nordsjofrakt AB to 1998). *Web:* www.rabt.se

Name	Flag	Year	GT	DWT	Loa	Bm	Drt	Kts	Type	Remarks
Transfalcon	Nis	1993	4,081	5,697	104.4	16.2	6.4	14	Cc	ex Falcon-08, Stella Pacific-98
Transnjord *	Gib	1995	2,997	3,182	97.3	16.2	5.9	15	Cc	ex Maryam-07, Alrek-03, I/a Julia Lehmann

* owned by subsidiary Transatlantic Container Shipping, Sweden.
Also see Ferry Section.

Transmarine Management ApS   Denmark

Funnel: Dark blue with narrow yellow and blue bands on brapd white panel below narrow black top. *Hull:* Dark blue with red boot-topping. *History:* Founded 1982 as Transmarine ApS to 1986. *Web:* www.transmarine.dk

Name	Flag	Year	GT	DWT	Loa	Bm	Drt	Kts	Type	Remarks
Amanda	Prt	2005	4,811	6,954	119.1	16.9	6.8	14	Tch	ex Pakize S-05
Amarant	Prt	2003	4,814	7,157	119.1	16.9	6.8	14	Tch	
Amber 1	Cyp	1997	3,159	4,999	99.9	15.4	6.3	12	Tch	ex Amber-07, Fortune Athena-98

Transnautic Ship Management   Estonia

Funnel: White with narrow pale blue top or * white with red eight-pointed wheel and narrow red top. *Hull:* Green or * blue with black boot-topping. *History:* Founded 2005 as subsidiary of Estonian-owned AS Pakri Marine Investments (formed 2004). *Web:* www.transnautic.ee

Name	Flag	Year	GT	DWT	Loa	Bm	Drt	Kts	Type	Remarks
Kaisa	Mlt	2005	3,183	4,528	90.0	15.2	5.3	12	C	ex Aspoe-08
Sisu Castor *	Atg	1999	2,599	3,500	92.8	15.9	4.9	15	Cc	ex Jan Mitchell-08, Bermuda Islander-04, Waaldijk-99

Torbulk Ltd. Sea Ruby. *David Walker*

Torso Rederi AB. Windstar. *F. de Vries*

Transonega-Shipping Joint Stock Co. Grand. *Oliver Sesemann*

Union Transport Group PLC. Union Moon. *David Walker*

Name		Flag	Year	GT	DWT	Loa	Bm	Drt	Kts	Type	Remarks
Sisu Cursa *		Atg	1998	2,599	3,459	92.8	15.9	4.9	15	CC	ex Georg Mitchell-08, Scheldedijk-04, Batavier IX-00, Scheldedijk-99, Batavier VII-99, I/a Scheldedijk

Also owns several coastal tankers based in West Africa.

Transonega-Shipping Joint Stock Co   Russia
Funnel: *White with red over blue bands, black top.* **Hull:** *Various colours.* **History:** *Founded 1994 and controlled by Government of The Russian Federation.* **Web:** *None found.*

Name		Flag	Year	GT	DWT	Loa	Bm	Drt	Kts	Type	Remarks
Amur-2511	(2)	Rus	1986	3,086	3,127	115.7	13.4	4.0	10	Cc	
Galan	(2)	Rus	1978	2,473	2,893	114.0	13.0	3.6	10	C	ex Volgo-Balt 209-07
Grand	(2)	Kna	1974	2,516	2,863	114.0	13.0	3.6	10	C	ex Volgo-Balt 180-97
Volgo-Balt 210	(2)	Rus	1978	2,516	3,165	113.9	13.0	3.6	10	C	

Tristar Shipping BV   Netherlands
Funnel: *White with yellow dart symbol on blue disc, narrow black top.* **Hull:** *Dark blue with red boot-topping.* **History:** *Founded 2002.* **Web:** *www.tristarshipping.com*

Name	Flag	Year	GT	DWT	Loa	Bm	Drt	Kts	Type	Remarks
Blue Bay *	Atg	2006	2,545	3,800	88.6	12.5	5.4	13	Cc	
Blue Sea	Nld	2008	2,993	4,504	90.0	14.0	5.7	12	Cc	
Blue Sky	Nld	2003	2,545	3,836	88.6	12.5	5.4	13	Cc	
Blue Star	Nld	2004	2,545	3,820	88.6	12.5	5.4	12	Cc	

* owned by subsidiary Tristar Shipping GmbH & Co KG, Germany

Tschudi Shipping Co AS   Norway
Funnel: *Black with white over blue diagonally divided shield on broad red band.* **Hull:** *Red with red boot-topping.* **History:** *Founded 1883 and operating in partnership as Tschudi & Eitzen until 1984, then Tschudi & Eitzen AS to 2003, when partnership arrangement was dissolved.* **Web:** *www.tschudishipping.com*

Name	Flag	Year	GT	DWT	Loa	Bm	Drt	Kts	Type	Remarks
Muuga	Iom	1995	2,658	3,200	90.7	15.9	4.6	16	Cc	

Also owns two larger chartered-out container ships.

Rederiet Otto Danielsen/Denmark
Funnel: *Green with white 'OD'.* **Hull:** *Grey with red boot-topping.* **History:** *Founded 1944 and amalgamated with Tschudi Shipping Denmark ApS in 2005.* **Web:** *www.ottodanielsen.com*

Name	Flag	Year	GT	DWT	Loa	Bm	Drt	Kts	Type	Remarks
Eva Danielsen	Bhs	1986	3,113	4,279	88.6	15.7	6.6	13	Cc	ex BBC Germany-02, Industrial Caribe-01, BBC Germany-01, Ranginui-99, Zim Bangkok-94, Anke-93, Global Express 4-89, Anke-88, Falcon-88, Anke-87
Maj Danielsen	Bhs	1985	3,120	4,107	88.6	15.7	6.5	13	Cc	ex Tinto-96, Band Aid Star-86, I/a Tinto
Otto Danielsen	Bhs	1985	3,120	4,100	88.6	14.5	6.5	13	Cc	ex Libra-96, Dorado-93, Band Aid Express-86, Dorado-85

Estonian Shipping Co Ltd/Estonia
Funnel: *White with white 'ESCo' on light blue band, some with narrow black top.* **Hull:** *Black, grey, brown or dark green with red boot-topping.* **History:** *Founded 1940 and acquired 2002 by Tschudi & Eitzen AS and owned since 2003 restructuring.* **Web:** *www.eml.ee*

Name	Flag	Year	GT	DWT	Loa	Bm	Drt	Kts	Type	Remarks
Dirhami	Est	1996	2,658	3,200	91.0	15.8	4.6	16	Cc	
Kalana	Est	1996	2,658	3,274	90.7	15.9	4.6	16	Cc	
Kurkse **	Est	1997	2,658	3,250	90.7	15.9	4.6	14	Cc	
Valga *	Mlt	1979	8,545	4,600	139.6	19.2	6.6	17	Ro	ex Waalhaven-94, Aleksandr Osipov-92
Viljandi *	Mlt	1978	8,545	4,600	139.6	19.2	6.6	17	Ro	ex Merwehaven-93, Viljandi-92, Boris Buvin-92, Uniroller-91, Boris Buvin-91

Managed by Tschudi Ship Management AS (www.firstbaltic.ee) or * by Baltic Mercur Ltd, Russia (www.mercur.spb.ru)
** owned by subsidiary Tschudi Lines Baltic Sea AS (founded 1992 as Teco Lines AS to 2007 (www.tschudishipmanagement.ee)

Egil Ulvan Rederi AS   Norway
Funnel: *White with houseflag (orange with white 'U' on green square).* **Hull:** *Orange or dark blue with red boot-topping.* **History:** *Founded 1919.* **Web:** *www.ulvan-rederi.no*

Name	Flag	Year	GT	DWT	Loa	Bm	Drt	Kts	Type	Remarks
Feed Halten	Atg	1992	1,999	3,186	81.2	12.4	5.2	11	Cc	ex Halten-08, Fiducia-05, Paphos-99
Feed Stavanger	Atg	1997	2,863	4,163	90.5	13.6	5.7	13	Cc	ex Bremer Unitas-08, Unitas-H-03, Geestborg-01, I/a Unitas-H
Feed Tromso	Nor	1998	1,791	1,725	62.0	13.0	4.7	-	Cp	ex With Junior-09
Feed Trondheim	Atg	2002	3,925	4,633	99.9	16.0	5.1	-	Cc	ex Oeland-08, Lolland-02
Mikal With	Nor	2002	1,252	1,200	55.4	13.0	4.7	12	Cp	
With Junior	Nor	2009	2,362	2,000	66.7	14.6	5.3	12	Cp	

Uman Rederi AB   Sweden
Funnel: *Dark blue with yellow 'U' inside yellow ring between narrow yellow bands.* **Hull:** *Dark blue or † light grey with red boot-topping.* **History:** *Founded 1952.* **Web:** *www.umanshipping.com*

Name	Flag	Year	GT	DWT	Loa	Bm	Drt	Kts	Type	Remarks
Hellevik	Swe	1975	1,957	1,537	82.1	12.8	4.2	13	Bu	ex Schwaneck-91
Lister †	Gib	1997	2,863	4,113	85.0	13.6	5.7	13	Cc	ex Graneborg-07
Listervik	Gib	1996	2,863	4,112	85.0	13.3	5.7	13	Bu	ex Ida Rambow-05
Listerland	Swe	1994	2,735	4,267	89.6	13.2	5.7	11	Bu	ex Pioneer-04
Sterno	Swe	1970	1,300	1,370	75.7	11.0	3.6	12	Bu	ex Seto-84, Ostestrom-83, Mariona-72, I/a Ostestrom (conv C-84)

Unibaltic Sp z oo
Poland

Funnel: *Blue with white anchor symbol, black top.* **Hull:** *Dark blue with white 'UniBaltic' or red with red or black boot-topping.* **History:** *Founded 2003.*
Web: *www.unibaltic.pl*

Name	Flag	Year	GT	DWT	Loa	Bm	Drt	Kts	Type	Remarks
Amaranth	Nis	1980	4,382	5,858	118.4	15.5	6.3	13	Tch	ex CT Sun-06, Coppelia-92 (len-98)
Ametysth	Pol	1991	1,716	3,232	83.5	13.7	5.5	11	Tch	ex Marianne Theresa-07, Else Terkol-95
Amonith	Nis	1972	1,843	3,460	82.7	13.0	6.4	13	Tch	ex Astra-03, Perko-91, Selma-90, Pointe de Lervily-74, Bras-74
Azuryth	Nis	1982	3,922	6,125	104.3	16.7	6.8	12	Tch	ex Vivaldi-05, Echoman-97
Thurkus	Nis	1991	2,561	3,284	88.0	12.6	5.3	-	Cc	ex Marie Christine-08

Unifeeder A/S
Denmark

Funnel: *White with blue and red 'U' symbol.* **Hull:** *Owners colours.* **History:** *Founded in 1977.* **Web:** *www.unifeeder.com*

One of Europe's largest feeder container ship operators, currently with about 26 chartered vessels including some up to 1,500 TEU.

Union Transport Group PLC
UK

Funnel: *Red with white 'UT'.* **Hull:** *Light grey or blue with red or black boot-topping.* **History:** *Founded 1946 as Union Transport (London) Ltd to 1987.*
Web: *www.uniontransport.co.uk*

Name	Flag	Year	GT	DWT	Loa	Bm	Drt	Kts	Type	Remarks
Peak Bergen *	Brb	1986	1,543	2,376	87.7	11.0	3.9	10	Cc	ex Union Titan-10
Peak Oslo *	Brb	1985	1,543	2,376	87.7	11.0	3.9	10	Cc	ex Union Sun-10
Union Bronze	Iom	2010	1,900	2,625	87.5	11.3	4.2	-	C	
Union Diamond	Iom	2009	2,967	4,450	89.9	14.4	5.8	-	Cc	
Union Elisabeth **	Nld	1997	1,905	2,665	88.6	12.6	4.0	10	Cc	ex Elisabeth S-97
Union Emerald	Iom	2010	1,900	2,625	87.5	11.3	4.2	-	C	
Union Gem	Iom	1991	2,236	3,222	99.7	12.5	4.3	11	Cc	ex North Sea Trader-01
Union Gold	Iom	2010	1,900	2,625	87.5	11.3	4.2	-	C	
Union Moon *	Brb	1985	1,543	2,362	87.7	11.1	3.9	10	Cc	
Union Neptune *	Brb	1985	1,543	2,376	87.7	11.1	3.9	10	Cc	
Union Pearl	Iom	1990	2,236	3,222	99.7	12.5	4.3	11	Cc	ex Bromley Pearl-95
Union Pluto	Iom	1984	1,530	1,762	82.5	11.4	3.5	10	Cc	ex Phonix I-95, Phoenix-94, Osterberg-87
Union Ruby	Iom	2010	2,967	4,450	89.9	14.4	5.8	-	Cc	
Union Saturn	Iom	1991	2,236	3,263	99.7	12.5	4.3	11	Cc	ex Short Sea Trader-01
Union Silver	Iom	2010	1,900	2,625	87.5	11.3	4.2	-	C	
Union Topaz *	Brb	1985	1,543	2,362	87.7	11.0	3.9	10	Cc	ex Bromley Topaz-92, Union Topaz-90

* owned and managed by A/S Ersco (Continental Ship Management AS), Norway or ** for Rederij H. Steenstra, Netherlands.

Unisea Shipping BV
Netherlands

Funnel: *White with dark blue 'U' on white diamond on dark blue square.* **Hull:** *Dark blue with red boot-topping.* **History:** *Founded 2005.*
Web: *www.uniseashipping.com*

Name	Flag	Year	GT	DWT	Loa	Bm	Drt	Kts	Type	Remarks
Beaumagic	Nld	2007	2,545	3,800	88.6	12.5	5.4	12	Cc	I/a Beaumajor
Beaumaiden	Nld	2008	2,545	3,800	88.6	12.5	5.4	12	Cc	
Beaumare	Nld	2008	2,545	3,850	88.6	12.5	5.4	12	Cc	
Beaumaris	Nld	2007	2,545	3,800	88.6	12.5	5.4	12	Cc	
Beautrader	Nld	2009	5,132	7,210	118.1	15.9	6.5	13	Cc	
Beautriton	Nld	2009	5,132	7,210	118.1	15.9	6.5	13	Cc	
Beautriumph	Nld	2008	5,132	7,218	118.1	15.9	6.5	13	Cc	
Beautrophy	Nld	2009	5,132	7,120	118.1	15.9	6.5	13	Cc	

Unitas Schiffahrts GmbH
Germany

Funnel: *Black with black 'U' on broad white band edged with narrow red bands or with houseflag (white with black 'U' between red bands), or charterers colours.* **Hull:** *Dark green with red boot-topping.* **History:** *Founded 1991.* **Web:** *www.unitas-h.de*

Name	Flag	Year	GT	DWT	Loa	Bm	Drt	Kts	Type	Remarks
Gerd	Atg	2003	7,660	9,500	134.6	21.5	7.1	18	CC	ex Javi-07, B.G. Ireland-06, I/a Gerd
Herm	Atg	2004	7,660	9,368	134.7	21.5	7.1	18	CC	
Iduna	Cyp	2007	7,112	8,820	125.2	21.7	7.8	17	CC	I/a Euro Sound
Marstan	Atg	2000	6,368	8,627	132.3	19.4	7.3	-	CC	ex B.G. Rotterdam-09, Marstan-01
SITC Melody	Deu	2009	8,074	10,600	153.7	21.5	6.9	-	CC	I/a Unisky
SITC Miracle	Atg	2010	8,970	10,600	153.7	21.5	6.9	-	CC	I/a Unisea

United European Car Carriers
Norway

Funnel: *Yellow with white 'UECC' on four small blue diamonds, blue top.* **Hull:** *Light grey with blue or black 'UECC' on superstructure, pink boot-topping.*
History: *Founded 1992 as United European Car Carriers (Norway) AS, a joint venture between Nippon Yusen Kaisha, Japan and Walleniusrederierna AB, Sweden.*
Web: *www.uecc.com*

Name		Flag	Year	GT	DWT	Loa	Bm	Drt	Kts	Type	Remarks
Auto Baltic *		Fin	1996	18,979	6,165	138.5	22.7	7.1	20	V	ex Transgard-07 (conv Rop-07)
Auto Bank *		Fin	1998	19,107	7,629	138.8	22.7	7.1	20	V	ex Serenaden-07 (conv Rop-07)
Auto Bay *		Fin	1997	19,094	7,630	138.8	22.7	7.1	20	V	ex Heralden-07 (conv Rop-07)
Autopremier	(2)	Prt	1997	11,591	4,443	126.9	18.8	6.2	20	V	
Autopride	(2)	Prt	1997	11,591	4,442	126.9	18.8	6.2	20	V	

Union Transport Group PLC. Union Saturn. *David Walker*

Unitas Schiffahrts GmbH. Gerd. *Allan Ryszka Onions*

Name		Flag	Year	GT	DWT	Loa	Bm	Drt	Kts	Type	Remarks
Autoprogress		Prt	1997	11,591	4,442	126.9	18.8	6.2	20	V	
Autoprestige		Prt	1999	11,591	4,442	126.9	18.8	6.2	20	V	
Autoracer	(2)	Prt	1994	9,693	3,933	119.9	18.8	6.0	20	V	
Autorunner	(2)	Prt	1994	9,693	3,933	119.9	18.8	6.0	20	V	
Autosky	(2)	Prt	2000	21,010	6,670	140.0	22.7	7.4	20	V	
Autostar	(2)	Prt	2000	21,010	6,670	140.0	22.7	7.4	20	V	
Autosun	(2)	Prt	2000	21,094	6,670	140.0	22.7	7.4	20	V	

Operated by United European Car Carriers Unipessoal Lda, Madeira.
* chartered from Rettig Group Ltd Bore, Finland qv
Also operates four larger car carriers and three chartered-in vessels.

United Marine Dredging Ltd   UK

Funnel: *Blue with blue outlined 'UMD' on broad white band.* **Hull:** *Light grey with green boot-topping.* **History:** *Founded 1983 as United Marine Aggregates Ltd by Tarmac Roadstone Holdings Ltd (later Tarmac Marine Ltd) until 1987 merger with Pioneer Aggregates Ltd.* **Web:** *www.uma.co.uk*

Name		Flag	Year	GT	DWT	Loa	Bm	Drt	Kts	Type	Remarks
City of Cardiff	(2)	Gbr	1997	2,074	2,730	72.0	15.1	4.6	11	Dss	
City of Chichester	(2)	Gbr	1997	2,074	2,730	72.0	15.1	4.6	11	Dss	
City of London	(2)	Gbr	1989	3,660	5,989	99.8	17.5	6.3	12	Dss	
City of Westminster	(2)	Gbr	1990	3,914	6,604	99.9	17.7	6.3	12	Dss	

United Marine Management Ltd   Estonia

Funnel: *Yellow with two-tone blue 'UMM' on white diamond on blue flag.* **Hull:** *Red with black boot-topping.* **History:** *Founded 1994 and separated from Euro-Baltic Shipping Services in 2005.* **Web:** *www.umm.ee*

Name	Flag	Year	GT	DWT	Loa	Bm	Drt	Kts	Type	Remarks
Agat	Atg	1984	2,723	3,980	98.5	13.5	5.1	10	Cc	ex Svendborg-04, Navaro
Akai	Atg	1985	2,740	2,785	98.3	13.5	5.3	11	Cc	ex Alk-05, Kamilla-04
Alma	Atg	1985	2,730	2,947	98.3	13.6	4.3	10	Cc	ex Emsbroker-04, Huemmling-01, Belida-99, Huemmling-99, Belida-96, Helena I-96, Almaris-94
Argo	Atg	1985	2,729	2,814	98.3	13.5	4.5	11	Cc	ex Arno-06, Jonas-04, Pegwell Bay-98, Altair-95
Gala	Atg	1989	2,867	4,289	88.2	13.6	5.8	11	Cc	ex Fehn Star-07, Arklow Vale-04
Gerd	Atg	1993	2,650	4,250	89.0	13.2	5.7	12	Cc	ex Heide O-08, Baltic Tara-07, Morgenstond I
Glen	Atg	1990	2,827	4,299	88.2	13.6	5.8	11	Cc	ex Fehn Moon-07, Arklow Valour-05
Golf	Atg	1991	2,827	4,299	88.3	13.7	5.8	11	Cc	ex Wilster-07, Arklow Villa-02
Heli	Est	1993	2,735	4,200	89.6	13.2	5.7	12	C	ex Katja-05, Helia-08
Lena	Rus	1995	2,345	3,400	82.5	12.7	5.3	11	Cc	ex Suderfeld-01, Pasha-98
Maya	Atg	1982	2,318	3,346	99.8	11.4	4.6	10	Cc	ex Cambrook-02, Lena Wessels-87
Nemo	Atg	1987	1,473	2,097	79.0	10.9	3.9	10	Cc	ex Scotia-03, Feed Star-03, Scotia-03, I/a Meise
Trine	Atg	1986	3,448	4,139	101.5	15.2	3.8	12	Cc	ex Katrin-09, I/a Odin (conv Cp-09)
Vudi	Deu	1981	1,939	2,890	88.0	11.3	4.7	11	Cc	ex Tafelberg-04, Helga-92

A/S United Shipping & Trading Co (Uni-Tankers A/S)   Denmark

Funnel: *Blue with large white square containing white swan outline on blue square above black 'UNI-TANKERS'.* **Hull:** *Blue with red boot-topping.* **History:** *Founded 1985 and Uni-Tankers subsidiary formed 1991.* **Web:** *www.uni-tankers.dk*

Name	Flag	Year	GT	DWT	Loa	Bm	Drt	Kts	Type	Remarks
Arctic Swan	Pan	1970	2,428	4,237	98.9	12.5	6.4	12	Tch	ex Nordstar-96, Lindtank-91, Ottawa-89, Jessica-88, Ottawa-84
Dane Swan	Dis	1980	840	1,165	64.2	11.2	3.3	11	T	ex Lotus-99, Beckenham-95

Also owns 5 larger tankers (15-24,700 dwt)

Universal Marine Service (Unimars)   Latvia

Funnel: *Blue with three blue waves on white disc.* **Hull:** *Blue with red boot-topping.* **History:** *Founded 1994.* **Web:** *www.unimars.lv*

Name	Flag	Year	GT	DWT	Loa	Bm	Drt	Kts	Type	Remarks
Alkiona	Vct	1981	2,120	2,950	82.5	12.8	5.1	12	Cc	ex Dorothea-09, Mehaanik Krull-03, Mekhanik Krull-92
Asteropa	Mlt	1980	2,061	2,730	82.5	12.6	5.4	12	Cc	ex Marvita-09, Mariana-03, Sterno-02, Markes-00, Stella Arctic-96, Vik-93, Alkes-89, Miniland-88, Mustola-84
Blankenese	Atg	1984	2,882	4,200	99.8	14.6	5.2	11	Cc	ex Eembaltic-99, Blankenese-99 (len-90)
Elektra	Vct	1981	2,120	2,950	82.5	12.8	5.1	12	Cc	ex Cailin-09, Kapten Voolens-03, Kapitan Voolens-92
Meropa	Mlt	1981	2,120	2,950	82.5	12.8	5.1	12	Cc	ex Vivita-09, Konga-03, Kapten Konga-01, Yuriy Klementyev-91
Taigeta	Dma	1980	2,061	3,085	82.4	12.8	5.1	12	Cc	ex Baltic Sky-09, Marlen-05, Bolero-05, Borre-00, Borne af Simrishamn-97, Svarte-91, Ann-Mari-90, Ann Ragne-86, Repola-84
Uniland	Vct	1982	3,720	6,179	84.2	17.0	8.4	11	C	ex Midland 21-07, Giulia-04, Cecilia I-96, Cecilia Smits-88

managed by subsidiary Uniship Ltd, Latvia (founded 2004)

USC-Barnkrug Gbr   Germany

Elbdeich Reederei GmbH

Funnel: *White with narrow black top or charterers colours.* **Hull:** *Blue or green with red boot-topping.* **History:** *Subsidiary founded 2005.* **Web:** *www.elbdeich-reederei.de*

Name	Flag	Year	GT	DWT	Loa	Bm	Drt	Kts	Type	Remarks
Deneb	Atg	1994	3,992	5,350	101.1	18.4	6.5	15	Cc	ex OOCL Neva-98, Deneb-98, Rhein Partner-98, Rhein Liffey-95, Deneb-94

United European Car Carriers. Auto Bay. *Phil Kempsey*

USC-Barnkrug/Elbdeich Reederei GmbH. Elbtrader. *Hans Kraijenbosch*

Name	Flag	Year	GT	DWT	Loa	Bm	Drt	Kts	Type	Remarks
Louise Borchard	Atg	2006	7,532	8,724	126.9	20.4	7.8	18	CC	ex Gracechurch Sun-09, Elbdeich-06
Elbmarsch	Cyp	2007	7,532	8,692	127.0	20.4	7.8	18	CC	ex Candelaria del Mar-08, Elbmarsch-07
Elbcarrier	Atg	2007	8,246	11,165	139.6	20.2	6.5	18	CC	
Elbfeeder	Atg	2008	8,246	11,157	139.6	20.2	6.5	18	CC	
Elbmaster	Atg	2009	7,170	8,510	131.5	19.2	7.7	-	CC	
Elbstrand	Atg	2009	7,589	8,530	139.6	20.2	6.5	18	CC	
Elbstrom	Atg	2009	7,541	8,600	139.6	20.2	6.5	18	CC	
Elbtrader	Atg	2008	8,246	11,174	139.6	20.2	6.5	18	CC	
Jade	Atg	2010	6,586	8,200	-	-	-	-	CC	
Ruth Borchard	Atg	2007	7,532	8,685	126.8	20.4	7.8	18	CC	ex Gracechurch Venus-10, Elbinsel-07

Also see Reederei Heinz Moje.

Reederei Hinsch
Funnel: *White with black top.* **Hull:** *Blue with red boot-topping.* **History:** *Subsidiary founded 1860 as Reederei Alfred Hinsch KG to 1996.* **Web:** *www.reederei-hinsch.de*

Name	Flag	Year	GT	DWT	Loa	Bm	Drt	Kts	Type	Remarks
CCL Shidao	Atg	2008	7,464	8,110	129.6	20.6	7.4	-	CC	ex Jackeline-H-08
Libertas-H	Atg	2007	7,532	8,540	127.0	20.4	7.8	18	Cc	ex CMA CGM Safi-09, Libertas-H-08
Novitas-H	Atg	1995	2,899	3,950	99.3	16.2	4.9	14	CC	ex Ady-03, Bell Ady-97 (len-95)
Paritas-H	Atg	2009	7,541	8,450	127.0	20.4	7.8	-	Cc	
Veritas H	Atg	1995	2,899	3,950	97.8	16.4	4.9	15	CC	ex Regulus-97, Veritas H-96

H & H Bereedereungs GmbH & Co KG
Funnel: *White with black 'HH' on blue/white diagonally quartered houseflag above narrow black band, black top.* **Hull:** *Blue with red boot-topping.* **History:** *Subsidiary founded 2005 and operates as a joint venture with Elbdeich Rederei.* **Web:** *None found.*

Name	Flag	Year	GT	DWT	Loa	Bm	Drt	Kts	Type	Remarks
Anna-Lisa	Atg	2008	7,464	8,113	129.6	20.6	7.4	-	CC	
Daroja	Cyp	1997	3,266	4,155	91.0	15.7	5.7	14	Cc	ex Muntediep-05, Lengai-02
Marjesco	Atg	1997	3,601	4,649	98.3	15.7	5.7	15	Cc	ex Middeldiep-05, Tyr-03

Reederei Heinz-Georg Voge GmbH & Co KG
Funnel: *Blue with white 'V' between narrow white bands, black top.* **Hull:** *Light grey with green above pink boot-topping.* **History:** *Subsidiary founded 1942 as Reederei H-G Voge KG.* **Web:** *www.reederei-hgvoege.de*

Name	Flag	Year	GT	DWT	Loa	Bm	Drt	Kts	Type	Remarks
Johanna	Gbr	1999	6,363	7,131	121.4	18.2	6.7	16	CC	
Robert	Gbr	2006	9,981	12,257	134.4	22.5	8.7	18	CC	ex Birkaland-08, I/a Robert
WEC Dali	Deu	2001	9,981	11,391	134.4	22.5	8.7	18	CC	ex Berit-09, Holland Maas Habana-05, Berit-04, Miriam Borchard-04, I/a Berit
WEC Sorolla	Gbr	2005	9,981	11,269	134.4	22.5	8.7	18	CC	ex Partnership-09

Also owns one larger feeder container ship.

Utkilen AS   Norway
Funnel: *White with blue 'A' inside 'U' symbol between narrow blue bands or with white 'U' on broad blue band.* **Hull:** *Red with red or black boot-topping.* **History:** *Founded 1940 as Anders Utkilens Rederi AS to 2007.* **Web:** *www. Utkilen.no*

Name	Flag	Year	GT	DWT	Loa	Bm	Drt	Kts	Type	Remarks
Bergstraum	Nis	1996	6,045	9,494	123.6	19.2	7.2	14	Tch	
Christina	Nis	1996	6,045	9,494	123.0	19.2	7.2	13	Tch	
Fjellstraum	Mlt	1997	3,726	5,846	100.0	16.5	6.8	15	Tch	ex Multitank Bolognia-08
Fjordstraum	Mlt	1996	3,726	5,846	100.0	16.5	6.7	15	Tch	ex Bow Bahia-08, Multitank Bahia-05
Fostraum	Nis	1991	2,470	2,910	85.0	13.0	5.5	14	Tch	
Havstraum	Nis	1991	4,931	7,975	115.1	18.3	7.0	14	Tch	
Kilstraum	Nor	1988	2,894	4,618	85.7	15.4	6.2	12	Tch	
Latana	Nis	2000	9,960	15,990	142.2	22.0	8.8	14	Tch	
Listraum	Nis	1991	3,998	6,519	101.7	18.3	7.0	14	Tch	
Nordstraum	Nor	1985	2,898	4,165	85.7	15.2	6.2	12	Tch	
Rystraum	Nis	1977	4,070	6,433	110.6	16.6	6.9	14	Tch	ex Chimiste Sayid-88, Chimiste Louisiana-77
Saltstraum	Nor	1980	1,881	2,533	80.2	13.0	5.2	13	Tch	
Solstraum	Nis	1990	3,998	7,013	101.7	18.3	7.0	14	Tch	
Sundstraum	Nor	1993	3,206	4,794	96.4	15.3	6.2	13	Tch	ex Maj-Britt Terkol-96,
Sydstraum	Nor	1981	1,881	2,550	80.2	13.0	5.2	12	Tch	
Vikstraum	Nis	1981	5,985	6,693	129.6	19.4	7.0	14	Tch	ex Snark-95, OT Acid-90

V-Shipping Spolka z oo   Poland
Funnel: *White with blue 'V'.* **Hull:** *Grey with red boot-topping.* **History:** *Not confirmed.* **Web:** *None found.*

Name	Flag	Year	GT	DWT	Loa	Bm	Drt	Kts	Type	Remarks
Barbara D	Pol	1966	409	624	57.4	7.2	2.5	9	C	ex Neuenbrok-08 (len-85, len/deep-78)

Vaage Ship Management AS   Norway
Funnel: *Orange disc on light blue top separated by narrow white wavy band from dark blue base.* **Hull:** *Blue with red boot-topping or dark green with black boot-topping.* **History:** *Founded 2006.* **Web:** *www.vaageshipman.no*

Name	Flag	Year	GT	DWT	Loa	Bm	Drt	Kts	Type	Remarks
Anne	Bhs	1995	2,035	2,800	90.6	13.8	4.3	13	CC	ex Seawheel Venture-09, Alette-05, Heereborg-04 Bermuda Islander-99
Berit	Gib	1996	1,864	2,516	82.4	11.5	4.8	12	Cc	ex Aldebaran-07, Hav Aldebaran-06, RMS Aldebaran-04, I/a Aldebaran
Kine	Bhs	1996	2,060	3,000	88.5	11.4	5.0	-	Cc	ex Countess Julia-07, Svenja-05

Utkilen AS. Saltstraum. *N. Kemps*

Vaage Ship Management AS. Liv Kristin. *F. de Vries*

Name		Flag	Year	GT	DWT	Loa	Bm	Drt	Kts	Type	Remarks
Kristin D		Bhs	1997	2,035	2,850	90.6	13.9	4.3	13	Cc	ex Seawheel Express-08, Jetstream-05, Heerestraat-04
Kryssholm		Nis	1975	1,075	1,066	58.7	11.0	3.8	10	Lv	ex Jago-08, Frohavet-06, Holstein Express-04, Caroline-04, Trans Holm-89 (conv Cp-89, len-78)
Liv Kristin		Gib	1984	1,843	2,348	80.1	12.7	4.2	11	Cc	ex Fehn Carrier-06, Westerems-05, Sea Clyde-01, Petena-98
Nina		Bhs	1997	1,864	2,516	82.5	11.5	4.8	12	Cc	ex Andromeda-07, Hav Andromeda-06, RMS Andromeda-04, I/a Andromeda
OOCL Nevskiy		Atg	2001	9,981	11,386	134.4	22.8	8.7	18	CC	I/a Jan
Orion		Gib	1996	2,035	2,800	90.6	13.8	4.3	13	CC	ex Heereplein-03 Batavier VIII-00, Heereplein-99
Rita		Gib	1985	1,843	2,325	80.0	12.7	4.2	10	Cc	ex Sea Waal-06, Triton Navigator-01, Lys Crown-99, Ettina-97
Sofie N *		Nld	1999	2,999	5,647	95.1	13.2	6.2	12	Cc	ex Alessia C-08, Alessia-08
Solvi A *		Nld	1999	2,999	5,647	95.1	13.2	6.2	12	Cc	ex Claudia C-08
Terneskjaer		Nor	1974	882	914	55.6	11.0	3.8	10	C	ex Sveafjord 1-08, Sveafjord-08, Risvaer-03, Heggholmen-95, Trans Sund-93 (len-79)
Torill		Gib	1988	1,524	2,183	73.8	11.5	4.4	11	Cc	ex Fehn Trader-06, Arklow Marsh-04
Tove		Gib	1996	1,864	2,517	82.4	11.4	4.8	12	C	ex Arcturus-07, Hav Arcturus-06, RMS Arcturus-04, Arcturus--96
WEC Navigator		Gib	1997	3,999	5,865	100.0	18.2	6.6	17	CC	ex HMS Navigator-08, Pacer-07, Portlink Pacer-06, Merino-04, Gracechurch Meteor-02, Merino-97

on charter to Carisbrooke Shipping Ltd qv

Rederi AB Vaderotank — Sweden

Funnel: *White with black ships wheel.* **Hull:** *Light blue with black boot-topping.* **History:** *Founded 1991 as Rederi AB Vadero Tank , but since 2006 subsidiary of Philippines-based Vadero Ship Management Inc.* **Web:** *www.vaderoshipping.se*

Name	Flag	Year	GT	DWT	Loa	Bm	Drt	Kts	Type	Remarks
Harpa Doris	Nis	2009	1,446	1,800	69.5	11.5	4.8	-	Tch	ex Vadero Trym-09
Kaprifol **	Cyp	2000	1,845	2,802	89.4	12.2	5.1	11	Tch	ex Vedrey Kattegat-08, Crescent Connemara-07, Crescent Oratuna-05, Oratuna-02
Vadero Highlander	Nis	2003	1,300	1,862	78.8	10.5	4.3	-	T	ex Clipper Highlander-08, Crescent Highlander-06, Montipora-04, Kerem D-03 (conv Tch-08)
Vadero Linnea *	Nis	1989	7,421	12,325	145.4	19.9	8.4	14	Tch	ex Hummel-08
Vedrey Hallarna †	Gib	2005	1,207	1,773	78.6	10.5	4.2	11	Tch	ex Pulathane-07

* owned by subsidiary Linnea Shipping A/S, Norway.
** managed by Sea Tank Chartering AS, Norway or † by V. Ships (UK) Ltd.

Scheepvaartbedrijf Van Dam — Netherlands

Funnel: *White with black ships wheel.* **Hull:** *Light blue with black boot-topping.* **History:** *Founded 1996.* **Web:** *www.vandamshipping.com*

Name	Flag	Year	GT	DWT	Loa	Bm	Drt	Kts	Type	Remarks
Andrea	Nld	2006	2,409	3,650	82.5	12.5	4.9	11	Cc	
Anet	Nld	2007	3,990	6,000	110.8	14.0	6.3	13	Cc	
Ankie	Nld	2007	2,518	3,638	90.0	12.5	5.3	13	Cc	
Carolina	Nld	2008	2,409	3,697	82.5	12.5	4.9	11	Cc	
Elise	Atg	2007	1,917	3,075	80.3	12.5	4.7	11	C	I/a Future
Leonie	Nld	2007	2,528	3,638	90.0	12.5	5.3	13	Cc	
Lianne	Atg	2007	1,903	3,075	79.9	12.5	4.8	11	C	I/a Maya-2
Susanne	Nld	2004	2,409	3,200	82.5	12.5	4.9	11	Cc	
Sylvia	Atg	2008	1,917	3,075	80.3	12.5	4.7	11	C	

Rederij Van Dijk — Netherlands

Funnel: *Black with black castle tower between two narrow red bands on broad white band.* **Hull:** *Managers colours.* **History:** *Founded 1998.* **Web:** *www.vandijkshipping.com*

Name	Flag	Year	GT	DWT	Loa	Bm	Drt	Kts	Type	Remarks
Dagna	Nld	2005	3,990	6,000	110.8	14.0	6.3	13	Cc	
Helga	Nld	2009	8,999	12,016	143.0	18.9	7.9	-	Cc	
Imke	Nld	2006	3,990	6,000	110.8	14.0	6.1	14	Cc	

Managed by Wagenborg Shipping BV

Vargon Shipping AB — Sweden

Funnel: *Blue or * white with brown 'G' and brown top.* **Hull:** *Dark blue with red boot-topping or * dark brown with light grey boot-topping.* **History:** *Not confirmed.* **Web:** *None found.*

Name	Flag	Year	GT	DWT	Loa	Bm	Drt	Kts	Type	Remarks
Tango	Swe	1976	1,155	1,472	67.0	11.7	4.3	11	C	ex Nordking-08
Tinto *	Swe	1977	1,191	1,550	74.8	10.6	3.3	11	C	ex Frakto-89, Tinto-83 (len-80)

Vassilev Maritime Transport Joint Stock Co — Russia

Funnel: *Blue with white triangle on red disc on white square.* **Hull:** *Blue with red boot-topping.* **History:** *Founded 2003.* **Web:** *www.vassilevmaritime.com*

Name		Flag	Year	GT	DWT	Loa	Bm	Drt	Kts	Type	Remarks
Chalna	(2)	Rus	1989	3,952	5,150	138.8	16.7	3.7	11	C	ex Volgo-Don 5102-94
Chupa	(2)	Rus	1986	3,935	5,150	138.8	16.7	3.7	11	C	ex Volgo-Don 5096-94
Ladva	(2)	Rus	1988	3,952	5,150	138.8	16.7	3.7	10	C	ex Volgo-Don 5101-94
Loukhi	(2)	Rus	1988	3,952	5,150	138.3	16.7	3.7	10	C	ex Volgo-Don 5100-94

Name	Flag	Year	GT	DWT	Loa	Bm	Drt	Kts	Type	Remarks
Pryazha	(2) Rus	1989	3,952	5,150	138.8	16.7	3.7	11	C	ex Volgo-Don 5104
Pudozh	(2) Rus	1990	3,952	5,150	138.8	16.7	3.7	11	C	ex Volgo-Don 5106-94
Shoksha	(2) Rus	1989	3,952	5,150	138.8	16.7	3.7	10	C	ex Volgo-Don 5103-94
Solikamsk	(2) Rus	1979	3,991	5,462	138.3	16.5	3.4	10	C	ex Volgo-Don 229-05

Manages or operates up to 52 ex-Russian coastal ships, some through Turkish subsidiary on a seasonal basis, including others based in Mediterranean and Black Seas as well as the Russian inland river system.

Anthony Veder Rederijzaken BV — Netherlands

Funnel: *Blue with white 'A' over red 'V' on blue diamond on red band or blue with blue 'U' on broad red band ('Unigas' pool).* **Hull:** *Orange-red with red or grey boot-topping.* **History:** *Founded 1988 as Anthony Veder & Co BV.* **Web:** www.anthonyveder.com

Name	Flag	Year	GT	DWT	Loa	Bm	Drt	Kts	Type	Remarks
Coral Carbonic	Nld	1999	1,825	1,786	79.4	13.8	4.0	12	Lpg	
Coral Favia	Nld	2001	4,048	4,314	99.9	17.0	5.8	14	Lpg	
Coral Ivory	Nld	2000	5,831	6,875	116.0	16.0	7.8	-	Lpg	ex BW Helen-08, Baltic Viking-05
Coral Leaf	Nld	2008	5,441	6,175	108.0	16.8	7.5	14	Lpg	
Coral Lophelia	Nld	2006	5,469	6,175	108.0	16.8	7.5	14	Lpg	
Coral Meandra	Nld	1996	4,054	5,000	92.4	15.3	6.6	14	Lpg	
Coral Methane	Nld	2009	7,833	6,150	117.8	18.7	7.2	-	Lng	
Coral Millepora	Nld	1997	4,054	5,000	92.4	15.3	6.6	14	Lpg	
Coral Obelia	Nld	1996	3,853	4,150	92.4	15.3	6.6	14	Lpg	
Coral Palmata	Lbr	1994	5,821	5,704	115.3	16.8	8.1	-	Lpg	ex Tarquin Rover-00, l/a Val Metavro
Coral Pavona	Lbr	1995	5,821	5,632	115.3	16.8	8.1	-	Lpg	ex Tarquin Navigator-00
Coral Rigida	Nld	2000	5,489	6,073	107.9	16.8	7.5	15	Lpg	
Coral Rubrum	Nld	1999	5,469	6,148	108.0	16.8	7.5	15	Lpg	
Prins Johan Willem Friso	Nld	1989	3,862	4,905	97.3	15.9	6.0	14	Lpg	

Associated with BV United Gas Carriers 'Unigas' International

SIA Vega Ship Management — Latvia

Funnel: *White.* **Hull:** *Blue with red boot-topping.* **History:** *Founded 2000.* **Web:** *None found.*

Name	Flag	Year	GT	DWT	Loa	Bm	Drt	Kts	Type	Remarks
Vega	Lva	1976	2,219	2,560	81.4	13.5	5.0	13	Cc	ex Sea Fox-05, Tinka-03, Taras-96, Ikaria-86

Rederiet Vega AS — Denmark

Funnel: *Green.* **Hull:** *Red with red boot-topping.* **History:** *Not confirmed.* **Web:** *None found.*

Name	Flag	Year	GT	DWT	Loa	Bm	Drt	Kts	Type	Remarks
Vega	Dis	1975	1,872	1,372	75.5	11.8	5.0	12	C	ex Nina Bres-07

Vega-Reederei Friedrich Dauber GmbH & Co KG — Germany

Funnel: *Buff with white 'V' on broad black above red bands, narrow black top.* **Hull:** *Black or * green with red or black boot-topping.* **History:** *Founded 1919.* **Web:** www.vega-reederei.de

Name	Flag	Year	GT	DWT	Loa	Bm	Drt	Kts	Type	Remarks
Beluga Meditation	Gib	2008	8,971	10,700	154.9	21.5	7.0	18	CC	
Beluga Movery	Gib	2007	8,971	10,750	154.9	21.5	7.0	18	CC	ex Beluga Modesty-08, Esprit-07
Kosterberg	Gib	1999	1,999	3,271	90.0	12.5	4.8	10	T	(rblt/conv Cc-06)
Mell Seraya	Lbr	2008	7,170	8,279	132.7	19.2	7.7	17	CC	ex Vega Sonja-09
Spica †	Lib	2008	9,996	11,807	139.1	22.6	8.8	18	CC	
Sullberg	Gib	1994	1,999	3,280	89.5	12.5	4.8	10	T	(rblt/conv Cc-07)
Vega Aquila	Lib	2009	9,961	12.015	139.1	22.6	8.8	18	CC	l/a Solitas H
Vega Azurit	Lib	2008	9,957	13,684	147.9	23.3	8.5	19	Cc	
Vega Davos **	Lbr	2006	7,464	8,272	129.5	20.6	7.4	15	CC	
Vega Dolomit	Gib	2007	7,170	8,279	132.7	19.2	7.7	17	CC	ex X-Press Monte Rosa-08, BCL Izabela-08, l/a Vega Dolomit
Vega Fynen	Atg	2006	9,957	13,742	147.9	23.3	8.5	19	CC	
Vega Gotland	Atg	2006	9,957	13,608	147.9	23.3	8.5	19	CC	
Vega Mercury	Lib	2009	9,957	13,702	147.9	23.3	8.5	19	CC	
Vega Nikolas	Lib	2008	9,996	13,600	147.9	23.3	8.5	19	CC	
Vega Sachsen	Lib	2008	9,957	13,742	147.9	23.3	8.5	19	CC	
Vega Saturn	Lib	2008	9,957	13,621	147.9	23.3	8.5	19	CC	
Vega Scorpio	Atg	2010	9,750	11,500	139.1	22.6	8.8	18	CC	
Vega Spinell	Gib	2007	7,170	8,524	132.7	19.2	7.7	17	CC	ex X-Press Matterhorn-08, l/a Vega Spinell
Vega Stockholm	Lbr	2006	7,464	8,306	129.6	20.6	7.4	16	CC	
Vega Topas *	Atg	1999	9,030	10,968	135.7	22.5	8.6	18	CC	ex Cape Coldbek-04
Vega Virgo	Gib	2010	9,750	11,500	139.1	22.6	8.8	18	CC	
Vega Zirkon	Lib	2007	7,170	8,279	132.7	19.2	7.7	17	CC	ex X-Press Monte Bianco-08, l/a Vega Zirkon

** managed for FHH Fonds Haus Hamburg GmbH & Co KG, Germany or ** for Suisse International Capital (Germany) GmbH.*
† managed by Reederei Wolfram Sabban GmbH & Co KG.
Also one larger container ship and 13 bulk carrier newbuildings between 32,200-118,000 dwt for 2010-11 delivery.

Vega-Reederei Friedrich Dauber GmbH. Sullberg. *Oliver Sesemann*

Vega-Reederei Friedrich Dauber GmbH. Vega Stockholm. *Allan Ryszka Onions*

Name		Flag	Year	GT	DWT	Loa	Bm	Drt	Kts	Type	Remarks

Venus Shipping ApS — Denmark

Funnel: *Dark blue with blue 'V' on 7-pointed star, black top.* **Hull:** *Dark blue with white 'SHIPPING.DK', red boot-topping.* **History:** *Founded 1997 as Venus AsS to 2003.* **Web:** *www.venusshipping.dk*

Name		Flag	Year	GT	DWT	Loa	Bm	Drt	Kts	Type	Remarks
Dan Fighter		Dmk	1988	852	1,260	64.3	10.5	3.4	10	C	ex Zuiderzee-04, Carolina-98, Feran-91
Dan Supporter		Mlt	1987	2,749	3,173	94.5	15.9	5.0	14	Cc	ex Mosa-06, Triton Loga-98, Jan Becker-99
Dan Viking		Dmk	1986	1,139	1,601	79.1	11.4	3.3	12	Cc	ex Geertje-05, Anne S-98
SDK Italy		Dmk	1982	2,657	4,056	90.0	14.0	6.3	11	Cc	ex Matua-09, Forum Rarotonga-06, Rarotongan Rover II-01, Maelifell-00, Katya-93, Alex-91, Stenholm-91
SDK Spain		Dmk	1986	1,525	1,860	74.3	12.4	3.7	10	Cc	ex Sea Box-09, Gorch Fock-05, RMS Scotia-00, Gorch Fock-99

Rederi AB Veritas Tankers — Sweden

Funnel: *Cream with blue 'T' inside 'V' on white square, narrow blue top.* **Hull:** *Blue with red boot-topping.* **History:** *Founded 1983.* **Web:** *www.veritastankers.se*

Name		Flag	Year	GT	DWT	Loa	Bm	Drt	Kts	Type	Remarks
Astina		Swe	2006	7,636	11,283	128.2	19.6	8.1	14	Tch	I/a Besiktas Iceland
Astoria		Swe	1999	8,886	12,712	137.4	21.5	8.0	14	Tch	
Astral		Swe	2006	7,636	11,317	128.2	19.6	8.1	14	Tch	ex Besiktas Finland-07

Rederij C Vermeulen — Netherlands

Universal Marine BV

Funnel: *White with blue over yellow over black bands.* **Hull:** *Green with red boot-topping.* **History:** *Parent founded in 1982 and subsidiary in 2001 as Upstream Marine BV to 2004.* **Web:** *www.universalmarine.nl; www.scheepvaartcv.com*

Name		Flag	Year	GT	DWT	Loa	Bm	Drt	Kts	Type	Remarks
Amazon River		Nld	2007	9,940	13,619	147.9	25.3	8.5	19	CC	ex Papuan Gulf-09, I/a Amazon River
Amur River		Cyp	2009	9,940	13,760	147.8	25.3	8.5	19	CC	
Mekong River		Cyp	2008	9,940	13,760	147.8	25.3	8.5	19	CC	
Mell Senoko		Cyp	2008	9,940	13,749	147.8	25.3	8.5	19	CC	ex Yangtze River-10, Australia Star-09, Yangtze River-08
Norjan		Lux	2007	8,407	11,256	129.3	19.0	8.7	16	Cc	ex Sloman Sprinter-09, Norjan-07
Normed Antwerpen		Atg	2008	8,407	11,184	129.3	19.0	8.7	16	Cc	
Normed Rotterdam		Lux	2007	8,407	11,145	129.3	19.0	8.7	16	Cc	ex Bosphorus-07
Orinoco River		Cyp	2007	9,940	13,760	147.8	25.3	8.5	19	CC	
Pearl River		Cyp	2007	9,940	13,760	147.8	25.3	8.5	19	CC	ex CMA CGM Sierra-09, Pearl River-08
Tiger Power		Cyp	2007	9,940	13,705	147.8	25.3	8.5	19	CC	ex Vaal River-09
Vento di Levante		Cyp	2007	9,940	13,627	147.8	25.3	8.5	19	CC	ex Hudson River-09, Emirates Adam-08, Hudson River-07
Vento di Maestrale		Nld	2006	9,940	13,640	147.9	25.3	8.5	19	CC	ex Eagle 2-08, Surinam River-06
Yellow River		Cyp	2007	9,940	13,702	147.8	25.3	8.5	19	CC	ex Qatar Swift-09, Emirates Meru-08, Yellow River-07

Managed by subsidiary Universal Shipping BV, Netherlands.
Also manages two larger container ships and two 22,000 dwt bulk carriers with four 57,000 dwt bulk carriers on order..

Vestland Rederi AS — Norway

Funnel: *White.* **Hull:** *Red with red black boot-topping.* **History:** *Founded 1998 and subsidiary 2002.* **Web:** *www.vestlandmarine.eu*

Name		Flag	Year	GT	DWT	Loa	Bm	Drt	Kts	Type	Remarks
Saturn I		Mlt	1992	2,450	3,720	87.9	12.8	5.5	12	Cc	ex White Sea-09, Saturn-05, MSC Bahamas-03, Saturn-02, MSC Bahamas-00, Saturn-98
West Stream		Bhs	1979	1,834	2,550	80.2	13.0	5.2	13	Tch	ex Golfstraum-98

Managed by subsidiary Vestland Marine Sp z o.o, Poland.
Also owns two offshore supply ships.

VG-Shipping Oy — Finland

Funnel: *Blue with irregular shaped white panel.* **Hull:** *Dark blue or blue with black boot-topping.* **History:** *Parent Meriaura Oy founded 1986 and shipping subsidiary formed 1997.* **Web:** *www.vg-shipping.fi*

Name		Flag	Year	GT	DWT	Loa	Bm	Drt	Kts	Type	Remarks
Aura	(2)	Fin	2008	3,238	4,700	101.8	18.8	4.7	13	Chl	
Mirva		Gib	1985	3,951	5,414	105.6	15.9	6.0	12	C	ex Uni 4-04, Heca Timber-03, Global Spirit-03, Evangelia IV-01, Baltic Sun-95, Merak-87, Annie Cosyns-87, I/a Wappen von Barssel

owned or managed by subsidiary Meriaura Oy, Finland (Founded 1986 – www.meriaura.fi)

Rederi AB Vidar — Finland

Funnel: *Dark blue with white 'V' symbol (shortened on one side).* **Hull:** *Dark blue with red boot-topping.* **History:** *Founded 1999.* **Web:** *www.vidarshipping.fi*

Name		Flag	Year	GT	DWT	Loa	Bm	Drt	Kts	Type	Remarks
Frida		Fin	1985	1,587	1,901	82.0	11.3	4.2	10	C	ex Scot Pioneer-07, Silvia-98
Helga *		Fin	1984	1,391	2,280	79.8	11.1	4.1	9	Cc	ex Confidence-03, Christiaan-98, Mouna-93
Nina		Fin	1987	2,006	2,723	82.0	12.7	4.5	10	Cc	ex Ursula G-06, Claus-02

* managed by Meriaura Oy, Finland (see under VG-Shipping Oy above)

Vista Shipping Agency AS — Estonia

Funnel: *White.* **Hull:** *Green with red boot-topping.* **History:** *Founded 1993.* **Web:** *www.vista.ee*

Name		Flag	Year	GT	DWT	Loa	Bm	Drt	Kts	Type	Remarks
Scanlark		Vct	1985	1,361	1,520	75.0	10.8	3.7	11	C	ex RMS Scanlark-09, Oland-06, Drochtersen-98

Name		Flag	Year	GT	DWT	Loa	Bm	Drt	Kts	Type	Remarks
Setlark		Vct	1983	1,281	1,572	74.9	10.6	3.4	10	C	ex RMS Setlark-08, RMS Duisburg-05, Rhenus-97
Snowlark		Vct	1984	1,289	1,555	74.9	10.6	3.4	10	C	ex RMS Snowlark-08, RMS Walsum-05, Mosa-98

Jan Vogelsang — Germany

Funnel: None. **Hull:** Brown/red with black boot-topping. **History:** Founded 1995. **Web:** None found.

Name		Flag	Year	GT	DWT	Loa	Bm	Drt	Kts	Type	Remarks
Jan/V		Atg	1985	1,749	2,218	80.7	12.6	4.2	12	Cc	

Joint-Stock Co Volga Shipping — Russia

Funnel: White or white with blue over red bands, black top. **Hull:** Various colours including light grey, blue and green with red boot-topping. **History:** Founded 1843 as United Volga River Shipping Co to 1984. **Web:** www.volgaflot.com

Name		Flag	Year	GT	DWT	Loa	Bm	Drt	Kts	Type	Remarks
Aleksandr Marinesko *	(2)	Rus	1984	1,785	1,776	86.7	12.3	3.0	10	C	ex ST-1303-94
Bakhtemir	(2)	Rus	1978	1,522	1,755	82.0	11.9	3.3	8	Cc	
Kapitan Babushkin	(2)	Rus	1984	1,785	1,777	86.7	12.3	3.0	10	C	ex ST-1306
Kapitan Ezovitov **	(2)	Rus	1984	3,070	3,377	107.4	16.7	3.5	10	C	
Kapitan Galashin	(2)	Rus	1983	1,719	1,652	86.7	12.3	3.0	10	Cc	ex Steamer-1-??, ST-1301-94
Kapitan Kuznetsov	(2)	Rus	1984	1,719	1,652	86.7	12.3	3.0	10	C	ex ST-1304-99, Steamer-4-96, ST-1304-94
Professor Volskiy	(2)	Rus	1982	2,491	3,100	114.1	13.5	3.7	10	C	ex STK-3007
Rusich-1	(2)	Rus	2003	4,970	5,485	128.2	16.5	4.3	11	C	
Rusich-8 †	(2)	Mlt	2007	4,970	5,460	128.2	16.5	4.3	11	C	
Sibirskiy-2101	(2)	Rus	1980	3,409	3,172	128.4	15.6	3.0	10	Cc	
Starovolzhsk	(2)	Rus	1979	1,522	1,260	82.0	11.9	2.8	10	Cc	
STK-1002	(2)	Rus	1983	1,408	1,706	82.0	11.6	2.5	10	C	
Ufa		Rus	1997	2,914	3,835	96.3	13.6	5.2	11	Cc	ex Nikolay Smelyakov-03
Volga-44	(2)	Mlt	2001	4,953	6,207	139.9	16.4	4.7	10	C	
Volgo-Don 236	(2)	Rus	1980	2,990	3,853	107.1	16.5	3.7	10	C	
Volgo-Don 240	(2)	Rus	1980	2,990	3,530	107.1	16.5	3.5	10	C	
Volgo-Don 5046	(2)	Rus	1975	3,989	5,150	138.8	16.5	2.8	-	C	
Zelenga	(2)	Rus	1978	1,522	1,810	82.0	11.6	2.8	10	C	

* managed by Steamer Ltd., Russia or ** by Volga-Neva Joint Stock Co.
† managed by Inok NV, Belgium (www.inok-nv.com)

Volga-Don Shipping Joint Stock Co — Russia

Funnel: White with blue over red bands, black top. **Hull:** Various. **History:** Founded 1993. **Web:** www.vdp.ru

Name		Flag	Year	GT	DWT	Loa	Bm	Drt	Kts	Type	Remarks
40 Let Pobedy	(2)	Blz	1985	2,466	3,135	114.0	13.2	3.7	-	C	
Ataman Platov		Mlt	1996	2,914	4,237	96.3	13.6	5.5	11	Cc	ex Neman-01
Don 1	(2)	Mlt	1996	3,796	4,400	100.7	16.2	4.8	11	Cc	ex Don-08
Don 2	(2)	Mlt	1996	3,796	4,400	100.7	16.2	4.8	11	Cc	ex Voronezh-08
Don 3	(2)	Mlt	1996	3,796	4,400	100.7	16.2	4.8	11	Cc	ex Aksaiy-08
Don 4	(2)	Mlt	1997	3,796	4,400	100.7	16.2	4.8	11	Cc	ex Temernik-08
Ermak		Rus	1995	2,813	3,837	96.3	13.6	5.2	11	Cc	ex Lava-03
Sormovskiy-43	(2)	Rus	1981	2,466	3,134	114.0	13.2	3.4	10	C	
Sormovskiy-121	(2)	Blz	1982	2,466	3,134	114.0	13.2	3.7	10	C	
Sormovskiy-122	(2)	Blz	1984	2,466	3,134	114.2	13.2	3.7	10	C	
Sormovskiy-123	(2)	Blz	1985	2,466	3,155	114.0	13.2	3.7	10	C	
Sormovskiy-3006	(2)	Blz	1982	2,491	3,100	114.1	13.5	3.7	10	C	
Sormovskiy-3066	(2)	Rus	1990	3,048	3,391	118.7	13.4	4.1	10	Cc	
Volgo-Balt 241	(2)	Blz	1982	2,516	3,150	113.9	13.2	3.6	10	C	
Volgo-Balt 248	(2)	Blz	1984	2,516	3,193	113.9	13.2	3.6	10	C	
Volgo-Don 203	(2)	Blz	1977	4,863	5,859	138.3	16.5	3.8	10	C	
Volgo-Don 205	(2)	Blz	1977	3,959	4,019	138.3	16.5	2.9	10	C	

Ernst-August Von Allworden — Germany

Funnel: White with white diamond over two red bands on broad black band. **Hull:** Light grey with red boot-topping. **History:** Founded 1987. **Web:** None found.

Name		Flag	Year	GT	DWT	Loa	Bm	Drt	Kts	Type	Remarks
Petuja		Deu	1997	6,362	7,200	121.4	18.2	6.7	16	CC	ex Joanna Borchard-00, I/a Petuja

Vroon BV — Netherlands

Funnel: White with three light blue wavy lines at base of dark blue 'V', narrow blue top or charterers colours. **Hull:** Red or black with red boot-topping. **History:** Founded 1890. **Web:** www.vroon.nl

Owns and operates fleet of larger vessels including container ships, car and bulk carriers, also a large fleet of offshore vessels.

Iver Ships BV

Funnel: White with blue tick inside narrow red square outline. **Hull:** Red with red boot-topping. **History:** Founded 2007. **Web:** www.iverships.com

Name	Flag	Year	GT	DWT	Loa	Bm	Drt	Kts	Type	Remarks
Iver Bitumen	Gib	2009	5,384	6,586	109.9	18.2	6.7	12	Ta	
Iver Balance	Gib	2010	5,384	6,100	109.9	18.2	6.7	12	Ta	
Iver Beauty	Gib	2010	5,384	6,100	109.9	18.2	6.7	12	Ta	
Iver Best	Gib	2010	5,384	6,100	109.9	18.2	6.7	12	Ta	

Name		Flag	Year	GT	DWT	Loa	Bm	Drt	Kts	Type	Remarks

Newbuildings: Four further 6,100 dwt asphalt/bitumen tankers for 2011 delivery (Iver Blessing, Iver Bliss and two others)
Also operates 13 product tankers between 37,200 and 46,800 dwt

Livestock Express BV

Funnel: *White with blue 'LE' and narrow blue top.* **Hull:** *Grey with blue 'LIVESTOCK EXPRESS', red boot-topping.*

Name		Flag	Year	GT	DWT	Loa	Bm	Drt	Kts	Type	Remarks
Angus Express		Phi	1998	4,752	4,200	103.1	16.8	6.3	-	Lv	ex Stella Alnilam-08, Alnilam Prima-08, Alnilam-03
Bison Express		Phl	1995	6,442	4,570	122.1	16.4	5.7	17	Lv	(len-99)
Brahman Express		Phl	2002	7,727	5,650	133.4	15.9	6.2	16	Lv	
Buffalo Express		Phl	1983	2,374	1,600	81.8	14.0	4.1	12	Lv	(len-84)
Devon Express		Phl	1997	6,159	3,656	116.6	15.9	5.3	16	Lv	
Friesian Express		Phi	1982	5,218	5,557	108.6	17.2	7.8	16	Lv	ex Kala Mona-94, Ryusei Maru-88 (conv R-95)
Hereford Express		Phi	1982	4,634	6,187	96.7	17.4	6.9	12	Lv	ex Dealco 1-04, Cosmo Star-98, Rimba Star-88, Pacific Star-87 (conv C-97)
Kerry Express		Phi	1980	3,246	3,862	86.0	14.0	6.6	12	Lv	ex Camira-04 (conv C-94)
Lincoln Express	(2)	Phi	1987	3,183	1,748	85.4	14.0	3.5	13	Lv	ex Felicia-04, Vanessa-96, Leeward Express-94, Vanessa-93 (conv Ro-96, len-90)
Murray Express		Phi	1995	1,762	1,559	73.5	11.4	3.8	9	Lv	ex Cimbria-04
Sahiwal Express	(2)	Phi	1990	2,725	4,675	91.5	16.2	4.3	12	Lv	ex Lis E-04, Elisabeth-97, Elsborg-93, Elisabeth-92 (conv C/Ro-99)
Shorthorn Express		Phl	1998	6,872	4,422	116.6	15.9	6.0	16	Lv	

Vyborg Shipping Co Ltd   Russia

Funnel: *Black or * black with two narrow and very broad white bands.* **Hull:** *Black or * green with red boot-topping.* **History:** *Founded 2007 as subsidiary of UK-based Oslo Marine Group.* **Web:** *www.oslo.ru*

Name	Flag	Year	GT	DWT	Loa	Bm	Drt	Kts	Type	Remarks
OMG Gatchina *	Mhl	1995	5,624	6,985	109.7	17.8	7.2	12	Cc	ex Walsertal-07
OMG Tosno	Mhl	2000	5,658	6,847	109.7	17.8	7.0	12	Cc	ex Norheim-08

Newbuildings: Ten 7,000-7,500 dwt general cargo and four 7,987 gt feeder container ships on order for 2010-11 delivery.

W & R Shipping BV   Netherlands

Funnel: *White with narrow blue top.* **Hull:** *Dark blue with red boot-topping.* **History:** *Founded 2006.* **Web:** *www.wrshipping.nl*

Name	Flag	Year	GT	DWT	Loa	Bm	Drt	Kts	Type	Remarks
Anne Dorte	Nld	2009	2,610	3,500	88.3	13.0	5.4	-	Cc	
Crown Mary	Nld	2009	2,610	3,500	88.3	13.0	5.4	-	Cc	
Crownbreeze	Nld	1999	2,548	3,620	87.8	12.5	5.4	13	C	
Monica *	Nld	1989	1,994	3,015	83.3	12.6	5.0	11	Cc	ex Itasca-04, Sambre-98
Thea Marieke	Nld	2001	2,311	3,171	82.5	12.4	5.3	11	Cc	ex Nordic Bianca-07, Korsar-05, Athos-05
Tina	Nld	2009	2,610	3,500	88.3	13.0	5.4	-	Cc	

* *managed for Monica Shipping BV (founded 2004 – www.msmonica.nl)*

Wagenborg Shipping BV   Netherlands

Funnel: *Black with two narrow white bands. Managed vessels with individual owners colours including † white with yellow 'FG' symbol on blue band.*
Hull: *Owned vessels - light grey with broad red band and white 'WAGENBORG', black boot-topping. Managed vessels - various including light grey, blue, green or red with red or black boot-topping.* **History:** *Founded 1898 as E Wagenborg's Scheepvaart en Expeditiebedrijf NV to 1972 and as Wagenborg Scheepvaart BV to 1987. Parent granted royal seal and renamed Royal Wagenborg in 1998.* **Web:** *www.wagenborg.com*

Name	Flag	Year	GT	DWT	Loa	Bm	Drt	Kts	Type	Remarks
Adamas	Nld	2010	2,437	3,754	82.5	12.5	5.5	12	Cc	
Aerandir	Nld	2009	2,545	3,850	88.6	12.5	5.4	10	Cc	
Alana Evita	Nld	2009	2,281	3,261	89.0	11.8	5.1	11	Cc	
Anet	Nld	2010	8,999	12,000	143.0	18.9	7.9	16	Cc	
Ashley	Nld	2000	2,056	2,953	89.0	12.5	4.3	10	Cc	ex Hydra-07
Avalon	Nld	2009	2,545	3,850	88.6	12.5	5.4	-	Cc	
Cristina **	Nld	2009	2,409	3,750	82.5	12.5	5.4	11	Cc	
Diamant	Nld	2005	2,437	3,670	82.5	12.5	5.4	11	Cc	
Diezeborg	Nld	2000	6,219	8,867	133.4	15.9	7.1	15	Cc	ex MSC Marmara-03, Diezeborg-01
Dintelborg	Nld	1999	6,235	8,865	133.4	15.9	7.1	15	Cc	ex MSC Dardanelles-04, Dintelborg-01
Dongeborg	Nld	1999	6,205	9,000	133.4	16.6	7.1	15	Cc	
Drechtborg	Nld	1999	6,219	8,865	133.4	16.6	7.1	15	Cc	ex Normed Rotterdam-05, Drechtborg-03, MSC Skaw-02, Drechtborg-00
Ebroborg	Nld	2010	7,196	10,750	137.9	15.8	8.0	-	Cc	
Edenborg	Nld	2010	7,196	10,750	137.9	15.8	8.0	-	Cc	
Eemsborg	Nld	2009	7,196	10,750	137.9	15.8	8.0	-	Cc	
Eemshorn	Nld	2008	3,990	6,000	110.8	14.0	6.1	-	Cc	
Egbert Wagenborg	Nld	1998	6,540	9,150	134.6	16.5	7.1	16	Cc	ex MSC Bothnia-03, Egbert Wagenborg-02
Emma	Nld	2007	2,528	3,500	90.0	12.5	5.3	13	Cc	
Emuna	Nld	2009	2,992	4,500	90.0	15.3	5.6	-	C	
Erieborg	Nld	2009	7,196	10,750	137.9	15.8	8.0	-	Cc	
Gelre	Nld	1992	1,576	2,249	81.7	11.0	4.1	12	C	
Hekla	Nld	2009	2,281	3,150	89.0	11.8	5.1	-	Cc	
Helenic	Nld	2008	2,281	3,150	89.0	11.8	5.1	-	Cc	
Helga	Nld	2010	8,999	12,000	143.0	18.9	7.9	16	Cc	
Hudsonborg	Nld	2006	4,206	6,100	113.8	14.4	6.0	12	Cc	

Name	Flag	Year	GT	DWT	Loa	Bm	Drt	Kts	Type	Remarks
Humberborg		Nld	2006	4,206	6,053	113.8	14.4	6.0	14	Cc	
Hunteborg		Nld	2006	4,206	6,100	113.8	14.4	6.0	14	Cc	
Hunzeborg		Nld	2005	4,206	6,100	113.8	14.4	6.0	14	Cc	
Hydra		Nld	2007	2,281	3,150	89.0	11.8	5.1	11	Cc	
Isis		Nld	2007	3,990	6,000	110.8	14.0	6.1	13	Cc	
Jade		Nld	2010	2,300	3,250	90.0	11.8	5.0	-	cc	
Jan van Gent		Nld	2010	8,999	12,000	143.0	18.9	7.9	16	Cc	
Jeannette		Nld	2007	3,990	6,000	110.8	14.0	6.1	13	Cc	ex Anet-09
Jolyn *		Ant	2007	2,528	3,568	90.0	12.5	5.3	13	Cc	
Kelt		Nld	2009	2,409	3,750	82.5	12.5	5.5	12	Cc	
Kliftrans		Nld	1997	2,224	3,132	88.0	12.5	4.6	11	Cc	ex Ambassadeur-06
Laganborg		Nld	2008	4,695	7,433	122.3	14.4	6.5	13	Cc	
Lauwersborg		Nld	2007	4,695	7,433	122.3	14.4	6.5	13	Cc	
Lingeborg		Nld	2008	4,695	7,433	122.3	14.4	6.5	13	Cc	
Loireborg		Nld	2008	4,695	7,433	122.3	14.4	6.5	13	Cc	
Maimiti §		Nld	2001	2,224	3,155	88.0	12.5	4.6	11	Cc	ex Nordfjord-09, Sagitta-05
Maineborg		Nld	2001	6,585	9,150	134.6	16.5	7.1	16	Cc	
Marietje Andrea		Nld	2009	3,956	8,200	126.2	15.2	7.0	-	Cc	
Marietje Deborah		Nld	2005	2,409	3,200	82.5	12.6	5.4	11	Cc	
Marinda		Nld	1999	1,999	2,815	89.5	12.4	4.3	10	Cc	ex Aquila-09, Hansa Bremen-04
Marneborg		Nld	1997	6,540	9,150	134.5	16.5	7.1	16	Cc	
Mary Christina *		Ant	1998	2,224	3,155	87.9	12.5	4.6	11	Cc	ex Sirocco-04
Merel-V		Nld	2006	2,409	3,200	82.5	12.6	5.4	11	Cc	
Metsaborg		Nld	2002	6,585	9,150	134.6	16.5	7.1	16	Cc	
Michiganborg		Nld	1999	6,540	9,105	134.6	16.5	7.1	16	Cc	
Mila		Nld	2006	2,528	3,638	90.0	12.5	5.3	13	Cc	ex Iselmar-07
Miska		Nld	1974	916	1,401	79.9	9.0	3.0	10	C	ex Deo Gratias-09, Deo Volente-95, Maria-92, Pia-82, Cargoliner II-81
Mississippiborg		Nld	2000	6,540	9,150	134.6	16.5	7.1	16	Cc	
Missouriborg		Nld	2000	6,585	9,150	134.6	16.5	7.1	16	Cc	
Moezelborg		Nld	1999	6,540	9,200	134.6	16.6	7.1	16	Cc	
Morraborg		Nld	1999	6,540	9,200	134.6	16.5	7.1	16	Cc	
Munteborg		Nld	1998	6,540	9,200	134.5	16.6	7.1	16	Cc	
Namai		Nld	1998	4,446	6,324	111.8	15.0	6.3	13	Ccp	
Noorderkroon †		Nld	2008	2,343	4,500	90.0	14.4	5.8	-	Cc	
Normed Gemlik		Nld	2004	3,991	6,063	111.4	13.4	5.7	12	Cc	ex Altena-04
Panda		Nld	2001	2,080	2,953	89.0	12.4	3.5	10	Cc	
Panta Rhei		Nld	2009	2,409	3,750	82.5	12.5	5.4	-	Cc	
Priscilla		Nld	2009	2,281	3,250	89.0	11.8	5.0	-	Cc	
Reestborg	(2)	Nld	1994	9,168	7,285	140.0	20.5	6.3	17	CC	
Reggeborg	(2)	Nld	1994	9,168	7,285	139.8	20.5	6.3	17	CC	ex Levant Elbe-96, Reggeborg-95
Robijn		Nld	2008	2,528	3,623	90.0	12.5	5.3	-	Cc	
Samira		Nld	2004	1,435	1,700	80.0	10.5	3.6	10	Cc	I/a Hansa London
Sandettie		Nld	2004	2,088	2,934	89.0	12.4	4.4	-	Cc	
Sirocco		Nld	2004	3,991	6,033	111.4	13.4	5.7	12	Cc	
Sprinter		Nld	2008	2,528	3,623	82.5	12.5	5.5	11	Cc	
Tucana		Nld	2008	2,545	3,783	88.6	12.5	5.4	-	Cc	
Vaasaborg		Nld	2000	6,130	8,700	132.2	15.9	7.1	14	Cc	ex Normed Hamburg-03, Vaasaborg-00
Vancouverborg		Nld	2001	6,351	9,900	132.2	15.9	7.1	15	Cc	
Victoriaborg		Nld	2001	6,361	9,850	132.2	15.9	7.1	15	Cc	
Virginiaborg		Nld	2001	6,361	9,600	132.2	15.9	7.1	15	Cc	I/a Volgaborg
Voorneborg		Nld	1999	6,170	8,700	132.2	15.9	7.1	14	Cc	
Westewind		Nld	2003	2,080	2,815	89.0	12.4	4.4	10	Cc	ex Agenor-08, Hilja Marjan-05
Willeke		Nld	2000	1,435	1,680	80.0	10.4	3.4	10	Cc	ex Hansa Parijs-06
Zeeland		Nld	2010	2,281	3,250	89.0	11.8	5.0	-	Cc	

* managed by Berg Maritime Management Ltd, Ireland or † by Flinter Management BV, Netherlands.
** managed for Willem Doorduin or § for Dekker Scheepvaart CV, Netherlands
Also owns and operates some larger vessels, tugs and domestic ferries.
See Esmeralda Schiffahrts GmbH, Germany.

Odd Wagle A/S   Norway

Funnel: Blue with blue 'W' on broad white band. **Hull:** Bluewith red boot-topping. **History:** Founded 1936 as Rolf Wagle A/S to 1963. **Web:** www.rolf-wagle.no

Name	Flag	Year	GT	DWT	Loa	Bm	Drt	Kts	Type	Remarks
Lill	Cok	1972	1,394	1,678	76.7	11.8	4.2	11	C	ex Heidi-02, Clipper II-86, Silke Riedner-85, Bottensee-81
Linda	Nis	1972	2,586	3,263	90.0	14.5	5.5	11	C	ex Norunn-02, Marine Trader-94, Gimo Trader-92, Gimo Celtica-90, Sandnes-89, Ringen-88, Laxfoss-87, Hofsa-86, Bonaventure II-84, Atlantic King-81, Shaikah Al Quraichi-79, Atlantic King-78, Nad King-75, Korneuburg-72
Line	Nis	1976	2,973	3,850	93.7	14.5	6.1	12	C	ex Swift-02, Bell Swift-97, Jan-91, Arfell-90, Jan-87
Lisbeth	Nis	1972	1,583	1,985	75.0	11.8	4.6	11	C	ex Carolina-02, Bellatrix-89, Thies-84

Wagenborg Shipping BV. Drechtborg. *Hans Kraijenbosch*

Wagenborg Shipping BV. Jan van Gent. *Hans Kraijenbosch*

Wagenborg Shipping BV. Sandettie. *Hans Kraijenbosch*

Name	Flag	Year	GT	DWT	Loa	Bm	Drt	Kts	Type	Remarks
Liv	Nis	1977	3,674	4,341	99.8	16.0	5,8	13	C	ex Peter Knuppel-01, Zim Black Sea-01, Peter Knuppel-00, Maersk Tempo-91, Peter Knuppel-87, City of Salerno-86, Peter Knuppel-84, Katherine Borchard-83, Peter Knuppel-82, Eurobridge Link-80, Peter Knuppel-78

Operated and managed by subsidiary Sia Wagle Ltd, Latvia (founded 2003)
Also operates 16 other coasters on charter from various other owners.

Thomas Wang A/S   Denmark

Funnel: *White with black 'Ø' symbol, black top.* **Hull:** *Black with red boot-topping.* **History:** *Founded 1986.* **Web:** *www.wang.dk*

Name	Flag	Year	GT	DWT	Loa	Bm	Drt	Kts	Type	Remarks
Baltic Betina	Mlt	1983	2,647	3,235	90.0	14.0	5.6	13	Cc	ex Cap Anamur-05, Andra-04, Arnarfell-94, Sandra M-89, Sandra-87, Band Aid III-85, Sandra-85
Baltic Sea	Nis	1977	2,282	2,560	81.4	13.4	5.0	13	Cc	ex Carina-89
Dyna Bulk	Dis	1985	2,719	3,900	90.4	14.0	6.3	14	Cc	ex Heimglimt-07, Tucana-05, Rangitikei-96, Lisa Heeren-92, Santa Paula-90, Lisa Heeren-89, Band Aid II-85, Lisa Heeren-85

Operated by subsidiary Nygaard Shipping A/S, Denmark

Warnecke Schiffahrt GbR   Germany

Funnel: *White with houseflag (white with pale blue border and red centre square).* **Hull:** *Dark green with red boot-topping.* **History:** *Founded 2004 to take over Gerhard Warnk GmbH & Co.* **Web:** *None found.*

Name	Flag	Year	GT	DWT	Loa	Bm	Drt	Kts	Type	Remarks
Montis	Deu	1985	1,649	1,631	82.5	11.3	3.5	10	Cc	ex Premiere-02
Suntis	Deu	1985	1,564	1,815	82.5	11.3	3.6	10	Cc	

Reederei Hans Peter Wegener   Germany

Funnel: *White with red 'W' above pale blue sea or charterers colours.* **Hull:** *Red with red boot-topping.* **History:** *Not confirmed.* **Web:** *www.hpw-shipping.de*

Name	Flag	Year	GT	DWT	Loa	Bm	Drt	Kts	Type	Remarks
Carina	Deu	1990	5,796	6,350	122.0	19.0	6.9	16	CC	ex Containerships III-99, Carina-90
Spica	Deu	1994	7,550	8,932	151.1	19.7	7.4	21	CC	ex Melfi Italia-04, Containerships IV-03
Wega	Deu	1996	7,550	8,912	151.1	19.7	7.4	21	CC	ex Containerships V-09, I/a Wega

Also see Containerships Group under Eimskip EHF (The Iceland Steamship Co Ltd)

Andrew Weir & Co Ltd   UK

Funnel: *Cream with white-edged broad blue band on buff top section.* **Hull:** *Back with red boot-topping.* **History:** *Founded 1896 as Andrew Weir & Co to 1945 and Andrew Weir Shipping & Trading Co Ltd to 1957.* **Web:** *www.aws.co.uk*

Name	Flag	Year	GT	DWT	Loa	Bm	Drt	Kts	Type	Remarks
Dartmoor	Mlt	1998	9,146	9,950	133.7	22.7	7.7	18	CC	ex CMA CGM Estrella-08, Maersk Felixstowe-06, Ridvan Ozerler-03

Also see Foreland Shipping in Ferry Section.

Werkendam Shipping Co CV   Netherlands

Funnel: *Buff with blue band.* **Hull:** *Blue with red boot-topping.* **History:** *Founded 2004.* **Web:** *None found.*

Name	Flag	Year	GT	DWT	Loa	Bm	Drt	Kts	Type	Remarks
Filia Ariea	Nld	2008	2,199	2,950	90.0	13.8	4.4	-	C	
Filia Nettie	Nld	2008	2,199	2,950	90.0	13.8	4.4	-	C	

Uwe Werner   Germany

Funnel: *White with white shield on gold panel.* **Hull:** *Blue with red boot-topping.* **History:** *Not confirmed.* **Web:** *None found.*

Name	Flag	Year	GT	DWT	Loa	Bm	Drt	Kts	Type	Remarks
Karina W	Deu	1983	1,022	1,113	74.5	9.5	2.9	10	C	ex Sheila Hammann-06, RMS Anglia-96, Sheila Hammann-92

Gerhard Wessels   Germany

Funnel: *White with white 'W' on blue traditional ship silhouette (with amidships superstructure and fore/aft masts).* **Hull:** *Blue with white 'WESSELS', red boot-topping.* **History:** *Founded 1977.* **Web:** *www.wessels.de*

Name	Flag	Year	GT	DWT	Loa	Bm	Drt	Kts	Type	Remarks
Argos	Lbr	2007	2,452	3,666	87.9	12.8	5.5	11	C	
Butes	Lbr	2010	2,452	3,675	87.9	12.8	5.5	11	C	
Clavigo	Atg	1992	2,446	3,735	87.9	12.9	5.5	10	Cc	
Echion	Lbr	2010	2,452	3,675	87.9	12.8	5.5	11	C	
Faust *	Deu	1997	2,997	4,444	99.9	12.8	5.7	13	Cc	ex German Express-97
German Bay *	Atg	1997	2,997	4,450	99.9	12.8	5.7	13	Cc	
German Sky *	Nld	1995	2,997	4,450	99.9	12.8	5.7	13	Cc	ex Dutch Sky-01, German Sky-97, Rhein Pilot-96, German Sky-96
Gorky	Atg	1997	2,914	3,387	93.3	16.5	5.2	10	Cc	ex Transworld I-00
Herakles	Lbr	2008	2,452	3,682	87.9	12.8	5.5	11	C	
Jason	Lbr	2008	2,452	3,686	87.9	12.8	5.5	11	C	
Kastor	Lbr	2007	2,452	3,671	87.9	12.8	5.5	11	C	
Marten	Deu	2009	2,997	4,450	99.9	12.8	5.7	13	C	
MCL Express	Atg	1999	3,787	4,800	93.3	16.5	6.3	14	Cc	ex Planet-01, Pannon Sky-00

Gerhard Wessels. Pamir. *M. Beckett*

Gerhard Wessels. Wotan. *David Walker*

Name		Flag	Year	GT	DWT	Loa	Bm	Drt	Kts	Type	Remarks
Melas		Lbr	2009	2,452	3,675	87.9	12.8	5.5	11	C	
Michael A		Atg	1993	2,514	3,560	87.7	12.8	5.5	11	Cc	ex Peary-07, Larnaca Bay-99, Fischland-97
Nestor		Lbr	2008	2,452	3,675	87.9	12.8	5.5	11	C	
Nordstern		Atg	1994	2,446	3,702	87.9	12.9	5.5	11	Cc	
Paganini		Atg	2007	2,971	4,247	89.9	15.2	5.6	12	Cc	
Pamir		Atg	1995	2,061	3,002	88.5	11.4	5.0	11	Cc	
Parma		Atg	2001	2,999	4,247	89.9	15.2	5.6	12	Cc	
Parsival		Atg	1995	2,061	3,007	88.5	11.4	5.0	11	Cc	
Pasadena		Atg	2001	2,993	4,250	89.9	15.2	5.6	12	Cc	
Pascal		Atg	2001	2,999	4,263	89.9	15.2	5.6	12	Cc	
Peleus		Lbr	2009	2,452	3,675	87.9	12.8	5.5	11	C	
Perle		Deu	1998	2,983	4,200	89.9	15.2	5.5	12	Cc	
Peru		Deu	1998	2,993	4,279	90.6	15.2	5.6	12	Cc	
Petersburg		Atg	2001	2,914	4,322	93.3	16.5	5.6	14	Cc	
Pex		Atg	2001	2,995	4,267	89.9	15.2	5.6	12	Cc	
Poet		Atg	1997	2,997	4,444	99.9	12.8	5.7	13	Cc	ex German Feeder-00
Pollux		Lbr	2008	2,452	3,689	87.9	12.8	5.5	11	C	
Pommern		Atg	1994	2,061	3,006	88.5	11.4	5.0	11	Cc	
Posen		Atg	1993	2,514	3,560	87.7	12.8	5.5	12	Cc	ex Seaprogress-99, Usedom-97
Potosi		Atg	1995	2,506	3,657	87.9	12.8	4.5	12	Cc	
Prasident		Atg	1995	2,061	3,004	88.5	11.4	5.0	12	Cc	
Pur-Navolok		Cyp	1997	2,446	3,720	87.9	12.8	5.5	11	Cc	
Rheinfels		Atg	1991	2,381	3,700	88.8	12.8	5.5	11	Cc	
Telamon		Lbr	2009	2,452	3,675	87.9	12.8	5.5	11	C	
Theseus		Lbr	2009	2,452	3,667	87.9	12.8	5.5	11	C	
Tinsdal		Deu	1998	2,983	4,250	89.9	15.2	5.5	12	Cc	
Wes Bar		Atg	2010	3,660	5,500	103.5	15.2	-	12	C	
Wes Beam		Atg	2010	3,660	5,500	103.5	15.2	-	12	C	
Wes Platte		Atg	2010	3,660	5,500	103.5	15.2	-	12	C	
Wes Profile		Atg	2010	3,660	5,500	103.5	15.2	-	12	C	
Wittenbergen		Cyp	1992	2,381	3,700	87.9	12.8	5.5	10	Cc	
Wotan		Deu	1996	2,997	4,450	99.8	12.8	5.6	13	Cc	

Newbuildings: four 10,585 gt feeder container ships for 2010 delivery and eight further 3,660 gt coasters for 2011-12 delivery.
*Owned by subsidiaries Wessels Reederei GmbH & Co KG (founded 1989) or * by Wesco Shipping GmbH & Co KG (founded 1998)*

W-O Shipping Group BV/Netherlands
Funnel: *White with blue symbol.* **Hull:** *Red with red boot-topping.* **History:** *Founded 2002 jointly by Wessels Reederei GmbH & Co KG and OMCI Germany GmbH & Co KG (subsidiary of Orinoco Marine Consultancy India - founded 1996).* **Web:** *www.w-o-shipping.com*
Operates several larger tankers and manages nine 13,200 dwt tankers for Wolbern Group KG.

Westco AB   Sweden
Funnel: *White with white 'Westco' on blue disc or charterers colours.* **Hull:** *Blue with red boot-topping.* **History:** *Founded 1989.* **Web:** *www.abwestco.se*

Name		Flag	Year	GT	DWT	Loa	Bm	Drt	Kts	Type	Remarks
Wilson Star		Swe	1989	5,627	4,452	107.5	17.2	6.1	15	Rop	ex Mini Star-03

John H Whitaker (Holdings) Ltd   UK
Funnel: *Black with white 'W' on white-edged black disc on red and green flag beneath narrow red and green bands or black with flag.* **Hull:** *Black or dark blue with red boot-topping.* **History:** *Founded 1949.* **Web:** *www.whitakertankers.com*

Name		Flag	Year	GT	DWT	Loa	Bm	Drt	Kts	Type	Remarks
Humber Endeavour		Gbr	1981	380	650	60.8	6.1	2.4	8	T	ex Fleet Endeavour-92
Humber Pride		Gbr	1979	380	650	60.8	6.1	2.4	9	T	
Humber Princess		Gbr	1979	380	650	60.8	6.1	2.4	9	T	
Humber Progress		Gbr	1980	380	650	60.8	6.1	2.4	9	T	
Jaynee W	(2)	Gbr	1996	1,689	2,901	75.3	12.8	5.2	10	T	
Keewhit		Gbr	2003	1,241	2,332	77.2	11.9	5.0	-	T	ex Recep Mercan-04
Whitchallenger		Iom	2002	2,965	4,580	85.0	15.0	6.3	10	T	
Whitchampion		Iom	2003	2,965	4,450	85.0	15.0	6.2	10	T	
Whitdawn		Gbr	1989	1,646	2,675	78.5	12.6	4.9	10	T	ex Blackrock-07
Whitonia	(2)	Iom	2007	4,292	7,511	101.1	18.0	6.0	-	T	
Whitspray		Gbr	1969	899	1,321	64.6	11.1	3.4	10	T	ex Bristolian 93 (len-71)
Wilberforce		Iom	2007	1,055	1,561	62.4	12.0	3.8	8	T	

Reederei Andre Wieczorek GmbH & Co KG   Germany
Funnel: *White.* **Hull:** *Blue with black boot-topping.* **History:** *Founded 1985 as Seeschiffahrt Andre Wieczorek to 2005.* **Web:** *www.wieczorek-ship.de*

Name	Flag	Year	GT	DWT	Loa	Bm	Drt	Kts	Type	Remarks
Egon W *	Atg	2004	2,409	3,200	82.5	12.5	4.9	11	Cc	ex Iselmar-05
Elke W	Atg	2006	2,409	3,206	82.5	12.5	4.9	11	Cc	ex Stern-07
Frank W	Atg	2006	2,528	3,638	90.0	12.5	5.4	13	Cc	ex Storm-08
John Mitchell	Atg	1997	3,999	5,865	100.0	18.2	6.6	16	CC	ex HMS Goodwill-06, Uwe Kahrs-04, Maersk Messina-99, Uwe Kahrs-98
Lilly Mitchell	Atg	1993	4,193	5,401	111.1	16.2	6.6	16	Cc	ex BCL Joanna-07, Stade-05, Atlantik-03, Gracechurch Harp-02, Atlantik-01, Birgit Jurgens-97

John H Whitaker (Holdings) Ltd. Whitonia. *Phil Kempsey*

Reederei Andre Wieczorek GmbH. Yvonne. *Hans Kraijenbosch*

Name	Flag	Year	GT	DWT	Loa	Bm	Drt	Kts	Type	Remarks
Marc-Andre *	Atg	2007	2,528	3,568	90.0	12.5	5.3	13	Cc	
Yvonne *	Ant	2008	2,528	3,500	90.0	12.5	5.3	13	Cc	

operated by Wagenborg Shipping BV qv

Charles M Willie & Co (Shipping) Ltd UK

Funnel: Blue with Welsh flag (red dragon on white over green halves). **Hull:** Dark blue with red boot-topping. **History:** Founded 1938 as Charles M Willie & Co to 1978. **Web:** www.williegroup.co.uk

Name	Flag	Year	GT	DWT	Loa	Bm	Drt	Kts	Type	Remarks
Celtic Ambassador	Gbr	1994	3,739	5,788	92.8	17.1	6.5	13	Cc	ex Lucy Borchard-06, Celtic Ambassador-05, Fairwind-96, Celtic Ambassador-94
Celtic Carrier	Gbr	1985	2,565	3,020	89.1	13.0	4.6	11	Cc	ex Buxtehude-06, Rita-95
Celtic Challenger	Gbr	1990	2,642	3,100	90.0	13.0	4.6	12	Cc	ex Atlantic Coast-08, Apus-03, Anke Ehler-98
Celtic Commander	Gbr	1993	3,840	5,833	92.8	17.2	6.5	13	Cc	ex Johanna Borchard-06, Celtic Commander-05, Fairway-96, Celtic Commander-94
Celtic Endeavour	Gbr	1985	2,568	3,070	88.0	12.8	4.3	10	Cc	ex Wahlstedt-06, Hampoel-02, Wahlstedt-97, Monika Ehler-95
Celtic Forester	Gbr	1985	2,564	3,050	87.9	12.8	5.0	11	Cc	ex Jork-06, Anita B-01, Spica-94
Celtic Fortune	Bhs	1984	2,119	3,042	92.1	11.5	4.7	11	Cc	ex Birgit Sabban-04
Celtic Freedom	Bhs	1986	2,120	3,028	92.1	11.5	4.7	10	Cc	ex Marlies Sabban-06, Petra Gunda-95
Celtic King	Gbr	1999	4,015	6,250	99.4	17.2	6.4	15	Cc	ex Emily Borchard-07, Celtic King-03
Celtic Mariner	Bhs	1986	1,957	2,886	87.9	11.5	4.7	11	Cc	ex Muhlenberg-06
Celtic Navigator	Gbr	1990	2,660	3,240	90.0	13.0	4.6	11	Cc	ex Atlantic Sea-08, Hera-03
Celtic Pioneer	Gbr	1985	2,561	3,065	87.9	12.9	4.6	11	Cc	ex Leeswig-06, Claus Jurgens-93
Celtic Spirit	Bhs	1976	2,978	4,001	91.1	14.6	6.8	13	Cc	ex Gardsky-03, Isnes-94, Dollart-87
Celtic Venture	Gbr	1990	2,606	3,647	88.0	13.0	5.2	11	Cc	ex Radesforde-06, Johanna-98
Celtic Voyager	Bhs	1985	1,957	2,890	88.0	11.3	4.7	11	Cc	ex Waseberg-05

Wilson ASA Norway

Funnel: Light blue with dark blue 'W' interrupting dark blue band on red edged broad white band, black top. **Hull:** Light blue or dark grey with white 'WILSON', red boot-topping. **History:** Founded 2000 to take over coaster assets of Euro Carriers AS, formed in 1993 as a joint venture between Paal Wilson & Co (founded 1942) and AS Kristian Jebsens Rederi (founded 1929). Wilson share sold to Jebsen in 1996, but Euro Carriers then acquired by Wilson in 1997. Jebsen is no longer related. **Web:** www.wilsonship.no

Name	Flag	Year	GT	DWT	Loa	Bm	Drt	Kts	Type	Remarks
ECL Challenger **	Brb	1995	3,833	4,635	100.6	16.5	5.9	15	Cc	ex Stephan J-06, Mekong Pioneer-06, Stephan J-00
ECL Commander	Brb	1997	3,850	4,766	100.6	15.5	5.9	15	Cc	ex Doris-08, APL Coronado-06, P&O Nedlloyd Trinidad-06, Doris J-00
Ferro †	Bhs	1991	1,986	3,504	88.2	14.2	5.0	12	Cc	
Jumbo	Bhs	1987	1,998	3,697	88.2	14.2	5.0	12	C	
Leiro	Bhs	1981	2,468	3,053	97.9	13.7	4.5	11	C	(len-86)
Lindo	Bhs	1982	2,468	3,580	98.1	13.7	5.2	11	C	(len-86)
Plato	Brb	1989	1,990	3,677	88.2	14.0	5.3	12	C	
Pluto	Bhs	1986	1,998	3,697	88.1	14.0	5.0	10	C	
Salmo	Bhs	1979	2,171	3,225	91.6	14.1	5.1	11	C	(len-83)
Tinno	Bhs	1991	1,986	3,504	88.2	14.2	5.0	12	Cc	
Torpo †	Bhs	1990	1,986	3,504	88.2	14.2	4.9	12	Cc	
Wilson Bar	Mlt	1979	3,967	6,105	107.0	15.0	6.5	13	C	ex Wilson Korsnes-02, Korsnes-00, General Ricarte-92, Korsnes-88 (len-83)
Wilson Bilbao *	Cyp	1992	2,446	3,735	87.9	12.8	4.5	10	Cc	ex Niklas-08, Padua-99
Wilson Blythe	Mlt	1995	2,446	3,713	87.9	12.8	5.5	11	Cc	ex Kapitan Drobinin-04
Wilson Borg	Mlt	1994	2,446	3,714	87.9	12.9	5.5	11	Cc	ex Northern Linanes-02
Wilson Bremen	Mlt	1992	2,446	3,735	87.9	12.8	5.5	10	Cc	ex Helen-08, Pandora-99
Wilson Brest	Mlt	1995	2,446	3,712	88.0	12.9	5.5	11	Cc	ex Northern Lesnes-02
Wilson Brugge	Mlt	1996	2,446	3,694	88.0	12.8	5.5	11	Cc	ex Northern Larsnes-03
Wilson Cadiz	Brb	1999	2,997	4,450	99.9	12.8	5.7	13	Cc	ex Dutch Sun-06
Wilson Caen †	Brb	1998	2,999	4,452	99.9	12.8	5.7	13	Cc	ex Dutch Navigator-04
Wilson Clyde	Brb	1998	2,997	4,450	99.9	12.8	5.7	13	Cc	ex Dutch Trader-4, Admiral Sun-01
Wilson Cork †	Brb	1998	2,999	4,444	99.9	12.8	5.7	13	Cc	ex Dutch Express-04
Wilson Dover	Atg	1993	2,480	3,269	87.5	13.0	5.1	12	Cc	ex Hanseatic Spring-07, P&O Nedlloyd Spring-05, Anna J-05, Admiral Sky-01, Anna J-01, MF Egypt-99, Intermodal Egypt-96, Anna J-93
Wilson Dvina	Atg	1992	2,481	3,221	87.4	13.0	5.1	12	Cc	ex Hanseatic Swift-06, P&O Nedlloyd Swift-05, Heide J-05, Eastmed-02, Zim Eastmed-02, MF Carrier-99, Intermodal Carrier-96, Rhein Carrier-95, Heide J-93
Wilson Elbe	Mlt	1993	1,589	2,682	82.4	11.4	4.8	9	Cc	ex Johann-07, Heinrich Bojen-98
Wilson Ems	Brb	1995	989	1,536	72.5	9.5	4.1	11	Cc	ex Fundo-07, Preussen-95
Wilson Fjord	Brb	1977	2,764	3,283	95.2	13.8	4.9	13	Cc	ex Victoria-02, Continental Alpha-94, Commodore S-94, Scott Survivor-92, Commodore Enterprise-87
Wilson Gaeta	Brb	1998	2,446	3,750	87.9	12.9	5.5	10	Cc	ex Hermann Sibum-06, Northern Lake-02
Wilson Garston	Brb	1989	2,270	2,801	82.3	12.5	4.9	11	Cc	ex Hanseatic Sun-05, Pionier-03
Wilson Gdansk	Brb	1993	2,514	3,610	87.8	12.9	5.5	11	Cc	ex Carrier-05, Seaprincess-98, Rugen-97
Wilson Ghent	Mlt	1996	2,446	3,670	88.0	12.8	5.5	11	Cc	ex Northern Loknes-04

Charles M. Willie & Co. Celtic Endeavour. *David Walker*

Charles M. Willie & Co. Celtic Fortune. *David Walker*

Name	Flag	Year	GT	DWT	Loa	Bm	Drt	Kts	Type	Remarks
Wilson Goole	Mlt	1995	2,446	3,712	88.0	12.9	5.5	11	Cc	ex Northern Loftnes-02
Wilson Grimsby	Brb	1993	2,506	3,650	87.7	12.8	5.5	11	Cc	ex Express-05, Seapride Spirit-98, Poel-97
Wilson Grip	Mlt	1996	2,446	3,680	87.9	12.9	5.5	10	Cc	ex Northern Liftnes-02
Wilson Harrier	Mlt	1993	2,811	4,206	91.2	13.8	5.8	12	Cc	ex Laura Helena-08
Wilson Hawk	Brb	1994	2,811	4,206	91.2	13.9	5.8	12	Cc	ex Haugo-06, I/a Niels
Wilson Heron	Mlt	1994	2,901	4,206	91.2	13.8	5.8	12	Cc	ex Garmo-08, I/a Ilka
Wilson Humber	Brb	1999	3,092	4,250	89.9	15.2	5.2	12	C	ex Marble Bay-05, I/a Stone
Wilson Husum	Brb	1998	3,092	4,250	89.9	15.2	5.2	13	C	ex Marble Sea-05, I/a Marble
Wilson Lahn	Atg	2001	1,559	2,500	83.2	11.0	4.7	12	Cc	ex Moravia-04
Wilson Leer	Mlt	1996	2,246	3,695	87.9	12.9	5.5	10	Cc	ex Northern Langnes-02
Wilson Leith	Mlt	1997	2,446	3,695	88.0	12.8	5.5	11	Cc	ex Northern Launes-02
Wilson Lista	Atg	1994	2,446	3,717	87.9	12.8	5.5	12	Cc	ex Wani Venture-04, Venture-02, Sea Severn-01, Venture-00, MSC Venture-99, Lys Trader
Wilson Maas	Brb	1998	1,169	1,863	78.3	9.5	4.4	12	Cc	ex Purdubice-01
Wilson Main	Brb	1990	1,690	1,857	82.5	11.4	4.5	10	Cc	ex Pola-04, Heinke-98
Wilson Malm	Mlt	1980	3,967	5,995	107.0	15.0	6.5	13	C	ex Garnes-02, General Campos-92, Garnes-86 (len-83)
Wilson Malo *	Cyp	1978	4,061	6,350	105.6	14.9	6.8	11	Cc	ex Blankenes-95, Black Sea-93
Wilson Mar	Mlt	1985	6.483	9,655	122.5	18.5	7.6	13	C	ex Selas-05, Sider Sky-02, Zapata-00, Cynthia Green-97, Zapata-96, Iron Toi-95, Lex Cerezo-94, Liria-89
Wilson Marin	Mlt	1978	3,949	5,800	105.7	15.4	6.9	13	B	ex Fromnes-03, Framnes-98 (len-84)
Wilson Mersin	Cyp	1981	3,937	6,186	106.9	15.0	6.7	13	C	ex Ramnes-04, Raknes-95, Eemnes-92, Raknes-86
Wilson Mo	Mlt	1975	3,658	5,790	102.0	15.6	6.9	13	B	ex Rocknes-02, Alexis-99, Rocknes-93
Wilson Mosel	Mlt	1993	1,589	2,694	82.6	11.4	4.8	9	Cc	ex Neermoor-07
Wilson Reef	Mlt	1975	3,842	6,258	103.5	16.1	7.0	12	B	ex Refsnes-03, Saint Brevin-00, Refsnes-83
Wilson Rhine	Brb	1998	1,169	1,850	78.3	9.5	4.4	10	Cc	ex Lovosice-00
Wilson Riga	Brb	1976	3,890	6,085	103.6	16.0	7.0	12	B	ex Risnes-03, General Luna-90, Ronnes-85
Wilson Ross	Mlt	1975	3,883	6,258	103.5	16.1	7.6	12	B	ex Rossnes-04, Saint Brice-00, Rossnes-82
Wilson Rouen	Brb	1976	3,885	6,258	103.6	16.0	6.9	13	B	ex Rafnes-03, General Garcia-89, Rafnes-86
Wilson Rough	Mlt	1976	3,885	6,258	103.6	16.0	7.0	13	B	ex Radnes-04, Lugano-89, Radnes-84
Wilson Ruhr	Brb	1997	1,169	1,831	78.3	9.5	4.4	12	Cc	ex Pilsen-01
Wilson Saar	Brb	1996	1,043	1,687	73.2	9.5	4.4	10	Cc	ex A. Wetzel-01
Wilson Saga	Cyp	1998	4,197	6,254	112.7	15.2	6.5	13	C	ex Borealnes-03, I/a Boreal
Wilson Skaw	Bhs	1996	4,197	6,254	112.7	15.2	6.6	13	C	ex Elianna-02, Langenes-98
Wilson Split	Brb	1977	3,885	6,258	103.6	16.0	6.9	13	B	ex Reksnes-08, General Valeriano-92, Reksnes-86
Wilson Stadt	Mlt	2000	4,200	6,463	112.7	15.2	6.7	12	C	ex Linito-06
Wilson Sund	Cyp	1999	4,200	6,274	112.7	15.2	6.7	12	C	ex Isnes-05
Wilson Tana	Mlt	1977	4,907	7,174	110.6	17.6	7.0	15	Cc	ex Husnes-02, Hook Head-93, Sumburgh Head-90
Wilson Tees	Mlt	1997	2,446	3,695	88.0	12.8	5.5	11	Cc	ex Northern Lurnes-02
Wilson Trent	Cyp	1980	4,924	7,160	110.6	17.6	7.0	12	C	ex Hernes-04, Rora Head-93
Wilson Tyne	Mlt	1980	4,913	7,107	110.6	17.6	7.0	12	C	ex Hordnes -03, Barra Head-96
Wilson Waal	Brb	1999	1,169	1,850	78.3	9.5	4.4	12	Cc	ex Podebrady-02

Newbuildings: Eight 4,500 dwt and eight 8,000 dwt general cargo vessels for 2010-11 delivery.
Owned. Managed or operated by Wilson Ship AS (founded 1997), Wilson Management AS (founded 1991 as Jebsens Thun Management AS to 1995 and Jebsens Management AS to 1998) or Wilson Ship Management AS (founded 1988 as Jebsens Ship Management to 1989 and Jebsens Ship Management (Bergen) AS to 1998)
* owned or managed by WEC - Wilson Euro Carriers AS (founded 1998 as Jebsens EuroCarriers AS)
** owned by Euro Container Line AS (formed 2006 jointly by subsidiary Wilson Euro Carriers AS and Eimskip)
† managed for parent Actinor Shipping ASA.

Wind   Netherlands

Funnel: *Blue.* **Hull:** *Blue with red boot-topping.* **History:** *Founded 1990 as Jan Wind Shipping BV to 2008.* **Web:** *www.wind.nl*

Name	Flag	Year	GT	DWT	Loa	Bm	Drt	Kts	Type	Remarks
Aniek	Atg	1978	1,008	1,559	65.8	10.7	4.3	11	C	ex Agnes-06, Expansa II-85
Layla *	Atg	1975	1,010	1,559	65.9	10.7	4.3	10	C	ex Blue Moon-04, Elina-97, Elina B-90, Elisabeth Holwerda-87 (rblt-08)
Lida	Atg	1974	992	1,482	65.3	10.8	4.2	11	C	ex Vissersbank-90, Spray-86, Arina Holwerda-81 (rblt-99)
Suzie Q	Atg	1983	1,980	3,008	81.7	14.0	5.4	11	C	ex Johanna Trader-02, Vrouwe Johanna-95,

* managed for Layla Shipping BV (founded 2004 – www.mvlayla.nl)

Wind Shipping ApS   Denmark

Funnel: *White.* **Hull:** *Blue or red with red boot-topping.* **History:** *Founded 1993.* **Web:** *www.windship.dk*

Name	Flag	Year	GT	DWT	Loa	Bm	Drt	Kts	Type	Remarks
Atiu	Cok	1990	3,113	3,487	92.7	15.1	5.6	12	Cc	ex Irbe Loja-08, Angola Express-07, Bristol Strait-05, Marie-Therese-03, Straits Joy-98, Wotan-96, Frank Konecny-95
Drawa	Pol	1978	1,575	1,500	84.3	10.8	3.8	10	Cc	ex Amstelborg-99, Rhein-90, Rheintal-88
Irbe Venta	Lva	1985	2,816	2,923	91.3	13.8	4.4	11	Cc	ex Sophie O-06, Bremer Anna-04, Aros News-02, Nioba-97, Bremer Import-91, Nioba-89, Rudolf Karstens-87
Tenedos	Pan	1980	2,854	3,124	95.7	13.5	4.8	10	Cc	ex Hermod-08, Gutshof-01, Hermod-00, Herm J-89

Also see Jan Stepniewski I S-Ka Sp z oo, Poland and Baltramp Shipping Sp z oo.

Name	Flag	Year	GT	DWT	Loa	Bm	Drt	Kts	Type	Remarks

Reederei Gebr Winter GmbH & Co KG — Germany

Funnel: *White.* **Hull:** *Black with red boot-topping.* **History:** *Founded 1991 as Schiffahrtskontor Reederei Gebruder Winter to 1999.* **Web:** *www.winter-ship.de*

Name	Flag	Year	GT	DWT	Loa	Bm	Drt	Kts	Type	Remarks
Carat	Cyp	2009	9,983	12,270	140.7	23.2	8.7	18	CC	
Celtic	Cyp	2009	9,000	12,200	140.7	23.2	8.7	18	CC	
Ceres	Cyp	2009	9,000	12,200	140.7	23.2	8.7	18	CC	
Cimbria	Deu	1998	3,999	5,350	101.1	18.7	6.6	15	CC	ex Comet-08
Condor	Cyp	2009	9,000	12,200	140.7	23.2	8.7	18	CC	
Conger	Atg	1995	3,999	5,207	101.2	18.5	6.6	15	Cc	ex Holger-05, UB Lion-97, Holger-95

Newbuildings Three further 9,000 gt feeder container ships on order for 2010-11 delivery.:
Also owns 13 larger container ships.

Reederei Heino Winter KG — Germany

Funnel: *White or charterers colours.* **Hull:** *Blue with red boot-topping.* **History:** *Founded 1988.* **Web:** *www.ing-buero-winter.de*

Name	Flag	Year	GT	DWT	Loa	Bm	Drt	Kts	Type	Remarks
Beluga Endurance	Atg	2005	9.611	12,806	138.1	21.0	8.0	15	C/hl	
Beluga Energy	Atg	2005	9.611	12,806	138.1	21.0	8.0	15	C/hl	
Beluga Expectation	Atg	2005	9.611	12,806	138.1	21.0	8.0	15	C/hl	
Beluga Fighter	Atg	2007	9.611	12,782	138.1	21.0	8.0	15	C/hl	
Mareike	Deu	1996	5,544	7,061	117.9	19.4	7.5	16	CC	ex Wellington Express-02

Wisby Tankers AB — Sweden

Funnel: *Dark blue with red ' ' on broad white band.* **Hull:** *Dark blue with grey boot-topping.* **History:** *Founded 1999.* **Web:** *www.wisbytankers.se*

Name	Flag	Year	GT	DWT	Loa	Bm	Drt	Kts	Type	Remarks
Wisby Argan	Nis	2009	4,500	7,400	116.4	15.0	6.8	13	T	
Wisby Verity	Swe	2004	4,295	7,479	116.4	15.0	6.8	13	T	
Wisby Wave	Swe	2009	4,263	7,478	116.4	15.0	6.8	13	T	

Newbuildings: Three further 7,400 dwt tankers on order.

Wrist Group A/S — Denmark

Funnel: *White with black 'W' inside red ring.* **Hull:** *Black with red boot-topping.* **History:** *Founded 1953 and sold 2007 to equity fund group 'Altor'.* **Web:** *www.wrist.com*

Name	Flag	Year	GT	DWT	Loa	Bm	Drt	Kts	Type	Remarks
Otilia	Dmk	1989	5,525	8,828	113.4	18.0	8.3	13	T	ex Tarnsund-05
OW Aalborg	Dis	2005	3,021	3,522	90.5	14.6	5.4	11	Tch	ex Clipper Barolo-08, Crescent Barolo-05
OW Atlantic	Dis	2002	4,341	6,019	103.2	15.0	6.8	14	T	ex Keilir-08 (len-03)
OW Baltic	Dis	2005	2,143	3,813	83.4	12.9	5.7	-	T	ex Octavia-08
OW Copenhagen	Dis	2006	3,021	3,548	83.4	12.9	5.7	11	Tch	ex Clipper Barbera-08
OW Scandinavia	Dis	2006	2,143	3,807	84.4	12.9	5.7	-	T	ex Olina-06
Sinbad	Nis	1981	5,582	8,145	112.7	17.5	8.2	14	C/T	ex Kemira-04
Sunbeam *	Pan	1975	318	420	43.3	8.1	3.0	9	T	ex Nosal-91
Tinka	Pan	1972	2,097	3,205	91.3	13.7	5.3	12	T	ex Inka-90

Newbuildings: Two 4,250 dwt and two 8,000 dwt tankers on order for 2010 delivery.
*Owned by subsidiaries OW Bunker & Trading AS (founded 1981 – www.owbunker.com) and OW Tankers AS (founded 2008) or * Alba Shipping Ltd A/S (founded 1982 - www.albaship.com).*

Zagranperevozk VF — Russia

Funnel: *White with dark blue anchor symbol or orange.* **Hull:** *Black with red boot-topping.* **History:** *Founded 2000 and controlled by the Government of The Russian Federation.* **Web:** *www.volgaflot.com*

Name	Flag	Year	GT	DWT	Loa	Bm	Drt	Kts	Type	Remarks
Bersut *	(2) Rus	1980	1,522	1,755	82.0	11.8	3.4	8	Cc	
Bratislava *	Rus	1994	2,446	3,718	87.9	12.8	5.2	12	Cc	
Druzhba Narodov	(2) Rus	1979	2,827	3,146	118.8	13.2	3.7	11	C	
Ivan Shchepetov	(2) Rus	1994	3,376	3,186	102.3	16.4	4.2	13	Cc	
Kapitan Belodvortsev *	(2) Rus	1986	1,628	1,209	85.9	12.2	2.6	10	C	ex ST-1376-86
Krasnovidovo	(2) Rus	1980	1,522	1,625	82.0	11.6	2.5	-	Cc	
Professor Tronin	(2) Rus	1984	1,766	1,777	86.7	12.3	3.0	10	Cc	ex ST-1308-98
Roskem	(2) Rus	1990	1,814	2,831	89.1	12.4	4.2	10	T	ex ST-1349-04 (conv C-04)
Roskem 1	(2) Rus	1990	1,814	2,821	86.7	12.0	4.2	10	T	ex Aleksandr Demidov-04, ST1345 (conv C-04)
Sergey Losev	(2) Rus	1983	2,466	3,134	114.0	13.2	3.7	10	C	ex Sormovskiy 46-92
Sibirskiy-2129 *	(2) Rus	1983	3,415	3,052	128.4	15.4	3.2	11	Cc	
Sormovskiy-44	(2) Rus	1981	2,484	3,134	114.2	13.2	3.4	10	C	
Sormovskiy-3048	(2) Rus	1982	3,041	3,135	119.2	13.4	3.8	11	Cc	ex XVII Syezd Profsoyuzov-92
Sormovskiy-3049	(2) Rus	1982	3,041	3,134	119.2	13.4	3.8	10	Cc	ex XI Pyatiletka-92
Sormovskiy-3050	(2) Rus	1983	3,041	3,135	118.8	13.4	3.8	10	Cc	ex 0065 Let Sovetskoy Vlasti-93
Sormovskiy-3051	(2) Rus	1984	3,041	3,134	119.0	13.0	3.8	11	Cc	
Sormovskiy-3052	(2) Rus	1984	3,041	3,134	119.2	13.4	3.8	10	Cc	
Sormovskiy-3053	(2) Rus	1985	3,041	3,134	119.1	13.4	3.8	11	Cc	
Sormovskiy-3054	(2) Rus	1985	3,041	3,134	119.1	13.4	3.7	10	Cc	
Sovietskaya Rodina	(2) Rus	1979	2,827	3,146	118.8	13.2	3.7	11	C	

Name		Flag	Year	GT	DWT	Loa	Bm	Drt	Kts	Type	Remarks
Volga-35	(2)	Rus	1995	4,955	5,885	139.9	16.7	4.5	10	C	
Volgo-Don 238	(2)	Rus	1980	2,968	3,853	107.1	16.5	3.7	10	C	
Volzhskiy-7	(2)	Rus	1984	3,070	3,709	107.4	16.7	3.7	10	C	
Volzhskiy-8	(2)	Rus	1984	3,070	3,709	107.4	16.7	3.7	10	C	
Volzhskiy-10	(2)	Rus	1984	3,070	3,546	107.4	16.7	3.6	10	C	(short-95)
Yakov Vorobyov	(2)	Rus	1985	2,466	3,135	114.0	13.0	3.7	10	C	

*managed by Volga-Neva Ltd, Russia or * by JSC Volga Shipping (www.volgaflot.com)*

Zirkel Verwaltungs GmbH Germany

Funnel: *Dark blue.* **Hull:** *Dark blue with red boot-topping.* **History:** *Founded 1994 as Helmship GmbH.* **Web:** *www.zirkel-services.de*

Amica		Atg	1993	2,400	3,300	85.4	12.6	5.2	13	Cc	ex Tainui-01

Wilson ASA. Ferro. *N. Kemps*

Wilson ASA. Wilson Reef. *C. Lous*

Index

Flinter Groep. UAL Africa. *Hans Kraijenbosch*

Name	Pg	Name	Pg	Name	Pg	Name	Pg	Name	Pg	Name	Pg
Fletum	67	Fri Tide	124	Giessenborg	90	Hako	130	Helga	203	Ijsseldijk	162
Fleurgracht	171	Fri Wave	124	Gina R	173	Halland	132	Helgafell	159	Ilka	52
Flevodijk	162	Frida	136	Gina	122	Hamilton Strait	76	Helgaland	111	Ilse	136
Flevogracht	173	Frida	201	Girvas	147	Hamlet	33	Helgoland	132	Imel Abdena	63
Flinteramerica	95	Friedrich Russ	158	Gitana	49	Hammerodde	8	Helgoland	18	Imi	132
Flinterarctic	95	Friesedijk	162	Gitana	53	Hamnavoe	10	Heli194		Imina	70
Flinteratlantic	95	Friesian Express	203	Gitta Kosan	125	Hamra	100	Helle	114	Imke	198
Flinterbaltica	95	Friesland	18	Glen	194	Haneburg	150	Hellevik	191	Impala	81
Flinterbay	95	Frifjord	124	Global Earth	71	Hanna C	74	Helma	151	Ina	56
Flinterbelt	95	Frigg Sydfyen	25	Global Hebe	99	Hanna	47	Helmut	117	Independent	188
Flinterbirka	95	Frigg	95	Global Hekate	99	Hanne Danica	96	Helmuth Rambow	152	India	56
Flinterboreas	95	Frigga	50	Global Helena	99	Hanne Theresa	111	Helse	178	Indian	130
Flinterborg	95	Frisia Aller	106	Global Helios	99	Hannelore	186	Helsinki	63	Industrial Cape	120
Flinterbothnia	96	Frisia I	25	Global Hemera	99	Hanni	144	Henan Scan	159	Industrial Century	120
Flinterbright	96	Frisia II	25	Global Hera	99	Hanoi	67	Hendrika Margaretha	173	Industrial Champ	120
Flinterbrise	96	Frisia Inn	106	Global Hermes	99	Hans Lehmann	128	Hendrik-S	174	Industrial Crescent	120
Flintercape	96	Frisia IV	25	Global Hestia	99	Hans Specht	66	Henneke Rambow	152	Industrial Dart	120
Flintercarrier	96	Frisia Lahn	106	Global Lake	71	Hanse Confidence	184	Henny	96	Industrial Dawn	120
Flinterclear	96	Frisia Spree	106	Global Libra	72	Hanse Courage	184	Henriette	130	Industrial Destiny	120
Flintercoast	96	Frisia V	25	Global Moon	72	Hanse Spirit	184	Henrike Schepers	112	Industrial Diamond	120
Flintercoral	96	Frisian Lady	66	Global Ocean	72	Hanse Vision	184	Henry Schulte	164	Industrial Dolphin	120
Flintercrown	96	Frisian Sky	67	Global River	72	Hanseatic Sailor	66	Hera	60	Industrial Dream	120
Flinterdijk	96	Frisian Spring	66	Global Sea	72	Hanseatic Scout	66	Herakles	206	Industrial Eagle	120
Flinterduin	96	Frisian Summer	66	Global Star	72	Hanseatic Sea	66	Hereford Express	203	Industrial Egret	120
Flintereems	96	Frisian Sun	67	Global Sun	72	Hanseatic Spirit	66	Herm J	120	Industrial Leader	66
Flinterforest	96	Frisian Trader	70	Global Taurus	72	Hanseatic Star	66	Herm Kiepe	160	Ines	105
Flinterfortune	96	Frisiana	66	Globia	100	Hanseatic Swan	66	Herm	192	Ines Bolten	63
Flinterfury	96	Frisium	66	Gloria	109	Hanseatic Trader	66	Hermann Scan	70	Inga H	153
Flinterhaven	96	Froan	59	Glory	56	Hanseduo	184	Hermann W	183	Inga Lena	152
Flinterhunze	96	Frontier Challenger	95	Glory	72	Hansen Scan	70	Herrentor	150	Ingeborg Pilot	95
Flinterjute	96	Fryken	46	Golf	194	Hansewall	184	Hertfordshire	60	Ingrid Jakobsen	79
Flinterland	96	Furioso	168	Golo River	100	Happy Bee	162	Hestia	128	Ingrid	79
Flinterlinge	96	Furnas	120	Gongora	128	Happy Bird	162	Hjaltland	10	Ingrid	99
Flintermaas	96	Futura Carrier	173	Gooteborg	90	Happy Bride	162	Hjordis	125	Ingunn	124
Flintermar	96	Fykan	142	Gorky	206	Happy Eagle	162	Hoburgen	129	Ingvild	176
Flinterrachel	96	Gaastborg	90	Gotaland	33	Happy Fellow	162	Hogeland	160	Innes	95
Flinterrebecca	96	Gabriella	42	Gotaland	56	Happy Girl	162	Hohebank	152	Inowroclaw	22
Flinterschelde	96	Gala	194	Gotland	132	Happy Harrier	162	Hoheplate	152	Inzhener Plavinskiy	139
Flinterspace	96	Galan	191	Gotland	70	Harilaid	30	Hoheriff	152	Iogann Makhmastal	139
Flinterspirit	96	Galaxy	36	Gotland	112	Harmony	152	Hohesand	152	Irafoss	86
Flinterspring	96	Galileusz	42	Gotland	14	Harpa Doris	198	Holandia	56	Irbe Venta	212
Flinterstream	96	Galway Fisher	93	Gotlandia	14	Hartland Point	22	Holger Dansk	33	Irene	105
Flintersuomi	96	Gammagas	170	Gotlandia II	14	Hartwig Scan	70	Holland Klipper	165	Irene Theresa	111
Flintersurf	96	Gardenia	40	Gouweborg	90	Hascosay	10	Hollum	67	Irene V	99
Flinterwave	96	Gas Pioneer	162	Goyen	165	Hathor	152	Holmfoss	86	Iris 1	174
Flinterzee	96	Gas Renovatio	162	Gracechurch Jupiter	120	Haugaard Scan	159	Holstentor	178	Iris Bolten	63
Floragracht	173	Gaschem Atlantic	106	Grachtborg	90	Haukur	134	Hrossey	10	Irtysh 1	116
Florence	105	Gaschem Atrice	162	Graf Uko	125	Hav Dolphin	109	Huckleberry Finn	42	Irtysh 2	116
Floretgracht	171	Gaschem Baltic	106	Granat	55	Hav Marlin	109	Hudson Strait	76	Isabella Kosan	125
Floretgracht	173	Gaschem Ben Flor	162	Grand	191	Hav Snapper	109	Hudson	104	Isabella	116
Floria	60	Gaschem Caribic	106	Grasmere	131	Hav Zander	109	Hudsonborg	203	Isabella	42
Fokko Ukena	63	Gaschem Dollart	106	Green Bergen	100	Havblik	59	Huelin Dispatch	114	Isar Highway	120
Fonnland	133	Gaschem Hunte	106	Green Cooler	100	Havglott	59	Huelin Endeavour	114	Isartal	111
Forester	158	Gaschem Ice	109	Green Explorer	100	Havhelt	59	Humber Endeavour	208	Isidor	74
Forseti	50	Gaschem Isar	106	Green Fast	133	Havstein	59	Humber Fisher	95	Isis	204
Fort Azov	97	Gaschem Jade	106	Green Freezer	100	Havstraum	196	Humber Pride	208	Isis	47
Fort Knox	97	Gaschem Jumme	106	Green Frost	100	Heather C	74	Humber Princess	208	Islander	70
Fort Ross	97	Gaschem Mosel	106	Green Ice	102	Hebridean Isles	10	Humber Progress	208	Islandia	109
Forte	129	Gaschem Pacific	106	Green Iceland	102	Hebrides	10	Humber Viking	16	Islay Trader	93
Forte	134	Gaschem Phoenix	106	Green Karmoy	102	Hege	52	Humberborg	204	Isle of Arran	10
Fortes	168	Gaschem Rhone	106	Green Klipper	102	Heidi	176	Hunteborg	204	Isle of Inishmore	24
Forth Fisher	93	Gaschem Shinano	106	Green Neptunic	102	Heike Lehmann	128	Hunze Trader	70	Isle of Lewis	10
Fortunagracht	173	Gaschem Weser	106	Green Nova	102	Hein	117	Hunzeborg	204	Isle of Mull	10
Fortunia	56	Geert K	120	Green Ocean	102	Heinrich Essberger	90	Hunzedijk	162	Ivan Ryabov	139
Forum Fiji II	150	Geest Trader	124	Green Spring	102	Heinrich G	99	Hurst Point	22	Ivan Shchepetov	213
Forza	152	Geise	67	Green Summer	102	Heinrich J	120	Husky Racer	152	Ivan Zhdanov	49
Fostraum	196	Geja C	74	Green Tromso	102	Heinrich Sibum	168	Husky Runner	152	Iver Balance	202
Frakt	159	Gelre	203	Green Winter	102	Heinrich	148	Hydra	204	Iver Beauty	202
Frakto	159	Genca	34	Greetsiel	62	Heinz Schepers	112	Hyundai Britania	159	Iver Best	202
Fram	24	Georg Essberger	90	Greta C	74	Hekla	203	Hyundai Buffalo	159	Iver Bitumen	202
Frances Wonsild	138	Georgina PG	72	Greta Kosan	125	Hela	60	Ibiza Cement	117	Ivy	144
Francop	56	Gerarda	96	Greta	116	Helane	91	Ice Bird	62	Jacaranda	63
Frank W	208	Gerd Sibum	168	Grietje	109	Helas	129	Ice Moon	62	Jacobus Broere	90
Franklin Strait	76	Gerd	192	Griftborg	90	Heleen C	74	Ice Runner	62	Jacqueline	105
Franz Schulte	162	Gerd	194	Grimm	134	Helen	53	Ice Star	186	Jade C	74
Frelon	53	Gerda	151	Grinna	133	Helena Kosan	125	Ice Sun	62	Jade	104
Freya	112	Gerda	152	Groningerland	18	Helena Sibum	168	Iceland Cement	117	Jade	196
Freyja	95	Gerhard G	99	Gryf	42	Helene	160	Icelandica Hav	109	Jade	204
Fri Lake	124	Gerhein G	99	Gudrun	83	Helene G	99	ID Trader	60	Jago	59
Fri Moon	124	German Bay	206	Gute	8	Helene H	112	ID Tuxpan	60	James Prior	151
Fri Ocean	124	German Sky	206	Hafentor	150	Helene	173	Ida Theresa	111	Jamina	100
Fri Sea	124	Germania	106	Hagen	63	Helene	176	Ida 114		Jamtland	178
Fri Sky	124	Germanica Hav	109	Hagland Bona	102	Helenic	203	Idannus	167	Jan D	134
Fri Star	124	Gertrud G	99	Hagland Borg	102	Helga	201	Ideaal	49	Jan D	83
Fri Stream	124	Gertrud	83	Hagland Boss	102	Helga	55	Iduna	192	Jan Sniadecki	42
Fri Sun	124	Geulborg	90	Hajo	81	Helga	198	Ijsseldiep	108	Jan van Gent	204

Name	Page	Name	Page	Name	Page	Name	Page	Name	Page	Name	Page
Jan/V	202	Kalliope	148	Kliftrans	204	Lammy	173	Lisbeth	204	Magnolia 1	76
Jana	100	Kanhave	25	Klostertal	120	Lana II	167	Lisco Gloria	14	Mai Mols	25
Jana	116	Kapella	36	Knock	62	Lana	167	Lisco Maxima	14	Maido	106
Jana	144	Kapitan Abakumov	147	K-Ocean	123	Lancer	178	Lisco Optima	14	Maike D	83
Janet	111	Kapitan Babushkin	202	Kolguev	139	Landia	130	Lisco Patria	14	Maike	52
Janina	174	Kapitan Belodvortsev	213	Kollund	68	Landy	138	Liselotte Essberger	90	Maimiti	204
Janina	122	Kapitan Boldyrev	49	Komarno	114	Langeland	132	List	84	Main Highway	120
Janne Wonsild	138	Kapitan Ezovitov	202	Komet III	81	Langenes	134	Lister	191	Maineborg	204
Jannie C	74	Kapitan Galashin	202	Kong Harald	24	Lantau Bay	124	Listerland	191	Maingas	106
Jansum	67	Kapitan Konkin	147	Kongsvaag	102	Lantau Beach	124	Listervik	191	Maj Danielsen	191
Jarikaba	165	Kapitan Konshin	49	Koningsborg	171	Lantau Bee	124	Listraum	196	Maja	173
Jason	206	Kapitan Kozhevnikov	147	Konstantin		Lantau Breeze	124	Little Ann	131	Majala	134
Jaynee W	208	Kapitan Kuroptev	139	Paustovskiy	140	Lantau Bride	124	Little Jane	133	Malachit	91
Jeannette	204	Kapitan Kuznetsov	202	Kopernik	42	Lantau Bridge	124	Liv Kristin	198	Malena	178
Jens M	132	Kapitan Lus	139	Koralia	60	Lappland	111	Liv	206	Malene	50
Jerome H	111	Kapitan Mironov	139	Korgelaid	30	Lara	116	Liva Greta	151	Malmnes	186
Jessica B	56	Kapitan Ryntsyn	139	Koriangi	147	Larch	144	Livarden	139	Malou Theresa	111
Jetstream	124	Kapitan Sosenkov	49	Kornett	84	Larsediep	112	Liverpool Viking	16	Malta Cement	117
Jette Theresa	111	Kapitan Yakovlev	139	Korsika	63	Largo	129	Livia	130	Malte B	62
Jevenau	178	Kappagas	170	Kossau	178	Largo II	156	Livland	134	Malte Rambow	152
Jo Spirit	144	Kaprifol	198	Kosterberg	199	Largona	156	Lizrix	156	Malvern	131
Joan	91	Karel	147	Kovera	147	Lark	52	Lizzie Kosan	125	Manannan	24
Joanna Borchard	79	Karen C	74	Kraftca	34	Larkspur	40	Lodella	151	Manfred	83
Joerg N	183	Karin Lehmann	128	Krasnovidovo	213	Latana	196	Loenerdiep	108	Mangan	123
Johann Philipp Specht	66	Karin Rambow	152	Krasnoye Sormovo	49	Laura Ann	84	Lofoten	24	Maple	144
Johann	112	Karin Schepers	112	Krempertor	178	Laura	125	Loireborg	204	Marathon	49
Johanna	174	Karin	114	Kristin C	74	Laura-H	125	Lokys	148	Marc-Andre	210
Johanna C	74	Karin	56	Kristin D	198	Lauren C	74	Lolland	132	Marcel	63
Johanna Desiree	102	Karina C	74	Kristin Schepers	112	Lauwersborg	204	Lomur	134	Marchaser	130
Johanna Russ	158	Karina Danica	96	Kristina Theresa	111	Lavina	116	Lona	130	Mare	55
Johanna Schepers	112	Karina G	99	K-River	123	Lavinia	130	London Bridge	131	Mare	144
Johanna	196	Karina Theresa	111	Kronprins Frederik	33	Laxfoss	86	Lone Bres	136	Mare	173
Johanne	111	Karina W	206	Kroonborg	90	Layla	212	Longchamp	131	Mareike	213
John Augustus		Karina	122	Kruckau	178	Leandra	116	Longstone	22	Maren Mols	25
Essberger	90	Karla C	74	Kryssholm	198	Lecko	186	Lontano	152	Marfeeder	130
John Mitchell	208	Karl-Jakob K	120	K-Stream	123	Leeswig	132	Loodiep	108	Marfret Mejean	130
John-Paul K	120	Karmsund	136	Kuban	114	Leiro	210	Lord of the Isles	10	Marfret Niolon	130
Joker	178	Karsnes	165	Kugelbake	78	Leistein	148	Lore Prahm	102	Margareta B	160
Jolanda	156	Kaspar Schepers	112	Kukkelborg	67	Lelie	71	Lotus	170	Margaretha	112
Jolanta	74	Kasteelborg	79	Kurkse	191	Lemo	97	Lotus	71	Margita	181
Jolyn	204	Kastor	206	K-Water	123	Lena	109	Louise Borchard	196	Margrete C *	74
Jomi	132	Kate C	74	K-Wave	123	Lena	194	Loukhi	198	Marguerite	105
Jonathan Swift	24	Kate	167	Kwintebank	150	Lenaneft-2066	49	Loya	77	Mari	168
Jongleur	55	Katharina B	160	Kyholm	25	Lenglo	74	LS Anne	125	Maria Elise	112
Jonsen	132	Katharina Siemer	168	La Rochelle	58	Leona	68	LS Christine	125	Maria K	136
Jopi	168	Katharina	116	Laakdiep	112	Leonid Khotkin	147	LS Concorde	125	Maria Schepers	112
Jork	132	Katherine Borchard	81	Labici B	132	Leonid Leonov	140	LS Eva	125	Maria Sibum	168
Jork Ranger	58	Kathy C	74	Ladoga-3	50	Leonie	198	LS Jamie	125	Maria Theresa	111
Jork Reliance	58	Kati L	68	Ladoga-5	50	Leonora Kosan	125	Lucy Borchard	79	Maria	109
Jork Ruler	58	Katja	116	Ladoga-8	50	Leopard	136	Lucy PG	72	Marianna Kosan	128
Jorvik	96	Katre	122	Ladva	198	Lesley PG	72	Luhnau	178	Marianne Danica	96
Josefine	79	Kaunas	14	Lady Carina	173	Lettland	134	Lunamar	108	Marianne K	120
Jotagas	170	Kazakh	147	Lady Christina	173	Leuvediep	108	Luro	186	Marianne	91
Joy	84	K-Breeze	123	Lady Clarissa	173	Lexus	170	Lynx	136	Marie Christine	173
JRS Canis	160	KCL Ballerina	122	Lady Claudia	173	Leybucht	67	Lyrika	55	Marie Lehmann	128
JRS Capella	160	KCL Banshee	122	Lady Elena	170	Lezhevo	147	Lys Point	105	Mariella	42
JRS Carina	160	Keewhit	208	Lady Elena	162	Lia-C	129	Lysblink	79	Marietje Andrea	204
JRS Castor	160	Kegums	59	Lady Helene	173	Lian	130	Lysbris	79	Marietje Deborah	204
JRS Merkur	160	Keizersborg	79	Lady Hilde	162	Lianne	198	Lysfoss	79	Marin	130
JRS Pegassus	160	Kelarvi	147	Lady Inger	173	Liberta	81	Lystind	79	Marina	122
JSV Yaiza	124	Kelly C	74	Lady Irina	173	Libertas-H	196	Lysvik	79	Marinda	204
Juergen K	120	Kelt204		Lady Isabel	173	Lida	212	Maas Trader	70	Marinus	170
Julia	116	Kendal	131	Lady Kathleen	162	Lieke	136	Maas Viking	16	Marion K	123
Julia	18	Kento	147	Lady Kirsten	173	Liepajas	128	Maasborg	171	Maris	133
Julie C	74	Keret	147	Lady Magda	173	Lifana	118	Maasdiep	108	Marit	59
Julietta	116	Kergi	74	Lady Margaux	162	Lifter	178	Madeleine	105	Marita M	132
Jumbo	210	Kerry Express	203	Lady Marie Christine	173	Lijun C	74	Maersk Anglia	16	Marja	112
Jumbo Challenger	118	Keswick	131	Lady Martine	162	Liliana	174	Maersk Delft	16	Marjatta	125
Jumbo Spirit	118	Kevin S	122	Lady Mathilde	125	Lill	204	Maersk Dover	16	Marjesco	196
Jumbo Vision	118	Kholmogory	139	Lady Mathilde	173	Lilly Mitchell	208	Maersk Dunkerque	18	Mark Prior	151
Jummetor	150	Khudozhnik		Lady Menna	173	Lincoln Express	203	Maersk Erimo	63	Markborg	90
Jupiter I	139	Vetrogonskiy	140	Lady Nola	173	Linda Marijke	96	Maersk Exporter	18	Marlene	183
Jutland	132	Kiara	122	Lady Nona	173	Linda	125	Maersk Ferrol	97	Marlin	78
Jytte Bres	134	Kikke C	74	Lady Nora	173	Linda	204	Maersk Flanders	18	Marne	178
Kaami	132	Kilstraum	196	Lady Nova	173	Lindo	210	Maersk Flensburg	152	Marneborg	204
Kadri	122	Kine	196	Lady Olga	173	Line	204	Maersk Fuji	70	Marnedijk	162
Kagu	58	King of Scandinavia	14	Lady Stephanie	164	Linge Trader	70	Maersk Fukuoka	71	Marschenland	63
Kaie	122	Kinne	186	Lagan Viking	16	Lingeborg	204	Maersk Funchal	152	Marstan	192
Kaili	122	Kirsten K	136	Laganborg	204	Lingediep	108	Maersk Importer	18	Marsus	151
Kaisa	188	Kirsten	83	Laguepe	171	Lingedijk	162	Magda D	83	Marten	206
Kaja	122	Kivach	147	Laguepe	53	Link Star	100	Magda	129	Martha Russ	158
Kalana	191	Kizhi	147	Laguna	130	Linnau	178	Magdalena	91	Martin	52
Kalevala	147	Klaipeda	46	Laila 5	97	Lis Weber	111	Magdalena	112	Marus	160
Kalina	134	Klazina C	74	Laila II	55	Lisa C	74	Magdalena	47	Mary Christina	204
Kalitva	131	Klenoden	153	Laima	151	Lisa D	83	Magellan Planet	152	Mary Wonsild	138
Kalkvik	186	Klevstrand	139	Lamaro	130	Lisa S	156	Magellan Star	152	Matua II	162

Name	Page
Mauritz	104
Max	174
Max Mols	25
Max Planck	106
Maxima	116
May	144
Maya	194
Mazarine	12
MCC Chalice	68
MCL Alger	104
MCL Antwerpen	104
MCL Express	206
MCL Trader	131
MCL Tunis	90
MCP Alstertal	109
MCP Altona	109
MCP Amsterdam	108
MCP Bilbao	108
MCP Blankenese	109
MCP Famagusta	109
MCP Goteborg	109
MCP Graz	148
MCP Hamburg	109
MCP Harburg	109
MCP Kopenhagen	108
MCP Linz	148
MCP London	108
MCP Nicosia	109
MCP Pachna	109
MCP Paphos	109
MCP Rotterdam	108
MCP Salzburg	148
MCP Vienna	148
MCP Villach	148
Mecklenburg-Vorpommern	33
Medaegean	71
Medangara	71
Medarctic	71
Medbalkash	71
Medbaykal	71
Medbothnia	71
Medcaspian	71
Medemborg	90
Medonega	71
Medum	67
Meg	147
Mekhanik Brilin	139
Mekhanik Fomin	139
Mekhanik Kottsov	139
Mekhanik Kraskovskiy	139
Mekhanik Makarin	139
Mekhanik Pustoshnyy	139
Mekhanik Pyatin	140
Mekhanik Semakov	140
Mekhanik Tyulenev	140
Mekhanik Yartsev	140
Mekong River	201
Mekong	67
Melas	208
Melfi Caribe	178
Mell Saraca	106
Mell Saujana	184
Mell Seletar	62
Mell Sembawang	106
Mell Senang	62
Mell Senoko	201
Mell Sentosa	106
Mell Seraya	199
Melody	97
Melusine	12
Memel	63
Mercandia IV	36
Mercandia VIII	36
Mercator I	159
Merchant	33
Mercs Mihintale	159
Merel-V	204
Meridiaan	173
Merit	91
Merita	49
Meriwa	134
Merle	144
Merle	183
Merle	91
Merlin	102
Mermaid	70
Meropa	194
Mersey Fisher	95
Mersey Viking	18
Merwe Trader	71
Merweborg	90
Merwedijk	162
Metallica	152
Metsaborg	204
Mette Mols	25
Michael A	208
Michael J	120
Michelle C	74
Michelle	102
Michiganborg	204
Midas	100
Midnatsol	24
Midsland	18
Mie Mols	25
Mikal With	191
Mike	46
Mikhail Cheremnykh	140
Mikhail Dudin	140
Mikhail Lomonosov	140
Mila	204
Milady	67
Milford Fisher	95
Mimer	100
Mina	139
Minerva	102
Minka C	74
Miramar	67
Miranda	100
Miriam Borchard	152
Miriam	83
Mirjam C	74
Mirva	201
Misana	100
Misida	100
Miska	204
Mississippiborg	204
Missouriborg	204
Mistral	100
Mistral	156
Mistral	164
Mistral	133
Moezelborg	204
Molo Sun	123
Molo Trader	123
Mondena	134
Monica	203
Monica C	74
Monika Muller	133
Monnik	42
Monsoon	164
Monsunen	60
Mont St. Michel	8
Monte	84
Montis	206
Moondance	12
Moormerland	63
Moresby Express	136
Morgenstond I	171
Moritz Schulte	164
Mornes	186
Morraborg	204
Morskoy-14	49
Mostein	148
Mosvik	123
Mozart	99
MSC Bahamas	95
MSC Longoni	68
Muhlenau	178
Muirneag	10
Multitank Badenia	46
Multitank Britannia	47
Mungo	47
Munsterland	18
Munteborg	204
Murray Express	203
Musketier	67
Muuga	191
Myras	97
Myrte	59
Nadja	116
Nadja	122
Nadvoitsy	147
Najade	173
Najaden	153
Nakhodka	131
Namai	204
Nanuk	178
Naruksovo	131
Natacha C	74
Natali	83
Nataly I	167
Nathalie Ehler	84
Nathalie	79
Nautica	55
Naven	186
Navigable	49
Navigare	49
Navita	49
Neckar Highway *	120
Nedland	123
Neerlandic	184
Nekton	152
Nemo	194
Nemuna	168
Nena	77
Nephrit	104
Neptun	106
Neptun	112
Neptunus	170
Ness	117
Nestor	128
Nestor	208
Neuburg	124
Neutor	150
Nevskiy-22	140
New Hayatsuki	165
New Hirotsuki	165
New Takatsuki	165
Newcastle	174
Nickerie	165
Nicola	116
Nicola	122
Nicole C	74
Nidaroe	167
Niels Stevns	183
Nigel Prior	151
Nikar G	99
Niklas G	99
Nikolay Psomiadi	131
NileDutch Cabinda	158
NileDutch Nordica	158
Nils B	62
Nils Dacke	42
Nils Holgersson	42
Nimbus	170
Nina 1	55
Nina Bres	136
Nina	104
Nina	130
Nina	198
Nina	201
Nirint Pride	159
Noblesse C	76
Noest	66
Nomadic Bergen	74
Nomadic Hjellestad	74
Nomadic Milde	74
Noorderkroon	204
Noorderkroon	96
Nor Feeder	159
Nor Viking	159
Norbank	26
Norbar II	136
Norbay	26
Norcape	26
Nord	46
Nordanhav	186
Norderau	178
Nordersand	67
Nordertor	150
Nordfjell	132
Nordfjord	97
Nordgard	153
Nordhav	136
Nordic Amanda	186
Nordic Chantal	59
Nordic Copenhagen	138
Nordic Diana	96
Nordic Erika	96
Nordic Glory	174
Nordic Helsinki	138
Nordic Oslo	138
Nordic Stockholm	138
Nordic Victory	174
Nordica Hav	109
Nordjarl	136
Nordkap	125
Nordkapp	24
Nordkyn	136
Nordland I	160
Nordland	108
Nordlandia	18
Nordlink	22
Nordlys	24
Nordnorge	24
Nordskott	132
Nordstar	186
Nordstern	208
Nordstjernen	24
Nordstrand	93
Nordstraum	196
Nordvaag	136
Nordvaer	136
Nordvik	136
Noren	46
Norgas Alameda	170
Norgas Camilla	170
Norgas Carine	170
Norgas Cathinka	170
Norgas Challenger	170
Norgas Chief	170
Norgas Energy	170
Norgas Napa	170
Norgas Orinda	170
Norgas Pan	170
Norgas Patricia *	170
Norgas Petaluma	170
Norgas Shasta	170
Norgas Sonoma	170
Norgas Trader	170
Norgas Traveller	170
Norgas Voyager	170
Norholm	159
Norjan	201
Norking	26
Norland	86
Norma J	120
Norman Arrow	25
Norman Bridge	25
Norman Leader	25
Norman Voyager	25
Normandic	114
Normandie Express	8
Normandie Vitesse	8
Normandie	8
Normed Amsterdam	183
Normed Antwerpen	201
Normed Bremen	183
Normed Gemlik	204
Normed Rotterdam	201
Norne	159
Norqueen	26
Norrland	68
Norrona	33
Norrvik	70
Norsky	26
Norstone	142
Norstream	26
Norsund	159
North Express	83
Northsea Trader	71
Nortic	111
Nosi	77
Nossan	186
Nostalgic	165
Notos	72
Nova Bretagne	165
Nova Caledonia	165
Nova Flandria	165
Nova Galicia	184
Nova Terra	165
Nova Zeelandia	165
Novatrans	49
Novitas-H	196
Novomar	108
NST Amalia	164
NST Amalia	72
NST Leoni	72
NST Natasja	72
Nural Stevns	183
O M Aestatis	131
O M Autumni	131
O M Humorum	131
O M Imbrium	131
Oak	144
Oak	40
Oberon	53
Oberon	83
Ocean Bird	151
Ocean Primero	128
Ocean Primus	128
Ocean Prism	128
Ocean Prize	128
Ocean Team	183
Oceanstar	186
OCT Challenger	88
Odergas	106
Odertal	105
Odin Sydfyen	25
Oerd	42
Ofelia	30
Ohlau	178
Okapi	95
Okko Tom Brook	63
Oland	56
Oleander	173
Oleander	40
Olesya	116
Olivia	116
Olivier Stevns	183
Olympic-A	47
Olympus	170
Omegagas	170
OMG Gatchina	203
OMG Tosno	203
Omskiy-100	140
Omskiy-105	131
Omskiy-107	131
Omskiy-114	49
Omskiy-115	49
Omskiy-116	49
Omskiy-117	49
Omskiy-121	49
Omskiy-122	49
Omskiy-125	131
Omskiy-130	49
Omskiy-131	49
Omskiy-132	140
Omskiy-133	140
Omskiy-134	140
Omskiy-135	140
Omskiy-137	140
Omskiy-14	131
Omskiy-140	140
Omskiy-141	140
Omskiy-141	140
Omskiy-205	131
Omskiy-207	131
Omskiy-98	140
Omskiy-99	140
Onarfjell	144
Onarfjord	144
Onda	114
Onego	147
Onego Breeze	188
Onego Merchant	108
Onego Mistral	109
Onego Monsoon	109
Onego Passat	109
Onego Ponza	84
Onego Spirit	144
Onego Traveller	108
Onego Zonda	109
Onyx	124
OOCL Narva	81
OOCL Neva	56
OOCL Nevskiy	198
OOCL St. Petersburg	118
Oostvoorne	160
Oostzee	144
Opal	104
Opal	91
OPDR Cadiz	164
OPDR Las Palmas	164
OPDR Lisboa	164
OPDR Tanger	164
OPDR Tenerife	164
Ophelia	47
Opus	165
Orabelt	167
Oradana	168
Oraholm	168
Orahope	168
Orakota	168
Oralake	152
Oraness	168
Orarikke	131
Orarose	131
Orasila	168
Orasund	168
Oratank	170
Orateca	170
Orcana	96
Orestina	116
Orinoco River	201
Orion A	47
Orion	144
Orion	198
Orso	62
Ortviken	30
Osa	56
OSC Rotterdam	108
OSC Victoriadiep	108
OSC Vlistdiep	108
Oscar Wilde	24
Oslo	63
Ostanhav	186
Ostanvik	122
Osteborg	90
Ostenau	178
Ostend Spirit	25
Osterbotten	134
Osterems	86
Ostermarsch	67
Ostfriesland	18
Ostgard	153
Ostrand	30
Otilia	213
Otto Danielsen	191
OW Aalborg	213
OW Atlantic	213
OW Baltic	213
OW Copenhagen	213
OW Scandinavia	213
OXL Lotus	183
OXL Nomad	183
OXL Samurai	183
Pacific Dawn	106
Pacific Egret	68
Pacific Grebe	68
Pacific Heron	68
Pacific Pintail	68
Pacific Sandpiper	68
Paganini	208
Paimpol	105
Paivi	114
Palatine	12
Palessa	105
Pallas Ocean	148
Pamir	208
Pampero	106
Panagia	106
Pancaldo	106
Panda PG	72
Panda	204
Pandora	114
Pangani	151
Panta Rhei	204
Pantanal	106
Panthera	106
Paper Moon	72
Paper Star	72
Paramar	106
Paranga	106

Name	Page	Name	Page	Name	Page	Name	Page	Name	Page	Name	Page
Silja Festival	36	Sormovskiy-3048	213	Stella Virgo	183	Stolt Tern	176	Tango	198	Tinka	81
Silja Serenade	36	Sormovskiy-3049	213	Stella Wega	183	Storfoss	86	Tanja	112	Tinnes	117
Silja Symphony	36	Sormovskiy-3050	213	Stellanova	118	Storoe	71	Tanja	129	Tinno	210
Silva	134	Sormovskiy-3051	213	Stellaprima	118	Storrington	174	Tanja Kosan	128	Tinsdal	208
Silver River	81	Sormovskiy-3052	213	Stena Adventurer	34	Stortebeker	67	Tanja	129	Tinto	198
Simone	93	Sormovskiy-3053	213	Stena Baltica	34	Strami	132	Taranto	63	Tista	125
Sina B	63	Sormovskiy-3054	213	Stena Britannica	34	Stroombank	151	Tarnbris	181	Tistedal	88
Sinbad	213	Sormovskiy-3055	142	Stena Britannica	36	Stropus	148	Tarndal	181	Tiwala	84
Sine Bres	136	Sormovskiy-3056	142	Stena Caledonia	34	Sturgeon	76	Tarnfors	181	Tiznit	124
Singeldiep	108	Sormovskiy-3057	142	Stena Carisma	34	Suderau	178	Tarnhav	181	Toli	77
Sirius	47	Sormovskiy-3058	142	Stena Carrier	34	Sudertor	150	Tarnholm	181	Tom Sawyer	42
Sirius	99	Sormovskiy-3060	133	Stena Danica	34	Sule Viking	142	Tarnsjo	181	Tomke	86
Sirocco	204	Sormovskiy-3063	139	Stena Europe	34	Suledrott	142	Tarnvag	181	Tommy	183
Sirrah	162	Sormovskiy-3064	142	Stena Explorer	34	Sulevae	142	Tarnvik	181	Tone	176
Sirte Star	104	Sormovskiy-3066	202	Stena Forecaster	34	Sullberg	199	Taroudant	152	Tongan	123
Sisu Canopus	55	Sormovskiy-3067	142	Stena Forerunner	34	Summity	95	Tasman	96	Topas	105
Sisu Capella	55	Sormovskiy-3068	139	Stena Foreteller	34	Sun Bird	106	Tatjana	116	Topas	130
Sisu Castor	188	Sormovskiy-40	49	Stena Freighter	34	Sun Leader	84	Taurine	12	Topi	168
Sisu Cursa	191	Sormovskiy-41	133	Stena Germanica	34	Sun Vita	47	Tekhnolog Konyukhov	140	Tor Baltica	16
SITC Dalian	90	Sormovskiy-42	133	Stena Hollandica	34	Suna	147	Telamon	208	Tor Begonia	16
SITC Express	59	Sormovskiy-43	202	Stena Hollandica	36	Sunbeam	213	Tellus	170	Tor Belgia	16
SITC Friendship	114	Sormovskiy-44	213	Stena Jutlandica	34	Sundstraum	196	Telma Kosan	128	Tor Bellona	16
SITC Melody	192	Sormovskiy-45	147	Stena Leader	34	Sunergon	152	Telnes	117	Tor Botnia	16
SITC Miracle	192	Sormovskiy-48	147	Stena Lynx III	34	Sunmi	132	Tempest	76	Tor Britannia	16
SITC Moderation	59	Sormovskiy-49	133	Stena Nautica	34	Sunnanhav	186	Tenedos	212	Tor Corona	16
Sitc Passion	105	Sormovskiy-50	147	Stena Navigator	34	Sunnanvik	122	Tenna Kosan	128	Tor Dania	16
SITC Prestige	130	Sormovskiy-53	133	Stena Nordica	34	Sunnmore	136	Tera	53	Tor Ficaria	16
Sitc Progress	105	Soul Sound	171	Stena Partner	36	Suntis	206	Terneskjaer	198	Tor Finlandia	16
SITC Prospect	130	Southern Pasifika	105	Stena Pioneer	36	Suoyarvi	147	Ternland	181	Tor Fionia	16
SITC Qingdao	90	Southern Phoenix	178	Stena Saga	36	Superfast VII	40	Tertnes	117	Tor Freesia	16
Sjard	67	Sovietskaya Rodina	213	Stena Scandinavica	36	Superfast VIII	40	Tessa Kosan	128	Tor Futura	16
Skadi	50	Spaarnediep	108	Stena Scanrail	36	Superiority	95	Tessa PG	72	Tor Hafnia	16
Skaftafell	67	Spaarnedijk	162	Stena Seafarer	36	SuperSpeed 1	12	Tetuan	123	Tor Humbria	16
Skagenbank	151	Speciality	95	Stena Trader	36	SuperSpeed 2	14	Thames	188	Tor Jutlandia	16
Skalva	129	Spica	199	Stena Transfer	36	Superstar	40	Thames Fisher	95	Tor Magnolia	16
Skane	33	Spica	206	Stena Transporter	36	Supremity	95	Thames Highway	120	Tor Minerva	16
Skania	42	Sprinter	204	Stena Traveller	36	Susan Borchard	152	Thamesteel 1	46	Tor Petunia	16
Skantic	111	St. Catherine	42	Stena Voyager	36	Susan K	136	Tharsis	56	Tor Primula	16
Skarpoe	71	St. Cecilia	42	Sterno	191	Susann	173	Thea B	160	Tor Selandia	16
Skirner	122	St. Clare	42	Stevns Pearl	183	Susanne Theresa	111	Thea Marieke	203	Tor Suecia	16
Skog	79	St. Faith	42	Stina Kosan	128	Susanne	162	Thebe	128	Torill	198
Skulptor Anikushin	142	St. Helen	43	Stinnes Passat	84	Susanne	198	Theda	70	Tornator	67
Sky Vita	47	Stabben Junior	174	STK-1002	202	Suurhusen	63	Thekla	116	Tornedalen	134
Skylge	181	Stability	95	STK-1003	142	Suzanne	105	Theodora	183	Tornes	117
Sleipner	122	Stadt Berlin	184	STK-1004	142	Suzie Q	212	Theseus	128	Torpo	210
Sletringen	59	Stadt Celle	184	STK-1005	139	Sv. Apostol Andrey	114	Theseus	208	Torrent	188
Sloman Producer	170	Stadt Dusseldorf	184	STK-1007	159	Sv. Georgiy		Thetagas	170	Tour Margaux	88
Sloman Provider	170	Stadt Emden	184	STK-1008	159	Pobedonosets	114	Thor Athos	151	Tour Pomerol	88
Sloman Trader	170	Stadt Flensburg	184	STK-1009	142	Sv. Knyaz Vladimir	114	Thor Blue	78	Tove	198
Sloman Traveller	170	Stadt Goslar	184	STK-1012	142	Svanur	134	Thor Elisabeth	184	Toyvo Vyakhya	147
Sloterdiep	108	Stadt Hamburg	184	STK-1020	139	Svartfoss	86	Thor Falcon	184	TPC Classic	183
Smaragd	181	Stadt Hameln	184	STK-1026	139	Sveabulk	112	Thor Gitte	184	TPC Dream	183
Smaragd	130	Stadt Hannover	184	STK-1028	142	Sveanord	112	Thor Hanne	184	TPC Eagle	183
Smaragd	62	Stadt Hemmoor	63	STK-1029	139	Sveatind	167	Thor Hawk	184	Tracer	173
Snaefell	24	Stadt Lauenburg	184	STK-1031	142	Sven	152	Thor Ingeborg	186	Tradenes	117
Sneekerdiep	108	Stadt Luneburg	184	STK-1036	142	Svendborg	60	Thor Inger	186	Trader	129
Snow Star	186	Stadt Munchen	184	Stoc Marcia	174	Svilas	129	Thor Irene	186	Trader	178
Snowlark	202	Stadt Rendsburg	184	Stolt Acacia	174	Svir142		Thor Leader	78	Tramontane	53
Soave	124	Stadt Rotenburg	184	Stolt Aguila	174	Svyataya Elena	83	Thor Liberty	78	Trans Agila	171
Sofia	116	Stadum	178	Stolt Avocet	174	Svyatitel Aleksiy	114	Thor Libra	78	Trans Alina	72
Sofie N	198	Stapelmoor	63	Stolt Ayame	174	Swalinge	79	Thor Light	78	Trans Alrek	171
Sofie Theresa	111	Star Aruba	123	Stolt Azalea	174	Swallow	52	Thor Pacific	78	Trans Arctic	165
Sofrana Surville	134	Star Bird	151	Stolt Azami	174	Swami	132	Thor Pioneer	79	Trans Carrier	167
Sofrana Tourville	105	Star Bonaire	123	Stolt Botan	174	Swan Diana	188	Thor Spirit	79	Trans Dania	165
Solanjo	131	Star Curacao	123	Stolt Cormorant	174	Swanland	188	Thor Spring	79	Trans Emerald	165
Solent Fisher	95	Star	36	Stolt Dipper	174	Swe-Bulk	181	Thor Swan	186	Trans Fjell	165
Solikamsk	199	Staris	129	Stolt Egret	176	Swedica Hav	109	Thor Sydfyen	26	Trans Fjord	165
Solombala	50	Starovolzhsk	202	Stolt Fulmar	176	Swegard	153	Thor Venture	79	Trans Frej	171
Solstraum	196	Stas	142	Stolt Gannet	176	Swift	52	Thresher	76	Trans Holm	165
Solveig K	123	Steenbank	151	Stolt Guillemot	176	Syam	147	Thule	160	Trans Odin	171
Solvi A	198	Steenborg	160	Stolt Hikawa	176	Sydfart	112	Thunder	178	Trans Scandic	165
Solway Fisher	95	Steersman	95	Stolt Jasmine	176	Sydgard	153	Thurkus	192	Trans Sea	165
Solymar	106	Stefan K	120	Stolt Kestrel	176	Sydland	123	Tidan	186	Trans Sund	165
Somers Isles	118	Stefan Sibum	168	Stolt Kikyo	176	Sydstraum	196	Tiger Power	201	Trans Vik	165
Sommen	46	Steffi C	74	Stolt Kite	176	Sylve	74	Tilda Kosan	128	Transandromeda	132
Sonja C	74	Steinau	178	Stolt Kittiwake	176	Sylvia	198	Tim	114	Transanuna	53
Sonoro	152	Steines	117	Stolt Lily	176	Sylvia	59	Tim B	183	Transeuropa	22
Sophia Kosan	128	Stella J	120	Stolt Pelican	176	Symphorine	12	Timbus	158	Transfalcon	188
Sophia	83	Stella Kosan	128	Stolt Petrel	176	Syn Mira	60	Timca	34	TransFighter	40
Sormovskiy-117	49	Stella Lyra	183	Stolt Puffin	176	Syn Mizar	60	Tina C	74	Transjorund	53
Sormovskiy-121	202	Stella Maris	183	Stolt Quetzal	176	Syn Zube	60	Tina Theresa	111	Translandia	18
Sormovskiy-122	202	Stella Maris	66	Stolt Razorbill	176	tadt Bremen	184	Tina	203	Translubeca	22
Sormovskiy-123	202	Stella Moon	66	Stolt Shearwater	176	Taigeta	194	Tina	56	Transmar	106
Sormovskiy-3001	142	Stella Orion	183	Stolt Skua	176	Taipan	123	Tingo	88	Transnjord	188
Sormovskiy-3003	142	Stella Polaris	183	Stolt Suisen	176	Tallin	63	Tini71		TransPaper	40
Sormovskiy-3006	202			Stolt Teal	176	Tananger	136	Tinka	213	TransPine	40

Name	Pg	Name	Pg	Name	Pg	Name	Pg	Name	Pg	Name	Pg
Transporter	173	Union Diamond	192	Veritas H	196	Volgo-Balt 231	148	Wes Beam	208	Wilson Marin	212
TransPulp	40	Union Elisabeth	192	Verity	93	Volgo-Balt 232	148	Wes Platte	208	Wilson Mersin	212
TransReel	40	Union Emerald	192	Vermland	60	Volgo-Balt 235	148	Wes Profile	208	Wilson Mo	212
TransTimber	40	Union Gem	192	Verona	129	Volgo-Balt 236	148	Weser Highway	120	Wilson Mosel	212
Transwing	133	Union Gold	192	Vesborg	26	Volgo-Balt 237	148	Weserdijk	162	Wilson Reef	212
TransWood	40	Union Moon	192	Vesteralen	24	Volgo-Balt 238	142	Wesertor	150	Wilson Rhine	212
Traveller	173	Union Neptune	192	Vestland	95	Volgo-Balt 239	148	West Carrier	95	Wilson Riga	212
Trelleborg	33	Union Pearl	192	Via	112	Volgo-Balt 240	148	West Stream	201	Wilson Ross	212
Trenden	153	Union Pluto	192	Via Mare	8	Volgo-Balt 241	202	Westerhaven	71	Wilson Rouen	212
Tri Frakt	159	Union Ruby	192	Victoria C	74	Volgo-Balt 243	133	Westerkade	71	Wilson Rough	212
Tri Star	47	Union Saturn	192	Victoria I	40	Volgo-Balt 244	133	Westerland	84	Wilson Ruhr	212
Trica	34	Union Silver	192	Victoria Kosan	128	Volgo-Balt 245	148	Western Carrier	63	Wilson Saar	212
Trine Theresa	112	Union Topaz	192	Victoria Scan	71	Volgo-Balt 246	139	Western Cruiser	63	Wilson Saga	212
Trine	194	Univoyager	123	Victoria	116	Volgo-Balt 248	202	Western Island	63	Wilson Skaw	212
Trollfjord	24	Uniwind	123	Victoria	97	Volgo-Don 203	202	Western Steamer	63	Wilson Sky	148
Trollnes	117	Uno	60	Victoriaborg	204	Volgo-Don 205	202	Western Trader	71	Wilson Split	212
Trones	117	Uphusen	63	Victorine	12	Volgo-Don 236	202	Westewind	204	Wilson Stadt	212
Troubadour	55	Uranus	78	Victress	93	Volgo-Don 238	214	Westgard	153	Wilson Star	208
Trout	76	Urd	33	Vidi	112	Volgo-Don 240	202	Westvoorne	160	Wilson Sund	212
Troy	46	Ursine	12	Vigo	148	Volgo-Don 5046	202	Westwind II	53	Wilson Tana	212
Tucana J	120	Uta	116	Vigoroso	168	Volgo-Don 5065	142	Whitchallenger	208	Wilson Tees	212
Tucana	204	Uttum	178	Viire	30	Volgo-Don 5076	142	Whitchampion	208	Wilson Trent	212
Tulos	147	V. Ushakov	83	Viking Cinderella	42	Volgo-Don 5077	142	Whitdawn	208	Wilson Tyne	212
Tuna	186	Vaasaborg	204	Viking XPRS	42	Volgo-Don 5080	142	Whitonia	208	Wilson Waal	212
Tuxpan Reef	150	Vadero Highlander	198	Viking	24	Volgo-Don 5084	142	Whitspray	208	Windena	188
Twaite	76	Vadero Linnea	198	Vikingdiep	108	Volgo-Don 5088	142	Widor	114	Windermere	164
Twister	76	Valbell	90	Vikstraum	196	Volgo-Don 5091	142	Wiebke	109	Windstar	188
Tycho Brahe	33	Valda	151	Viktor Taratin	147	Volgo-Don 5105	142	Wiebke D	83	Winona	116
Typhoon	76	Valencia	97	Viljandi	191	Volgoneft-301	50	Wight Light	43	Wisaforest	108
Tyumen-1	153	Valentin Pikul	142	Ville	168	Volkers	56	Wight Sky	43	Wisby Argan	213
Tyumen-2	153	Valentine	12	Villum Clausen	8	Volkhov	114	Wight Sun	43	Wisby Verity	213
Tyumen-3	153	Valga	191	Vilnius	16	Volo	158	Wilberforce	208	Wisby Wave	213
UAFL Express	56	Valiant	93	Vina	112	Volo	60	Wilhelmine Steffens	102	Wisdom	49
UAL Aberdeen	96	Vana Tallinn	40	Vindoe	71	Volzhskiy-10	214	Wilke	67	Wisdom	72
UAL Africa	96	Vancouverborg	204	Vinga Helena	181	Volzhskiy-33	148	Willeke	204	Wisteria	40
UAL America	74	Vanessa C	74	Vinga Safir	181	Volzhskiy-40	142	Willy	150	With Junior	191
UAL Angola	108	Vanguard	159	Vinga	112	Volzhskiy-44	142	Wilma	109	Wittenbergen	208
UAL Antwerp	74	Vanino	55	Vingatank	181	Volzhskiy-47	142	Wilson Aberdeen	63	WMS Amsterdam	162
UAL Capetown	74	Vanquish	112	Viola	122	Volzhskiy-50	142	Wilson Amsterdam	63	WMS Groningen	162
UAL Coburg	108	Vans Queen	148	Virginiaborg	204	Volzhskiy-7	214	Wilson Antwerp	63	WMS Harlingen	162
UAL Congo	78	Vantage	152	Virma-2	114	Volzhskiy-8	214	Wilson Aveiro	63	WMS Rotterdam	162
UAL Cyprus	108	Varangerfjord	178	Virtus	168	Voorneborg	204	Wilson Aviles	63	WMS Vlissingen	162
UAL Europe	74	Varmido	71	Visby	14	Voornedijk	162	Wilson Avonmouth	63	Wolin	42
UAL Gabon	74	Varnadiep	108	Viscount	55	Vossborg	78	Wilson Ayr	63	Wolthusen	63
UAL Lobito	96	Varnebank	151	Viscount	93	Vossdiep	108	Wilson Bar	210	Wotan	208
UAL Malongo	156	Vasadiep	108	Vissersbank	151	Vudi	194	Wilson Bilbao	210	Xenia	116
UAL Rodach	108	Vasiliy Klimov	147	Visten	46	Vyg	148	Wilson Blythe	210	X-Press Matterhorn	118
UAL Texas	96	Vasiliy Malov	142	Visurgis	168	Waal Trader	71	Wilson Borg	210	X-Press Monte Bianco	118
UAL Trader	96	Vasiliy Shukshin	142	Vita	47	Waaldijk	162	Wilson Bremen	210	X-Press Monte Rosa	118
UBC Cartagena	109	Vastanvik	122	Vitta Theresa	112	Walter Hammann	102	Wilson Brest	210	Yakov Vorobyov	214
UBC Cebu	109	Vechtborg	90	Vivara	88	Wani Logger	90	Wilson Brugge	210	Yamburg	150
UBC Cork	109	Vechtdiep	108	Vladimir Noskov	147	Wani Point	90	Wilson Cadiz	210	Yara Gas I	71
UBC Manzanillo	108	Vedette	93	Vliedlep	108	Wani Will	90	Wilson Caen	210	Yara Gas II	71
UBC Maracaibo	108	Vedrey Barfodh	131	Vlieland	18	Wappen von Augsburg	104	Wilson Clyde	210	Yara Gas III	71
UBC Mariel	108	Vedrey Freene	90	Vlistborg	90	Wappen von Bayern	104	Wilson Cork	210	Yasmine	12
UBC Miami	108	Vedrey Hallarna	198	Vodla	114	Wappen von Berlin	104	Wilson Dover	210	Yellow River	201
UBC Mobile	108	Veendijk	162	Volente	152	Wappen von Bremen	104	Wilson Dvina	210	Yuko	46
UBC Moin	108	Veerseborg	78	Volga	147	Wappen von Dresden	104	Wilson Elbe	210	Yvonne K	120
UBC Montego Bay	108	Veersediep	108	Volga-35	214	Wappen von Flensburg	104	Wilson Ems	210	Yvonne	210
UBC Montreal	108	Veersedijk	162	Volga-4002	147	Wappen von Frankfurt	104	Wilson Express	102	Zaan Trader	71
UBC Moon	108	Vega	199	Volga-4004	147	Wappen von Hamburg	104	Wilson Fjord	210	Zamoscvorechye	140
UCT Elizabeth	104	Vega Aquila	199	Volga-4006	147	Wappen von Leipzig	104	Wilson Gaeta	210	Zara	116
UCT Ellis	104	Vega Azurit	199	Volga-4007	147	Wappen von Munchen	104	Wilson Garston	210	Zeeland	204
UCT Elwood	104	Vega Davos	199	Volga-4011	50	Wappen von Nurnberg	104	Wilson Gdansk	210	Zelenga	202
UCT Engle	104	Vega Dolomit	199	Volga-44	202	Wappen von Stuttgart	104	Wilson Ghent	210	Zephyr	76
UCT Espen	104	Vega Fynen	199	Volgo-Balt 102	50	Warber	173	Wilson Goole	212	Zeus	128
UCT Everad	104	Vega Gotland	199	Volgo-Balt 107	50	Warnow Carp	71	Wilson Grimsby	212	Zeus	96
Ufa 202		Vega Mercury	199	Volgo-Balt 136	134	Warnow Perch	71	Wilson Grip	212	Zeya	68
Ugra	114	Vega Nikolas	199	Volgo-Balt 179	97	Warnow Trout	71	Wilson Harrier	212	Zillertal	122
Ukrainets	147	Vega Sachsen	199	Volgo-Balt 19	55	Wasaborg	95	Wilson Hawk	212	Zuiderdiep	108
Ulla Scan	184	Vega Saturn	199	Volgo-Balt 190	55	Waterway	55	Wilson Heron	212	Zuzanna	174
Ullswater	164	Vega Scorpio	199	Volgo-Balt 195	134	Wawel	30	Wilson Holm	68		
Ulrike F	97	Vega Spinell	199	Volgo-Balt 201	142	WEC Dali	196	Wilson Hook	148		
Ulrike G	99	Vega Stockholm	199	Volgo-Balt 204	142	WEC Goya	117	Wilson Horn	68		
Ulriken	142	Vega Topas	199	Volgo-Balt 210	191	WEC Majorelle	49	Wilson Hull	148		
Ultramar	106	Vega Virgo	199	Volgo-Balt 211	142	WEC Navigator	198	Wilson Humber	212		
Ulusland 1	147	Vega Zirkon	199	Volgo-Balt 215	142	WEC Rubens	97	Wilson Husum	212		
Ulysses	24	Vega	199	Volgo-Balt 220	147	WEC Sorolla	196	Wilson Lahn	212		
Umgeni	156	Vela	47	Volgo-Balt 223	147	WEC Van Eyck	97	Wilson Leer	212		
Umiavut	173	Velox	93	Volgo-Balt 225	133	WEC Van Gogh	47	Wilson Leith	212		
Undarum	131	Velserdiep	108	Volgo-Balt 226	147	WEC Velaquez	133	Wilson Lista	212		
Unden	46	Velserdijk	162	Volgo-Balt 227	147	WEC Vermeer	97	Wilson Maas	212		
Undine	12	Vento di Levante	201	Volgo-Balt 228	148	Wega	206	Wilson Main	212		
Uniland	194	Vento di Maestrale	201	Volgo-Balt 229	148	Welsh Piper	76	Wilson Malm	212		
Unimar	67	Vera	133	Volgo-Balt 230	148	Werder Bremen	59	Wilson Malo	212		
Union Bronze	192	Verdi	99			Wes Bar	208	Wilson Mar	212		